MUSIC AND BROADCASTING IN IRELAND

Music and Broadcasting in Ireland

Richard Pine

FOUR COURTS PRESS

Set in 10 on 13 point Janson for
FOUR COURTS PRESS LTD
7 Malpas Street, Dublin 8, Ireland
e-mail: info@four-courts-press.ie
http://www.four-courts-press.ie
and in North America by
FOUR COURTS PRESS
c/o ISBS, 920 N.E. 58th Avenue, Suite 300, Portland, OR 97213.

ISBN 1–85182–842–7 hardback
ISBN 1–85182–843–5 paperback

A catalogue record for this title
is available from the British Library.

Printed in England
by MPG Books, Bodmin, Cornwall

For Patricia:
marvellous musician,
wonderful woman

Contents

Appendix on accompanying CD:
Recordings of works by Irish composers in RTÉ Sound Archives
[compiled by Richard Pine and Joan Murphy]

Illustrations

Plates 1–16 occur between pages 130 and 131; plates 17–31 occur between pages 290 and 291; plates 32–45 appear between pages 450 and 451.

1 Vincent O'Brien, 2RN's first Music Director.
2 The 'Station Orchestra' – late 1920s.
3 W.A. Manahan's Dance Band.
4 J.M. Doyle, Principal Conductor of the Radio Éireann Orchestra.
5 Michael Bowles, Principal Conductor and Music Director.
6 1943 concert programme with Jelly d'Aranyi's autograph.
7 Adrian Boult's autograph for his concerts on 26 and 27 April 1942.
8 León Ó Broin, Secretary of the Department of Posts and Telegraphs.
9 P.J. Little, Minister for Posts and Telegraphs.
10 Renzo Marchionni, leader, RÉSO.
11 Jean Martinon.
12 Milan Horvat, Principal Conductor, with pianist Charles Lynch, c.1955.
13 RÉSO, Gaiety Theatre, with Milan Horvat, Principal Conductor, c.1953.
14 Eimear Ó Broin.
15 Tibor Paul, Principal Conductor and Music Director.
16 Igor Stravinsky in Dublin, 1963.

17 Programme for the RÉ Music Festival, 1963.
18 Seán MacRéamoinn with the RÉ mobile recording unit, 1950s.
19 Fachtna Ó hAnnracháin, Terry O'Connor and Nancie Lord.
20 Arthur Nachstern.
21 Sleeve of the RÉSO's recording of the National Anthem.
22 The RÉ Singers with Hans Waldemar Rosen, 1955.
23 The RÉ Singers with Hans Waldemar Rosen, 1965.
24 Seán Ó Riada.
25 Ciarán MacMathuna.
26 The RÉLO with conductor Dermot O'Hara, 1955.
27 A.J. Potter.
28 Sketch by A.J. Potter for his 'Tostal overture'.
29 The Rowsome family.
30 The RTÉLO 25th anniversary concert, with leader Jack Cheatle and conductor Robert Murphy, 1973.
31 Leaders of the RTÉSO/NSO: (a) Geraldine O'Grady; (b) Colin Staveley; (c) Audrey Park; (d) Alan Smale.

CREDITS

22 *Irish Times*; 12–16, 23–25, 29, 33–5, 40b, 40f RTÉ Stills Library.

Foreword

As well as editing this series on 'Broadcasting and Irish Society', Richard Pine has written both its first and its final volumes. With *2RN and the origins of Irish radio*, he revealed neglected aspects of an early, momentous act of the Irish Free State. That story and his telling analysis of its significance illuminated the politics of the early years of independence while exploring radical questions that continue to agitate our political and cultural life. Richard Pine modestly describes *Music and broadcasting in Ireland*, the final volume of this series, as an index to the 70 years that began with the establishment of 2RN, and not as a comprehensive treatment of 'all the events, activities and personalities' that constitute the history of music-making for radio and television.

While his reserve is admirable, others will welcome this book as a uniquely well-documented account of a most significant strand of Ireland's cultural experience in the twentieth century. It is an impressive work of record which includes, for example, the texts of the 1958 radio series 'Composers at Work'; a survey of works by Irish composers, performed by decade, since 1938; and transcripts of the verbal submissions made to the PIANO review group in the 1990s. As an institutional history, it deals with the people, the politics and the policies of 2RN/RÉ/RTÉ and the external bodies with which broadcasting engaged since 1926. It is based on new research into the earliest struggles for funding, the establishment of both the RÉSO and the Light Orchestra, and the role of Radio Éireann in helping to create both the Dublin Grand Opera Society and the Wexford Festival. While recognizing that RTÉ has been 'the chief motor of musical development' in Ireland, Richard Pine argues that the broadcasting organization had acted 'at times [as] a brake on that development'.

Music and broadcasting in Ireland will be an essential reference for future historians of our music making and culture in the twentieth century. Its title nods to *Music in Ireland* which Aloys Fleischmann edited in 1952. In the foreword to that book Sir Arnold Bax expressed the wish that Ireland 'might establish a musical culture worthy of her wonderful folk heritage' while Fleischmann judged that 'Since the first world war the main advances have been due to the development of broadcasting and more recently to the increased importance attached to music as a school subject …' Half a century on, Richard Pine salutes the achievements of those who showed the nerve and dedication to cultivate music in and through broadcasting since the 1920s. But the past is indeed another country, and the question now is whether we are doing things differently enough for a larger, wealthier and more educated society. Ireland today speaks with pride – and without irony – of its musical industry. Technology promises transformation of broadcasting, and marketing is the business of pleasing the customer. *Music and broadcasting in Ireland* presents us with a timely analysis – one that helps clarify questions about policy and action for an age when it appears that music, broadcasting and education are all to be tested first and foremost by the measures of 'value added'.

Adrian Moynes
Managing Director
RTÉ Radio

Preface

This is not a book of reminiscences, and for this reason I have interviewed only those who could materially add to the facts at my disposal. Where my own memories of events seemed to justify indulgence in reminiscence, I trust that I have kept this to the minimum. When I started work in RTÉ in 1974 many of those whom I met had a working memory of the organisation stretching back to the 1940s and 50s. Reading the files available to me, I realise how important the continuity of that working experience can be, but at the same time how fragile that continuity can be in the context of changing technologies and, indeed, of broadcasting policies.

In providing the narrative that follows, I have borne in mind several factors which might influence the objectivity with which it has, I trust, been written: chiefly, my experience as RTÉ's Concerts Manager 1974–1983. The day-to-day encounter with visiting soloists and conductors was one of the most enriching elements of the work, as was the close association with principal conductors of the RTÉSO (Albert Rosen and Colman Pearce) and leaders Colin Staveley, Audrey Park and Alan Smale. Working everyday with the members of what is now Ireland's National Symphony Orchestra was an immense privilege which, as will transpire in the course of this book, it was painful to relinquish. Work with the RTÉLO/CO was equally stimulating, especially collaborating with Gareth Hudson on the introduction of the 'Music For Fun' family concerts. Knowing, and working with, the Academica String Quartet also provided personal and, at times, viscerally exciting, musical rewards. Less encouraging was my relationship with the Director of Music, Gerard Victory, with whom I found it difficult and frustrating to work, despite his extraordinary charisma as a creative intelligence: I hope that whatever criticisms are made of him in chapter 6 are purged of any personal feeling in connection with the, at times, acrimonious nature of our working relationship.

For a broadcasting station which has inevitably become increasingly visible through the public performances of its orchestras and ensembles, the invisibility of certain unsung heroes has condemned them to obscurity: it is therefore necessary to give due credit to the sound engineers and radio producers who have brought the performing groups to the listening audience: they include Tommy Warren, Éamonn Timoney, Anto Timoney, Jim MacHale, Venetia O'Sullivan, Dennis Suttill and John Hughes. Administrative personnel in the Music Department, such as Laurie Cearr, Maureen Donohoe and Gareth

highly talented musician), provided a service which was sel-
ed by the wider public, while successive orchestra managers,
gh, Frank Murphy and Frank Young, exercised both responsi-
rity which is seldom acknowledged. Others, by virtue of their
isibility, feature more distinctly in the course of this book.

Perhaps the most grievous aspect of any manager's job is the death of colleagues, and over that decade (and since) it has been my sad duty – but I would
also call it an honour – to have attended the funerals of so many fine musicians
whose work has enriched Ireland's cultural life.

This is therefore not a 'social' history. In 1989 Michael Dervan, editor of
Music Ireland, asked whether there would ever be 'such creatures' as historians
of the RTÉSO.[1] This particular creature has chosen the path of institutional
history, in the course of which, it is hoped, the personalities, the policies, the
aspirations will come to life.

In anticipation of the fiftieth anniversary of the founding, in 1948, of the
National Symphony Orchestra (as the Radio Éireann Symphony Orchestra),
RTÉ commissioned Pat O'Kelly to compile his commemorative *The National
Symphony Orchestra of Ireland 1948–1998: a selected history*. As will be clear, I am
greatly indebted to Pat O'Kelly for his largely pioneering work in establishing a chronicle of the players, conductors and administrators (myself among
them) associated with the NSO, and of the works they performed. I have not
attempted to emulate that work: instead, using material that was not available
to Pat O'Kelly at the time, I have concentrated more on the policies and the
politics of the organisation which was responsible for those performances, in
order to highlight the systemic strengths and weaknesses to which I refer in
my Introduction.

In one respect, however, I do emulate Pat O'Kelly. He began his 'selected
history' with a personal reminiscence of performances which were important
to his musical development. My own 'top twenty' performances which I have
witnessed in Ireland include thirteen orchestral or chamber music events
involving RTÉ. At the risk of boring those who are too young to have witnessed them, or unfortunate enough to have missed them, and in the hope of
reviving memories among those who were there, I will list them in chronological order:

– the cycle of Beethoven string quartets performed by the Aeolian Quartet
in the Rupert Guinness Hall, Dublin, in 1969; at the conclusion of the
series, there was that kind of silence from the audience, before the massive applause, which indicates an occasion of awesome magnitude;

1 *Music Ireland* 4/7, July–August 1989.

- Charles Lynch's performance of the complete Beethoven symphonies in the transcription for piano by Liszt, on four consecutive Saturdays in January 1971, in the Examination Hall of TCD;
- Pascal Rogé's two lunchtime recitals in the TCD Examination Hall in 1971 during the Dublin Arts Festival, when he played the Liszt sonata in B minor and Schumann's 'Carnaval' (I was privileged to have organised both these and Lynch's Beethoven recitals);
- Smetana's opera *The Bartered Bride* conducted by Albert Rosen at the DGOS in 1971;
- Janácßk's opera *Kátya Kabanová*, also conducted by Albert Rosen, at the 1972 Wexford Festival;
- Liszt's 'Totentanz' played by John Ogdon with the RTÉSO at the Gaiety Theatre in 1973;
- John O'Conor's performance of Beethoven's 'Diabelli Variations' in the studio of Charles and Carol Acton, prior to his appearance with the work at the Wigmore Hall, in January 1974;
- the Berg violin concerto played by Kyung-Wha Chung with the RTÉSO, conductor Colman Pearce, during the Dublin Festival of Twentieth-Century Music, 1974, at St Patrick's College, Drumcondra;
- the Brahms violin concerto played by Mincho Minchev with the RTÉSO, conductor Colman Pearce, at the St Francis Xavier Hall, Dublin, in 1976 – Minchev played a Guarneri 'del Gesù' which had been lent to him by the estate of Joseph Szigeti, and the performance was far superior to that in the Gaiety Theatre a year later, when he played the 'Baron Wittgenstein' Stradivarius;
- Olivier Messiaen's 'Turangalîla-symphonie' performed by the RTÉSO under Albert Rosen, in the presence of the composer, in the SFX in 1976 during that year's Twentieth-Century Festival – the piano and *ondes martenot* soloists were the composer's wife and sister-in-law;
- for pure enjoyment and excitement, Albert Rosen's lightning performances of the overture to 'Russlan and Ludmilla' at various venues as the encore to the RTÉSO's 1976 European tour programme;
- the performance by Victor Malirß(then principal horn of the RTÉSO) of the four horn concertos of Mozart in a single concert, with the New Irish Chamber Orchestra in St Audoen's Church, Dublin, in 1976;
- Micheál O'Rourke's all-Chopin programme at the RDS in 1976;
- the Lutosaawski cello concerto played by Heinrich Schiff and the RTÉSO, under the composer's baton (SFX), at the Twentieth-Century Festival in 1978;
- performances by the Academica Quartet from their appointment in 1978, especially Schubert's 'Death and the Maiden';

- Benjamin Luxon's performance of Schubert's song cycle 'Winterreise' in 1978 at the Wexford Festival, interrupted by a workman inadvertently walking on stage;
- A.J. Potter's opera *The Wedding*, performed by Irish National Opera with the RTÉCO under Proinnsías O'Duinn at the Abbey Theatre in 1981;
- Philip Martin's performance of Brahms' first piano concerto at the NCH in 1981, which revealed depths of his playing and musicality that previously had only been hinted at;
- Suzanne Murphy as Violetta in the DGOS production of *La traviata* in 1983;
- the cycles of Nielsen and Bruckner symphonies by the NSO conducted by Bryden Thomson at the NCH in 1985–6. At the end of each symphony, Thomson held the score aloft, as much a part of the performance, and of the salute to the composer, as the playing itself.

These memories recall the triumphs which can be achieved when the best management creates and cultivates the best environment within which artistic expression can flourish. This is the chief purpose and aim of arts management, in its facilitative role, in relation to both individual events and concert seasons. Even so, volatility of temperament can destabilise an ensemble, and in a symphonic concert the relations between and within individual orchestral sections, the orchestra as a whole and the conductor – and of course, in a concerto, the soloist – in interpreting and giving voice to a succession of possibly quite diverse musics, can on occasions such as these transcend the ordinary. They can also condemn it to remain just that – the ordinary – or worse. This inherent danger of oscillation between success and failure illustrates the polarity of views on management structures and the culture of management. Thus one commentator states that 'creativity and innovation disturb [the order necessary to achieve targets]. Hence, organization tends to be inhospitable to creativity and innovation';[2] while another believes that 'conflicts arise out of ideas also, in organizations established to promote creative individuals, but such organizations are to a certain extent designed to allow for conflict'.[3] Both views reflect aspects of RTÉ's experience with music-making over the decades, but the latter would probably prevail in today's environment.

In order to emphasise the problems of polarity and mutual ignorance, I would add to all these instances of 'classical' triumphs, without apology for the repetition, what I wrote in my Preface to the Thomas Davis Lectures which I edited for RTÉ Radio 1 in 1998:

---

2 Theodore Levitt, quoted in B.-A. Vedin, *Corporate culture and creative management* p. 90. 3 Ibid.

I met Micho Russell only once, at the Clifden Community Arts Week in 1986, when the guest of honour was Siobhán McKenna, on what proved to be her last public engagement (she already knew that she was dying). After some introductions had been made in the school-room [of Clifden Community School], the two were fortuitously left alone, Siobhán on an improvised stage, Micho some yards away on a bench, each getting a feel for the space in which they would perform the following morning, among schoolchildren. Each was aware of the other, yet, each timidly embarrassed by the presence of a greatness not their own, they silently acknowledged their situation with a wry smile and a coy nod of the head. Then, Micho took from his pocket his tin whistle, and played a slow air. It was his greeting, for which words were inadequate and perhaps out of place, and it filled the whole world, crossing boundaries and language barriers as it did so, and meeting Siobhán's 'eye of the mind', as his own eye could not. To say that it was one of the most poignant moments I have ever witnessed is almost pointless, because its significance lies not in what it meant – and will always mean – for me, the silent onlooker, but in the fact that codes and syntax can be unravelled and negotiated by gestures and state-ments more powerful than those imposed on us by conventional wis-dom and orthodox behaviour.[4]

If that kind of occasion is hardly possible in our modern world, it may not be due to the displacement of Micho's kind of music by 'classical' music, although many consider that to be the cause, creating a gap between the two genres. Christian de Quincey, writing in the *Irish Times* in 1970, thought that 'when we talk of reviving traditional music or preserving it, it is this gap, threat-ening to isolate us for ever from the past, which we must confront'.[5] I have written extensively elsewhere about 'the gap'; [6] suffice it here to say that it is a treacherous place to work, but, as de Quincey says, a necessary one.

---

4 R. Pine (ed.), *Music in Ireland, 1848–1998* (1998), p. 15.   **5** 'Traditional music tomorrow, 1: ori-gins vs. integration', *Irish Times*, 30 December 1970.   **6** Cf. R. Pine, *The diviner: the art of Brian Friel* (1999), pp. 25–31.

ACKNOWLEDGMENTS

My first debt is to Bob Collins who, as Director-General, invited me to under-take the general editorship of the series 'Broadcasting and Irish Society' and to write the present volume. I regret that he had retired from his position before this book could appear. I am also indebted to his successor, Cathal Goan, who has given his continuing support to the project, and to Peter Feeney, RTÉ's Head of Public Affairs Policy, and Adrian Moynes, now Managing Director of Radio, for their interest and advice.

This book could not have taken its present form if it were not for the per-sonal contributions by Fachtna Ó hAnnracháin who, with León Ó Broin (Secretary of P&T), virtually created the RÉ Symphony Orchestra in the years 1947–61, and by Eimear Ó Broin, who was appointed Assistant Conductor in 1953 and conducted that orchestra more often than almost any other person. Their insights and profound knowledge of those years have transformed what would otherwise be a strict chronology into a record of challenge and excite-ment in the creation and nourishment of a vital musical entity. The revelation in the P&T files of the heroic work undertaken, often in the most unhelpful circumstances, by Fachtna Ó hAnnracháin puts deeply in his debt everyone who cherishes the NSO of today.

The fact that Charles Acton wrote music reviews and music journalism over a period of almost forty years establishes him as the most consistent – as well as the most trenchant – commentator on Irish musical life during the years to which the core of this book is devoted, and his views and judgements will be encoun-tered frequently. While his colleagues at other newspapers and magazines (such as Fanny Feehan at *Hibernia*, Robert Johnson at the *Irish Press* or Mary McGoris at the *Irish Independent*) wrote of the same events, their coverage was less con-sistent and less comprehensive, and although they are quoted in the present text, it is the contribution of Acton and the *Irish Times* itself, to the shaping of pub-lic opinion of Irish music-making, that remains pre-eminent.

The archivist in charge of RTÉ Written Archives, Brian Lynch, has been a mine of information: without his ability to locate material long thought to have been lost, this book would hardly have been possible. The present and past staff of the RTÉ Sound Archives (Ian Murray, Ian Lee, Rob Canning and particularly Joan Murphy, who not only guided me through the intricacies of the catalogue but also established the template for the information in the Appendix); the successive Managers of the RTÉ Sound Library/Archives (Majella Breen and Malachy Moran); and the staff of the RTÉ Reference and Illustrations Library, have all been co-operative and enthusiastic. Niall Doyle (Director of Music) and the staff of the Music Department gave advice and support. Tom Quinn, Secretary to the RTÉ Authority, made available details of its deliberations in the 1960s. In particular Brian O'Rourke, now General Manager of the NSO, who has been a central figure in Irish music-making for so many years, gave freely of his time, patience and advice in shaping the early mindset of this book.

I also wish to thank Dr Dermot Rattigan of UCD who presented the 1988 radio series 'Composers in Conversation'; Professor Harry White of UCD and Dr Joseph Ryan of Athlone Institute of Technology (formerly of the Army School of Music), whose work, although I criticise it extensively in this book, has done much to focus, and stimulate, attention on the theme of music and nationalism; Axel Klein, for advance copies of aspects of his research; Eve O'Kelly and Jonathan Grimes of the Contemporary Music Centre, Dublin; Philip Shields (librarian of the Royal Irish Academy of Music); John O'Conor (Director of the RIAM and former chair of the PIANO Review Group); John Horgan (member of the PIANO review group); Maura Eaton (Director of the Music Board of Ireland), for making available material from the PIANO Review Group; David Byers (Chief Executive of the Ulster Orchestra); Patrick Blanc, brother of the late James Blanc; Jonathan Browner, Maureen Lemass and Ita Beausang (whose *Anglo-Irish Music, 1780–1830* is a model of research which few could hope to emulate) – her musical sleuthing on a small but vital matter was beyond any call of duty that I might have uttered. Pat O'Kelly's assistance has already been greeted and acknowledged in my preface.

At Four Courts Press, both Michael Adams and Martin Fanning have, since the inception of 'Broadcasting and Irish Society', provided totally professional support and co-operation.

I am particularly anxious to thank Carol Acton, Sarah Burn, Brian Lynch, Eimear Ó Broin, Fachtna Ó hAnnracháin and Brian O'Rourke for reading and commenting on sections of this book, and to Toner Quinn for publishing versions of chapters 1 and 6 in the *Journal of Music in Ireland.* I am grateful to them all for their assistance, and for correcting some factual errors. I am, of course, solely responsible for any that may remain.

A note on sources

During the 1980s, many files in the RTÉ Music Department were inadvertently destroyed when an off-campus storage facility was discontinued. The implications of that destruction for a history of this kind are incalculable; chief among the identifiable *lacunae* are the files relating to the tenures of the principal conductorship of the RTÉ Symphony Orchestra by Tibor Paul (1961–7) and Albert Rosen (1968–81), which has made it difficult in the case of the former, and almost impossible in that of the latter, to reconstruct their artistic policy in relation to recruitment, programming and choice of artists. Nevertheless, it has been possible, by cross-reference to extant files relating to other areas, and in other locations, to detect some of the activity in the Music Department in this period. A further 'missing link' is the absence of much information relating to the Dublin Grand Opera Society 1960–80, and to all but the earliest years of the Wexford Festival. Consequently, the sections of this book which address RTÉ's relations with these bodies concentrate on their establishment in, respectively, the early 1940s and the early 1950s. A significant discovery has been the files relating to the campaign in the 1950s to have the RÉ Light Orchestra relocated in Cork, which reveal the eventual establishment of a string quartet in the city to have been a far more complicated and controversial affair than has been commonly believed.

All files described as 'P&T' are original documents of the former Department of Posts and Telegraphs and are now located in RTÉ Written Archives, as are files described as 'RTÉ Music Department'. Where I have quoted from sensitive material relating to persons still living, I have used the formula 'name withheld' to protect the identities of those persons. Unattributed quotations in the text are taken from unnumbered or untitled Music Department files. Material from the records of the RTÉ Authority is part of the RTÉ Authority papers. The archives of the late Charles Acton and the late A.J. Potter remain in private collections. Quotations from the written submissions to the PIANO Review Group, and transcriptions made by me from the tape recordings of the oral hearings held by the Group in November 1994, were taken from the PIANO Archive in the custody of its former Secretary, Maura Eaton.

The tables in the text listing preformances of works by Irish composers have been assembled from available data, including extant concert programmes, Music Department music diaries, newspaper files, etcetera. Some performances have eluded detection, and not all dates of performances are complete, despite extensive enquiry and research. The author and publishers would welcome any additional information that may come to light.

Abbreviations

BBCNI	BBC Northern Ireland
BBCSO	BBC Symphony Orchestra
CBSO	City of Birmingham Symphony Orchestra
CCÉ	Comhaltas Ceoltóirí Éireann
DGOS	Dublin Grand Opera Society
DOS	Dublin Operatic Society
EBU	European Broadcasting Union
Finance	Department of Finance
GPO	General Post Office (Dublin)
ICO	Irish Chamber Orchestra
IFMAP	Irish Federation of Musicians and Allied Professions
LPO	London Philharmonic Orchestra
LSO	London Symphony Orchestra
MAI	Music Asociation of Ireland
NCH	National Concert Hall
NG2	Stanley Sadie (ed.), *New Grove Dictionary of Music and Musicians*, second edition, 2001.
NICO	New Irish Chamber Orchestra
NSO	National Symphony Orchestra
P&T	Department of Posts and Telegraphs
R&R	Rathmines and Rathgar Musical Society
RAM	Royal Academy of Music (UK)
RCM	Royal College of Music (UK)
RDS	Royal Dublin Society
RÉ	Radio Éireann
RÉLO	Radio Éireann Light Orchestra
RÉSO	Radio Éireann Symphony Orchestra
RIAM	Royal Irish Academy of Music
RLPO	Royal Liverpool Philharmonic Orchestra
RPO	Royal Philharmonic Orchestra (London)
R(T)É	to refer to the organisation before and after the creation of Radio Telefís Éireann
RTÉ	Radio Telefís Éireann
RTÉCO	Radio Telefís Éireann Concert Orchestra
RTÉLO	Radio Telefís Éireann Light Orchestra
RTÉSO	Radio Telefís Éireann Symphony Orchestra
SFX	Saint Francis Xavier Hall (Dublin)
TCD	Trinity College, Dublin
TD	Teachta Dála (Member of the Dáil)
UCC	University College, Cork
UCD	University College, Dublin

Introduction

[handwritten: • music area of RTÉ neglecteduhen compared to others]

It is in the nature of a large and complex organisation that it contains both the seeds of achievement and the critics of its success; both dynamic creativity and collective conservatism; both the intellectual means of change and institutional resistance to change. In the case of a broadcasting organisation, the very fact that it is concerned with the vital matter of communication heightens the tensions between the warp and the weft running across each other within the fabric of the organism – its systemic structures, its hierarchies, its personnel, and even the physical layout of its buildings.

It can be argued that its engagements with its publics merely extend and replicate these internal exchanges, discussions and antagonisms, since a broadcaster is in many ways a mirror of the organic culture of its society – not only its radio and television audiences but also its political masters, its critics, its enemies (or 'begrudgers') and those who comment upon its operations, including the sometimes envious non-electronic media.

This can be less than obvious in the case of what Pierre Bourdieu has called 'doxic societies' – 'that which goes without saying because it comes without saying'[1] – which could be taken as a definition of the societies in which public service broadcasting is taken for granted. Certainly the creation, performance and transmission of music is no different from other broadcasting functions in this respect, and the book which follows could, in many details and in many directions, be an analogy of RTÉ's activity in the areas of sport, religion, education, drama or current affairs: where competition for limited resources; difference in styles, outlook or persuasions; the clamour of cultures to find expression and to relate to one another; the very methods of communication and presentation – underlie, impinge upon and affect the satisfactions of entertainment or intelligence.

That purely orchestral music is wordless should not obscure the fact that music as communication is intimately concerned with language, whether that language be available as verbal sound (spoken or sung), or as a system of concepts or notions to be encoded, transmitted and decoded by non-verbal means. Brian Friel's plays – most explicitly, *Dancing at Lughnasa* (and most recently *Performances*) – explore the intimate relationship between language and music in such a way as to bring before us the idea of music as 'meta-language', a sec-

[1] As discussed in D. Sutton, *Memories cast in stone* (1988), p. 58.

[handwritten: • Argument that orchestral music had, seen as communicator because no words]

xxiii

ond or 'other' symbolic system which refers to, and comments upon, the first.[2] For most Irish audiences, witnessing the early radio broadcasts by the fledgling Radio Éireann studio orchestra, and then its first major series of public concerts from 1941 onwards, musical language was an almost new and unknown quality which could be accessed and assessed not merely in cultural terms but also in terms of the excitement it produced, as listeners became aware of a novel experience in communication and a previously unheard symbolic system. The opportunity to compare and contrast this system with what they knew of indigenous music would have provided grounds for making decisions – or at least establishing viewpoints – on the preferability of one cultural genre to another, or alternatively for simply placing them beside one another in the mindset of the listener. Thus created, images of sound would take up residence in that mindset, never entirely to be dislodged and always to exert some influence, however minimal, upon it.

Since the creation of a symphony orchestra, and its sustenance and growth over a period of more than seventy-five years, is the single most important achievement of RTÉ in the field of music, it occupies the central place in this book (as described in chapters 2, 3, 6 and 7). But, as chapter 1 makes clear, the 'classical' genre is by no means the only consideration, nor is the symphonic repertoire the only subject within that genre: as chapter 5 emphasises in impressive detail, RTÉ, since its inception, has been the backbone of music-making in Ireland; the provision of musical and broadcasting facilities for the performance of opera, light music, chamber and choral music (both established and contemporary), and for the composition of music in many genres, has been a significant feature of Ireland's national and international musical presence. Recently the question has been asked: 'Would there ever have been a symphony orchestra without the pre-existence of RTÉ?'[3] Since the undeniable fact is, that 2RN, in parallel with many other comparable broadcasting organisations in Europe, did establish an incipient orchestra, the question may seem superfluous. Yet, the larger question of what constitutes an *Irish* orchestra, or indeed a *national* orchestra in any country, would become intimately connected with the nature and role of broadcasting. This allows us to re-focus on the simpler question, of whether, in hindsight, a modern symphony orchestra and a modern broadcasting organisation are necessarily obvious or natural bedfellows.

A further complication arises in regard to the question of heritage. At the outset of 2RN, the musical 'heritage' of Ireland was a hotly disputed area, the

---

2 Cf. B. Friel, *Dancing at Lughnasa* (1990), p. 71: 'The air is nostalgic with the music of the thirties. It drifts in from somewhere far away – a mirage of sound – a dream music that is both heard and imagined; that seems to be both itself and its own echo.' 3 Cf. John Horgan, member of the PIANO review group, 1994, oral hearing 19 November 1994 (PIANO Archive).

[handwritten: Also poses the question of what makes the symphony Irish or inane]

only surety being that the Irish were an inherently musical nation and that therefore music belonged at the heart of broadcasting. What was actually meant by 'music' and 'nation'? Would 'music' as a meta-language provide any answers? These and similar questions will be encountered throughout this book, and it is my purpose here to emphasise that it cannot hope to be exhaustive – not least, due to the significant gaps in the records – but that its bias towards 'classical' music and the symphonic repertoire is inevitable, given the weight of extant evidence – since, by virtue of its activity from 1926 onwards, RTÉ has unquestionably become the custodian not only of valuable national assets in the form of its performing groups, but also of a newly minted national heritage in the form of its Sound Archive and its several music libraries.

While this book has not been written *ad hominem*, there are many stories waiting to be told, in which certain pivotal personalities take their place, but at the core of the narration, imperatively, are the regular performances by the performing groups, and the creation of audiences for broadcasts and live concerts, as well as the presence and commentary of critics. However much the issues such as management of resources are teased out, the transmission of cultural experiences remains the key element. Behind that, however, there is one cardinal point: that no one has ever honestly addressed the question of the RTÉSO/NSO as the heart of Irish music-making, and this narrative seeks to do justice to the many issues raised by that question.

The provision and indeed the collection of non-'classical' or 'traditional' music, for which RTÉ has been widely acclaimed, has been better documented than has that of 'classical' music to date. Nevertheless, insofar as it is within my competence, I have given attention to the broadcasting of 'traditional' or indigenous music for two reasons. Firstly, because I believe that – to give two brief examples – the presence of a musician such as piper Leo Rowsome on the Irish airwaves is as significant as the presence of a musician such as pianist Charles Lynch; similarly, the presence of the Aughrim Slopes Céilí Band on those airwaves is as significant as the presence of the Dublin Chamber Orchestra. Secondly, because the questions raised by Seán Ó Riada in his performances and in his radio series *Our Musical Heritage*, about the relationship of Irish 'traditional music' to other musical genres, are as pertinent today as they were forty years ago, or indeed over 100 years ago when the concept of an 'Irish National School of Music' was first debated. The appearance of the proceedings of the 'Crossroads' conference (1996) – 'tradition and change in Irish traditional music' – is sufficient evidence of that. As Sir William Harcourt, then the leader of the Liberal Party in Britain, exclaimed in dismay when he encountered Irish delegates at the 1898 Welsh Eisteddfod, 'Is there an Irish Question in music also?'[4]

---

4 *Freeman's Journal*, 5 January 1898. At the same period, G.B. Shaw reported that William O'Brien,

It would, however, be both ridiculous and pretentious to suggest that the following book could address comprehensively all the events, activities and personalities that constitute the history of music and broadcasting in Ireland since 1926. But it does claim to be an index to the ideas and aspirations, as they are demonstrated in the extant records, of the officials of 2RN/RÉ/RTÉ and their critics over that seventy-five-year period. In particular, to give as detailed a scenario as possible of the early period in each instance – the hiring of artists, the association with 'outside bodies', and the relationship of music-making to broadcasting.

It is, of necessity, a large book because, in order to do justice to these themes, over such a wide canvas, it was necessary to give exhaustive treatment to previously unknown files which would otherwise not come to public attention by such means, however much they may be subsequently studied by doctoral candidates. One reason (apart from constraints of space) for giving less attention to the concert programmes and critical reviews of recent years is that these events still live in the memories of concert-goers and are largely in the accessible public domain, whereas events before, say, 1980 may be thought of as part of a dimmer past or even prior to the experience of the younger audience today.

Because RTÉ has become this large and complex organisation, one must look not only at its *management of culture* – for example, the day-to-day and year-to-year planning and administration of its orchestras – but also at the *culture of its management*, since it can be argued that it has not only been the chief motor of musical development but also at times a brake on that development. From the inception of broadcasting in Ireland until the establishment in 1960–1 of RTÉ as a semi-state, quasi-autonomous body under a government-appointed Authority,[5] all employees of Radio Éireann were civil servants, subject to all the conditions and constraints of the civil service. The management of an orchestra and the practice of the profession of musician were thus both enabled and constrained by such conditions. This was an inevitable trap: organisational culture has been defined as 'the collective programming of the mind which distinguishes the members of one organization from another';[6] the sometimes

a nationalist MP, had 'told the people of Dublin to demand "that Irish music shall be heard and honoured on Irish soil before the music of Italy and Germany"', on which Shaw commented: 'The thing is impossible at present. The best modern music is the fruit of a complex culture which no Irishman can enjoy today in his own country ... If Ireland were to set about honouring Irish musicians tomorrow, what would she do? Would she go to the only class that is nationally alive: the peasantry ... whose unwritten tunes made the best real music? Not a bit of it: she would go to the educated class – a class nationally dead, and artistically as sterile as Sodom and Gomorrah; pick out some plausible imitator of the hated foreigner; and then desperately pretend to think him a great Irish composer': *The Star*, 11 October 1889.   **5** Radio Éireann and Telefís Éireann existed in parallel, in a curious symbiosis until 1966 when the organisation was integrated under its new title, Radio Telefís Éireann.   **6** G. Hofstede, *Cultures and organizations: software of the mind* (1991), p. 180.

bafflingly Byzantine procedures of Radio Éireann/RTÉ would, under any other dispensation, have produced a similar mindset managing a similar set of processes. Conformity to civil service regulations may or may not impede artistic progress, but the equation of the artistic temperament with that of clerical and even of strategic executives will inevitably tend to inhibit the artist more than it will leaven the clerk.[7]

The available files make it clear that an immense sea-change took place from 1960, once RTÉ became, effectively, its own master, even though there were those in its offices who hankered for the protective clothing of the civil service intellectual uniform. Responsibility for one's own affairs – as the Irish Free State itself was discovering at the time when 2RN was set up – means not only balancing the books and safeguarding standards, but also having a view on future direction and relationships. When broadcasting was a division of the Department of Posts and Telegraphs, the enemy was the Department of Finance. In RTÉ, Finance is within; so too are Personnel and Staff Relations, and the culture of management of such a highly prized national asset as the National Symphony Orchestra has to do as much with the organisation's overall fiscal wellbeing as with artistic standards and vision. The fact that, after the advent of television in 1961–2, Music Department remained hermetically sealed within the Radio Division, with little access to the screen, was a major error of judgement on the part of the architects of the new RTÉ, which was only rectified in the creation of a non-aligned Music Division in 1998.

In any organisation, management displays tendencies influenced by class, education and political and family affiliations and loyalties. Professional competence is a major factor, but can be easily oriented by these tendencies, since 'a management culture is essentially about values which indicate how to produce achievement … Culture refers to the mixture of values – typically expressed as habits, conventions, beliefs and precepts – which typify a community'.[8] When I joined the RTÉ Music Department in 1974 as Concerts Manager, few of the staff had professional qualifications or experience relating to their function; all had some musical reason for holding their posts: the Director of Music and his assistant were composers; one of the senior radio producers had been a bandmaster; another was a church organist; another had been a singer at Sadler's Wells. I myself had been a concert promoter, but had

---

7 As a newcomer to RTÉ in 1974, I was shocked to discover that, as the author of a letter to the Editor of the *Irish Times*, I had disregarded a regulation requiring me to secure permission to publish it: the letter was concerned with neither music nor broadcasting. As John Horgan has discussed in *Broadcasting and public life: RTÉ news and current affairs* (2004), the operation of Section 31 of the Broadcasting Act made it impossible for RTÉ to carry interviews with members of Sinn Féin, even if the subject of the interviews was as innocuous as beekeeping. 8 W. Kingston, *Strengthening the management culture* (1994), p. 12.

no training in arts administration. Today, that department (now a Division) is mostly staffed by highly professionalised people in highly specialised functions. The aspirational and tentative previews of the 1960s and 70s have been over-taken by pragmatic, measured and more deeply informed forecasts, yet the instinctive flair required for the performance of an arts-related function remains essential, even in that specialised climate.[9]

Experts in the management field recognise that there is an argument 'between those who believe that efficient and effective management is based largely on universal principles, practices and general know-how which can (and should) be transferred to any country, and those who advocate that manage-ment as a philosophy and/or process is essentially or substantially culture-bound'.[10] From my own experience I would favour the latter view, because in Ireland, as I see it, it is quite unlikely that one can operate on 'universal prin-ciples' without allowing one's 'culture' to intervene. It is still too early to say that Ireland is an 'organic' society in the sense that there should be a near-opti-mal match between nationhood, culture, organisational behaviour and human resources[11] – debates over political and social issues such as neutrality, divorce and abortion, and major questions of self-determination within the EU, all affect the way we think about, and organise, our lives in music, however sub-liminally. Music is one way in which we give order to the expression of our experiences, and as such it is always potentially divisive. In Marie McCarthy's words, broadcast music, because of the power of the medium, 'assist[s] in cre-ating and circumscribing spaces of identity that in a sense determine cultural ... horizons'.[12]

As the authors of *Sit Down and Be Counted* – the incisive account of their resignation from the young RTÉ organisation in the late 1960s – observed, 'the real political problem of our contemporary world is that of the meaning of authority ... There is one notion of authority which we might call "author-ity as power" and this, we believe, is what dominates the mind of the Director-General. There is another notion, of "authority as service", which we think ought to prevail'.[13] The history of RTÉ's direction of music-making since 1926 makes it clear that a balance between those two notions of authority has been

---

9 Cf. P. Clancy, *Managing the cultural sector: essential competencies for managers in arts, culture and heritage in Ireland* (1994), p. 5: 'One recent guesstimate is that 70 per cent of the competencies needed for management are generic and 30 per cent are specific to a particular job and/or organ-isational climate ... A distinction has also been made between levels of competencies, distinguishing between basic competencies fundamental to the job and "high performance competencies" which are associated with superior performance.' **10** B. Richman, 'Significance of cultural variables' (1965). **11** Cf. M. Warner, 'Culture, organizational behaviour and human resource management: a critique' (1995). **12** M. McCarthy, *Passing it on: the transmission of music in Irish culture* (1999), p. 26. **13** J. Dowling, L. Doolan and B. Quinn, *Sit down and be counted* (1969), p. 303. They are of course referring specifically to the Director-General of the time, T.P. Hardiman.

a managerial minefield through which the administration of the performing groups and their activities has found its way.

The additional point needs to be made, that RTÉ of its very nature has become, since its separation from the civil service, a micro-climate of its own devising. A recent report by the Music Board of Ireland analyses the 'Structure of the Music Industry' into the categories of Creation (including composers and performers), Facilitation (including managers), Production (including concert promoters) and Distribution (including media and concerts).[14] In order to manage its commissioning, performance and broadcasting of music, RTÉ has developed 'competencies' in all these fields and as such is a self-enclosed and self-referential environment, with all the freedom and the dangers of freedom that that entails.

---

14 Music Board of Ireland, *The economic significance of the Irish music industry* (2003), p. 3.

CHAPTER I

Musical life in Ireland in the

AN INCIPIENT NATIONAL RADIO SERVICE

To appreciate the way in which Irish radio has attempted to serve the needs of music itself, and to serve the needs of its listeners by means of music, it is necessary to understand why the inception of radio in Ireland in 1926 – four years after the Irish Free State came into existence – was so tentative and vulnerable. And to appreciate the condition of musical life in Ireland in the 1920s it is necessary to understand what had occurred – or failed to occur – in the preceding 120 years, and especially in what I have called elsewhere 'the silent century'.[1] This preliminary chapter addresses these two issues.

Radio broadcasting was introduced to the Irish Free State in 1926, at a time of serious political instability and uncertainty[2] and a fallow period for musical activity. (Broadcasting in Northern Ireland by the BBC had begun two years previously.)[3] In the aftermath of the war of independence, the Anglo-Irish Treaty and the civil war, Ireland remained a deeply divided society, with on one side the 'pro-Treaty' parties, led by Cumann na nGaedheal and W.T. Cosgrave, striving to create a stable, civil society capable of repairing the damage of the past ten years, and on the other the 'anti-Treaty' section of public opinion, which crystallised in May 1926 with the formation by Éamon de Valera of Fianna Fáil, a party which declined to take its seats in Dáil Éireann until August 1927.[4]

In such circumstances – as the broadcasting authorities in many other European states discovered when establishing their own national radio services at this time – the transmission of potentially divisive or inflammatory programmes, even news reports, and particularly discussion of current affairs, was to be avoided. Even in Britain, where the BBC was to become symbolic of national identity and tradition, the General Strike of 1926 had represented a political crisis of considerable destabilising potential, which inhibited the devel-

---

1 In a documentary series 'Music, place and people', Lyric fm, 7 February 2000.   2 Cf. R. Pine, *2RN and the origins of Irish radio* (2002).   3 Cf. R. Cathcart, *The most contrary region* (1984).   4 Cf. J. Praeger, *Building democracy in Ireland* (1986). Dáil Éireann: the lower house of representatives ('deputies') in the Irish Parliament.

opment of this genre of programming.[5] In Ireland, the fledgling radio station '2RN'[6] which grew into Radio Éireann in 1937 and eventually into Radio Telefís Éireann, could not provide anything approaching a comprehensive news and current affairs service until after the second world war.[7]

The classic definition of media analysis by Harold Lasswell should serve us here: 'who says what, by what means, to whom and with what effect?'[8] If we connect this with Sidney Verba's observation, that 'political culture regulates who talks to whom and who influences whom',[9] we begin to appreciate the reasons for the tentative approach to *all* forms of broadcasting on the part of the Department of Posts and Telegraphs (P&T), even those such as 'music' that might have been considered anodyne and unlikely to attract ideological comment.

There was, in fact, considerable exploration of competing ideologies within the process of establishing 2RN, with the Postmaster-General[10] maintaining a strong anti-British bias which was both political and cultural, and, when the decision had been taken to proceed with the radio station, this was carried over into Dáil debates where the schedule content was discussed extensively.

In the absence of current affairs programming, the radio schedule came to be dominated by music and by talks on a variety of subjects judged to be of an 'improving' nature. It might therefore be assumed that 'music' would provide a safe substitute for more dangerous topics, by soothing the savage breast of civil disruption. This, however, was not the case, and the sameness and repetition in much of the music broadcast in the early years of 2RN and Radio Éireann concealed an ambiguity and a divergence of opinion as to what 'music' actually might be in the Irish social, cultural and political contexts, a divergence which continues to the present day and will reappear often in the course of this book. The availability of music on Irish radio, whatever the quality of transmission and reception, was a phenomenon both exciting and frightening, and would be recognised as part of 'conveying the culture of the country', as P.J. Little, one of the most progressive ministers responsible for broadcasting, put it.[11]

In 1926 Irish classical musicians were not numerous. The most eminent figure to emerge since 1850, Charles Villiers Stanford, who spent his entire career in Britain, had died in 1924; the next most senior, Herbert Hamilton Harty, who featured extensively in the early years of Irish radio, was in his mid-for-

5 Cf. A. Briggs, *The history of broadcasting in the United Kingdom*, vol. 1 (1961), pp. 245, 329–51. 6 The Dublin Broadcasting Station was identified by its 'call-sign', designated by international authority as '2RN': cf. Pine, op. cit., pp. 1–2, 40. 7 Cf. J. Horgan, *Irish media: a critical history since 1922* (2001) and John Horgan, *Broadcasting and public life*, op. cit. 8 H. Lasswell, 'The structure and function of communication in society' (1948). 9 S. Verba, 'Conclusion: comparative political culture' (1965). 10 Later, Minister for Posts and Telegraphs. 11 Dáil Debates (henceforth, DD), vol. 121, 25 May 1950, col. 617.

ties, and making an international career for himself as conductor of the Hallé Orchestra, with whom he was to appear in Dublin several times from 1923. Arnold Bax, English-born but *hibernior ipsis hiberniis*, was in the midst of his love affair with Ireland, which had evoked, among many other works, his *In Memoriam [Patrick Pearse, 1917]*, commemorating leaders of the 1916 rising with whom he had been familiar. The most notable and powerful of the native musicians working in Ireland was John F. Larchet, then aged forty-two, who simultaneously held a professorship of composition at the Royal Irish Academy of Music (RIAM), the professorship of music at University College, Dublin, was musical adviser to the army, director of music examinations in secondary schools, and music director and conductor of the Abbey (National) Theatre. In 1928 Larchet would inherit the mantle of the central figure in Irish musical life over the past forty-five years when the Neapolitan composer and professor of piano at the RIAM, Michele Esposito, retired at the age of seventy-three.

Therefore, when Douglas Hyde spoke at the inauguration of 2RN on 1 January 1926, we must take this musical context into consideration:

> A nation has never been made by Act of Parliament. A nation is made from the inside itself, it is made, first of all, by its music, songs, games and customs.[12]

Thus, radio could be expected to become a vehicle for nation-building, with indigenous music and songs – which had been regarded as the lifeblood of Irishness for at least a century – as its primary material. More than the fabric of the built environment was in need of 'reconstruction', as this era in modern Irish history can be called: so too was the self-esteem of the Irish psyche, the sense of identity which was being stimulated by the notion of 'Irish-Ireland'.[13] In 1903 Fr Richard Henebry, who repudiated the eighteenth-century harper Turlough Carolan for associating with Italian musicians, had stated: 'the more we foster modern music, the more we help to silence our own'.[14] Henebry was central to efforts to preserve traditional music as a living tradition without respect for, and at the expense of, other musical forms. This is a mindset that

---

12 The full text of Hyde's speech is in Pine, *2RN*, Appendix 2 (ii).   13 A valuable parallel is to be found in the concept of 'Negritude' promoted in Africa in the mid-twentieth century; cf. Léopold Sédar Senghor, 'Negritude: a humanism of the twentieth century': 'Who would deny that Africans ... have a certain way of conceiving life and of living it? A certain way of speaking, singing and dancing; of painting and sculpturing, and even of laughing and crying? ... Negritude is ... the sum of the cultural values of the black world'. Cf. also Amilcar Cabral, 'National liberation and culture': 'A people who free themselves from foreign domination will be free culturally only if ... they return to the upward paths of their own culture, which is nourished by the living reality of its environment, and which negates both harmful influences and any kind of subjection to foreign culture'.   14 R. Henebry, *Irish music* (1903), p. 14.

has perdured: indeed recently the Director of the Irish Traditional Music Archive, Nicholas Carolan, has said:

> People involved in ethnic music are not looking at classical music, they don't see it in fact, they don't recognise its existence, because they have a music system that to them is closed, fully satisfying ... Oral tradition music is a closed system – world – that is satisfied with its own structures.[15]

Hyde, who was to become the first President of Ireland in 1938, had been one of the first in recent times to articulate the cultural project of ousting British influence in Ireland when, in 1892, he had delivered a lecture to the National Literary Society on 'The Necessity for De-Anglicising the Irish People':

> Our music too, has become Anglicised to an alarming extent. Not only has the national instrument, the harp ... become extinct, but even the Irish pipes are threatened with the same fate ... If Ireland loses her music, she loses, what is, after the Gaelic language and literature, her most valuable and most characteristic expression. And she is rapidly losing it.[16]

(Hyde was no doubt gratified that from 1940 the pre-eminent piper Leo Rowsome broadcast frequently on Radio Éireann – see below, pp. 325–6.) Hyde's speech in 1926 was echoed by composer Frederick May ten years later: 'If it is true that great art is always part of a tradition, it is also true that such a tradition cannot be created self-consciously or by state decree. It comes from richness of life, and the most we can do is to help to bring this richness into being'.[17]

The expectation that radio could serve the cultural agenda of Irish nationalism was partially exemplified when, in 1925, an appointments board had entrusted the job of creating 2RN to Séamus Clandillon,[18] a *gaeilgeoir* [gaelic speaker] who had been associated with Patrick Pearse, and a noted performer and collector of Irish songs, who himself was to perform regularly on the new station, both *solo* and with his wife Mairéad ní Annagáin. Yet that same board had also appointed, as Music Director, Dr Vincent O'Brien, at that time organist of Dublin's Pro-Cathedral and a noted composer. Although he demonstrated a strong commitment to the fostering of traditional Irish music, O'Brien's *métier* was firmly in what we would today call the 'classical' genre. In the years up to Clandillon's dismissal from 2RN in 1934, he and O'Brien oversaw the development of a schedule which focussed not only on 'traditional' Irish music and songs, but also on the entire gamut of 'classical' music, including opera.

15 In 'Off the Shelf', RTÉ Radio 1, 1 July 1998. 16 As quoted by H. White, 'Nationalism, Colonialism ...' (2001), p. 266. 17 F. May, 'Music and the Nation' (1936). 18 Cf. Pine, *2RN*, pp. 139–40.

The limited resources available to Clandillon and O'Brien severely restricted the scope of what they could achieve in either genre, but the fact that they had an unspoken – or at least unwritten – commitment to both genres points us towards a consideration of the status of music of all types in Ireland at the time that the broadcasting service was brought into existence.

IRONIES

Harry White has recently written:

> The art tradition [in music] maintained a fragile but unbroken presence in Ireland in spite of the hostile division [between colonial and ethnic ideologies of culture] which plagued its existence ... One might say that, beneath the surface level of nationalist ideologies in Ireland [in the later nineteenth century], a certain amount in the service of the European aesthetic was being achieved.[19]

Of course, the tradition of which White speaks is generically European rather than British, and therefore it could hardly be said that antipathy to that tradition was a sign of hostility to Britain, which, until the time of Elgar (1857–1934), had had little more than a tangential and minimal role in the development of western music – being, as some Germans called it, *das Land ohne Musik* [the land without music].[20] In Ireland, that lack was even more pronounced and, as White puts it, 'music lay remote from the Anglo-Irish intellect'.[21] Nevertheless, White's argument is that, however slightly and inadequately, 'art' or 'classical' music survived the separation which had developed in nineteenth-century Ireland, between itself and indigenous or 'traditional' musical culture. That separation of the two genres stemmed from the rejection of imposed or colonial culture by those seeking independence, or at least a distinct cultural identity for Irishness. It was, essentially, an unnecessary separation, and after the mid-eighteenth century its painful divisiveness set up obstacles to any cross-fertilisation between Irish and non-Irish musical idioms. The last phase of Irish society in which there had been such exchanges was the mid-eighteenth century, when Italian musicians such as Geminiani and Francesco Scarlatti mingled with those of the native traditions such as Turlough Carolan and resulted in music which, however marginal, represented a high point of what we might call 'baroque traditional'. It is only in the past forty years, following the brief genius of Seán Ó Riada (see below, chapter 4), that

19 White, 'Nationalism, Colonialism ...', p. 267. 20 O. Schmitz, *Das Land ohne Musik* (1920); cf. also B. Rainbow, *The land without music* (1967). 21 Cf. H. White, *The keeper's recital: music and cultural history in Ireland, 1770–1970* (1998), pp. 14, 29, 33.

such dialogue between musical genres could once more be essayed on a professional and intensive level.[22]

In the eighteenth century, the concept of the 'protestant nation' had enabled the 'Ascendancy' – or at least its intellectual wing – to encourage the idea of an Ireland led by itself, the culmination of which was 'Grattan's Parliament' immediately preceding the Act of Union of 1800–1 which abolished the Irish legislature. In the nineteenth, conversely, a 'Catholic nation' was envisaged, having the goal of separation founded on difference. Leading up to (and after) independence, despite the impetus given to cultural nationalism by writers of protestant descent –Thomas Davis, Sir Samuel Ferguson, Yeats, Lady Gregory, Synge – the remnants of this 'protestant nation' fitted badly with the new project of a state which was predominantly 'Irish-Ireland'. The division between musical genres, which became most intense as the momentum of cultural nationalism reached its peak at the end of the nineteenth century, meant that cultural allegiances were bracketed with political affiliations. With the advent of political independence, those who espoused the classical tradition in music (and who could therefore be expected to be mainly unionist, or at least non-republican, in their political sympathies) were in a severely isolated minority, identified in the popular mind with the remnants of the 'Ascendancy' clustered around the Royal Dublin Society and the Dublin suburbs of Ballsbridge, Rathmines and Rathgar, their cultural interests being ringed round by legislation such as the Censorship of Films Act, 1923, and the Censorship of Publications Act, 1929, as well as the prohibition of divorce in 1925.[23] One former minister responsible for the RÉ orchestra would even say that the existence of foreign musicians in the orchestra was 'for the benefit of a few old fogies in Rathmines'.[24]

---

22 When part of this chapter appeared in *Journal of Music in Ireland* (3/3, January–February 2003) this contention was criticised by Patrick Zuk (*JMI* 3/5, July–August 2003) who asserted that it was 'demonstrably false', asking 'What of the works of O'Brien Butler and O'Dwyer? What of the very fine *Sreath do Phiano* [suite for piano] and *Trí Amhráin* [three songs] by Fleischmann, two extremely interesting and wholly successful attempts to forge a compositional idiom rooted in folk music?' To cite work by two almost unknown composers which hardly merit revival and belong decidedly to a side-road of Irish musical history, and two admittedly fine works by Fleischmann which, however, are not the most significant works in his output, hardly amounts to negating my broader contention that Ó Riada's own work was the first major milestone in the attempt to re-introduce these two idioms to one another. One must acknowledge, however, that in some quarters O'Brien Butler was highly regarded: Edward Martyn, writing in 1912, thought that 'his interesting experiments, after his being saturated by the folk music tradition, entitle him to be the father of Irish composers' – 'The Gaelic League and Irish music', *Irish Review*, 1 (March 1911–February 1912), 449–51.   23 When Dermod O'Brien, cousin of Lord Monteagle, solicited subscriptions for the provision of a new library at the RIAM, one correspondent told him that the Anglo-Irish were 'considered to be "foreign" by people with such distinctively Irish names as de Valera and Blythe': Maurice Headlam to O'Brien, 27 November 1934 (RIAM archive).   24 James Everett, DD, 142, 10 November 1953, col. 1776.

The incipient radio station was to reflect both the diversity and the divisiveness of the musical idioms which either flourished or languished in Ireland in the late 1920s, and it remains true that the entire history of RTÉ up to the present gives us intimate signals of the difficulties, the ironies and the challenges to be met in any attempt to provide a service in musical terms which accommodated all these idioms and sought a balance and a harmonious coexistence between them, as in the larger Irish society.[25]

Chief among these are the *ironies*, by which I mean the lack of a shared referential context within which concepts such as 'national' music or 'cosmopolitan' music might be understood: it is ironic, principally, that most of those (Bunting, Petrie, Joyce, Hudson, Pigot and Goodman) who had striven to ensure the survival of the ethnic musical traditions – the collectors whose work is so well documented since the time of the Belfast Harpers' Festival – should have come originally from the very class or cultural background which was anathema to the proponents of that ethnic culture, and that it was their legacy which would be debated in the new Ireland.

The fact that the survival of Irish ethnic or indigenous music was threatened by some kind of cultural erosion in the Irish imagination is the second irony of this aspect of musical history. The need to collect the surviving music of the harpers by bringing them together in Belfast in 1792 and writing down their atonal music – which did not lend itself to notation – in a mode which would make it accessible to other forms of musical performance,[26] highlights the rapidity with which the fortunes of this musical idiom had declined since the time of Carolan, only half a century previously. It still appears difficult to establish the fact that the act of writing down the melodies of traditional music inevitably changes its nature, as in all translation – so much so that Bunting relates the difficulties encountered by Geminiani when he attempted, unsuccessfully, to do so.[27] The collectors had no choice but to impose the laws of tonal form on what Moore himself called 'a lawless kind of music'.[28] This has been the central fact of music collecting: as Bartók observed, the original collectors could not but fail, because they lacked the essential tool: a recording machine[29] – which would become the key to the early success of Radio Éireann's collection of that material.

25 When Harry White refers to 'a *cultural* predicament, borne out by the consignment of traditional music to Raidió na Gaeltachta and art music to FM3 [the precursor of Lyric fm]' ('The conceptual failure of music education', 1997) he is making a forced example of a broadcasting strategy which I believe is unnecessary if one takes the entire spectrum of RTÉ programming into account. 26 This is discussed by M. McCarthy, 'Music education and the quest for cultural identity in Ireland, 1831–1989' (1990); cf. also B. Breathnach, *Folk music and dances of Ireland* (1971), p. 111: 'A great many of Bunting's airs are set in keys which the harpers could not have used; more surprisingly, his music is speckled with accidentals, for which they lacked strings.' 27 T. Ó Canainn, *Traditional music in Ireland* (1978), p. 8. 28 Quoted in J. Ryan, 'Nationalism and music in Ireland' (1991), p. 133. 29 B. Bartók, *Collected essays* (1976), p. 10.

The essence of traditional music, in contrast to 'classical' music, is its invisibility. The qualitative difference between the two has defied any significant intercourse between them, since the matter of translation is irresoluble. Tomás Ó Canainn discusses the elements of Irish traditional music in terms of the *personality* of the individual singer or player and the *location* or *context* in which the tune is played or sung. And he quotes the musicologist Albert Lord on the singers of epic poetry in the Balkans which, he says, could be applied to an Irish *sean-nós* (old style) singer: 'the singer of tales is at once the tradition and an individual creator'.[30] This is anathema to the classical style, where, despite the interpretative dimension to performance, the textual statement of the score (with the possible exception of the cadenza) remains supreme.

Collection of fragile material – fragile because of its vulnerability to attrition, erosion, supersession and neglect – is a recurring fact of Irish traditional music. Writing of the activities of Radio Éireann's mobile recording unit of the 1950s, Breandán Breathnach stated that the resultant programmes 'initiated a veritable new era of discovery ... Here indeed was a revival, or at least a reversal of the decline which had set in more than four score years previously'.[31] Among the collectors in this second 'golden age' were Proinsías Ó Conluain, Séamus Ennis, Seán MacRéamoinn, and Ciarán MacMathuna, whose *A Job of Journeywork* and *Mo Cheol Thú* have introduced and popularised Irish music for generations of radio listeners. Yet, in Breathnach's view, this new impetus to the appreciation of the musical heritage had, by the late 1960s, become imperilled by the very medium which had initiated it:

> there can be little doubt that the survival and renewal of traditional music depend on its dissemination by radio and television, but as yet the authorities in charge of these two media have given little evidence of their awareness of the high role they could play in this field.[32]

The use of this material by nineteenth-century arrangers need not concern us here, except to say that it laid the foundation for the modern-day arrangement of these and similar melodies commissioned by Radio Éireann from composers such as Redmond Friel, Éamonn Ó Gallchobhair, A.J. Potter and others. But we should note that the revival of interest in this particular body of tunes did not ensure the survival of the Irish folk idiom *per se*. The Great Famine of 1845–9 took such a toll on the rural population by way of death and emigration that the greatest of the mid-century collectors, George Petrie, saw yet again a danger of the extinction of an entire culture. Believing that 'the melodies of my country ... are ... the most beautiful national melodies in the world' and acti-

30 T. Ó Canainn, op. cit., pp. 1–3, 49. 31 B. Breathnach, op. cit., p. 130. 32 Ibid.

vated by 'a deep sense of their beauty, a strong conviction of their archaeologi-
cal interest, and a consequent desire to aid in the preservation of remains so honourable to the national character of my country', Petrie conceived of the immediate need 'to gather from amongst the survivors of the old Celtic race,
innumerable melodies that would soon pass away for ever', since 'the total extinction of their ancient language would be, inevitably, accompanied by the loss of
all that, as yet unsaved, portion of their ancient music which had been identified with it'.[33] The fact that this would continue to be the case when Radio Éireann's mobile recording unit went on the road in the 1950s is a salutary reminder
of the absence of Bartók's recording machine in previous centuries.

It was in the 1790s, just before the congress of the harpers in Belfast, that
Jean Baptiste Leclerc had examined the role of music in the context of nationalist France:

> The problem is ... the restoration of an equilibrium between the towns-
> folk and the countryfolk, or rather the discovery of a halfway point at
> which music will serve to restrain the former and advance the latter.[34]

Leclerc considered that in revolutionary France, at any rate, cosmopolitan
music was already too decadent to be worthy of sustenance, whereas the rural
tradition was 'still pure enough to deserve protection'. In Ireland, at the same
time, music of all kinds was under threat, its vibrancy as much in question in
the cities and towns as it was in the villages and homesteads, and this distinction between rural and urban societies in Ireland has been reflected in the tastes
and *mores* disclosed on RTÉ radio and television since their inception. The
basic irony was that the Irish, held since the time of Giraldus Cambrensis to
be innately musical, seemed to give no demonstrable indication of that musicality. The absence of music education (either in performance or appreciation)
may even be the greatest irony of all, since it was predetermined by this assumption that a musical people can behave musically *ad libidem* without external
stimulus. And, without the deliberate inculcation of a properly articulated policy on the role of music in broadcasting, underlying assumptions and prejudices were allowed to direct whatever programming policy there might have
been, and to contribute to the dearth of Irish composition. As will be seen in
chapter 5, Dáil debates frequently featured heated exchanges as to what type
of music should, or should not, constitute the RÉ schedule.

It has been cogently argued by both Harry White and Joseph Ryan that the
subordination of music, as a pure art form, to the demands of nationalism, from

33 C. Petrie in C.V. Stanford (ed), 'Introduction' to *The Complete Collection of Irish Music*, pp. v–viii.
34 Quoted by J. Ryan, 'The tone of defiance' (2001), pp. 206–7.

the time of Thomas Davis onwards, was the cause of this *caesura* in the creation of music for its own sake, and of the rise of a meagre musical standard at the service of literature. They attribute this to the demands and vagaries of nationalism, and do not seem to acknowledge that, in Irish musical history, the existence of *sean-nós* music is cognate with, and indivisible from, that of orality and poetry – a point borne out by Seán O'Boyle:

> As a people we Irish have always looked upon music in much the same way as the philosophers of ancient Greece. Throughout the Middle Ages we shared with the rest of Europe certain Greek ideas: a conception of music as consisting essentially of pure, unencumbered melodic line, and the idea of melody intimately linked with words, especially in matters of rhythm and metre.[35]

White and Ryan argue that the impetus of cultural separatism placed an onus on music which enforced a concentration on genres such as the *ballad* as a vehicle for emphasising the distinctiveness of innate Irish musicality and difference (exemplified by the *Melodies* of Thomas Moore) and that this inhibited the development of music by Irish composers in the European mainstream.[36] This argument has also been equally vigorously countered by Patrick Zuk and Barra Ó Séaghdha, in a debate which centres on the meaning and interpretation of 'nationalism' and on the relationship of the 'classical' or 'art' music of Europe to the 'traditional'or indigenous music of Ireland – a relationship which has bedevilled our understanding of either genre, and which has been at the heart of broadcasting in Ireland since it began.[37]

The one genre that one might expect to have emerged (as it did for example in Poland and Hungary in similar circumstances)[38] as a vehicle for cultural nationalism was *opera*, a powerful marriage of words and music in which romantic composition could support a vigorous libretto advocating heroism, defiance and separatism. Yet almost no operas of this kind emerged in nineteenth-century or early twentieth-century Ireland, and those that did were produced under circumstances which made their purpose ambiguous at least. For example, Stanford's *Shamus O'Brien* (1896, based on J.S. Le Fanu), with a 1798 theme, was billed as a romantic *comic* opera, and while, at the time of the centenary of '98, it became the most accessible Irish opera of its era, it raised more ques-

---

35 S. O'Boyle, *The Irish song tradition* (1976), p. 19.   36 Cf. White, *The keeper's recital*; 'Nationalism, colonialism …'; Ryan, 'Nationalism and music in Ireland', and 'Nationalism and Irish music'; 'The tone of defiance'.   37 P. Zuk, review of *Musical constructions of nationalism*, *Journal of Music in Ireland*, 2/2 (January–February 2002 and 2/3 March–April 2002), and 'Music and nationalism', *JMI*, 3/5 (July–August 2003); Barra Ó Séaghdha, 'Harping on', a review of *The keeper's recital* (1999).   38 Cf. M. Murphy, 'Moniuszko and musical nationalism in Poland' (2001).

tions as to the nature of Irishness and of rebellion than it could satisfy. Sullivan's unfinished opera, *The Emerald Isle*, coming four years after *Shamus O'Brien* and based on the same theme, also with a semi-comic treatment, suggests that a genre might have developed which would have addressed this most serious of topics in an ambivalent but nevertheless instructive manner. In my opinion, three Irish-language operas which have recently been cited as evidence of a lively compositional atmosphere in the early twentieth century – Thomas O'Brien Butler's *Muirgheis* (1903), Robert O'Dwyer's *Eithne* (1909) and Geoffrey Molyneux Palmer's *Sruth na Maoile* (1923) – do not amount to a significant corpus or school of composition in the field of music drama.[39]

As Gerard Victory observed, the Tailteann Games of 1924 saw a peak in operatic activity, with performances of *Sruth na Maoile*, *Shamus O'Brien* and *Shaun the Post* by critic H.R. White (writing as 'Dermot McMurrough') – the latter having a place in the repertory of the Carl Rosa Opera for some time, and also being broadcast by RÉ in 1960, but 'public interest failed. The incipient tradition was crushed for a time – possibly the roots were too fragile and too remote from the great international power house of opera to persuade the Irish people that their prejudice against native opera could be overcome'. Nevertheless, as Victory mentions, this 'tradition' was 'the most intensely "Gaelic" wing of Irish culture which best continued to foster what activity there was in a genre that many considered alien'[40] – the successors being Éamonn Ó Gallchobhair, a ballad opera by Seán Ó Riada, and more recently James Wilson, A.J. Potter and Victory himself.

Almost simultaneous with the predominantly literary renaissance, directed largely by Yeats and Synge through the medium of the National (Abbey) Theatre, *film* became a much more powerful and effective medium for the propagation of nationalist sentiment and ideology, in productions such as *The Lad from Old Ireland* (1910), *Rory O'More* (1911), and *For Ireland's Sake* (1912) – all of them concerned with eviction, suppression and the unjust persecution of the Irish by English troops – and, coinciding with the tenth anniversary of the Easter Rising and depicting the war of independence, *Irish Destiny* (1926).

It would not be until the late 1950s and the 1960s, with a trilogy of films relating to the 1916 Rising, that music (composed by Seán Ó Riada) would team up with film to provide a compelling basis for the exploration of modern Irish identity. Brian Boydell's scores for four films by Patrick Carey and Vincent

39 Nevertheless, cf. A. Klein, 'Stage-Irish, or the national in Irish opera, 1780–1925' (*Opera Quarterly* 21, 2005, forthcoming) where a case is made for a 'tradition' of Irish opera-writing; the author identifies approximately 280 operas in the period under review, mainly of 'internationalist' character, with 30 'which are central to the theme and period covered by this article' – i.e., 'national' in character. **40** G. Victory, 'Irish opera in this century', programme note for A.J. Potter's *The Wedding*, Abbey Theatre, 1981.

Corcoran, might arguably also belong in this category.[41] The use of the tune 'Roisin Dubh' (Dark Rosaleen) on French horn at the opening of Ó Riada's music for George Morrison's film *Mise Eire* ['I am Ireland'] (1959) is a particularly effective example of introducing an ancient melody to an Irish orchestral work.

A further argument needs to be made which Ryan and White do not seem to have addressed: the fact that the espousal of a nationalist agenda does not necessarily mean that its followers should turn their backs on other cultural manifestations. In Finland, which had a similar history to that of Ireland in the early twentieth century – a war of independence followed immediately by a civil war – the nationalist imperative in cultural terms had produced many compositions which were either directly or indirectly inspired by the specificity of Finnish identity, most of them taking elements of the national epic poem *Kalevala* (1835) as their source (an inspirational work which made W.B. Yeats deeply envious that Ireland had no equivalent to act as a cultural stimulus). But this was possible because, since the mid-1880s, Finland had enjoyed a vigorous growth in its musical infrastructure, which, while at the service of nationalism, was also able to sustain an interest in the classical genre *per se*, and had its first major manifestation in Sibelius' *Kalevala*-based *Kullervo* symphony (1890).

Ireland produced no Sibelius or Grieg, no Bartók or Kodály, whose genius could be placed equally at the service of the mainstream western musical tradition and at that of the cultural nationalism of their country. Stanford and Harty certainly did write 'Irishly' – to use Bax's vivid expression[42] – but their works in this vein were distinct from those written with the British concert audience in mind. Stanford's 'Irish' Symphony (no. 3, 1887),[43] his six orchestral Irish Rhapsodies, the Irish Concertino, and an organ sonata titled 'Celtica', are, like his various settings of Irish tunes for chamber ensembles, sentimentally effective. (In addition, he wrote many songs using Irish airs and many settings of words by figures in the Irish Literary Renaissance such as Alfred Perceval Graves.) Stanford's work oscillates between the music of his native land and the predominantly Brahmsian style of continental Europe. It is explicit in the slow movement, entitled 'Caoine' [lament], of his clarinet sonata, giving an unmistakeably Irish flavour to what is certainly a very Brahmsian work.

---

41 Boydell's film scores were (for Patrick Carey) *Yeats Country* (1965), *Mists of Time* (1967) and *Errigal* (1968) and (for Vincent Corcoran) *Ireland* (1965). **42** 'In part at least I rid myself of the sway of Wagner and Strauss and began to write Irishly, using figures and melodies of a definitely Celtic curve, an idiom which in the end was so much second nature to me that many works of mine have been called Irish or Celtic when I supposed them to be purely personal to the British composer, Arnold Bax': A. Bax, *Farewell my youth* (1992), p. 41. **43** Stanford was severely criticised for stealing a motif from Brahms for the opening of the third movement of the symphony. Brahms's fourth symphony was performed in 1886, Stanford's third the following year. But Stanford rejected the criticism, explaining that he had found the motif in the Petrie collection of folksong as a 'Lament for the Sons of Usnach': *Pages from an unwritten diary* (1914), pp. 262–3.

Harty's output, by contrast, was far more limited, but his own 'Irish' Symphony (1904) and his tone poem 'With the Wild Geese' (1910) – the latter of which would be frequently played by the Radio Éireann orchestras over the years – display a more deeply felt sense of Irishness, contrasted with Stanford's employment of Irish material as a more routinely regional phenomenon: that is, when Stanford wrote 'Irishly' he regarded Ireland as a region; when Harty wrote 'Irishly' he regarded Ireland as a country.

But perhaps the most inexplicable fact of Irish music education and music-making in the twentieth century is that there appears to have been almost no attempt to utilise, as an educational tool, the much vaunted stock of folk music in the same fashion as that adopted in Hungary by Bartók and Kodály, the latter giving his name to a 'method' which originated in 1925, and which he expressed as follows:

> If the child is not filled at least once by the life giving stream of good music during the most susceptible period – between his sixth and sixteenth years – it will hardly be of any use to him later on. Often a single experience will open the young soul to music for a whole lifetime. This experience cannot be left to chance; it is the duty of the school to provide it.[44]

Much lip service has been paid in Ireland to this method of inculcating an awareness, even a love, of music by means of the folk songs of one's own country, but the effective refusal to implement it, despite the availability of radio (with, from 1943, Cór Radio Éireann and from 1953 the RÉ Singers – see below, chapter 5) as a vehicle for its dissemination, amounts to a display of post-colonial embarrassment at the expense of the Irish heritage. As Frederick May would write in 1952, 'It is doubtful if any nation with such a wonderful storehouse of traditional music has made such a negligible contribution to art music as we have'[45] – that is, not only was such a storehouse a source of educational material, but also a means by which to create 'art music'. Yet May (perhaps because he was conscious of his Anglo-Irish roots) did not insist that such music had to be placed at the service of any ideology: it was 'an unwarrantable premise' that 'all good music must be demonstrably nationalist in feeling'[46] –

44 'Children's Choruses' in *Selected writings of Zoltán Kodály*, quoted in *New Grove 2*, 13/722. Cf. Breathnach, *Folk music and dances*, pp. 126–7: 'It is strange that one should have to appeal to a people to become acquainted with its own music, and that folk music should have to fight for a hearing against art music ... In this great body of folk music we possess what should naturally be the basic musical language of the country. Students coming to a serious study of music should already have a knowledge of it. Without that knowledge, musicians in Ireland may compose music, but except in a purely geographical sense it is nonsense to hold that they can compose Irish music'. **45** F. May, 'The composer in Ireland' (1952), p. 169. **46** Ibid.

a point on which Bax himself appears to have agreed: 'whether nationalism in art is a desirability can be a matter for non-stop debate'.[47]

While I would not wish to push the following example to any categorical conclusion, the case of J.M. Synge points us towards an understanding of how music in Ireland might have taken a different direction at the beginning of the twentieth century, if circumstances and inclination had been in favour. Classically trained as a violinist at the RIAM, where he played in the orchestra and, under the tutelage of Sir Robert Prescott Stewart, also won a scholarship for composition,[48] Synge was actively composing both the libretto and the score of an opera, with the title (one of the oldest traceable Irish themes) of 'Eileen Aroon',[49] right up to the time that he left Ireland for study in Germany in 1893. In Germany, he discovered that his talent for music was outweighed by his fear of solo performance, and he became instead one of the leading figures of the Literary Revival and a founder of the Abbey Theatre. Otherwise his innate sympathy with all aspects of country life – speech, customs, rhythms – and his considerable musicality might have enabled him to create operas as powerful as his own play *Riders to the Sea* was to become at the hands of Ralph Vaughan Williams,[50] as was evident in Louis Lentin's production of the opera for RTÉ Television in 1988.[51]

In 1902 Synge attended *Diarmuid and Grania*, a play by W. B. Yeats and George Moore, at Dublin's Gaiety Theatre.[52] In the interval, he heard part of the audience singing

> some of the old popular songs. Until that moment, these songs had never been so heard, sung by so many people together to the old, lingering Irish words. The whole auditorium shook. It was as if we could hear in these long-drawn notes, with their inexpressible melancholy, the death-rattle of a nation.[53]

---

47 A. Bax, Foreword to Fleischmann, *Music in Ireland* (1952). **48** Cf. R. Pine and C. Acton (eds.), *To talent alone* (1998), pp. 202–4, 207–10. One of Synge's biographers, W.J. McCormack, disputes this significance attributed to Synge: 'While historians of the RIAM are understandably keen to emphasise the extent of Synge's commitment to music, the surviving evidence does not include enough to warrant laments for a lost composer': *Fool of the family: a life of J.M. Synge* (2000), p. 84. **49** 'Eileen Aroon' – or 'Eibhlín a Rún' or 'Darling Eileen' – was the subject of a set of variations for harpsichord as early as 1746 by Matthew Dubourg, who led the orchestra at the first performance of *Messiah*. **50** For a consideration of Synge's interest in music, cf. A. Saddlemyer, 'Synge's soundscape' (1992). **51** The production of *Riders to the Sea* featured Sarah Walker [Maurya], Yvonne Brennan, Kathleen Tynan, Hugh Mackey [Bartley], Mary Sheridan de Bruin, and was conducted by Bryden Thomson. A previous radio recording (1969) featured Ruth Maher [Maurya], Minnie Clancy, Bene MacAteer, Peter McBrien [Bartley], June Croker and the RTÉ Choral Society. **52** Moore later admitted that the choice of Edward Elgar as the composer of the incidental music for the play was due to the fact that there was no Irish composer capable of the task with the exception of one living in Paris – the reference was to Augusta Holmès. **53** Quoted

Synge's recollection is poignant for two reasons: firstly, because, like Petrie before him, he believed that this form of expression was symbolic not only of the 'nation' but also of its extinction;[54] and secondly, because it represented the too-late advent of such an expression in a venue to which it was culturally alien – the home of so-called 'art music'.

Harry White has argued that Synge's perception acknowledged 'the metaphorical status of "Irish music" [which] almost always eclipses the actual condition of the music itself', and that the main metaphor is that of *song*[55] – a metaphor which we found Douglas Hyde employing on the opening night of Irish radio. Thus, music comes to be representative of something other than itself – or 'indentured' as both White and Ryan call it.[56]

As we shall see, all these ironies had a profound effect on the new generation of composers in Ireland in the 1930s, 40s and 50s (and even later), who might have been expected to write music in the 'European aesthetic' for performance and broadcast by the only cultural organ capable of presenting their work to the larger Irish audience – Radio Éireann.

MUTUAL DENIAL

For music, which is a social act, to thrive and develop, it requires political stability, financial security and an educated audience. None of these has been enjoyed by the music profession in Ireland for any length of time sufficient to allow a concrete infrastructure – or a significant level of creation, performance or appreciation – to develop. The various phases of political change since the mid-eighteenth century have, for example, placed a burden on music by putting it in a context in which uncertainty and anxiety are the key characteristics. So overall, each initiative in Irish musical history has been a fresh endeavour, a beginning again, to solve the perennial problem which in itself has never been adequately defined. In each case, individuals and small groups of volunteers have set out to supply a specific need which keeps asserting itself, because up to recently there has been no coherent policy on behalf of government, or the educational system or the music profession as a whole, as regards the nurturing of musical creativity, the development of a music industry or even the appreciation of music and its social role. As we shall see, whether by accident or design, RTÉ positioned itself at the centre of this serendipitous and haphazard process.

by Seamus Deane (in Deane's translation from Synge's original French text), in 'Synge and heroism' (1985), p. 62. **54** Cf. Petrie, op. cit., p. viii: '"The land of song" was no longer tuneful, or, if a human sound met the traveller's ear, it was only that of the feeble and despairing wailing for the dead'. **55** White, 'Musical constructions', pp. 258 and 264. **56** White in 'Nationalism, colonialism …', p. 259; Ryan in 'A tone of defiance', p. 207.

The greatest irony of all is that the mutual ignorance and suspicion of 'classical' and 'traditional' musicians – which we find in broadcasting as in all other artistic formats – is due in large measure to their self-descriptions. 'Classical' suggests the existence of a *canon* supported by *training* and *elevation*, and conferring superiority on its practitioners; it has cosmopolitan and class connotations. 'Traditional' suggests a less tangible and more flexible style, associated more with the countryside than the city, with informality as its main energy and with community (rather than class) connotations. Both 'classical' and 'traditional' styles of music have their own hierarchies, however. The main difference might at first be thought to be the question of *application*, since conventionally the learning of 'classical' musicianship is a matter of rigorous inculcation of rules and procedures, whereas 'traditional' musicianship is incapable of being *taught* in the same sense, because it cannot be reduced to a set of rules: the mere fact that it is not readily amenable to notation being perhaps the characteristic which separates it from 'classical' forms. It is, moreover, tragic that few can recognise the fact that both genres have their own style of musical literacy but that each is of a different order (a fact revealed in respect of Irish music by Seán Ó Riada in *Our Musical Heritage*, his groundbreaking RTÉ radio broadcasts in 1962 – see chapter 4).

As Fintan Vallely has shown,[57] the idea of classical music as a superior form of expression and subject of appreciation has been institutionalised since the sixteenth century, with the result that other forms of music, especially folk and popular music of all kinds (most notably because the grassroots nature of folk music empowers it as a vehicle of resistance), became something to be respected, and indeed feared, for their emotional and sentimental significance, something to be 'refined' before it ever reaches the palace or, in more modern times, the drawing-room and the concert hall. It is instructive to note Michael Bowles's view that the distinction between the two genres is 'unsound':

> It is not rooted in music but in politics. It germinated naturally in the days of Daniel O'Connell and then of the Young Irelanders … consciously fostered and deliberately exploited during the struggle towards political separatism … It has now reached its logical apogee … No public man, however eminent or of whatever party-political allegiance, would dare say a word against what he understands Irish music to be.[58]

Bowles's point would become crucial in the political choices to be made in the early days of 2RN, and would be manifest in Dáil debates throughout the developmental period of Radio Éireann in the 1940s and 50s.

57 *Journal of Music in Ireland*, 2/5 (July/August 2002) 14.   58 'Irish music and real Irish music', *Irish Times*, 26 March 1981.

Between the two styles, a most invidious epithet inserts itself: that of 'art music'. I first encountered this term, as a description of a particular form of music for concert performance, when the late Dr Gerard Victory discussed the nature of the many arrangements made for the RTÉ Singers by composers such as Éamonn Ó Gallchobhair, Redmond Friel and A.J. Potter. 'Art music' was an *arrangement* of a 'traditional' melody so that it became suitable for the concert platform, and was thus elevated from the indigenous genre to the artificial, classical, sphere. Such arrangements were analogous to, and cognate with, those of Hungarian folk music by Bartók and Kodály. While this may be a respectable convention and a commonly accepted epithet, the implied connotation, that certain forms of music are 'artless' until they are elevated to a condition of art is, to me, repulsive and fundamentally divisive.

Breandán Breathnach brought to the fore the essential nature of traditional music (the antiquity of which has always been stressed by the collectors) by pointing out that its 'tradition' (literally 'handing down') consists in its being passed on from one age to the next. (The anxiety expressed by Petrie et al., that its survival should be ensured for future generations, is the last gasp of such a handing down, relying as it does on an emergency action rather than an organic and systemic *transitus*.) Breathnach observed that what constituted this 'tradition' was the *heritage* of Ireland,[59] and, since it is clear that the 'classical' genre is not part of the older Irish heritage, it is disappointing that a term such as 'heritage music' was not adopted in preference to that of 'traditional', as the dominant way of signalling indigenous Irish music. When Seán Ó Riada, in *Our Musical Heritage*, introduced a recording of an uilleann piper with the words 'This is the authentic voice of the eighteenth century' there was palpable pride in his voice.[60]

Michele Esposito, professor at the RIAM 1882–1928, felt that too much lip-service was paid to 'traditional' music and not enough to the techniques and craftsmanship of the European mainstream. 'What is "Irish" music? Is Brian Boru's march Irish music? Well, give me the composer's score and I'll play it. But you can't. You can only give me a melody sixteen bars long; no harmony, no expression.'[61] One can readily understand the frustration of a classically trained Italian composer when confronted with this central dilemma of Irish music: the linear defeated by the cyclic. Charles Acton, music critic of the *Irish Times*, discussing the inclusion of traditional tunes in Harty's 'Irish' symphony, recalled Constant Lambert's similar epigram, 'to the effect that there was nothing you could do with a folk tune except repeat it louder or softer or in another way because it was complete in itself ... What of Harty's first

---

59 Breathnach, op. cit., p. 1. **60** S. Ó Riada, *Our Musical Heritage* programme 5 – transmitted 11 August 1962: RTÉ Sound Archive tape no A608. **61** *Freeman's Journal*, 19 February 1906.

movement, with "Avenging and Bright" [and] "The Croppy Boy" as first and second subjects? I must admit that for me both are such definite and strongly known tunes that I find it very hard to hear them as symphonic material rather than as two fine tunes in their own right.'[62]

Esposito – to whom Harty would have submitted his symphony for comment and approval – insisted that Irishness in music was inherent rather than acquired, and said:

> If your Irish composers use every modern device of the orchestra their music will be none the less Irish ... The music that the future will call Irish will be written by Irishmen and will be Irish by virtue of something of his race-consciousness which his music will set free – no matter what his creed or political opinions may be. They will be 'national' in the same way that Dvořák and Grieg and Brahms are national. My advice to Irish composers is to master their art as musicians to the fullest possible extent, then go back to the wonderful store of folk-melodies and build them into their music.[63]

When the late Joan Trimble first read this quotation in 1998, she told me that this expressed exactly her ambitions as an Irish composer: attempting to be Irish yet at the same time European.

Bartók argued similarly that

> in our case it was not a question of merely taking unique melodies in any way whatsoever, and then incorporating them – or fragments of them – in our works, there to develop them according to the traditionally established custom. This would have been mere craftsmanship and could have led to no new and unified style. What we had to do was to grasp the spirit of this hitherto unknown music and to make this spirit (difficult to describe in words) the basis of our works.[64]

The separatist thought in Irish music was expressed most lucidly and eloquently by two composers who were central to Radio Éireann's development: Éamonn Ó Gallchobhair (1910–82) appears to have opposed Bartók's viewpoint, asserting that 'the Irish idiom expresses deep things that have not been expressed by Beethoven, Bach, Brahms, Elgar or Sibelius – by any of the great composers',[65] and went on to say (almost as if he were replying to Esposito),

62 C. Acton, 'Harty's Symphony', *Irish Times*, 20 April 1981; Acton was reviewing the recording of Harty's symphony and 'Comedy Overture' by the Ulster Orchestra, conducted by Bryden Thomson (ABRD 1027). 63 *Freeman's Journal*, 19 February 1906. 64 Bartók, *Collected essays*, p. 332. 65 *Ireland Today*, 1 (1936).

What can the professor do with a perfect lyric like the 'Derry Air'. He can look at it, divide it into its component parts and so on, but technical analysis is useless before the complexity of its unity. All the technique of modern Europe will not achieve a thing like this lyric – its roots lie far underneath the superficiality of objective thought.[66]

Seán Ó Riada (1931–71) also commented graphically on the divided mind of Irish music in a now legendary exchange of letters with Charles Acton, when he said:

Very broadly ... there are on this small island two nations: the Irish (or Gaelic) nation, and the Pale. The Irish nation, tiny as it is at the moment, has a long, professional literary and musical tradition. The Pale, on the other hand, has a tradition of amateurishness.[67]

To Ó Riada, the concept of 'development' in a musical work was uninteresting or unnecessary, compared to the simplicity and ornamentation of the melodic line. In *Our Musical Heritage* he said:

By emphasising 'traditional' I mean the *un*touched, *un*arranged, *un*diluted, *un*Europeanised, *un*Westernised, *un*-dressed up, native, orally transmitted music which is still, to the best of my knowledge, the most popular type of music in this country ... Irish music is *not* European music ... Not alone is Irish music not European music, but it is quite remote from it. It is, indeed, much closer to some forms of oriental music than to European music. Therefore, the first thing we must do, if we are going to try and understand it, is to forget all about European music. Its standards are not Irish standards, its style is not Irish style, its forms are not Irish forms and so on.[68]

The enigmatic figure of Stanford appears here as one who might have been able to reconcile these seemingly opposing views. In 1899 he spoke on the teaching of music in elementary schools, and advocated that

What should be taught is national music, folk music, the music which since the earliest times has grown up amongst the people. Without the

---

66 Ibid.   67 Seán Ó Riada, 'An open letter to Charles Acton' in Harris and Freyer, *The achievement of Seán Ó Riada* (1981), p. 151–2. The 'Pale' was the area of Leinster, around Dublin, which was effectively under British control; those excluded from, or resistant to, the power of the British administration gave rise to the expression 'beyond the Pale'. 68 Seán Ó Riada, *Our Musical Heritage* – first programme, transmitted 6 April 1963; the extant tapes in the RTÉ Sound Archives differ in significant detail from the text of the programmes as published (Fundúireacht an Riadaigh/Dolmen Press, 1982, ed.Thomas Kinsella). RTÉ Sound Archives tape 00604.

foundation of such music, no healthy taste can be fostered. From all times it has been the germ from which great composers have come. The British Isles have the greatest and most varied storehouse of national music in existence. The English, strong, solid and straightforward; the Welsh full of dash and go; the Scotch a mixture of the humorous and poetic, full of strongly marked rhythm; the Irish is the most remarkable literature of folk music in the world – there is no emotion with which it does not deal successfully, and none has more power of pathos or fire.[69]

We must not overlook what Stanford wrote about nationalism in music: he pointed out that, in the later nineteenth century, composers began to ask wherein lay the strength, as well as the international domination, of German composers, 'what was the fundamental factor on which the Germans depended for their inspiration. And the answer', said Stanford,

> was on their 'nationality'. This led composers to a further inquiry – the perplexing search for the existence of *a musical sanction* for their activity. This search was taken up eagerly in many countries and it resulted in the rediscovery of folk-song.[70]

A 'SCHOOL OF IRISH MUSIC'?

As Marie McCarthy notes, 'Fragmented and differing definitions of "Irish" music brought major obstacles when defining a national musical image that was all-encompassing.'[71] Setting aside the question of whether one can 'define' Irishness in music, and whether an all-encompassing image is desirable, it must be observed that from the late nineteenth century onwards, a debate has been in train as to whether there should, or could, be an 'Irish school of music', or a 'school of Irish music'. In 1900 Brendan Rogers, debating under the title 'An Irish School of Music', referred to 'those who consider that Irish music should stop short in its development … who anathematise all such modern inventions as cantatas, overtures, symphonies, sonatas as … utterly unsuited to the Irish temperament and genius'.[72] Nine years later, Annie Patterson urged fellow composers to 'endeavour to work out a distinctive school of our own',[73] while in 1913 W.H. Grattan Flood concluded his *History of Irish Music* with 'the hope that ere long a school of national Irish music will be founded', quoting A.P. Graves to the effect that if that did not happen, 'we shall assuredly forfeit our

---

69 Quoted by J. Ryan in 'Nationalism and music in Ireland'. **70** C.V. Stanford and C. Forsyth, *A history of music* (1925), p. 209. **71** McCarthy, *Passing it on*, p. 111. **72** *New Ireland Review*, 13 (March–August 1900). **73** *Journal of the Ivernian Society*, 2 (September 1909).

national birthright of song; for, Antaeus-like, our musicians have lost their power since they have been lifted from the touch of their native earth'.[74] To bring such views and aspirations – irredentist, antiquarian, autochthonic, forward-looking, and ruminatory, and all powered by at least a sense of the cultural nationalism that preceded independence – into harmonious discourse has proved largely impossible, not least because of the changing nature of Irishness, or perceptions of Irishness, over the past century: as J.S. Kelly puts it, 'the developing objective reality of a nation is forever moving out of range of the subjective imagination that tries to encompass it'.[75]

The experience of division, of an unnecessary separation and separateness of the two styles, has been a chief factor in creating the mindset of modern Irish musicians, which has permeated broadcasting: John Kinsella, Head of Music in RTÉ 1983–8, told the author that

> when I began attending weekly Editorial Board meetings as Gerard Victory's Deputy and subsequently on my own behalf as Head of Music I was very surprised to encounter, fairly frequently, hostility from certain department heads towards the whole notion of having this expensive and irrelevant music thing attached to RTÉ. Some openly stated they could do better things with the money and others regarded it as something which had been imposed on the country by invaders from across the water and had nothing to do with Irish culture.[76]

The hostility may well be attributed not only to nationalist or xenophobic sentiment but also to the poverty of the Irish education system in respect of music, which effectively deprives most schoolchildren of an introduction to both Irish and non-Irish musical experience or inspiration.

Only a few composers, such as Seán Ó Riada and more recently Seóirse Bodley, Shaun Davey, Micheál Ó Suilleabháin and Bill Whelan, who feature in the later chapters of this book, have attempted to translate the experiences of either style for the benefit of the other. That expression of Stanford's, '*a musical sanction* for their activity', resonates throughout the consciousness of Irish composers attempting to find different ways of being Irish and of being composers.

Throughout its history, RTÉ has carried an implicit responsibility for sustaining all forms of music, yet it has seldom been in a position to bring them forward together, or to achieve more than a fleeting introduction of one to the other. Usually, the practical barrier has been that of training. Works such as

74 W.H. Grattan Flood, *A history of Irish music* (1913), p. 336.   **75** J.S. Kelly, 'The political, intellectual and social background to the Irish Literary Revival' (1971), conclusion, p. vi.   **76** J. Kinsella, e-mail to the author, 8 November 2003.

Rolf Liebermann's 'Concerto for Jazz Band and Orchestra' or Matyas Seiber's 'Improvisations for Jazz Band and Symphony Orchestra', (both performed by the then RTÉSO in 1979 in an ill-conceived 'Gala Concert of Symphonic Jazz'), suffered because the 'classical' players and the 'jazz' players had little common ground on which to establish a satisfactory performance.

Harry White has referred to expressions such as 'the intelligence inside sound' as 'shibboleths of Western culture',[77] where 'Western' presumably means *concerned with the European (and North American) mainstream*. Broadcasting in Ireland, as a form of education, has attempted to introduce its audiences to an understanding of that 'intelligence', as Brian Boydell indeed did in his radio talks for younger listeners from the 1940s onwards. It thus becomes possible for us to regard a shibboleth less as an exclusivist term defining 'us' and 'them' and more as an enabling persuasion. To say, as White does, that 'those edifices of Western culture which authorise the conventional understanding of music's pre-eminence play no part in the private history of most Irish men and women'[78] is to insist that the only effective means of meeting that intelligence is by way of a Western edifice, at the door of which there is a gatekeeper of fashion and tradition. He goes on to say that 'Hundreds of thousands of school-goers pass through the structures of Irish education, a significant fraction of whom might reasonably develop skills of musical perception without which a universe of intelligent sound remains inaccessible.'[79]

White's assumption is that the 'structures' are unequal to the task but, if that is the case, it does not necessarily mean that it is impossible to inculcate skills of musical perception. It does mean, however, that not only have the schools systems (put in place in Ireland by the British administration between 1830 and 1878) proved unsuited to the inculcation of 'Western' skills for the youth of Ireland, but also that the change of administration in 1922 implicitly decided that music *of all kinds* was not a priority for emergent Ireland. If there is a failure of procedure, it stems from a failure of intent and indeed a failure of imagination, at a time when the gravest decisions were being taken as to the political, social, economic and cultural future of the country.

For Harry White to have spoken in his 1995 address to MEND[80] of 'the absence of art music from the Irish mind', and to wish for the creation of an 'informed listenership',[81] is to overstate the case, since those in Ireland who can listen to 'art music' will inevitably remain a small minority, as they would in any other country. In her study of the Celtic Renaissance, Jeanne Sheehy paid almost no attention at all to the phenomenon of music,[82] while in *The Irish Mind*,

77 White, 'Conceptual failure', p. 103.   78 Ibid.   79 Ibid., p. 108.   80 Music Education National Debate hosted by the Dublin Institute of Technology.   81 White, 'Conceptual failure', pp. 104, 110. 82 Jeanne Sheehy, *The rediscovery of Ireland's past* (1980).

Richard Kearney and his contributors tacitly exclude the notion that music contributes to the Irish consciousness or creative process.[83] It is indicative also of the perception of music within RTÉ itself that the major ideological critique of the organisation, *Sit Down and Be Counted* by Jack Dowling, Lelia Doolan and Bob Quinn, should have ignored the subject of the station's musical policy and output, although Quinn has recently written with insight of the establishment by RTÉ of its classical music radio channel, Lyric fm.[84] Furthermore, in 2003 a multi-disciplinary conference entitled 'Re-Imagining Ireland: Transformations of Identity in a Global Context' failed to include any consideration of classical music. Raymond Deane, already fêted for his article on the status of the Irish composer,[85] suggests that 'the omission was deliberate, and raises the suspicion that classical music quite simply didn't fit in with a template of Irish identity that covertly lay behind the selection procedures for the event'.[86]

White's point, however, is more serious:

> The current projection of Ireland's musical culture ... is an emphatic repudiation of Western art music, which is a pretty stiff price to pay for the technical finesse and bravura of *Riverdance* and *A River of Sound*. I realise that it has become almost *de rigueur* to insist that all music is of the same specific gravity, but I am not persuaded by such political correctness in musical matters: almost any significant work from the art tradition renders such insistence absurd. Not that *Riverdance* should be sneezed at: snobbery will avail nothing in discriminations between different kinds of music.[87]

White would seem to be unaware of, or unconcerned by, the debate in the 'Crossroads' conference which was largely occasioned by *A River of Sound*, and oblivious to the fact that his reference to 'significant work' immediately condemns him for the snobbery which he disavows. That RTÉ should have been the forum in which both *Riverdance* and *A River of Sound* were conceived, once more points to the contentious, and potentially divisive, area in which the competing claims of musical taste are to be confronted and debated.

THE NINETEENTH-CENTURY LEGACY

During the nineteenth century in Ireland, all forms of music suffered a debilitating decline in energy and sense of direction. Throughout the nineteenth,

---

83 R. Kearney (ed.), *The Irish mind: exploring intellectual traditions* (1985). 84 B. Quinn, *Maverick: a dissident view of broadcasting today* (2001), pp. 207–19. 85 'The honour of non-existence – classical composers in Irish society' (1995). 86 'Identity on parade' (2003). 87 White, 'Conceptual failure', p. 104.

and for most of the twentieth, century, the indigenous music of Ireland was regarded as in danger of imminent extinction, so much so that in 1926 – the year of 2RN's establishment – Donnchadh Ó Braoin (a future schools' inspector of music) wrote of the silence of the Irish countryside 'broken only by the quavering ineffectual sound of a shattered, forgotten and self-doubting tradition'.[88] Even as late as the 1970s, Breandán Breathnach was uttering a dire warning that the heritage was about to be lost, for want of a proper means of maintaining it – a situation hopefully retrieved (in all senses) by the establishment in 1987 of the Irish Traditional Music Archive.

If folk music was in danger of extinction, conversely 'classical' music was ever on the threshold of being born. It is no longer valid to regard the slump in the fortunes of 'classical' music as being due to the exodus of the rich and powerful following the Act of Union, since we now know that the middle classes moved rapidly to fill the places of the so-called Ascendancy, and to create and maintain a new musical tradition, with the vice-regal court as its hub.[89] But it was decidedly middle class, and its musical fare (largely oriented towards the Church of Ireland's interests) was a poor reflection of that available at the charity concerts which had enlivened Dublin in the eighteenth century.

For most budding performers and composers in nineteenth-century Ireland, exile to London or further afield was the norm, since the size of the audiences in Dublin, Cork or Belfast, and the lack of an appropriate infrastructure, severely limited the opportunities for making a living. The pianist and composer John Field (born Dublin; 1782–1837), the singer Catherine Hayes (born Limerick; 1825–61), the opera composers Michael Balfe (born Dublin; 1808–70) and William Vincent Wallace (born Waterford; 1812–65), the composer and academic Sir Charles Villiers Stanford (born Dublin; 1852–1924), the pianist, composer and conductor Sir Herbert Hamilton Harty (born Hillsborough; 1879–1941) and the singer John McCormack (born Athlone; 1884–1945) are merely the most prominent examples of Irish-born musicians whose talents could not have been sustained at home. Others include the pianists George Osborne (born Limerick; 1806–93), Arthur O'Leary (born Tralee; 1834–1919) and Michael Quarry (born Cork; 1840–1906), the composers Victor Herbert (born Dublin; 1859–1924) and Charles Wood (born Armagh; 1866–1926) and the singer Harry Plunkett Greene (born Bray; 1865–1936). Those born outside Ireland of Irish parentage such as composers Sir Arthur Sullivan (born London; 1842–1900) and Augusta Holmès (born Paris; 1847–1903) and singer Denis O'Sullivan (born San Francisco; 1868–1908) had little or no incentive to work in Ireland.

---

88 'School music' in *Irish School Weekly*, 77 (15 May 1926). 89 Cf. Derek Collins, 'Music in Dublin, 1800–1848' (1998).

One of the few composers to stay and flourish was Sir Robert Prescott Stewart, but, to appropriate White's and Ryan's term, he was 'indentured' unashamedly to what I have called 'the Protestant triangle'[90] of Trinity College, Dublin and the two cathedrals, in all of which he held the position of organist simultaneously. Almost all his works were conservative and at the service of the protestant faith, academe and the Crown. Yet if we look elsewhere there are a few examples of a close relationship between composition and the literary revival – most notably and ironically, from the pen of an Italian, Michele Esposito, the only really significant composer to work in Ireland between 1882 and 1928. Esposito's cantata *Deirdre* sets words by T.W. Rolleston, and he collaborated with A.P. Graves on the song-cycle 'Roseen Dhu' and the operetta *The Post-Bag* (subtitled 'A Lesson in Irish'). With Douglas Hyde he collaborated on the one-act opera *The Tinker and the Fairy* which had first been conceived as incidental music to Hyde's play *An Tincéir agus an tSidheóg* and was first performed in 1902 in George Moore's garden in Dublin's Ely Place, with Hyde and Sinéad ní Fhlannagáin (later the wife of Éamon de Valera) in the title roles. (At one point Esposito was working on an opera on the 'Deirdre' theme in collaboration with George Moore, James Cousins and George Coffey.)

The paucity of large-scale works is therefore due to a combination of factors: famine, emigration, the continued suppression, or at least segregation, of the Catholic population, poor infrastructure, and a small audience which, to agree with White, was *not* an 'informed listenership'. One could hardly disagree with the telling point made by Joseph Ryan: introducing a CD by the RTÉ Concert Orchestra entitled 'Romantic Ireland' he writes:

> It is perhaps not surprising that an emerging nation should look early to establish its own distinctive culture and it is equally not surprising that a people with a divided musical heritage should engage with shorter forms. This has been the Irish experience, with composers writing in the equivalent of the short story rather than the novel.[91]

We might say, with James Joyce, 'history is to blame'. As a gross simplification, the conservative, urban Protestant section of the population, whether it was unionist or separatist in political inclination, looked for its intellectual nourishment to the cultural diet of Britain and Europe, which included the mainstream symphonic, oratorio and operatic traditions (the two former dominated by Germany, the latter by Italy), whereas the nationalist, or republican, Catholic, rural section of the population looked to elements unmistakably Irish

90 'Music, place and people', op. cit., programme 6, 7 February 2000. 91 Sleeve note to 'Romantic Ireland': Marco Polo DDD 8.223804.

for its sense of identity. Both sectors, ironically, were looking to something of which they were unsure and which did not necessarily offer them what they needed. Both sectors would discover that they in fact had to invent that diet in order to sustain their ideas about identity and about where that sense of identity might lead them.

It may not be entirely true, as Harry White asserts, that Irish music was 'the absolute expression of nationalist feeling, aesthetics and culture',[92] but it *was* the way of saying that its proponents and executants were gaelic, Catholic, rural and nationalist. To espouse 'classical' music was not only a statement about education and class, but, perhaps, a way of saying that one did not wish to be associated with the culture of gaelic Ireland.

When Joseph Ryan argues that 'music became indentured to political events'[93] he is in fact eliding several arguments to arrive at such a position. It is partially, although not exclusively, true that 'composers, promoters and auditors [elected] between insularity and cosmopolitanism' in their choice of diet.[94] One could rarely effect a *transitus* between the two. Yet the argument put in such a nutshell does not allow us to see the broad range of cultural, social and political factors, nor the concomitant range of options. Nevertheless, it is fair to say that to live in a culturally and politically emergent country, with an as yet undefined but immensely potent sense of nationalism, exerted considerable pressure on the creative imagination of composers and performers as well as on the attitudes of their potential audiences, as we shall see from the anxieties of the composers featured in 'Composers at Work' (1958: see chapter 4). Nationalism not only wanted independence, but in its cultural dimension it also wanted to assert its own identity and difference. That the rejection of things English meant, in effect, turning one's back on the music of Germany and Italy was merely another of the ironies of the age.

Patrick Zuk suggests that the idea of a composer 'indentured' to nationalism might lead us to

> imagine that Irish composers worked under the expectation of producing compositions such as their counterparts in the Soviet Union felt constrained to write – paeans of praise to de Valera or odes in celebration of the Shannon Scheme, perhaps. There is nothing of this nature to be found in the work of Irish composers.[95]

This is crassly self-evident, although in later years RTÉ did commission works from Seán Ó Riada to mark the anticipated death of de Valera, and the Irish

---

92 White, 'Musical constructions', p. 257. 93 Ryan, 'The tone of defiance', p. 207. 94 Ibid. 95 *Journal of Music in Ireland*, 2/3 (March–April 2002) 27.

American Cultural Institute also commissioned a symphony from A.J. Potter (his second) to commemorate him. Yet there *was* quite definitely a constraint felt by Irish composers which endures to the present day, exemplified in the case of the Irish-absorbed Arnold Bax writing 'Irishly'. Several of the composers whose work was important to the development of Radio Éireann experienced and expressed this creative dilemma.

One of them, Aloys Fleischmann (1910–92), one of the most eminent of twentieth-century Irish composers, gave personal evidence of this dilemma when he wrote in 1936

> Unless his music is confined to arrangements of traditional tunes, or at most to sets of variations on these tunes, he [the composer] may indeed risk being classed as Anglo-Irish, even as anti-Irish.[96]

This is not an 'indenture', in the sense that Ryan and White have used the term, but it does suggest a form of mental constriction, and reveals that at the core of the cultural dilemma lay an anxiety about the nature of Irishness, and about 'how to be Irish'. The context of an emergent nation, with an emergent medium such as radio at its disposal, tied the artist to the responsibility of articulating an 'other' entity that could only be imagined because it had not yet come to be. I therefore think that Ryan is correct when he contends that

> to be clearer about what you are not rather than what you are is not a peculiarly Irish trait; it is evident in all separatist movements. But it was particularly pronounced in Ireland due to the dominance of the imported culture. Irish culture came to be defined by what it was not; it was not progressive, nor European, and decidedly it was not British. This mode of thought led to the insularity and cultural protectionism which inhibited aesthetic endeavour throughout the first half of the twentieth century.[97]

In Fleischmann's case we become aware of the ambiguities of identity. While his words of 1936 suggest that he wanted to escape the straightjacket of 'traditional tunes' – at least occasionally – one of his former students has said that his 'sense of [national] duty ... influenced his early compositions. He was firmly on the side of those (few) composers who saw Irish art music deriving its inspiration from Irish roots rather than those who looked to Europe and the exciting experiments going on there'.[98] The answer, for Fleischmann, lay in-between: 'We have on the one hand a tradition in folk-music, on the other

96 A. Fleischmann, 'Ars nova: Irish music in the shaping' (1936). 97 Ryan, 'Nationalism and music in Ireland', p. 276. 98 Declan Townsend in Ruth Fleischmann (ed.) *Aloys Fleischmann, 1910–1992* (2000), p. 54.

hand a half developed art-music which is for the most part alien ... What we need is a Gaelic art-music which will embody all the technique that contemporary music can boast and ... be rooted in the folk-music spirit'.[99]

Similar evidence of this search for the way to be Irish, or to write 'Irishly', can be found among composers from the 'Anglo-Irish' tradition such as Frederick May and Brian Boydell, who – May in his String Quartet (1936) and Boydell in his Violin Concerto (1953–4) – wrote the two works of mid-twentieth-century Ireland most committed to the international genre and most free of Irish influence of any kind. Both May and Boydell commented profoundly on the question of coming from an Anglo-Irish culture and discovering Irishness by means that were not immediately apparent or available to them in their early years. (Boydell in particular was adamant that it would have been dishonest of him to follow Stanford in writing an 'Irish' Symphony.) The fact that they expressed these apprehensions during a Radio Éireann series, 'Composers at Work' in 1958, is an eloquent mid-century mark of the use of the medium for cultural reflection (see chapter 4). Both these composers could, however, exhibit emotions, underpinned by cosmopolitan craftsmanship, which were unmistakably Irish – for example in May's 'Songs from Prison' (1941) and Boydell's 'In Memoriam Mahatma Gandhi' (1948). Boydell would subsequently recall that

> there was an accent upon what almost became chauvinism, a period during which contemporary Irish composers were expected to write specifically Irish things. It was in that connection that I coined a phrase which caused a lot of amusement, 'the plastic shamrock'. By that, I meant stuff turned out for the unthinking public ... All this sort of stuff with a pseudo-Irish flavour. If you look back at the composers of the late forties you will find that we were more or less equally divided into two camps. There were those people who were following what I might call the Stanford-Harty Anglo-Irish tradition, in which Irish folk songs were married in a curious mésalliance to Brahmsian Teutonic textbook harmony. Again there were those of us who wrote in a more international idiom. And here arises the difference between what one wants to write and what one is told one ought to write.[1]

If Irish composers were not 'indentured' to literature and nationalism, therefore, they were – and are – quite obviously and self-consciously constrained in much of their work to address a singular aspect of Irish affection which has man-

99 Fleischmann, 'The outlook of music in Ireland'. **1** C. Acton, 'Interview with Brian Boydell' (1970), pp. 97–111. Brian Boydell, interviewed by Michael Taylor in 1989, also said that 'Aloys Fleischmann ... came over to our side': 'An interview with Brian Boydell' in G. Cox et al. (eds), *The life and music of Brian Boydell* (2003), p. 80.

ifold repercussions, for which there was a precedent in literature. In fiction and drama, for example, *the land* – both as a physical space and as a spiritual, mythological presence – exercised a powerful influence on both the factual and emotional content in work stretching from Edward Martyn's *The Heather Field* (1899) through Yeats's *Cathleen-ni-Houlihan* (1902) with its irredentist celebration of 'four green fields', George Moore's *The Untilled Field* (1903) and Padraic Colum's *The Land* (1905) to Denis Johnston's *The Moon in the Yellow River* (1931) (which *was* set against the background of the Shannon Hydro-Electric installation), John B. Keane's *The Field* (1965) and Brian Friel's *The Mundy Scheme* (1969) with its plot to solve the country's economic ills by selling the west of Ireland to grave-hungry Americans as the ultimate resting-place.

Irish painters, too, sought an identity that was determined to a large extent by landscape. Thus Paul Henry (whose work has become synonymous with the landscapes of counties Galway and Mayo) combined a sense of 'national identity, the West as somehow the quintessential Irish landscape [and] the nature of our relationship to the land' as continuing, and inter-related, emotional and cultural issues.[2] For Henry and many other painters at the turn of the twentieth century, 'landscape as "place" became all important' in the 'rise of a national art, the nature of which was never satisfactorily defined'.[3] S.B. Kennedy underlines the fact that where the literary movement had a political agenda, among painters there was a 'divergence between, on the one hand, those who strove for Modernism and, on the other, those who sought a more narrowly based national art – a divergence that preoccupied Irish painting till after the Second World War'.[4] The parallel with Irish composers could hardly be more clear.

As Paul Dromey has written, in an article on 'style and authenticity' in traditional music, 'Vernacular landscapes reflected the pre-eminence of locality in the lives of people … [and] local styles of singing and playing music are essentially part of the same vernacular tradition … Development of these music landscapes probably mirrored broad topographical features in the sense that the landscape's physical features and settlement patterns conditioned the flow of people and traditions in it and through it'.[5] This would be hugely evident in the work of the early RÉ collectors and of Seán Ó Riada, as demonstrated in the regional variations of singing and fiddling in *Our Musical Heritage*.

In music the same paradigm therefore informs much of Irish composition. The continuing affective subscription to the legend of the Children of Lir is celebrated first in Moore's 'Silent, Oh Moyle', arranged by so many subsequent composers (including Ó Gallchobhair), in the opera *Sruth na Maoile* (1923) by Stanford's pupil Geoffrey Molyneux Palmer, in Harty's eponymous and word-

2 S.B. Kennedy, 'Introduction' to *Paul Henry* (2003), p. 5. 3 Ibid., p. 6. 4 Ibid. 5 In F. Vallely (ed.), *The companion to Irish traditional music* (1999), p. 389.

less suite for soprano and orchestra, and in Larchet's orchestral 'By the Waters of Moyle'. Geographical specificity is evident in Harty's 'Variations on a Dublin Air' and his 'Londonderry Air' and in the individual movements of his 'Irish' symphony; in Norman Hay's symphonic poem 'Dunluce' (1921); in Stanford's 'Cushendall' and 'The Fisherman of Lough Neagh and what he saw [Irish Rhapsody no. 4]'. There is a distinctly Irish flavour in the latter's 'The Voyage of Maeldune', while topographical dedication is continued in Bax's 'Connemara Revel', Maconchy's 'Toombeola' and Duff's 'Meath Pastoral'. Bax introduced a mythical suffusion into his tone poems 'Cathaleen-ni-Houlihan', 'Into the Twilight', 'In the Faery Hills' and 'The Garden of Fand'. More recently Seán Ó Riada's 'Banks of Sullane', Seóirse Bodley's second symphony 'I Have Loved the Lands of Ireland' (also written *in memoriam* Padraig Pearse),[6] Elaine Agnew's 'Ballyvaughan' and – to return to specific thematic inspiration – Shaun Davey's 'The Brendan Voyage' and 'The Relief of Derry Symphony' (and Kevin O'Connell's complementary 'From the Besieged City') have borne out this continuing presence not only of a *sense* of place, but of *place itself*, personified by mythical personality both general and specific. John Kinsella noted that his Symphony no. 4 (dedicated to the then RTÉ Director-General, Vincent Finn) is 'a sound sketch of each of the four Irish provinces … Munster with its high peaks and broad and fertile grasslands, Connacht with its contrasts of warmth and sharply etched horizons, Ulster where human tragedy overshadows all other impressions and Leinster where, historically, there has been such strong centralisation of the Irish psyche'.[7]

In this list of works by Irish composers, there is no suggestion (although it has been asserted to the contrary)[8] that *all* works by *all* Irish composers are 'indentured' to, or constrained by, a sense of Irishness or an inescapable devotion to Irish traditional music, but it is definitely clear that a *sense of place* is perhaps stronger among Irish composers than among composers of many other

6 The sub-title is derived from a twelfth-century poem spoken by Columcille: 'I have loved the lands of Ireland, I speak truth; it would be delightful to spend the night with Comgall and visit Canice': David Greene and Frank O'Connor (eds), *A golden treasury of Irish poetry* (1967). 7 J. Kinsella letter to Vincent Finn, 4 September 1990. In thematic terms, this echoes the structure of Daniel McNulty's Sinfonietta no. 1 (The Four Provinces). 8 In 'Music and nationalism' (*Journal of Music in Ireland* 3/5, July–August 2003) Patrick Zuk stated that I had suggested, in the cases of Bodley and Kinsella, that they 'experienced constraints to compose "Irishly"' and that 'both composers answered decisively in the negative', Bodley replying that his idea in the second symphony 'was to go back to the sources of Pearse's inspiration in Irish myth rather than simply compose a work glorifying the revolution … It is certainly not simply a piece of Irish Nationalism, unless the view is a very superficial one'. I did not, at any point, imply, or intend to imply, that Bodley was influenced by any sense of nationalism, since this would bring me into agreement with the highly debatable theses of White and Ryan discussed, and dismissed, above; rather, Bodley's statement bears out my fundamental point, that 'I Have Loved the Lands of Ireland', as a reference to 'Pearse's inspiration in Irish myth', is cognate with many other works by Irish composers which bear witness to the continuing affect of this sense of place.

societies in which identity is a less divisive and contested issue. Paul Henry offers a painterly insight: 'what always strikes me about the Irish landscape is its other worldliness. There's an air of mystery about it'.[9] The expression *dinnseanchas* (the lore of place-names) has led Séamus Heaney to speak of a 'country of the mind' in which place-names constitute a mental landscape,[10] especially for the exile, and this is evident also in the work of Irish composers.

E.J. Moeran, interviewed in 1947 by Éamonn Andrews (a future chairman of RTÉ), said that the new symphony on which he was working was inspired by the mountains of Kerry, that walking the mountains allowed him to 'think out the tunes'.[11] In the same year Arnold Bax, also interviewed by Andrews, said that the Irish atmosphere in his work was 'derived from the mountains, woods and streams of Ireland itself', and that he had learnt Irish 'in order to get to the depths of Ireland'. His favourite among his works was 'The Garden of Fand' 'which is considered the most Irish of all'. 'Is that why it's your favourite?' 'Probably, yes'.[12] One can detect, in both their expressions, that *rhythm* and *cadence* might be inspired by, or derived from, those of the rivers and mountains; of course, they might have received equal inspiration from those of Germany or Switzerland but the fact remains that one, Anglo-Irish, and the other Irish by adoption, chose these particular landscapes from which to derive, or upon which to base, their pastoral image of sound.

As Agnew said of 'Ballyvaughan', it is 'simply an expression of my experience in Co. Clare, which is one of the most scenic and beautiful counties in Ireland',[13] while Ian Wilson says of his 'Timelessly This' that it was inspired by a stone circle at Drumskinney, Co. Fermanagh, which 'provoked me to consider the events that these stones and others like them had witnessed during their long existence. I imagined celebration and rituals, and always the constancy of the presence of the stones, surrounded by, but seemingly unaffected by, a halo of passing time'.[14] And Frank Corcoran, who, as an avant-garde composer, might be expected to write outside the general corpus of 'Irish' composition, has said that 'I am a passionate believer in Irish dream-land-scape … [the] polyphony of history … No Irish composer has yet dealt adequately with our past. The way forward – the newest forms and techniques – is the way back to deepest human experience'[15] – an example of the searching for collective memory that Jung called *anamnesis*. The simplicity of Agnew's statement and the affective linguistic resonance of Wilson's and Corcoran's, indicate the range of emotions that can be evoked by the land of Ireland in the mindscape of Irish

9 Quoted in S.B. Kennedy op. cit., p. 6.   **10** S. Heaney, 'The God in the Tree – early Irish nature poetry', in the RTÉ radio series *The Pleasures of Gaelic Poetry* on cassette RTÉ MC 93, 1985; also printed in Heaney's *Preoccupations*.   **11** RTÉ Sound Archives tape no. AA5882.   **12** Ibid.   **13** In Hilary Bracefield, 'The Northern composer: Irish or European?' (1996), p. 258.   **14** Ibid., p. 259. **15** *Irish Times*, 22 September 1995.

composers – competing emotions, when one contrasts the beauty of the land with the inhospitable aspect which caused repetitive famine and emigration or the gnawing need to own the land on which one lived.

THE NINETEEN TWENTIES

By the end of the nineteenth century, musical life in Ireland was dull. An initiative to improve the opportunities for, and the standard of, performance was the Dublin Feis Ceoil. Just as the literary movement had led to the establishment of the Abbey as a playwright's theatre, to counter the crudity of the prevailing performances of melodrama, so in musical circles influential figures came together to set up an Irish festival modelled on the Welsh Eisteddfod. The Feis Ceoil in fact came from within the National Literary Society, and it was at a 1894 meeting of the Gaelic League (founded 1893) that Dr Annie Patterson urged its creation. Its early circumstances bear out the remark attributed to Brendan Behan, that the first item on the agenda of any organisation is to have a split, since some among the original founders considered that the Feis would not sufficiently protect and promote Irish musical culture, and thus led to the founding of a separate organisation, An tOireachtas; both bodies had Annie Patterson at their head. (One wonders what might have been the direction of the Feis if the original intention, to have Stanford as its President, had been realised.) By 1919 Hester Travers Smith was calling for 'a musical league' to emulate that of the recently established Dublin Drama League – apart from the RDS, the Dublin Oratorio Society and the Rathmines and Rathgar Musical Society 'we have no definite musical enterprise which we can count on'.[16]

One of the most interesting facets of the Feis was its stipulation that in the prize for composition each movement of a symphony must incorporate an Irish melody, resulting in both Esposito's and Harty's 'Irish' symphonies. The main works which emanated from the Feis, and, later, the Oireachtas and associated initiatives were (in addition to these symphonies) Esposito's cantata *Deirdre*, his song cycle 'Roseen Dhu' and the two short operas *The Tinker and the Faery* and *The Post-bag*. In addition to his symphony, Harty won prizes annually from 1899 to 1904, with his violin sonata, two string quartets, two *fantasiestücke* for piano trio, and a 'Romance and Scherzo' for cello and piano. And, commissioned by the Oireachtas, came two Irish-language operas, *Muirgheis* by O'Brien Butler in 1903 and *Eithne* by Robert O'Dwyer in 1909–10 – a tradition to be continued in commissions from the revived Oireachtas to Éamonn Ó Gallchobhair in the 1950s.[17] The indecision and divisiveness of the musical

16 'A musical league for Dublin' (1919). 17 An tOireachtas na Gaeilge was held in most years in

situation vis-à-vis national identity is demonstrated in the case of O'Dwyer's *Eithne* by the critic Harold White, who asked what reason there could be for writing an opera in Irish – a question which he answered for himself fourteen years later with his own opera, *Seán* [or *Shaun*] *the Post*.

Stanford had exhibited the frustration experienced by an Irish composer in a recently discovered letter written to his old teacher in Dublin, Sir Robert Stewart, at the time when his opera *The Veiled Prophet* – based on Moore's 'Lalla Rookh' – was being produced in Hannover in 1881: 'It is an Irishman's work on an Irish poet's story, but there is unfortunately no opening for a prophet (even a 'veiled' one) who writes opera, in his own country'.[18] And as Harty had bluntly said, 'Ireland offers [the music student] no scope'.[19] Thus the inevitable exile continued. In 1936 Aloys Fleischmann had to say that its reputation for an innate musical culture was ill-founded and, in fact, Ireland had become 'a land that is literally music-starved'.[20]

One would not go as far as Joseph Ryan, who asserts that 'even Stanford's industry does not alter the sorry fact that the nineteenth century cannot supply a single Irish work of enduring quality'[21] – but the argument about the viability of Irish composition is more accurately exhibited in the fact that in 1924 the critic H. L. Morrow said 'Ireland has not produced a single symphony of any account: not even a piano concerto'.[22] (In the same year Esposito, writing to Harty, referred to the composers of Ireland collectively as 'Vincent O'Larchet' – the implied disparagement linking the about-to-be-appointed Music Director of 2RN with the rising musical star of the day.)[23]

Music education was provided by the RIAM (founded 1848), the Cork School of Music (the first municipal school of music in the British Isles, founded in 1878) and the Municipal School of Music in Dublin, originally founded in 1890 and administered on behalf of Dublin Corporation by the RIAM (until 1905 when it was transferred to the Corporation's Technical Education Committee).[24]

The advent of the Free State meant that a training school was necessary for military music, thus creating a new source of musicians in wind and brass under the tutelage of Colonel Fritz Brase, recruited from Germany by Larchet among others, and his assistant and successor Christian Sauerzweig. Brase was to become an influential figure in Irish music-making until his death in 1940, being an outspoken member of the Radio Éireann Advisory Board in the 1930s.[25] These play-

the period 1897–1924 and was revived in 1939. **18** Stanford to Stewart, 2 January 1881 (RIAM Archives). **19** H. Harty, *Early memories* (1979), p. 34. **20** Fleischmann, 'Ars nova'. **21** Ryan, 'Nationalism and music in Ireland', p. 463. **22** *Irish Statesman*, 19 April 1924. By implication, my quibble with Ryan would include Morrow, to the extent that I would place value on Stanford's piano concerto and of course his symphonies, and on the cello concertos of Victor Herbert. **23** Quoted by Mary O'Sullivan, 'The legacy of Michele Esposito' (1991). **24** Cf. Pine and Acton, op. cit., pp. 234–43; Jim Cooke, *A musical journey, 1890–1993* (1994). **25** Brase (1875–1940) had studied with Reinecke at Leipzig, and had been sponsored by Joachim and Bruch for further study

ers facilitated the custom of augmenting the orchestras in Dublin from the military, although the problems of style, intonation and tuning would recur.

Although there was no overt intention to allow it, a class division did enter the music education system. The RIAM was, in theory, open to all, but its fees, and the fact that its classes were held in the daytime, effectively excluded working people and the less affluent. This in turn meant that its teaching concentrated on the piano, violin and voice, to the neglect of wind and brass playing in general. The discontent experienced among the leaders of Dublin's major bands, at a time of general decline in the standard of band performance, had been the chief factor in the request to the RIAM by the Corporation to establish the Municipal School, specifically for the education of 'artisans'. However, the fact that the two establishments were physically separate and that severe managerial problems made themselves evident, did little to improve this class division, which the existence of the Army School of Music reinforced. The recruitment of brass players to the Radio Éireann Orchestra was exclusively from the Army bands up to 1943 when the first civilian horn player, Frank Murphy, was appointed.[26]

Spurred on by the huge success of visits to Dublin by the Hallé Orchestra under Hans Richter in 1897, '98 and '99, Esposito established a professional co-operative orchestra of sixty-one players, the Dublin Orchestral Society, modelled on the *Società Orchestrale della Scala* in Milan, with financial guarantees from well-wishers including Edward Martyn. The first concert was given on 1 March 1899 at the Royal University, in what is now the National Concert Hall (today the home of RTÉ's National Symphony Orchestra), and in the following fifteen years it gave over 200 concerts, approximately five or six each season in the university and later the Gaiety Theatre (which would be the venue for decades for RTÉ's Subscription Concerts), and, from 1905, over twelve concerts each year on Sunday afternoons at the Antient Concert Rooms in Great Brunswick (today, Pearse) Street (adapted by the Antient Concert Society from an existing building in 1843).[27] It depended (as had all previous orchestral endeavours) on the availability of wind and brass players from the bands of the police and the army, and was to founder in 1914 when many of these were transferred away from Ireland to wartime duties. An attempt to revive

at the Royal Academy of Music in Berlin. In 1911 he became bandmaster of the Kaiser's Life Regiment, with which he performed for many heads of state, the audience for his final concert in 1917 including the Kaiser and Generals von Hindenburg and Ludendorff. In addition to a symphony and other works, he arranged and orchestrated six Irish rhapsodies, each including a number of airs and dances, three of which were arranged for symphony orchestra. Brase composed an orchestral suite in four movements, 'From my Country' which was performed by the Dublin Philharmonic in 1931, and 'Irlandia', a suite in four movements, which the Philharmonic played in 1932. In May 1935 he was awarded the title 'Professor of Music' by Adolf Hitler, the first person outside Germany to be thus honoured. **26** Later, Manager of the RTÉCO and subsequently Manager of the NCH. **27** Cf. *To talent alone*, pp. 96–7.

the orchestra in 1926–7 was frustrated by the collapse of Esposito during a rehearsal. Frederick May observed that, through the Dublin Orchestral Society, Esposito had introduced the symphonies of Brahms, 'then regarded as relatively modern', and César Franck's symphony, as well as contemporary works such as Debussy's 'L'après-midi d'un faune'.[28]

This was not the only orchestra active in Dublin but it was the only one attempting to set professional standards. In 1925 Larchet had conducted an 'Orchestral Recital' at the RDS with an unspecified orchestra, with a programme of Mozart's Serenade in G for strings, Grieg's Elegiac Melody, an arrangement of the canzonetta from Mendelssohn's string quartet op. 12, Beethoven's first symphony and, with Rhona Clark as soloist, Schumann's piano concerto. Nevertheless, it was an isolated occurrence, and Larchet had pointed to the fact that there was almost no public opportunity to hear the works of the great composers: 'Except for occasional visits from some of the British orchestras, there has been no performance of any importance or educative value in Dublin for ten years [since the collapse of the Dublin orchestra]. This means that most of the people have no knowledge of Strauss, Brahms, and the great volume of modern orchestral music.'[29] This was the climate of ignorance in which Vincent O'Brien was to attempt to introduce 'serious' music to the listeners of 2RN and to audiences at his earliest concerts.

In the later 1920s Larchet and Brase were involved in the formation of the Dublin Philharmonic as a successor to the Dublin Orchestral Society, and this overlapped the creation of the 2RN orchestra. Both required the services of extra players from the Army bands. The Philharmonic's inaugural concert in 1927 – eight months before Vincent O'Brien's for 2RN – celebrated the centenary of Beethoven's death with two performances in Dublin's Theatre Royal of his 'Choral' symphony and his Mass in D (specifically stating that it was presented in conjunction with the no. 1 Army Band), since it was both a choral society (the choral concerts being conducted by Turner Huggard) and a symphony orchestra. (See Table A for the Dublin Philharmonic Society Orchestra, 1927 and Table B for 1935.)[30]

The Philharmonic built swiftly on its initial success, with performances featuring Berlioz' 'Symphonie fantastique' and Tchaikovsky's first piano concerto in October 1927 (soloist Rhoda Coghill), Mendelssohn's oratorio *Elijah* (December 1927), Liszt's 'Faust Symphony', Richard Strauss's 'Tod und

28 F. May, 'Radio Éireann Symphony Concerts' (1952), p. 280. 29 J. Larchet, 'A plea for music' (1923). It is instructive to note, a few years earlier, the apprehension of Hugh Lane, that 'only the presence in Ireland of a representative selection of international contemporary art could ensure that the country developed its own distinctive school of painters': Robert O'Byrne, *Hugh Lane, 1875–1915* (2000), p. xi. Cf. also pp. 41, 50, 54, 58, 63, 76. 30 The soloists for the symphony were Mamie Dingle, Norah Lough, William Mulcahy and Patrick Duffy and, for the Mass, Lilian Swan, Norah Lough, William Mulcahy and T.W. Hall.

Verklärung' and the première of Harold White/Dermot MacMurrough's 'Autolycus' (January 1928), Tchaikovsky's sixth symphony and the Elgar cello concerto (soloist Ida Starkie-O'Reilly, March 1928) and, at the same time that 2RN was celebrating the event, a concert to mark the centenary of Schubert's death in 1928 with the 'Unfinished' symphony and the Mass in B flat.

Meanwhile, Harty had brought the Hallé orchestra to the Theatre Royal in March 1923 with Berlioz' 'Carnaval romain', Beethoven's seventh symphony, Richard Strauss's 'Don Juan' and a selection of shorter orchestral items including 'Siegfried's Rhine Journey' (Wagner). The Hallé was in Dublin again in January 1925, with Berlioz' overture 'Beatrice and Benedict', Brahms' first symphony, Stanford's Irish Rhapsody no. 1 and Wagner's 'Siegfried Idyll' and, later in the year, with his own 'With the Wild Geese' and Mozart's aria 'Dove sono' (sung by his wife, Agnes Nicholls), Wagner's overture to *Die Meistersinger* and Schubert's C major symphony. The following year, Harty brought his own chamber orchestra to play two concerts with works by Bach (including the double violin concerto), Mozart, Holst, Elgar (the Serenade for Strings), and Esposito's 'Neapolitan Suite' for strings.

Thus, by the time that Vincent O'Brien began to attempt 'symphony concerts' with his tiny 2RN studio band, Dubliners had already started to become reasonably accustomed to a large-scale orchestral fare for which they had been starved for the last ten years. The Philharmonic continued in existence until 1936, and its demise may in turn have encouraged Radio Éireann to put in place the series of Public Concerts inaugurated by Michael Bowles in 1941.

There were thus many inherent frustrations awaiting 2RN as it set out to provide a musical service to the Irish listener in the late 1920s. Chief among these were the lack of an orchestra, lack of adequate music education, and a dearth of composers. The major problem in Irish music education remained, and was to be the greatest obstacle to Radio Éireann's own role, as it has been in every other musical initiative in modern Ireland: the school system, or lack of it as far as music is concerned. At the same time that 2RN was being set up, Larchet said:

> Our system of music education is not merely wrong, it is fundamentally unsound. From the primary and secondary schools all the way up through the circuitous paths and byways of individual teaching and private endeavour, the whole mental attitude is at variance with common sense ... Music is generally pushed into the darkest corner of the curriculum.[31]

As a result of the lack of education, in the view of conductor and musicologist Eimear Ó Broin, 'the lack of understanding of music as a creative intelligence in Irish society' continues to impede its development today.[32] The energies of

31 Larchet, op. cit.   32 RTÉ interview 6 April 1982, RTÉ Sound Archive tape no. AA2231.

Table A: Dublin Philharmonic Society Orchestra

Inaugural Concert, 26 March 1927

1st Violins	2nd Violins	Violas
Joshua Watson	Nancie Lord	George Brett
Petite O'Hara	Mr W. Casey	Constance Bell
Edith Alton	Pearl Duffin	Mrs Heycock
Alice Brough	Maeve Gerrard	May Lord
Nora Bridge	Mabel Kenny	Mrs E.J. Little
Kitsy Franklin	Ethel Moore	Mrs Montgomery
Louie Hayden	Bridgid O'Connor	Maureen O'Brien
Peggy Martin	Moireen O'Connor	Noel Reid
Eleanor Redddy	Mrs Scott	Jeannie Russell
Gilbert Smyly FTCD	Josephine Tisdall	
Walter Starkie FTCD	Miss M. Watts	
Muriel Starkie	Miss O. White	
Lorna Thompson	Mr R. Grove-White	

Cellos	Double Basses
Joseph Schofield	Mr R. Bell
Ida Starkie	Mr W. Cheatle
Dora Alton	Mr Boardman
Miss* Dargan	Rhoda Coghill
Nora Dowse	Miss Simpson
Miss N. McLoughlin	
Miss O'Meara	
Mrs Moylan	
Mrs Stokes	
Mrs Woodworth	
Mrs Williams	

Flutes	Oboes	Clarinets	Bassoons
Corporal E. Harty	Comdt. C. Sauerzweig	Sgt. F. Ashton	Corporal R. Davies
Private T. Pim	Private J. Marshall	Private M. Egan	Private R. Persse

Horns	Trumpets	Trombones	Timpani
Corporal J. Gallagher	Sgt. T. McCurtin	Private W. Stanford	Private J. Clare
Private N. Gibbons	Private H. Tracey	Private P. Feeney	
Private M. Dolan		Private J. Cameron	
Private J. Barrett			

The exclusive use of army personnel in the wind and brass sections should be noted; Richard Persse and Nicholas Gibbons (see Table B) were to become long-standing members of the RÉSO. Of the string players, Alice Brough, Nancie Lord, Maud Aiken and Zach Lee (see Table B) would be stalwart members of 2RN/R(T)É orchestras, while double-bass player Rhoda Coghill would be the station (piano) accompanist for forty years.

*Players were often reluctant to give their first names on concert programmes. Where the first name is unknown, the prefixes [Miss], [Mrs] and [Mr] have been added to indicate gender.

the eighteenth century had been debilitated by the lacklustre nineteenth, its passion sapped rather than heightened by cultural politics. In 1926 significant pressure was thus being exerted on the direction to be taken by 2RN and its provision of music, which was not only to become an aesthetic revolution but also to elicit a series of social expectations bordering often on the political, making the development of a national orchestra a widely debated and deeply divisive issue.

Table B: Dublin Philharmonic Society Orchestra, 23 November 1935

1st Violins	*2nd Violins*	*Violas*
Nora Kiernan	Bessie O'Harte-Bourke	Maud Aiken
Alice Brough	Mrs J.W. Scott	May Lord
Miss R. Christopher	Hazel de Courcy	Mrs F.M. Montgomery
Mrs Fitzgerald Draper	Miss C. Ellard	Miss C. Bell
Mrs M.S. Heycock	Miss E. Hiland	Rita Broderick
Miss M. Kenny	Miss I. Orpen	Edith Coplin
Mrs. J MacDonagh	Miss K. Rankin	Mrs Egan
Miss E. Moore	Miss A.M. Reid	Miss E. Woods
Miss E. Mann	Mrs R. Seale	
Miss J. Murphy	Miss K. Simpson	
Miss M. O'Connor	Miss J. Tisdall	
Mrs Pike	Miss V. Wilkinson	
Miss Bloom-Pollock	Miss M. Ward	
Miss A. Stoer		
Miss L. Thompson		

Cellos	*Double Basses*
Ida Starkie-O'Reilly	Zach Lee
Mrs N. Stokes	Mr H. Bell
Miss D. Alton	Miss Simpson
Viola McCarthy	Mr J. Kennedy
Miss N. Gilbert	
Myrrha Jephson	
Miss U. Lord	
Miss K. O'Meara	
Miss Retz	

Flutes	*Oboes*	*Clarinets*	*Bassoons*
Corporal E. Harty	Private J. Marshall	Sgt. F. Ashton	Corporal R. Persse
Private P. Crosby	Private F. Slockett	Private E. Kelly	Private P. Donnelly

Horns	*Trumpets*	*Trombones*	*Timpani*
Corporal N. Gibbons	Private J. Owens	Private P. Feeney	Private J. Curtis
Private W. Somers	Private R. Gallagher	Private C. Ashmore	
Private P. Hendrick		Private J. Cameron	
Private J. Barrett			

CHAPTER 2

Making a start, 1926–46

The programme on 1 January 1926, the opening night of 2RN, was, with the exception of Douglas Hyde's inaugurating speech, exclusively musical. Music would be the predominant type of programming during the early years, and the call upon the work of the Station Orchestra would be extremely heavy. Although it was supplemented by gramophone records, dance bands, céilí bands and solo performers from all genres, as well as relays of BBC concerts (when they could be afforded),[1] the centrality of the orchestra to the programming needs of 2RN was immediately obvious. The role of the broadcasting orchestra – from the initial 'Station Trio' to the National Symphony Orchestra (NSO) – has continued to be central and contentious up to the present day.

The principal fact of the period under review in this chapter is that, whatever its internal weaknesses, P&T encountered enduring problems with the over-riding Department of Finance which restricted its attempts to grow the orchestra according to its perceived needs. This was evident from the outset. If one takes the point of view of P&T, as the department responsible for providing a varied and interesting schedule for its listeners, Finance was unnecessarily restrictive and failed to understand these needs; if one takes Finance's point of view, as the department responsible for managing a seriously sick economy, P&T was asking for far more than could be afforded or warranted. It is thus quite possible to regard the initial provision of the 'Station Trio' as incompetent and inadequate, an installation which was ill-conceived – as P&T itself would very soon admit – but it is also possible to regard the strategy of P&T in seeking increases in the size of the orchestra, and in the facilities available to it, as one of stealth, given that its requests would almost always be resisted, and usually refused, by Finance. Although Ronan Fanning, in his history of the Department of Finance, comments that 'the Wireless Telegraphy Act of 1926 [which created 2RN] illustrates the powerlessness of the Department of Finance successfully to resist new expenditure when political considerations affecting national prestige were adjudged paramount',[2] the work of P&T in growing the orchestra is a classic case of the 'art of the possible' as it strove to

---

1 For the cost and frequency of BBC relays carried by 2RN, see Pine, *2RN*, pp. 43–4, 130, 154, 158. 2 R. Fanning, *The Irish Department of Finance, 1922–58* (1978), p. 112.

establish the idea that this aspect of broadcasting was, in fact, a matter of 'national prestige'. It would be almost twenty years before P&T would explicitly acknowledge that its orchestra was 'in essence Ireland's State Orchestra'.

As Michael Heffernan, Parliamentary Secretary at P&T, was to write to his Minister, Ernest Blythe, in 1931:[3]

> The long discussion which has taken place on this matter is indicative of the difficulties of running Governmentally an undertaking of this nature which has mainly the entertainment of the public for its object ... If the persons responsible for broadcasting programmes constantly encounter unsurmountable opposition from the Department of Finance, the temptation eventually is to adopt the attitude of just letting things slide and perhaps stagnate. They will lose all initiative and resiliance [*sic*].[4]

As I have observed elsewhere,[5] the economy of the fledgling state was in such a serious condition that the Dáil was debating the establishment of a radio service, with set-up costs of approximately £10k and running costs of £20k per annum, on the very day that Ernest Blythe, as Minister for Finance, had secured a reduction of one shilling in the weekly old age pension – one of the most controversial fiscal measures in the history of the State. Blythe's determination to balance the books meant, in his words, 'carrying out the most drastic economies',[6] and when, in October 1927, Blythe himself took on the extra portfolio of P&T, the infant broadcasting service cannot have viewed its new political master with any enthusiasm.

That the Oireachtas decided, in these economic circumstances, to establish the radio station at all was an act of faith in which, in more modern terms, we might recognise the embrace of cost-benefit analysis: a recognition that the social costs of *not* having such a service outweighed the financial costs of providing it. To some, the radio service was an expensive luxury, to others a dangerous medium; townsfolk would regard it in a different light from rural dwellers; possessing a valve radio – more powerful than a mere inexpensive crystal set – was a mark of relative affluence and a possible cause of envy among neighbours.

Throughout Europe and North America, radio stations were being set up, many of them incorporating a broadcasting orchestra. The German stations had the first such – with Mitteldeutscher Rundfunk (Leipzig) in 1924, closely

---

3 Ernest Blythe held the P&T portfolio in addition to that of Finance, 1927–32. 4 Heffernan to Blythe, 27 April 1931, P&T file 119/55/2 dated 9.12.29–7.11.31, 'Advisory Committee proposal to increase personnel of Station Orchestra'. 5 Pine, *2RN* pp. 126–30. 6 DD, 3, 3 April 1924, col. 2866.

followed by Berlin in 1925; Milan, Prague and Brno followed suit in 1925 and national stations did likewise in Denmark and Finland in 1926 and 1927 respectively. Although the BBCSO was not established until 1930, an 'Augmented Wireless Orchestra' functioned from 1924, with Elgar and Harty as its conductors. In the USA, the *New York Times* reported on 14 June 1928 that 'Science is becoming musical and music is becoming scientific. When man soared, music soared with him, because the airplane provided new materials for instruments. Businessmen and engineers now discuss casually the intricacies of Scriabin or the lyricism of Beethoven because radio, as a big American industry, has centred their attention on music. Thanks to modern inventions the human ear has developed more rapidly than any other part of the body'.

In Ireland, the establishment of 2RN was succeeded briefly in 1927 by '6CK' in Cork, and although there was no official studio band, director Seán Neeson secured the services of musicians such as Aloys Fleischmann senior, and his wife the distinguished pianist Tilly Fleischmann,[7] violinist Feruccio Grossi, brothers William and Gerard Shanahan (whose family had a music shop in the city), the Army No. 2 Band with its conductor Arthur Duff, and Neeson's own wife Geraldine. On occasions he could assemble a small chamber orchestra. Grossi, William Shanahan and Duff were to feature prominently in RÉ's musical life in Dublin.

We must also remember that radio was an almost completely unknown quantity in Ireland at this time, and therefore there was considerable speculation and debate as to what its social and educational uses and benefits (or possibly its disadvantages) might be. In September 1926 the Secretary of P&T, P.S. O'Hegarty, had already sufficient insight to write to his opposite number in Finance about the status of the nuclear orchestra:

> I want to stress also a point which I have urged on you repeatedly with regard to the whole of the broadcasting undertaking, and that is that we have been in the position of experimenting with a totally new thing with no experience anywhere in Ireland [*nb*] to guide us. All proposals we make are therefore in the real sense only tentative … because we could not know until the thing had been in operation what exactly would be required, and in practice we found we required much more … than we had provided for.[8]

The lack of clarity – which seems absurd to us today, but at the time was quite understandable – led to a lack of judgement as to what resources would be nec-

7 For Frau Tilly Fleischmann, see Pine and Acton, *To talent alone*, pp. 505–6. 8 O'Hegarty to Boland [Secretary of Dept of Finance], 27 September 1926, P&T file 119/55/1, dated 27.4.26–22.1.27, 'Station Orchestra'.

essary. It is quite possible that the recruitment of a trio of instrumentalists was regarded as sufficient, simply because comparable 'orchestras' were equally small or almost so (the orchestra at the Abbey Theatre would have been a major exception to the rule).

As far as the orchestral side of the equation was concerned, the opening years of 2RN indicate an internal debate in P&T, followed by an external argument between itself and Finance, on the analysis of the cost-*effectiveness* of the musical schedule: did the provision of more players 'merely' result in a higher musical standard, at a higher financial cost, without necessarily proving that broadcasting's social needs were being ameliorated? Ironically, given today's debates on the role and value of public service broadcasting, it was the advent of sponsored (commercial) programmes which provided the necessary financial means to increase the number of players (below, p. 64).

FIRST RECRUITMENTS

Initially (and before the appointment of either the Station Director or the Musical Director), P&T (at that time, the Post Office) had 'asked for authority for three members of Orchestra "to take part in the tests"' which had preceded the opening of the station.[9] This was 'sanctioned' (a significant and enduring term) by Finance on 2 September 1925.[10] The three instrumentalists were the members of 'Clery's Instrumental Trio',[11] a salon band which played in the tea-rooms of Clery's department store in Dublin's O'Connell Street and had presumably been chosen due to its proximity to the General Post Office (which was the headquarters of P&T) and to the nearby studios of 2RN in Little Denmark Street.[12]

The employment of musicians of this genre, however musically expert they might be, was to place a question mark over the assumptions upon which O'Hegarty's 'tentative proposals' were based. In 1930, when the trio had expanded to a sextet, the Station Director, Séamus Clandillon, would write to O'Hegarty in support of an increase in numbers:

> We must be able to offer the people something better than we have been doing up to the present. I do not mean this as in any way a disparagement of the work done by our very capable sextet. Still the fact remains that in practically any London café, and even in some Dublin restau-

9 Post Office letter of 4 August 1925: no longer extant, reference in P&T letter to Finance, 23 June 1926, file 119/55/1; for the tests, see R. Pine, *2RN*, pp. 142–5. 10 Finance letter to P&T F.81/1/25: evidence as in note 9. 11 Aileen Doyle, Bessie O'Harte Burke and Chrissie Fagan – Doyle and Fagan would become members of the RÉ orchestra. 12 Cf. Pine, *2RN*, p. 142.

rants it is possible to get a band of the same strength and combination as the Dublin Station Orchestra. After four and a half years working, we should be able to get beyond the strength of a café band.[13]

In the 1930s, a similar argument would be adduced to justify the expansion of the Station Orchestra to 19, 23 and 39 players, in 1947 to warrant its reconstitution as a Symphony Orchestra of 62 players, and in the 1980s to make the case for the establishment of the NSO, with 93 players, an expansion from the RTÉ Symphony's then complement of 72.

Clandillon had been appointed Director in November 1925 at a salary of £750, a month after Vincent O'Brien had been appointed to the part-time post of Musical Director at a salary of £400.[14] O'Brien was one of the most noted musicians in Ireland at the time,[15] deeply involved with the Palestrina Choir at Dublin's Pro-Cathedral, and a trainer of voices such as John McCormack and James Joyce.[16] His duties consisted of selecting the music programmes for the orchestra (in conjunction with the leader), selecting the performers (vocal and instrumental soloists and ensembles), part-time rehearsing and conducting and, as the orchestra expanded, adjudicating on auditions. The fact that O'Brien's was a part-time post was to be a source of serious operational problems both for himself and for the organisation.

The original Station Trio, renamed one month later as 'Station Orchestra',[17] consisted of Rosalind Dowse and Frederick Treacy (violins) and Viola O'Connor (cello). On 8 January (one week after transmission started) P&T, immediately realising that the trio was insufficient for its needs, requested and obtained the extra post of Pianist who also became leader,[18] Vincent O'Brien having previously stated that 'the Orchestra should consist of four as a minimum'.[19] Unlike the situation with a conventional symphony orchestra, the piano was an essential component in this small band, since it added weight to the thin string sound and, by means of transcription, supplied the missing orchestral tone of the wind and brass instruments. This addition represented the beginning of the process in which the ball would be tossed

13 Clandillon to O'Hegarty 14 June 1930, P&T file 119/55/2. **14** Cf. Pine, *2RN*, pp. 138–40. **15** Cf. Pine, *2RN*, pp. 138–9. **16** In 1902, when McCormack was eighteen, he 'walked into his choir in the Pro-Cathedral ... and I asked Mr O'Brien to allow me to sing for him with a view to obtaining a place in the cathedral choir. I sang *Believe Me, If All Those Endearing Young Charms*. When I had finished, Mr O'Brien said "You'll do"'. Quoted by Liam McAuley, 'An Irishman's Diary', *Irish Times*, 1 May 1998; of Joyce, O'Brien said 'a lovely tenor, before turning to writing' (ibid.). **17** The ensemble would go by various names – such as 'The Radio Éireann Orchestra', or the 'Dublin Station Orchestra' – none of which was officially sanctioned, until its transformation as the 'Radio Éireann Symphony Orchestra' in 1948. **18** P&T to Finance P.7445/24, and Finance to P&T file153/11/25: no longer extant: reference in Finance to P&T 17 May 1926, E.78/5/25, file 119/55/1, 'Station Orchestra – 27.4.26–22.1.27'. **19** P&T to Finance, 8 January 1926: reference in P&T to Finance, 23 June 1926, ibid.

backwards and forwards between the two departments on the issue of what had or had not been authorised in relation to the orchestra and what was, or was not, a musical necessity. Mindful of its responsibility for fiscal rectitude, Finance would immediately maintain that this authority was the basis of 2RN's musical output, thus occasioning an inaugural row between itself and P&T that would continue for decades.

The pianist-leader was Kitty O'Doherty, from Derry. However, in March it was recognised that, whatever about her musical skills, which were considerable, she was not a satisfactory leader, and the position of leader was transferred from 1 May 1926 to Viola O'Connor's sister, Terry, a violinist who had joined the band to replace Frederick Treacy on 20 March, thus making the leader's position as first violinist as conventional as in most orchestras. O'Hegarty wrote 'even to a philistine like myself she does appear to be a musician of much more than average capacity'.[20] A former member of the cinema orchestras at the Bohemian Picture House in Phibsboro and, from 1925, at the Capitol, Terry O'Connor remained as leader of the RÉ orchestra until 1945, a formidable figure who went on to maintain her central place in music-making in Ireland as founder of the Dublin String Orchestra in 1939, and as conductor of the R&R until her retirement in 1976 at the age of seventy-eight. Kitty O'Doherty remained as pianist-accompanist until 1939, when she was succeeded by the legendary Rhoda Coghill, but she continued to be in constant demand as an accompanist for studio recordings for many years.

The 'tentative' or 'guesswork' nature of the original assumptions is borne out by the fact that the Leader and Pianist had at first been engaged on a salary of £4.10.0 and it had immediately been realised that they would be required to work far longer hours than the other members of the orchestra and should therefore command a higher salary. They were now to be paid £7.10.0 in respect of a 36-hour week, and the second violinist and cellist received £4.10.0 in respect of a 21-hour week. In addition to the superiority of the leader's position, her extra pay was in respect of assisting the Music Director in a librarian capacity. O'Hegarty stated 'it would not be practicable to replace her unless by engaging the services of a cross-Channel Artiste at a high figure'.[21] In the case of the pianist-accompanist, the extra hours and pay reflected the fact that she was also required to play for solo recitalists and as *répétiteur* for opera choruses. But Finance seemed unwilling to acknowledge the enormous workload of the leader of the orchestra as well as that of the part-time Musical Director: 'The Minister observes that it is proposed that the leader of the Orchestra should act also as an assistant to the Musical Director and that the salary of the

20 P&T to Finance, 12 October 1926; P.S.O'Hegarty to Terry O'Connor, 12 January 1927, ibid.
21 O'Hegarty to Boland (draft) on P&T file 119/55/1.

leader should be increased. The Minister is not satisfied on the information before him that this post is necessary'.[22]

O'Hegarty had to plead with Finance for the necessary increase:

> I quite appreciate the standing objection to increasing a Civil Servant's salary within a year of his engagement, but that objection cannot possibly be reasonably applied to the cases which have cropped up in broadcasting, where actual experience and circumstances which we could not possibly have foreseen have modified very considerably our ideas of what is needed. I will agree, if you like, that the first proposals might have been more carefully considered, but that cannot vitiate the necessity for the revised proposals, made after actual experience of what is required.[23]

The Secretary of Finance, H.P. Boland, added to the departmental letter rejecting the case for the increase in these salaries a handwritten postscript of some significance:

> If we begin to accept artists' valuation of their own worth as the basis of our rates of pay we will get on to a slippery slope. And once we advance pay up to a certain figure for an individual on grounds of personal merit we will never again get below it – especially where women are concerned. Some artists on their merits may be desirable: none are [*sic*] indispensable.

To this, O'Hegarty responded:

> I agree that normally we cannot be at the mercy of any employee. But in every call of life people with outstanding qualifications are in a position to insist that their outstanding qualifications shall be specially recognised, and that is particularly the case with artists. There appears to be no doubt that the acting Leader, as Leader-Violinist, and the Pianist, as Pianist-Accompanist, are at the top of their profession, are specially and exceptionally fitted for what we want, and that they will require to give an attendance of from 30 to 36 hours per week. It appears furthermore … that if we let them go we shall not succeed in getting their places filled satisfactorily at a lower figure than that which I suggest.[24]

Three months later he would warn Boland: 'The sudden resignation of any member of the Orchestra would throw the ensemble out of gear, and with the "Artistic temperament" it is liable to happen at any moment'.[25] There was no sick leave entitlement, no pension or terminating gratuity, and the annual leave

22 Ibid. 23 Ibid. 24 O'Hegarty to Boland, 27 September 1926, ibid. 25 Ibid., 7 December 1926.

of twelve days was unpaid. (The basic salary of full-time rank-and-file players in the RTÉ orchestras in 2003 was €540 per week.)

By comparison, the members of the orchestra at the Metropole Cinema in Dublin's O'Connell Street were paid £8 for a 33-hour, full-time, week; those in the La Scala Theatre, also in O'Connell Street, were less well-off, with £6.10.0 for the same hours, while those in the Grafton Cinema (in Grafton Street) fared considerably better, the leader receiving £10 and the pianist and cellist £8 and £9 respectively, for only 28½ hours. Comparability is much more difficult today, when such resident bands have all but disappeared. Indeed, the advent of talking pictures was already making it more difficult for musicians to earn a living by such means, and, as we shall see, this change in circumstances was to be felt within Radio Éireann itself.

The 2RN rank-and-file players were part-time, since it was assumed that they could earn extra money by freelance playing, outside the hours of rehearsal and broadcasting, but in effect this proved almost impossible because the dance bands and theatre and cinema orchestras in which they might have worked were in fact playing at the same time as the broadcasting station. It is a little known fact that the 2RN players had to stay on until the end of transmission each night, whether or not they were required to play, in order to perform the national anthem at closedown, and perhaps equally unappreciated that, as recording equipment did not come into use until the mid-1930s, all broadcasting was 'live'. It is clear from a comment by O'Hegarty that P&T regarded the situation as advantageous to itself: 'the salaries ... are the minima for which suitable musicians could be obtained, and from enquiries which have been made they compare favourably with those paid in the Cinemas and Theatres in Dublin'.[26] The terms and conditions of employment, as well as the salaries, would be a matter of major contention between management and players up to the end of the 1990s.

Thus when, in April 1926 (less than four months after 2RN had come on air), P&T asked for permission to increase the orchestra from four to seven players, Finance presented a stony expression. 'It is observed that ... the Musical Director was apparently satisfied with an Orchestra of four'.[27]

Not only does this letter, signed by H.P. Boland, Secretary of Finance, carry an implicit question – why, then, is an increase necessary, only three months after it was considered *un*necessary? – but it also betrays an attitude which P&T would, rightly or wrongly, interpret as contemptuous, as well as dismissive, of what it was trying to achieve:

It is noted that the present proposal to increase the number in the Orchestra from four to seven has been made in accordance with rec-

26 O'Hegarty to Boland, 27 April 1926; O'Hegarty to Boland, 27 September 1926, P&T file 119/55/1. 27 Ibid.

ommendations of musical experts. This information is not however sufficient in itself to enable the Minister to form a judgement on the proposal. He accordingly desires to know what new circumstances have arisen to warrant an increase in the number previously suggested by the Musical Director and on what grounds the musical experts base their recommendations.[28]

It would be several years, and after several changes in personnel and personalities, before P&T and Finance reached an understanding of how 'the information' should be couched so that the Minister could be satisfied on the points of any proposal.

The identity of the experts is unknown, but it is likely that they included John F. Larchet and Fritz Brase, as a member of the Radio Éireann Advisory Board – a body which would frequently come into conflict with the Department and which had already become a subject of political resistance within the mindset of the civil servants.[29]

Thus, when it came to increasing the size of the orchestra, O'Hegarty had to insist once more on the provisional nature of the planning for 2RN:

> Four was the number then contemplated, purely as a minimum, for actual working, and the Post Office letter [of 8 January 1926] ... states definitely 'The Musical Director reports that the Orchestra should consist of four as a minimum, viz. 1 leader and 3 orchestra.' It will be seen, therefore, that at no period was either three or four put forward as anything but a bare experimental minimum. In actual practice the Orchestra of four was found to be unsatisfactory and ineffective, and numerous complaints were made of the inadequacy, which the Minister found to be well founded.[30]

BROADCAST PROGRAMMES

Vincent O'Brien supplemented his orchestral items with a wide range of what one might describe as 'salon' music. A typical evening's broadcast in the period 1926–30 might be:

8.00p.m.:	Time and tuning note [to enable wireless sets to adjust to the station's frequency]
8.05:	New Gramophone Records
8.15:	Clery's Instrumental Trio with excerpts from *Carmen* (Bizet)
8.30:	Songs from Joseph O'Neill

28 Ibid. 29 Cf. Pine, *2RN*, pp. 158–62. 30 P&T to Finance, 23 June 1926, file 119/55/1.

8.40:	Orchestra: 'Hymn to the Sun' (Rimsky-Korsakov)
9.00:	Songs from Florrie Ackermann (contralto)
9.10:	Solo violin: Rosalind Dowse
9.20:	Songs (Joseph O'Neill)
9.35:	Clery's Trio, with two Irish airs
9.45:	Songs from Florrie Ackermann
9.55:	Orchestra: excerpts from *The Gondoliers* (Sullivan)
10.05:	Weather forecast

By the mid-1930s, the schedule had become slightly more varied, but not enough to quell criticism of its 'sameness'; this programme is from 13 March 1937:

5.30:	Garda Síochána Band
6.25:	The Home Doctor (talk)
6.35:	Sgáthán na nGaedheal ['the mirror of the Gael']
6.45:	News
7.00:	Aughrim Slopes Céilí Band
8.00:	Symphony Concert (conducted by George Hewson)[31]
	Programme: Overture, 'In der Natur', Dvořák
	'New World Symphony', Dvořák
	Concerto for two pianos, K. 365, Mozart (soloists Dorothy Stokes and Alice Bell)
	Legend in C, Dvořák
	Capriccio Italien, Tchaikovsky
	Irish Melody, 'The Maid of Mourne Shore'.

The succession of artists passing through 2RN's original studio in Little Denmark Street and, from October 1928, in the GPO, would have been a cross-section of musicians in Dublin City, with a small but increasing number of soloists and bands coming in from the country. As we shall see (in chapter 5), many bands came from the country at a loss, since twenty guineas was the maximum Clandillon was permitted to pay. Among the first to broadcast were W.A. Manahan's band and the Dick Smyth Céilí Trio. Dublin bands, such as the St James's Brass and Reed Band, which broadcast from 2RN as early as 1926, had easier access to the airwaves. Among classical musicians regularly in the schedules in the mid-1930s was Victor Love (1890–1946): an organist,

---

31 1881–1972: organist at Armagh Cathedral, 1916–20, St Patrick's Cathedral, Dublin (where he was also choirmaster) 1920–60, Trinity College, Dublin, 1927–72 where he was also professor of music 1936–62, and professor of organ at the RIAM.

musicologist, composer, teacher and pianist, who had given the first Irish performance of the second Rachmaninov concerto with the LSO under Harty at
Sir Stanley Cochrane's private concert hall (still extant) at Woodbrook in 1930,
he gave a noted series of Beethoven sonatas on Radio Éireann in 1937–8.[32]

Another source of talent was the RIAM, which, as soon as 2RN was on the
air, O'Brien asked to provide two one-hour programmes, the first of Bach, the
second of Beethoven – suggesting that he was at that early stage unaware of
either the students' stamina for performance or that of the listeners. Some
members of the RIAM's board were hesitant about the idea, but one, Sir John
Irwin, urged that the RIAM should allow its students to broadcast on 2RN: 'I
consider it the duty of a State-aided institution such as this to assist the
Government Broadcasting Station ... It is a favourable opportunity of appealing to a much larger audience ... and giving the Irish public generally proof
of the high standard of the teaching.'[33] The Academy's advice was taken, and
a much reduced and more varied programme resulted, with pianist Rhona Clark
(later Marshall), a leading student of Esposito, becoming on 15 March 1926
the second Irish student to broadcast.[34] She played the *andante* and *finale* from
Beethoven's 'Appassionata' Sonata, and provided the orchestral accompaniment for her colleagues Alice and Sheila Brough in the *largo* and *allegro* from
Bach's concerto for two violins.[35] Another RIAM student, Harold Hope
Johnston, sang Brahms's 'We Wandered' and Mendelssohn's 'On Wings of
Song'. In the same week, another group of RIAM students gave a second concert – the collective fee in each case was five guineas. In later years, Radio Éireann would take live relays from the Aberdeen Hall of the Gresham Hotel of
the RIAM's Student Musical Union, which gave many concerts both in public and private from its foundation in 1905.[36]

As I have noted elsewhere,[37] 2RN took relays of BBC concerts, amounting
to over thirty-five hours in 1926, but the cost of these was considerable –
£14–15 per hour – and the fluctuation in the number of hours broadcast (14
in 1927, 23 in 1928, 5½ in 1929) suggests that they were only availed of when
Clandillon had the money in hand.

Studio performances of opera in 1928–9 featured Donizetti's *La fille du rég-
iment*, Offenbach's *Les contes d'Hoffmann*, Mozart's *Figaro*, Verdi's *Il trovatore*,
and Balfe's *The Rose of Castille* (which would be the opening work of the
Wexford Opera Festival, performed by the RÉLO in 1951). Soloists frequently
included Joan Burke (half-sister of W.T. Cosgrave, and a teacher at the Leinster

---

32 For further details of Love's career, see Pine and Acton, *To talent alone*, pp. 243, 251, 352, 505.
33 Quoted in Pine and Acton, p. 362. 34 The first, Dina Copeman, had played on opening night:
cf. Pine, *2RN*, pp. 149–50. 35 Alice Brough (1905–2002) was, at the time of her death, the longest
lived student of the RIAM and the oldest surviving member of the RÉSO. 36 Cf. Pine and Acton,
pp. 322–36. 37 Pine, *2RN*, pp. 43–4, 130, 154, 158.

School), J.C. Browner,[38] and William Lemass.[39] In the mid-1930s operas in studio performance included a second production of *Les contes d'Hoffman*, Gounod's *Romeo and Juliet* (twice in 1933), Puccini's *Madama Butterfly* and *La bohème*, Verdi's *La traviata* and *Aida* (1933 and 1934), Wallace's *Maritana* and Flotow's *Marta*.

One area that provided musical controversy, and inhibited 2RN from providing a fuller schedule, was that of jazz: at the risk of repeating what I have written elsewhere,[40] it should be noted that, from the late 1920s to at least the mid-1940s, there was considerable resistance to the public performance of jazz on moral grounds – that it was un-Irish and un-Catholic – and this objection extended to its being broadcast. Maurice Gorham recalled that in 1944 a member of the Committee of Inquiry (a successor to the Advisory Committee) had 'contended that good American dance music was being kept out by the Minister's sweeping ban on "jazz and crooning"' (see also chapter 5).[41]

CONCERT ACTIVITY

Despite the small size of his 'orchestra', Vincent O'Brien was determined to provide his listeners, as well as the concert-going public, with a symphonic repertoire which far outstripped the capacity of the Station quartet or sextet. For this purpose he resorted to the conventional strategy by means of which Dublin had provided itself with such music throughout the nineteenth and early twentieth centuries – a basic band, augmented by string players (largely educated at the RIAM) and by wind and brass players who were in the military and police bands, most of whom, after independence in 1922, came from the Army School of Music and had received their earliest training at the

38 John Christopher Browner won the gold medal for bass solo at the 1904 Feis Ceoil; he sang Mephistopheles to John McCormack's Faust (in Gounod's *Faust*) on several occasions, and appeared with the Carl Rosa Company for some time; he made several gramophone recordings of operatic arias and Irish ballads. He died in 1944. I am indebted to Jonathan Browner for this information. 39 Lemass (1890–1973), a first cousin of future Taoiseach Seán Lemass, had been a boy soprano in the Palestrina Choir, had won first prize at the Feis Ceoil in 1905, and had studied opera with Vincent O'Brien, joining the Walter McNally Opera Company; he combined a professional singing career with secretaryship of the Society of the Irish Motor Industry; he was also an organiser of the Meath Hospital fund-raising concerts, a governor of the RIAM 1932–42 and President of the Bohemians. For the Dublin Operatic Society he sang in *La bohème* (Puccini), *Lurline* (Wallace), *The Bohemian Girl* (Balfe) and Valentine in *Faust* (Gounod) opposite Heddle Nash in the title role, and was later a committee member of the DGOS. He also recorded Irish songs with the Army no. 1 Band under Brase. (I am indebted to Maureen Lemass for this information regarding her father.) Thus, although neither Joan Burke nor Lemass was politically inclined, the families of the two sides of the political divide were represented in these 2RN broadcasts. 40 Cf. Pine, *2RN*, pp. 164–6. 41 M. Gorham, *Forty years of Irish broadcasting* (1967), p. 143.

Municipal School of Music. In effect, therefore, 2RN provided a minuscule band in the form of the string-trio-plus-piano for most of its broadcast output, and a quite different, *ad hoc*, orchestra for its public performances and its occasional symphonic broadcasts. It would not be until the Station Orchestra had reached a figure of twenty-three players (in the late 1930s) that it could be said to represent the core element of a true orchestra which would be capable of augmentation to a satisfactory level, but still a 'chamber' rather than a 'symphony' orchestra.

Just as the Dublin concerts by the Hallé Orchestra in 1897 and 1898 had provided a spur to Esposito to establish the Dublin Orchestral Society, so may its return visits in 1923–7 have prompted Vincent O'Brien in his own endeavours in the first public concert by the vastly augmented 2RN Orchestra on 26 November 1927, when, in Dublin's Metropolitan Hall, it performed Weber's *Euryanthe* overture, Beethoven's first symphony, Saint-Saëns' 'Danse macabre' and Respighi's ballet suite 'La boutique fantasque' (after Rossini), in addition to vocal items from Bellini and Mozart sung by Glyn Eastman (bass), 'Carolan's Concerto' played by Arthur Darley (violin), the Civil Service Choir and Séamus Clandillon himself singing Irish songs – as he had done on the opening night of 2RN.[42]

Throughout the nineteenth century, Dublin audiences – composed largely of the upper and middle classes and frequently joined by the Lord Lieutenant – had heard concerts consisting of overtures, concertos and symphonies punctuated by what we might today regard as 'light' items, usually vocal, amounting more to a 'variety' programme than a modern, solidly classical, affair. Thus the menu for this inaugural concert by 2RN indicates that musical fare had not changed in the past quarter-century and programmes bore little relationship to the conventional layout of overture-concerto-interval-symphony which predominates in most symphony concerts worldwide today.

Besides the Hallé concerts, the Dublin Philharmonic continued to flourish, so that O'Brien's brave endeavour was not entirely without competition – indeed, most of those playing in the Philharmonic would have been the players who augmented the 2RN band. In December 1928 the Philharmonic gave an all-Wagner concert; in February 1929 Nancie Lord played the Tchaikovsky violin concerto (the other works on the programme were Dvořák's 'Carnival overture', Richard Strauss's 'Till Eulenspiegel' and Beethoven's third symphony); the following month its programme included Ina Boyle's 'Magic Harp' rhapsody which was repeated in November of that year, when the amazingly virtuosic and versatile Commdt. Sauerzweig performed Weber's clarinet concerto;[43] in February

---

42 Coincidentally, the Hallé played in Dublin again in 1947, just before the creation of the RÉSO.
43 Sauerzweig was an adept performer on almost all the instruments of the orchestra, and on one

1930 pianist Jean du Chastain (who had taught at the RIAM 1928–9) played the first Liszt concerto in a concert also featuring his own 'Comedy Overture'; a month later, White/MacMurrough's cantata 'Hymn of St Patrick at Tara' had its first performance, alongside Sullivan's 'Golden Legend'. Later in 1930, Harty would return to Dublin to conduct the Philharmonic in a programme largely dedicated to Wagner, but also including a Mozart symphony and the Schumann piano concerto (soloist Fred Stone).

Other ventures by Vincent O'Brien included concerts at the beginning and end of 1928 to commemorate the centenary of the death of Schubert. That on 29 January, in addition to songs by Schubert sung by Jean Nolan, also featured Terry O'Connor as soloist in Saint-Saëns' 'Introduction and rondo capriccioso'. That on 24 November (close to Schubert's death-date of 19 November) was an all-Schubert programme, with the overtures to *Rosamunde* and *Alfonso und Estrella*, the symphony no. 3 in D, the ballet music from *Rosamunde*, a minuet and polonaise, and the 'Marche Militaire' from the orchestra; songs ('Litanei', 'Die Allmacht', 'Erlkönig', 'Du bist die Ruh', 'Wiegenlied' and 'Ständchen [Serenade]') from P.J. Duffy (baritone), and 'An die Musik', 'Nacht und Träume', 'Wohin?', 'Ave Maria' and 'Die junge Nonne' from Elizabeth Mellor (soprano), with a fifteen-minute address by Adelio Viani, the professor of singing at the RIAM, who had also sung at the Philharmonic's commemoration of Schubert.

Other programmes in 1928 featured Beethoven's eighth symphony, selections from Sullivan's *The Tempest*, Harty's 'Irish Symphony', Respighi's 'The Fountains of Rome' and Tchaikovsky's '1812' overture.

'Orchestral and Vocal Recitals of Irish Music' were also promoted by the Royal Dublin Society to mark St Patrick's Day 1929; they were held on the afternoon and evening of 18 March. Although the orchestra for these concerts was not billed as '2RN', it is a reasonable assumption that it represented a typical augmented 2RN ensemble such as Vincent O'Brien (the conductor on this occasion) employed in his own public concerts and monthly symphonic broadcasts (see Table C). They featured Harty's overture 'To an Irish Comedy' (usually titled 'Comedy Overture') and his tone poem 'With the Wild Geese', Stanford's Irish Rhapsody no. 6 with soloist Terry O'Connor, White/ MacMurrough's ballet music 'The Shepherd's Dream', harp solos by Annie Fagan, and songs: Josephine Curran sang arrangements of 'Silent, O Moyle!' (Herbert Hughes), 'A Stóirín Bán' (Larchet), 'The Little Red Lark' (Stanford), 'Song of the Leannán Sidhe' (with Larchet's orchestral accompaniment), MacMurrough's setting of Alice Meynell's 'The Shepherdess', Harty's setting

---

occasion at the Queen's Hall, London, he played (with piano accompaniment) the Mendelssohn violin concerto, the Weber clarinet concerto, an oboe concerto and a work written by himself which required him to play fifteen different instruments.

of Cathal O'Byrne's and Cahir Healy's 'The Lane o'the Thrushes' and Charles Wood's setting of A.P. Graves's 'The Cuckoo Madrigal'; Patrick Kirwan sang 'A Bhruinnillín Bheusach [Polite Little Maiden]', 'Cnocáinín Aerach Chill Mhuire [The Airy Little Hill of Kilmurry]', 'Norah O'Neale' and 'The Ninepenny Fidil' (both arranged by Hughes); Michael Gallagher sang 'The Song of the Kings' (a setting of Oliver St John Gogarty's Tailteann Prize Ode by Louis O'Brien), 'Inghean an Phailitinigh [The Palatine's Daughter]' (Hughes), 'Bán-Chnuic Éireann Óigh [The Fair Hills of Virgin Ireland]' (Hardebeck) and Stanford's setting of Winifred Letts's 'The Bold Unbiddable Child'. Of the entire programme, only poet Alice Meynell was not Irish. In later years, the Radio Éireann Light Orchestra would give an annual concert of Irish music for St Patrick's Day.

These concerts constitute an impressive display of the admittedly limited range of Irish composition available at the time, and of the use of Irish literary material by Irish composers. Harty's and Stanford's orchestral works were (and remain) major features of the repertoire (Stanford's original songs and arrangements are today becoming better known), while Larchet's orchestral setting of the 'Song of the Leannán Sidhe' is characteristic of his intimate small-scale engagement with traditional music which would become such an important feature of Radio Éireann's output, as were the many arrangements by Belfast-born Herbert Hughes (1882–1937), one of the founders in 1904 of the Irish Folksong Society. Wood (1866–1926), also Belfast-born and best known today for his Anglican church music, was in fact a prolific collaborator with Graves in the arrangement of folksong, and the presence on the programme of settings of poems by Graves and Gogarty indicates the close connection and collaboration of writers and composers in the period of cultural awakening known as the Celtic (or 'Literary') Revival. That lyrical works, traditional airs and texts by such a political writer as Cahir Healy could sit comfortably together on such a patriotic occasion as St Patrick's Day, only seven years after independence, is a sign of positive optimism about the mixed cultural heritage of the Free State.

The music critic of the *Irish Times* ('Obbligato'), reviewing the first of O'Brien's concerts, considered that the string tone was weak but that the wind players (supplied by the Army School of Music) achieved a good balance – a surprising aspect, perhaps, given that the styles of playing in the symphonic and band repertoire, as well as the pitch of the instruments, were likely to diverge significantly. Nevertheless, 'Obbligato' pronounced 'the quality of the playing in all departments was excellent and we have an orchestra that is worthy of high praise' and conveyed the fact that Clandillon had indicated that there would be further such events.[44]

44 *Irish Times*, 28 November 1927.

However, there had been a small audience, and although concerts did continue for two years, they were suspended until the advent of the Irish National Music League in 1932, when, on 1 December, in the Mansion House, the '2RN Symphony Orchestra' played Dvořák's 'Carnival' overture, after which William J. Lemass, who was becoming a popular and frequent broadcaster on 2RN, sang two songs; this was followed by Dvořák's symphony 'From the New World', harp solos by Annie Fagan and the entr'acte to the opera which had featured at the Tailteann Games of 1924, *Shaun the Post* by White/MacMurrough. After the interval came Rimsky-Korsakov's 'Sheherazade', followed by two more songs from Lemass, and Elgar's first suite of 'The Wand of Youth' before the concert concluded with the National Anthem. This concert and others,[45] described characteristically as 'Orchestral and Vocal Concerts', were organised – and subsidised – by the Irish National Music League (an initiative by baritone P.J. Duffy), which urged: 'Join the League and help to promote good music at popular prices'. Tickets were 6*d.* and the members of the League contributed £4–5 towards the costs. Maurice Gorham records that co-operation with the League ceased, due to the fact that its members were agitating for the provision of a concert hall in Dublin, to which the Government was unable to give its support.[46]

Many of the players listed in Table C would have a long association with Radio Éireann: Terry O'Connor, Rosalind Dowse and Alice Brough have already been mentioned; Nancie Lord will re-appear as soloist and leader in this and subsequent chapters. Maud Davin would resign in 1931 to become Director of the Municipal School of Music, retiring in 1934 to marry Frank Aiken, Minister for Defence 1932–45 and External Affairs 1951–4 and 1957–69; she was a long-time Chair of the RIAM in the 1950s and 60s. Chrissie Fagan, Kathleen Pollaky and Clyde Twelvetrees would be long-term members of the orchestras, and Chris Kiernan remained in the RÉ orchestras for thirty-five years. Kiernan had studied at the RIAM with Achille Simonetti; when he died in 1977 Michael Bowles commented that 'Ireland in the 1920s was not exactly the Promised Land for a young man who had to earn his crust as a professional violinist', and Kiernan was typical of his generation in that he found work in the orchestra of the Pillar Picture House where, in 1925, Harty heard him and gave him a position in the

45 For example, Thursday 7 February 1933 when the programme was: the overture to Mozart's *The Marriage of Figaro* and his piano concerto in A (soloist Douglas ffrench-Mullen); three songs from Kitty Fagan; Ponchielli's 'Dance of the Hours'; Tchaikovsky's 'Nutcracker Suite'; three piano solos (Douglas ffrench-Mullen – including Mendelssohn's 'Andante e rondo capriccioso'); Weber's 'Invitation to the Waltz'; three more songs from Kitty Fagan; 'Leslie Seymour's' Suite for Strings; Percy Grainger's 'Molly on the Shore'; National Anthem. A further concert was given on 21 March 1933. 'Leslie Seymour' was the pen-name of Seymour Leslie, a member of the Leslie family of Glaslough, Co. Monaghan, who organised charity concerts on behalf of the Adelaide Hospital. 46 Gorham, op. cit., p. 107.

Hallé. In the early 1930s he returned to Dublin because 'he and his wife thought that, everything considered, Dublin would be a healthier place in which to bring up a family' and he wanted to be part of the Irish orchestral naissance. He was the first male player to have a regular job with RÉ, and became leader of the second violins when the then octet was enlarged, besides acting as orchestral librarian. He also had his own quintet which broadcast 'café-style' music (thus in effect replacing the original personnel and repertoire of the 'studio band'), and was teaching at the Municipal School. Bowles commented that 'orchestras … tend to exist in a more or less sub-acute condition of near-hysteria, part of their normal function of purveying excitement to audiences, but they cannot exist without a leaven of players like Chris Kiernan, simple, clear-minded, steady in action, with a saving sense of humour'.[47]

Many of the others who augmented the orchestra came from the RIAM and were members of families such as the Starkies, Pottertons and Coplins who were ubiquitous presences in Dublin musical life; Bay Jellett (a sister of the painter Mainie) had her own ensemble, which for decades played at the RDS annual Horse Show. Of the wind and brass players, the vast majority (the exceptions were Adolphe Gébler, Herbert Leeming and Joseph Thwaites) were members of the Army bands.

They would also continue to appear in Philharmonic concerts, which in 1933–4 featured visiting soloists such as Australian pianist William Murdoch (1888–1942) who was a chamber-music partner of Albert Sammons and Lionel Tertis; Russian pianist Vitya Vronsky (1909–92), a pupil of Schnabel; and violinists Isolde Menges (1893–1976, a pupil of Leopold Auer) and Adela Fachiri in the Beethoven concerto, which would also be memorably performed by her sister, Jelly d'Aranyi, a few years later.[48]

This indicates that it is by no means true that the Radio Éireann concerts in the late 1920s and the first half of the 1930s were the sole orchestral fare available to Dubliners, and certainly makes it clear that the Philharmonic was providing concert-goers with artists of a significant international calibre.

ENLARGEMENT

Up to this point, the Station Orchestra had consisted of six players: the original quartet plus violinist Moira Flusk and Maud Davin, viola.[49] In November 1929

47 M. Bowles, 'Chris Kiernan, an appreciation', *Irish Times*, 17 January 1978. **48** Menges herself had been the first player to record the complete Beethoven concerto. **49** Moira Flusk was still playing in the orchestra in 1963, and had written to the Administration Manager 'I am the only orchestra member who contributed to the opening of the Broadcasting Station and am now contributing to the opening of the Televison Station!'

the Broadcasting Advisory Committee recommended 'That the Station Orchestra should be permanently strengthened' and Clandillon was asked to prepare a report.[50] (At the same meeting Col. Brase had suggested that, in addition to the Spanish and Italian language lessons being broadcast by Walter Starkie, he should also be asked to give illustrated musical lectures. It was also agreed (again, at Brase's suggestion) that there should be more dance music, with an extension of broadcasting hours up to 11.30pm on Thursday and Saturday nights for this purpose, and that the Army No. 1 Band would broadcast at least twice monthly.)[51]

The recommendation of the Advisory Committee is a useful example of what happens when wishful thinking encounters reality. Clandillon's manuscript report stated that 'For permanent augmentation of our present orchestra Mr O'Brien is of opinion that in order to preserve purity of tone and delicacy of character the strings only should be permanently augmented. In any case if brass is at any time to be introduced the strings must be augmented to preserve the balance.'[52] O'Brien proposed two additional first violins, two additional second violins, one extra viola, one extra cello and one double bass – each player would cost an extra £4.10.0 per week except the bassist, for whom £7 should be provided. The total extra cost per week would amount to £34, thus more than doubling the total cost to £71 and the total complement to thirteen.

(Clandillon's use of the word 'augmentation' is confusing, since conventionally augmentation is taken to mean temporary additions to an existing ensemble for a specific concert, whereas 'permanent augmentation' in fact meant the expansion of that ensemble on a permanent, or at least long-term, basis.)

As far as the musical quality of performances is concerned, the proposal was impeccable, but there was obviously a fundamental problem regarding quantity. Clandillon's report continued: 'Mr O'Brien considers there is no augmentation possible between this and full orchestra. He thinks this band might be brought up to full orchestral strength on two nights a week by the addition of the following instruments, to be paid for on an engagement basis £1.1.0 per engagement, or two guineas weekly each, to cover rehearsals'. These wind instruments were to be: one flute, two clarinets, two cornets (trumpets), two horns, one oboe, one bassoon, two trombones, plus a timpanist and percussionist – a total of twenty-six players, which would not be approached until 1936.

50 P&T file 119/55/2. 51 The members of the Committee were: the folksong collector, Senator Ellen Costello (Tuam), Col. Fritz Brase, F.T. Clarke, T.A. Grehan, J.J. Halpin, Sir John Irwin, S. MacNiocaill, John Ryan, C. Ó Raghallaigh, and D. O'B MacAteer. 52 Ibid. Leaving aside the question of balance between the various 'sections' of this tiny orchestra, it is worth reflecting that, even in the late 1920s it may have been possible for the microphones to convey to the radio listener a sound much more orchestral than that created in the studio. Richard Morrison (*Orchestra: the LSO*, 2004, p. 48) states that pre-1914 recordings by the LSO under Artur Nikisch were made with two first violins, two seconds, one viola, one cello and one bass, 'with the minimum of woodwind, brass and percussion'.

Table C: Musicians regularly performing in the augmented 2RN orchestra

First Violins
Terry O'Connor, *leader*
[Miss] M. Delaney
Muriel Starkie
Eleanor Reddy
[Miss] N. Bridge
Raymond Potterton
Richard Kiernan
Arthur Franks
Nancie Lord
Madeleine Mooney

Second Violins
Rosalind Dowse
[Miss] M. O'Connor
[Miss] R. Christopher
[Miss] A. Feeley
[Miss] D. Garrett
Alice Brough
[Mr] B. Wilson
Bay Jellett
Christopher Kiernan
Patrick Oakley

Violas
Maud Davin
[Mrs] M. Egan
Edith Coplin
[Mr] J. Munro

Celli
Viola O'Connor
Chrissie Fagan
Kathleen Pollacky
[Mr] W. Reidy
Clyde Twelvetrees

Basses
[Mr] R. Bell
[Mr] J. Titherington
[Mr] ? Bishop
Zachariah Lee

Flutes
[Mr] E. Harty
[Mr] P. Crosby
[Mr] F. Slockett, *piccolo*
Herbert Leeming
Thomas Browne

Oboes
[Mr] J. Marshall
[Mr] T. Clarke
Commdt Sauerzweig,
cor anglais

Clarinets
Frederick Ashton
[Mr] M. Egan
[Mr] J. O'Rourke
Adolphe Gébler

Bassoons
[Mr] R. Davies
[Mr] L. Fennelly
Richard Persse

Horns
[Mr] J. Gallagher
[Mr] R. Hendrick
Nicholas Gibbons
[Mr] J. Barrett

Trumpets
[Mr] J. Owens
[Mr] C. Hatch

Trombones
[Mr] M. Sheppard
[Mr] J. Hazlewood
[Mr] J.Reddy
Joseph Thwaites

Tuba
[Mr] T. Dunne

Timpani
[Mr] J. Clarke

Harp
Annie Fagan

Percussion
[Mr] J.Curtis

Having this band twice weekly in addition to the permanently augmented strings will mean a total extra cost of £58.18.0 per week in addition to our present weekly cost. The augmentation to full orchestra could be continued for 6 months each year, being dropped in Summer. Overtime would be payable to the string players for extra attendances over 21 hours per week. The programme on augmented nights would be mainly orchestral, and would involve the attendance of Mr O'Brien as conductor, as would also the rehearsals.[53]

Up to that time, the Station Orchestra was substantially augmented, largely from the Army School of Music, for a monthly symphony concert. Brase had suggested to the Advisory Committee that there should be full orchestra three times a week, but Clandillon's report indicates that Vincent O'Brien thought this impractical. It is not clear whether the wind and brass players (to be hired on a per-concert basis) would continue to be recruited from the Army players, and it can be surmised that the proposal also indicates the beginning of a policy of encouraging non-Army musicians.

However, in a separate memo, four days later, Clandillon spelt out the situation as regards O'Brien's existing workload:

> The difficulties against the proposed augmentation are so great as to be practically insurmountable. Mr O'Brien has at present an Opera each fortnight and a Symphony Orchestra each month. A new Opera involves twelve rehearsals for chorus and two for Orchestra and principals. At present we have 'Madame Butterfly' and 'La Tosca' in preparation. An opera already in the repertoire involves one rehearsal for principals and orchestra and two chorus rehearsals. Each Symphony Orchestra takes six rehearsals. Under these circumstances Mr O'Brien could not possibly rehearse full orchestra for two performances per week. To accomplish one performance per week, Mr O'Brien would require one rehearsal, which would mean Station Orchestra would have to be paid overtime as they in addition would have to do their two ordinary rehearsals. Outside all augmentation, Mr O'Brien thinks that the first thing that should be done is to provide a permanent bass player, with the Station strings. The services of a really competent man would come to £7 per week. This augmentation should be made at any rate. The proposal of having full orchestra even weekly would take away from the novelty of the Symphony Orchestra performance. Mr O'Brien is personally opposed to this type of augmentation under our present circumstances, and he proposes as the best solution of this difficulty that we do Symphony Orchestra monthly, and smaller full orchestra also monthly, leaving a fortnight between the performances. This would leave time for thoroughly rehearsing the music undertaken by all these combinations.[54]

53 Clandillon's report, dated 16.xii.29, is on file 119/55/2. 54 Clandillon to O'Hegarty, 20 December 1929, ibid.

(Again, there is ambiguity and confusion in the expression 'smaller full orchestra', suggesting that the administration had not at this stage decided what constituted a 'full orchestra' or a 'Symphony Orchestra'.)

This made it clear that while there was a very strong musical argument for increasing the size of the orchestra, the Advisory Committee's idea that the workload and output could be increased was unrealistic. However, with the weekly cost of the existing orchestra at £37.10.0, it was hardly likely that there would be much support for an increase of over 150%. The departmental response was immediate: 'The total increased cost would be prohibitive … It is suggested, as an alternative, that the existing Station Orchestra (five strings) remain unchanged, but that a full Orchestra, constituted as set out in your report, should be put on twice a week for six months. [This would cost approximately £700.] This is about the limit of expenditure which could be put up to Finance for sanction and, further, the increase to full Orchestra for two nights a week would probably be about as much as Mr O'Brien could handle in present circumstances.'[55] Thus we find the first explicit departmental recognition of what it could hope to obtain by way of approval from Finance for a major increase in funding.

Obviously the Advisory Committee asked for more information, as the department then provided the following three options: Plan A, doubling the existing strings, would cost £942 per annum; Plan B, growing the existing band to 'full orchestra' of 24–6,[56] would cost £2168. Both options were considered prohibitive, but Plan C, which had been agreed by both Clandillon and O'Brien in the interim, was to add a double bass, double the existing strings on two evenings and to hire full orchestra once a month for six months, which would cost a total of £528 above present costs. O'Hegarty signed this in January 1930, noting: 'Practically all Programmes depend upon the support of a good Orchestra, and the arrangements now proposed would greatly strengthen the volume and tone of the orchestral performance, and, moreover, the "doubled" strings would constitute an excellent foundation upon which to build up the "Full" Orchestra and the Symphony Orchestra'.[57]

However, this did not please the Committee, and O'Hegarty told the Minister on 3 February that

> Colonel Brase expressed his extreme dissatisfaction with the suggestion that the augmentation of the strings should be confined to two days a week, and said that from the point of view of efficiency and working cohesion of the Orchestra the arrangement would be quite useless. He

---

55 Ibid.   56 4 first violins, 4 second violins, 2 violas, 2 celli, 1 bass, 1 flute, 2 clarinets, 2 trumpets, 2 horns, 1 oboe, 3 trombones and a timpanist.   57 File 119/55/2.

said that nothing less than putting on the extra strings every night – and engaging players on a full-time basis – would be satisfactory. The financial difficulties were explained to the Committee and it was urged ... that it would be better to put forward and carry through a proposal involving only moderate expenditure than to fail to carry through proposals involving heavy expenditure .... The Committee, however, strongly supported Colonel Brase and would not accept the proposal for augmentation on two days a week. There is no doubt that from a musical standpoint the proposal for augmentation on two days is unsatisfactory, and if the financial difficulty could be overcome it would be best to go for the full time increase.[58]

Finance's response was predictable: it rejected the proposal for a full-time 'bass violin' on the grounds that the player would not in fact be needed full-time and should be hired as and when required. How Finance came to this conclusion is unclear, but it was obviously based on its own brand of musical logic, as was the following statement: 'In the view of an tAire [the minister] the appointment of "permanent" members of the Orchestra should not be encouraged as it makes it difficult to maintain the freshness and variety in production which is essential, if public interest in performances is to be retained ... In any event the rate of pay proposed is excessive having regard to prevailing conditions surrounding the employment of musicians'.[59] The increase in string players was deferred until the high-power station at Athlone came on stream, but £30 per month was sanctioned for six months for extra wind players.

Clandillon responded vigorously:

This is quite contrary to fact and to the usual practice. The oftener players work together in an orchestra, the greater cohesion and balance is obtained. For instance, in the case of our own sextet, they were really six months playing together before they became a proper cohesive unit. It is only by constant playing together that orchestral playing becomes perfected. Consequently the occasional engagement of players, instead of making for improvement, has really a weakening effect on the performance of an Orchestra, and it is strongly my view, and the view of the Musical Director, that the engagements should be permanent. The increase should be precedent to the establishment of the High Power Station, so that we may not repeat the mistake which was made at the opening of the Dublin Station of starting with inadequate numbers and an inadequate programme, merely on grounds of economy ... If we open

58 Ibid.   59 Finance to P&T, 27 May 1930, E.78/2/30, ibid.

... without being able to show a definite advance in our orchestral programmes, we are thereby inflicting a serious check on the possibility of
obtaining fresh revenue by licences.[60]

Clandillon had contacted the BBC in Northern Ireland, and learned from
Godfrey Brown, the Station Musical Director, that the orchestra in Belfast had
thirty permanent players: 12 strings, of whom one could also play drums; 8
woodwind and 8 brass, one timpanist and one harp; the piano accompanist also
played percussion and one of the three trombonists also played double bass;
another trombonist also played tuba, while the timpanist also played flute: 'we
find it very advantageous for some of the members to be double handed'. They
worked twenty-four hours per week, with six-day liability; the minimum salary
was £300 and the first horn was paid £500, plus two weeks' paid holiday, and
one month sick leave.[61] By comparison the basic pay in the Dublin orchestra
was £234, with the leader and accompanist receiving £390.

Clandillon was thus able to say that 'the rate of pay is moderate compared
with that prevalent in regularly established orchestras, and even in the present
straitened circumstances of musicians, we will not get the best musicians at
smaller rates, as the good ones will always find a place somewhere at decent
rates of pay, and we do not contemplate loading up our Orchestra with second-rate musicians'. He did not say – perhaps because it was unclear even to
him – that in any case the type of musician needed for the symphonic repertoire would by no means be necessarily found in the pool of casual players in
the city's cinemas and theatres.[62]

Armed with Clandillon's arguments, O'Hegarty was able to go back to
Finance with renewed persuasion:

An increase of the Station Orchestra is of fundamental importance to
the development of broadcasting programmes, and it is urged that the

---

60 Clandillon to O'Hegarty, 14 June 1930, ibid. 61 Godfrey Brown to Clandillon, 2 June 1930,
ibid. 62 We should not, however, dismiss the orchestras of the silent cinemas as low-grade:
Éamonn Ó Gallchobhair observed that 'People assume that music in the silent cinema was provided by a pianist knocking as much noise as possible out of a honky-tonk piano. It really wasn't
at all like that. Any cinema with pretensions had its orchestral ensemble great or small. They were
very proud of their music and they spent a lot of money on it.' Ó Gallchobhair was pianist in the
Capitol and was paid 'five times the salary of a school teacher'. He recalled that in the 1930s the
Capitol had two orchestras, an 18-strong big band and a relief band of 7. Other cinemas installed
organs which could simulate the sound and weight of woodwind. 'This was a magnificent chance
for music education. The public ... paid their shilling or 1s. 6d. and could ... hear orchestral music
from 3 in the afternoon until 11 at night. The music was taken from the ends of the earth: the
operas of Meyerbeer, music by Mussorgsky and Villa-Lobos, music from North America, Mexico,
music from Algiers, [music] by people like Gabriel Pierné ... The Grafton Cinema boasted that
their music library turned over once a year': É. Ó Gallchobhair, 'Éamonn Ó Gallchobhair remembers', 13 January 1980, RTÉ Sound Archives tape no. LAA 376.

question cannot be deferred any longer without detriment to the reputation of the Dublin Station ...There has been a decrease in licence
fees last year. That, it is believed, is mainly due to the want of programme development. If the service fails to satisfy public demand in this
respect the effect upon revenue will be serious. ... There is no doubt of
the public demand for a larger Station Orchestra. This demand has been
expressed from time to time in letters and articles in the daily press and
Wireless Journals and it is strongly and unanimously supported by the
Broadcasting Advisory Committee ...

   Whilst it is not suggested that the standard of salaries, etc. set by the
BBC should be followed here, it is evident that the BBC attaches much
importance to the value of permanent orchestras of really first class players and it is extremely unlikely that such instrumentalists can be obtained
in Dublin at lower rates than those at present being paid to the members of the 2RN orchestra.[63]

To which his counterpart in Finance retorted on the subject of advisory committees:

They are always presuming to be executive bodies and unfortunately
we find that the Departments to which they are attached are not always
sufficiently strong to resist that tendency. We are not without apprehensions that this is what is happening in the case of the Broadcasting
Station and your letter gives definite colour to the impression that in
your Department there is an inclination to adopt, as a matter of course,
what the Advisory Committee think should be done ... We have never
heard any adverse criticisms of the present Orchestra and if the symphony concerts for which we have given authority are provided once a
month we cannot see what justification there is for this other proposal.
If an augmentation of the staff of the Station could be shown to be necessary in order to maintain the interest of licence holders such would
be a convincing argument with us. But we think that anyone who follows broadcasting closely knows well that what anchors licence holders
is not what the Station gives as a regular programme every night but
what it gives on exceptional occasions. Personally, I know people who
for the sake of the football matches alone would not give up their sets
and others who will keep them on merely for the sake of hearing the
symphony orchestra once a month. It is these exceptional features in
the programme of the Station and not necessarily the regular pro-

63 O'Hegarty to Finance, 14 July 1930, ibid.

gramme from night to night which keep up the revenue of the Station. I am afraid that if we agreed now to the proposal in your letter for the employment of the seven additional instrumentalists it would, so far as we are concerned, mean recognising them as a permanent feature, because once they were in they would not be got out again. *The fact that augmentation of the Orchestra may make it better would not be a sufficient justification in our eyes, unless it can be shown to be absolutely necessary.* You could go on, no doubt, making additions in this way all of which would have to be admitted as embellishments, but from our point of view they would be luxuries.[64]

O'Hegarty's reply is masterly: not wishing to be seen as the lackey of the Committee, anxious to align himself with the prevailing wisdom among government ministers as to their irritating nature, yet determined that he can prove his case:

I have a poor opinion of the value of Advisory Committees of any kind. Such Committees when comprised of outsiders should have no voice nor place in state administered services. The Broadcasting Advisory Committee is, however, a statutory body and we must make the best of it. We do not adopt the recommendations of the Committee as a matter of course – we are most of the time explaining why we cannot carry out their suggestions – and we would not go to you on a recommendation of the Committee if we disagreed with it. In the present case the Committee is only voicing an opinion which has been held for a long time by ourselves – that a good orchestra is essential to programmes generally and that the present piano sextet is not an orchestra in the ordinary sense of the word – that is an ensemble of strings, woodwind and brass … It has exhausted its possibilities and no longer satisfies listeners whose standards of comparison have been extended by experience of the programmes of other Broadcasting Stations. We cannot get away from these comparisons and we must therefore try to improve the standard of our own programmes so far as our resources permit. I do not share your view that it is the occasional first class programme or particular programme items which listeners consider when estimating the merits of a Station. It is not the intermittent peak point of merit but the average level of merit which maintains the continued interest of listeners, and it is continued interest alone which induces people to keep on with wireless. There is no doubt whatever that the general standard

64 Boland to O'Hegarty, 3 October 1930, ibid., my emphasis.

of any Station's programme depends very largely upon its orchestra, and judged by this standard we fall short ... It lacks the variety and brilliance of an orchestra with 'wind' and its attempts to perform music which is usually scored for a full orchestra are unsatisfactory.[65]

The arrival of sponsored programmes permitted the increase. By early 1932 O'Hegarty was confidently predicting their success: 'Apart from Government policy in the matter ... the probabilities so far as concerns the advertisers are on the side of considerable development of Broadcasting Advertising. It is universal in America, it is extending on the Continent, and if we were now in a position to do so we could conclude a three to five years contract on very favourable terms for a service from the High Power Station.'[66] In the interim of the exchanges between O'Hegarty and Boland, Michael Heffernan had met the Advisory Committee, who had pointed out that a freelance orchestra of seventeen players, including wind, was being used by the promoters of sponsored programmes and had made 2RN's sextet sound ineffective. Heffernan agreed:

We look upon the existing Orchestra as ... only an orchestra in name ... Since the introduction of sponsored programmes, the Station Orchestra has, in a sense, been thrown into the shade by the larger orchestra employed by Radio Publicity Limited (the organisation which arranges the sponsored programmes). There are, perhaps, certain advantages in the competition which has thereby arisen, but there are also disadvantages which I believe will ultimately outweigh the advantages. I feel that in the end, should we decide to continue the policy of sponsored programmes, the musical side would be best provided by an augmented Station Orchestra for which a substantial charge could be made to the sponsored programme people, thereby increasing our broadcasting revenue without any additional expenditure.[67]

O'Hegarty therefore wrote to Boland proposing that an additional £930 for an augmented orchestra should be provided for a trial period, during which the players could be hired out to the sponsored programmes and thus eliminate the extra cost, and might even earn a profit. However, the question arose as to whether the existing 'band' should be disbanded and a fresh start made by a completely new recruitment, and this was to cause personnel problems of some magnitude. 'Is it intended to disband the existing orchestra[?]' asked Boland. 'If so, what is the justification for wiping out this orchestra? We have not been told that there has been any adverse criticism of this orchestra'.[68]

65 O'Hegarty to Boland, 2 January 1931, ibid. 66 O'Hegarty to Boland, 1 March 1932, ibid. 67 Heffernan to Blythe, 27 April 1931, ibid. 68 Boland to O'Hegarty, 18 February 1932, ibid.

Blythe was bound to see the financial logic of such a development, even if the musical reasons eluded him, and agreed that the increased number of players could be authorised, provided that there was no increase in the overall budget for broadcasting. Nevertheless, it was not for almost another year that the increase took place, due to the further deterioration in the economy during 1931.

By mid-February 1932, Finance was still displaying the negative attitude to the orchestra which was fuelled by far more than a concern for fiscal rectitude. The lack of understanding of the nature and function of an orchestra, which was becoming clear in the minds of those responsible for its day-to-day administration, was a major obstacle on the path of real development. 'In the sense that variety is essential in nightly programmes is it not better to have the Sextet only on some nights and a full Orchestra on others than to have the sameness of a full Orchestra every night?'[69] In reply, O'Hegarty set out yet again the complement of nineteen now required, and attempted to meet Finance half-way in respect of its persistent quest for 'variety':

> The present orchestra would not entirely disappear as a unit. Various instrumental combinations can be made up from the augmented Orchestra, e.g. String Quartette, full String Orchestra (without wind). There is no question of criticism of the present orchestra as such; the criticism is entirely of its inadequacy … It is quite unsuitable for performance of general orchestral music and the least the Station should have is an orchestra on the lines of the local BBC stations like Belfast, Manchester, Glasgow, Cardiff. At present we have during the winter with Sponsored Programmes, Operas, etc., an augmented orchestra on about four nights a week, but it is impossible to organise and to keep together an orchestra in this way. It means that the persons engaged have not regular or full time work and they must seek outside engagements as well with the result that the personnel of the orchestra is constantly changing. It is always only a 'scratch' Orchestra, here to-day and gone tomorrow, and no satisfactory standards of performance can be attained under such conditions. An orchestra must be a permanently organised unit with fixed personnel always playing together. This, to my mind, is all so self-evident that it scarcely needs explaining.[70]

Another term which caused confusion was 'combinations': it can be argued that a fixed complement of players, such as the conventional symphony orchestra, with an established balance between the various sections, was the most

69 Ibid.   70 O'Hegarty to Boland, 1 March 1932, ibid.

appropriate, efficient and musically satisfying format for (in this case) the symphonic repertoire; this, however, runs counter to the idea of a flexible use of members of that ensemble for the purposes of other repertoires. At this stage there seems to have been no concept of the Station Orchestra as a monolithic body of performers, and indeed the idea of the highly flexible use of players from a 'pool', drawn for whatever purpose, as required by a variety-led schedule, would be promoted again in the 1950s and even later.

With the Athlone high-power station due to come on-air on 1 November, O'Hegarty on 1 October was still seeking permission to undertake the new recruitment, while Finance, for its part, was continuing to ask whether this was merely an augmentation of the existing sextet or a completely new recruitment – a crucial point being the employment status of the extra players. The new Minister for P&T, Senator Joseph Connolly, proposed a termination of the existing players, who would then be eligible to audition for the new orchestra.[71] Furthermore, a gender differentiation was to be introduced in the rates of pay – a discrimination against women that would remain in force for decades: the leader and pianist would continue at £7 per week, but where the rank-and-file male players were to receive £5, females were to get £4.[72] And the standard Civil Service ban on married women was to become a formal feature of the conditions of employment:

> The Minister for Finance feels that the appointment of married women is not desirable and should be prohibited. He is prepared to recognise, however, that, having regard to the need for recruiting the best material procurable for the Orchestra there may be reasons why married women should not be altogether excluded. At the same time he is of the opinion that if married women are now recruited it will not be practicable to impose and implement a condition that women who are single at the time of appointment to the Orchestra should retire on marriage. While not wishing to press his view on this point, the Minister trusts that the arrangements for recruitment will obviate the employment of married women. If they do so, a condition should be attached in each case that the appointee will retire on marriage.[73]

Consequently, advertisements appeared in the national newspapers on 5 and 7 November in Irish and English, stating that 'Women on marriage may be

71 O'Hegarty to Boland, 1 October 1932, ibid. 72 P&T to Finance, 2 November 1932
73 Boland to P&T, 2 November 1932, ibid. In the Dáil on 9 December 1931 deputy Eámonn Cooney (Fianna Fáil, Dublin North) had asked Michael Heffernan 'if he was aware that at present the staff [of the orchestra] consisted solely of women who were comparatively well off otherwise' – DD, 40, col. 2586.

required to resign'. However, as Maurice Gorham recorded, 'there has never been a time when there were no married women in Radio Éireann. The first Woman Organiser [Mairéad ní Ghrada] was married; so was her successor [Kathleen Roddy].[74] Some of the best-known and most effective members of the staff were married women ... When the dramatic repertory company was formed ... special exemption was granted, on the grounds that some women's parts demanded the maturity that only a married woman could have; but the question of women in the orchestras caused constant difficulty'.[75]

An appointments board consisting of J.F. Larchet, Vincent O'Brien and Annie Patterson (a pioneering composer and lecturer in Irish music) scrutinised a total of 232 applications and reported that 'as the quality of the local talent forthcoming was so good, it was decided to eliminate applications from persons resident outside the country'.[76] It was the last occasion for many years on which such confidence in 'local talent' could be so sure. 65 applicants were interviewed, and among those not recommended for appointment were (for the position of piano accompanist) Arthur Duff, Éamonn Ó Gallchobhair and Victor Love, the first two of whom were to figure largely in RÉ's later output. Duff was also unsuccessful in seeking the post of organist, as was Desmond Fitzgerald, while a future leader of the RÉLO, Jack Cheatle, was turned down for a violin post.

The Minister continued his opposition to the appointment of married women by refusing to accept the recommendation confirming Terry O'Connor and Kitty O'Doherty in their existing posts, until prevailed upon by O'Hegarty who wrote: 'In [the opinion of the board] these ladies are so essential as to outweigh the objections to the employment of married women'.[77] Connolly accepted this, with the qualification 'That it be definitely understood that if & when there is available a sufficiently qualified musician to take the place of either a married woman member of the orchestra whose husband is in a position to provide adequately for her, or a woman member of the orchestra who might be termed a "Pin Money" earner, the replacement will take place'.[78] Quite apart from present-day issues of equality, the Minister's view is a salutary example of how the question of musical policy, and that of quality, might be over-ridden by a negative perception of women in the workplace.

Appointments were made, on a two-year contract, of twelve men and five women in addition to the existing leader (Terry O'Connor) and accompanist

74 Maurice Gorham records that Kathleen Roddy, who worked in RÉ 1929–54, was a singer who had won prizes at the Feis Ceoil and had recorded Irish songs for HMV: op. cit. p. 70. 75 M. Gorham, op. cit., p. 32. Even as late as 1962, Audrey Park received an automatic notification from the Civil Service Commissioners that her employment with RTÉ was terminated due to her marriage to Archie Collins (*Sunday Review*, 28 January 1962). 76 P&T file 139/58 'Orchestra – Selection Board Report to an tAire 1932 – 30.8.33'. 77 O'Hegarty to Connolly, 23 December 1932, ibid. 78 Connolly to O'Hegarty, 28 December 1932, ibid.

(Kitty O'Doherty). As Maurice Gorham wryly observes, 'the real reason for the expansion of the orchestra' was the need to be heard well abroad, 'rather than the devotion to the art of music or deference to the importuning of Colonel Brase'.[79] As we shall see, it was the reason once again in 1947, when a short-wave radio service, directed at the Irish overseas, was contemplated.

By the end of 1934, P&T could inform Finance that 'all the members of the orchestra have given most satisfactory service and as an orchestra of the present strength, at least, is indispensable for the maintenance of the standard of programmes I am to seek the sanction of the Minister for Finance for renewal of the Agreements of all the present members for a further period of 12 months'.[80] Finance, however, wished the contracts to be extended for only six months,[81] while, in July 1935, P&T itself was placing another major question mark over the status of the orchestra by announcing that the new Director of Broadcasting, T.J. Kiernan, who had replaced Clandillon in 1935,[82] 'is at present considering the general question of the organisation of the Orchestra'.[83] Kiernan had been seconded from the (then) Department of External Affairs, to which he would return in 1941.[84] During this hiatus, the employment of the orchestra was renewed on a three-monthly basis until Kiernan's proposals were submitted to Finance in January 1936.

RE-ORGANISATION

Clearly O'Hegarty had taken the opportunity of Kiernan's appointment to obtain an objective, but at the same time informed, view of the strengths and weaknesses of the orchestral establishment, and Kiernan was given an extremely clear brief:

> Please furnish your observations generally on the position in regard to the Station Orchestra – its constitution, personnel, working, programme value, etc ... The existing Orchestra of 19 (including the pianist) costs about £5,000 a year and you should please consider whether any reduction of this expenditure would be possible.[85]

79 M. Gorham, op. cit., p. 84. 80 de Brit to Boland, 21 December 1934, P&T file 119/55/4, 'Station Orchestra – Appointment of augmented orchestra of 19. Correspondence with Finance re agreements etc., 3.3.33–17.4.36'. 81 Finance to P&T, 2 March 1935, ibid. 82 For the circumstances of Clandillon's departure from 2RN, see Pine, 2RN, pp. 156, 174–5. 83 P&T to Finance, 22 July 1935, ibid. 84 T.J. Kiernan (1897–1967) was a career diplomat who had served in the Irish High Commission in London; after leaving Radio Éireann he was Irish Minister to the Vatican 1941–46, High Commissioner (later Ambassador) to Australia 1946–55, West Germany 1955–56, Canada 1956–60 and Washington 1960–64, where he was responsible for planning the visit to Ireland of President John F. Kennedy. After retirement he became director of the American Irish Foundation in New York. 85 P&T internal memo, 21 June 1935 on P&T file 119/55/5:

Four months later, Kiernan submitted a thirteen-page report. His proposals were far-reaching, utterly realistic and completely professional, and can be regarded as the founding document of orchestral policy in R(T)É. It was the first occasion on which the nature and status of the orchestra – which would grow into Ireland's NSO – had been given such clear-sighted consideration. Although he had not 'grown up' within the broadcasting structures, Kiernan was clearly aware of the background to the situation and was able to form a view as to the unsatisfactory way in which it had been allowed to develop. He would have been aware that in 1937 Finance had quashed an initiative to establish, jointly, a national symphony orchestra and a national concert hall (an initiative which O'Hegarty himself considered to be 'entirely bad'):[86]

> thirty years ago or more a case might possibly have been made for State subsidisation of public musical performances … Although interest in music must have increased enormously, public attendances at Symphony Concerts, and consequently the necessity for such public concerts, has become smaller and will continue to decline. Is it any part of the State's duty to resuscitate a Victorian form of educational recreation[?][87]

Kiernan was probably also aware of the dissatisfaction which was being publicly expressed by those such as the young and talented composer Frederick May (1911–85) who could reasonably be expected to co-operate with, and benefit from, music broadcasting. May (then twenty-five) had written 'Anyone who reflects on the present state of music in Ireland is bound to be filled with the most profound depression'. Referring to 'a state of almost complete [musical] stagnation' May proferred the view that

> Since the establishment of self-government we have been suffering from a kind of spiritual exhaustion; the ugly sisters of politics and materialism have claimed our souls, and the arts, like Cinderella, have gone unregarded. They have been thought of as, at the best, a barely tolerable luxury, and there has been no vital connection between them and the life of the nation as a whole.[88]

At the outset of his report, Kiernan went some way towards displaying an appreciation of this view, addressing the central artistic problem which was also systemic:

'Dublin Station Orchestra – Reorganisation sanctioned by Finance 6 April '36. Expenses in connection with Selection Board, and employment of Lieut J.M. Doyle as Temp Conductor, 6.4.36–29.7.36'. **86** Quoted in Brian P. Kennedy, *Dreams and responsibilities: the State and the arts in independent Ireland* (1990), p. 41. **87** Department of Finance memorandum S 101/13/36, quoted by Kennedy, ibid., p. 43. **88** F. May, 'Music and the nation'.

> The beginning and the end of an orchestra is the Conductor. The
> Conductor must be fresh and vital and be capable of taking command
> of his team and inspiring enthusiasm. The conductor's enthusiasm and
> energy are reflected in the performance of the orchestra. The first ques-
> tion to pose in relation to the Station Orchestra is not, is it big enough
> or too big, or a bad combination, or weak in spots, or badly placed; but,
> what sort is the conductor?[89]

Kiernan highlighted the chaotic method – or lack of it – by which the weekly
rehearsal and performance schedule was organised:

> Doctor O'Brien is a part-time official. He rehearses on certain mornings;
> and the leader on those occasions is Miss O'Connor. On the night of
> broadcast, Miss O'Connor may conduct, and Mr Grossi [deputy leader]
> leads. Or Miss O'Connor conducts at rehearsal, and Mr Grossi leads; but
> when broadcasting the music, Doctor O'Brien may conduct and Miss
> O'Connor reverts to her place as leader. Music is interpreted by one con-
> ductor, at times, at rehearsal, and by another conductor at the time of
> broadcast. The changes of conductor involve a change of leader. The
> entire combination is demoralised and devitalised. The conductor at the
> rehearsal must conduct the broadcast. This difficulty in the Station has
> arisen from the part-time nature of the Music Director's appointment.[90]

O'Hegarty would have been the first to agree that this systemic fault had led
to a paralysis in artistic terms, which would lead further to claim and counter-
claim of the leader and deputy leader as to status and pay. The appointment
of Vincent O'Brien could most likely not have been achieved if the post of
Musical Director had been conceived as full-time, and, given the extent of the
responsibilities and of the musical proportion of broadcasting output, it is probable that it was realised at the outset that the post should have been full-time,
but that sanction would probably been withheld.

Kiernan recognised that, while considerable kudos attached to the fact that
a man of O'Brien's musical stature occupied the post, its demands were unfair
to someone who, however talented and experienced in certain areas, was constitutionally unable to fulfil all its requirements. Kiernan referred in a most
tactful manner to the fact that O'Brien had too often taken the line of least
resistance in lightening his arduous workload:

> He is imaginative but needs to be directed ... It should be part of the
> policy of the Station to discourage the playing of easy and well-worn

89 Kiernan memorandum, 9 September 1935, file 119/55/5. **90** Ibid.

music which had become the padding in the programmes – and many of the programmes became entirely pedestrian ... The Musical Director is the key man in this important part of the work of the Station. So far, his duties have been too diversified and too hazily defined to enable this work to be begun even in an elementary way ... The conductor at rehearsals should also conduct the rehearsed work in the transmission. This alone would involve 22 hours work a week for the Director of Music. The work involved in planning and choosing suitable programmes and selecting artistes and choosing their programmes would take 20 hours a week if properly done. As a 40-hour week is not accurately described as the work of a part-time Director of Music, it is probably proper that Doctor O'Brien should economise his labour at the expense of conducting at rehearsals and broadcasts. Yet this is a highly important factor in the success of the orchestral parts of the programmes; and economy in this direction is unwise ... Doctor O'Brien is competent to [select the orchestral programmes] & 20 hours a week devoted to it (exclusive of luncheon intervals) would be well repaid. I do not think he should be retained beyond the age of 65.[91]

Kiernan identified two cardinal facts about 2RN's musical output: that it was repetitive, and that its standards were too low. In pointing to O'Brien's responsibility in this regard, he was also identifying an organisational flaw which would recur in the cases of Michael Bowles and Tibor Paul: that one person should not occupy the positions of both music director and principal conductor. Not only would the dual mandate be too onerous, but it could lead to clouded judgement and, more seriously, to conflation of powers.

Kiernan's report also emphasises (and here he may have gone somewhat outside his brief, but instructively so) that the control of live performance of 'classical', 'light' and 'traditional' music by both the resident orchestra and outside contributors was an integrated part of the Musical Director's duties, and that what the listening public heard was therefore governed by that person's choices and decisions:

> The tone of musical appreciation in Ireland can be raised through the influence of the radio but this cannot be done by drifting along the lazy line ... In broadcasting Irish music, and encouraging a fair standard of playing and some composing, it is even more important that the Musical Director should select and reject, instead of accepting what is offered.

91 Ibid. In fact O'Brien had already reached the age of sixty-five and was to remain in position for a further five years.

It is easy to fill programmes with quarter hours of submitted material, such as Traditional Fiddle, Pipes, Melodeon, and to list the players and give each a regular turn. Only the best players should be engaged, and a combination programme of, say, a traditional singer, fiddler &c. would be a better arrangement than a quarter-hour for each player. Combination programmes involve much more Station work. Many kinds of combinations can be devised but it does seem that the ideas will have to originate with the Directorate, as contributing artists have shown little imagination and initiative. The standard of broadcasting in Ireland is so low that broadcasters have become almost incorrigibly dull and repetitive and it will require an amount of effort to repair the damage which the establishment of broadcasting has caused in Ireland by lowering cultural standards.[92]

The last sentence was damning, and must be read as intentionally so. Kiernan was now the Director, and it is clear that he intended to take control of the situation and to introduce the standards and safeguards which he considered necessary, if Irish radio was to observe its public service remit. Kiernan had already acted on the question of selection of artists:

This has been done in a haphazard manner, probably partly because the Director of Music was not made solely responsible, without intervention from the Director of Broadcasting, for the choice. I have made him solely responsible; but finding repetition of artistes, some of poor-grade competence, I asked Doctor O'Brien to grade all musical contributors. In this I think he has found a difficulty, owing to his personal knowledge of the artistes as men and women rather than as artists.[93]

This suggests that Clandillon had interfered with O'Brien's choices of performers – a supposition which is probably well-founded – and it also points to Kiernan's own possible lack of expertise in this area (although, as in Clandillon's case, his wife, Delia Murphy, was a distinguished ballad singer). Kiernan was in effect arguing that O'Brien was too weak to refuse work to those he knew well, even if he knew that they were not up to standard. Approximately eighty auditions took place each month, and Kiernan reckoned that one in a hundred reached 'a mediocre standard' and that 'the remainder are definitely bad'. He was introducing a 'Newcomers' Hour', and would try to establish County Committees to weed out poor talent from among the applicants for audition. If Kiernan's figures were correct, however, they do underline the perennial

92 Ibid. 93 Ibid.

problem that was said to afflict Clandillon and O'Brien in their choice of performers: that less than one adequate performer came forward each month. As
we shall see, there would be serious problems with falling standards in performance of traditional music in particular. It did not, however, prevent importuning by young hopefuls. Clandillon once (at least apocryphally) asked what
he could do to stop persistent applications from a particular source and was
advised to respond 'Silent, O'Boyle, be the roar of thy daughters'.

Kiernan now reached his central proposal, which would mark the first major
shift in musical practice since 1926:

Proposal for the appointment of a Conductor of the Orchestra

The present position is not satisfactory. Miss O'Connor, leader of the
Orchestra, is a competent leader but not a Conductor. Doctor O'Brien
is not an entirely satisfactory conductor. As the Conductor must work
with the Orchestra for 22 hours a week and should also be free to attend
staff meetings and discuss broadcast productions and should be available when outside bands such as Brass and Reed Bands are broadcasting, his hours of work would normally be 30 per week. I recommend
that a young Conductor, qualified as such, should be appointed. It has
struck me that possibly some arrangement could be made with the
Department of Defence which would enable the Station to have the
services of a Conductor who would not remain long enough in the
Station to become stale. The suggestion is that the Department of
Defence should lend one of the younger of the Army Band Conductors
to the Broadcasting Station for one year or two; then withdraw him and
lend another for a year, or two. It seems wise to centralise in the Army
Bands the proviso of the few first-class Conductors for whom there is
any employment in Ireland.[94]

And Kiernan suggested that guest conductors should also become part of
the musical fabric: 'as music is the most important part of the programmes,
and variety and freshness are of great importance, it is suggested that permission should be given to the Director, within his discretion, to invite Guest
Conductors for not more than twelve concerts in a year at an aggregate outside cost for conducting of £72'.[95] This proposal would have far-reaching effects
which were both advantageous and damaging.

Given the resistance to increases in the orchestral budget, it is perhaps surprising that P&T obtained sanction from Finance for a full-time conductor,
on a salary of £400, 'whose duties will be to take charge of the Orchestra for

94 Kiernan memorandum, ibid. 95 Ibid.

all rehearsals and programmes, and to co-operate, so far as may be necessary, in the arrangement of programmes for the Orchestra with the Musical Director who will be responsible, as heretofore, for the general organisation of the musical programme as a whole'.[96] One must assume that the advent of Kiernan carried considerable weight outside his department. Even more surprisingly, Finance also agreed to another of Kiernan's proposals, that the orchestra should increase from nineteen to twenty-three players – the additions being an extra cello, clarinet, horn and trumpet which, together with the conductor's salary, would cost approximately £1500 to implement. But it would not concede Kiernan's strongly argued point that there should be no discrimination in rates of pay based on gender.

In response to advertisements for the new posts, over 400 applications were received, and preliminary auditions were held by Vincent O'Brien and Stuart Redfern, sub-leader of the BBC Northern Ireland Orchestra. The shortlisted candidates were interviewed by Sir Hamilton Harty, Godfrey Brown from BBCNI and O'Brien. (Larchet had been invited to sit on the selection board but was unavailable.) Meanwhile, unofficial approaches were made to the Department of Defence to solicit the secondment of Lieutenant James Doyle from the Army School of Music for a period of one year. Doyle took up duty on 21 July 1936 and remained for exactly twelve months, returning to the Army until December 1938, when he was again seconded to Radio Éireann, this time for two years; he became the first Irish Director of the Army School of Music in 1947.

Born in 1906 into a musical family, Doyle obtained the B.Mus. at UCD in 1934 and had also studied with Esposito at the RIAM, where he followed his mother and aunt in winning a Vandeleur Scholarship. He had been at the Army School of Music since 1924, and two years later had become conductor of the Army No.1 Band, with whom he won the band competitions at the Tailteann Games in 1928 and 1932. Just before his appointment to 2RN he had conducted at the Dublin Operatic Society and had deputised for Brase in a performance of Beethoven's 'Choral' symphony with the Dublin Philharmonic Society, which had continued to give concerts up to 1936. He later transferred his operatic allegiance from the DOS to the DGOS, becoming its Music Director and conducting many productions.[97] Opinions of Doyle's conducting were uniformly positive. Writing in 1951, Denis Donoghue gave his view that Doyle was 'a fine man, tall and well-built. As a conductor, he has all the manly virtues, competence, clarity and strength. He has the clear-cut approach of one who knows his score intimately, and none of his actions are [*sic*] either arbitrary or casual. Everything he does while conducting an orchestra means something definite'.[98]

96 Boland to O'Hegarty, 6 April 1936, ibid. **97** Doyle conducted all four of the DGOS operas in its first (Spring 1941) season, and continued to conduct until 1958. **98** *Irish Times*, undated

At Doyle's death in 1997 one of his successors in the Army School of Music, Commandant Fred O'Callaghan, would recall 'great musical experiences' under Doyle's baton: 'the sheer excitement ... of so many operatic performances: Verdi's *Otello* ... or *Aida*, their drama underlined with such a sure touch, the orchestral palette aglow, singers inspired and audience absorbed'.99 John McCormack had described him as 'most brilliant and exhilarating' and Fred O'Callaghan wrote that 'his direction was always informed and secure, his baton work elegant, purposeful and supremely legible. And he had that mysterious ability of some conductors to make his musicians feel at times that they were surpassing themselves, that they were achieving what in other circumstances would have seemed impossible'.1 Thus Doyle clearly met the criteria established by Kiernan in his report ('taking command of his team and inspiring enthusiasm').

Doyle's choice of repertoire was characteristic of what we have already noted in the programmes of Vincent O'Brien: a willingness to present his audiences with unusual works. As Fred O'Callaghan recalled: 'his programmes were not over reliant on sure-fire classics and romantics ... he would often lead us into the charming byways of Massenet, Chabrier, Turina and others. I remember too an impressive performance of Nielsen's fourth symphony at a time when that composer was scarcely known here.'2

Doyle had the advantage that Kiernan, as the author of the document which reorganised the orchestra, would have appreciated its musical needs, as Doyle made these evident to him. Thus, only three months after his secondment, Doyle succeeded in persuading Kiernan that a further increase was necessary. As Kiernan wrote to O'Hegarty:

> The Orchestra of 23 players is a considerable improvement on the earlier combination but a large amount of music has to be edited for it. This has always been so here. A composer writes for a bigger orchestra. The Conductor (now), Music Director (before), revised the composer's work by cue-ing i.e. transposing the 2nd flute part to be played by one of the First Violins, the 2nd oboe part by a second violin or viola, the 2nd bassoon part by the 2nd cello. We have only one trombone and most works are written for two or three. A first and third (i.e. two) trombones are necessary. It still is necessary on occasions to introduce the piano into the Orchestra to supply the missing double wind, when it is impossible to cue the score.3

cutting [1951] (Acton Archive). **99** *Irish Times*, 20 October 1997. **1** Ibid. **2** Ibid. Doyle continued to work with the RÉSO as a guest conductor up to the early 1960s, regularly conducting *Messiah* at Christmas time, but also introducing several new works by Irish composers, such as T.C. Kelly's 'Three Pieces for Strings' (1949), Beckett's Rhapsody no. 1 (1959), and McNulty's Sinfonietta (1961). **3** Kiernan to O'Hegarty, 16 October 1936, P&T file 119/55/6: 'Station

CELEBRITY CONCERTS

In the 1937–8 season, when Doyle had returned to the Army, Kiernan and O'Brien decided on a short series of celebrity concerts at Dublin's Gaiety Theatre, as a way of reviving music-making by Radio Éireann (as 2RN had now been officially renamed). Three foreign conductors, two of them of considerable renown – Frank Bridge and Constant Lambert – were engaged, and one Irish conductor-composer, Aloys Fleischmann, who would conduct an all-Irish concert.

On 20 February 1938 the Korean composer Ahn Eak Tai (1905–65), conducted his symphonic fantasy 'Korea', a work that was banned in his own country, which incorporated into the finale the (South) Korean national anthem,[4] which he himself had recently written, and which was intended, as the programme note explained, to express 'national suppression, leading to revolution in 1920 and ending with the March for Freedom'. The programme began with Beethoven's 'Egmont' overture and also included Schubert's 'Unfinished' symphony, and Mozart's piano concerto in C minor K.491, played by the up-and-coming British pianist Maurice Cole. Typical of the long and varied programmes which still featured vocal items, it also presented songs by Donizetti ('Una furtiva lagrima'), Mozart ('Il mio tesoro') and others from the eighteen-year-old Irish singer Hubert Valentine, a student of Vincent O'Brien, whose voice was to be commended by both Gigli and Tauber; in 1938 he left Ireland to live in the USA, where he became a well-known musician, broadcasting frequently on RTÉ up to the mid-1970s during his visits home.[5]

Fleischmann's concert, on 24 April, included E.J. Moeran's Rhapsody no. 2 (1924), Ina Boyle's 'Colin Clout' (1920), Elizabeth Maconchy's Piano Concertino (1930), with Charles Lynch as soloist, the première of Frederick

Orchestra – proposed addition of four further positions, 16.10.36–1.2.37'. Kiernan had also initiated a system of monitoring programmes by two means. Up to this point, senior management had been required to listen personally to the entire output: 'In order to regularise this nightmare an informal method has been devised of asking selected listeners to report occasionally on broadcast items … In addition to the reports received from listeners to whom these forms are sent, it is now part of the duty of three members of the staff (Mr Hughes, Mr MacDonagh and Miss Roddy) to make nightly reports which are given to the Director in the morning after the broadcast. It is recommended that it should be an important part of the work of the Musical Director to check the broadcasts of musicians so that future engagements may be offered strictly on merit'. Thenceforth, programme report slips, annotated by the responsible individual, would be filled each evening until at least the late 1950s. Kiernan also initiated a primitive form of listener survey by means of questionnaire, which revealed that orchestral music was not very popular: cf. M. Gorham, op. cit., p. 116. **4** Previously sung to the tune 'Auld Lang Syne'. **5** Valentine served four years in the US army during World War 2, giving concerts to the troops in the Philippines, the Pacific islands and Australia. He subsequently resumed his singing career in the USA and Canada, and presented a programme of Irish classical music, 'Music from Ireland' on Boston Radio WCRB during the 1970s and '80s.

May's 'Spring Nocturne', and Fleischmann's own 'Three Songs for Tenor and Orchestra' (1935) sung in English by Heddle Nash, at that time one of the pillars of the fledgling Glyndebourne opera and one of Elgar's chosen interpreters of 'The Dream of Gerontius'.[6] The 'Three Songs', which had been first performed at UCC in 1935 in Irish, and under their Irish title 'Trí hAmhráin', were immediately recognised as one of the most original and important works by an Irish composer at that time. Written under the pen-name 'Muiris Ó Rónáin' (which suggests Fleischmann's desire to emulate Bax's 'Dermot O'Byrne' in an attempt to present himself more 'Irishly'), the songs were 'an attempt … to set Irish poems to music in a way that will reflect the true nature of the people's songs. This is not the old traditional music, however, as we understand it, but art-music of today imbued with the old traditional spirit'.[7] Frederick May greeted the songs as combining 'remarkable lyrical beauty with deep intensity of feeling', representing 'one of the highlights of contemporary music in Ireland'.[8]

These concerts were sufficiently successful to justify repeating the formula in the 1938–9 season, with visiting conductors Arthur Hammond, Walton O'Donnell from BBCNI and Manuel Rosenthal. An additional celebrity concert – albeit from the studio – was conducted by Hamilton Harty. O'Donnell's soloist in Beethoven's third concerto was the veteran pianist Walter Rummel (1887–1953), who had worked (and had an affair) with the dancer Isadora Duncan, was a friend of Debussy and had visited Dublin as early as 1926.[9] Rosenthal's soloist was Lily Laskine (1893–1988), the outstanding harpist who was the dedicatee of Roussel's 'Impromptu' for harp (1919) and had worked with Koussevitsky and at the Lamoureux concerts; she would later collaborate with flautist Jean-Pierre Rampal for over four decades; the previous year, 1938, she had recorded Ravel's 'Introduction et Allegro' with Marcel Moyse and the Pro Arte Quartet; in Dublin she played Pierné's 'Concertstück' (1903).

Of these visitors, Bridge, Lambert, Rosenthal and Harty must be considered the most prestigious, a signal that RÉ intended to present its orchestra in the best possible light, working with conductors of high international calibre. Bridge (1879–1941), a pupil of Stanford at the Royal College of Music (RCM) in London, had deputised for Henry Wood at the London Promenade Concerts, and had conducted opera at the Savoy Theatre and at Covent

---

6 Fleischmann had been unable to persuade Nash to sing the songs in Irish – cf. Séamus de Barra, 'The music of Aloys Fleischmann: a survey' (2000), p. 329. 7 Original programme note for the first performance, quoted in Séamus de Barra, ibid., p. 328. The pen-name had been suggested to Fleischmann by Daniel Corkery: ibid., p. 327. 8 F. May, 'The music of Aloys Fleischmann' (1949). 9 Walter Starkie's wife told a friend that 'I was so afraid of him [Rummel] … he is so alarming … He is such a chaser of women': quoted in Ann Saddlemyer, *Becoming George: the life of Mrs W.B.Yeats* (2002), p. 345.

Garden, parallel with his career as a composer, in which he displayed qualities akin to those of Bax and John Ireland.

The bohemian Englishman, Constant Lambert (1905–51), had been a pupil of Vaughan Williams (for composition) and Malcolm Sargent (for conducting) at the RCM; he is probably best known today for his massive, exotic setting of Sacheverell Sitwell's *Rio Grande* (1927);[10] he was commissioned by Diaghilev to compose *Romeo and Juliet* for the *ballets russes* in 1926, the same year that he co-recited Walton's *Façade* with Edith Sitwell. At the time he came to Dublin, he was working extensively as a music critic and, like Bridge, was conducting at Covent Garden. Eimear Ó Broin recalls that on his return visit in 1943 he directed a 'stunning' performance of Tchaikovsky's fifth symphony but that at the *fermata* before the coda in the *finale* the audience, thinking the work had ended, interrupted with applause. This concert also featured an unusual work, excerpts from Rimsky-Korsakov's unfinished opera *Stenka Razin*. On this occasion Michael Bowles complained that Lambert, 'an inveterate alcoholic', had 'almost drunk Blackrock dry'.[11]

The French composer Manuel Rosenthal (1904–2003), who worked in every musical genre, especially choral and sacred music, was a close associate of Ravel, who encouraged his conducting career which began in 1928 with the Orchestre Pasdeloup (with which Tibor Paul was to work in the 1960s). From 1934 to 1939 he was associate conductor with the newly formed National Radio Orchestra of France, and after the second world war he returned as its chief conductor, working also with the Orchestre National. Later his career took him to North and South America, including the Metropolitan Opera in New York, and the music directorship of the Seattle Symphony, and he made definitive recordings of Debussy and Ravel; he has been described as 'one of those who shaped the concept of the 20th-century repertoire'.[12] He was professor of conducting at the Paris Conservatoire, 1962–74.

Harty (1879–1941) has been described as 'the Irish Toscanini',[13] but his Irishness is evident not in his conducting but in his compositions. Following his early successes as a piano soloist and accompanist, and as a prizewinner in composition at the Feis Ceoil, his conducting skills had become evident when he was invited by Hans Richter to conduct the London Symphony Orchestra in his tone poem 'With the Wild Geese' in 1911, leading to his engagement by the LSO in the 1912–13 season. (He brought the LSO to Dublin in 1913

---

10 Commercially recorded in 1930 by the Hallé Orchestra under the composer, with Harty as piano soloist. 11 E. Ó Broin, interview with the author, 17 April 2002; Blackrock was the suburb of Dublin where Lambert was staying. 12 Marcel Marnat, 'Manuel Rosenthal', *New Grove Dictionary of Music and Musicians* 2nd edn., [henceforth *NG2*] ed. Stanley Sadie (London: Macmillan, 2001), vol. 21, p. 702. 13 Philip Hammond, RTÉ Radio 1 documentary on Harty, 1979, RTÉ Sound Archives, tape no. LAA1154.

to perform at Woodbrook, near Bray.) Success followed at Covent Garden, the Liverpool Philharmonic and then the Hallé, which appointed him permanent conductor in 1919, the relationship lasting until 1933. In 1939 he was still at the peak of his reputation as one of the most popular and sought-after conductors internationally, but in ill health – well enough, however, to conduct the première of 'The Children of Lir' (which he had completed the previous year), with Isobel Baillie as the wordless soprano soloist, with the BBC Symphony, on 1 March. Harty had been involved with 2RN/Radio Éireann since its inception, and so, near the end of his life, this involvement with its orchestra must have seemed very fitting.

One might reasonably infer that the invitations to four conductors of such different backgrounds and styles as Bridge, Lambert, Rosenthal and Harty, at this delicate phase of the orchestra's development, was a planned series of meetings between the orchestra and some of the most interesting and eminent conductors available to Irish radio and its publics.

After J.M. Doyle's first term with the orchestra (1936–7), he was replaced by Lieutenant Dermot O'Hara for one year; Doyle then returned to the post for 1939 and 1940, when he was succeeded by Captain Michael Bowles.[14] Meanwhile studio concerts continued under the batons of Vincent O'Brien, Fritz Brase, Godfrey Brown (now retired from BBCNI) and Dermot O'Hara, who was to have a long association with the orchestras, particularly the RÉLO from its foundation in 1948.

IRISH COMPOSERS

It is important to note that the concert conducted by Fleischmann on 24 April 1938 is indicative of the fact that a policy was being put in place whereby an Irish work would be performed at the majority of concerts, and almost exclusively by a contemporary composer. This was particularly so during the period of Michael Bowles's principal conductorship and, later, under Fachtna Ó hAnnracháin as Music Director. Between January 1938 and January 1948, at least fifty-six works by twenty-one Irish composers (of whom eighteen were living)[15][16] received a total of eighty performances (see Table D[a]). This policy would be reinforced when 'Prom' concerts began in 1953.

14 Bowles had joined the Army School of Music in 1932 as a cadet bandmaster, and was commissioned as a second lieutenant in 1936, the year in which he obtained the B.Mus (first class honours) at UCD.   **15** If we allow the inclusion of Arnold Bax as an Irish composer. Although Bax himself (above, p. 12) described himself as a *British* composer, he did so in the context of writing 'Irishly', and had consciously adopted an Irish *persona*; furthermore, he had a considerable amount of Celtic blood from Cornish ancestors: Hilary Boyle (his cousin), letter to the Editor, *Irish Times* 6 June 1973 (this contradicts the statement by James Barry [Séamus de Barra] that he was 'with-

Of the living composers whose works featured in the public concerts from 1941 to early 1948, five (Bax, Boyle, Larchet, White/MacMurrough and Moeran) could be regarded as senior figures, while the remainder, under fifty years of age, were junior, up-and-coming composers, the direction of whose work was as yet unclear. As one might expect, the larger-scale works came mainly from those who were no longer alive – Harty and Stanford in particular: Harty's 'Irish' Symphony (which had two performances in this period) and 'With the Wild Geese' (three performances), as well as 'The Children of Lir', were clearly the most substantial Irish works in the concert programmes. That the work of Harty received consistent attention during these years (with twelve performances of seven different works) is an indication of the esteem with which he was regarded, and of the interest evinced by Bowles and his superiors in bringing his works before the public. Of the two concertos by Moeran, that for violin, performed at least twice by Nancie Lord,[17] is acknowledged as a fine work; however, that for cello, performed by Moeran's wife, Peers Coetmore, gave Bowles himself some cause for reflection, and near the end of his life he gave Gareth Costello this insight: 'Jack [Moeran] was committed to Peers for the cello concerto because he had written it as a "wedding present". Later, he revised downward his opinion of the quality of the work and the quality of Peers as a virtuoso cellist'.[18] Bowles's own 'Divertimento', when performed by the BBCSO in 1945, was considered to be 'good, deft light music, most ably scored … Irishry is prominent in the style, but happily not lush in the "begorra" manner'.[19]

In hindsight, Fleischmann, Maconchy and May were 'the ones to watch', although none of them was to deliver any substantial body of orchestral work,

out any Celtic connections whatever' (*Counterpoint*, November 1979). One should, however, note the view of Axel Klein, that 'it is … a pity that a Celtic impressionist such as Arnold Bax … could not claim Irish heritage … Bax can not be considered an Irish composer as such': 'Roots and directions in twentieth-century Irish art music' pp. 172–3. (Klein, who excludes Bax from his Irish discography, nevertheless *includes* Tommaso Giordani as an 'Irish' composer by virtue of long residence in Dublin: A. Klein, *Irish classical recordings*). I could not agree with Joseph Ryan, that Bax's 'characteristic intensity' 'was merely an infatuation' and that for Bax, as for Moeran, 'the genuine regard for the country and its musical heritage was but an occasional influence': Ryan, 'The tone of defiance', p. 206.   **16** Hardebeck died one month after the performance of 'Seoithin Seo' in 1945.   **17** Michael Bowles stated ('The birth of the R.É.S.O.', 1973) that Arthur Catterall (who had given the première at the Proms in London in 1942) had been engaged to perform the work in Dublin but had died a few weeks prior to the concert; however, it is generally agreed that Moeran had intended Nancie Lord to give the Irish première; Eimear Ó Broin (interview with the author, 17 April 2002) recalls that Moeran rehearsed her, with Charles Lynch providing – at sight – a piano reduction of the orchestral parts from the composer's manuscript score.   **18** Michael Bowles, interview with Gareth Costello, 19 December 1997. Aloys Fleischmann described Moeran as 'one of the few major composers who have lived and worked here, with any real understanding of the people and of their traditional music': 'The music of E.J. Moeran' (1951).   **19** W.R. Anderson, *Musical Times* (June 1945).

Fleischmann because he felt inhibited to some extent by the Irish context and by the lack of performance opportunities, Maconchy because she devoted herself mainly to the genre of the string quartet, and May because his unfettered imagination was tragically undermined by persistent illness from the mid-1950s, with his string quartet (1936) and 'Songs from Prison' (1941) his only major output; 'Sunlight and Shadow' (1955) was his last, and his only post-war, composition.

The enigmatic figure of Éamonn Ó Gallchobhair, whose relationship both to the 'classical' genre and to the broadcasting station itself was complex and idiosyncratic, is worth noting in the context of Tables D (a) and (d). In his programme notes for 23 January 1944 Frederick May (who wrote excellent notes for Radio Éireann for several years) said of Ó Gallchobhair's 'Machtnamh': 'The composer himself has suggested a line of Yeats as a fitting subtitle [for] this work, "Lines written in dejection". The use of the first bar of the National Anthem as a motif and general musical trend suggest[s] that the work is perhaps a "political commentary" in music'. In the light of Ó Gallchobhair's adherence to 'Irish-Ireland' it points towards a potential divisiveness in musical matters that in fact took place only in the minds of composers such as Ó Riada and Ó Gallchobhair himself. This was not the first epiphany of Ó Gallchobhair on the Irish airwaves. As early as 1937, when he was only twenty-seven, he had featured significantly in a special programme devoted to his own music. As Kiernan wrote to O'Hegarty:

> It is desired to broadcast a special programme of new Irish compositions by Éamonn Ó Gallchobhair on November the 18th and to invite Mr J. J. Delamere as Guest Conductor … The proposed broadcast is of considerable importance from the point of view of the cultivation and encouragement of newly composed Irish music.[20]

This was followed by further concerts in January and March 1938:

> These concerts will each last one hour and will consist of new compositions by an Irish composer Éamonn Ó Gallchobhair. This composer works entirely with an organisation called An Ceol Cumann, founded some years ago for the development of orchestrated forms of Irish music, and to encourage and guide Irish composers working in this field … Mr Ó Gallchobhair is not willing to permit us to have his music conducted by any other Conductor except the Ceol Cumann Conductor. He points out that a very close bond of understanding between the composer and

---

20 Kiernan to O'Hegarty, 7 October 1937, file 119/55/9: 'Station Orchestra – occasional augmentation of: Finance Section, 23.1.33–17.4.39'.

Table D (a): Works by Irish composers performed by the Radio Éireann Orchestra,
January 1938–January 1948*

	Year of Composition	Date(s) of Concert(s)		
Arnold Bax [1883–1953]				
Overture to a Picaresque Comedy	1930	20.02.44	24.11.46	
In the Faery Hills	1909/21	12.11.44		
Piano solos		23.02.47		
Michael Bowles [1909–98]				
Three pieces for orchestra		13.11.41		
Suite of Irish dances		29.10.42		
Divertimento for Strings		06.02.44	29.10.44	
Prelude, Scherzo and Impromptu		13.11.41	09.03.47	
Brian Boydell [1917–2000]				
Magh Sleacht				
[The Plain of Prostrations]	1947	05.09.47	05.11.47	
Ina Boyle [1889–1967]				
'Colin Clout'	1921	24.04.38		
The Wild Geese	1942	18.11.47	25.01.48	
Arthur Duff [1899–1956]				
Irish Suite for Strings	1940	30.10.41	11.03.43	23.03.47
Aloys Fleischmann [1910–92]				
3 songs for tenor and orchestra	1935/37	24.04.38		
Suite, The Humours of Carolan	1941/44	20.02.44		
Overture, The Four Masters	1944	25.06.44	29.10.44	26.01.47
Clare's Dragoons	1945	09.09.45		
The Fountain of Magic	1946	19.10.47		
Redmond Friel [1907–79]				
6 Airs for Orchestra		29.01.42		
The Battle of the Blackwater		25.06.44		
3 songs for baritone		09.09.45		
Carl Hardebeck [1869–1945]				
Two Irish Airs		16.10.41		
Seoithin Seo [lullaby]		28.01.45		
Hamilton Harty [1879–1941]				
Songs	–	15.05.39		
The Children of Lir	1938	11.12.41		
Comedy Overture	1906/08	29.10.42	27.01.46	
With the Wild Geese	1910	10.12.42	24.11.46	20.07.47
Violin concerto	1908	25.03.43		
Irish Symphony	1904/15	14.11.43	26.11.44	09.09.45
		18.11.47		
John Field Suite	1939	28.01.45		

J.F. Larchet [1884–1967]				
Songs	–	11.12.41		
Songs	–	28.11.43		
Lament for Youth	1919/39	08.06.47		
Dirge of Ossian and MacAnanty's		26.10.47		
Reel	1940			
March	1947	08.06.47		
Dermot MacMurrough				
[Harold White] [1872–1943]				
The Opium Smoker	c.1940	26.02.42		
Overture, Autolycus	1928	25.03.43		
Elizabeth Maconchy [1907–94]				
Piano concertino	1928/30	24.04.38		
Puck Fair	1943	11.02.45		
Theme and variations	1942/3	13.01.46		
Frederick May [1911–85]				
Scherzo	1933	26.06.42	27.06.42	
Lyric Movement for strings	1943	19.03.44	18.11.47	
Spring Nocturne	1938	24.04.38	29.10.44	
Songs from Prison	1941	22.12.46		
E.J. Moeran [1894–1950]				
Violin Concerto	1937/41	--.03.42	??.10.43	05.03.44
		29.10.44		
Cello Concerto	1945	25.11.45		
Rhapsody no. 2	1924/41	24.04.38	12.03.42	22.06.47
Whythorne's Shadow	1931	08.12.46		
Máire Ní Scolaí				
4 Songs		25.03.43		
Vincent O'Brien [1871–1948]				
Miniature Overture		00.05.41		
Peadar. Ó Cillin				
Dreacht do Cheolfhuin Bhig		18.11.47		
B.Walton O'Donnell [1887–1939]				
Songs of the Gael	1924	11.11.45		
Éamonn Ó Gallchobhair [1910–82]				
Machtnamh	1944	23.01.44		
Andante and allegro [Sleachta na n-Annalacha]		25.06.44		
Lament for Owen Roe		09.09.45		
'Leslie Seymour' [Seymour Leslie]				
Fugal Fantasy		30.09.47		
Charles Villiers Stanford [1852–1924]				
Irish Rhapsody no. 1	1902	15.10.42	28.10.45	
Irish Rhapsody no. 4	1913	15.06.45		

*Records are incomplete – these are the performances which can be established from extant sources.

Summary: 21 composers, 56 works, 80 performances

Table D (b): First performances by the Dublin Orchestral Players
*of works by Irish composers, 1941–50**

John Beckett [1927–]	
A Short Overture	23.05.44
Brian Boydell [1917–2000]	
Tone poem, 'Laish'	08.06.43
House of Cards – Satirical Suite	23.05.44
Sleep Now	01.03.45
Symphony for strings	30.10.45
Ballet suite, The Buried Moon	02.03.50
Ina Boyle [1889–1967]	
Elegy from a Virgilian suite	30.11.50
Edgar Deale [1902–99]	
Ceol Mall Réidh	29.05.47
Joseph Groocock [1913–97]	
Ricercari for strings	08.05.48
T.C. Kelly [1917–85]	
3 pieces for strings	14.06.50
Havelock Nelson [1917–96]	
Irish Fragment – Supplication	25.03.41
Strgs of the Earth and Air	17.02.42
Poème for harp and orchestra	08.06.49
Overture for a special occasion	16.06.49
Caoimhín Ó Conghaile	
An Sreath Sígael [Tipsy Suite]	19.12.47

*source: Frederick May, 'First Performances of Works by Irish Composers 1935–1951'
in A. Fleishmann, *Music in Ireland*

Table D (c): Performances by the Dublin String Orchestra
*of works by Irish composers, 1940–44**

Arthur Duff [1899–1956]	
Suite for strings	04.11.40
Music for strings	06.10.41
Meath Pastoral	06.11.44
John F. Larchet [1884–1967]	
Dirge of Oisín and Macananty's Reel	15.04.40
Carlow Tune and The Tinker's Wedding	06.10.41
Frederick May [1911–85]	
Lyric movement	15.02.43
Eamonn Ó Gallchobhair [1910–82]	
Andante and allegro	04.11.40
Joan Trimble [1915–2001]	
In Glenale	09.02.42

*source: Frederick May, 'First Performances of Works by Irish Composers 1935–1951',
in A. Fleischmann, *Music in Ireland*.

conductor is necessary and that the person who conducts must be animated with the same spirit as the composer, and have a close understanding of what is intended in the music which he is to interpret.[21]

The Ceol Cumann orchestra had been founded by Arthur Darley 'for the purpose of playing concerted Irish music ... This started the setting of Irish music in chamber style.'[22] It broadcast on Radio Éireann from 1926 until 1969. Coming to Dublin the young Ó Gallchobhair found himself inspired by W.B. Yeats's ambition, 'to make this again a proud people' and joined the orchestra and its smaller quartet or quintet as a pianist (other members were Cormac McGinley, violin and Seán Delamere, cello, who also conducted the orchestra). 'I found that there was hardly any Irish music in existence for such a combination and I wrote 250 instrumental quartet or quintet numbers and I set 200 songs with quartet or quintet accompaniment'.[23] The group specialised in Celtic music – that is, not only Irish, but Scots, Welsh, Manx, Cornish and Breton music also, but Ó Gallchobhair regarded his work as predominantly 'Irish-Ireland'.[24]

Table D (d): Performances by An Ceol Cumann of works by
Éamonn Ó Gallchobhair, 1936–45*

The Singer – dance drama	01.11.36	[Padraig Pearse]
Casadh an tSugáin – mime for dancers	06.11.38}	[Douglas Hyde]
Good and Evil – metaphysical ballet	06.11.38}	
Peter Street – comedy mime	06.11.38}	
The Tall Dancer	06.11.38}	[ballet inspired by Joseph Campbell's poem]
Deirdre – procession for dancers	06.11.38}[25]	
Paul Henry Landscape – ballet	05.11.39	
Mise Eire – political mime	05.11.39	
Cathar Linn – dance drama	25.01.42	
Ceól-drama – Loscadh na Teamhrach [The Burning of Tara] – opera	29.11.43	
Ceól-Drama – Nocturne sa Cearnóg [The Nocturne in the Square] – opera	25.10.44	
Ceól-Drama – Traghadh na Taoide [Ebb-Tide] – opera	21.10.45	

*source: Frederick May, 'First Performances of Works by Irish Composers 1935–1951', in A. Fleischmann, *Music in Ireland.*[26]

---

21 Kiernan to O'Hegarty, 26 September 1937, ibid. 22 Éamonn Ó Gallchobhair, 'Éamonn Ó Gallchobhair remembers'. Ó Gallchobhair pronounced the word 'concerted' in the Italian style, *'concherted'*. 23 Ibid. 24 Ibid. 25 An Ceol Cumann also requested assistance from RÉ with this performance of ballet, in collaboration with the Keating Branch of the Gaelic League at the Gaiety Theatre. 26 May's listings are not entirely accurate and require checking against other sources.

However, chauvinism could also go too far, as Michael Bowles reveals in his comment on the work by Walton O'Donnell,[27] 'Songs of the Gael': 'not much of a piece but there was a ministerial "request" around this time for featuring Irish music, and we willingly scraped the barrel. The general state of musical skill in Ireland in those years was very sparse and complicated by the facile assertions of politically motivated characters, worst of all musicians like Jack Larchet.'[28]

PUBLIC CONCERTS

Unlike the previous secondments, Bowles's association with the orchestra lasted for seven years, and contributed enormously to its development, both musically and in relation to the concert-going public. His long tenure was due to the fact that his secondment from the Army ended in 1944, when he resigned his commission after being appointed to succeed Vincent O'Brien as Director of Music in addition to his post as conductor, in a competition in which the other applicant was Aloys Fleischmann. (Bowles had been Acting Music Director since 1941 when O'Brien had retired.) In 1952 Séamus Ó Braonáin recalled 'That these officers [Doyle and Bowles], whose musical training and experience were linked with Army bands, succeeded so well as conductors of a symphony orchestra is a fine tribute to their natural talents and abilities, and to their versatility and capacity for adapting themselves to cirumstances'.[29] In fact, it was Bowles's initiative which definitively shifted the status of the orchestra from its broadcasting function to one of consistent visibility as a platform-based entity:

> It was obvious that some sort of performance before a live audience was essential if we were all to avoid the onset of rigor mortis ... As often as not, the players were bored to death. 'O Gawd not those Henry VIII Dances (or Eine Kleine or Tales from the Vienna Woods) again!' They were perfectly reasonable in this, churning out the five programmes a week, 50 weeks a year, in an eccentrically-shaped attic space on the top of the GPO, lacking stimulation from the presence of an audience, not certain that anyone listened in or cared a hang what they played, except a few personal friends. 'De la musique par kilo' as Tom McGreevy used to say.[30]

Bowles relates that his proposal for a series of public concerts initially met with a negative response from Finance. 'This was perfectly understandable.

---

27 A conductor working with the BBC who had been with the BBCNI orchestra from 1937 until his premature death in 1939. 28 Interview with Gareth Costello. 29 S. Ó Braonáin, 'Music in the broadcasting service' (1952), pp. 198–9. 30 Bowles, 'The birth of the R.É.S.O.' Art critic Thomas McGreevy (1893–1967) was Director of the National Gallery of Ireland, 1950–64.

There was no concrete evidence that anyone listened to the Radio Éireann orchestra when it played "good" music; there was no evidence of a general public desire for orchestral concerts'.[31] He recalled that even Harty's concert on 15 October 1939 with the pianist Solomon [Cutner] playing Beethoven's 'Emperor' concerto had been poorly attended.[32] The new series of six fortnightly concerts was eventually sanctioned by Finance on condition that the cost did not exceed £90 per concert.

Nevertheless, its broadcast output would continue to be the principal criterion for assessing its workload: in 1945 Charles Kelly, then deputy director of broadcasting, was to record that 'We transferred [the Symphony concerts] to the Mansion House and later to the Capitol Theatre with a view to giving the public the benefit of them, but ... they were in essence broadcast programmes and an extension of our ordinary broadcasting activities'.[33] In hindsight, Bowles was unsure about the move from the Mansion House to the Capitol: 'in the small auditorium there was a "family" atmosphere. Between the audience and the players, there was a bond of sympathy and goodwill which contributes more than any other factor, even technical facility, to the enjoyment of music.' He found himself worrying if the audience fell below 1,400–1,500, 'when, three years before, we had been delighted and surprised with more than 400'.[34] But the public's expectation of regular concert series, and the orchestra's enthusiasm for meeting its audiences, would orient the policy of the whole organisation in this outward-looking direction. Not only did this development take the form of Subscription Concerts, which remain the backbone of the NSO's activity to this day, but Bowles also persuaded Radio Éireann that the orchestra should move out of its studio at the GPO in order to give 'studio concerts' in the hall of the Scots Church in Lower Abbey Street, so that a small audience could be accommodated. Over thirty years later, Bowles would say 'When I set up the Radio Éireann orchestra concerts in 1941, my objective was no more than raising the morale of the players. To play as they did, five days a week, 48 weeks a year, to an impassive studio microphone, was soul-destroying.'[35]

Even this move could not ameliorate all the orchestra's problems. As Bowles recalled:

> They were true musicians, liable to be excited by the music itself, no matter what circumstances they played in. With an honesty of purpose above and beyond the call of duty, they could, and often did, produce fine work. Unfortunately, the effect of this was invariably smudged in transmission. The studio equipment was too primitive for anything more

31 Ibid.   32 Bowles's memory was playing him false: Solomon had in fact played the first Tchaikowsky concerto.   33 Charles Kelly's departmental memo, 27 July 1945, file 10/57/2, originally A 9404/45.   34 *Irish Times*, 2 January 1967.   35 *Irish Times*, 8 April 1974.

complicated than a solo voice with piano accompaniment. Just before going on air with my very first programme to include a piano concerto, I remember a discussion on whether the microphone should be sited directly over the piano or 'over the middle of the woodwind somewhere' and whether the lid of the piano should be open or closed.[36]

Bowles's first series of fortnightly public concerts, in the Round Room of Dublin's Mansion House, was inaugurated on 16 October 1941 with Mozart's overture to *Don Giovanni*, the Irish première of Rachmaninov's 'Paganini Rhapsody', played by Charles Lynch, two Irish airs by Carl Hardebeck, and Beethoven's 'Eroica' symphony. The audience included the Ministers for P&T, Agriculture, Education and Justice, the Lord Mayor of Dublin, the Ministers [ambassadors] of Britain, Belgium, France, Germany and Spain, the Japanese, Swedish and Polish consuls, the Swiss *chargé d'affaires* and the Canadian High Commissioner. The choice of Lynch as soloist, a role he would perform again two years later when the concerts transferred to the Capitol Theatre, and once more when Public Concerts were reinstated in 1953, underlines his position at that time as the pre-eminent Irish international concert artist.

As the then Director of Broadcasting, Séamus Ó Braonáin, recalled in retirement,

> Having regard to previous experience there was every possibility of a flop and of course we all felt that the worst possible service we could do to music, to Radio Éireann itself, and generally would be to sponsor a rather ambitious effort such as this which might be doomed to failure … We need not have worried – there were about 300 people unable to gain admission on that first night.[37]

In late 1942, probably due to the huge success of these concerts, P.J. Little, the Minister for P&T, announced that he intended to increase the orchestra from twenty-eight players to forty, at an extra cost of £1,265. He considered this 'the minimum necessary to secure an adequate standard of performance'. He told the Dáil that he 'would like indeed to see an even larger augmentation, but at present circumstances do not admit of the proper utilisation of an orchestra of greater size in general programme work … With such a combination the status of Irish broadcasting would be immensely raised and, through the influence of the highly artistic and varied broadcasts which would become practicable, national musical effort and appreciation would be materially stimulated'.[38] (He also announced the formation of a 'radio chorus' – see chapter

36 Ibid.   37 S. Ó Braonáin, 'Seven years of Irish radio' (1949).   38 DD, 88, 26 November 1942,

5.) Little's announcement is a classic example of the congruence of, and confusion between, politically motivated decisions in cultural matters and the needs of a broadcasting orchestra: because the RÉ orchestra was also required to be a 'national' orchestra, it was subject to announcements of this kind which placed an undue, and probably unbearable, burden on its broadcasting function. Bowles who, as we shall see, had serious misgivings about expansion, recorded in 1967 that 'when the orchestra was being increased ... every prospective applicant in Ireland was already known at Radio Éireann ... The auditions produced nothing more than positive proof that there were not then available enough players to increase the orchestra beyond 40'.[39] In fact, 125 applications were received to fill the twelve new places,[40] but Bowles was clearly ineffective in signalling that the standard offered was largely unacceptable and that national (or nationalist) aspirations could not be fulfilled in the short term.

Not only did Bowles perform Irish works (with a broadcast series dedicated to 'Contemporary Irish Composers' featuring Larchet, May, Duff, Fleischmann, MacMorrough, O'Dwyer, Ó Gallchobhair, Geoffrey Molyneux Palmer, Redmond Friel and Hubert Rooney) but he was also responsible for introducing many from outside the conventional repertoire, most of which were contemporary. The basic repertoire featured overtures, symphonies and concertos by Beethoven, Brahms (the complete symphonies in the 1941–2 season), Tchaikovsky and Dvořák, a wide range of Mozart's works (including several performances of the symphony no. 35 – 'Haffner'), many works by Elgar and overtures and excerpts from Wagner's operas. Bowles introduced Irish audiences to works by Sibelius, Vaughan Williams, Delius, Rachmaninov and Prokofiev. Even Beethoven's 'Choral' symphony was instructive: when Bowles performed it in 1944, it was almost a decade since it had been heard in Dublin, and Eimear Ó Broin recalls that, although he was familiar with radio broadcasts of the work, he found 'that vast first movement was a revelation to a youngster like myself' when he first heard it live – 'even more so when preceded by the "Emperor" concerto played by Rhoda Coghill'.[41] The performance was noted for the fact that a quartet of Irish singers – Renée Flynn, Kathleen Uhlemann, Robert McCullagh and Frank Cowle – had been available, a fact vigorously asserted by Bowles in 1976, when Charles Acton opined

col. 2574. **39** *Irish Times*, 3 January 1967. **40** DD, 90, 19 May 1943, col. 283. **41** E. Ó Broin, interview with the author, 17 April 2002. G.B. Shaw, writing in the *Musical Times* in 1947 had made the same comment: 'Radio music has changed the world in England ... Fifty years ago I heard a Beethoven symphony once in a blue moon ... As to the ninth symphony, performances of it were extraordinary events separated by years. Today, with radio sets as common as kitchen clocks, the Eroica, the Seventh, the Ninth, are as familiar to Tom, Dick and Harriet as ... every street piano. So too are Mozart's three greatest symphonies'.

that 'a couple of decades ago we could not have fielded an adequate Irish quartet of soloists'.[42]

Eimear Ó Broin believed that Bowles was basing his programme choices on the model of the BBC Proms in London, which frequently involved concerts considerably longer than the norm today.[43] One such concert, on 11 December 1941, featured (in order of performance) the overture to the opera *Il Guarany* by the Brazilian composer Carlos Gomes (1836–96); a group of songs by Larchet sung by May Devitt; Dvořák's symphony no. 7; 'Caucasian Sketches' by the Russian Mikhail Ippolitov-Ivanov (1859–1935); Harty's 'The Children of Lir' with May Devitt;[44] and finally Berlioz' 'symphonie fantastique'. Not only is the concert notable for the inclusion of two unusual and unfamiliar works (Gomes and Ivanov) but for the performance of two substantial symphonies as well as the work by Harty. As Ó Broin observes, 'today an orchestra would collapse with a programme of that kind'.[45]

Works which are little-known today which featured in Bowles's schedule include the ballet music from *Céphale et Procris* by André Grétry (1741–1813); 'Carnival in Paris' by the Norwegian Johan Svendsen (1840–1911) dating from 1872, which had performances in 1941 and 1946; 'Fantaisie sur deux airs populaires angevins' (1892) by the short-lived Belgian, Guillaume Lekeu (1870–94); the 'Rondò arlecchinesco' by Ferruccio Busoni (1866–1924), better known for his arrangements of Bach; the 'Festival Overture' by Max Reger (1873–1916); and 'Les béatitudes' of César Franck which Jean Martinon conducted in 1947 with Our Lady's Choral Society and soloists Moira Griffith, Jean Nolan, Kathleen Uhlemann, Frank Walsh, Dermot Browner and Patrick Thornton.

Of near-contemporary works, Messiaen's 'L'ascension' (performed in 1947) was composed in 1932–3; John Ireland's piano concerto (1930) was performed in Dublin in 1944; Edmund Rubbra's 'Improvisations on Virginal Pieces by Giles Farnaby' was only four years old when it was played in Dublin in 1943, as were William Walton's overture 'Scapino' and Dag Wirén's third symphony; 'Summernacht', a suite for strings by the Swiss composer Othmar Schoeck (1915–86), was a completely new work when it was brought to Ireland by his compatriot Robert Denzler in 1947.

Bowles's intentions were very similar to those of Micheál mac Liammóir and Hilton Edwards in founding the Dublin Gate Theatre in 1928. Bowles

---

42 *Irish Times*, 4, 9, 13, 16 October 1976. Bowles mistakenly mentioned Rita Lynch in place of Renée Flynn. One of the soloists, Robert McCullagh (1905–2001) had been a chorister at St Patrick's and Christ Church cathedrals and was a Feis Ceoil gold medallist; he had first broadcast from 2RN in 1929. **43** E. Ó Broin, interview with the author, 17 April 2002. **44** The Dublin-born soprano May Devitt (*c.*1904–77) had enjoyed a career as a singer of opera in London, returning to Dublin in the 1940s to take leading roles at the DGOS in *Madama Butterfly*, *Carmen*, and *La bohème* as well as musicals such a *Showboat* in which she sang opposite Josef Locke, with whom she was having an affair at the time. **45** E. Ó Broin, interview with the author, 17 April 2002.

had acted briefly at the Gate in Shaw's *Back to Methuselah* in 1930 (and recorded that it was there that he first heard Debussy), and had recognised that the theatre 'brought 20th-century Europe into Dublin. That they did not also succeed, at that time, in bringing Dublin into the 20th century was not their fault. It was an enterprise that would have given Sisyphus a nervous breakdown'.[46]

The choice of repertoire was not without its critics, either in the 1940s or the 50s, especially at the hands of the many visiting conductors. John O'Donovan (who in later years wrote a long-lived column on music for the *RTÉ Guide*), while acknowledging that 'mine was the first generation in Ireland which was enabled to hear, while still in its early teens, more and better performances of the standard repertoire', also felt that in the 1950s 'the orchestra was playing far too much new music of the French and Scandinavian schools'.[47]

Bowles also introduced to his audience one of the most important musical figures of the time, the conductor Sir Adrian Boult. Boult (1889–1983) had been music director of the BBC since 1930, when its symphony orchestra was established. He was at this time becoming an international star, with immense power and prestige, especially with the British orchestras, and was to have a significant influence on the career of Bowles himself. His excellence as a conductor stemmed not from any showmanship but from his reserve in rehearsal, his devotion to the score, and the extreme economy of gesture in performance, which took away nothing from what he called 'the point of the stick'.[48] Boult had brought the BBCSO to world stature within a few years of its foundation, and these years were probably matched only by the period when Pierre Boulez was principal conductor (1971–5). Like Bowles himself in Dublin, Boult had stood aside in order to introduce great foreign conductors such as Ansermet, Walter, Mengelberg, Koussevitsky and Toscanini. For Bowles to have succeeded in attracting Boult to Dublin was equal to Boult's own achievement in securing these conductors for the fledgling BBCSO.

Boult's programme began with Elgar's overture 'Cockaigne' which, in an elegant gesture, he invited Bowles to conduct. It also included Frederick May's 'Spring Nocturne', which Eimear Ó Broin recalled as causing bewilderment in the audience, who greeted it with 'inward laughter and embarrassed applause'.[49] The concert was so successful that it had to be repeated the following day.

Another visiting conductor of note was the Scotsman Ian Whyte (1901–60), a pupil of Stanford and Vaughan Williams, who was head of music at BBC

46 Letter to the Editor, *Irish Times*, 2 February 1982. **47** 'Music on the air' (1976), pp. 141, 146. **48** The title of his 1971 film on conducting technique. **49** E. Ó Broin, interview with the author, 17 April 2002. The concert also featured the prelude to Act 3 of Wagner's *Die Meistersinger*, the Schubert-Liszt 'Wanderer Fantasy' with Louis Kentner as soloist, Delius' 'On Hearing the First Cuckoo in Spring', Brahms' first symphony and Vaughan Williams' overture 'The Wasps'.

Scotland 1931–45, during which time he established the BBC Scottish Symphony Orchestra. He was responsible for guiding the early careers of Alexander Gibson, Colin Davis and Bryden Thomson (who was to become Principal Conductor of the RTÉSO). Whyte was a Scottish Nationalist, and it is believed that this counted against him in the upper echelons of the BBC in 1950, when he was strongly tipped as successor to Boult. Eimear Ó Broin, who noted his especial skill in conducting Dvořák and Sibelius, recalls his comment to the RÉ orchestra: 'Ye may be a bigger orchestra than mine in Glasgow, but I wish ye played as well in tune!'.[50]

The Irish and Irish-based soloists in these concerts were well-known to their audiences: in many cases they were teachers, and in all cases the intimacy of Dublin musical life meant that they were accessible not only on the concert platform but socially. Of these, Charles Lynch (1906–84) had enjoyed a considerable career in Britain, where he had studied with York Bowen, Egon Petri and, for short but significant periods, with Benno Moiseiwitsch and Rachmaninov. In addition to his solo work, he had played with the legendary cellist Beatrice Harrison and her violinist sister May. Rachmaninov had invited him to give the first British performance of his piano sonata No. 1, and Bax had dedicated his fourth sonata to him. Wartime caused Lynch to retreat to Ireland, where, as we shall see, he became deeply involved in concert work and, as a conductor, in the DGOS, for whom he conducted fourteen operas between 1941 and 1944. Thereafter, he failed to resume his career in Britain but, as the pre-eminent Irish musician in terms of reputation and musical capacity, he made regular appearances with RTÉ, demonstrating, over the years, his remarkable breadth of taste, both in new works and the romantic repertoire. His career was, however, in the doldrums until a brief, late re-flowering in the 1970s when he gave several important series of recitals in Dublin and Cork, and held a part-time lectureship at UCC, where he gave many lecture-recitals, specialising in the French impressionist repertoire in which he excelled.

Rhoda Coghill (1903–2000), on the advice of Fritz Brase, had studied in Berlin with Artur Schnabel, one of the greatest piano interpreters of the age, whom she described as 'the most intellectual musician I ever encountered';[51] she had succeeded Kitty O'Doherty as Station Accompanist in 1939, a position she was to hold until her (compulsory) retirement in 1968, after which she was regularly re-engaged during the following decade. As an accompanist she earned the acclaim of Leon Goossens, Evelyn Barbirolli, Wanda Wiłkomirska and Josef Suk among many others. As a concerto soloist she had played with the Dublin Philharmonic, under Brase, and many times with the new RÉ

---

50 E. Ó Broin, interview with the author, 17 April 2002.   51 RTÉ Sound Archives tape no. BB1940.

orchestra. She was also a double-bass player and a poet, with two collections to her credit,[52] and as a composer she made many settings of poems by her contemporaries, such as Padraic Colum and Æ (George Russell), besides her rhapsody *Out of the Cradle Endlessly Rocking* for tenor, choir and orchestra (1923) – a setting of poems by Walt Whitman – and her 'Rhapsody' for piano and orchestra.[53] Bowles would later say that Lynch and Coghill 'were as much a box-office attraction as almost any celebrity from England'.[54] In the 'Bowles era' Lynch played at least eight concertos (on approximately an annual basis)[55] and Coghill at least six.[56]

Other 'local' artists who were adroitly balanced vis-à-vis the visitors were Clyde Twelvetrees, an English cellist settled in Dublin who had joined the orchestra and was also teaching at the RIAM – he played the Saint-Saëns and Dvořák concertos and the Tchaikovsky 'Rococo Variations' during the Bowles era.[57] Another member of the orchestra, Arthur Franks, played the Brahms and Mozart D major violin concertos, while Isidore Shlaen, a Jewish refugee who found a temporary home in the orchestra, performed the Mendelssohn, Beethoven and Glazunov violin concertos.[58] Kerry-born Pat Ryan, who in 1945 was principal clarinettist with the Hallé, played the Mozart concerto. An unusual feature of a concert in 1945 to commemorate the centenary of the death of Thomas Davis was the first performance (conducted by the composer) of Aloys Fleischmann's 'Clare's Dragoons' with baritone Michael O'Higgins, featuring the warpipes played by Joan Denise Moriarty, better known in later years as the founder of Irish National Ballet.[59] The dramatic nature of the entrance of the warpipes from the body of the auditorium onto the orchestra stage – witnessed by the President and Mrs. O'Kelly, members of Dáil and Senate and the judiciary – was particularly effective and was spoken of by its audience for many years thereafter.[60]

The presence of top-class visiting soloists on the Dublin platform assured audiences that they were witnessing the local orchestra at work with artists at the highest level. The fact that Radio Éireann was prepared to finance the

52 *The Bright Hillside* (1948) and *Time Is a Squirrel* (1956). **53** *Saoirdhréacht gaedhealach do'n phianó* (Baile atha Cliath: Oifig an tSoláthair, 1942). **54** M. Bowles, interview with Gareth Costello. **55** Rachmaninov's 'Paganini Rhapsody' (twice), Rachmaninov's second and third concertos, Brahms' first and second concertos, and the concerto by John Ireland. **56** Beethoven's fourth and fifth concertos, Brahms' second, the concertos of Grieg and Schumann and César Franck's 'Symphonic Variations'. **57** Twelvetrees (1875–1956) taught at the RIAM, 1902–19 and 1945–56. He was principal cellist of the Hallé 1921–38. **58** He subsequently played in the BBCSO. **59** The composer relates that *c.*1971 'it was considered for one of the [RTÉ] Gaiety concerts, but rejected because of the difficulty imposed by the need for centrally-placed steps to enable the piper to mount the stage, on the grounds that the fire chief would rule out any interference with freedom of movement at the top of the parterre [stalls]': A. Fleischmann to Charles Acton, 25 January 1981 (Acton Archive). **60** Cf. Ruth Fleischmann, op. cit., pp. 292, 296–7, 332. The overture was performed in London by the LPO under Maurice Miles in 1957.

engagement of such artists indicates that it was anxious to give its own players the *frisson* of musical satisfaction that almost always results from these encounters. Among visiting violinists, Max Rostal (1905–91), a pupil of Carl Flesch whose teaching assistant he became, had been the youngest professor at the Berlin Hochschule (1930–33) before moving to London to work at the Guildhall School of Music (1944–58) where he taught Yfrah Neaman and members of the Amadeus Quartet. (The intimacy of the musical world is underlined by the fact that Neaman was one of the teachers of Mincho Minchev, who in his turn was to astound Irish audiences in the 1970s and 1980s.) Rostal played the Dvořák concerto in 1945. Jean Fournier (1911–2003), the brother of cellist Pierre, was a pupil of Enescu and recognised as an important soloist and chamber music player; he was to return to Dublin in 1950 to play the Bach double concerto with his eighteen-year-old student Geraldine O'Grady. Henry Holst (1899–1991) was one of the most experienced string players of his era: he had been appointed leader of the Berlin Philharmonic (under Furtwängler) at the age of twenty-four and in 1941 had founded the Philharmonia Quartet in Britain. He played twice in Dublin in this period: the Brahms concerto in 1945 and the Sibelius two years later; he would also be part of the auditioning process for the new orchestra. Jelly d'Aranyi, a great-niece of Joachim, and a major figure in music-making in London at that time, gave what Eimear Ó Broin considered to be the finest solo performance of those seasons in the Beethoven violin concerto: 'a deep commitment to the work, a close-knit rapport with the orchestra which displayed an intellectual concept of the work'.[61]

Among visiting pianists, Moura Lympany, Ginette Doyen (the wife of Jean Fournier), Harriet Cohen and Julius Katchen were outstanding young international soloists. Lympany (b.1916) had studied with, among others, Paul Weingarten and Tobias Matthay, and in 1938 had beaten Yakov Flier and Arturo Benedetti Michelangeli to win second place (Gilels came first) at the Ysaÿe Piano Competition in Brussels. (In Dublin she played the second concerto of Saint-Saëns, and appeared with the RTÉSO in Croydon, in its first European tour in 1976.) Katchen (1926–69), although only twenty-one when he came to Dublin to play the first Brahms concerto with Jean Martinon, already had an international reputation since childhood; he was later the teacher of the young Pascal Rogé, who has impressed Irish audiences many times since his Irish concerto début in 1972. The Hungarian Louis Kentner (1905–87), brother-in-law of Yehudi Menuhin, was, in 1942, at the height of his powers, widely recognised as a supreme interpreter of Bartók as well as Chopin and Liszt; in 1956

---

61 E. Ó Broin, interview with the author, 17 April 2002. D'Aranyi was a friend of W.B. and George Yeats, whom she visited during her several visits to Dublin, and who were aware of spiritualist attempts during 1933 by d'Aranyi's sister Adila to locate the missing concerto by Schumann which the composer was anxious for Jelly to locate and perform: Saddlemyer, *Becoming George*, p. 473.

he would give the première of the Tippett concerto; he was later the teacher of Irish pianist Hugh Tinney.

The cellist Paul Tortelier (1914–90) had played under Koussevitzky in the Boston Symphony 1937–39 and, when he appeared in Dublin in June 1947, had just been engaged by Beecham to play 'Don Quixote' at the Richard Strauss festival in October, which was to launch his international career and which he was to play (with his violinist son, Jan Pascal and violist Constantin Zanidache) in Dublin in 1979.[62] Beatrice Harrison played the work with which she is most closely associated, the Elgar cello concerto, in 1943. The oboist Leon Goossens (1897–1988), who taught at both the RCM and RAM, had joined the LPO on its foundation in 1932 and was at this time acclaimed worldwide as the finest oboist of his day, with many works written for him, including the Vaughan Williams concerto (1944) – on this occasion (January 1947) he played the very new concerto by Richard Strauss, as well as an arrangement by Barbirolli of a work by Pergolesi.[63] The Russian singer Oda Slobodskaya (1888–1970) was another artist of huge international significance: an established star at the Mariinsky Theatre in St Petersburg, she came to Europe in 1922 (and went to South America in 1936), appearing regularly at Covent Garden and on the BBC in concert performances of opera including Shostakovitch's *Lady Macbeth of Mtsensk*. In addition to the 'Liebestod' from Wagner's *Tristan und Isolde*, her appearance in Dublin also featured songs by Rimsky-Korsakov, Balakirev and Mussorgsky.[64]

In 1949 Séamus Ó Braonain, having retired as Director of Broadcasting in 1947, could comment that 'If I were asked for my opinion as to the most spectacular and successful effort in the shape of a programme ... it would not be the ever-popular ... "Question Time" but the series of public symphony concerts'.[65] And almost twenty years later his successor, Maurice Gorham, writing in 1966–7, could justifiably record that the series of concerts from 1941 to 1947 'is still looked back to by Dublin music-lovers as a Golden Age'.[66]

---

62 He also conducted the orchestra in 1958 in a programme that included his own 'Symphonie Israelienne' and his wife, Maud, playing a Boccherini cello concerto. 63 On a later occasion, Goossens played a Marcello concerto with the RÉ Light Orchestra under Dermot O'Hara, and insisted on playing the rest of the concert with the orchestra as second oboe: Eimear Ó Broin, interview with the author, 4 August 2003. 64 She had previously sung in Dublin with the Philharmonic on 3 February 1934, in a concert which also featured violinist Adila Fachiri as soloist in part of Berlioz' 'Damnation of Faust'. 65 Ó Braonáin, 'Seven years of Irish radio'. Audiences also had the opportunity of hearing fine instruments: Holst and Rostal both played instruments by Giuseppe Guarnieri ('del Gesù'), considered to be the finest example of the Guarnieri family's work in Cremona in the late-seventeenth and early-eighteenth centuries and superior in most instances (depending on the repertoire) to that of his Cremonese contemporary Antonio Stradivari. 66 Gorham, op. cit., p. 126.

Table E: Members of the Radio Eireann Orchestra, 1945

First Violins	Second Violins
Terry O'Connor	Christopher Kiernan
Nancie Lord	Arthur Franks
Ferruccio Grossi	Posy Shreider
Madeleine Mooney	William Shanahan
James Chapman	Patrick Oakley
Rosalind Dowse	Jack Cheatle
Moira Flusk	J.P. McCurtain

Violas	Cellos	Double Bass
Walter Hall	Clyde Twelvetrees	Zach Lee
Máire Larchet	Christine Fagan	Robert Bushnell
Thomas Collins	Kathleen Pollaky	

Clarinets	Oboes	Flutes	Bassoons
Adolphe Gebler	Joseph Murphy	Thomas Browne	Richard Persse
Frederick Ashton	Hugh Doherty	Raymond Brewer	Sylvester McCormack
Herbert Leeming			

Horns	Trumpets	Trombones	Timpani
Nicholas Gibbon	Herbert Treacy	Joseph Thwaites	Stanislaus Stack
Harry Wood	Joseph Cassells	Patrick Feeney	
Liam McGuinness			
Frank Murphy			

At this stage, the orchestra still contained several players who had been with 2RN since its inception or very shortly after (O'Connor, Lord, Grossi, Dowse, Flusk, Lee) and many who would remain in either the RÉSO or the RÉLO for many years thereafter (Hall, Shanahan, Cheatle, Larchet, Fagan, Pollaky, Murphy, Cassells) besides several who had been members of the army bands and had found their place in the symphonic repertoire. In 1972 the Director-General presented long-service awards to twelve employees of RTÉ, of whom nine were orchestral musicians who had each given twenty-five years' service: Robert Bushnell (double bass, RTÉLO), Joseph Cassells (trombone RTÉLO), James Chapman (violin, RTÉSO), Jack Cheatle (leader, RTÉLO), Walter Hall (viola, RTÉSO), Máire Larchet (viola, RTÉSO), Liam McGuinness (horn, RTÉLO), Frank Murphy (manager, RTÉLO and formerly a horn player), and William Shanahan (violin, RTÉSO).

CHAPTER 3

New departures, 1947–62

'A SORT OF NATIONAL SYMPHONY ORCHESTRA'

Michael Bowles's success with the public concerts was, in fact, the beginning of his ultimate downfall. Dublin's Mansion House held an audience of 750, and the concerts were sold-out – so much so that tickets, costing 1s. 6d. to 2s. 6d., were limited to four per queueing customer. By 1943 the concerts moved to the much larger auditorium (over 2000 seats) of the Capitol Theatre in O'Connell Street. For concerts at the Mansion House, Bowles augmented his basic orchestra of 26 up to 51–2. For the Capitol, he could recruit another ten players, making a total of 61–2, the size that the new permanent orchestra would reach in 1948. In the interim, over a period of six years, he had persuaded Radio Éireann to increase the permanent complement to 37–9, which he regarded as the maximum practicable position. Most of the string players were semi-professionals who had played under Brase in the Dublin Philharmonic Orchestra, while the wind and brass continued to come from the army, again having had plentiful experience under their regular bandmaster in a different guise in the Philharmonic, as well as in the now weekly studio concerts from Radio Éireann. Eimear Ó Broin remembers in particular the sensitive playing of one, Daniel O'Reilly, who was to become principal clarinet in the RÉLO,[1] but problems of intonation and generic differences in repertoire continued to present obstacles to the integration of strings and wind, as did the recruitment of players from Dublin's numerous dance bands.

Thus, the increased interest in the concerts led in turn to a belief that the size of the permanent orchestra could legitimately be increased from its present number of 37–9 to, perhaps, 55–60 players, since the extra cost could largely be met by a reduction in the number required to augment for the public concerts.

Bowles's successes thus exacerbated the issue of whether broadcasting, or public performances, was the orchestra's, and the organisation's, priority, and it heightened the discussion as to whether the broadcasting service should employ the 'national' orchestra. There is no doubt (as we have seen from Charles Kelly's remarks) that RÉ saw the orchestra as having principally a

---

1 E. Ó Broin, interview with the author, 17 April 2002.

broadcasting function, to which the function of playing to a live audience was secondary. This is also displayed in the remarks of the incoming minister, James Everett, in 1948, who told the Dáil:

> To encourage the dissemination of musical knowledge – while providing an audience for the orchestra – invitations are issued each week to the public to participate – free of charge, in the symphony concerts broadcast from the orchestra's studio in the Phoenix Hall.[2]

This made it clear that the Phoenix Hall was a *studio* rather than a concert hall; that the audience was present, by invitation, as a witness to the broadcast being made. The conceptual difficulty, for those who wanted to see an expansion of the orchestra beyond broadcasting needs, was that, with the suspension of the Public Concerts in 1947, there was no opportunity to attend symphony concerts as of right. The new symphony orchestra was, and would be for the next five years, firmly within the control of broadcasters, and most of its conductors in that period would be personnel from other European broadcasting stations whose work was almost exclusively with radio orchestras.

In the view of Patricia Herbert, who performed piano concertos in the Phoenix Hall in the 1940s and 50s and in the SFX in the 1960s, 'the Phoenix Hall, whatever its limitations, provided for the first time the technical resources of a studio with facilities for audience participation', designed to service a radio audience rather than those physically present. Writing in 1973, she believed (like her husband, Eimear Ó Broin) that 'music has been over-influenced by the concept of public performance to the neglect of the many unexplored possibilities of the technologies of radio and television'.[3] There was certainly a strong case to be made for an orchestra, either national or municipal, being based in Dublin and organised quite separately from RTÉ and its studio orchestra; there was also a case to be made for the vibrancy of programming, for listeners and the non-paying audience-in-attendance, that was not dependent on box-office receipts, which in turn affected the musical tastes of the paying public. Certainly the repertoire in those years (both before and after the foundation of the RÉSO) was adventurous. In fact in 1947, with the complement of players still fixed at forty, we find Jean Martinon conducting a contemporary programme with Carlo Pizzini's 'Al Piemonte', Florent Schmitt's 'Tragédie de Salome', Stravinsky's 'Rag Time' and Richard Strauss's 'Bourgeois Gentilhomme'. A month later, he presented Fleischmann's 'Fountain of Magic', alongside Prokofiev's 'Classical' symphony, Brahms' first, and Marcel Landowski's symphonic poem 'Edina' (1946). In the same year Edmond Appia

2 DD, 112, 20 July 1948, col. 817. 3 *Irish Times*, 18 April 1973.

gave another all-Irish programme, with Fleischmann's overture 'Four Masters', Ina Boyle's 'Wild Geese', Duff's 'Drinking Horn' suite, May's 'Lyric Movement' for strings, Harty's 'Irish Symphony' and Peadar Ó Cillín's 'Dréacht do Cheolfhuirinn Bhig [Piece for Small Orchestra]'. The distinct radio connection was emphasised in Appia's concert a month later, of 'Music by Composers of the Suisse Romande', featuring Pierre Wissmer's 'Le bal chez Sylvie', Roger Vuataz' 'Petit concert' and Aloÿs Fornerod's 'Le voyage de printemps'.4

Looking back from the perspective of 1980, Charles Acton recalled that in 1957 he heard works by Khatchaturian (two), Boydell (three), Victory (two), Bodley (two), Reidy/Ó Riada (three), Shostakovich (his tenth symphony), Pizzini, Martinů, Gordon Jacob, Blomdahl, Rossellini, Gabrieli, Honegger, Françaix, Turina, Vuataz, May, Francesco Mander and Monteverdi's *Il ritorno d'Ulisse*. He commented 'In those days ... the RÉSO ... directed by Fachtna Ó hAnnracháin, had a 20th-century standard of superlative quality and a livelier repertoire in Dublin than orchestral concerts had in London',5 his point being that programming in the 1970s had been far less adventurous. His claim about London concerts was not unfounded: in the early 1950s, before William Glock became controller of music at the BBC, representatives from the BBC had travelled to Dublin to discuss with Ó hAnnracháin how RÉ succeeded in presenting such a wide and varied repertoire.

Growth in the orchestra of the order envisaged by P.J. Little could not be achieved by recruiting Irish players alone – it was acknowledged that it would be necessary to audition abroad; as Bowles put it, 'seven or eight players from abroad [would be] a welcome and refreshing addition, large enough to make its presence felt but not so large as to disturb the indigenous flavour of the orchestra ... As I saw it, with patience and the development of young native talent, we could look forward to having, in ten years or so, an Irish orchestra establishment securely rooted in a healthy musical life'.6 This was to be the cause of serious debate both within RÉ and in public (especially in the Dáil) as sides were taken as to whether Ireland should be aiming to have an all-Irish orchestra or to employ foreign musicians in addition to Irish.

However, Bowles's moderate perspective was not shared by Patrick Little (1884–1963), previously parliamentary secretary to de Valera 1933–39, and Minister for P&T from September 1939 until January 1948 when Fianna Fáil lost office. Unlike two of his predecessors – Joseph Connolly and Gerald

---

4 Eimear Ó Broin (interview with the author, 8 February 2004) recalled that Wissmer, who was a balance and control engineer with the Suisse Romande, proposed to instruct 2RN's own sound engineers in the techniques of broadcasting music, during courses in Geneva; it appears that nothing came of this proposal. 5 *Irish Times*, 7 November 1980. 6 Bowles, 'The Birth of the RÉSO'.

Boland[7] – who evinced no interest whatsoever for radio, Little was a deeply cultivated man with a very strong interest in radio and particularly in music, both 'classical' and 'traditional'. TD for Waterford County 1927–54, he was passionately interested in the arts,[8] and the credit for the establishment of the Arts Council/An Chomhairle Ealaíon (of which he was subsequently appointed director in 1951, while still a member of the Dáil) is shared by Little and Thomas Bodkin. Eimear Ó Broin recalled that Little 'had a strong belief in the power of radio to bring about considerable social and economic developments in the state. There was a small group of individual civil servants who shared this conviction and were supportive of such a concept in twentieth-century administration ... He was one of the few Irish politicians who had a vision of, and a belief in, the idea of a European Community as we know it'.[9] P.S. O'Hegarty had retired as Secretary of the Department in 1944 and was succeeded briefly by Joseph Cremins and then by León Ó Broin (father of Eimear);[10] Little (and later Erskine Childers who was Minister 1951–54 and again 1966–69) and Ó Broin (who, in his former post in Finance, had already supported Bowles's applications for extra funding) were to exert a transformation of the orchestral scene which it would be difficult to overestimate.

In Bowles's words, the Minister took the view that

> with the end of the war in Europe and the large number of musicians presumably needing employment, there could be formed in Ireland, right away, an orchestra as large and as good as any in the world. It seemed very much like looking a gift horse too firmly in the mouth, but I had many misgivings about this, and said so. Unfortunately, I had neither the years [n]or the self-assurance to lay down the law ... Obediently, I drafted proposals for a full-scale establishment: a 60-piece symphony orchestra, to be complemented as needed from a 22-piece 'light music' orchestra.[11]

Almost thirty years later, Bowles would say that 'the proposal was megalomaniac, an oversize, a misfit in the community, and this could account for the fact

---

7 Connolly was Minister for P&T 1932–3, and Boland 1933–6.   **8** He published poems under the pseudonym 'M.J. Labern' in the *Capuchin Annual* and was the model for the hero of Yeats's story 'Where There Is Nothing' (1896); his eccentric older brother, Philip, was an associate of George Russell (Æ) and published *Thermopylae and other poems* (1915).   **9** E. Ó Broin, 'Music and broadcasting' (1998), p. 115.   **10** Ó Broin had been a Principal Officer in the Department of Finance when, in 1940, in anticipation of civil disruption in the wake of a possible German occupation of Ireland, he was appointed a commissioner for counties Galway and Mayo; at the end of the Second World War he became Assistant Secretary at P&T and Secretary in 1948, having been transferred by de Valera at the request of P.J. Little; on his appointment as Assistant Secretary, Joseph Cremins had told him 'I am leaving the mantle of culture to you': interviews with Eimear Ó Broin, 3 May 2002 and 4 August 2003.   **11** Bowles, op. cit.

that the orchestra establishment staggered from one crisis to another during the next twenty years'.[12] He described the decision as a 'basic flaw': 'the orchestra had been enlarged too much too soon: it could not be assimilated comfortably and was a sort of oedema in the musical life of the country as a whole'.[13] On another occasion he had written 'An orchestra is a social organism, not a synthesis of talented players'.[14]

Whether or not the Minister actually believed that a world-class orchestra could be founded in such a way, or even understood what was meant by 'world-class', is debatable, but certainly the unrealistic view prevailed, fuelled by Little's own enthusiasm and by innate feelings of national pride, that this was at least a possibility. Accordingly, a press statement was issued announcing that

> it has been decided to extend the present Radio Éireann Orchestra of 39 which was engaged on a part-time basis and which has given such valiant service in every type of programme for years past to a Radio Éireann Symphony Orchestra of 61 players, and a salon orchestra of 22, both on a full-time basis. It is intended that the Radio Éireann Symphony Orchestra will be employed exclusively in the performance of first class music, and that the salon orchestra will provide programmes of the lighter type – giving especial attention to programmes of Irish dance music, incidental music for plays etc.[15]

On another chauvinistic note, the Minister's announcement then added the Irish diaspora into the broadcasting equation by announcing the establishment of

> the short wave service ... for transmission to distant countries, and specially countries where Irish people and their descendants are most numerous. We shall aim at giving the Irish abroad, and other sympathetic listeners, programmes of music and speech which will keep them in touch with the best that is to be found in Ireland. In addition we intend to broadcast news bulletins which will give a day to day picture of Irish events and activities, so that the constant listener may follow the everyday story of the new Ireland, spoken with its own voice.

It was also envisaged, as Little told the Dáil, that on occasions the two orchestras 'will be brought together to form a sort of national symphony orchestra,

12 *Irish Times*, 8 April 1974. 13 *Irish Times*, 14 February 1973. 14 *Irish Times*, 3 January 1967. 15 P&T file 95/55/1 [originally W 3677/47]: 'Recruitment of Musical Staff – general procedure approved by An tAire, 10.2.47–5.6.47'. The complement for the RÉSO is variously given as 61 or 62: the discrepancy is due to the fact that the accompanist, Rhoda Coghill, was sometimes included in the overall figure. The BBCNI Light Orchestra in 1949 had a complement of 16 players.

capable of giving an adequate performance of the most important works and works outside the capacity of the largest orchestral combinations we have hitherto been able to assemble'.[16] One can detect here a nervous anxiety, firstly, that music should have a central place in expressions of Irishness, and secondly, that, as far as possible, music-making in Ireland should encompass as much of the repertoire as circumstances permitted.

Thus the political dimension of music – the presentation and promulgation of forms of Irishness – was present in the background to this enlargement. But the conceptual difference between the two orchestras, as stated, meant that for decades – until the repositioning of the RÉLO as the RTÉ Concert Orchestra in 1978 – there would be an assumption that 'programmes of the lighter type' could not in themselves be regarded as 'first class music', with a concomitant reluctance on the part of listeners and audience to give due attention to the RÉLO's broadcasts and public appearances. In 1951, Brian Boydell would acknowledge 'tremendous improvements which we must recognise with gratitude', but he would express his condescension to the idea of 'light music' in scathing terms: 'The Light Orchestra has been formed so that the energy of the Symphony Orchestra is no longer wasted on the kind of sounds which blend so well with bacon and cabbage'.[17] A year later, he had changed his diet but not his views:

> No orchestra which sets out to give first class performances of the great masterworks of the repertoires can afford to waste its time and energy on hack work which every broadcasting station seems bound to provide in the form of meal-time concerts for those who prefer to eat their sausage and mash to the background of light music.[18]

Boydell may not have intended to give the impression that the work of the RÉ Light Orchestra was a waste of time and energy, but he certainly conveyed his view that the only music worthy of attention was the 'great masterworks', and that, by default, 'light music' was something to be dismissed as second-rate. This would become an unconscious prejudice on all sides: thus a Dáil deputy would pick up on the fact that, after extensive laudatory reference to the Symphony Orchestra, Erskine Childers (as Minister for P&T) had said: 'The light orchestra also progresses'. The deputy 'thought that a very poor tribute to the conductor and members of that orchestra who have done so much for light music in this country and who have done so much for Radio Éireann in making it as popular as it is … If the people are to appreciate the music played

---

16 DD, 105, 23 April 1947, col. 1296. **17** B. Boydell, 'The future of music in Ireland' (1951). **18** B. Boydell, 'Orchestral and chamber music in Dublin' (1952), p. 223.

by the symphony orchestra, they will only be educated into a love of that type of music by such an orchestra as the Radio Éireann Light Orchestra'.[19] The same thoughtless prejudice would extend even to critics of repute: thus Michael Dervan of the *Irish Times*, referring to Proinnsías Ó Duinn, wrote that 'There is something very peculiar about the fact that Ireland's greatest living conductor spends his time preparing and performing light music with the RTÉ Concert Orchestra'.[20]

RECRUITMENT

Planning for the new orchestras proceeded during early 1947. On 10 February Ó Broin advised the Minister:

> The Department recommends strongly that all the Orchestra positions should be advertised, that is those filled by the existing Orchestra as well as the new positions. If any suitable people are got from abroad, it is possible that it will be desirable to change some of the present Orchestra in their positions or even to put them down to the second Orchestra. Apart from this certain of the present members are of an age when they cannot be expected to maintain their efficiency (e.g. Grossi is 71, Twelvetrees 72, Lee 68, Leeming 67) and obviously they cannot be continued until they drop from old age. You will recollect that when Dr Vincent O'Brien was retired the reason given to him was that we could not keep people after 70. It would be inconsistent now to retain those who are well over that age ... Even if nothing can be got by way of gratuity for the older members of the Orchestra whose services may have to be terminated the Department feels that the position must be faced and that they must be let go ... It is also felt in regard to the new Orchestra that while we should not insert age limits in the advertisements (to let us see what material is forthcoming) we should not appoint any members over 40 (if suitable people under that age are available) and that we should lay down a condition requiring the members to retire at 60 years of age.[21]

Once again, a conceptual bias in favour of the larger orchestra is evident in the expression 'put them *down* to the *second* orchestra', as it would also be found in the denomination in the Department's collective mind of 'No. 1 and No. 2 orchestra'.

---

19 Brendan Corish (Labour, Wexford), DD, 134, 6 November 1952, col. 1150. **20** *Irish Times*, 31 July 1985. **21** Ó Broin to Little, 10 February 1947, P&T file 95/55/1.

It was later agreed that the retiring age would be sixty-five. It was proposed not only to maintain the wage differential between men and women, but also to have a differential between the orchestras: the players in the Symphony were to receive £8.10.0 (men) or £7.10.0 (women), with the leader getting £11 if a man or £10 if a woman; those in the Light were to receive £7.10.0 or £6.10.0 with £9 or £8 for the leader. Advertisements were to be placed in the Irish dailies, including the northern *Irish News* and *Belfast Telegraph*, and in two London dailies, with smaller announcements in the main journals of Paris, Geneva and Rome.

Predictably, the old problem of whether to stand down the existing players and, where appropriate, invite them to re-audition for the new jobs resurrected itself. In mid-March Séamus Brennan,[22] Director of Broadcasting, minuted a meeting with the orchestra:

> Orchestra object to the humiliation of having all the positions in the two orchestras advertised for open competition; they hold that it would amount to a public announcement that the members of the existing orchestra were unfit for their jobs and had been sacked. They object to having to undergo auditions; they say that not one of them could face audition happily under such circumstances ... Many of them have undergone several auditions to hold their present posts; they object to yet another.[23]

Another, more serious, problem now also arose which would cause severe *angst* among musicians and administrators for decades: the issue of the employment of foreigners. This was not only a matter of whether Irish jobs should be kept for Irish people, but also one of standards: if there were insufficient Irish players of an adequate standard, should the posts be filled by foreigners who met that standard, or by Irish players who fell below it? Brennan's note from the same meeting recorded that 'they object to aliens being admitted to any competition for the new orchestras. They state that in France and Belgium, for instance, no musician who is not a national can secure a position'. In an attempt to mollify the musicians, the Minister met them and assured them that the existing posts would not be advertised.[24]

However, it had already been decided that

22 The Irish name 'Ó Braonáin' and the English form 'Brennan' are used interchangeably, as they appeared in Ó Braonáin's own usage.   23 Departmental memo by S. Brennan, 15 March 1947, ibid.   24 There was in fact a long tradition of foreign players, especially violinists, working at the RIAM as *teachers*, e.g. Guido Papini, Achille Simonetti, Adolf Wilhelmj, Joshua Watson, and, in Cork, Ferruccio Grossi who was now a member of the RÉ orchestra; apart from playing in quartets and in Esposito's Dublin Orchestral Society concerts, they were not threatening the livelihood of Irish musicians who depended on performance for their income.

when the new applicants have been tested and selected, both the new and the present members will be placed temporarily in the No. 1 or No. 2 Orchestra in the positions for which they are considered suitable. During a trial period the performances of all the members will be observed under actual working conditions. Changes may be made as considered desirable for the purpose of trial in the members' positions in each Orchestra or from one Orchestra to the other. At the end of the trial period the selections for the two Orchestras will be made definitely and the members selected for retention will be appointed to the positions it is proposed to offer them in either Orchestra.[25]

This memo was written by Matt Doherty, who was to become a central figure in the development of the orchestras in his position as Establishment Officer, the chief personnel administrator in the department. As to the question of foreign musicians, Doherty recorded:

We have no desire to admit to the Orchestras artists from outside the country if a sufficient number of fully qualified people were available at home. But the Orchestra must recognise that with an increase in the number of members required from 39 to 83 it is unlikely that all the positions can be filled by fully qualified people at home. The admission of a certain number of outsiders must, therefore, be regarded as a possibility.[26]

In the outcome, insufficient numbers of Irish applicants, of whatever standard, came forward for the positions in the two orchestras, when auditioned by Michael Bowles, Fachtna Ó hAnnracháin, Charles Kelly and Henry Holst (see Table F). It is notable that although there were more than enough Irish applicants for most of the wind and brass sections (mainly because the Minister had given tacit agreement to the suggestion that personnel of the army bands would be given preferential consideration and could, if appointed, carry over their army service)[27] the number of string players available – even if they had been up to standard – was well below requirements.

In fact, of the 332 Irish and British applicants,[28] 131 were called for audition and of these, only 16 were considered qualified, thus underlining the need to look more widely for suitable players[29] – that is, 16 out of 48 left 32 to be found elsewhere. This represented a major conceptual and social, as well as

---

25 Departmental memo by Matt Doherty, 18 February 1947, ibid. 26 Ibid. 27 Secretary of Dept. of Defence to Charles Kelly (P&T), 28 February 1947; Ó Broin to Defence, 7 March 1947, ibid. 28 Unfortunately we have no separate record of Irish as distinct from British applications. 29 P&T file 95/55/4, originally W 11541/47, information prepared by Ó Broin for the Minister, 25 June 1947, in anticipation of Parliamentary Questions the following day.

Table F

	Number of posts to be advertised	Number of Irish applicants
Violin	18	16
Viola	7	2
Cello	5	3
Double bass	4	3
Flute	1	2
Oboe	1	0
Clarinet	1	4
Bassoon	1	1
Horn	2	3
Trumpet	3	7
Trombone	1	4
Tuba	1	2
Percussion	2	1
Harp	1	0
TOTAL	48	48

musical, challenge to P&T, the Dáil and Irish society. The feeling against foreign players ran very deep, to an extent which may surprise us in today's climate of relative openness to economic migrants and asylum seekers, and it manifested itself in the most visible fashion, by way of parliamentary questions to the minister (PQs). Thus in June 1947 (as soon as the expansion of the orchestras had been mooted), Oliver J. Flanagan, independent TD for Laois-Offaly, asked the Minister 'if he is aware of the dissatisfaction among Irish musicians regarding the decision to recruit foreign musicians to fill certain vacancies' and 'if he is satisfied that this decision is, in all the circumstances, justified; and if he will state whether, in order to foster and encourage suitable native talent for the orchestra, he will consider the establishment of a suitable school for training musicians'.[30] On the same day, Alfie Byrne, another independent TD (Dublin North-East) and a past and future Lord Mayor of Dublin, put the question more bluntly: in view of the fact that the Radio Éireann musical authorities had stated that Irish musicians were not up to the required standard, would the Minister 'state what new facilities he proposes to offer to Irish musicians to acquire the standard demanded by the Radio Éireann authorities and so ensure constant remunerative employment for native talent'.[31] Six years later, when the debate on this issue was still as heated, and perhaps even more intense, Flanagan would declare:

30 DD 107, 26 June 1947, col. 314. 31 Ibid.

If there is ever a change of Government and if I have any say either to or within that Government the first people who will go will be those foreigners employed in Radio Éireann. I want to dissociate myself entirely and completely from any hand, act or part in the provision of employment by Radio Éireann for those aliens brought in by the Minister and encouraged by the present director of broadcasting. It is against the wishes of the majority of the people who hold licences for radio-sets that these people should be employed in Radio Éireann. It is disgraceful and improper. No Irish Government should tolerate the employment of aliens in preference to our own. I would prefer a thousand times over to have no orchestra than to use the talents of those aliens brought in here entirely against the wishes of the Irish people. I want to make it very clear that it is not the wish of this side of the House that these people be employed there. If there is a change of Government they may understand that and may take this as notice to quit, as they will be the first people to be shifted and removed.[32]

In reply, Little acknowledged the dissatisfaction 'particularly among unsuccessful candidates', and, having stated that he had no reason to question the decisions of the selection board and that 'there is no alternative to going outside the country for performers of adequate standard', announced that he had 'arranged that a limited number of vacancies shall be reserved for a further competition'. As far as training was concerned, 'it is not the function of the Broadcasting service to provide such facilities ... Facilities for students of music already exist in Dublin and elsewhere ... and, apart from these, the Department of Education arranges special summer courses for advanced students of music in which the Broadcasting service co-operates'.[33] As we shall see (below, pp. 172–86), music education was by no means adequate, and within a few years Radio Éireann would find itself involved in detailed negotiations in an attempt to improve the situation. By the time that Erskine Childers had become Minister, it was felt that 'a system of annual auditions ... is the only safeguard against criticism of Radio Éireann for importing foreign musicians, and if it is to achieve its purpose the examining board must contain a preponderance of outside judges'.[34]

PLANS FOR MICHAEL BOWLES

Up to now, there has been some confusion as to the circumstances in which Bowles vacated his position. In order to find the foreign players, it was agreed

32 DD, 142, 11 November 1953, cols. 1932–3. 33 DD, 107, 26 June 1947, cols. 314–15. 34 Director of Programmes to Controller, 19 May 1953, on Music Department 'Waterford' file dating from 1947.

that he was to travel throughout Europe. This was partially achieved by auditions held in Brussels, Zurich, Bern, Rome, Lisbon and Paris, which, in Bowles's recollection, resulted in the recruitment of thirty-five players, which was obviously sufficient for current needs.[35] In fact, Bowles, on his departure, left these names on lists which then had to be verified by his successor. But, in addition, Bowles was to have two years' paid leave of absence to develop his conducting career, which would be partly achieved by setting up reciprocal arrangements with European broadcasting stations, by means of which conductors would be exchanged: Bowles had already conducted the BBCSO twice in April 1945,[36] and had brought the Swedish conductor Sixten Eckerberg from Gothenburg. Slightly later, Léon Ó Broin had suggested that Edmond Appia (Ernst Ansermet's assistant at the Orchestre de la Suisse Romande in Geneva), should be engaged as a further step in establishing exchanges. Fachtna Ó hAnnracháin, Bowles's successor as Music Director, believes that Bowles's skills as a conductor – limited at that stage to his experience with the army bands and with his small symphony forces – would have been enlarged and deepened if he had been able to fulfil the terms of his contract.[37]

In fact, it was envisaged that Bowles would work abroad under a noted conductor, and that, if possible, an exchange would be effected whereby his mentor, or some conductor associated with the mentor's establishment, would come to Dublin to direct concerts. Authority had been obtained to pay a visiting conductor £1,000–1,200 per annum for this purpose.[38] It is clear that Ó Broin expected Bowles to return as a conductor, but that if this did not materialise, another Irish conductor should be identified. 'While the advantages of having a conductor of European reputation here for a time are of course immense, it would appear a desirable eventual aim that we should have an Irish conductor with wide experience but at the same time with a firm ground-work in regard to Irish music and an Irish outlook generally'.[39] It can thus be inferred that Ó Broin realised the difficulties that might arise if the fortunes of the orchestra were to be placed exclusively in the hands of foreign conductors, and if Irish talent were not to be encouraged.

Ó Broin argued that, rather than advertise the position, he should seek advice from his opposite numbers in the UIR (the forerunner of the European Broadcasting Union); Germany 'is out of the picture at the moment while the

35 Bowles, 'The birth of the RÉSO'. 36 22 April 1945 from the BBCSO studio in Bedford: Smetana, overture *The Bartered Bride*; Beethoven, piano concerto no. 5 (soloist Clifford Curzon); Sibelius, symphony no. 1. On 24 April: Dvořák, overture 'Carnival'; Bowles, Divertimento for Strings; Harty, 'With the Wild Geese'. In addition, Bowles had conducted the BBCNI Orchestra and the BBC Scottish Orchestra in Glasgow. 37 Fachtna Ó hAnnracháin, interview with the author, 11 September 2002. 38 Ó Broin to Little, 21 October 1946, P&T file 229/56/1: 'Guest Conductor Symphony Orchestra Oct 1946–July 1947'. 39 Ibid.

emphasis in Italy appears to be on opera-conducting'.[40] Ó Broin's thoughts therefore turned somewhat naturally towards France, although his ideal – which he appears to have acknowledged as incapable of realisation – would have been to secure visitors of different styles in the persons of Boult, Ansermet and Charles Münch. The interim post of Music Director, responsible for administration but with no conducting duties, was offered to the unsuccessful candidate from the 1944 competition, Aloys Fleischmann, who accepted it, subject to the condition that he could conduct four out of the ten public concerts each season, which was unacceptable to RÉ. In the event, there was no further discussion on this point, since Fleischmann had sought, and had been refused, leave of absence from UCC, and was not prepared to resign his professorship in favour of a temporary post.[41]

Although Ó Broin gave the Minister the option of leaving vacant the post of Music Director so that the position could be reviewed on the return of Bowles, there is also evidence (from a fragment of an unsigned draft memo dating from the same period as Ó Broin's communication to the Minister) that the authorisation to bring in a foreign conductor during Bowles's absence 'has to some extent influenced [Bowles] to decide finally on a step which has been in his mind for some time, viz., that his talents and tastes and, in fact, his ambitions lie rather in the line of conducting than in that of administration and that he wishes to make his future career in music as an orchestral conductor'.[42] The fragmentary note went on to urge that, 'having regard to the almost complete absence of young talented musicians of Captain Bowles' type in Ireland – young people with initiative, courage, vision, powers of composition, knowledge of Irish and an Irish outlook generally – we must make every effort to secure that Captain Bowles' services are not lost to Ireland'. In the outcome, through a collision of Bowles's temperament with the civil service mind and the musical personality of his replacement, Jean Martinon, Bowles would, in fact, be lost.

Bowles's CV was prepared in order to promote his case with potential foreign mentors; it stated that he had conducted the majority of studio concerts and public concerts for the past six years, that he had also been responsible during that time for all other music ouput from RÉ, and that he had made many arrangements of Irish airs 'and some original work', as well as organising and training Cór Radio Éireann. He frequently gave broadcast talks and had been a music examiner for the Department of Education for the past four years.

Ó Broin did pursue the possibility of Bowles working in Geneva under Ansermet, the latter then to take concerts in Dublin but, although Ansermet expressed some interest in doing so, his schedule would not permit it. Similar

---

40 Ibid.   41 Ó Broin to Fleischmann, 27 December 1946; Fleischmann to Ó Broin, 6 January 1947; Ó Broin to Fleischmann, 8 January 1947; Fleischmann to Ó Broin, 8 January 1947, ibid. 42 Ibid.

consideration was given to (in descending order of interest) Münch, Paul Paray, Louis Fourestier, Manuel Rosenthal, Eugène Bigot, Gaston Poulet, and Roger Desormières, indicating that Ó Broin's focus was becoming increasingly French. Eventually, after discussions with Henry Barraud (who, as well as a composer whose work was played often in Dublin, was Music Director of French Radio), it emerged that 'easily the best of the younger school is Jean Martinon',[43] and that Martinon was interested in a six-month period in Dublin.

While Martinon's work with the RÉSO was inestimable, one can only speculate what the level of development might have been, had Ó Broin succeeded in engaging a conductor of the stature of Ansermet or Münch, bearing in mind that these great names of the concert platform and the recording studio were specialists in radio broadcasting.

Ó Broin then reported to Little that Bowles should in fact be appointed 'Conductor of the main orchestra' and released on exchange to radio stations in Italy and Switzerland (the latter under Ansermet's guidance) for six months each, while also being free to seek freelance engagements in London and Paris for a further six months; and Martinon would be brought in for six months: 'he would build up the new orchestra and leave it in a position to hand over to the exchange conductors'. This should coincide with advertisements for the enlargement of the existing orchestra and the creation of a new 'salon' orchestra, including the conductor of the latter.[44] In fact, Little rejected the proposal to appoint Bowles as conductor, thus removing him from a position to which he could otherwise have returned, but retaining him as Music Director, with an interim appointee in the post. It was already understood that Martinon had a subsequent engagement in Montreal from October 1947, so that there was no question of his settling in Dublin for any protracted period. Ó Broin reported that 'I ... saw Captain Bowles and I gave him an outline of the proposed arrangements. He was satisfied generally'.[45]

Bowles always maintained that it was understood that, on his return to Dublin, he would resume his post as Principal Conductor – a fact confirmed by Fachtna Ó hAnnracháin.[46] Thus it was a shock to him, on a return visit to Dublin during his leave of absence, to discover that Martinon, who had been working with the orchestra since mid-1946, was widely regarded as the heir-apparent. It is also clear that Bowles did not know of Little's decision regarding the future of his appointment.

43 Ó Broin, ms. note at Hôtel Claridge, Paris, n.d., ibid. As this note is undated, it is unclear whether it predates Martinon's first concerts in Ireland, which began in mid-1946. It seems unlikely that Martinon could have been engaged by RÉ so quickly, so it must be assumed that when Ó Broin made his enquiries in Paris, Martinon had already started his work with the old orchestra and that he was not as completely unknown a quantity as the note suggests. 44 Ó Broin to Little, 21 November 1946, ibid. 45 Ó Broin departmental memo, 10 December 1946, ibid. 46 Fachtna Ó hAnnracháin, interview with the author, 11 September 2002.

Martinon (1910–76), a pupil of Charles Münch for conducting and Albert Roussel for composition, was a recently released prisoner of war, who was busy in the re-establishment of French musical life; he had first come to Dublin as a stand-in for the indisposed Münch in March 1946, making such an impression that he was immediately re-engaged for a series of concerts in 1946–8. (In the concert of 18 September 1946 he conducted his 'Stalag IX (*Musique d'exil*)'[47] which he had composed in 1941 in the prison camp near Cassel where he had formed a choir and a small orchestra, and had been transferred from grave-digging duties to writing music for camp entertainments.) It was in Martinon's concerts that some of the most outstanding visiting soloists had been heard – Katchen on 8 June 1947 with the Brahms piano concerto no. 1, Tortelier on 22 June 1947 with the Haydn cello concerto in D, Jean Fournier (another Münch protégé) on 6 July 1947 with the Mozart violin concerto K.218 and Martinon's own 'Concerto giocoso' (1937), and Ginette Doyen two weeks later with the Ravel piano concerto.

It can be appreciated that Martinon quickly became very popular with the public, whom it was essential to please if the launch of the new orchestra in February 1948 was to be a success. Martinon had charmed Irish people with his declaration 'Why, you could make Dublin another Salzburg! You could have a yearly music festival of European importance here. Dublin is so beautifully situated and attracts so many summer visitors, and the people obviously love music'.[48] However, Martinon's interest in the less well known aspects of the repertoire did not always meet with popular success: the critic and teacher Joseph O'Neill observed that a rare performance of César Franck's 'Les béatitudes' with Our Lady's Choral Society in 1947 encountered 'a deplorable lack of support. Apparently Dublin audiences only want to hear one great [choral] work, namely Handel's *Messiah*'.[49]

At the time, Frederick May noted that at the Department of Education's music summer schools 'every score M. Martinon interpreted blazed into an incandescent flame of beauty, and without a doubt he has left an indelible impression on the minds of his students'.[50] On Martinon's death in 1976 the critic and journalist John O'Donovan recalled that Martinon 'created the impression of a man who was complete master of himself, whose head gov-

---

47 'The opening depicts the sordid atmosphere of the camp; the tramp of clumsy military boots forms a recurring rhythm. In the slow movement, the exile expresses his sadness and longing for home. The *Vivo* describes the ironical good-humour with which the prisoners lighten their tasks, and one hears the folk tunes of many French provinces which the soldiers sang and whistled through the camp; a note of some hope is introduced with the popular song "J'irai revoir ma Normandie." Then the sad atmosphere of the prison camp returns. Such sentiments will find an echo in many lands, our own included': Grace O'Brien, 'Can Dublin become an Irish Salzburg?', *Irish Press*, 6 September 1946. **48** Ibid. **49** J. O'Neill, 'Music in Dublin' (1952), p. 257. **50** 'The composer in Ireland' (1952), p. 165.

erned his heart, who shrank from sloppiness and who was too fastidious to play to the gallery'.[51] Martinon's ability not only to comprehend the music but to convey its inner meaning, first to the players and then to the audience, was a skill noted by many:

> I often felt as I came away from a concert conducted by Jean Martinon … that if I were the composer of a complex and tricky score I would rather have him give the first performance than many a more illustrious practitioner. For, although limited in his emotional range, he was a superb technician and, like Pierre Boulez, could lead an orchestra with ease and confidence through the densest maze … He had the rare knack of being able, at one and the same time, to display his ability and to disarm the resentment that ability arouses at close quarters and he was second to none at fitting mailed fists with velvet gloves … Jean Martinon's chief contribution to the RÉSO lay in his being the first conductor to hold the players' interest and respect over an extended period. He never exasperated them with inefficiency, never alarmed them with doubts about his being able to cope with any emergencies in a public concert.[52]

The slight sense that O'Donovan's recollection was not entirely one of approval is borne out by Eimear Ó Broin, who acknowledged that Martinon was 'a brilliant interpreter of the French Impressionists – with an expressive, clear-cut, dynamic, interpretative style of conducting', but was 'more matter-of-fact, correct, precise and brisk', and 'not as fine an interpreter as Hans Schmidt-Isserstedt' in the classical and romantic repertoire.[53] Nevertheless, as Brian Boydell recalled, Martinon was 'the first really good conductor we had here … He was an absolute revelation. Not only did he make the orchestra play like they'd never played before, but also he was terribly encouraging [to young composers]'.[54] At Martinon's death Charles Acton wrote that he was 'still affectionately and gratefully remembered here for his special work in virtually making our Symphony Orchestra … He was strict, even stern, but that was what was wanted, and he quickly earned the respect and admiration of the whole orchestra'.[55]

At Martinon's concert on 31 October 1947 (which featured Messiaen's 'L'Ascension, 4 méditations symphoniques' [1932–3]) Séumas Brennan referred to the fact that Martinon would be returning to Dublin for concerts with the new orchestra in 1948. These included the inaugural concert of the RÉSO on 14 February 1948 in its new home, the Phoenix Hall. As Bowles ruefully observed, almost twenty years later:

51 J. O'Donovan, 'A musician's musician', *RTÉ Guide*, 12 March 1976. 52 Ibid. 53 E. Ó Broin, interview with the author, 17 April 2002. 54 B. Boydell interviewed by Michael Dervan, *Irish Times*, 17 March 1992. 55 *Irish Times*, 2 March 1976.

When he arrived in Dublin, M. Martinon, to my very naïve surprise, became a focus for those resentments, always latent and unavoidably cumulative around any performing arts administration, especially in music. He suddenly found himself in the position of being my rival as a conductor in Dublin and we both found ourselves the centre of a quarrel to which neither of us had contributed in any personal sense.[56]

Although it is misleading to state, as does *New Grove 2*, that Martinon 'held [a] residential principal appointment … 1947–50',[57] it was the *de facto* case that he was regarded as having principal status. Martinon went on to hold principal positions with the Concerts Lamoureux in Paris (1951–57), the Israel Philharmonic (1957–59), the City of Düsseldorf orchestra (1959–63) and the Chicago Symphony (1963–69) which commissioned his fourth symphony, 'Altitudes' (1966) to mark its 75th anniversary.

A draft departmental announcement of the re-organisation of the music department stated that

> During his [Bowles's] absence, the principal orchestra programmes will be directed during limited periods by various continental conductors. The first of these will be ~~very probably~~ M. Jean Martinon of Paris, who is already known in Dublin. He conducted the Radio Éireann Orchestra at public and studio concerts last year and was in charge of the class for conductors at the Department of Education Summer School … It has been decided to divide the responsibilities of Music Director and principal conductor of the orchestra. We are advertising, therefore, the post of Music Director tenable for a period of up to two years. The position will be reviewed on Capt. Bowles' return to Ireland.[58]

The salary of the Music Director would be £800 as advertised in February and March 1947. Fachtna Ó hAnnracháin, a choral conductor who had worked with the Keating Branch of the Gaelic League and also with Cór Radio Éireann (an *ad hoc* group of 20–4 voices), took up this temporary position in June 1947.

This announcement made it clear that, initially, conductors were to be recruited from abroad, and it underlines the suggestion that Bowles was being moved out of the way to facilitate this, even though initially Ó Broin hoped that Bowles would return in eighteen months' or two years' time. Bowles must have been quite naïve to have accepted the leave of absence, if he thought that he could also continue to conduct in Dublin to any significant extent, and the fact that, when he attempted to return after six months, he was instructed to

56 *Irish Times*, 3 January 1967. 57 Noel Goodwin, *NG2*, 15/936. 58 P&T file 95/55/1.

complete the remaining eighteen months of that leave, indicates that his use-fulness to the organisation had been exceeded. It explains why he evermore harboured a resentment against RTÉ which continued up to the fiftieth anniversary celebrations of the NSO in 1998, shortly before his death.

With Michael Bowles on the verge of resignation, as he began to realise that his position within P&T was vulnerable to the point of being untenable, Fachtna Ó hAnnracháin, as Acting Music Director, became responsible not only for all programme output but also for the implementation of the orchestras, which included obtaining a regular slot for their concerts in the still haphazardly organised broadcasting schedule. Bowles had left only a few outlines of his plans for the new orchestras, having, as Ó hAnnracháin put it, 'kept the big questions in his head'. Renzo Marchionni, from Florence, had been nominated by Bowles as leader, and Bowles had indicated a number of visiting conductors to take charge during his anticipated absence of two years. Ó hAnnracháin recalled that 'it was clear that if it was to happen it must happen quickly – within a couple of months – and it was important to get names down on paper'.[59] As the dispute between Bowles and the department deepened, the overseas auditions ceased, and thus the likely intake from Italy, Germany and elsewhere, which had already found Marchionni himself, became more remote. Marchionni was described by John O'Donovan as combining 'great charm with great dignity ... a dazzling technician ... [who] could unobtrusively shepherd his flock to safety while the conductor was driving them towards disaster'.[60]

During this period, the orchestra certainly expressed a sense of grievance, but this had more to do with their conditions of employment than with their relationship with Bowles. The orchestra had grown to a total of 37–40 in the Bowles era. The main ground for complaint was that the wartime conditions had forced up the cost of living and that their conditions of employment meant that they were unable to look for freelance work elsewhere. The representatives of the orchestra met Charles Kelly, then deputy director of broadcasting, and pointed out that 'having regard to the standard of work they were doing and the hours they were supposed to work, they were very badly remunerated by comparison with other orchestras in Dublin [such as those of the Capitol and Theatre Royal] and with dance bands – not to mention the rates paid to the Belfast BBC Orchestra'.[61] Players in BBCNI at that time were paid a minimum of £11.11.0 per week, with annual pay rising to £1500–2000. It was also pointed out that the members of the Hallé Orchestra worked 25 hours per week (as against 30 in Dublin); enjoyed full sick pay up to three weeks; and were paid £10 per week for rank-and-file players.

59 Interview with Fachtna Ó hAnnracháin, 11 September 2002. **60** J. O'Donovan, 'Music in the Air', p. 149. **61** C. Kelly, departmental memorandum of meeting on 27 July 1945, P&T file 10/57/2: 'Orchestra – claims for improvement in pay and conditions'.

Brennan made enquiries and informed the Secretary that the Capitol orchestra worked 22 1/2 hours per week, playing the same programme eighteen times, and were paid from £5.1.0 to £9. At the Theatre Royal the orchestra worked 23 1/2 hours and were paid from £6.12.0 to £8.10.0 for a seven-day week, with two shows daily. 'It is obvious from the foregoing that compared with these two rather ordinary theatre orchestras the Radio Orchestra, *which is in essence Ireland's State Orchestra*, is very badly circumstanced in regard to emoluments and required min. and max. hours of attendance and conditions generally'.[62]

> The comparison or contrast [with the Dublin cinema orchestras] becomes ludicrous when we consider the high-class and varied programmes our orchestra has to play and the standard of performance which is expected of them. Our very weak position in the matter has had and is likely to have many unfavourable reactions. There seems to be an air of restlessness and dissatisfaction among the members generally which is certain to have a bad effect on their work and to add to the already numerous difficulties of the Music Director and Conductor. We recently lost Posy Shreider, one of the best of our new recruits, and there is grave danger that we may lose others, particularly as Belfast and other BBC orchestras are likely, in the near future, to get going in full strength once more [i.e. at the end of the war]. And it is always the best who will get the chance of going. The poor opinion the musicians have of our jobs was reflected in the very small number of good class applicants for three posts advertised recently ... £5 (woman) and £6 (man) is small enough, but the probationary figures of £4 (woman) and £5 (man) would frighten off anyone ... The whole question of salaries and conditions generally would need to be considered without delay and substantial improvements effected – otherwise we'll be left eventually with an orchestra of mediocrities and all the valuable building up of the standard of performance which we have been doing in the past few years will have been thrown away.[63]

Brennan felt it sufficiently important to confer with his opposite number in Belfast, where he met George Marshall, successor to Godfrey Brown. The advice in relation to conditions is enlightening: 'Sir Adrian Boult and the authorities generally feel that it is very necessary for the members, in order that they may keep fresh, [to] have time for recreation, for reading and studying their music, for private practice, etc.'[64]

62 Brennan to Ó Broin, 20 September 1945, ibid.; my emphasis. 63 Brennan to Ó Broin, 20 September 1945, ibid. 64 Brennan to Ó Broin, 15 October 1945, ibid.

However, while discussions on the matter were taking place, events were overtaken by the announcement of the expansion and repositioning of the existing orchestra and the creation of the Light Orchestra.

It should be noted that financial restrictions operated across the board. Gorham records that there was no provision whatsoever for petty cash for incidental expenses,[65] and frequently the administrative staff put their hands into their own pockets when entertaining their opposite numbers. On the occasion of his conference with the BBC officials, Brennan had to write that

> our position in Radio Éireann without any expenses fund is humiliating in the extreme. The amount of such expenditure in a year would be small, but would be of inestimable value from the standpoint of national prestige and the maintenance of the right sort of relations with the BBC and the artistic world. Why should personal entertainment be at the expense of an official who comes up against it in the course of his work and why should he have to seek Dept of Finance sanction when there is a Director to see that the expenditure is justified? … We are at the beginning of a season of Symphony Concerts, with visiting artists coming to most of them. Expenditure of this kind will inevitably fall on myself and the Music Director … Captain Bowles has nothing but his salary, which for the Music Director of a National Radio Station is not high. Something must be done at once to right this position – otherwise we may lose the good name for hospitality that we are supposed to have.[66]

In fact, on grounds of expense, the Department took the drastic step of suspending Public Concerts from January 1948 (when the Phoenix Hall became available for studio concerts with an audience) until their restoration in 1953, thus removing this particular source of grievance among the administrative staff. The measure was part of the new government's Economy Campaign in 1948–9, which required every department to make cuts – in the case of the orchestras, of the order of £8,000. A cut in the actual numbers of the RÉSO was avoided, on the grounds that 61 was the minimum complement for a symphony orchestra (the BBCSO had 98 and the Concertgebouw 120), but it is surprising that the RÉLO was not axed, which was certainly considered as a possibility. As P&T informed Finance, 'the cutting off of 20 posts would … leave the orchestras in such an unbalanced condition that they would not correspond to any recognised musical combination and could only be compared to a Gaelic football team without backs or forwards'.[67]

---

65 Gorham, op. cit., pp. 166–7. 66 Brennan to Ó Broin, 15 October 1945, file 10/57/2 [originally A 9404/45]: 'Orchestra – Claims for improvement in pay and conditions'. 67 P&T to

Thus, with the cessation of public concerts, music policy took two steps forward and one step back, as it put in place two new orchestras but prevented them from playing before any substantial live audience. Despite the new vigour with which orchestral activity was undertaken, the RÉSO was effectively relegated to being a broadcasting-oriented, studio-based group. Shortly after his retirement Séumas Brennan was to write that 'I consider that not alone should the fortnightly concerts in Dublin ... be resumed, but that in addition what is really our national and only Orchestra should tour the country regularly, as the BBC, Hallé and other orchestras do in England'.[68] This was only the second time that the RÉ orchestra had been acknowledged as a 'national' entity, a recognition which would not be formally made until it was reconstituted as the National Symphony Orchestra in 1990.

FACHTNA Ó HANNRACHÁIN AS MUSIC DIRECTOR

From the time of his appointment in June 1947, Fachtna Ó hAnnracháin worked intensively with León Ó Broin and Matt Doherty to implement the results of the auditions, which he had been attending before the date of his appointment. Ó hAnnracháin feared that unless the auditions could achieve a viable number of satisfactory appointments, pressure would be exerted to reduce the plans to more manageable proportions. 'When uncertainty arises, the natural reaction is to see what you can do without'.[69] The most likely outcome would be a decision to concentrate on the Symphony and to postpone the creation of the Light Orchestra, but Ó hAnnracháin believed that that would be a wrong decision because it was part of Bowles's overall plan to have the two orchestras working in parallel: if the Light were not proceeded with, there would be a serious danger that musical needs for which the Symphony was not suitable would not be met. It was his task, together with Doherty and Ó Broin, to secure agreement with that viewpoint. Ó hAnnracháin recalled that Ó Broin asked him 'Do you really believe that we can do this – make two orchestras out of the single small orchestra that we have now? – and will they both survive?' It was a gamble, which time has proven to have been a correct guess, but in late 1947 it cannot have been at all clear that it would succeed.

The urgency of the situation was underlined by the fact that, if a starting date was not decided, many of the foreign musicians to whom offers had been made would take up work elsewhere. 'It was only in a post-war situation that people were willing to uproot themselves', Ó hAnnracháin recalled.[70] Thus

Finance, 29 November 1948, P&T file 175/58/5, 'Economy Campaign – Orchestras May 1948–Feb. 1949'. **68** S. Ó Braonáin, 'Music in the broadcasting service', p. 202 **69** Fachtna Ó hAnnracháin, interview with the author, 11 September 2002. **70** Ibid.

the date of 14 February 1948 was chosen for the inaugural concert of the RÉSO. Considering that it coincided with the change of government, this was fortuitous, since it was believed (wrongly) that the incoming Minister was inclined towards a total review of the existing plans. Fortunately the incoming players had been engaged and had arrived in Ireland before the new government took office, so that on that score there could be no reversal of policy.

In the meantime Bowles, believing that he had been supplanted, had resigned impetuously, telling the *Irish Times* 'I do not wish to discuss the reason for my resignation from Radio Éireann except to say that it is not of recent origin'.[71] This somewhat cryptic comment might be explained by the fact that, in conversation with Gareth Costello late in his life, Bowles adverted to the fact that there had been complaints from the orchestra about his 'bad language', and that 'things were getting not exactly difficult but sticky in the Department'.[72] Bowles was an irascible man ('Inarticulate and impotent, I just blew up and offered my resignation')[73] and, despite his undoubted skills as an artistic planner, and to a lesser extent as a conductor, his abrasive manner cannot have endeared him to his superiors. He himself put it thus:

> I was becoming increasingly tense and over-defensive in Dublin about this time [1945]. I did not know exactly why. Indeed I did not think in detail about any specific reason beyond the usual unpleasant captiousness of musical life in Dublin, where plain Mike Bowles from the plains of Boyle or whatever [Bowles in fact hailed from Riverstown, County Sligo] had got away with musical eminence without being beholden in any way to the former 'Establishment', mostly Anglo-Irish, of the spirit if not in strict provenance.[74]

It is worth noting that, in Bowles's admittedly embittered recollection, he could regard the masters of the new state as 'Anglo-Irish [in] spirit' – that is, emulating their own former colonial masters; in particular, one assumes, he meant O'Hegarty and his successors Cremins and Ó Broin, as the mandarins of the broadcasting establishment. It may help to explain why Bowles felt he had been supplanted by Martinon who, in their eyes, would have been a more attractive, exotic specimen. But it is difficult to see how Bowles could have expected to occupy any principal conducting position with the new orchestra at the outset, if he were to abide by the terms of his leave of absence. He also demonstrated his naïveté in other matters when he looked back from 1967 and admitted that he had not sought publicity for the Public Concerts: '"The ret-

---

71 *Irish Times*, 16 January 1948.   **72** Michael Bowles, interview with Gareth Costello, 19 December 1997.   **73** *Irish Times*, 14 February 1973.   **74** Interview with Gareth Costello.

icence of the public servant" was my guiding notion ... The reticence was misguided. I did not understand at that time that music-making of any kind is, of
its nature, a public act. For executant musicians, as for politicians, public relations are next to professional ability as an essential part of their function'.[75]

Maurice Gorham records that after the change of government in 1948,
Bowles approached the incoming Minister to request a re-examination of his
position, and was offered a six months' conducting engagement once the existing schedule of visiting conductors had run its course, but that eventually nothing transpired. In the following year, the Minister held 'a confrontation in his
presence between Bowles and his supporters and officers of P&T and Radio
Éireann' which resulted, after a four hours' discussion, in Bowles being offered,
and accepting, a concert in the Phoenix Hall.[76] Bowles was rarely to conduct
again in Dublin thereafter: in January and March 1950 (those resulting from
the 'confrontation'), 'after which he had an enthusiastic and sustained ovation
from both the audience and musicians';[77] in March and April 1954, and in
September 1955. Bowles, with Sir Adrian Boult's encouragement, subsequently
became Conductor of the New Zealand Orchestra on a three-year contract
1950–3, and Conductor of the Indianapolis Philharmonic and Professor of
Conducting at Indiana University, writing a book on conducting.[78] When he
returned to Ireland in 1970, he and his wife opened a guest house in Roscarbery
in West Cork and he was appointed chairman of the Cultural Relations
Committee. He had at least two engagements with the RTÉ Singers in 1977
and 1978, and in January 1977 conducted the RTÉSO in concerts in Dublin
and Cork, which many of those involved found to be far from satisfactory.[79]

Following Martinon's six-month period, Ó Broin anticipated that a visiting conductor would be found in Italy, and pursued (unsuccessfully as it turned
out) the candidacy of Armando La Rosa Parodi, reporting to Little that 'our
Minister in Italy has wired that "after serious and discreet enquiries nothing
unfavourable is known of him either morally or politically"'.[80] Following the
Italian, the next six months would be taken by Jean Meylan: 'this man appears
to be on the young side and not to have a great deal of experience. He is also
placed very low on a list of Swiss conductors which I got confidentially from
the Swiss Broadcasting Service. On the other hand he has sent forward a strong
recommendation from Paul Kletzki who is, after Toscanini, the world's greatest conductor'.[81] Meylan would, in fact, undertake several successful concerts

---

75 *Irish Times*, 2 January 1967. 76 M. Gorham, op. cit., pp. 170–1. 77 Pat O'Kelly, op. cit.
78 *The art of conducting*; the English edition was *The conductor: his artistry and craftsmanship* with
an introduction by Sir Adrian Boult (London: Bell, 1959). 79 Moeran, Sinfonietta; Rachmaninov,
'Paganini Rhapsody' (soloist John O'Conor); Dvořák, symphony no. 8. 80 Ó Broin to Little, 25
April 1947, file 229/56/1. 81 Ibid. Meylan was at that time thirty-two years of age; Kletzki's recommendation included the statement: 'I am convinced that he is capable of creating, building up

in Dublin, although the next visitor, after Martinon, was another Swiss, Edmond Appia. Swiss radio (like that of France) would be a recruiting ground for many years for R(T)É, with Pierre Colombo working with the RTÉSO as late as 1980.[82]

POLITICAL AND MUSICAL CHANGE

1948 was a very significant year in Irish musical and political history. Two years previously, Radio Éireann had acquired its first dedicated concert studio, the Phoenix Hall, originally built in Dame Court (between Exchequer Street and Dame Lane) by the Irish Hospitals Sweepstakes which were now moving to larger premises. On 30 January the hall was officially inaugurated for public use by the Minister, P.J. Little, in what was to be his last duty in office. Edmond Appia conducted Schumann's first symphony and the Grieg piano concerto with Patricia Herbert as soloist. Accommodating an audience of 3–400, it would be the home of the RÉSO for the next fifteen years. Two weeks later, on 14 February, the new Radio Éireann Symphony Orchestra gave its first concert (Martinon conducted Brahms' 'Academic Festival Overture', Fauré's 'Masques et bergamasques' and Hindemith's contemporary 'Mathis der Maler'), while the Light Orchestra made its first studio broadcast from Portobello Studios in the Dublin suburb of Rathmines, on 1 March. In the interim, the general election on 4 February had brought to the Dáil ten TDs representing Clann na Poblachta (founded by Seán MacBride), mainly at the expense of Fianna Fáil, and, with a consequent shift in the balance of power, on 18 February John A. Costello of Fine Gael was elected Taoiseach of the first coalition government, ending sixteen years of continuous government by Éamon de Valera and Fianna Fáil. P&T's new political master was James Everett of the Labour Party. By the end of the year, the Music Association of Ireland had been founded, with the aims of establishing a national concert hall and of improving music education, and the Republic of Ireland Act had resolved the constitutional position of the country and a republic was finally in place, giving full effect to the Constitution adopted in 1937.

Political changes would have repercussions for the work which was being undertaken within P&T to establish the Symphony and Light Orchestras on

and developing into a symphonic orchestra any body of musicians placed under his charge'. After over 25 years' absence from Dublin, Meylan returned in 1986 with a programme including Frank Martin's 'Petite symphonie concertante' (Denise Kelly, harp; John O'Sullivan, harpsichord; Linda Byrne, piano) but Charles Acton disliked his performance: 'It was hard to believe that Mr Meylan was conducting the same orchestra that had played Bruckner for Bryden Thomson as they did only a week before': *Irish Times*, 19 July 1986.   **82** Colombo (1914–2000) worked with the chamber orchestras of Geneva 1950–68, was chief conductor of the Suisse Romande 1955–79, and was President of the UNESCO Rostrum of Composers 1958–79.

the best possible basis. James Everett (1890–1967) had none of P.J. Little's enthusiasm for music which had been such an encouragement to O'Hegarty and Ó Broin. A former trades union official, he was elected to the Dáil in 1922, holding his seat until his death; he had been central to a split within Labour in the mid-1940s which resulted in the temporary formation of the separate National Labour under Everett's leadership, gaining five seats in the 1948 election before re-joining the main Labour Party. As Minister for the next three years he showed little interest in, or support for, music in P&T, beyond his obvious obligation to speak up for the activities of his department in their entirety. The irony is that while he did not in fact reverse the policy that had been put in place (and actually allowed Ó Broin to resist the cuts required by the Economy Campaign), and while he even spoke supportively of the ongoing measures during Dáil debates – especially when introducing the annual estimate for his department – he was utterly dismissive of what was being attempted and, later in opposition, virulently offensive about the same endeavours that he had had to champion while in office.

Ó Broin, in his memoirs, states, somewhat surprisingly, that on the opposition benches Everett 'had shown some antipathy to Paddy Little's ideas. But in office he revealed none of this to me; and he reversed nothing. When presenting his first broadcasting estimate, he said that, being a new boy, he wanted to give an adequate trial to the enlargement that had taken place'.[83] But Everett, besides hating classical music, was in particular trenchantly opposed to the employment of foreigners, and gave an undertaking to this end in the Dáil: 'It is my intention to limit the introduction of foreign players to the necessary minimum'.[84] In the cases of most contributors to the Dáil debates, the main cause for concern (the result of a vigorous campaign against foreigners by the musicians' union, IFMAP)[85] was the availability of jobs for Irish people, rather than that of musical standards, which many did not seem to accept as a valid reason for excluding Irish players. But in Everett's case it was both a social and a cultural issue: back in opposition in the early 1950s, he made explicit his contempt for the Symphony Orchestra, saying that it was full of foreigners, and that it would be 'torture' for him to listen to it.[86]

> Deputy Briscoe: Can anybody imagine a Deputy of this House admitting publicly that to listen to a symphony concert would be the infliction of torture on himself?
> Deputy Everett: You are in favour of the foreigner.[87]

83 Ó Broin, *Just like yesterday*, pp. 176–7. 84 DD, 12 July 1949, col. 628; Everett nevertheless could only go so far as saying that foreigners would still be required where Irish players of sufficient standard were unavailable: ibid., cols. 625–6. 85 Irish Federation of Musicians and Allied Professions. 86 DD, 142, 10 November 1953, col.1788. 87 Ibid.

Everett's ability to equate the presence of foreign musicians, or the concept of non-Irish music in general, with a form of torture represents one of the high points of xenophobia in the new state, more extreme even than Oliver Flanagan's provincialism or IFMAP's protectionism.

Everett would not be alone: a future Taoiseach, Liam Cosgrave, would state in 1952 that 'we can listen in to any station in Europe and hear an orchestra from another country but, at the moment, the Radio Éireann Orchestra is some sort of international orchestra broadcasting from Radio Éireann. I think it is only right that our people should have the best standard available and an orchestra with a first-class reputation, but it should be composed of Irish musicians'.[88] This intellectual sleight of hand, suggesting that because the orchestra was international in composition it was therefore a foreign agent operating on Irish soil, was followed next day by Cosgrave's Fine Gael colleague, Sir Anthony Esmonde (Wexford), who stated 'I think we are all agreed that it is highly undesirable that we should employ all these foreign artistes ... I say that we should not have any foreign artistes. Surely we can form an Irish orchestra wholly consisting of Irish personnel ... We have waited long enough to get on the air and to get our own control of the air, and let us use it for the Irish people.'[89] The question of quality *versus* quantity would elude all those whose principal purpose in speaking on these matters in Dáil Éireann was to give widespread evidence of their laudable chauvinism at the expense of any understanding, or acceptance, of foreign values. It particularly highlights Bowles's telling point about the political analogy of music-making.

It cannot be stressed too much that the creation of two orchestras at this time was part of a carefully worked out policy to meet a wide variety of musical needs by means of both broadcasting and concert activity. It again underlines the prescience of Bowles as both administrator and musician, capable of the artistic vision that had been lacking in the Department up to that time, even though, in the opinion of Eimear Ó Broin, Bowles himself 'did not appreciate the effectiveness of broadcasting as communication – he was more oriented towards public performance'.[90]

But to achieve it was almost impossible: the first step was to transfer players of sufficient calibre from the existing RÉ orchestra to constitute the foundation of the Light, since 'it was crucial that the Light would not be second-rate'.[91] Ó hAnnracháin's first move was to persuade Jack Cheatle, first appointed in 1943 and then playing number two in the RÉ orchestra, to become leader of the Light. Coming from a background in the Theatre Royal and the DGOS,

88 DD, 134, 5 November 1952, col. 954. **89** Ibid., 6 November 1952, cols. 1161–2. **90** Interview with E. Ó Broin, 4 August 2003. **91** F. Ó hAnnracháin, interview with the author, 11 September 2002.

having played extensively with the Dublin Philharmonic, and directing his own 'salon orchestra', he was ideal for the new position, 'a very steady man' with 'a vast experience in light music'.[92] Cheatle was hesitant, but eventually agreed to Ó hAnnracháin's proposal. He was to lead the RÉLO for twenty-four years, and to be part of its growth in stature as it became one of the world's most versatile and successful radio orchestras.

Surveying the developments of 1947–8, Ó hAnnracháin commented that 'although it has not been found possible yet to bring both orchestras up to the full strength envisaged, nevertheless the availability of two orchestras in place of one opened up great possibilities in the orchestral field …Both the Radio Éireann Symphony Orchestra and the Radio Éireann Light Orchestra are yet in their infancy, and a long road lies ahead. In all modesty, however, it may be said that the formative stage has been completed with success'.[93]

Speaking of the twice-weekly concerts, he could claim that 'many thousands have availed themselves of the opportunity of seeing and hearing the first permanent Irish Symphony Orchestra'. Nevertheless, critics such as Frederick May could write (in 1951) that 'for the past twenty-nine years a native Government has been in power in Ireland, and though the period may be comparatively short, it is surely long enough to have enabled us to hammer out a certain policy with regard to music here, and the conditions governing its survival and development'.[94] As far as 'the art of the possible' was concerned, the 'modesty' and 'infancy' of which Ó hAnnracháin spoke were to be superseded at the time of the NSO's golden jubilee in 1998, when Ó hAnnracháin could write with justifiable pride of the change from a time 'of a shortage of orchestral players, of considerable financial and administrative restrictions, of a dire lack of suitable performing venues and of many doubting Thomases' to a period of growth in which he and his successors were able 'to confront and overcome obstacles'.[95]

However, Ó hAnnracháin's diplomacy in his public statement of 1948 in fact masked a deep-seated unease concerning the state of the two orchestras which he had just brought into existence. Ó Broin's question – 'Can we do it?' – must have resonated as he prepared schedule after schedule of orchestral layouts which continued to show that there was still a considerable – and perhaps an impossibly long – way to go before they could be brought up to the full complements of 61 and 22, and, moreover, that those complements would actually represent an acceptable musical standard. As would prove the case with the expansion of the RTÉSO into the NSO in 1990 and subsequent years, the harmonisation of incoming players into an integrated orchestra was a matter

92 Ibid. **93** *Radio Éireann Yearbook 1948.* **94** 'The composer in Ireland' in A. Fleischmann, *Music in Ireland*, p. 164. **95** F. Ó hAnnracháin, 'Introduction' to P. O'Kelly, *The National Symphony Orchestra* (1998).

Table G: Radio Éireann Symphony Orchestra, 1948

First Violins	Second Violins		
Renzo Marchionni	James Chapman		
Nancie Lord	Rosalind Dowse		
Arthur Nachstern	Christopher Kiernan		
William Shanahan	Luigi Corbara		
Zola Cirulli	Carmel Lang		
Monica Condron	Una Kenny		
Alfonso Evangelisti	Peggy Roche		
Alice Brough	John MacKenzie		
Suzy Luthi	Daphne Garratt		
Dora Hall	Mrs C—Salvadori		
Violas	Cellos	Basses	
Máire Larchet	vacant	Robert Bushnell	
Walter Hall	Clyde Twelvetrees	Zach Lee	
Wilson Formica	Christine Fagan		
Thomas Collins	Kathleen Pollaky		
Mr M— Gavagnin	Mollie Concannon		
Feruccio Grossi	Emer Lang		
Angela Egan	Nancy Doyle		
Edith Coplin	Una Lord		
Flutes	Oboes	Clarinets	Bassoons
Thomas Browne	Léon Thonon	Adolphe Gébler	Richard Persse
Herbert Leeming	Joseph Murphy	vacant [Army]	P— Donnelly
Horns	Trumpets	Trombones	Tuba
Leopold Laurent	Herbert Treacy	Novemo Salvadori	T— Dunne
Harry Wood	Joseph Cassells	Joseph Thwaites	
Gernod Essig	Charles Parkes	Patrick Feeney	
Nicholas Gibbons			
Timpani	Percussion	Harp	
Stanislaus Stack	Patrick O'Regan	Síle Larchet	

of technical skills, musical temperament, personalities and the orchestra's relationship with its principal conductor, and therefore departures were common
as it became necessary to 'let go' players who had proved unsatisfactory. The
chief anxiety was that insufficient players could be found to fill the places of
those who had to leave.

Because it had not in fact been possible to recruit the full numbers (due to
inadequate native players and a smaller intake of foreigners than had been
hoped for), deputies were engaged on a casual basis to augment the core of
each orchestra. However, since those deputies were local players who had been
adjudged inadequate for the initial intake, they were, by definition, sub-stan-

Table H: Radio Éireann Light Orchestra, 1948

First Violins	*Second Violins*	
Jack Cheatle	Patrick Oakley	
Fanny Feehan	Bessie O'Harte Bourke	
Moira Flusk	Miss M—McMahon	
Doris Lawlor		

Violas	*Cello*	*Bass*
Charles Maguire	Aileen Cheatle	Thomas Mathers
Kathleen Rankin		

Flute	*Oboe*	*Clarinets*
Thomas Stewart	Hugh Doherty	Thomas Cole
D— McGlynn		

Horns	*Trumpets*	*Trombone*
Frank Murphy	D— P Kelly	C— Brennan
Liam McGuinness	D— Rowe	

Percussion	*Piano*	
Val Keogh	Eileen Braid	

dard. Thus, when resisting Finance's demands for cost reductions, Ó Broin was in the awkward position of acknowledging that 'the substitutes engaged are entirely too weak in qualifications to give the necessary balance and for a few key positions it has been found impossible to get players of adequate standard in the country even to act as substitutes … There are also a few players in the combination whose ages range from 69 to 74 years. They are being kept on at the moment only through sheer necessity but age will make their retirement imperative very shortly'.[96]

Ó hAnnracháin had asked Martinon to submit a confidential report on the RÉSO; Martinon told him 'Since the facilities for musical education and training in this country are not yet developed to a high degree … there are at present many musicians who are not sufficiently qualified to take their place in it. While I do not expect the same standard of performance from this orchestra as I would from one of the major continental orchestras, I have placed a mark (+, -, ?) after the name of each musician: + signifying satisfactory, ? signifying doubtful, – signifying completely inadequate'. Martinon's list had thirty-one satisfactory players (twelve foreign and nineteen 'home'), eleven 'doubtful' and fifteen 'completely inadequate'.[97] It can have been uncomfortable to say the least for Ó hAnnracháin to be told that only half his symphony orchestra was

---

96 Ó Broin to Finance, 29 November 1948, file 175/58/5. 97 Martinon to Ó hAnnracháin, 20 October 1948, ibid.

of satisfactory standard, and that a quarter was 'completely inadequate', especially when the only sections without 'passengers' were the first violins and the
sole member of the clarinets, Adolphe Gébler, who was still being joined on
an *ad hoc* basis by an army player.[98]

As far as the RÉLO was concerned, Ó hAnnracháin had already alerted Ó
Broin to the fact that it could not be treated casually: 'It is extremely difficult
for a conductor to get good results. It is sometimes overlooked that we require
in the Light Orchestra players of the same calibre almost as those we need for
the Symphony Orchestra. If we do not succeed in getting good players for the
Light Orchestra I fear it will get a bad reputation which will be as difficult to
eradicate as was that of the old Radio Éireann Orchestra'.[99] It would be a further five years before a significant intake of German players (see below, pp.
186–96) would put an end to his years of anxiety.

MUSIC ASSOCIATION OF IRELAND

At the time, however, severe criticism, of a constructive nature, was levelled at
RÉ by the newly formed Music Association of Ireland (MAI). Shortly before
its formation, four of its founders – Aloys Fleischmann, Frederick May, Brian
Boydell and Michael McMullin (its inaugural secretary) – had written to the
Minister for P&T, challenging RÉ's capacity to make appointments such as
those of Music Director, and its policy in making musical judgements.

> In view of the immense importance of choosing the right men [*sic*] for
> positions which have such an influence on the future of music in Ireland,
> it is hoped that the Minister will use his influence to see that expert
> musical opinion is consulted before any such appointments are made …
> It is also urged that the powers of the Director of Music should be sub-
> ject to collective advice, since absolute dictatorial power in musical mat-
> ters has already proved an obstacle in the way of a healthy progress of
> artistic development, through the pursuing of a narrow individual pol-
> icy, with consequent bitterness and discontent.[1]

---

98 Gébler was a Czech Jew who had run a grocery shop in Wolverhampton, England, before coming to Dublin in 1930. He was the father of the novelist Ernest Gébler, the father-in-law of Edna
O'Brien and the grandfather of the novelist Carlo Gébler. He also composed incidental music,
for example for the Dublin Gate Theatre's production of *Julius Caesar* in 1934. He had been an
unsuccessful applicant during the re-auditioning process for the orchestra in 1932 (P&T file
139/58). **99** Ó hAnnracháin to Ó Broin, 25 August 1948, ibid. **1** 28 April 1948, file 118/55/1:
'Music Association of Ireland – Representations about Music Department of Radio Eireann
24.4.48–22.2.51'.

It can only be assumed that the reference to 'narrow individual policy' was aimed directly at Michael Bowles, as the occupant of both positions. The letter was copied to the ministers for education, social welfare and foreign affairs.

An immediate point needs to be made about the MAI's relationship with RÉ during this period and up to the 1970s, by which time the MAI seems in any case to have begun to decline in vigour and sense of purpose: within R(T)É the MAI was commonly regarded as having been founded by a clique of largely Anglo-Irish citizens who saw 'classical' music as their personal prerogative, were unconvinced of the propriety of native government, and of RÉ in particular as the custodian of the new symphony orchestra, and regarded themselves as entitled to berate its administration for shortcomings which, if their view were sustainable, would be largely cultural in nature. The most vocal of these were Brian Boydell, Anthony Farrington (who succeeded McMullin as secretary) and Olive Smith, who later gained national renown as one of the founders of the Irish Youth Orchestra.[2] In later years, Gerard Victory would regale the author with an account of Boydell in the RÉ offices in the GPO in Henry Street, banging the unattended reception desk with his walking stick 'in the manner of an Anglo-Irish squire trying to attract the attention of the natives' – an occurrence which is far from likely, but which illustrates the suspicion with which the MAI and officials in RÉ might regard one another. Ironically, therefore, the 'native' Irish, in a position of authority within RÉ, were perceived in some quarters as the protectors, or even the usurpers, of a cultural genre which was not natural to them and which would flourish better in the hands of those to whom it more properly belonged. This potential gulf would, in time, be bridged by the invaluable and far-sighted co-operation between the MAI and RTÉ in the Dublin Festival of Twentieth-Century Music.

There was, however, a more deep-seated reason for the RÉ officials to look with some jaundice on this letter, which also suggested, somewhat ineptly, that lack of musical expertise in recent appointments might have been further tinged by favouritism. In rebuttal of this letter, León Ó Broin pointed out that

> This is definitely a suggestion of corruption on the part of public officials … This attack may be due partly to the fact that two of the signatories (Messrs Boydell and May) were unsuccessful applicants for positions in the Broadcasting Station. Professor Fleischmann was actually offered the position of Temporary Music Director … He refused it mainly because the job was an administrative one and he wished to be allowed to conduct public symphony concerts as well. We had engaged

2 In the opinion of Eimear Ó Broin, 'Olive Smith saw herself as the Boadicea of the lobby': interview with the author, 3 May 2002.

other conductors and had made up our minds that Fleischmann was not good enough as a conductor. In any event we wanted once and for all to separate the duties of Music Director and Conductor ... All the boards were heavily weighted with musical experts. Even if the administrative officials who formed a small minority on each board had such a disregard for their public responsibilities as Messrs Fleischmann and company appear to think them capable of, they would have to accept the decision of the Board as a whole.[3]

Boydell had in fact applied unsuccessfully for the posts of Music Director and Assistant Music Director, and May had been a candidate for the post of Temporary Music Director.[4] It seems, from the way the MAI handled its discussions with RÉ and the Minister, that its chief anxiety, as represented by Boydell and Fleischmann in particular, was that the direction of the new orchestra should be in the safest possible hands, and it was widely considered that one of its chief (but unwritten) aims was to effect the removal of the orchestra from the control of RÉ.[5] One cannot help noticing, however, that the terms adopted to express this concern exhibit more than a little condescension and, at times, a level of hectoring by which the personnel in RÉ refused to be drawn.[6]

By July 1948 the MAI had written two major parts of its overall inaugural manifesto, promoting itself as the body most suitable to represent the interests of classical – or as it termed it, 'serious' – music in Ireland. These related to 'Broadcasting' in general and 'The Orchestra' in particular, and continued the insinuating tone of remonstrance that had already riled Ó Broin:

> At present the music profession in Ireland is ultimately almost entirely dependent upon broadcasting. Apart from organist posts in churches, where remuneration is inadequate for a livelihood, and teaching, Radio Éireann is the only regular source of employment for serious musicians

---

3 Ó Broin to Everett, 20 July 1948, ibid. The interview board which had appointed the Temporary Music Director had consisted of León Ó Broin, Robert Brennan (Director of Broadcasting), John F. Larchet, Michael Bowles, Jean Nolan (singing teacher and former registrar of the Feis Ceoil) and G.P. Hewson, Professor of Music at TCD; Hewson had been the only member of the board supporting the appointment of Brian Boydell. The same panel – minus Bowles – had handled the appointment of the Assistant Music Director. Robert Brennan (1881–1964) had succeeded his namesake as Director of Broadcasting in mid-1947 but would hold the post for less than two years; he had commanded the troops who seized the town of Wexford in the 1916 Rising and had been Irish Minister in Washington for nine years (having been instrumental in setting up the Department of External Affairs). He later became a director of the *Irish Press*. Brennan was succeeded in 1948 by Charles Kelly. 4 Doherty to Kelly, 6 May 1948; Kelly to Doherty, 7 May 1948, ibid. 5 Eimear Ó Broin, interview with the author, 3 May 2002. 6 On one occasion Edgar Deale had apologised for the manner in which the officials in P&T had been hectored by members of a MAI delegation: Eimear Ó Broin, interview with the author, 4 August 2003.

... Radio Éireann does, and will for some time to come, exercise a virtual monopoly in the field of the public performance of music ... Owing to this position of decisive importance, the musical organisation of Radio Éireann is a matter of national concern.[7]

(Even thirty years later, RTÉ's Director of Music would acknowledge that 'the fact is that RTÉ monopolises perhaps 80 per cent of any market that exists in Ireland for musicians'.)[8]

The memorandum put forward the view that 'the office of Director of Music at Radio Éireann is one of the most important and influential cultural positions in the country' (to which Ó Broin's marginal note reads 'agreed'). 'It is his business to direct musical policy and taste in as progressive a manner as possible' ('agreed'). 'The office of Director of Music should be distinct from that of conductor of the orchestra' ('agreed').

Ó Broin could not, however, 'agree' with the MAI's notion that 'The Minister should be advised by an independent advisory body of competent musical opinion', as he believed that the existing Advisory Committee, of which Fleischmann was a member, was the most appropriate body to make judgements. When the MAI wrote: 'It cannot be too strongly urged that musical appointments and decisions be put into the hands of musicians who are qualified to exercise judgement in them. In the past they have been too much in the control of Civil Service and political interests', Ó Broin pencilled 'What grounds for this[?]'.

> Though there have been many good performances given from Radio Éireann, there have also been far too many bad ones, some of which would not be considered creditable even for amateurs ... One is sometimes left wondering what musical standards, if any, are required in order to broadcast from Radio Éireann, or by what system engagements are given ... There has been at least one case of a foreigner being accorded several series of engagements for the transmission of what can only be described as lamentable tom-foolery.

The memorandum also said that 'The comparative absence of the more inferior kinds of commercialised music from Radio Éireann programmes is a feature of them that must be whole-heartedly applauded, and we hope that this policy will continue', and it criticised sponsored programmes for lowering standards. Finally, it criticised the day-to-day practices in studio work, and Ó Broin noted, 'We agree with this generally'.

7 MAI Memorandum, section (ii), ibid. 8 Victory to Personnel Director, 23 March 1978.

Turning to the Orchestra, the memorandum continued:

> An Irish Symphony Orchestra giving regular public concerts, not only in Dublin but in provincial centres, should be regarded as a national necessity. Orchestral music is one of the greatest art media of the present day, and no nation that aspires to take its place in European culture can afford to be without it. Nor can Irish music or musicians ever hope to thrive or to attain a level comparable with that of other countries in the absence of a good and properly directed orchestra ... Until there is some other National Orchestra, that of Radio Éireann must be regarded as fulfilling the functions of one.[9]

The suggestion that Ireland should aspire to a condition of nationhood in cultural terms, so that Emmet's epitaph might be written, must have been deliberate.[10]

On the discontinuation of public concerts it said: 'That ... the city of Dublin and the country [should] be deprived of all that results from public symphony concerts is a gesture unworthy of an enlightened and responsible government'. Apart from a music advisory board, the MAI wanted visiting conductors appointed for two-year periods, and recommended Jean Martinon for a long-term engagement.

> There has ... been a case where a foreign conductor has been imported and paid an unusually large salary, and has obtained results a great deal inferior to those that could have been obtained by a number of Irish conductors. An incompetent man of this sort can reverse in a week all the progress that has been made during months of hard work and training under capable predecessors, and such a blunder is inexcusable ... The engagement of a certain number of instrumentalists from abroad is necessary as long as there is a shortage of first-class players here. This shortage is due to the absence of opportunities for the great mass of the population of becoming acquainted with or aware of music in general, and of orchestral music in particular; to a lack of facilities for learning various instruments; and to the absence of prospects sufficiently encouraging to induce young people to take up an orchestral instrument or a musical career.

9 MAI memorandum, section (iii), file 118/55/1.   10 In 1803 Robert Emmet, after a failed insurrection, having been condemned to death, asked that his epitaph be not written until Ireland had taken her place 'among the nations of the world'. In college debating societies the motion 'That Emmet's epitaph can now be written' was frequently tabled at least into the 1970s.

1 Vincent O'Brien, 2RN's first Music Director, at the time
of the concert marking his retirement.

2 The 'Station Orchestra' – late 1920s.

3 W.A. Manahan's Dance Band made the first test broadcast from the
2RN studio in Little Denmark Street, 17 December 1925.

4 J.M. Doyle, Principal Conductor of the Radio Éireann Orchestra, on secondment from the Army School of Music.

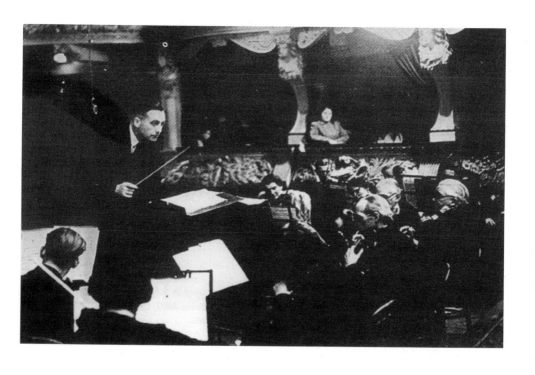

5 Michael Bowles, Principal Conductor and Music Director.

CAPITOL THEATRE

RADIÓ ÉIREANN

I CUIRTEAR ÓS BUR SCOMAIR

CEOL SIANSAC

CEOL-FUIREANN

RADIÓ ÉIREANN

UAIR SA SCOICTIGIS

Dia Domnaig, 12ad Mí na Nodlag, 1943

3.15 p.m. :: :: Luac 3p.

6 1943 concert programme with Jelly d'Aranyi's autograph: 'To dear Terry O'Connor with gratitude for her beautiful leading'.

RaDió éiReann

ceól siansać
Ceól-Ḟuiɲeann RaDió Éiɲeann

*

AMRÁN NA bFIANN

EDWARD ELGAR: Réaṁ-ċeól "Cockaigne" op 40

BRAHMS: Sianɼa a 1 i min-ġléaɼ C   op 68
    (1) Poco sostenuto—Allegro
    (2) Andante sostenuto
    (3) Un poco Allegretto e grazioso
    (4) Adagio

Soɼ 15 nóiṁeataí

WAGNER: Réaṁ-ṁíɼ Don tɼíoṁaD ġníoṁ,
    "Die Meistersingers"

SCHUBERT-LISZT: Fantasia "Der Wanderer" op 15
FREDERICK MAY: Scherzo
    LOUIS KENTNER
    'na aonaɼ aġ an bPianó

DELIUS: "Aɼ cloɼ na cuaiċe Don ċéaD uaiɼ lá Eaɼɼaiġ"

R. VAUGHAN-WILLIAMS:
    Réaṁ-ċeól Don tSpaɼċ "The Wasps"

DÁ Ṗinġin LuaċAN ĊLÁiR

7 Adrian Boult's autograph for his concerts on 26 and 27 April 1942:
'All good wishes & thanks for a grand show'.

8 León Ó Broin, Secretary of the Department of Posts and Telegraphs.

9 P.J. Little, Minister for Posts and Telegraphs.

10 Renzo Marchionni, inaugural leader, RÉSO.
11 Jean Martinon: although never appointed 'Principal Conductor',
he was crucial in the formation of the RÉSO.

12 Milan Horvat, Principal Conductor RÉSO, with pianist Charles Lynch before a Prom concert, Gaiety Theatre, Dublin, *c.*1955.

13 RÉSO, with Milan Horvat, Principal Conductor and leader
Renzo Marchionni, Gaiety Theatre, Dublin, *c.*1953.

14 Eimear Ó Broin conducting the RTÉ Light Orchestra (formerly the Radió Éireann Light Orchestra) at its 21st anniversary concert, held at the Abbey Theatre, 25 May 1969.

15 Tibor Paul, Principal Conductor and Music Director.

16 Igor Stravinsky, with (*on left*) Leo Donnelly and (*right*) Tibor Paul,
Geraldine O'Grady and Robert Craft at St Francis Xavier Hall,
Dublin, June 1963.

Summing up his reaction to this memorandum, Ó Broin told the Minister 'The only point in the letter to which I think we could not agree is the suggestion that the musical organisation of Radio Éireann should be in the hands of a board of "competent and progressive musicians". Advice on musical matters is very useful … but the direction of musical policy in the Station must be exercised by some person or persons who have executive and financial responsibility to the Minister'.[11]

Although Ó Broin did not consider it necessary to meet the MAI, this Memorandum was discussed by an MAI delegation with the Minister, at the Minister's insistence, on 25 October and referred to the Advisory Committee. Everett's decision is indicative of his determination to fulfil his ministerial mandate, regardless of his personal prejudices. Prior to the meeting, the MAI had written to the Minister:

> The Association has come into being largely as a result of the atmosphere of new endeavour that has coincided with the change of government, and of the example of co-operation set by the new Government and its apparent willingness to receive suggestions and representations from various sections of the community … Hitherto no such body has existed, and the progress of music in Ireland has been dependent on the limited efforts of isolated individuals or of small independent institutions; or, what is more serious, it has been in the hands of persons whose main interests and qualifications have lain in other directions. This is particularly true in the case of Radio Éireann, which not only plays so decisive a part in the musical life of the nation, but is the mirror by which our standards, civilisation and ideals are reflected abroad. The [MAI] believes that the musical organisation of Radio Éireann should be in the hands of a board of competent and progressive musicians.[12]

The MAI deputation consisted of Edgar Deale, Brian Boydell, Brendan Dunne, and Michael McMullin. Matt Doherty's minute of the meeting records that

> What the Association was really concerned about was that the positions of permanent Music Director and permanent Conductor were so important they were 'terrified' lest the posts would be filled without the Minister being quite sure that he had the very best advice it was possible to obtain … Mr Ó Broin put it to the deputation that a body like

11 Ó Broin to Everett, 20 July 1948, ibid. 12 McMullin to Everett, 5 June 1948, ibid. The inaugural Council of the MAI for 1948 consisted of: Brian Boydell, Patrick Delany, Brendan Dunne, Edgar Deale, Aloys Fleischmann, Anthony Hughes, Madeleine Larchet, Nancie Lord, Frederick May, Terry O'Connor, Joseph O'Neill, Olive Smith, Dorothy Stokes and William F. Watt.

the MAI would not be the proper one to make a selection for an important musical post from perhaps its own members and that if they did it
might be the cause of breaking up their Association. The deputation
appeared to see the force of this.[13]

Furthermore, 'Mr Ó Broin asked would the MAI be prepared to sponsor a
series of public concerts with the broadcasting orchestra. The deputation
appeared to be somewhat taken aback at this (no funds, etc.) but promised to
consider it'. Here the Minister made a personal intervention which Doherty
recorded as follows: 'Before the interview concluded the Minister said that the
country people in general were not in favour of all this high class music and as
representative of all interests it might well be that he would have to listen
favourably to the demands for a curtailment instead of an increase in the facilities for such music'.

The MAI record of the meeting, while not differing in significant detail
from Doherty's version, displays different priorities:

The interview was opened by Mr Deale who, as a prelude, emphasised
that the policy of the Government on matters of musical culture should
be dictated by a recognition of the value of these things in themselves,
and not by a consideration of musical returns. Since we were a new State
it was important to lay a sound foundation if we were to take our proper
place among cultured nations; that it was up to the present Government
in particular to make an impression in this sphere, and that they should
be prepared to spend more money on music. Mr Deale compared this
country with Finland which also has a population of three million but
which maintains several orchestras and subsidises composers ... Mr Ó
Broin ... asked whether the Association would take over the public concerts. Mr McMullin replied that we could scarcely afford such a venture, but that it would be worth the Association's while to approach the
Corporation and any other possibly interested parties with the suggestion of their support ... Regarding the appointment of a permanent conductor ... Mr McMullin repeated that the opinion of the orchestra
should in this case be consulted. Mr Ó Broin said that it would be wrong
in principle to allow the station employees to have a hand in the appointing of their superiors. He agreed, however, when it was put to him by
Mr Deale, that the attitude of the members of the orchestra to the conductor was important, but would give no undertaking that their opinion might be consulted even unofficially. Mr McMullin said that if the

13 Doherty memo, 28 October 1948, ibid.

orchestra had been consulted in certain cases, and in one case in particular, serious errors could have been avoided. Mr Ó Broin admitted
that one large error had occurred. [A large question-mark appears beside
this section of the note on the departmental file.][14]

Despite attempts by the MAI to start up a series of concerts in the new year
of 1949, for which RÉ would supply the orchestra and the MAI would be
responsible for other costs, the initiative came to nothing, chiefly because the
MAI sought an indemnity from RÉ that the orchestra had been consulted and
was willing to take part as an integral part of its broadcasting duties, which
RÉ refused to give as it considered it to be an unnecessary undertaking.[15] In
fact, given the complications that would arise when the orchestras demanded
supplementary fees where an outside body was charging admission, it was a
very reasonable request for clarification. Nevertheless, two months later the
MAI began to organise a festival to mark the Bach bicentenary, and the RÉSO
and Cór Radio Éireann performed the B minor Mass at the Metropolitan Hall
on 29 September 1950 (with the Culwick Choral Society)[16] and an orchestral
and choral concert on 20 October with the Clontarf Choral Society, conducted
by Sixten Eckerberg.

NEW BLOOD

Among the many foreign musicians who now came to Ireland was violinist Arthur
Nachstern (1911–99), who was born of Polish parentage in Odessa, where he
studied at the conservatoire with Peter Stolarski (the teacher of Milstein and
Heifetz) and had played the Glazunov concerto with the composer conducting.
When his family returned to Poland, Nachstern continued his studies at the
Warsaw Conservatoire where he, Witold Lutosławski, Andrzej Panufnik and
Witold Małcuzynski were known as the 'Four Musketeers'. Lutosławski
(1913–94) and Panufnik (1914–91) went on to become world-famous composers
(both of them coming to Dublin for memorable concerts), Małcuzynski

---

14 Dublin Corporation subsequently stated that it was not empowered to give financial assistance
in such a manner. **15** Departmental memos of meetings with MAI, 29 November, 12 December,
22 December, 11 January 1950, ibid. **16** Conductor, Otto Matzerath; Margaret Field-Hyde
(soprano), Anne Wood (contralto), Ronald Bristol (tenor), Owen Brannigan (bass) with John
Beckett playing a harpsichord made in Dublin in 1776 by Ferdinand Weber, on loan from the
National Museum. The orchestra was augmented by two trumpets in D, played by George Eskdale
and Bramwell Wiggins of the LSO. The Festival also included a lecture on the B minor Mass by
Joseph Groocock, two recitals of organ and vocal items at the Methodist Centenary Church and
a lecture on 'Cantatas and Orchestral Works of J.S. Bach' by Brian Boydell. Matzerath was a conductor with the Radio Symphony Orchestra of Frankfurt.

(1914–77) carved out a Lisztian career as a piano virtuoso (he also gave memorable performances in Dublin and Cork), and Nachstern spent over thirty years as a deputy leader and backbone of the RÉSO, initially making a strong first desk alongside Marchionni;[17] as Eimear Ó Broin recalled, they had 'a very fine way of rehearsing – they could work at different types of bowing for different situations – if Schmidt-Isserstedt said "you just play and find the bowing that suits you individually", they would work out a unanimity of bowing'.[18]

After graduation, Nachstern was a member of the Warsaw Philharmonic and the opera orchestra, the Cracow Philharmonic and the orchestra of the Vienna radio service. He had had an audition for the BBC Northern orchestra which, however, had no vacancy, and in early 1946 he was working with the Santa Cecilia Orchestra in Rome, where his father, also Arthur, had set up as a lawyer. Why the Nachsterns, senior and junior, considered Ireland to be a suitable destination for Arthur's talents is unclear, but in January 1946 – that is, before any decision had been taken to establish the RÉSO – the father was writing to a firm of solicitors in Dublin: 'Having no acquaintance in Dublin and having no address of an orchestra or philharmonia, I prey you by your leave to make me the favour and send by post the added letter my sons to a director of a great orchestra or to Philharmonia' (*sic*).[19] Another letter, to a firm of solicitors in Cork, suggests a certain level of desperation on the part of Nachstern's father: 'I know that above mentioned matter is no relation to attorneys but as I have no acquaintances in Eire I turn myself to you as colleague of profession. I mark that I want to assign £200 for your fee in this matter' – a very considerable sum for the job of effecting an introduction of this kind. In the 'added [i.e. accompanying] letter my sons' Arthur junior stated that 'now I should like to establish myself in Ireland'.

Michael Bowles was sufficiently interested to request T.J. Kiernan (now in Rome) to obtain 'an authoritative report on his ability',[20] León Ó Broin decided that he should be asked to submit a formal application, and he was eventually appointed in June 1947, making, in Eimear Ó Broin's recollection, 'a great team with Marchionni'.[21]

A difficulty arose two years later when Nachstern realised that other foreigners in the orchestra were in receipt of a 'foreigner allowance' which had been offered as an inducement, but was officially described as a measure to

---

17 Nachstern was temporary deputy leader (in place of Nancie Lord) in 1953; he subsequently played as no. 3 (behind Marchionni and Max Thöner) and again became no. 2 after Thöner's departure in 1956. After Marchionni's resignation in 1959 he was acting leader; he occupied the no. 2 position for most of the 1960s and 1970s until his retirement in 1976, after which he was retained as a deputy rank-and-file player until 1992 when he was 81. **18** E. Ó Broin, interview with the author, 17 April 2002. **19** Arturo Nachstern, Avvocato, Rome, to Messrs McCracken, Dublin, 5 January 1946. **20** Bowles to Department of Foreign Affairs, 2 February 1946. **21** E. Ó Broin, interview with the author, 4 August 2003.

facilitate relocation from countries other than England, in cases where the player was ostensibly also maintaining his original home. (Nachstern's papers showed that he had been officially resident in England at the time of his appointment.) Nachstern's application for this allowance stated that 'I have to start from the very beginning to provide a home for my aged father and mother, our home having been completely destroyed with all our property in Warsaw', and pointing out that he could not get extra work in Dublin as he was not eligible to join the musicians' union.[22] Ó hAnnracháin supported the application:

> Nachstern is an excellent player and if he decides to leave we shall have great difficulty in getting as good a man to take his place … Is it not a fact that Nachstern is really more entitled to a 'displacement' allowance than most of the other continental musicians – many of whom were fairly comfortably placed in their own countries [?][23]

Although the application was refused, it elicited the view of the Director that the union's attitude to foreigners was indefensible: 'We should do all we can to combat this ban … We should make it clear … that we cannot allow our orchestras to be divided into sheep and goats. If the members want the Federation to represent them it must represent all of them and not simply make outcasts of the continental people'.[24]

Ó hAnnracháin persisted: his view of the situation would be reiterated again and again over the next decade and beyond, as Radio Éireann confronted the problem of making Ireland a sufficiently profitable destination in both financial and social terms.

> I feel that we shall lose Nachstern if we do not do something for him quickly as the demand for musicians in South Africa and South America and the salaries and conditions offered in these places will result in his leaving us just as De Groote and D'Erbée left. We can ill afford to lose an excellent violinist like him and hence I strongly recommend that an allowance be granted to him.[25]

Nachstern in fact settled comfortably in Dublin, and was one of many immigrant musicians such as Victor Maliř, Gilbert Berg and János Fürst, who applied for naturalisation and received Irish citizenship. In Nachstern's case some amusement was caused by his taking advantage of the encouragement

---

22 Nachstern to Broadcasting Director, 31 January 1949. 23 Ó hAnnracháin to Director, 3 February 1949. 24 Director to Ó Broin, 22 February 1949. 25 Ó hAnnracháin to Director, 5 May 1949. De Groote, a Dutch cellist and D'Erbée, a Belgian oboist, were part of Bowles's recruitment.

to have one's name in Irish in the telephone directory: it appeared as 'Art Óg Nachstern'. His solid playing became one of the most dependable aspects of the 'old guard' of these immigrants, as the wealth of experience and the technical assurance of continental European playing began to have an effect on younger and less experienced Irish players. He recalled that the mixture of nationalities, and of musical styles, in the orchestra led to 'heated differences, as many were hot-headed (and sometimes hot-blooded to boot), with minds of their own – but the diversity of the membership brought freshness and vitality to the life of the orchestra'.[26]

In later years Nachstern was to recall that 'the achievements of the early years of the RÉSO laid a firm foundation for what we know today as the National Symphony Orchestra. Looking back, we were very fortunate: as a country we were small, musically we were not known internationally, yet such a wealth of brilliant conductors and musicians – some of them world-famous – were coming to Ireland and giving us the benefits of their experience'.[27]

VISITING CONDUCTORS V. A PERMANENT CONDUCTOR

The period immediately preceding and immediately following the début of the RÉSO in fact highlighted both the benefits and the disadvantages of the policy of bringing in visiting conductors. As already signalled, in addition to the series of concerts by Jean Martinon in 1947, the Swiss conductor Edmond Appia (1894–1961) began to make a number of appearances. He had begun his career as a violin soloist, leading the Geneva Opera House orchestra and then the Suisse Romande 1932–5, after which he was permanent conductor at the Geneva Radio from 1938. He conducted two of the final public concerts in the Capitol Theatre: that on 7 December 1947 introduced the four-year-old Concerto for Orchestra by Béla Bartók, as well as the prelude to d'Indy's opera *Fervaal* and André de Ribaudpierre in the Brahms violin concerto; that on 25 January 1948 was almost equally unusual, with a concertino for strings by Pergolesi, Ina Boyle's 'Wild Geese', Beethoven's seventh symphony and Georges Tessier as violin soloist in Lalo's 'Symphonie espagnole'.[28]

Probably the most distinguished of the visiting conductors at this time was Hans Schmidt-Isserstedt (1900–73), Generalmusikdirektor at the Deutsche Oper in Berlin since 1944. His concerts in 1948 and 1949 included the recently composed Vaughan Williams oboe concerto (soloist Léon Thonon), the first

---

26 A. Nachstern, 'Music and memories: 50 years of the Symphony Orchestra', 15pp. typescript, 1997. 27 Ibid. 28 Appia's catholic musical taste, which encompassed early French and Italian composers as well as modern work, is reflected in his posthumous *De Palestrina à Bartók: études musicologiques* (1965).

piano concerto (1939/42) by Alan Rawsthorne (who was to teach alongside Schmidt-Isserstedt at the Summer School of 1949) with soloist James Gibb. Schmidt-Isserstedt's value to the RÉSO was the fact that he was rapidly gaining a reputation as a trainer of radio orchestras: he was working at this stage with the Norddeutscher Rundfunk-Sinfonieorchester in Hamburg and was to remain its chief conductor until 1971. Like Adrian Boult, he 'aimed at a transparent orchestral text and strict rhythmic precision, rejecting all superfluous gestures and mannerisms',[29] which accounts for his inclusion, in addition to contemporary works, of classics such as Haydn's 'Oxford' symphony and Mozart's fortieth, K.550, on which a young orchestra would be expected to cut its rhythmical and tonal teeth.

At the same time, another rising star, Carlo Zecchi (1903–84), took his first concerts in 1949 and 1950,[30] which concentrated on the romantic repertoire with Beethoven and Brahms (first symphony), and all-Tchaikovsky and all-Schubert programmes without soloists. Zecchi, a student of Busoni and Schnabel, was both a pianist and a conductor with an extensive range of international guest engagements, who had made his début in 1941 and was professor of piano at Santa Cecilia, Rome. His many recordings made him a household name in the 1950s and 1960s. He taught at the Department of Education/RÉ's summer schools in the 1950s, and at the Salzburg Mozarteum, where one of his students for both piano and conducting was Daniel Barenboim.

Mosco Carner, later to earn distinction as a musicologist and biographer of Puccini, was less successful in his 1947–48 concerts with a performance of Bruckner's difficult fourth symphony, although he too presented little-known works such as Shostakovich's first symphony, Mahler's 'Kindertotenlieder' (with baritone Robert Irwin) and Dallapiccola's 'Piccolo concerto' for piano (1939/41) performed by Ilona Kabos (at that time the wife of Louis Kentner). It is believed that Carner was the main target of the virulent criticisms of one of the visiting conductors, which had been voiced by the MAI.

One of Bowles's exchanges had been with the Swedish radio conductor Sixten Eckerberg, who returned to Dublin for five concerts in January 1949. These featured music quite unusual for Irish audiences, and almost amounted to a mini-festival of modern and Scandinavian works, with the English-based Franz Reizenstein playing his own piano concerto (1941),[31] and Sweden represented by the symphonic variations for piano and orchestra by Gunnar de Frumerie, the nineteenth-century Franz Berwald's 'Sinfonie sérieuse', and Eckerberg's own first symphony. Later, in 1953, he gave another work of early twentieth-century Sweden, the interlude from Stenhammar's cantata 'Sången'

29 H. C. Worbs, in *NG2* 22/540. **30** He would return in 1958 and 1966. **31** His work is today championed by his former student, Dublin-born Philip Martin.

(1921). Also in 1949, Martinon was once again in evidence, with Stravinsky's 'Firebird' and the première of Walter Beckett's 'Pastoral and Scherzo'.

Nineteen-fifty witnessed more out-of-the-way repertoire in a studio concert when Jean Fournier led his former pupil Geraldine O'Grady in the Bach two-violin concerto under the baton of Edouard Lindenberg, who also included the 'Firebird' and Henry Barraud's 'Offrande à une ombre' (1942) in his programme. He was followed in two concerts by the Polish Matteo (Mateusz) Gliński, a composition student of Max Reger and a conducting student of Arthur Nikisch at the Leipzig Conservatory, and of Tcherepnin and Glazunov in Petrograd. Based in Rome at this time, he brought with him 'Tre Cantate d'amore' by the nineteenth-century Luigi Rossi, Casella's 'Paganiniana', and Pizzetti's prelude to *Edipo*, and, from his own country, the instrumental version of Szymanowski's 'Kurpie' songs (with the RIAM violin teacher François d'Albert), Moniuszko's symphonic poem 'Bajka', and his own symphonic poem based on Liszt's melodrama 'The Blind Singer'. The almost obligatory Haydn symphony (no. 104, 'London') also featured, as did Elgar's homage to the conductor's homeland, the symphonic prelude 'Polonia', seldom heard today.

1951 saw the Dutchman, Albert van Raalte, in three concerts, accompanying a return visit by Tortelier in the Schumann concerto and François d'Albert in the Mendelssohn. Again, Mozart's K.550 symphony and Brahms' first featured in his programmes.

Winfried Zillig (1905–63) gave three concerts in 1953. A composition student of Schönberg, he had worked as a conductor in several opera houses, including Düsseldorf, Essen and wartime occupied Poznań, and had latterly been working with the radio orchestra of Frankfurt (Hessischer Radio). Later he would become music director of Norddeutscher Rundfunk. Although he was a vigorous proponent of contemporary music, and one of the first to introduce the music of Schönberg and others of the second Viennese school (and was himself a composer of music regarded at the time as 'difficult'), his first two programmes in Dublin were unexceptional (Mahler's fourth symphony with Celestine Kelly, soprano, receiving its first Irish performance, and an all-Tchaikovsky evening), but his third was characteristic of his personal interests, with excerpts from Berg's *Wozzeck* (Ilse Zeyen, soprano), Schönberg's first chamber symphony and Zillig's own 'The Nearness of the Beloved'. In 1988, Seóirse Bodley would recall these concerts as one of the foundations of his musical education.[32]

As an example of a musician from a comparable cultural background to that of Ireland, one might cite Ivo Cruz (1901–85), the Portuguese composer and

32 S. Bodley, 'Composers in Conversation' with Dermot Rattigan, 1988, RTÉ Sound Archives tape no. AA4346.

conductor, who, after study in Germany, had founded the Lisbon Philharmonic in 1937 and was appointed Director of the Lisbon Conservatoire the following year, remaining there until retirement in 1971. Cruz' concentration on the major choral and orchestral repertoire with the Lisbon orchestra, and his parallel foundation of an organisation ('Pro Arte') to promote Portuguese musicians, is similar to the work of Esposito and Brase with the Dublin Orchestral Society and Dublin Philharmonic and of numerous initiatives such as the Irish 'Pro Arte' orchestra and the Dublin Orchestral Players. After protracted negotiations, he conducted in Dublin in 1953, with a programme including his own piano concerto no. 2 – the '"symbolist poem" Lisbon' (soloist Dinorah Elvas Leitao) – an overture by his compatriot Carlos de Seixas (1704–42) and Brahms' second symphony.

The impression one gathers from this repertoire is fourfold: firstly, a determination to meld the various elements of the orchestra into a common musical intelligence and common tonality by means of assiduous attention to the basic classical and romantic repertoire; secondly, to introduce new work to both players and audience, including that of contemporary Irish composers (see Table J); thirdly to make available some of the best international conducting talent in order to entertain and instruct, and fourthly to feature, in particular, conductors involved in the development of broadcasting orchestras.

The policy was not without its critics. Writing in 1951, Brian Boydell had said

> Within the orchestra there must arise a feeling of belonging to a community in which each individual feels a sense of responsibility for its achievements. To bring this about, the players must be treated as responsible human beings with a hand in their own destiny, and they must have leadership in the person of a really good permanent conductor.[33]

The terms of this observation were, in fact, congruent with MAI thinking, to which it is therefore reasonable to assume that Boydell was a major contributor, so much so that, when Fachtna Ó hAnnracháin received from the MAI's Anthony Farrington a letter with similar wording, he wondered whether the MAI was not being used 'to further aims which are purely personal'. However, at a subsequent meeting both Boydell and Fleischmann made it clear that neither had any personal interest in the question of the conductorship of the orchestra. 'I discussed the article in "The Bell" with Mr Boydell and … he admitted, that as far as conductors were concerned, his main worry was that we might appoint a bad permanent conductor'.[34] Farrington's letter also pointed out that

33 B. Boydell, 'The future of music in Ireland', loc. cit.   34 Ó hAnnracháin to Kelly, 24 January

There are, at present, many faults in the orchestra, of which you are no doubt aware and which are the subject of constant discussion among the musical public; the eradication of these faults is really not the business of any one conductor who is here merely on a visit and the continuance of these faults can only have a disheartening effect upon a body of musicians who should be keyed up to the highest level of inspiration and enthusiasm in order to give of their best and to bring credit to our country ... Nothing much is being done to bring on Irish conductors. If the existing policy is to continue we shall have in the future an orchestra made up partly of foreigners and partly of nationals operating under a succession of foreigners. By what stretch of the imagination could such an orchestra claim to be Irish? We should like to see a first-class Irish orchestra working under a first-class Irish conductor by say 1960 but the present policy could not possibly achieve such a result.[35]

Asked for a response, Ó hAnnracháin told Charles Kelly:

The RÉSO has made steady progress under guest-conductors. It might, of course, make still greater progress under a 'permanent' conductor – provided the 'right person' could be found. It is not easy, however, to find such a person. We have had a number of fine musicians on the podium in the Phoenix Hall during recent years; yet, it appears that not one of them would be acceptable to *all* current schools of musical thought! The difficulty to find a suitable 'permanent' conductor is, however, no argument against trying to find one. I think we can truly say that we have been looking round for a suitable man, and I myself have had some discussion on the matter with some of these conductors we have been most satisfied with here. It is a matter on which we should be glad to have views from any representative musical body, however, and I think it might be no harm to invite the MAI to make suggestions which could be considered ... Really of course potential [Irish] conductors should go for training abroad if possible; this would be far better than learning 'on the RÉSO itself'.[36]

Asked for his opinion, Roibéard Ó Faracháin (deputy Director) told Kelly in characteristically sceptical terms:

1951, File 118/55/3 'Music Association of Ireland – Suggestions for appointment of permanent conductor and Asst Conductor 29.12.50–4.2.53'. **35** Farrington to Ó Broin, 29 December 1950, ibid.; Farrington wrote from 19 Dawson Street, the premises of the Royal Irish Academy, of which he was Secretary. **36** Ó hAnnracháin to Kelly, 24 January 1951, ibid.

It certainly raises once more a problem which has so far eluded a completely satisfactory solution. No Irishman is at present qualified to conduct the RÉSO permanently. Is there one known to us, or is it possible that competition might discover one, with so conspicuous a gift that his training should be paid for, and his future employment guaranteed? And if there is or might be such a person, is it possible in Government finance, with or without special legislation, to provide for all or part of the cost of his training? ... I cannot see any way in which a group of Assistant conductors could be employed over any extended period.[37]

As Kelly passed these on to Ó Broin, he added 'It is so obvious that we should, if possible, have a permanent conductor, and preferably an Irishman, that the MAI are pushing an open door'.[38]

On foot of this, Ó Broin met Farrington, Fleischmann and Boydell, and noted that

The advantage of a permanent conductor of the Symphony Orchestra over the present system would be in the view of the MAI to create a new spirit within the orchestra, inspire leadership and infuse the players individually with an urge to improvement for the sake of the orchestra as a whole, spirit and standard being closely related. Initially for a period of about five years, a 'builder-conductor' would be required, a first-class man of technical rather than interpretative brilliance, who would make of the orchestra a technically brilliant instrument.[39]

However, he pointed out to the MAI representatives that, for radio listeners, novelty was necessary – 'new names, new interpretations etc.' Moreover, 'There could be no absolute departure from the present system because the most a suitable conductor would stay in Dublin would be 7 months in any year. There was considerable risk involved, the risk of signing on a flop or a man with a limited repertoire, and the fear that a long-term contract might induce indifference ... In selecting a man the views of the orchestra could not be relied on, since there was generally as much divergence of opinion there as among the musical public.'

Moving on to the alleged 'faults' in the orchestra,

The MAI, while admitting that the orchestra had shown great improvement over the past few years, asserted that many faults were still to be

---

37 Ó Faracháin to Kelly, 29 January 1951, ibid. 38 Kelly to Ó Broin, 31 January 1951, ibid. 39 Ó Broin memo, 2 March 1951, ibid.

detected, and these not only among the Irish players. Under a succession of temporary conductors bad players need not make an effort to improve nor could short-term conductors in the time available to them eradicate obvious deficiencies in certain sections and in discipline. On the other hand, a permanent conductor would be interested enough to insist on their elimination. Furthermore, a permanent conductor would demand the liberty to choose his materials.

It would be over thirty years before an incoming principal conductor would demand sweeping changes in the NSO's personnel, with consequences which were far from favourable.

In mid-1950 the editor of the *Irish Times*, R.M. Smyllie, writing under his pen-name 'Nichevo', asked why no principal conductor had been appointed, and why few British conductors were invited,[40] to which Ó Broin responded:

It is easy to confess that we would have British conductors more frequently if they were, as a class, of better material, but it is well known, even in Britain, that the blight that has fallen on so many other British institutions has fallen also on their orchestras and conductors. Their conductors are, by and large, poor stuff and those who are good, like Beecham and Barbirolli, we could not pay enough to bring over, even if they were willing to conduct what is a relatively small and not well known combination. We find it better business to go to the Continent.[41]

But he took the opportunity of pursuing the Minister on the issue:

It is a very remarkable fact that the orchestra has become self-confident as a result of the careful nursing we have given it in the last three or four years and by obtaining as conductors for it men who, the most critical players in the orchestra themselves had to confess, were for the most part excellent ... Assuming that we thought Departmentally that the appointment of a permanent conductor was desirable, what would your personal reaction be? Would you be prepared to distinguish between a conductor and an ordinary instrumentalist to the extent of allowing a permanent conductor in, whereas you have placed an embargo of foreign players save as substitutes? ... There would always be the risk that the 'permanent' conductor might not prove popular with either the orchestra or the public or with both, whereas under the present dispensation if we happen to light upon a bad temporary man we can always console ourselves by the thought that he won't be long with us.[42]

40 *Irish Times*, 24 and 30 June 1950. 41 Ó Broin to Everett, 28 June 1950, file 118/55/3. 42 Ibid.

Everett does not appear to have responded. A year later, when the situation had yet to be resolved, Farrington wrote again to the Minister, pointing out once more that

> A really good symphony orchestra must be something more than a collection of individual instrumentalists: it must have a collective personality. In rare cases, this personality has arisen from within certain orchestras; but the RÉSO is made up of so many diverse types that this is very unlikely to happen in this case. The mixed personality of the RÉSO must be welded into a team with both personality and a collective desire to achieve a common goal of perfection ... In choosing the right conductor for the position envisaged, it is suggested that the most important qualifications should be technical excellence, personality and universal musical sympathies. The specialist is not suitable.[43]

At the same time, Frederick May, while acknowledging 'the vast improvement which has taken place in recent years' in the RÉSO,[44] also pointed out that

> the conductors [were] either English or continental, with an Irish conductor getting only a very occasional engagement if an interval should arise between the termination of one foreign conductor's period of engagement and the start of another. Although this policy undoubtedly makes for interest and variety, it is none the less certain that the lack of a permanent conductor promotes a feeling of restlessness and instability.[45]

Former Director of Broadcasting Séumas Brennan concurred, in an article published in the same volume as May's:

> There has been no permanent conductor of the Orchestra since the resignation in 1948 of Michael Bowles ... I feel that a permanent conductor should be appointed as soon as possible. A succession of foreign conductors coming across for a month or two months is obviously highly expensive – more expensive, I should say, than the loss on public concerts. Apart from this, a conductor is only getting the feel of the orchestra, getting to know its weaknesses and its strengths, when he departs to be succeeded by another who has to commence learning the same lesson.[46]

---

43 Farrington to Everett, March 1952, ibid. 44 May, 'The composer in Ireland', p. 165. 45 May, 'Radio Éireann Symphony Concerts', p. 283. 46 S. Brennan, op. cit., p. 203.

Table 7: Orchestral works by Irish composers performed by the RÉSO,
February 1948-December 1958

	Year of composition	Date(s) of concert(s)		
Arnold Bax [1883–1953]				
Piano Concerto	1918	29.09.53		
Tintagel	1919	22.07.58		
Walter Beckett [1914–96]				
Irish Rhapsody no. 1		25.06.57	20.10.57	
Pastoral and Scherzo		01.04.49	14.02.54	
Triple Fantasy		14.04.50	07.11.54	
Seóirse Bodley [b. 1933]				
Ceol do Théadaibh	1952	15.01.56		
Movement	1956	--.03.56	21.07.56	04.11.56
Salve Maria Virgo	1957	27.10.57	12.10.58	
Brian Boydell [1917–2000]				
Five Joyce Songs	1948	--.--.48		
In Memoriam Mahatma Gandhi	1948	20.07.48		
Buried Moon	1949	24.01.54		
Violin Concerto	1953/54	01.10.54	30.01.55	
Wooing of Etáin [2]	1954	31.10.54		
Megalithic Ritual Dances	1956	12.02.56	03.07.56	14.10.56
Elegy and Capriccio	1956	14.03.56	28.01.58	
Meditation and Fugue	1956/57	20.01.57	21.06.57	
Ina Boyle [1889–1967]				
The Wild Geese	1942	09.01.55		
Arthur Duff [1899–1956]				
Echoes of Georgian Dublin	1955	18.11.56	18.03.58	
Meath Pastoral	1940	10.02.57		
Drinking Horn Suite	1953	09.02.58		
Brendan Dunne				
Scherzo		09.02.48	09.10.53	
John Field [1782–1837]				
Piano Concerto no. 3		23.04.54		
Piano Concerto no. 4	1814	21.06.57		
Piano Concerto no. 1	1799	20.06.58		
Aloys Fleischmann [1910–92]				
The Golden Bell of Ko	1947	12.10.48		
Eilís nic Dhiarmada Rua	1944	13.09.49		
An Cóitín Dearg	1951	16.10.51	17.01.54	
Biogadh & Marbhra Eogain Ruaidh Ui Neill		23.04.54		
Hamilton Harty [1879–1941]				
Fair Day	1904	17.10.54		
Comedy Overture	1906	19.01.58		
Irish Symphony	1904	28.02.58		
With the Wild Geese	1910	08.04.50	24.05.50	
Children of Lir	1938	14.11.54		

T.C. Kelly [1917–85]

Three pieces for strings	1949	16.02.54	17.02.54	30.10.55
		08.09.57		
Variations on a traditional air	1949	17.02.57	17.06.58	

J.F. Larchet [1884–1967]

Dirge of Ossian and	1940	25.10.53	
Macananty's Reel			
By the Waters of Moyle	1957	27.01.57	13.10.57

Daniel McNulty [1920–96]

Divertimento		26.10.58

Frederick May [1911–85]

Songs From Prison	1941	02.10.53	26.09.58	
Spring Nocturne	1937	07.02.54		
Sunlight and Shadow	1955	22.01.56	07.09.56	26.03.57
Lyric Movement	1939	03.02.57		

E.J. Moeran [1894–1950]

Symphony in g minor	1937	02.09.58

Havelock Nelson [1917–96]

Sinfonietta		06.03.51

Éamonn Ó Gallchobhair [1900–82]

Homage to Mangan		--.01.50

J.J. O'Reilly [1905–83]

Tone Poem, 'Oluf'	1954	--.10.55	08.01.56
Remembrance – Nocturne	1958	16.02.58	

Seán Ó Riada [1931–71]

Olynthiac Overture	1955	07.09.56	07.10.58	
Banks of Sullane	1956	12.07.57	10.11.57	
Hercules Dux Ferrariae	1957	13.09.57	12.11.57	28.03.58

A.J. Potter [1918–80]

Rhapsody under a High Sky	1950	17.06.52	06.11.55	24.09.57
Piano Concerto	1952	25.09.53		
Overture to a Kitchen Comedy	1950	17.06.52	11.02.53	25.10.53
		19.10.58		
Variations on a Popular Tune	1955	06.02.55	21.10.56	12.09.58
Tostal Overture		24.05.56	28.10.56	11.11.56
Fantasia Gaelach	1952	02.02.58		
Finnegan's Wake	1958	02.02.58		

C.V. Stanford [1852–1924]

Irish Rhapsody no. 4	1913	05.02.56
Prelude to *The Travelling Companion*	1916	02.11.58

Gerard Victory [1921–95]

Elegy and March	1951	26.03.54
Piano concerto		08.11.55
Movements from Oiche Bealtaine		26.01.58
Charade overture		29.01.57

Summary: 22 composers (of whom, 16 living), 63 works, 100 performances

As John O'Donovan recalled, 'There was one school of thought which held that the orchestra would never be really good until it had a permanent chief conductor. He could get to know the orchestra thoroughly ... and do whatever was needed to strengthen weaknesses and plug loopholes. The problem was where to get a dual-purpose conductor of sufficiently high standard, a man who was an efficient trainer of orchestras (a profession in itself) and at the same time capable of achieving aesthetically satisfying performances ... Once or twice it seemed that the very man to fill the bill had come on the scene. I was convinced that Carlo Zecchi and ... Constantin Silvestri were just what the orchestra needed and one day indignantly asked the Director of Music, Fachtna Ó hAnnracháin, why he hadn't grabbed them. His reply was to this effect: "If *you* can persuade them to come and then find the money to pay them, you'll be doing us all a good turn"'.[47]

The points were well made. In 1948 Brian Boydell himself had taken the rostrum twice, in order to direct the premières of his own 'Five Joyce Songs'[48] and 'In Memoriam Mahatma Gandhi'; Brendan Dunne, whose own Scherzo (from his Symphony in C) had been performed earlier in 1948, conducted Schubert's 'Great' C Major symphony on New Year's Eve 1948 and appeared again in 1953;[49] as noted above, Michael Bowles returned for two concerts in early 1950; Havelock Nelson directed the first performance of his Sinfonietta in March 1951; J.M. Doyle conducted *Messiah* at Christmas 1951 and 1952; and in 1953 (after May's article had been published) Aloys Fleischmann gave an all-Bax concert shortly before the composer's death.

The situation for Irish or Irish-based conductors improved slightly in the 1952–3 season: Boydell conducted seven concerts for schoolchildren; J.M. Doyle conducted at Tuam, Maynooth and the Phoenix Hall. Arthur Duff, who had joined Radio Éireann as a sound controller, from the Army where he had been a conductor, had four studio concerts and in the opinion of many deserved more such work on the strength of his demonstrable conducting ability; he had impressed both Martinon and Arnold Bax with his direction of the composer's work, and had a wide range of Russian works at his command, including the 'smaller' Tcahikovsky symphonies and those of Borodin.[50] But Duff, although a highly talented musician, and a composer of note, was beginning to show signs of the alcoholism which would contribute to his death three years later,

47 J. O'Donovan, 'Music on the Air', pp. 147–8. The Romanian conductor Constantin Silvestri (1913–69) appeared with the R(T)ÉSO on at least three occasions in the 1960s, including one with violinist Isaac Stern which is generally considered to have been one of the most outstanding concerts ever given by the orchestra; he had come to western Europe in 1956 and was conductor of the Bournemouth SO 1961–69. **48** 'Five settings of poems by James Joyce' op. 28 was first performed in 1946 with the composer accompanied by Joseph Groocock, piano; this was the orchestrated version, op. 28a. **49** Brendan Dunne was a frequent conductor of the amateur Dublin Orchestral Players. **50** Information from Eimear Ó Broin, 4 August 2003.

and Matt Doherty informed Maurice Gorham that 'Mr Ó hAnnracháin would not propose to ask him to conduct more than four concerts in any year'.[51] Hans Waldemar Rosen, soon to join the staff as Director of the RÉ Singers, had conducted a choral concert and a Phoenix Hall studio concert, while Éamonn Ó Gallchobhair had also made one studio appearance. In the same season the Czech conductor Vilem Tausky, recently appointed Music Director of Welsh National Opera, had taken the orchestra to Sligo;[52] Boyd Neel, the English conductor for whose orchestra Britten had written his 'Variations on a theme of Frank Bridge', had given a concert including a talk in the Phoenix Hall; Jean Meylan had directed five concerts in June, and another conductor with considerable radio experience, Pierre-Michel le Conte, who would have a long association with the orchestra, had introduced himself with four concerts in December–January.[53]

It is clear from these bare facts that almost the only occasions on which Irish conductors featured were those when they conducted their own works or those of other Irish-oriented composers. It was only in 1952 that the Music Department in Radio Éireann began to make room for two young Irish conductors, Eimear Ó Broin and Sydney Bryans, the former of whom made his début on 26 August, and was to be closely associated with both orchestras for the remainder of his career. And it was from early 1951 that Irish audiences were introduced to the Croatian, Milan Horvat, who was to become Principal Conductor from August 1953.

Meanwhile, Charles Lynch – not without a degree of self-interest – also observed that where, during the recent war, Irish pianists had plentiful concerto engagements with the orchestra, since the inception of the Phoenix Hall concerts, 'foreign and especially French conductors and soloists have been much to the fore, and Irish artists have not been engaged to anything like the same extent as hitherto. As a result the amount of available concert work, meagre at the best, has been still further reduced, and Irish soloists are finding it increasingly difficult to live.'[54]

Lynch was also correct: whereas he had played at least nine concertos with the orchestra in the decade to the end of 1947 (with Rhoda Coghill playing at

51 P&T file 200/53/2, '1) Question of employment of an assistant conductor; 2) report of Selection Board'. 52 Tausky (b. 1910) a Czech conductor who had worked extensively in opera, conducted the R(T)ÉSO frequently in both concert and opera, during the period when he was Music Director of the BBC Concert Orchestra (1956–66). 53 Pierre-Michel le Conte (b. 1921), who was a pupil of Eugène Bigot and Louis Fourestier, spent most of his career in French radio, including the conductorship of the ORTF Opera Orchestra 1960–73, and taught conducting at the Paris Conservatoire; he continued to work with the RTÉSO up to 1981, in 1977 scoring a particular triumph with César Franck's symphony in D minor in a concert which also included Seóirse Bodley's 'A Small White Cloud Drifts over Ireland'. 54 C. Lynch, 'The concert pianist in Ireland', (1952), p. 179.

least five, Clyde Twelvetrees and Arthur Franks two each, and Claud Biggs, Nancie Lord and Gerard Shanahan one each), he himself had only one engagement in the period 1948–52, although overall, in the decade to the end of 1957, he did almost sustain his previous level of engagements, with eight concertos, while rising stars Anthony Hughes and Florence Ryan (piano) had five and three respectively, and Geraldine O'Grady (violin) had two.[55] Apart from choral works, which, from 1951, increasingly featured Italian-trained soprano Veronica Dunne, RÉ's concerts, while making room for young Irish-born soloists, tended to be dominated by eminent visitors and the incoming principal players in the RÉSO who were anxious to maintain their public profile as soloists.

However, one can hardly fault the policy of continuing to introduce top-class soloists of the calibre of cellist André Navarra, violinists Max Rostal and Josef Szigeti (the latter joining the RÉSO for one of its first extended national tours in 1954),[56] horn Denis Brain, or pianist Shura Cherkassky, or re-introducing previous favourites such as Tortelier, Goossens, Katchen or Fournier. The problem – and it has remained a problem to the present day – is to achieve a balance between four categories or types of soloist: the visiting 'stars', of whose quality and status there is no question; visiting soloists of the second rank by virtue of their age or accomplishment; the best Irish soloists; and the up-and-coming Irish soloists who need to cut their teeth in terms of experience of audience presence and reaction. Too often a music director is tempted to pander to the box office by placing the 'star' performers before a paying public, and bestowing second-class status on others by restricting them to the studio or to less well-defined public engagements.

THE EARLY YEARS OF THE RÉLO

As already noted, there was a serious anxiety that the standard of the incipient RÉLO should be comparable to that of its senior sister, and that therefore it should not become a place of transfer for the RÉSO's unsatisfactory players,

---

55 Anthony Hughes (b.1928), a pupil of Bruno Seidlhofer in Vienna, made his début as a soloist with the RÉSO in 1947 and continued to appear with them on many occasions, in a wide range of repertoire including the premières of concertos by Potter and Victory, and in those of Beethoven, Mozart, Franck and Falla, parallel to his academic career as Professor of Music at UCD in succession to Larchet. Florence Ryan (b.1939), who studied with Ginette Doyen, Carlo Zecchi and Edwin Fischer, is widely regarded as a Mozart specialist, playing several of his concertos with the RÉSO since her début in 1954, as well as concertos by Beethoven and Chopin. Geraldine O'Grady (b.1932) has played as soloist with the RÉSO more than a dozen times, including the Boydell and Moeran concertos, and the Chausson 'Poème' which she performed in its European Tour of 1980. 56 Szigeti's tour, in which he played the Beethoven concerto, began in Dundalk, proceeding to Belfast, Derry, and Sligo before finishing at the Gaiety in Dublin. The concerto was preceded by Harty's 'Fair Day' and followed by Tchaikovsky's fourth symphony.

or, in return, merely a source of supplementary players for the RÉSO. The appointment of Jack Cheatle was therefore a major plank in Fachtna Ó hAnnracháin's planning for its success. When Cheatle died in 1979 after a short retirement, Charles Acton, writing of 'the deep respect and friendliness that he inspired' noted that

> whether in its maid-of-all-studio-work guise inside the station, or in its public concerts, or in the gramophone recording studio, the members of the orchestra gave of their best in a bewildering variety of music, from Wexford Festival Opera, to the 'Music of the Nation', to songs from the shows, to the Eurovision Song Contest, to almost anything else you can think of, because of the utterly professional devotion of Jack Cheatle …. The RTÉCO remains his monument.[57]

That summing up is an excellent indication of the range of the Light/Concert Orchestra's repertoire and the extent of its broadcasting commitments, to which might be added the fact that in 1950 the RÉLO took over the role of the RÉSO in the conducting course of the Summer School, and in the 1960s performed, among others, A.J. Potter's ballets 'Careless Love' and 'Gamble, No Gamble' with Irish National Ballet.

In the 1970s I coined the expression: 'The RTÉ Concert Orchestra is one of the most distinguished and versatile broadcasting orchestras in the world', which has subsequently appeared in most of its publicity literature. This description was disputed, on at least one occasion, by Michael Dervan, who succeeded Charles Acton as music critic of the *Irish Times* in 1986, who called it 'gushy',[58] but if an Irish critic (who might well be unfamiliar with the international phenomenon of the radio orchestra *per se*) is uncomfortable with the acclaim accruing to the RTÉCO, the orchestra's record, which includes winning the EBU's 'Nordring' radio prize in three successive years, speaks for itself.

The foundations for this versatility were laid under Cheatle's long leadership and under its earliest conductors: Éamonn Ó Gallchobhair, who was appointed after public competition and remained in the post for only one year;[59] Dermot O'Hara, who had come second in that competition and then succeeded him in 1949, and would conduct the orchestra in the first seasons of its residency at the Wexford Festival from 1951; and Eimear Ó Broin, who shared the bulk of the conducting duties with O'Hara after his appointment as Assistant Conductor in RÉ in 1953, and up to the RÉLO's re-organisation in 1962.

The inaugural broadcast consisted of 'dance music', illustrating another of Ó hAnnracháin's anxieties, namely the criticisms of RÉ's broadcasting of céilí

57 *Irish Times*, 29 December 1979. 58 *Irish Times*, 21 July 1990. 59 Ó Gallchobhair, by his own admission, was not a success as conductor of the RÉLO: 'Éamonn Ó Gallchobhair remembers', loc. cit.

music of extremely variable quality. A twenty-two piece céilí band might seem a contradiction in terms, or might at least merit the type of criticism that would be levelled at céilí bands in general by Seán Ó Riada a decade later; but performances of Irish dance music, by professional players of an assured standard, would do much, at least, to allay the censure which RÉ was incurring on a regular basis in the one place that rural Ireland had a strong voice: Dáil Éireann. With arrangements by David Curry, who was working largely with BBCNI on the programme 'Irish Rhythms', traditional music would enjoy a renaissance. In 2002 Ó hAnnracháin would remark that these arrangements 'would not be regarded as suitable today, since another philosophy has developed, but it was acceptable to most people at the time, and since the interest in traditional music was very slight, it was important to counter the effects of bad céilí music which had predominated'.[60] As León Ó Broin was able at the end of 1948 to write to his opposite number in Finance, 'This combination has filled a long felt want in broadcasting. It was impossible to get Céilidhe music performed in a finished manner by outside combinations and the provision of music for variety was also a most difficult problem.'[61]

Barely a year later, Ó hAnnracháin had to point out that 'The RÉLO is the instrumental group which now supplies the bulk of our light music programmes and, as it should be our aim to build and develop these light programmes to the fullest extent – programmes of a kind which were beyond our resources before the advent of the Light Orchestra – no second-rate musicians should be employed by us in it, in any circumstances.'[62]

It would, however, be some years before this could be achieved. In 1952 the conductor Hubert Clifford, head of BBC Light Music and the instigator of 'Friday Night is Music Night', was asked for a confidential report, which identified as the main problem the fact that many of the wind and brass players came from army backgrounds and had poor intonation. 'Some of them lapse back into the outdoor style of playing which merely sounds rough and crude indoors, let alone in a small studio for a microphone.' Clifford made a detailed judgement on each player, picking out as thoroughly acceptable only the leader, the pianist (Eileen Braid) and Daniel O'Reilly (first clarinet): 'an artist who can phrase with musical intelligence and sensibility – the most reliable of all the wind players in the matter of pitch'. Others received severe verdicts: 'Intonation very poor indeed, tone poor. I doubt whether this player has ever played well, even when in his prime.' Cheatle possessed qualities that were lacking in most other players: 'a very good influence with the orchestra ... a musicianly player whose intonation was always accurate ... free from nervousness and uncer-

---

60 Ó hAnnracháin, interview with the author, 11 September 2002. 61 Ó Broin to Finance, 29 November 1948, file 175/58/5. 62 Ó hAnnracháin to Ó Broin, 4 January 1950, file 10/57/6. 63 Typescript, 5pp., July 1952.

tainty'. Clifford also criticised the restricted space and inadequate recording facilities of the orchestra's new home at the Portobello Studios (which subsequently became the headquarters of the RTÉ Singers).[63]

A measure of the way in which the RÉLO was perceived within P&T was the fact that the players – and Cheatle in particular – were unsuccessful for a number of years in seeking parity with the members of the RÉSO. Cheatle was granted an increase in salary from £9.10.0 to £10.10.0 per week, but 'The Minister [for Finance] is unable to agree that the pay of the Leader of the Light Orchestra should be equated to that of the pay of the Deputy Leader of the Symphony Orchestra'[64] which was £11. In one case in the following year Ó hAnnracháin was writing in what sounds like desperation: 'recently, Mr Charles Parkes, the 3rd trumpet of the Symphony Orchestra, tendered his resignation. We had in mind changing Mr Parkes to 1st trumpet in the Light Orchestra where the trumpet situation is so bad that it has now become a joke even amongst the other musicians of both our orchestras. Mr Parkes did not like the idea of going to the Light Orchestra but he would have done so if we could have offered him an increased salary. The 1st trumpet is a very important person in all light-music combinations and Mr Parkes was well aware of this fact'.[65]

In the same memo, Ó hAnnracháin had to tell Ó Broin: 'the double-bass we have at present, Mr M—, is 78 years of age, an old man who has to be assisted frequently by other members of the orchestra to find even the piece of music that is being played, and who very often loses his place in a particular piece. This shows the desperate nature of the situation we have to contend with; a situation which, I suggest, would not be allowed to continue in any rational organisation'. Nearly a year later, Ó Broin was remonstrating with Patrick Lynch, assistant secretary to the government, 'Experience we are gaining every day about the versatility required for light orchestra work makes us more convinced than ever that there should be no differentiation between the salaries of the two orchestras ... We have bad gaps in the Light Orchestra which we feel cannot be filled unless the salaries are levelled out. The situation is now so bad that the competent players have become restive because of the danger to their reputations by indifferent performances and the conductor has actually demanded that the programmes of the Light Orchestra should for the present be left completely out of the night programmes'.[66]

At the same time, Ó Broin was advising Finance: 'During a recent visit to Switzerland the Music Director observed that a Light Orchestra was the high-

---

64 Finance to P&T, 23 September 1949, file 10/57/6. 65 Ó hAnnracháin to Ó Broin, 4 January 1950, ibid. Charles Parkes went to the Theatre Royal orchestra where he was paid £12 per week but rejoined the RÉSO at a later date. 66 Ó Broin to Lynch, 13 November 1950, file 10/57/7. For a similar situation in which Ó Broin invoked Lynch's aid, see p. 358.

est paid combination in that country which has symphony orchestras of a very high standard. Symphony orchestras perform the more important works but the musician in a Light Orchestra must be more versatile as he has to be capable of performing light modern music, music for variety, céilí music, etc.'[67] Finance did agree to an increase in salaries for the RÉLO, but there was still a £1 differential from the RÉSO, and even after the intervention of the Taoiseach (John A. Costello), stipulating that the two orchestras should have equal pay, Finance resisted the move until it was finally conceded at the beginning of 1951.[68]

The basic schedule of the RÉLO was daunting: it played four programmes each week: on Saturday nights a half-hour of Irish music, supplied by the many arrangers working as freelancers for RÉ; on Tuesday nights 'Music Album', a classical programme with mainly vocal items from rising stars such as Veronica Dunne and Dermot Troy; on Wednesday nights 'Masters of Melody' with popular old-style music; and on Thursdays 'Mainly Modern' which went in the other direction with jazz and contemporary pop, with contributors like the legendary saxophonist Johnny Devlin (better known in later years as an arranger and conductor), who was to be associated with the orchestra for five decades, and arrangers like Jimmy Watson from Glasgow whom Eimear Ó Broin remembers for his skilful work.

It was for this versatility and sheer hard work that the RÉLO was applauded from all sides: politicians, in particular, acknowledging their own general lack of appreciation of symphonic music, chose to single out the RÉLO, especially when it offered an 'Irish' alternative to the increasing attractions of 'pop'. Brendan Corish (Labour, Wexford; leader of the Labour Party, a former Minister for Social Welfare and a future tánaiste) was typical of many when he said, in 1958,

> If we want, and I think our intention should be, to try to get people away from canned music, hot music, real jazz music to decent music, the proper medium is the Radio Éireann Light Orchestra. One cannot go from bread to caviare with one quick jump. If it is the desire of the Minister and the Comhairle to get people to appreciate and enjoy reasonably good music, not heavy music, it ought to be done through the medium of an orchestra such as the light orchestra.[69]

Dermot O'Hara (1906–78) had been 'talent-spotted' by Col. Brase in his native Tralee, and had served his apprenticeship in the Army School of Music,

---

67 Ó Broin to Finance, 12 December 1949, ibid. **68** C. Kelly to Ó Broin, 15 February 1950; Finance to Ó Broin, 27 April 1950; Finance to P&T 24 January 1951, ibid. **69** DD, 167, 17 April 1958, col. 332. Comhairle Radio Éireann had been established as a first step in the devolution of responsibility for RÉ.

being seconded to RÉ to work with the orchestra 1937–8, immediately after becoming a commissioned officer. During this period he conducted the European broadcast on St Patrick's Day, 1938. Subsequently he conducted the No.1 Army Band until, with Michael Bowles's transfer to RÉ, he took up the latter's post with the band in Cork. At the end of 1948 he was given temporary work with the RÉLO and was recommended for retention in March 1949. 'Mr O'Hara has shown good promise as a conductor. He has shown a flair for conducting a Light Orchestra and his sense of the requirements in that type of music and his control of the players are good. He co-operates well with the different programme departments in the Station'.[70]

Unfortunately the proposal to appoint O'Hara full-time led to an example of prejudice in which, nevertheless, a note of caution might not have been amiss: in 1943 O'Hara had in fact been 'cashiered' or 'drummed out'[71] of the Army for drunkenness (a condition from which he made a full recovery), and Finance asked if he could therefore be suitable, as his name appeared on the Army 'Black List'. Ó Broin immediately took the sensible course of rebutting the implied suggestion that O'Hara was in any way unsuited to his new appointment: 'I would press you not to insist on his removal because of his delinquencies while in the Army ... I know from my own personal observation that he has most conscientiously kept his pledge since taking up duties with us. I have every hope that the reformation will continue.'[72] When O'Hara's (in every sense) probationary period ended the following April, Ó hAnnracháin reported: 'Mr O'Hara continues to progress; he takes a personal interest in the Light Orchestra and he has co-operated with the Music Department in an exemplary manner', to which Ó Broin added 'In a case of this kind it is most creditable for a man to overcome the craving for drink and instead of referring to the Black List we should be grateful to be in a position to help such a man by giving him congenial employment suitable to his abilities'.[73]

On O'Hara's death Charles Acton wrote: 'he was ... a brilliant musician of immense range and deep sensitivity though he never paraded the fact ... I am sure he would be glad to be remembered here for his often biting wit at least as much as for his infinite and unpublicised kindnesses.'[74]

O'Hara's relations with members of the RÉLO were not without their tempestuous side, however. An easily irascible man who carried on his sleeve the pain of his previous humiliation, O'Hara was wont to speak sharply to his players, giving little quarter and causing offence especially among the women. In 1956 RÉ received a unanimous objection by the RÉLO to his behaviour,

---

70 Ó Broin to Everett, 25 March 1949. 71 The author witnessed O'Hara's moving account of the procedure of 'drumming out' to which he was subjected. 72 Ó Broin to Ó Muimhneacháin, 18 July 1949. 73 Ó Broin to Everett, 25 April 1950. 74 *Irish Times*, 31 July 1978.

although on this occasion Matt Doherty appears to have believed and supported O'Hara's complete rebuttal of the allegations against his conduct.
Nevertheless, there was a build-up of tension, perhaps caused in part by the
fact that Eimear Ó Broin was now sharing the duties in what, for the past seven
years, had been O'Hara's exclusive preserve.

A mutual antipathy developed between O'Hara and Moira Flusk, at that
time playing in the second violins. He believed that she was inadequate, she
alleged that he was prejudiced in favour of the foreign members of the orchestra. There were several incidents when O'Hara lost his temper and, in Flusk's
words, 'used very rough language indeed'.[75] In Flusk's view O'Hara's prejudice
meant that 'the Germans can do no wrong and the Irish can do no right. A terrible atmosphere to work against'.[76] In particular, the foreign player with whom
she shared a desk – 'B' – was objectionable to her, and she claimed that O'Hara
overlooked B's faults, thus exacerbating a bad situation. As Flusk recounted it,

> From the time he ['B'] came, he drank and drank to excess during his
> work. He apparently decided he was indispensable and that it was a great
> country to keep a £16 a week job under such conditions. He duly went
> from bad to worse, being drunk 9 nights out of ten! Apart altogether
> from this I doubt if it would be possible to get someone less suited to
> the position, he had neither the background, the experience or the edu-
> cation. He was incapable of leading or counting bars ... He spent the
> whole morning, every morning, bowing parts to impress and was too
> drunk at night to play them. I have no prejudice against him because he
> was made leader [of the second violins] or that he is a foreigner. I have
> the greatest respect for some of these visitors who are an asset to the
> country, such as Egon Jauch – a gentleman – Eisenbrand, a fine artist
> and many others who being foreigners were horrified at [B]'s behaviour
> to me.[77]

It was a situation which O'Hara was probably unable to control, possibly
because of his own history, and because he was not suited to the managerial or
administrative element in a conductor's work. Temperamentally, he was an
artist who was described in the Radio Éireann Handbook for 1955 as 'a martinet [who] has fought like a tiger both with and for his orchestra. He is an
excellent practical musician who has a knowledge of every wind instrument in
the orchestra ... and a firm believer in the thesis that even trivial music must
be played well.'[78] One of the best examples of O'Hara's work is a series of

75 Arthur Duff to Ó hAnnracháin, undated note.   76 Flusk to Ó hAnnracháin, 19 November 1956.
77 Flusk to Ó hAnnracháin, 25 April 1959.   78 John Morrish, *Radio Éireann Handbook 1955*.

recordings that he made in 1960, shortly before his tenure with the RÉLO came to an end, with the tenor Dermot Troy, and just two years before Troy's premature death. Troy was, like Austin Gaffney, a pupil of Michael O'Higgins, who went on to sing as a lyric tenor at Covent Garden (where he had a small part in *La traviata* with Callas in the leading role), and then at the opera houses of Mannheim and Hamburg, earning acclaim in a variety of roles. In the words of Liam Devally (another pupil of O'Higgins) Troy 'did an immeasurable service for Irish music in that he showed us that an Irish tenor did not have to imitate the squeezed nasal sound that came from the 78s of a declining John McCormack'.[79] The variety of the recordings, from 'Finiculì finiculà' and 'Roses of Picardy' to Schubert's 'Serenade', indicates a distinctive voice which was excellently partnered by O'Hara and the RÉLO.

Another valuable indication of the work of both O'Hara and Ó Broin in the late 1950s is the series 'Concert Hall', in which the RÉLO was joined by the RÉ Singers and vocal and instrumental soloists in a variety programme that stretched from Beethoven's overture 'Prometheus' to Borodin's 'Polovtsian Dances' and the polka from Walton's 'Façade', from Redmond Friel's arrangement of a 'Derry Medley' (for the Singers) to three *chansons* by Ravel, from the romance from Chopin's first piano concerto (for a soloist such as Elgin Strub) to Handel's 'Ombra mai fu' sung by the young Bernadette Greevy. Indeed, during these years a number of emerging Irish artists such as David Lillis (violin), Mary Sheridan (contralto), and Veronica McSwiney (piano) featured in these and other programmes of the RÉLO, alongside newly established figures such as sopranos Winifred O'Dea and Veronica Dunne.

For the most part, the RÉLO remained behind its microphones in Portobello, but for St Patrick's day in 1958 (in what had become a succession of annual events marking the national holiday) a 'Concert of Irish Light Music' was given in the Gaiety Theatre, featuring singers Veronica Dunne, Deirdre O'Callaghan, Martin Dempsey and Richard Cooper, Dermot O'Brien's Céilí Band, and piper Leo Rowsome. Charles Acton remarked that the orchestra should be seen more often: 'They should have a valuable part to play in our musical life, both in providing good light music and suitable "popular classics", a field almost wholly ignored in Dublin. Light music has its own style of performance (which serious orchestras often cannot achieve) and Dermot O'Hara, on last night's showing, can be proud of a band of musicians who seem to have the style and to enjoy themselves in their work. And in A.J. Potter and Redmond Friel they have professional composers who are not afraid to write honest bread-and-butter music.'[80] The St Patrick's Day celebratory concerts

---

79 In a sleeve note for the commercial disc of these recordings issued in 1979 – RTÉ catalogue no. 56. Troy had won second prize in the 'Great Caruso' competition for citizens of the UK and Ireland. 80 *Irish Times*, 18 March 1958.

would in future years feature singer/harpist Mary O'Hara (1961) and actress Siobhán McKenna (1966).

MILAN HORVAT

While criticisms of the lack of a principal conductor were being voiced in the early 1950s, the authorities in Radio Éireann were in fact proceeding with the appointment of Milan Horvat (b. 1919), a graduate in law from Zagreb University and in music from the Zagreb Music Academy. His career had begun in 1945 as a pianist and choral conductor and he had become a conductor of the Zagreb Philharmonic in 1946, the post to which he returned after his five years in Dublin (he was appointed Director in Zagreb while still in Dublin, in 1957), and which he held concurrently with the principal conductorship of the Zagreb Opera 1956–66.[81] In the Dáil, Erskine Childers, as Minister for P&T, acknowledged the criticisms of the policy regarding visiting conductors, saying 'last July [1952] I decided that the indefinite continuation of the practice … would be bad for the Orchestra and to the disadvantage of young Irish players … Because of the excellence of the performances under his [Horvat's] direction, generously recognised by the musical public and his conspicuous enthusiasm and hard work I am satisfied that he is … highly suitable for the task of building up an Orchestra which will justify the assertion that we are a music-loving people'.[82] Horvat had been chosen because, in Childers' view, such a person 'would wish to make the reputation of the orchestra and his own', and stated quite unequivocally 'I have no limit to my ambition for the Symphony Orchestra. I am determined that we shall have one at least as good as the Hallé', also expressing the hope that the Hallé and the RÉSO could effect regular exchanges.[83]

Horvat was only thirty-four at the time of his appointment to RÉ, but he was clearly a rising star, whose concerts with the RÉSO had the same qualities as those of Martinon. He had first appeared in Dublin in 1949, and, in similar conditions to other visiting conductors, had spent extended periods in 1951 and 1952, including concerts in aid of the Adelaide Hospital, and for the first of what became a regular annual concert appearance by the RÉSO during the Wexford Festival. A series of three concerts in January 1953, typical of the pattern on which concerts by visiting conductors had been based, persuaded Fachtna Ó hAnnracháin that Horvat should be appointed from August 1953,

81 Horvat was subsequently principal conductor of the Radio Symphony Orchestra in Vienna 1969–75, and of the Zagreb Radio Symphony from 1975, principal guest conductor of the Lausanne Chamber Orchestra, and chief conductor of the symphony in Graz (1997–2000) where he has also taught conducting at the conservatoire since 1975. 82 DD, 139, 25 June 1953, cols. 2103–2104. 83 DD, 134, 6 November 1952, col. 1182.

and a relationship was begun with the RÉSO and with Irish composers which continued until early 1958.

Horvat's appointment coincided with the re-instatement of the Public Concerts, now called 'Proms', and the popularity of these two developments did much to raise the profile of the orchestra which, as the *Irish Times* remarked, 'is still struggling on its way to maturity ... Mr Erskine Childers voiced the hope last autumn that the RÉSO would eventually gain an international reputation. Such a wish, even if now a little visionary, should not be impossible to achieve, provided direction comes from the musicians and not from politicians with their smugly unrealistic ideas about national orchestras'.[84]

Horvat established a good working relationship with both orchestra and audience, telling the *Irish Times* that he found Dublin audiences 'sincere, appreciative of new works if they are sound, and untinged by snobbery, perhaps the greatest affliction known to music'.[85] The *Irish Times* did not hesitate to point out that Zagreb, with a population half the size of Dublin's, supported a permanent symphony orchestra, chamber orchestra and opera company, and two concert halls. It also put forward the opinion that 'Horvat may never be a Furtwängler or a Toscanini, but ... he speaks with the voice of authority ... He keeps an unrelaxing control on his players, and while some of them may object to his strict demands during rehearsals, they are ready to keep any grumbling to themselves, for they recognise the quality of his musicianship'.[86]

Horvat's own musical tastes inclined towards the classical and romantic repertoire, evidenced by his first concert as Principal Conductor on 11 September 1953 with the first Tchaikovsky piano concerto (soloist Shulamith Shafir, a pupil of Schnabel and Solomon) and Brahms's fourth symphony. This début marked the reinstatement of the Public Concerts, which now transferred to Dublin's Gaiety Theatre (where they were to remain until the advent of the National Concert Hall), thus making these live events available to an audience of 1200, whereas for the previous five years the Phoenix Hall had restricted numbers to 300, allowing Brian Boydell to comment that they were 'semi-private' affairs.[87] Horvat's next, on 25 September, gives an indication of a remarkable period of concerts which would feature new work by Irish composers (see Table J): the work on this occasion was A.J. Potter's piano concerto 'Concerto da Chiesa', which had won RÉ's Carolan Prize, and was performed by Anthony Hughes; his symphony was Beethoven's third. On 2 October Horvat followed this with May's 'Songs from Prison', sung by baritone Michael O'Higgins, and Mussorgsky's 'Pictures from an Exhibition'. During his first season 1953–4, Horvat presented works by Larchet, Fleischmann (the ballet suite 'An Cóitín

---

84 *Irish Times*, undated cutting (Acton Archive). 85 Ibid. 86 Ibid. 87 In A. Fleischmann (ed.), op. cit., p. 223.

Dearg'), Boydell (the ballet suite 'The Buried Moon'), May's 'Spring Nocturne', and Beckett's 'Pastoral and Scherzo', while Eimear Ó Broin introduced Gerard Victory's 'Elegy and March'. Horvat's symphonies were by Mozart, Beethoven and Berlioz, and his soloists included Denis Brain, probably the finest horn player in the world at that time (Mozart and Richard Strauss), the Irish piano duettists Joan and Valerie Trimble (Mozart),[88] and pianist Cor de Groot (Beethoven, 'Emperor').

In his next season, Horvat's programmes included Boydell's suite 'The Wooing of Etáin', Beckett's 'Triple Fantasy', Harty's 'The Children of Lir' with Veronica Dunne, Ina Boyle's 'The Wild Geese', Potter's 'Variations on a Popular Tune' and the revised version of Boydell's violin concerto which had been premièred the previous year by Jaroslav Vaneček with the composer conducting. Again, his symphonies were firmly in the classical and romantic mode, with Beethoven, Schubert, Tchaikovsky, Brahms and Dvořák, but his choice of soloists revealed a taste for the exotic, with Goossens playing oboe concertos by Cimarosa and Richard Strauss, André Navarra with the Schumann cello concerto, and, from the members of the orchestra, Max Thöner and Herbert Pöche in Mozart's Sinfonia Concertante K.364, which Horvat followed with a work with which he was to become particularly associated, Hindemith's 'Mathis der Maler'.

The 1955–6 season saw new work by J.J. O'Reilly, who was to become Principal of the Municipal School 1969–73 and the first teacher of pianist John O'Conor; his tone poem 'Oluf' (given twice in the year) was followed in 1958 by 'Remembrance – Nocturne', dedicated to Horvat. Premières of May's 'Sunlight and Shadow', Boydell's 'Megalithic Ritual Dances', Bodley's 'Ceol do Théadaibh [Music for Strings]' and 'Movement for Orchestra', Potter's 'Rhapsody under a High Sky' and 'Tostal Overture', Ó Riada's 'Olynthiac Overture' and Gerard Victory's piano concerto (soloist Anthony Hughes). The pattern continued in subsequent seasons, as did Horvat's relative conservatism with the symphonic repertoire (although he did include Borodin's second symphony, Prokofiev's fifth and Shostakovich's first and tenth) and his openness to experimental or unusual works from his soloists, such as Edith Farnadi with Bartók's second and third piano concertos, Austin Gaffney (a baritone soon to make a considerable mark) with Mahler's 'Kindertotenlieder', Margaret Hayes with Glazunov's violin concerto, and Vaneček with the Britten concerto.

'Horvat works his orchestra hard' said the *Irish Times*. 'He believes that if the players can be drilled through the works of Bach, Handel, Mozart and Haydn, interpretation and style can be perfected; and once the orchestra can learn easy control of itself, he feels it will be fit to try its hand at anything'.[89]

---

88 For details of Joan and Valerie Trimble, see Pine and Acton, *To talent alone*, p. 503.   **89** *Irish*

This, then, was the type of 'builder-conductor' suggested by the MAI, who would put the orchestra through a learning curve with the foundational repertoire – including the symphonies of Mozart and Haydn from the 'classical' era – that is not always found in the portfolio of more flamboyant *maestri*. On his departure, Horvat drew attention to the fact that broadcasting requirements imposed a minimum output of programme hours per week, thus reducing the time he would like to have had available for rehearsals, which were especially important for the younger, less experienced players. (This would be a feature of George Hurst's tenure of the position, leading to his abrupt departure.) Thus, while some concerts might be outstanding, unless a team could be trained to an acceptable level, consistency of performance would elude them.

Charismatic conductors, as distinct from the 'builder' type, raise both orchestral morale and public awareness, and as there has been only one Irish-born principal conductor of the Symphony Orchestra it can be stated as a general rule that those conductors have been a leading factor in the intake of foreign musicians. As P.J. Little, in opposition, said in the Dáil in 1949, 'until we have created the atmosphere by bringing in foreigners, we cannot expect to build the greatness which is in us and always has been as a musical country'.[90] Horvat, Tibor Paul, Albert Rosen and Alexander Anissimov have all contributed to 'create the atmosphere' in which musical excellence can be pursued. As we have seen, one of the problems which have arisen to impede the consistent development of the orchestra has been that of recruiting a successor to an outgoing principal conductor, and there have been periods (see chapter 7) when serious *lacunae* occurred in this development. One such followed the departure of Horvat, when Charles Acton observed that he had had insufficiently extended periods with the orchestra: in the year 1956–7 Horvat had conducted approximately one third of the RÉSO's total performances (opera included). The Vienna Philharmonic might survive in such conditions because 'it has a corporate personality which our orchestra has not yet had time to develop ... It seems clear that the orchestra needs a chief conductor who will not only conduct it for six months of the year, but who will do so for several unbroken periods'.[91] Where John O'Donovan had suggested Silvestri or Zecchi, Acton recommended Bryan Balkwill, whom he praised highly for his début concerts with the RÉSO after having had operatic triumphs with the RÉLO during six seasons at Wexford and with the RTÉSO for the DGOS.[92] A year later, with no successor in sight, Acton would attribute uneven standards in the RÉSO to

Times, loc. cit. **90** DD, 117, 8 July 1949, col. 521. **91** *Irish Times*, 15 February 1958. **92** Balkwill's operas for Wexford were *Don Pasquale* (1953), *La sonnambula* (1954), *Manon Lescaut* (1955), *Martha* and *La Cenerentola* (1956), *La figlia del reggimento* and *L'Italiana in Algeri* (1957) and *I due Foscari* (1958); at the DGOS he conducted *La bohème* (1955), *Le nozze di Figaro* (1957), *Don Giovanni* and *Tosca* (1958),

'the absence of continuous direction from a conductor with a high standard of technical discipline',[93] and the situation would remain unsatisfactory until the appointment of Tibor Paul after a further two years, the delay being most likely caused by fruitless negotiations between Fachtna Ó hAnnracháin and Carlo Franci, one of the most popular and successful visiting conductors from that period, whom Ó hAnnracháin had been on the point of engaging.

The almost analogic image of a series of highs and troughs would continue to be a feature of the R(T)ÉSO/NSO's relationships and experiences with its principal conductors, with one training period under a 'builder' being followed by one in which a more outward-looking personality would take control, after which more basic work (retrenchment or repair) will most likely become necessary – the succession of Kasper de Roo, Anissimov and Gerhard Markson illustrating this particularly well.[94]

ASSISTANT CONDUCTOR

Meanwhile, Eimear Ó Broin had been appointed assistant conductor (at a salary of £800) after a selection procedure involving twelve applicants, of whom seven were invited to a forty-minute audition on 29 June 1953. Most of these (Beckett, Ó Broin, Townshend and Victory) had attended the Summer School courses in conducting under Martinon or Schmidt-Isserstedt or both.

Walter Beckett, then living in Rome, where he was studying conducting on an Italian Government scholarship, elected to conduct Beethoven's first symphony. S.M. Bowyer, from Waterford, had from an early age played in his parents' travelling opera company (Bowyer Westwood) and had more recently worked as an organist in Ennis, Limerick and Waterford, where he was currently playing at the Dominican church and teaching at Presentation Convent. He chose the Schubert C major symphony. Sydney Bryans, who had already conducted both the RÉSO and RÉLO, and was currently music master at Mountjoy School and organist at the North Strand church, chose Schubert's 'Unfinished' symphony. J.M. Doyle, although invited, withdrew his name, as he said he could not be expected to undergo such a test in his present position as conductor of the Army No.1 Band. Eimear Ó Broin, son of León, had been studying at the Paris Conservatoire where, in addition to the conducting course with Eugène Bigot, who was, significantly, principal conductor of Radio France (with particular responsibility for the Orchestre Radio-Symphonique and the Orchestre National),[95] he attended classes by Messiaen and Nadia Boulanger,

93 *Irish Times* 1 July 1959. **94** Martyn Westerman, interview with the author, 3 March 2003. **95** E. Ó Broin, 'Music and Broadcasting' in Pine (ed.), *Music in Ireland*, p. 118. Ó Broin described

and was awarded *premier prix* for conducting. He had then spent a year in Munich, studying ballet and opera at the Staatsoper, and had been offered, but declined, a scholarship to Harvard. He had also conducted concerts of Irish music at the Studio Beromunster (Zürich), at the Suisse Romande, and the Monte Ceneri orchestra in Lugano. His test piece was Schumann's fourth symphony. Brian Uniacke Townshend, who had studied under Ernest Read (one of the most notable pioneers of the youth orchestra movement in Britain), and was now teaching at a school in Nottingham, directed Mozart's symphony no. 40. Gerard Victory had extensive experience as conductor of the choir and orchestra of the Keating Branch of the Gaelic League in succession to Fachtna Ó hAnnracháin, as well as acting as music director for many stage shows, including the annual pantomime at the Abbey Theatre since 1946, had conducted the Dublin Orchestral Players and the Cork Symphony Orchestra, and his own opera *An Fear a Phós Balbhán* at the Abbey earlier that year. He was currently working in RÉ as a talks producer. His chosen trial work was Beethoven's seventh symphony.[96]

The audition panel, consisting of Gorham, Horvat, Ó hAnnracháin and Arthur Grüber (from Hamburg), with whom Radio Éireann was in communication regarding the proposed intake of a large number of German musicians (below, pp. 186–96), considered that only Bryans and Ó Broin were suitable: Bryans would be offered a number of engagements but Ó Broin, as the clear leader on the assessment sheets, was given the appointment.[97] At the time of Horvat's appointment, Childers had already stated that part of Horvat's work would be the training of young Irish conductors, and that an assistant conductorship would soon be advertised, enabling the successful candidate to travel abroad for part of the year and who would in turn be responsible for the recruitment and advanced training of Irish musicians.[98] The press announcement dated 30 June 1953 now stated that 'under the plan which will enable young Irish conductors to work and study for a period with the Station's Principal Conductor and Guest Conductors, Eimear Ó Broin has been appointed Assistant Conductor'. Altogether, Ó Broin, in addition to his work with the RÉLO, would conduct the R(T)ÉSO in almost 150 concerts in the course of his career, more than any other conductor except Tibor Paul, Colman Pearce or Albert Rosen.

him as 'to French Radio what Adrian Boult was to the BBC'; he was adept in the works of Brahms and also 'the complex works of the Messiaen school': interview 4 August 2003. **96** P&T file 200/53/1, 'Staff vacancies – Assistant Conductor 1953 – applicants called for interview'. **97** P&T file 200/53/2. Bryans would subsequently conduct an average of two concerts each year up to 1961, and further concerts in 1968–69. Reviewing his concert on 16 May 1958, Charles Acton opined 'I remain convinced that Sydney Bryans has it in him to be a really good native conductor: it is up to him to realise his great potentialities' (*Irish Times*, 17 May 1958) – which were cut short by Bryans' early death. **98** DD, 139, 25 June 1953, cols. 2103–4.

The same announcement stated that John Reidy [Seán Ó Riada][99] had been appointed Assistant Music Director (in succession to Éamonn Ó Gallchobhair): he had been a member of the amateur Cork Symphony Orchestra and 'is also a composer of promise and has several interesting works to his credit'.

Eimear Ó Broin's Parisian experience had given him a love and understanding of French music that was to characterise his choice of repertoire over the thirty-six years of his association with RTÉ, and especially in the next decade, before his career was seriously undermined by Tibor Paul. He had already conducted Debussy's 'La Mer' with the RÉSO in 1952, and would give symphonies by Jean Revier, Roussel, d'Indy and César Franck, the piano concertino by Jean Françaix (with his wife, Patricia Herbert, as soloist),[1] Milhaud's 'La Création du Monde' and 'Suite Provençal', Saint-Saëns' 'Suite Algérienne' and his third violin concerto (with Margaret Hayes), Debussy's 'Images', the Ravel piano concerto (with Ginette Doyen), and Ibert's 'Divertissement'. In addition to a regular diet of classical and romantic symphonies, he would explore many modern and contemporary works, including Honegger (symphony no. 2 [1940–1] and no. 5 [1950]), Blomdahl (symphony no. 2 [1947]), the Stravinsky symphony in C (1938–40), Dag Wirén's serenade for strings (1937), Fartein Valen's 'Le cimitière marin' (1933–4), Werner Egk's 'Französische Suite' (1949), Michał Spisak's 'Serenade' (1939), Hindemith's 'Nobilissima Visione' (1938) and his symphony 'Die Harmonie der Welt' (1951), Hengk Badings' 'Symphonic Variations' (1936), Constant Lambert's 'Aubade Héroique' (1942), one of Siegfried Borris' six 'Intrada Serene' (1952) and Boris Blacher's 'Paganini Variations' (1947).

Ó Broin's soloists would include Veronica Dunne in Strauss's 'Four Last Songs', the young John Ronayne with Wieniawski's second violin concerto and the Bruch concerto in G minor, Erich Eisenbrand with Robert Volkmann's cello concerto, George Minne with Doppelbauer's organ concerto,[2] Gerard Meyer with the Dittersdorff harp concerto,[3] Herbert Downes in the Walton viola concerto and János Fürst in his compatriot János Viski's violin concerto (1955).

Ó Broin also demonstrated an affinity with Grieg (whose *Peer Gynt* music he conducted several times), Sibelius, Copland, and English composers such as Elgar, Delius, Peter Warlock and Lennox Berkeley (first symphony [1940] and Nocturne [1946]).

---

99 Although it is generally assumed that Reidy adopted his Irish name in the 1960s, after taking a decision to move to Cúil Aodha and to speak in Irish, Tomás Ó Canainn reveals that he had, since youth, employed the Irish form: T. Ó Canainn, *Seán Ó Riada: his life and work* (2003). **1** In the same concert she played Turina's 'Rapsoda sinfónica' for piano and strings. **2** Minne, a native of Ghent, was organist and choirmaster in Roscrea, Co. Tipperary at this time, and had been an unsuccessful applicant for the post of Assistant Conductor. In 1959 he became organist of the Roman Catholic Cathedral in Armagh. **3** Meyer, a French harpist, joined the orchestra in 1954, and married RÉSO horn player Ann Doyle, daughter of J.M. Doyle and Nancy Doyle (then in the RÉSO cello section).

Moreover, Ó Broin displayed his commitment to Irish composers with Duff's 'Meath Pastoral' and 'Echoes of Georgian Dublin', T.C. Kelly's 'Variations on a traditional air', Bax's 'Tintagel', Joan Trimble's 'Suite for Strings', Elizabeth Maconchy's 'Suite on Irish Airs', Victory's 'The Enchanted Garden', Antoinette Kirkwood's first symphony,[4] Bernard Geary's 'Provocations', and the premières of Ó Riada's 'Olynthiac Overture', 'Banks of Sullane' and 'Nomos 4' (soloist Charles Lynch), Daniel McNulty's 'Divertimento' (soloist also Charles Lynch), and Potter's 'Rhapsody under a High Sky' which he conducted several times.

ORCHESTRAL STABILITY

Parliamentary scrutiny of the RÉSO's management and recruitment policies continued meanwhile, with James Everett harrying Childers on several occasions with PQs asking how many non-nationals were employed, and what it cost to maintain the orchestra. Childers invariably replied that the number of non-nationals 'is not abnormal when compared with leading foreign symphony orchestras in countries with a longer history of concert development'.[5] He justified the annual cost of £40k by stating that the orchestra appeared throughout the country and combined with other music organisations 'for the benefit of all classes and particularly of school children on whom the future of music so much depends'.[6] When Everett asked 'Has the Minister's attention been drawn to the fact that it was agreed that no further foreigners would be employed to the detriment of native musicians?' Childers answered that 'every effort is made to recruit Irish nationals for the orchestra'.[7]

Throughout the 1950s we find continual reiterations of the fact that no suitable Irish players could be found or, in some cases, none whatsoever came forward for audition. This was especially true in the case of percussion and timpani, resulting in the employment of János Keszei, Fredemann Lembens and Kurt Goedicke. In that of trombonists, Kevin Roche (as orchestra manager) would find himself travelling to Europe, especially Germany, in the early and mid-1960s, using a network of professional associates, friends and ex-RÉ players to identify potential candidates. Apart from violins and celli, the rarer strings – violas and double-basses – also posed enormous problems, and in every case a justification had to be provided to the Department of Industry and

4 Kirkwood's symphony, in the style of Sibelius, has not received any subsequent performance in Ireland; she also wrote pieces for performance by the RÉLO. 5 DD, 130, 27 March 1952, col. 729. 6 Ibid. 7 Ibid.

Commerce before a permit could be issued under the Aliens Act 1935; when an objection was raised by IFMAP on behalf of Irish musicians deemed, or claiming, to be qualified, a regular riposte was issued to the effect that Irish applicants had not reached sufficient standard for permanent employment, even though they might be working on a temporary or deputy basis.

In the Light Orchestra, filling the position of harpist in 1964 caused difficulties as the preferred candidate, Catherine Michel from France (*premier prix* at the Paris Conservatoire as a pupil of Pierre Jamet), was only sixteen years of age. Of the possible Irish applicants, Una O'Donovan had just been appointed to the Concertgebouw and Nuala Herbert was professor at the RCM.[8] Even in Europe there was a shortage of harpists, as Roche reported that he had made 'extensive enquiries in Hamburg, Stuttgart, Munich and Amsterdam without success'.[9] A prejudice against working in the RTÉLO was even evident among Irish violinists who actually were eligible: when IFMAP objected to the appointment of Giulio Piccini on the grounds that 'we have been prompted ... by our certain knowledge of the professional competency of a member of this Federation ... which has been commented upon by a prominent conductor (non-Irish)',[10] the RTÉ personnel department was told 'all along it has been very difficult to get good violinists for the LO. Several young Irish violinists have actually refused to accept posts in this orchestra as they were interested in being members of the SO only.'[11]

The harp position in the RÉSO was also difficult to fill. Síle Larchet (daughter of John F. Larchet and sister of violist Máire) had been with the Liverpool Philharmonic for two years from 1946, and then joined the nascent RÉSO where she was paid £8 as opposed to £15 in Liverpool. Fachtna Ó hAnnracháin supported her application for an increase on the grounds that 'It is vital to have a good harpist ... We know the period of turmoil we endured before Miss Larchet's arrival.'[12] Ó Faracháin concurred: 'Miss Larchet's trump card is her indispensability. So far as I know there is no other harpist in Ireland who is qualified to play in a symphony orchestra, and the present salary would attract no foreign artiste.'[13] This was taken up by León Ó Broin as Secretary of P&T who wrote to Seán Ó Muimhneacháin, his opposite number in Finance: 'There is now the danger that Miss Larchet will again seek employment abroad where she would certainly be welcome, because it was only with difficulty that she was got back from the Liverpool Philharmonic who could not get a player up to her level to replace her.'[14] Either by accident or design, Síle Larchet's appli-

---

8 Nuala Herbert was the sister of Patricia Herbert and also a pianist; the sisters played the Mozart concerto for two pianos in 1957. 9 K. Roche to Controller of Programmes, 23 November 1964. 10 IFMAP to RTÉ 17 May 1961, File H/R/4/A–RTÉLO. 11 Ibid. 12 Ó hAnnracháin to Kelly and Ó Faracháin, 4 May 1949, P&T file 10/57/6, 'Orchestral Salaries'. 13 Ó Faracháin to Kelly, 11 May 1949, ibid. 14 P&T to Finance, May 1949, ibid.

cation in May 1949 coincided with her performance of Maurice Thiriet's 'Introduction, Chanson et Ronde' for harp and orchestra (1936) at the Phoenix Hall under the baton of Martinon on 18 May (which also included Martinon's 'Irish Symphony'), of which Joseph O'Neill wrote:

> It is always of special interest when an Irish instrumentalist takes a solo part with [the] Radio Éireann Orchestra. It is unique to have one playing the harp solo in a complicated modern work and Sighle Larchet is to be congratulated on her mastery of this instrument. The solo part was played with considerable technical skill and a fine rhythmic sense. Every variety of harp tone was exploited with success, from the light glissando to the full rich middle register.[15]

Predictably, this and other claims, including Jack Cheatle's request for parity with the leader of the Symphony, were rejected by Finance, the Minister stating that 'he considers that the present rates of pay ... are adequate by reference to ordinary standards'.[16] Since there were no 'ordinary standards' with which a comparison could be made, it is difficult to judge the real basis of the decision, other than that of financial constraint. Ó Broin rose to this challenge, writing to Ó Muimhneacháin 'For the life of me I cannot understand how you have come to the conclusion that the present rates of pay ... are "adequate by reference to ordinary standards". What are the ordinary standards to which you refer?' In regard to Cheatle, whose claim was rejected because Finance considered the comparison between the RÉLO and RÉSO to be inadmissible, 'will you kindly say with what orchestra(s) should we make comparisons? ... Were we to take a headline from any of the English orchestras we would not be going for such a modest increase as 30s[hillings] a week. In America the wages of musicians are a good deal higher than in England; in New York the minimum wage for an instrumentalist is £31 a week, in Chicago £30 and in Boston and Philadelphia £21. Miss Larchet has been offered a post in the London Symphony Orchestra at a much higher salary than she has here and will probably accept unless we give her some increase.'[17]

Following a meeting between P&T and Finance on 1 September 1949, Ó Broin wrote to Ó Muimhneacháin:

> I should like to keep before you the fact that you cannot deal with this body of musicians in exactly the same way as you would with an ordinary Civil Service group. They are temperamental and must be handled

---

15 *Irish Independent*, 21 May 1949. **16** Finance to P&T, 3 July 1949, file 10/57/6. **17** Ó Broin to Ó Muimhneacháin, 5 August 1949, ibid.

with tact and consideration. I would not of course give way to claims solely to placate temperamental people, but we must recognise that the number of symphony players is extremely limited ... The players know their value to us and apart from justice they have a strong lever to make us treat them fairly. Even if they did not leave – and I know that many of them could not afford to leave – we shall have constant trouble if justified grievances are allowed to remain. It is also the case that as we improve their standard of playing we increase their market value.[18]

Ó Broin's masterly summing up of both the civil service mentality and the imperative of growing an artistic endeavour within that mentality could not be better demonstrated.

Apart from providing places for suitably qualified Irish players, the chief anxiety for Ó hAnnracháin and Ó Broin was to make conditions sufficiently enticing to hold onto those immigrant players who proved satisfactory and, in many cases, vital to musical development. Another case which highlighted the anxieties and difficulties which Ó hAnnracháin had met in that of Arthur Nachstern was Maurice Meulien, who was appointed to the cello section of the RÉSO in 1950 (on the recommendation of Jean Fournet) and became section leader the following year on the resignation of Wolfram Hentschel.[19] Meulien was a *premier prix* at the Paris Conservatoire where he also won a *première medaille* for chamber music. With a brief interlude in 1958–9 when he was at the Orchestre National de l'Opéra Monte-Carlo, he was with the RÉSO until the exodus of some key players to join the newly formed Ulster Orchestra in 1966 (see below, pp. 446–8). Charles Kelly gave, as an example of overcoming prejudice against foreign players within the orchestra itself, the occasion when a visiting soloist did not materialise to rehearse the Dvořák concerto: Meulien 'offered to sit in as soloist for the rehearsal ... [and] gave a faultless performance entirely from memory, being loudly applauded by the rest of the orchestra. This incident did a great deal to convince Irish players of the gap between their musical standards and those which obtained abroad.'[20]

In 1953 Meulien was considering resignation to take up a post in Montevideo at a much larger salary (£85 p. m. compared to the £55 he was receiving from Radio Éireann), but was persuaded to stay. But again, in 1955, Ó hAnnracháin was pointing out to Doherty that Meulien was looking for a job elsewhere and that Horvat was extremely worried at the prospect of los-

---

18 Ó Broin to Ó Muimhneacháin, 5 September 1949, ibid.   **19** Hentschel had founded the Dublin String Quartet with François d'Albert, and after his departure from Ireland had established the Benthien Quartet, which visited Ireland several times, and recorded Boydell's first string quartet. **20** C. Kelly, 'Look back in pleasure' in L. McRedmond, op. cit., p. 25.

ing a player who was not only a fine cellist but also a very satisfactory section leader. He urged a salary increase, which was turned down on the grounds that it would lead to similar claims. A month later he was pointing out that 'Undoubtedly when Meulien was absent recently we realised with a shock how much we depend on him to keep the 'cello section together. Would you consider an increase of say 10/- a week? This would be very little indeed, in one way, but it would show Meulien that we recognise the very good work he is doing'. Again, Maurice Gorham rejected the proposal.

When Meulien resigned in 1958 to go to Monte Carlo, Tortelier was asked to recommend a replacement, but no one could be found, such was the rarity of players of this calibre throughout Europe at the time. There were no young Irish cellists of sufficient standard worthy of consideration for recruitment to either orchestra – another fact that would become excessively apparent throughout the 1960s and 1970s.

Ó hAnnracháin told his superiors:

> I had several discussions in Rome about the question of orchestral players, mainly with Maestro Salvatore Allegra. The position seems to be that if we could offer a salary equal to 5000 lire a day we could get really good musicians without any difficulty … The situation in regard to the Principal 'Cellist in the Symphony Orchestra is now very serious and I beg of you to consider the possibility of increasing the pay for this post, even temporarily. The Principal 'cellist is a key player in any Symphony Orchestra and is generally considered to be more important than any of the string section leaders, except the first desk of the 1st violins of course.[21]

The dismissive, almost contemptuous, tone of Roibéard Ó Faracháin's reaction belies the reputation he seems to have enjoyed for being supportive of Ó hAnnracháin's endeavours:[22]

> <u>Because</u> we are already paying a special salary to the Principal Viola <u>couldn't</u> we pay a slightly higher figure for a Principal Cello? [23] What an argument! I do wish I could emulate the MD's buoyant pertinacity in proposing disproportionate expenditure. Think of the years during which I have tolerated the absence of a full complement of proficient

---

21 Ó hAnnracháin to Ó Faracháin, 30 January 1959. Salvatore Allegra (1898–1993), a pupil of Cilea, was an Italian composer who was president of the Cassa Nazionale Assistenza Musicisti and honorary president of the Italian Musicians' Union. 22 Gerard Victory supportively, but wrongly, wrote of Ó Faracháin that he 'never tired in his efforts to serve the cause of the orchestras': 'Ó Riada on Radio' (1981), p. 46. 23 Meulien had intimated that he would return to the RÉSO if he had a higher salary.

Irish-speaking actors, simply because the money which would bring them in would be disproportionate to several other sorts of salary as well as to our general expenditure. And the years during which we have paid all our actors at lower average rates than the orchestral players.[24]

In 1958–9, Ó hAnnracháin's problems intensified with the resignation of Renzo Marchionni:

I am very concerned about the general situation in the RÉSO because of the forthcoming departure of Renzo Marchionni. Meulien was a key brick in the wall as it were and now a still more important brick is being removed. The re-engagement of Meulien at this crucial moment would have a stabilising effect on the whole Orchestra ... No matter how much individual views may differ, I think nobody here wants to see the RÉSO disintegrating and when the danger of such disintegration can be avoided by the expenditure of a very small sum of money.[25]

But again Ó Farácháin refused: 'I'm sorry, but I cannot support the MD's petition, sincere though I believe it to be. The trouble is that he is once more making a special plea, while we must view broadcasting needs as a whole ... How do we justify raising orchestral salaries while leaving others as they are?'[26]

A similar situation arose in the early 1960s in the case of timpanist Kurt Hans Goedicke, who was appointed in 1954 and promoted to Principal two years later, of whom Tibor Paul would say that he was one of the best timpanists in the whole of Europe. In 1962 Gerard Victory, Paul's assistant Director of Music, had to write to the Personnel Department in relation to Goedicke and percussionist János Keszei: 'Both are excellent players and within recent years no other timpani or percussion player of any quality appears to have come forward from Irish musicians ... At the moment there is considerable worry with regard to offers being made to foreign musicians ... by orchestras abroad, and it is very necessary to use every inducement to retain our best players.'[27] Eventually Goedicke, although he too had become a naturalised Irish citizen, was unable to refuse the offer of an appointment with the London Symphony Orchestra in 1964. Keszei had come to Dublin on a temporary (probationary) appointment in 1957, and had been confirmed as principal percussionist a year later, remaining until he joined the exodus to Ulster in 1966. 'This Hungarian refugee has proved a veritable "Deus ex machina",' wrote Ó hAnnracháin.[28]

---

24 Ó Farácháin to Gorham, 31 January 1959. 25 Ó hAnnracháin to Doherty and Ó Farácháin, 25 February 1959. 26 Ó Farácháin to Gorham, 27 February 1959. 27 Victory to D. Lucey, 5 December 1962. 28 Ó hAnnracháin to Doherty, 9 April 1958. When the LSO gave a concert in Dublin in 1981,

Goedicke was succeeded by Fredemann (Freddie) Lembens, who had been playing in the RÉLO since 1956, at the young age of nineteen. Playing at that time in the orchestra of the Kurfurstendammtheater, he had been recommended by his own father, Professor Hans Lembens, of Berlin, who was responsible for several other of his pupils joining the Irish orchestras, including timpanist Henning Knöbel and percussionist Joachim Weiland.

The financial situation regarding the rates of pay was serious, since the differential or 'special allowance' paid to non-Irish players was a cause of contention and disaffection. Ó Broin wrote in late 1949 that

> Apart from the continental musicians, the salaries of the Orchestras generally are still too low to enable the Department to face the criticism and pressure to which it is subjected. Outside bodies such as the Irish Federation of Musicians are making the most of the insufficient salary and differentiation between the home and foreign players in its efforts to foment unrest and there is no doubt that the attempts made by the Federation to create antagonism between the two sets of players will gain ground unless something is done to put all the salaries on a satisfactory level and to narrow the gap between the remuneration of the home and continental members.[29]

A further difficulty in the cold-war period of the 1950s was that of politics, which inevitably had a religious dimension. In 1955 the Catholic Archbishop of Dublin, John Charles McQuaid, had attempted to prevent a football match between Ireland and Yugoslavia from taking place, to demonstrate the church's attitude to the treatment of Cardinal Stepinač in Yugoslavia; when that failed, an attempt was made to dissuade fans from attending the match, on the grounds that the visiting team, coming from a communist country, would endanger Irish morals. Therefore when Matt Doherty interviewed Vitezslav (Victor) Maliř, at that time principal horn at Ljubljana, whom Horvat wished to appoint in succession to Leopold Laurent, he found it necessary to state that 'I [did not] discuss the question of politics. Mr Horvat has said that we might have his categorical assurance that Mr Maliř was not a communist and that he was only interested in his music.'[30] Horvat had written to Ó hAnnracháin that he had conducted two concerts in Ljubljana at which he had been impressed with Maliř's playing: 'lovely ton [*sic*], excellent technic and musicality ... He is certainly the best horn-player in Yugoslavia'.[31]

Charles Acton remarked that three former RTÉ players were in the orchestra: 'it was ... a joy to see back in Ireland Maurice Meulien (sub-leader of the cellos), Nuala Herbert (harp), Kurt Goedicke (timpanist). To see them here again is a measure of how we still miss them', *Irish Times* 10 April 1981. **29** Ó Broin to Finance, 12 December 1949, file 10/57/6. **30** Doherty memorandum 13 July 1954. **31** Horvat to Ó hAnnracháin, 10 May 1954.

Some immigrants simply passed through Ireland, leaving either because they had regarded their stay here as purely temporary, or because their qualifications earned them superior employment elsewhere; others found the social or working conditions uncongenial. A major source of complaint was the lack of opportunity for extra work, due mainly to the paucity of the musical environment. Thus John Franca, appointed temporary principal cello with the RTÉLO at the end of 1962, stayed a mere nine months. A pupil of Maurice Maréchal in Paris and also of Casals, he had played in the Leipzig Gewandhaus, the LSO, the Philharmonia, the RPO, the LPO, the London Mozart Players, the BBC Welsh, Covent Garden and Sadler's Wells orchestras, and had been principal with the Royal Ballet. He was anxious to secure freelance work in both chamber music and as a soloist, prompting Kevin Roche to observe:

> This raises the old question of outside engagements undertaken by staff musicians, but I think that we have always pursued the policy of encouraging serious musicians who undertake work of prestige value. We have always disapproved of our musicians undertaking dance-band engagements which have no prestige value and which take place at very late hours. André Prieur is perhaps the best example of a competent player who has successfully combined his position as a Principal player with a considerable amount of solo work, chamber music ensemble work and teaching. This has been achieved with our tacit approval and sometimes our active encouragement, and his present status in Ireland's musical life reflects credit on Radio Éireann.[32]

Prieur, as principal flute 1950–78, was also the director of the André Prieur Ensemble and, from 1970, conductor of the reconstituted New Irish Chamber Orchestra (see chapter 5). Comment had already been made on his abilities by Ó hAnnracháin, who had written, at a time when it seemed that Prieur might resign to take up the position of principal flute at Covent Garden:

> Prieur … is an outstanding flautist and also an outstanding all-round musician. Apart from his work in the Symphony Orchestra, he has played concertos [and] solos … Prieur has also proved successful as a teacher and he is the kind of man who could be expected to produce in due course flautists who would be able to fill any vacancies arising on the orchestral staff.[33]

It is, however, indicative of the stress experienced by orchestral musicians – especially principal players in the wind sections – that André Prieur suffered

32 Roche to Victory 23 October 1962. 33 Ó hAnnracháin to Gorham, 6 June 1957.

debilitating health problems in the 1970s, leading to his taking early retirement. While some left Ireland for health reasons, others sought work here: a Czech viola player working in the Iceland Symphony wrote that 'I am looking for a position in a slightly warmer country'.[34]

A coup by RTÉ was the recruitment in 1966 of Czech cellist Alban Berky, who came to Ireland with an extremely distinguished record as a soloist who had played in the Prague Radio Orchestra, the Bratislava Radio Symphony, RIAS Berlin, and the Slovak Philharmonic, where he was also a member of the Slovak Quartet. Described by Tibor Paul as 'a brilliant musician but a difficult man', Berky suffered not only from artistic temperament but also from another factor which caused RTÉ serious difficulty in dealing with eastern European musicians: the political situation which gave immense power to the national concert agencies in the communist countries, in this case Pragokonzert. Similar difficulties were experienced consistently with the agencies in other communist countries, such as Hungary and Yugoslavia. Although the agency eventually permitted Berky to take up the post of sub-principal in the RTÉSO from 1 September 1966, differences between himself and the principal, Vincenzo Caminiti, were irresoluble, and by April 1968 he had tendered his resignation with effect from 1 September that year.

Financial and political concerns were not the only reason for hasty departures. In January 1968 a cellist who had joined the RTÉSO three months earlier, had been convicted of common assault. The cryptic note by Redmond Walsh reads: 'He was caught redhanded by the Guards. Child of 5 or 6 involved. Guards did not want to bring child into court. [Department of] Justice wants to get aliens like this out of the country. They will contact him and give him a fortnight to leave'.[35] It is instructive that incidents of this kind, not unknown today, were taking place in the early 1960s, and also that musicians are not immune to this type of tendency.

Others stayed much longer, in some cases for most or all of their mature playing careers. Of the 'Prussian' intake, Heinz Jablonski was in the bass section of the RÉSO from the beginning of 1954 until mid-1961; similarly his colleague Egon Jauch, formerly at the Frankfurt Opera, the Volksoper Berlin, the Berlin Philharmonic and the symphony orchestra of the Berlin radio station RIAS, was appointed principal cello with the RÉLO in mid-1954, transferring to the RÉSO in 1957, where he remained until resigning at the end of 1962 to take up a place with the German-based Philharmonia Hungarica; Georg Gerike was a second violinist with the RÉSO from 1954 until reaching retirement age in 1967; flautist Hans Kohlmann was in the RÉSO from 1954 until his untimely death in 1976. Cellist Otto Pacholke preceded the 'Prussian'

---

34 Ondraček to Victory, 12 March 1971. 35 RTÉ Music Department file, name withheld.

intake, joining the RÉSO in 1952 from RIAS, and staying for ten years. Alfonso Evangelisti was appointed in 1948 and, with the exception of one year when he sought treatment for sciatica in Naples, remained in the RTÉSO as leader of the second violins up to his death in 1978. Vincenzo Caminiti came to Ireland aged thirty in 1959, became section leader in 1967 and resigned in 1977 to return to his native Palermo. Gilbert Berg came to Ireland in 1949 and remained until 1980.

MUSIC EDUCATION

The experience with recruitment of Irish and foreign musicians gave León Ó Broin considerable food for thought, not least because on several occasions he had to prepare answers for his Minister in reply to PQs in the Dáil and Seanad. Ó Broin correctly identified the poor standard of music education in Ireland as the chief reason for the failure of Irish-trained musicians to secure employment in the orchestras. This was widely perceived as a national problem – in 1952 Brian Boydell wrote that the only cure for 'a lack of real musicianship amongst instrumentalists in Ireland' was 'a complete reorganisation of musical education',[36] while critic Joseph O'Neill had observed the same problem in relation to music appreciation by the audiences which was vital to success in performance: 'Too often does it happen that adults who discover music for the first time are baffled by its complexities because of their lack of any elementary training.' He referred to 'the disappearance in adult life of the thousands of children from the primary and secondary schools who have been given a basic musical training'.[37]

In 1952, for example, O'Neill had written (in the same article):

> There can be no doubt about the fact that the love of music is not very deep-rooted in Irish people. By this I do not mean that music does not attract them. They have a superficial love of music and an emotional reaction to it, but the music must be both simple and familiar. The general public has never been able to cope with anything more *recherché* than an opera performance, and even this would need to be one of the stock specimens of the repertoire to ensure a following. Ireland's prolonged political struggle undoubtedly prevented the general public from taking a serious interest in music or other art forms. It is probably the primary cause of the escapist attitude of the people to the light entertainment of the cinema. With the disappearance of political concentra-

36 In A. Fleischmann, op. cit. p. 226. 37 Ibid., p. 261.

tion, however, the more intellectually minded people are seeking an absorbing interest, and if they are carefully guided there is no reason why music should not supply this need.[38]

The appearance of such a judgement, at a time when the MAI and others were clamouring for the re-introduction of the public concerts, can have done little to persuade the Radio Éireann authorities of a groundswell of public opinion on the matter.

The Royal Irish Academy of Music (RIAM) was at the lowest point in its history in the early 1950s, when it was just over a century old,[39] and the Municipal School of Music, established by the RIAM in 1890 at the request of Dublin Corporation, and by this time managed by the City of Dublin Vocational Education Committee (CDVEC),[40] was ill-situated to train orchestral musicians. A mutual rivalry and a mutual suspicion had grown up between the two institutions, based originally on class preconceptions: traditionally, the clientele of the Academy had been drawn, as one of its constitutive documents had stated, from among 'the children of respectable Irish parents'[41] – and its students acquired a genteel knowledge of predominantly piano, violin and singing; its daytime teaching hours and its high fees precluded the less well-off and those who worked for a living. To compensate for this situation, and to remedy the decline in the standards of the city's many brass and reed bands, the Municipal School had been founded specifically for the education of 'artisans', and focussed on wind and brass instruments. Thus the class differential between the two establishments was emphasised by the difference in the style and content of their curricula.

A departmental memorandum dating from 1959 referred to this problem in the following terms:

> The building up of the Radio Éireann Orchestras has been a painstaking and at times a heartbreaking task which has extended over the last 15 years or so. We have the problem that we have not got a teaching institution of conservatoire standard in this country. The Royal Irish Academy [of Music] should be of such a standard but it is not ... It could not concentrate on the higher work of finishing pupils for orchestral and solo standard. The Municipal School of Music is doing very good work in training, but as this School is under the Vocational Education Committee, which is mainly concerned with Technical Schools, it could

---

38 O'Neill, 'Music in Dublin', p. 260. 39 Cf. Pine and Acton (eds.), *To talent alone*, chapter 7. 40 Ibid., pp. 234–43; also, Jim Cooke, op. cit. 41 This expression was contained in the will of Elizabeth Coulson, whose donation to the RIAM of a considerable sum of money led to its reformation in 1889 – cf. Pine and Acton, pp. 155–65.

not aim to be a finishing school for musicians. Consequently, when we require replacements for members of either Orchestra, we are faced with holding auditions on the Continent, in Germany, France, Italy and other countries. We are making every effort to help music institutions to raise their standards but it is a very slow process.[42]

Thus, music education would be perceived as a cardinal problem in the development of an Irish orchestra *qua* Irish, yet one which was not immediately amenable to solution by those responsible for the RÉ orchestras. The same problem would recur in the 1960s and has not disappeared today.

In 1949 an attempt had been made by Radio Éireann to improve the situation with regard to the standard of teaching in the Municipal School. A meeting was attended by the Director of Broadcasting, Charles Kelly, his deputy Roibéard Ó Faracháin, Fachtna Ó hAnnracháin, and Joseph O'Brien, Director of the School, 'for the purpose of considering a draft scheme for the setting up of a Vocational Day School for Music'.[43] (Prior to the meeting, approaches had been made by Kelly and Ó hAnnracháin both verbally and by letter to the CEO of the CDVEC, Martin Gleeson, with a view to the appointment to the staff of the School of Renzo Marchionni, in order both to raise the standard of string teaching and to increase Marchionni's income. This appears to have been unsuccessful.) Although the 'scheme' had in-built faults, such as the intention to run the proposed school 'on lines obtaining for the various trades' – which would have continued the artisan-oriented style of education – there were signs that it would have made a significant inroad into the overall problem.

Approximately twelve students aged 14–16 were interested in enrolling for a four-year programme which would teach Irish, English and a third language (French, German or Italian), and mathematics, in addition to instrumental tuition and music theory.[44] Nine music teachers would be required, some of whom would be members of the RÉSO. It was envisaged that the CDVEC and the county councils would provide scholarships for the less well-off. Regional junior music schools might be established as feeder-schools as the scheme developed. Tuition would take place 9.30–4.30, Monday to Friday, with the afternoons being given over to 'orchestra and ensemble practice'. In the case of students making satisfactory progress, 'supernumerary employment in the Radio Éireann Orchestra would be available to them in their final year'. (This had

42 RTÉ Music department file, 1959. 43 'Scheme of Co-operation between Radio Éireann and Municipal School of Music with regard to the supply of adequately trained personnel for the Radio Éireann Orchestra', on a P&T file, number illegible. 44 This intention is very similar to that envisaged for the initial RIAM in 1848–56 – cf. Pine and Acton, op. cit., p. 57: 'a sound General Education in English and in the modern languages with the best musical instruction so that the entire education of the pupils may be conducted within the walls of the Academy'. The RIAM retained a teacher of Italian on its staff 1880–1917.

been planned by Ó hAnnracháin in his seating arrangements for the RÉSO, which provided for three or four students playing at the back desks of the first and second violin sections.) Furthermore, on graduation 'there would be a guarantee of employment in the Radio Orchestra if the pupil reached orchestral standard. This would be determined by final audition and interview'.[45]

Following the meeting, P&T debated whether to leave the matter with Gleeson or to attempt 'a pincer movement' by a simultaneous approach to the Department of Education; it was decided to wait for a reaction from the CDVEC.[46] Despite a further meeting, the result was a vacuum: 'I kept in touch with Mr Gleeson for some time after the discussion on 25th March, 1949,' Kelly wrote fifteen months later, 'but without getting anything satisfactory. I understand that the Vocational Education authorities regard the scholarship scheme for sending young musicians to the Continent as their solution of the problem for the time being'.[47] Since it was increasingly evident that the enforced emigration of young musicians, with or without scholarships, was *not* an appropriate solution, this response on the part of the CDVEC was a major disappointment to Radio Éireann.

However, a major breakthrough occurred in 1951, within a month of Erskine Childers taking office. Aware of dissatisfaction 'from the home members of the Orchestras and from TDs prompted by them and from Trade Union sources such as the Federation of Irish Musicians',[48] Ó Broin suggested that, simultaneously, Fachtna Ó hAnnracháin should seek recruits in conservatoires abroad, while

> we should make our requirements known to the teaching establishments at home and that the Minister should bring influence to bear on the Royal Irish Academy of Music to improve their teaching facilities. The teaching facilities generally are at present so poor that there would be no prospect whatever of bringing Irish musicians up to the standard needed unless some radical change was made. As an instance of the present weakness in the Academy ... it had as a cello Professor an old man now approaching 75 years of age [Clyde Twelvetrees] whose services were terminated by the RÉSO a couple of years ago on age grounds and who is obviously now quite incapable of handling the cello efficiently. It is also the case that some young people found on test to be unsuitable for the RÉSO have been employed as teachers in the Academy.[49]

45 'Scheme of Co-operation'. **46** Kelly to Ó Broin, ms. note, 21 February 1949, ibid.; Doherty to Ó Broin, 19 March 1949, ibid. **47** Kelly to Ó Broin, 8 June 1950, ibid. **48** P&T memo, July 1951, on P&T file 86/56 reg BC 12963/51 Royal, 'Royal Irish Academy of Music – improvement of teaching facilities'. **49** Ibid.

For its part, the RIAM had been struggling with the idea of change management in the period 1945–8, which focussed on a proposed radical reshaping of the institution with John F. Larchet in a new post as Director. The outcome was one of 'no change', with the Academy's governing body rejecting the appointment, since the proposed development would have given Larchet almost dictatorial powers.[50] Neverthless, from a recently discovered submission by the RIAM to P&T dating from 1948, it is evident that the institution was acutely conscious of its possible role in relation to Radio Éireann, if it could effect the necessary improvements in standards, on the basis of the proposed new scheme featuring Larchet as director.

> This new scheme will enable the Academy to enlarge its scope and influence, and to make better use of its position in improving the traditions and the standards of music in Ireland … The principal feature is the provision for a Director … who could himself take classes in modern composition and conducting, and undertake the training and development of orchestras within the Academy which would in time secure competent native talent for the Radio Éireann and other professional orchestras … The Governors are anxious to include in the teaching staff new members from the leading centres of music in Europe, who can bring to them the best of the modern ideas … The remuneration of the existing staff has not been increased since 1914 and is now pitifully inadequate. Many of the best graduates, who would have been welcome on the staff, have drifted elsewhere both in Ireland and England to better conditions … It is the leading institution for the teaching of music and the spread of musical culture in Ireland, and it hopes to be able to do even better work in the future than it did in the past. In the interests of musical education in Ireland the Governors think that they ought to organise Annual Summer Courses for Music Teachers. They have felt for some time that such work should be done by the Academy, but have hesitated to undertake it owing to the risk of serious financial loss.[51]

Two years later, the RIAM was sufficiently emboldened to promote the idea that 'the Academy should receive Government recognition as an Irish National Conservatoire, and be granted a sufficient measure of State assistance to enable it to fulfil that role'.[52] It was unlikely to achieve this under the coalition government, especially since the Municipal School was thinking along similar lines

---

50 Cf. Pine and Acton, op. cit., pp. 363–6; in fact the episode delayed the appointment of a Director at the RIAM until 1981. 51 P&T file 12963/51. The prospect of a summer school would bear fruition in the early 1960s after the cessation of the Department of Education's own scheme and that organised by Larchet at UCD. 52 RIAM memo, 8 November 1950, ibid.

at the same time, but when Fianna Fáil returned to power Childers proved eager to meet a RIAM delegation.

Fachtna Ó hAnnracháin had drawn attention to the fact that the RIAM had recently employed the Czech violinist Jaroslav Vaneček 'and that the standard of violin teaching has since improved immensely. Some of the musicians recommended for appointment by the recent Radio Éireann Board were pupils of this teacher. He has organised musicians in the Academy in such a way that he is able to say what pupils would be likely to be ready up to 1956 or 1957'.[53] Vaneček and his wife Kveta had come to Ireland to give a joint recital at the RDS; since they were unhappy with the situation in Czechoslovakia, they wished to remain in Ireland, in which they were sympathetically aided by the Czech Minister in Dublin, and, through the offices of Larchet, became teachers at both the RIAM (1949–55) and the Municipal School (1954–73); they were to be the 'parents' of several generations of Irish string players whose timbre, resonant of the string sound of *mittelEurop*, was to characterise the playing not only of the RTÉSO but also of the Irish Chamber Orchestra and its successor, NICO, well into the 1980s.[54] In 1953 Vaneček and Eimear Ó Broin had secured agreement from RÉ that the Portobello studio would be available for the nucleus of a training orchestra for strings (with about twenty participants) and this continued until 1958; envisioned expansion to embrace other instruments did not materialise, but violinists of the calibre of Audrey Park, Loretto McGrath and Mary Gallagher 'graduated' from this breeding ground which, like the Vanečeks' work in the Academy and the College, infused that 'atmosphere' so much espoused by P.J. Little.[55] It was the only instance in

53 Ibid. **54** Many of these players became members of the RÉSO. In April 1957 members of Vaneček's class at the Municipal School gave a concert (conducted by Terry O'Connor) of which, in Charles Acton's opinion, Margaret Hayes's performance of the Mendelssohn violin concerto was the highlight; he found that 'the characteristics of all the violinists are a very sure, brilliant tone, beautiful intonation and a really neat, lively crispness of playing' (*Irish Times*, 5 April 1957). In the same concert, Audrey Park played Mozart's third concerto. **55** Mary Gallagher was a member of the RÉSO for a short period, but appeared as soloist on several occasions, later becoming leader of NICO for ten years, and more recently of the Orchestra of St Cecilia. She gave her first concerto with the RÉSO and Eimear Ó Broin in 1959, playing Spohr's eighth concerto (which she had also played two years previously with the student orchestra [see preceding note]); Charles Acton (*Irish Times*, 3 January 1959) reported that 'her playing throughout was graceful, musical and in full keeping with the character of the work'; he would continue to notice her gracefulness, dignity and 'admirable lack of fuss' (ibid., 6 November 1961). After her performance of the Khatchaturian concerto in 1960 he wrote of her 'beautiful rich tone ... real authority and mastery ... This was no performance by a young promising player to be criticised with encouraging indulgence; here was assurance ... so that I might have been listening to an established master' (ibid., 4 January 1960). When she played Prokofiev's second concerto in 1966, Acton wrote: 'Her technique is sound, secure and impeccable ... a full ringing tone, the complete authority of knowing exactly what she was doing ... If a visiting violinist played it as Miss Gallagher did last night, we would exclaim at the formidable technique, be duly awed, and maybe even say we had nobody here who could play it equally well': *Irish Times*, 24 September 1966.

the history of R(T)É of the organisation actually putting resources directly into the training of its future players, and achieved the objective announced at its inauguration, of providing six places to students 'on a half-time basis while they continue their studies', with Park and Gallagher among them.[56] Simultaneously, the Arts Council advertised fourteen scholarships for wind instruments at the RIAM, since there was, as always, an even more pressing shortage in this area.

The same P&T memorandum continued:

> After discussion it was agreed that the best method of procedure appeared to be: ... to get all the information possible about the Academy affairs; see representatives of the Academy later (and also representatives of the Municipal School of Music) – put the Radio Éireann problem about music to them tactfully with information as to the number of vacancies likely to arise in Radio Éireann over a period and ask them what they would do to help. The Minister would like to be present at this discussion ... The Minister would perhaps discuss the matter with the Ministers for Finance and Education to try and enlist their support in putting the teaching of music in the Academy on a proper basis.

The most significant point about this initiative is that, as Minister for P&T, Childers had no responsibility for music education, but as Minister presiding over the fortunes of the country's two professional orchestras he had an anxiety about the quality of Irish musicianship. Identifying the RIAM as the principal source of potential players in the RÉ orchestras, he would therefore do whatever he could to improve its facilities, including an amelioration of its finances which at that time were in an extremely precarious condition. Childers immediately approached his opposite number in Finance, Seán MacEntee, in an attempt to persuade him to increase the annual government grant to the RIAM, which had stood at £300 p. a. since 1880.[57]

> Dear Seán ... I am writing to ask for your help and consent to some proposals which are related solely to the provision of musicians for the RÉSO and the RÉLO ... We are making arrangements with the Federation of Irish Musicians whereby they will not object to our employing continental players on short-term contracts but at the same

---

56 DD, 142, 10 November 1953, col. 1767. It should be noted that, since its inception in 1939, the Dublin Orchestral Players (originally called the Dublin Junior Orchestra) had had as its principal aim the provision of orchestral experience for prospective orchestral musicians, and as a breeding ground for Feruccio Grossi's and Constance Harding's Musical Arts Society Orchestra.
57 Cf. Pine and Acton, pp. 149–50, 369, 372–3.

time we have intimated to the Federation that we will do all in our power to improve the training of musicians at home. The RIAM provides very poor teaching facilities in the general sense and there seems to be no prospect of bringing Irish musicians up to the standard needed for Symphony Orchestra work unless some radical change is made ... It is believed, however, that much could be done to improve [the Academy's] work if action is taken of a tactful kind to bring the problem of training musicians for the Symphony Orchestra before their notice in a semi-official way. I have agreed with the Secretary of this Department that someone from Radio Éireann should approach a member of the Academy, like Mr Deale, whom we understand has the interest of the Academy at heart and is already disturbed at the present situation ... [At this point Childers also referred to the Municipal School.] It is not our intention to discuss the question of providing further finance for either institution because we believe that it may be possible to effect improvements without bringing in this factor ... If, as a result of these informal discussions, the financial question is raised to the point where we are certain that no further progress could be made without at least having your own view on this question we will cease all further negotiations until we have again approached you on the matter in order to consider ways and means of discussing the matter further. As you are aware the interest in Orchestral music in this country is very limited and we have not made anything like the progress of, for example, the English people in popularising good music throughout the country. While it is true that foreigners serve everywhere in countries where there are orchestras, the position is very serious here indeed. We are compelled to employ comparatively young married women in the RÉ orchestras and if we did not do so we would be unable to appoint a sufficient number of unmarried persons or older married people to maintain the Orchestra at its present strength.[58]

58 Childers to MacEntee, 30 July 1951, P&T file 12963/51. Childers was already fighting a departmental battle regarding married women: Ó Broin had stated that 'there were too many women in the Orchestras. Women were not physically capable of playing symphony music effectively. He also put it forward that as a principle married women should not be in the Orchestras ... The Minister said he had strong views about the desirability of keeping married women in professions like teaching and the arts. He asked that the point about getting rid of married women should not be pressed at present': minutes of a departmental meeting, 9 July 1951, P&T file 12963/51. It should be noted that it was a general rule throughout Europe in the 1940s and 1950s that orchestras were almost exclusively staffed by men, a position which changed gradually in the post-war period – for example in the Hallé under Barbirolli – but which remained unchanged in the Berlin Philharmonic until near the end of the twentieth century. Radio orchestras were more likely to employ women. Edgar Deale (1902–99) was a composer and singer, founder-member of the Music Association of Ireland and the Irish Association of Civil Liberty, and edited the first *Catalogue of*

As an example of delicate diplomacy, opening a channel of negotiation which history had already shown to be strewn with obstacles, Childers' letter could hardly be bettered. In reply, MacEntee told Childers that, having met a deputation from the RIAM in November 1950, he was about to give it a small increase in grant, but that he saw disadvantages in giving state assistance – presumably he regarded the eligibility of the RIAM, as a private body, to be questionable – but had nevertheless suggested that it should approach the CDVEC.[59]

This latter suggestion signals the beginning of a long-drawn-out episode during which Ó Broin, as the helmsman of the orchestras, contemplated and attempted to effect a merger between the RIAM and the Municipal School to form a national conservatoire – a manoeuvre which would remain frustrated and which would be a matter for public and private discussion to the present day.[60] Matt Doherty gave as his opinion 'that there is plenty of room for both the Academy and the Municipal School of Music and that their functions are separate but complementary to one another. The School trains pupils from the beginning and the Academy "finishes" them'.[61] Although he was not quite accurate in forming such a view, he had, perhaps unwittingly, exposed the notion that there was a differential in standards between the two schools. He considered the idea of the RIAM approaching the CDVEC as pointless: 'It would seem that the Academy cannot expect help from anywhere but a direct increase in its grant from the State, and the State should contribute whatever is necessary to make first-class teaching facilities available in this country'.[62] The lengths to which all concerned within P&T would go, on a matter which, strictly speaking was not within their remit and in which they had little expertise, is remarkable. Doherty continued:

> I suggest discussion should be had individually with some of the Governors of the Academy to find out what are their real difficulties, financial or otherwise, to ascertain whether they could appoint ... somebody who would have the qualifications and functions they intended in a Director and whether they could effect improvements with a small increase in the grant or perhaps without any increase ... There are such places as the Leinster School of Music which appears to have the same functions as the Academy and if any further assistance is being given to the Academy it should be considered whether any wrong would be done [to] places like the Leinster School.[63]

Contemporary Irish Composers. **59** MacEntee to Childers, 20 Mean Fomhair 1951, ibid. **60** Cf. John O'Conor, 'Towards a new academy' in Pine (ed.) *Music in Ireland*; R. Pine, 'In dreams begins responsibility' *Journal of Music in Ireland*, 2/3 (March–April 2002). **61** Doherty to Ó Broin, 22 October 1951, file 12963/51. **62** Ibid. **63** The Leinster School of Music is a private establishment, founded in Dublin in 1904 by Stanley Spenser Myerscough.

In the meanwhile, the Department of Finance had also realised that the rivalry between the RIAM and the Municipal School was a hindrance. MacEntee's predecessor in the 1948–51 coalition government, Patrick McGilligan, had written to General Richard Mulcahy, his opposite number in Education:

> If you think well of it, perhaps you would get your people to take up the matter with the [VEC] with a view to such co-ordination of activities between the School of Music and the Academy as would enable the Academy to obtain the finance they need; … It would be a pity if these two cultural institutions were to stand aloof from each other when, by co-operation, they could do more for music in the city and country.[64]

However, the CDVEC indicated in August 1951 that it would not subsidise the RIAM, especially as it expected to be improving and extending the Municipal School. The 'aloof' attitude of both institutions was in fact to impede the development of indigenous players for many years.

Nevertheless, by October 1951 Edgar Deale (referred to in Childers' letter to MacEntee, above) as the RIAM go-between with P&T, could report that the Academy had appointed several of the RÉSO principal players to its teaching staff: Roland Dufrane (oboe), Herbert Leeming (flute), Gilbert Berg (bassoon), Leopold Laurent (horn), and Novemo Salvadori (trumpet and trombone). 'I understand that the number of pupils is disappointingly small, which, in my opinion, is due to the fact that the Municipal School of Music can give tuition in these instruments much more cheaply'.[65]

When Childers met the RIAM deputation at the end of 1951,[66] he pointed out that, although he had no responsibility for financial affairs,

> he was anxious to discuss … how the Academy could help Radio Éireann and how Radio Éireann could help the Academy. Radio Éireann wanted to see a stream of first class Irish musicians coming along who could be recruited to the Radio Éireann Orchestras. Radio Éireann had recruited many first class musicians on the Continent and … the Academy should avail of the services of these musicians to a greater extent so as to train Irish musicians up to their own high standard so that in time the Radio Éireann Orchestras would be composed practically entirely of Irish musicians.[67]

64 McGilligan to Mulcahy, 23 November 1950, P&T file 12963/51. 65 Deale to Ó Broin, 26 October 1951, ibid. 66 The deputation consisted of John F. Larchet, Edgar Deale, Mrs W.J.M. Starkie (the mother of Walter Starkie) and Maud Aiken, wife of the Minister for External Affairs, one of Éamon de Valera's closest associates. 67 Minutes of meeting between P&T and RIAM, 7 December 1951, P&T file 12963/51.

Supplementing the Minister's opening statement, Ó Broin

> suggested that the Academy should provide expert tuition in every orchestral instrument and that it should endeavour to increase the number of pupils learning instruments other than the piano and violin. He said that there was [*sic*] 16 vacancies in the Orchestras at present and that vacancies will arise fairly frequently as musicians reach the age limit or leave for other reasons and the Minister mentioned that it was probable that the size of the Orchestras would be increased within say the next 10 years.[68]

Adverting to the recent appointment of the wind players from the RÉSO, and to the lower cost of tuition at the Municipal School, Larchet stated that 'the students of the Municipal School usually join Dance Bands but they would not generally be good enough for a Symphony Orchestra without further tuition'. Agreeing with this, Childers said 'that it seemed to him that the problem was one of getting the students of the Municipal School to continue their studies in the Academy. This could probably be effected by vocational guidance methods as no doubt a number of the students would prefer classical to band music … How are students to be attracted to the wood wind sections?' Edgar Deale said that in his opinion scholarships should be offered to promising students discovered at local centres (a nationwide examination system which the RIAM had established in 1894). The trouble was, however, that the Academy could not afford these scholarships which would have to be sufficient to pay for the students' accommodation in Dublin. 'The Minister said that he would look into the question of whether existing Local Government legislation permits of giving scholarships in music to persons desiring to attend the Academy'.[69]

As a result of this meeting, Childers persuaded MacEntee to increase the government grant to the RIAM, and at the same time it was noted that responsibility for supervision of the Academy's work should be undertaken by the Department of Education – again, the notion of a national conservatoire, combining the resources of both teaching institutions, was being contemplated. (As far back as 1936, Frederick May had called for a 'National Music Academy … work[ing] in the closest co-operation with our national broadcasting station' which would thus alleviate the broadcaster's problem of finding adequate resources.)[70] By May 1952 Ó Broin could confidently write that the improvements at the RIAM 'should transform the situation, so far as the brass and wood

---

68 Ibid. **69** Ibid. For the RIAM Local Centre system, cf. Brian Beckett, 'Tested teaching' (1998), pp. 297–321. **70** May, 'Music and the nation'. May would repeat his argument in his contributions to Aloys Fleischmann's symposium *Music in Ireland* (1952).

wind instruments are concerned and, together with Vaneček's work, should put the State well on the way towards fulfilling an undertaking we have given viz. that everything possible will be done to provide a supply of native players competent to fill vacancies as they occur in the Radio Éireann orchestras'.[71] As the recruitment of first-class foreign players to the orchestras raised the standard of performance, so too their participation in the RIAM raised not only standards but also awareness of the attractions of the instruments. Following those new teachers already mentioned, the RIAM saw the arrival of André Prieur (flute) in 1952, Victor Malíř (horn) and Michele Incenzo (clarinet) in 1955, in addition to string players Maurice Meulien and Erich Eisenbrand (both cellists) in 1952 and 1955 respectively, Heinz Jablonski (double bass, 1956), and violinists François d'Albert (1952) and Max Thöner (1955), the latter as a result of the resignation of Jaroslav Vaneček.[72]

Parallel to the negotiations with the RIAM and Municipal School, RÉ also sought to make improvements in the area that presented most difficulty, and *via* the channel from which it had traditionally, but temporarily, solved that difficulty: the Army School of Music. Although earlier files are no longer extant, it is clear from correspondence and detailed meetings with officials at the School that there was a continuing anxiety to bring about a long-term solution to the availability of Irish wind and brass players.[73] This was ameliorated by the fact that in May 1958 Kevin Boland was both Minister for Defence and Acting Minister for P&T,[74] but it was also caused by the fact that the intake of continental musicians, and the encouragement given to them to produce successful students at the RIAM, was not entirely fruitful, due not to their deficiencies but to the small numbers of pupils enrolling. An attempt had also been made in 1956 by the Municipal School to start a class for its own pupils combined with those of the Army, but 'this scheme did not prove practicable'.[75]

In his briefing document for the Minister, León Ó Broin made these points, still forced to acknowledge that 'we have no tradition in the teaching of classical music for orchestras'.[76] While the position had improved in relation to

71 Ó Broin departmental memo, 16 May 1952, P&T file 12963/51. **72** For an account of this resignation, and of difficulties concerning Max Thöner, cf. Pine and Acton, op. cit., pp. 371–2. François d'Albert (1918–99) was Hungarian born, becoming a French citizen in 1948; he was prodigiously talented as a young player, earning plaudits from Bronislav Huberman and Jacques Thibaud, and in Dublin he formed his own string quartet; after leaving Dublin he went to North America, eventually settling in Chicago, where he founded Chicago Conservatory College and became music director of the American Festival Orchestra, the Chicago Chamber Players and a guest conductor of the Chicago Symphony. **73** P&T File 86/5675/5: 'Army School of Music – suggested improvement of teaching facilities'. This had already been noticed by Erskine Childers who, in opposition in 1955, referred to the need for the Army School to provide musicians of concert standard: DD, 152, 6 July 1955, col. 287. **74** The Minister for P&T (December 1957–June 1959), Seán Ormonde, was unwell at this time. When ill health forced his resignation, he was succeeded by Michael Hilliard. **75** Doherty to Ó hAnnracháin, June 1958, file 86/5675/5. **76** Ó

string playing, 'the position about brass and wood-wind remains, however, entirely unsatisfactory'. An approach had been made earlier in 1954 to intro-duce some of the continental musicians from RTÉ into the Army School of Music, which had not proceeded – principally because, as the Army itself admit-ted, 'there was not sufficient enthusiasm at the higher levels in Defence',[77] and it was this which Ó Broin hoped Boland might re-examine and give effect to it. He was not to be successful – the scheme would 'not prove practicable'.

The approach of 1953–4 was initiated by Childers, and had been in the hands of Fachtna Ó hAnnracháin and Milan Horvat, who had met with Lt. Col. J.M. Doyle (now Director of the Army School) and his assistant (and even-tual successor) Commdt. J.P. Brennock. They had proposed that in addition to wind and brass, strings should also be taught: 'On the Continent, students of woodwind and brass instruments generally study a string instrument as well. This is done principally as a precautionary measure, because if a man should have any serious trouble with his teeth in later life, he might find himself unable to continue playing a "blown" instrument'.[78] Ó hAnnracháin told Maurice Gorham: 'We consider it vital to make the Army School of Music and the Army Bands attractive to boys of all classes, so that entrants do not consist exclusively of boys from the poorer families, as seems to be the case at present'.[79] As in the case of the RIAM from the late 1940s onwards, it was clearly necessary for RÉ to involve itself in a matter which, strictly speaking, was not a broadcast-ing function, in order to safeguard its musical future. As Ó Broin was to observe near the end of this episode (he was trying to make a case to his opposite num-ber in Finance): 'Radio Éireann through its orchestras has revolutionised the musical situation in Ireland. The revolution has to be kept going, It turns largely on the maintenance of standards in the orchestras and the continuous supply to them of trained native talent … Believe me, as a close observer of what is going on, that it is rather heart-breaking to try to maintain our orches-tras at any reasonable level at all.'[80] He pointed out that Swedish Radio had started its own school of music: 'If Radio Éireann had the money I would strongly counsel that they should follow suit. But they have not and will not in the foreseeable future.'

Boland gave his approval for the re-introduction of the scheme, and it had been made clear to the Army personnel that 'every effort [should] be made to overcome the obstacles which exist'.[81] Apart from a shortage of physical facil-ities, the chief obstacles were numbers, standards and time. The Army acknowl-edged that 'present intake of boys, while adequate in standard for Army Bands,

Broin to Boland, 23 May 1958, ibid. **77** Col. P. Hally, Adjutant General, reported at P&T–Defence meeting 4 July 1958, memo by M. Doherty, ibid. **78** Ó hAnnracháin to Gorham, 27 July 1954, ibid. **79** Ibid. **80** Ó Broin to MacInerney, 3 May 1960, ibid. **81** Department of Defence 'Memo for Conference 4/7/58', ibid.

are [*sic*] hardly of sufficiently high standard educationally and in intelligence to meet the requirements of symphony playing … A better class of boy is required … It was considered it would take at least six years to develop an average boy to the standard where he could commence to take his place in a symphony orchestra.'

A fresh meeting recognised that civilian teachers would be required, for which there were already precedents. It suggested that boys would be educated up to 'secondary Intermediate Cert. standard' which would be musically sufficient. There was some caution about whether advertising the new course at the Army School might attract more players than would be needed by RÉ, but, as Doherty wryly noted, 'I have no fear that more high class players will be available from the Army than we shall need. The Defence people did make the point that, being in the Army (fed clothed & paid!) they could afford to wait.'[82] This meeting had also recognised that, wearing both hats, Boland was determined that both sides should make it work.

The meeting had taken what one might describe as an actuarial approach to the situation, preparing a forecast of the vacancies that would occur in the RÉ orchestras (woodwind, brass, percussion and timpani) up to 1995. Of the 39 members of these sections, only 19 would be retiring in the next thirty-seven years, with none leaving before 1964.[83] However, if, as the meeting acknowledged, 'an all-round improvement in the standards of musical education and general education' were to be the necessary result,[84] then benefits would accrue to the Army above and beyond the creation of a better avenue of transit to RÉ; put another way, the benefits to RÉ would be outweighed by the actual costs of producing the small number of players it required. Since the briefing papers reveal that in the preceding years the numbers entering the Army School had been considerably less than those leaving, it must have seemed attractive to Defence to proceed with a scheme that would enhance its intake, and to this end it applied to the Department of Finance for recognition as a National School and for permission to employ extern teachers, which was backed up by a personal letter from Boland to James Ryan, Minister for Finance.[85] It was argued that 'the cost of the scheme was trifling in relation to the desirable national objectives aimed at'.[86] (The cost of extra teaching was estimated at £1,300 p.a.) The outcome was that Finance sat on the proposal for over a year, and rather than approving it, instead started an inquiry into why the number of Army bands, and the number of players in each band,

82 Ms. note on memo from Gorham to Doherty, 8 July 1958, ibid. 83 'Appendix A', Memorandum for meeting 4/7/58, ibid. 84 An Scoil Ceoil [Army School of Music] report of an internal committee, ibid. 85 Defence to Education, 2 February 1959; Boland to Ryan 3 February 1959; Boland to Ormonde, 3 February 1959, ibid. (Ormonde had resumed duties as Minister for P&T). 86 Hilliard to Boland 28 July 1959, ibid.

should not be reduced, on the grounds that 'Army bands were out of date as a source of music and that there was now no room for anything except the "Top Twenties" on one side and classical music on the other'.[87]

Eventually, a meeting of the RTÉ Authority on 27 June 1960 was informed that 'following protracted discussions', Finance approval had finally been granted, but a letter on this file from Matt Doherty (now, in 1963, in retirement) indicates that it had been overtaken by political and cultural *forces majeures*: nothing further was done to implement the scheme 'because of the preoccupation of Defence with the sending of troops to the Congo and because of the preparations for the starting of Television'.[88] When Doherty's letter provoked a re-examination of the proposal, Gerard Victory (at that time deputy Director of Music) informed the Directorate-General that 'within the next twenty to twenty-five years nine posts would fall vacant on age grounds ... No vacancies in the other 31 posts might arise for over 20 years but, of course, no one can predict the incidence of resignations for other reasons.' Also, the climate had changed: 'Prevailing world shortages have now affected string players more severely than wind. Good wind players are still fairly obtainable on our terms abroad, but string players are becoming more difficult to find.'[89] Victory was of the opinion that to proceed with this scheme was 'of secondary importance to the re-establishment of the Summer School of Music, for instance, or any educational assistance of a more embracing kind'. From the Army's point of view, permission could not be obtained to designate its school as a National School, and it resisted the suggestion that it should become a Vocational School and 'the matter died there'.[90]

PRUSSIAN STATE ORCHESTRA

Since the initial intake for the two new orchestras had been less than ideal, it must have come as a godsend to Fachtna Ó hAnnracháin when he received news in late 1952 that an extraordinary defection of musicians from east Berlin was being contemplated. He had been told by Hans Schmidt-Isserstedt that since the Prussian State Orchestra, which was the resident band for the Berlin Staatsoper, was now working in the eastern, Soviet-controlled, sector of the city, its members were to be compelled to reside, as well as work, in that sector. Consequently they were seriously considering a defection to a more con-

87 Report by Doherty of a meeting with Mr MacInerney (Dept. of Finance), 29 April 1960, ibid.
88 Doherty to Controller of Programmes, 19 November 1963, ibid. In August 1960 Irish troops had been sent as part of a peace-keeping force to the civil war in newly independent Congo, from which Katanga had seceded. 89 Victory to John Irvine, 12 December 1963, ibid. 90 Report by Leo Donnelly of a conversation with Mr O'Hara, Department of Defence, 16 January 1964, ibid.

genial environment (one recalls Ó hAnnracháin's earlier remark about people being prepared to uproot themselves). In January 1953 Ó hAnnracháin received the following confirmation from Arthur Grüber (a Hamburg-based conductor who had worked with the Hamburg State Opera at the DGOS in 1950 and 1951):[91]

> These musicians who have held out until now partly from idealistic loyalty to their institute and partly so as not to lose any service for a pension later on, now wish to continue their work in a place where it will not be influenced or disturbed by politics. The possibility is so unique that I hope it may be realised. These gentlemen all live in West Berlin and, therefore, it will be no problem for them to go over West Germany to Ireland. I expect that the event would receive the support of the West German authorities. Possibly you might like to discuss this with the German representative in Dublin. I request only that you remember in your correspondence to Berlin that letters are controlled.[92]

Ó hAnnracháin immediately requested authority to act on this information:

> An opportunity like this may never arise again in our time, and if we are to get the best players we must act quickly ... We have 8 vacancies at the moment[93] and this figure will have reached 9 by June ... It is proving increasingly difficult to manage in the Symphony Orchestra without triple wood-wind, and it is only by a miracle that we were able to put on last Sunday night's 'Prom' programme as advertised. In a recent memorandum I asked once again for the 4 extra wood-wind players which would solve this problem. This present opportunity makes it possible to increase the strings sections of both orchestras so as to achieve a satisfactory balance and perhaps a suitable Deputy Leader for the Symphony Orchestra could also be found.[94]

The chief negotiators from the German side were to be Egon Jauch and Herbert Pöche – the latter was to become a central figure in Irish music-making for two decades. Born in Berlin in 1905, he had studied viola at the State

91 Grüber conducted Mozart's *Don Giovanni* in the Spring Season, 1950, and Rossini's *Il barbiere di Siviglia* and Mozart's *Die Entführung aus dem Serail* in the Spring Season 1951. 92 Arthur Grüber to F. Ó hAnnracháin, 19 January 1953, P&T file 285/53/1, 'Orchestra – 1) Applications from members of Prussian State Orchestra for employment; 2) Applications for treble woodwind. Authority for auditions and engagements'. 93 3 violins and 1 viola in the RÉLO, 2 violins and 1 cello, plus 1 horn and 1 violin nearing retirement age, in the RÉSO. 94 F. Ó hAnnracháin, departmental memo, 29 January 1953, ibid. The final words suggest that he was finding Arthur Nachstern less than satisfactory in this post.

Academy there, had played in the State Opera 1925–42 before spending two years at the Hague and then returning to Germany as a member of the Gewandhaus Orchestra and Quartet in Leipzig; since 1946 he had been back in his old job in Berlin. 'I am healthy, my wife too. I like my profession from all my heart'.[95] Jauch had been born in 1906 in Wiesbaden, where his father was a violinist; a pupil of Max Rostal at the Munich Academy, he had worked in Ulm, at the Baden-Baden Philharmonic of Munich, in Leipzig and, since 1937, in Berlin as solo viola and *Kammervirtuos*. The experience and calibre of these – and indeed of almost all the German players who eventually arrived in Ireland – makes it clear why Ó hAnnracháin was so anxious to avail of this unique opportunity.

However, Ó hAnnracháin would face an uphill struggle in obtaining approval for an intake of such magnitude. Matt Doherty immediately pointed out that 'On two grounds we could not possibly face the employment of 31 further foreign musicians ... a) financial; b) the uproar that would arise if that number of foreign musicians were now imported and some Irish players dismissed'.[96] The Minister (Childers) had agreed that it was essential to add five violins,

> as no matter what is done to improve matters in the Gaiety by the addition of a canopy etc, the violin section will be unsatisfactory. He [Childers] would be prepared to face the importation of five violinists, if Irish players had not to be put off just now. On the same basis he would agree to the addition of a total of up to say 10 players to provide for weaknesses in other sections ... The Minister suggested that we should at once hold an audition for Irish players to keep matters right and that the standard to be set down for the examiners should be that of the regional BBC orchestras.[97]

The cost would be an extra £5,500, for which no provision had been made in any of the Estimates. The intake of fifteen players was, in fact, to be the total that Ó hAnnracháin would achieve. Doherty's next task, even with Childers' active support, was to face the Comhairle at its meeting of 21 February; he recorded:

> The Comhairle was not disposed to recommend an expenditure of £5,500 to get 10 players from [Berlin] with no offset by displacement of substitute players at home. They felt that foreign players would be

95 Herbert Pöche to Radio Éireann, 18 January 1953, file 285/53/1. 96 Doherty to M. Gorham, 5 February 1953, ibid. 97 Ibid.

available at any time. It was decided to get them on their merits and that
we should not now be rushed into this expenditure by the fear that if
the present chance of getting players were lost it would never recur …
The Minister agreed.[98]

(If Childers was in fact in favour of the proposed increase, it seems strange that
he would have 'agreed' with the opinion of the Comhairle, and it is possible
that Doherty more properly meant to say that the Minister appeared to
acknowledge this opinion, rather than concur with it.)

Temporarily deterred, Ó hAnnracháin continued to pursue the need for
extra woodwind, since the use of two players in each section was insufficient:

> Since I joined Radio Éireann in 1947 I have pointed out several times
> orally and in writing that we should have triple woodwind in the
> Symphony Orchestra instead of double woodwind as at present. The
> incessant troubles we have in the Symphony Orchestra trying to have
> the full set of players for each concert have become unbearable and I
> appeal once more for favourable consideration of this request. Herr
> Zillig recently told us all that the absence of these 4 players lowered the
> standard of the performance of the Orchestra out of all proportion to
> the numbers involved. It is not possible to get suitable outside players
> of these instruments and frequently we fail to find anyone at all, suit-
> able or unsuitable. The matter has come to a head in connection with
> the visit of the Munich State Opera and the situation is so bad that the
> German conductor who has been rehearsing Tristan, was restrained only
> with great difficulty from ceasing rehearsals and disclaiming all respon-
> sibility for the Orchestra's performance … As far back as 1947 Jean
> Martinon recommended triple woodwinds and every conductor of dis-
> tinction since has recommended likewise. These men are experienced
> in orchestral matters and know what they are talking about. A drama
> should not be put on the stage with some of the characters missing and
> this is more-or-less what we are expected to do with many orchestral
> works at present.[99]

This was to be vigorously supported by Horvat a couple of months later:

---

98 Memo by Doherty, 25 February 1953, ibid. 99 F. Ó hAnnracháin departmental memo, 17
April 1953, ibid. Hans Gierster and Robert Heger conducted the Munich State Opera productions of Wagner's *Tristan und Isolde* in the DGOS Spring season, Gaiety Theatre, April–May 1953.
Heger had conducted the Wagner Festival at Covent Garden in 1939 and was also acclaimed for
his recording of Richard Strauss's *Der Rosenkavalier* with Lotte Lehmann and Elisabeth Schumann.

> It is absolutely necessary to have three players in each woodwind sec-
> tion in the Symphony Orchestra otherwise I cannot guarantee any sat-
> isfaction because the quality of the casual players is very poor ... The
> gentleman who has been engaged as 2nd oboe for Friday's concert is
> incapable of playing, perhaps by reason of his great age[1]

– to which Ó hAnnracháin added:

> We just cannot be expected to carry on from day to day in a state of ter-
> ror lest the necessary instrumentalists cannot be available for our con-
> certs. During the last two weeks, we have been forced to run around
> from one jazz band to another to try and get a clarinet player, having
> failed to get one from Liverpool or Manchester.

It is typical of the cynicism with which Ó hAnnracháin's sense of urgency
was rebuffed, as well as the civil service professionalism with which increases
in expenditure had to be controlled, that Riobéard Ó Farachán, then controller of programmes, referred to this as 'one more instance of the Gorham
law of the inevitable expansion of the orchestras'.[2] Doherty suggested a compromise of two extra players, asking Ó hAnnracháin to nominate which instruments were most necessary: he chose bassoon and oboe.[3]

In fact the importation of foreign players was not always the answer to Ó
hAnnracháin's problems, as he himself admitted when dealing with the clarinet situation (although the problem was demonstrably more acute in the case
of wind and brass players): a foreign clarinettist had left the country without
warning, precipitating another crisis. According to Ó hAnnracháin, this player

> had not given satisfaction as a member of the orchestra. He had good
> tone and technique but at times he played in an extremely unmusical
> and stupid manner. I had intended recommending that he should not
> be kept on after his 12 month probationary period had expired but he
> has now relieved me of the necessity of doing this. We have been very
> unfortunate with clarinet players so far. Wolf Adler, a Hungarian, proved
> unsatisfactory and had to be let go; Raymond Malfait, a Frenchman,
> was unsatisfactory and left without notice just 2 years ago ... Last year
> we auditioned [in Rome] a very good Italian clarinet player from Naples,
> but he was unable to come for personal reasons and because the salary
> offered was too small. I have kept in touch with this man, Michele

---

1 M. Horvat, departmental memo, 4 June 1953, file 285/53/1. 2 R. Ó Farachán, comment on
Ó hAnnracháin's memo, ibid. 3 Doherty to Ó hAnnracháin, 24 April 1953, ibid.

Incenzo, and I believe he is now definitely interested in coming here if we can meet him in the matter of salary ... We cannot go on without a 1st clarinet and the very inferior player we are using ... will not be available after another fortnight as he is going to play in Butlin's Holiday Camp during the summer.[4]

A special salary of £15 per week was authorised, and as a result the RÉSO acquired the services of Michele Incenzo, who was to be one of the most outstanding players (and teachers) in the history of the orchestra. Meanwhile, despite Childers having approved the expansion of the woodwind, auditions held in July 1953 failed to identify any satisfactory players for the vacancies or the new positions in either orchestra.

By September 1953 the situation in Berlin was still open, and Horvat and Ó hAnnracháin were able to travel to meet the players in question – again, Herbert Pöche and his wife Katrin were crucial to the arrangement of the meetings and subsequent correspondence.

Our visit to Berlin ... was ... even more successful than we ever hoped it would be. Were it not for the very unsatisfactory political and economic situations in Berlin, most of the players we are now recommending for appointment would not dream of coming to Dublin at the salaries we are offering. Many of them are men of the highest standard in the music profession who have held important music posts for years. It is with regret that they have decided to leave Berlin but, having taken the decision, they now wish to make a complete break and make their homes in Ireland. Some others are young [and of] considerable talent and ability, whose future in Berlin would have been assured in normal times ... Every clause of the Conditions of Service had to be explained in full and many questions answered about living conditions in this country. Generally, the players would not come for a period of less than three years, but as this is comparatively short we agreed that we could meet the request ... We consider that at long last the opportunity has arisen of making a really good Symphony Orchestra here and it is an opportunity that may never again arise in our time. We can confidently say that if our recommendations are now accepted, only the normal comings and goings in any large group of musicians may be expected in the future and that no further large scale importation of players should be required.[5]

4 Ó hAnnracháin to Doherty, 5 May 1953, ibid. Incenzo went on to become an internationally famed teacher, with his base at the Academia di Santa Cecilia, Rome; he is the father of the singer/composer Vincenzo Incenzo. 5 M. Horvat and F. Ó hAnnracháin, joint memo, 14 October 1953, ibid.

In order to satisfy prospective employees from Germany about the living conditions in Ireland, a statement was issued incorporating typical financial facts with the Deutschmark equivalent (see Table K). It would later be alleged that these prices (also stated in *lire*) had been incorrect and that some players had been thus misled into thinking the cost of living was lower than it actually was. In early 1953 Renato Ferrerini, a tuba player, complained: 'I hope you will pardon me troubling you again, but I have to refer to the list of prices of cost of living sent to me ... before I accepted my position here. I find myself in very difficult financial position due to the fact that the actual prices of essential items of living cost are much above your list. I am very pleased to be in Ireland and would not like to be obliged to live [*sic*] the country but I truly cannot continue to manage to stay and continue to have my wife and myself worried trying to manage to live here on my present pay.'[6] Ó hAnnracháin recognised the reality of this: 'the group of Italian players who came here last summer were particularly severely hit by the increase in the cost of living because the details ... sent out to the Legation in Rome were, it seems, inaccurate ... They cannot help feeling that we did not play quite fair with them and I believe some of them would not have come here had they been aware of the actual position'.[7]

Horvat and Ó hAnnracháin recommended the appointment of nineteen German players,[8] of whom fifteen were to fill existing vacancies, thus having to make a case for only four new positions. Of the fifteen existing positions, five were already held by foreign players 'who have not given satisfaction'.[9] It was essential for Horvat and Ó hAnnracháin to stress that only the minimum number of foreigners was contemplated, since, in giving permission to travel, Gorham had made it clear to Childers that

> we have given an undertaking to the Orchestra Committee that a permanent player, even if he is not considered up to standard, will not be dismissed until he has been given every opportunity over a considerable period to improve. We know that it is your desire as it is ours that any deficiencies in the permanent Irish players should be put up with as far as possible and they should be allowed to continue until they work out their period of service.[10]

The recommendations would mean that the total number of players in the two orchestras would be 97, of whom 40 would be non-Irish, with three new

6 R. Ferrerini to RÉ, 2 March 1953, P&T file 10/57/6.   7 Ó hAnnracháin to Doherty 14 March 1953, ibid.   8 4 violins, 2 violas, 1 cello, 3 double basses, 1 flute, 1 oboe, 1 clarinet, 1 bassoon, 3 horns, 1 bass trombone, 1 tuba.   9 Ibid. In 1968, Kevin Roche would assert that 'we must have imported upwards of a 100 foreign musicians in the past 20 years, and I doubt whether more than half-a-dozen of them have been sub-standard': File H/R/4/A, 'RÉLO 1961–68'.   10 Gorham to Childers, 10 September 1953, ibid.

Table K [Exchange rate 11.74 DM = £1]

Income tax in Ireland:
> Standard rate 32.5%, but the first 1174 DM was charged at 16.25%
> Tax Relief – 20% of gross salary
> Personal allowance 1644 DM (3288 married)

Children's allowances:
> children over 16: 939DM;
> children under 16: first 2 children: 939DM,
> others 740DM

Dress allowance   117.4DM

The result is that a musician earning 131 DM per week [£11.3s.3d], which is the rate at present paid to ordinary members of the Radio Éireann Orchestra, would pay in Income Tax:

1019 DM per annum if single	485 DM if married with no children
185 DM if married with 1 child	32 DM if married with 2 children
Nil if married with 3 or more children	

Cost of living in Dublin

Food

Bread		0.35 DM	per kilo
Meat	Beef	2–3.3 DM	" "
	Mutton	2.38–3.57 DM	" "
	Bacon	3.03–4.87 DM	" "
Butter		3.89DM	" "
Coffee		7.14DM	" "
Tea		3.46DM	" "
Milk		0.42 per litre	
Luncheon	2.35 (average)		
Suits	factory cut:	106DM	
	tailor made:	164DM	
Overcoats	factory	103DM	
	tailor made	141DM	
Shirts		18DM	
Shoes		29DM	
Accommodation			
3–4 room flat (furnished)		23–35 DM weekly	
Full board and lodging		32DM weekly	
Partial board		23DM weekly	

---

posts being created in the RÉSO and four in the RÉLO. The situation was discussed at a meeting attended by Childers, Ó Broin, C.J. Brennan (chair of the Comhairle), Gorham, Horvat, Ó hAnnracháin and Doherty, after which Gorham wrote to Brennan that he agreed with the additional posts in the RÉSO but that the remaining additions seem to be mostly designed to provide for available foreigners without getting rid of regular Irish players who are not so good ... We have only recently announced that the auditions disclosed quite a healthy situation on the string side although the outlook was depressing for woodwind etc. I think in view of this it will be hard to justify bringing in violins and violas from Berlin. All our defences to these criticisms are going to be weakened by the uncontrovertible fact we are importing 19 Germans at the same time. In the eyes of the general public, Radio Éireann's value does not primarily depend on the amount or standard of the symphonic music that it broadcasts. Drama, variety, discussions, traditional music, and above all news are probably far more important for the station to try to raise its standards in these directions. In spite of my great sympathy with Mr Horvat's desire to produce an orchestra of international standing, I feel that to adopt all of these proposals would do Radio Éireann more harm than good.[11]

And in a characteristic outburst which typifies Childers's feelings about the role which music could play in the social and aesthetic life of post-war Ireland, he told Gorham and Brennan:

I cannot endure avoidable mediocrity. It is destroying the renaissance of this land more than any other single factor. The Comhairle will have full Ministerial support. If there is criticism I shall take responsibility for it but I would hope that the Comhairle will agree with the proposals. The Light Orchestra is not big enough. There should probably be a Ceilidhe Band. There are plenty of precedents [for bringing in foreigners], Czech beet sugar experts, English pilots, Danish cement technicians ... In view of the very major part serious music plays in Radio Éireann I would ask the Director to publish a full statement of what is being done about Irish music arrangements and describe plans for the Choir.[12]

Part of the 'mediocrity' was the fact that, while Irish musicians were seen to be more spontaneous and expressive, they did not have the grounding in technique that distinguished those trained in continental conservatoires. As far back as the 1890s Harty had noted 'that light-hearted facility and self-confidence which has always been the curse of native Irish musical talent' which could only be countered by serious and disciplined study.[13]

As a consummate politician who took Éamon de Valera as a mentor, Childers would most likely have recognised the political dimension of music

11 Ibid.   12 Ibid. In 1953 Radio Éireann also established the RÉ Singers (see below, chapter 5).
13 Harty, *Early memories*.

reflected in Frederick May's statement 'Though music is sometimes thought of as a thing withdrawn and apart from the world of every day, no art is so deeply intimate'.[14] Coming from a non-musical background, Childers had been initially hesitant about his role in relation to music, but as soon as he and his wife had started to attend RÉSO concerts as a matter of duty, they became deeply interested in, and excited by, musical activity; as President of Ireland, Childers would frequently attend not only 'Public Concerts' but also studio concerts in the St Francis Xavier Hall.[15] Looking back from the perspective of 1984, the *Irish Times* critic Charles Acton was to say 'Childers's impact on music both as Minister and as President was considerable ... [The restoration of] RTÉSO public concerts in the Gaiety (which had immense musical and public effect) came from him; ... he was the first Head of our State who helped to sell our musicians abroad (and at home) by the simple matter of inviting them to play in Áras an Uachtaráin ... I think it is important to *music* that our musicians get such formal encouragement'.[16]

Despite this, Gorham made strenuous efforts to resist the ministerial directive, attempting to restrain the initial German intake to twelve players, but Ó hAnnracháin argued persuasively that they should all come at once, since the first twelve would be insufficient to raise standards, with the consequent danger that they would leave Ireland. Gorham seems to have persuaded him to compromise on 14–15, plus Incenzo, the Italian clarinettist.[17] This would leave the RÉLO needing an extra cellist, a horn and a deputy leader, and the RÉSO needing a double-bassist. By the following year, he had not only succeeded in obtaining permission for the extra posts, but he had also been able to add four extra strings to the RÉLO.[18] The Comhairle agreed to the increase on 13 February 1954 and was fully supported by Childers on 24 February when he also wrote to Ó Faracháin

> My previous directions re the steps to be taken to assist Irish musicians are to be carefully followed. I wish to make it clear again that every candidate found satisfactory at the July audition must be appointed in September to one of the Orchestras or to form part of a new Orchestra. I am afraid this is a very easy commitment to honour from what I hear, so far as 1954 is concerned.[19]

At the same time, the 1953–4 intake enabled Ó hAnnracháin to re-assign some players (whose playing was not suitable for the symphonic repertoire)

---

14 F. May, 'Music and the nation', loc. cit. 15 Personal information to the author from Erskine Childers, 1974; his only musical *bête noire* was the harpsichord. 16 Acton to Fergus Linehan, 3 January 1984 (Acton Archive). 17 Gorham to Childers, 3 November 1953. 18 P&T File 285/53/3 'Symphony and Light Orchestras – Importation of players for 1954'. 19 Childers to Ó Faracháin, 24 February 1954, ibid.

from the RÉSO to the RÉLO, where they might be more effectively employed.

Not every Berlin player was a saviour of the orchestra. Temperaments and cultural differences, besides language problems, meant that misunderstandings occurred, often involving rows at rehearsals. On one occasion one of the German players, having been reprimanded several times for late arrival at rehearsal, sent the following apology: 'I have been absent of my duty, because I have been sick in the stomach … The reason for this illness seems to have been some no more quite fresh sausages, which I have eaten just the night before.'[20] On another occasion, the same player – 'D' – blamed his lateness on his alarm clock: 'I know, that occurred such thing at me not the first time, but I wish to say, that I myself am terrible sorry about those occasions. Please, you don't think so, that I am not serious enough in these things. I hope, that you think not bad about all these happenings.' After the Concerts Manager had complained about his attitude at work, 'D' wrote to Ó hAnnracháin:

> I am aware which big help and sympathy came from your person, that I simply can't believe that you are convinced that I am a trouble-maker. It would be so unwise for a thinking person as I claim for me, to bring in danger all those advantages you gave me. I can only assure you, that I live and die for music in <u>any</u> form, and I give in, that I might not be an ideal civil servant. I promis you again, that I cut down the fanatic musician and better up the civil servant.

Finally, Ó hAnnracháin had to acknowledge that '[D] appears to be another of the swans who has proved with experience to be a goose. We appear to have spent some hundred pounds on bringing him here – which shd. warn us for the future. All things considered we shd. perhaps help him to leave us!' Having spent four years' in RÉ's service, 'D' returned to a position in Germany in 1959.

The situation with some of the Irish players had also deteriorated. The most notable and distressing was that of Nancie Lord. Her official appointment dated from 1933 and, when Terry O'Connor resigned as leader in 1945, Lord was the unanimous choice of León Ó Broin, Michael Bowles and the Director of Broadcasting to take her place on a temporary basis. When she in turn stood down in 1948 to make way for Renzo Marchionni as leader of the newly constituted RÉSO, it was made clear that 'there was no complaint at any time about Miss Lord's qualifications as a musician but she was considered not to have the verve and the qualities of control desirable in a leader'.[21] (As we shall see, this would recur as a problem perceived by the administration in Radio Éireann as inherent in women players.) Her downward spiral following her voluntary

20 RTÉ Music Department file, name withheld.   21 Kelly to Ó Broin, 13 May 1949.

demotion to no. 2 position was, however, due not to musical reasons but to her relationship with Arthur Duff. Her passion for Duff may not have been entirely unrequited but it was certainly incapable of decent fulfilment, since Duff, as well as being a married and separated man, had been carrying on an affair in the late 1930s and early 40s with a woman called Peggy Gough (who was also involved simultaneously with poet Patrick Kavanagh). Duff's relationship with Ms Gough appears to have ended by the time that he became involved with Nancie Lord.[22] The social conventions or inhibitions of the time made it almost impossible for lovers in these circumstances to enjoy any domestic relationship, so that for both Peggy Gough and Nancie Lord their affairs with Duff had a built-in frustration which in Lord's case propelled her in the direction of alcohol as a solace – a prop she shared with Duff himself. Duff's death at the age of fifty-seven in 1956 may have pushed her over the edge, alcoholically speaking, since it is from 1957 onwards that we find a succession of deeply upsetting exchanges between herself and Fachtna Ó hAnnracháin and others in the RTÉ adminstration, up to her retirement in 1965. From these exchanges it is clear that her alcoholism was very advanced, so much so that in Ó hAnnracháin's opinion she was incapable of holding her position. Obviously she was a very distressed person, aware that her outstanding musicianship was being undermined: in her plea 'I love my work and try always to give of my best' there is the voice of one who knows that 'best' can hardly ever be achieved again. In Ó hAnnracháin's reply we note the sympathy and at the same time the managerial firmness of someone faced with the difficult task of protecting the integrity of the orchestra, as he observed that he was aware that she loved her work, but asked her to honour the pledges and promises which she had given some years ago, to overcome her drink problem.[23]

There is something very tragic about a musician, aware of her waning powers and increasing sickness, reviewing the rise and fall of her career, especially in so resonant and confined a society as Dublin in the 1960s, and it is a mark of the charity of RTÉ's managerial practice that Nancie Lord was retained until 1965, when she retired 'due to severe rheumatism in the left arm'. In a farewell note (no doubt drafted by Gerard Victory) Tibor Paul wrote diplomatically and with respect that although he had been in Ireland for only a few years, he was well aware of her magnificent work as Leader of the Orchestra's earlier years and that its successful development owed a great deal to her diligence and artistry.[24] Nancie Lord died in her teaching room at the RIAM (where she had been professor of violin since 1925) on 4 November 1966, at the age of sixty-four.

22 Cf. Antoinette Quinn, *Patrick Kavanagh: a biography* (2001), pp. 139–45, where the following Limerick by Kavanagh is recorded: 'There was an oul' devil called Duff/Whom I could not torture enough/He took from me one/ Who could give me high fun/And left me to mouth my old guff'. 23 Ó hAnnracháin to Lord, 15 April 1957. 24 Paul to Lord, 26 May 1965.

Table L: Radio Éireann Symphony Orchestra, 1954

1st Violins	*2nd Violins*	*Violas*
Renzo Marchionni	Alfonso Evangelisti	Herbert Pöche
Max Thöner	Rosalind Dowse	Máire Larchet
Arthur Nachstern	Christopher Kiernan	M. Gavagnin
Nancie Lord	Carmel Lang	Walter Hall
William Shanahan	Eileen Parfrey	Thomas Collins
Zola Cirulli	Joachim Stahr	Wilson Formica
James Chapman	Doris Lawlor	Shirley Pollard
Alice Brough	P. Antoni	Kathleen Green
Dora Hall	A. Hanley	Monica Maguire
Yvonne Bizet	Elias Maguire	
David Lillis		
Margaret Hayes		
Audrey Park		

Cellos	*Basses*
Maurice Meulien	Willy Clasen
Otto Pacholke	Rudolf Frei
Goar Theis	Edmund Novak
Christine Fagan	Heinz Jablonski
Kathleen Pollaky	Herbert Engel
Thomas Kelly	
Nancy Doyle	

Flutes	*Oboes*	*Clarinets*
André Prieur	Albert Solivérès	Michele Incenzo
Hans Köhlmann	Joseph Murphy	Adolphe Gébler
Thomas Browne	Sydney Egan	

Bassoons	*Horns*	*Trumpets*
Gilbert Berg	Leopold Laurent	Kurt Lengefeld
Dieter Prodöhl	Manfred Trauer	Domenico Benedusi
Richard Persse	Harry Wood	Joseph Cassells
Gernod Essig		
Nicholas Gibbons		

Trombones	*Tuba*	*Timpani*
Novemo Salvadori	Hartmut Pritzel	Stanislaus Stack
G. Franchi		
Rudolph Jannasch		

Percussion	*Harp*
Patrick O'Regan	Síle Larchet
Valentine Keogh	

Alcohol was not a problem in the case of Christine (Chrissie) Fagan, a veteran cellist who had first been appointed in 1936: here the difficulty was simply that age had diminished her playing powers to the point that in 1959, when all members of the cello section were required to re-audition as preparation for the appointment of a new section Principal, she was judged to be 'below appointment standard'. Again, a charitable view on the part of the Music Department, encouraged no doubt by an acute shortage of suitable replacements, prompted the opinion that 'to avoid causing her undue stress she should be told that her playing has caused concern but that if she endeavours to effect an improvement it is hoped to be able to retain her ... until she reaches the age of 60 [she was 55 at the time]'.[25] Five years later, Gerard Victory (assistant to Tibor Paul) would say that, due to the acute shortage of suitable cellists, Tibor Paul could not retire Chrissie Fagan, even though he was not satisfied with her playing.[26] The following year the situation had deteriorated again, but Riobéard Ó Faracháin could still say that

> I need much more information on such matters and the extent of the deterioration in the playing standards ... and also as to how the vacancies would be filled if they were created, i.e. would filling them mean bringing in more foreign players or would it mean bringing in young and inexperienced players?[27]

Victory responded

> She is ... lacking in concentration ... her playing is weak and the situation is aggravated in her case by the general lack at present of almost any first-class players in the section. This means that the existence of one very inadequate player has an even more serious effect than in a relatively strong section such as the first violins ... When the sub-principal, Mr Caminiti, was ill, Miss Fagan because of seniority has had to take over this position and was completely unsatisfactory. Regarding replacements for these players, Mr Paul has hopes of suitable young Irish players ... He intends to use every possible effort to avoid importing further foreign players for these posts.[28]

As previously noted, another long-serving member was Moira Flusk, who was able to boast of having played on the opening nights of both Radio Éire-

25 Audition Board report, May 1959. Chrissie Fagan had played in a student quartet at the RIAM with Nancie Lord, Alice Brough and May Lord. 26 Victory to Personnel, 16 January 1964. 27 Ó Faracháin to Victory, 8 February 1965. 28 Victory to Ó Faracháin, 12 February 1965. In fact, Ms. Fagan was necessarily retained until age 65, since the pre-1947 intake was entitled to remain up to age 65 if required.

ann (in 1926) and Telefís Éireann (in 1961). Officially on the staff since 1943, she received a negative report from Dermot O'Hara in 1950, who considered that her work in the orchestra had never been satisfactory. Nevertheless, by 1959 when she was working with the RÉLO, she too was exhibiting signs of stress, and Ó hAnnracháin considered her an unsatisfactory performer. Yet she wrote, successfully, to both Ed Roth, Director-General, and his successor Kevin McCourt, for retention which was granted up to 1963, after which Tibor Paul was agreeable, on occasions, to give her deputy work in the RTÉSO.

The situation had in fact become so grave that by 1959 Matt Doherty was writing to Ó hAnnracháin that 'with all these adverse recommendations on the cellists and other native players it is feared we are approaching a point in which we will have a nearly all foreign Symphony Orchestra and a mainly foreign Light Orchestra'.[29] When double-bassist Mario Pitzianti was recruited from the Teatro Carlo Felice in Genoa in 1958, Ó hAnnracháin's explanation was that no Irish double-bass players of acceptable standard were coming forward, and when Pitzianti left precipitously the next year (due to family illness) he was almost impossible to replace. The same year, when Brian Mack was appointed to the viola section (on the recommendation of Sir Thomas Armstrong, Principal of the RAM) Ó hAnnracháin's litany continued: 'Needless to say there is no suitable Irish viola player available for the vacancy'.[30] When Mack, in his turn, left in 1961 to take a position in the City of Birmingham Symphony, there was no one to replace him; it was fortunate that he returned later in the year and remained until 1966.

LEADERS

In 1961, when Joseph Groocock was commissioned by Foras Éireann to provide an overview of music in Ireland, he would observe that

> at present about half the players in the Symphony Orchestra are Irish musicians: the rest are imported from England and various continental countries. Our position seems to resemble that of England towards the end of the 19th century, when the London orchestras were composed to a large extent of foreigners. The reason however why so many foreigners came to work in English orchestras in the 19th century is that at that time there were very few good English players. We cannot plead with complete honesty that this is still true of Ireland, when it is a fact that good Irish instrumentalists are employed as rank-and-file players, even as leaders, by many English orchestras at the present day.[31]

29 Doherty to Ó hAnnracháin, 11 July 1959.   30 Ó hAnnracháin to CP, 7 November 1958.   31 J. Groocock, *A General Survey of Music in the Republic of Ireland* (1961), p. 78.

Groocock was not entirely accurate in his facts about the London orchestras at the end of the nineteenth century,[32] but his point was nonetheless well made, especially since he had in mind English-based Irish players such as John Ronayne and Hugh Maguire who enter our story at this point. Groocock went on:

> If we really desire to fill the greater part of our orchestral ranks with Irish players, then it is important that some of these musical emigrants should be encouraged to come back to the country of their birth. It is even more important that we should try to safeguard the future, and avoid further unnecessary emigration, by making conditions of employment in Ireland fully as attractive as those which our emigrants appear to enjoy in England.

The aspiration to see an all-Irish orchestra would always be far-fetched, but a crucial topic which exercised successive Directors of Music was that of the orchestra leader, a position which became extremely problematic in 1959 after the departure of Renzo Marchionni, who returned to Florence on a year's leave of absence (from which he did not return) to take up a better-paid post which would enable him to look after his ailing parents.[33] The next fifteen years were to demonstrate how difficult it is to find a musician with the appropriate qualities for the position of leader, as a succession of Irish players occupied the leader's seat, usually as 'guest leaders' whose ratification was permanently in question. Although this account of the leadership of the RTÉSO goes beyond the chronological confines of this chapter, it is important to understand the episode of these fifteen years as a single period of uncertainty leading up to the eventual appointment of Colin Staveley in 1974.

Anxious to secure a leader of Irish origin who had achieved international stature, Fachtna Ó hAnnracháin approached Hugh Maguire, probably the only person who met those criteria. Thirty-two years old at the time, Maguire, a member of a musical Dublin family, four of whom (Hugh, Charles, Elias and Monica) played in the RTÉ orchestras, had studied at the College of Music in Dublin and at the RAM, making his London début at the Wigmore Hall in 1947 at the age of twenty, before going on to study with Enescu in Paris. He was leader of the Bournemouth Symphony 1952–6, and then of the London Symphony Orchestra. 'He would like to return to Dublin for sentimental rea-

---

32 Cf. A. Stewart, *LSO at 90* (1995), p. 17 for a list of the inaugural members of the London Symphony Orchestra.   **33** The author has seen a note suggesting that Marchionni's resignation was due to the increasing presence on the rostrum of Tibor Paul, and the likelihood that he would be appointed Principal Conductor in succession to Milan Horvat, but there appear to be no grounds to substantiate this: at most, the likelihood of Marchionni resigning on such grounds may have accelerated his actual decision to return to Florence.

sons but the financial sacrifice would be too great. His present earnings are about £3,000 a year', Ó hAnnracháin reported.[34] (Marchionni's finishing salary was £1324.) Nevertheless, Maguire's interest was such that detailed negotiations took place, reaching the point at which he was prepared to accept a three-year contract on a salary of £2100, on the basis of which he resigned his position with the LSO, as he informed Ó hAnnracháin at 3.30pm on Sunday 26 April 1959. By midnight he had changed his mind and revoked his resignation: 'He had suddenly realised during the afternoon that he was on the point of making a very great mistake. He had been caught up in the romantic idea of returning to Dublin and he felt now he should not leave London,' Ó hAnnracháin wrote.[35] As Maguire himself expressed it:

> Even though I cherish a love for my native land and would love to be able to make some contribution to her musical heritage, my present position in the musical world prevents me from doing so just at this moment. I have reached a point in international music making where it would be detrimental to myself and to the London Symphony Orchestra were I to leave London now ... Emotion and reason were pulling in opposite directions and it has taken till now for me to discover which path I must follow.[36]

As Matt Doherty remarked, 'it would have been a land-mark in the history of the present Symphony Orchestra to have an Irishman of distinguished talents taking over its leadership'.[37] A year and a half later, Maguire was again contemplating the same move: 'It is seventeen years [*recte* sixteen] since I first came to London. I was seventeen years of age at the time and I still don't like living here. Now I know that if I don't return to Dublin soon, then it possibly won't happen until I'm a decrepit old man, by which time it will be too late for me to make my contribution towards building an orchestra in Dublin, of the highest standard, which I would dearly love to see.'[38] Again, negotiations failed, and Matt Doherty, acting Director of Broadcasting,[39] wrote to the Director-General (Roth) and the Chairman (Éamonn Andrews) 'It would have been a serious decision for him to take, to leave one of the main centres of musical activity to come to a country which has practically no tradition so far as classical music is concerned.'[40] This telling commentary on the status of the RÉSO at this point in

---

34 Ó hAnnracháin, departmental memo, 19 February 1959. 35 Ó hAnnracháin, departmental memo, 27 April 1959. 36 Maguire to Doherty, 27 April 1959. 37 Doherty to Maguire, 30 April 1959. 38 Maguire to Ó hAnnracháin, 3 November 1960. 39 Maurice Gorham had resigned in mid-1959 and left RÉ in early 1960. 40 Doherty to Roth, 28 November 1960, ibid. Hugh Maguire at this time sent Edward Roth a memorandum on the development of the orchestra, but unfortunately this appears to be no longer extant.

its development underlines the challenges still facing its administrators as they attempted to bring it to a new level of achievement. Hugh Maguire continued as leader of the LSO for a further two years, when he moved to the BBCSO 1962–8, and then succeeded Eli Goren as leader of the Allegri Quartet 1968–76.[41] In this role he performed frequently in Ireland, giving series of lecture recitals, thus beginning his 'contribution' to music-making in his native country, which was to find its orchestral dimension in his work with the Irish Youth Orchestra as musical director and conductor from 1970 until 1990, during which time the orchestra appeared in Europe and North America.

Having been disappointed in this direction, Ó hAnnracháin then turned to another young Irish violinist, John Ronayne, who had studied at the College of Music with Michael McNamara and John MacKenzie and had played in the trio at the Gate Theatre at the age of sixteen. At seventeen he had worked as a deputy in the RÉLO and in 1949, aged eighteen, he was transferred temporarily to the RÉSO. Asked to return to the RÉLO, he wrote that he appreciated the fact that the standard of the LO must be maintained, but stressed that, at the outset of his career, he needed to develop his experience of orchestral playing.

Unable to retain his post in the RÉSO, Ronayne was in the painful position of being forced to 'seek his experience elsewhere' – gaining a scholarship for further study, with Max Rostal at the Guildhall School of Music, before returning to Dublin for a year in 1953, when he again found employment with the RÉSO. Ó hAnnracháin had recognised his obvious talent, which would eventually come to fruition as one of the finest leaders the RTÉSO has enjoyed, and he was anxious to maintain a connection with Ronayne in what was to prove a difficult relationship, as Ronayne commuted between jobs in Dublin and London, waiting for the opening as a leader, which came at the point where talks with Hugh Maguire had broken down. From 1953 onwards, Ronayne had worked with the Boyd Neel and Covent Garden orchestras and with the LSO, and had been offered sub-leadership of the Liverpool Philharmonic. But Ó hAnnracháin did not take kindly to Ronayne's remark that Ireland needed players of distinction but seemed to ignore them when they offered themselves. Since Ronayne would not settle for anything less than the front desk of the RÉSO – which, as Ó hAnnracháin pointed out, would mean demoting Nachstern, Nancie Lord, Zola Cirulli and William Shanahan – there was therefore no position for him at that time. Now, in 1960, Ronayne was assistant or co-leader with the RPO, working with conductors such as

41 In 1976 Hugh Maguire joined the Melos Ensemble, until his retirement in 1991; during this period he was also leader of the Covent Garden orchestra and director of strings at the Britten-Pears School.

Beecham (who had appointed him), Monteux, Kempe, Reiner and Martinon. He had also made several broadcasts for Radio Éireann, including a performance of the Brahms G major sonata with his wife, pianist Elgin Strub,[42] and, with the RÉSO, the Wieniawski second concerto in 1958, the Bruch concerto in 1959 (both with Eimear Ó Broin at the Phoenix Hall), the Prokofiev second in a studio concert under Lawrence Leonard in 1961, and, at a 'Prom' in the Gaiety, the Tchaikowsky concerto in February 1960 during a return visit by Horvat (he would play it again under Wolker Wangenheim in 1964). Of one of his Dublin recitals, Robert Johnson, critic of the *Irish Press*, had written 'Mr Ronayne has all the attributes of a first-class performer: good, steady tone, extremely clean fingering and alert intonation. He has also a keen sense of style',[43] while in the *Irish Independent* Mary McGoris concurred: 'a violinist of impressive ability with assured technique, tone that is strong and firm, and a developed sense of style'.[44]

But Ó hAnnracháin was still not satisfied that Ronayne was the right person to fill the vacancy on a permanent basis, and he was offered four months' work as acting leader of the RÉSO, for which he took leave of absence from the RPO. During this period, it was proposed that Margaret Hayes, Mary Gallagher and János Fürst would occupy the sub-leader's chair on a rotating basis, 'with a view to finding out which would make the best D[eputy] Leader',[45] although this was not put into effect on any more than a casual and infrequent basis.[46] 'We can start considering what steps we should take to engage a suitable leader on a more permanent basis. As a national competition in Italy failed to produce a suitable man for Florence (hence the offer made to Marchionni) our task will not be an easy one', Ó hAnnracháin wrote to Ó Faracháin (now Controller of Programmes).[47] He was quite correct: after Ronayne's return to London, the next choice as leader was the young Geraldine O'Grady. Ó hAnnracháin's choice of words – ' a suitable man' – was also prophetic, as Radio Éireann now began a period of discussion and dispute as to whether a woman was capable of leading a symphony orchestra. It has been generally accepted that she was leader in succession to Terry O'Connor and Nancie Lord, thus establishing a tradition of women leaders which had been punctuated by the appointment of Marchionni. In fact, Geraldine O'Grady was not officially confirmed as Leader of the RÉSO, but occupied the leader's chair as 'guest leader' for a succession of temporary appointments from March 1960 up to the end

---

42 The broadcast was on 4 January 1958; Ms Strub is the grand-daughter of Bernhard Stavenhagen (1862–1914), one of the last pupils of Liszt; a pupil herself of Franz Osborn, who had studied with Schnabel, she was a prizewinner at the 1954 piano competition in Munich: RTÉ Music Department file, 'Ronayne 1'. **43** *Irish Press*, 12 January 1959. **44** *Irish Independent*, 12 January 1959. **45** Ó hAnnracháin memorandum, 2 February 1960. **46** Information to the author from Mary Gallagher, 8 February 2004. **47** Ó hAnnracháin to Ó Faracháin, 19 October 1959.

of 1963 (this coincided with her marriage), when she resigned in order to pursue the solo career which has since brought her such international acclaim.

It is probable that neither O'Grady herself nor Ó hAnnracháin envisaged a permanent appointment, and in fact in 1961 another approach was made to Hugh Maguire, again unsuccessfully. If it were not for her gender, O'Grady's single biggest obstacle as leader would have been her youth and relative inexperience with the standard repertoire, which is one of the most onerous responsibilities of the position, since it requires the preparation of scores for bowings in the strings, which only intense practical knowledge of the works in question can satisfactorily enable. In 1962, after the appointment of Tibor Paul as Principal Conductor, Roibéard Ó Faracháin told him that many visiting conductors were reluctant to work on a long-term basis with a woman leader, even though Paul himself wished to make O'Grady's tenure permanent. Recognising the combination of the inherent difficulties she was experiencing, with the fact that she was anxious to undertake solo work outside RÉ, Gerard Victory (now assistant to Paul) suggested in March 1963 that on a long-term basis her retention as leader might be damaging to her own real interests, as much as to those of Radio Éireann, since the task of controlling the orchestra as leader, combined with her relative lack of experience, had placed an unduly great strain on her. In the event, Geraldine O'Grady's eminence as an international solo artist placed her for several decades at the forefront of Irish music-making.

It would seem that the gender bias of that period was responsible for the notion that women were less capable than men of leading a symphony orchestra, but the question did not arise in the case of Audrey Park when, twenty years later, she became leader of the RTÉSO. The question of leadership itself was not in dispute, since Audrey Park had been leader of the RTÉLO since 1972, and frequent references had been made in departmental memos to the fact that she would probably make a good leader of the smaller orchestra. But, as Fachtna Ó hAnnracháin had observed in 1960, in relation to Geraldine O'Grady's tenure of the post, the general consensus of opinion was that a woman cannot fill the post of Leader adequately, no matter how good she may be as a performer, mainly due to the perceived problem that a woman would have a less commanding personality than a man.

When O'Grady indicated that she would leave the orchestra at the end of 1963, RÉ turned once more to Ronayne, who in the meanwhile had led the RPO on a tour of North America under Sir Malcolm Sargent. His appointment from 1 January 1964 was considered sufficiently significant for the new Director-General, Kevin McCourt, to advise Ó Faracháin 'In the event Ronayne is signed up … please ensure there is consultation with Public Relations as to planned effective publicity. Ronayne's return to Ireland woud be a coup by us and we should avoid newspaper leakage by publishing it ourselves fast and completely'.[48] The memo was characteristic of McCourt's sympathy with, and concern for, the fortunes of the RÉSO, which would engage him increasingly over the next few years. It was hoped that Ronayne would be able to persuade other Irish players working in London, such as Brendan O'Brien, to imitate his return to Dublin, but this proved only partially successful.

Once again, however, Ronayne's appointment was temporary and tentative, and in March 1965, after fifteen months in the post, he left to work with the Bayerischer Rundfunk orchestra; he would not return to the RÉSO until 1972. The leader's chair was occupied in rotation by János Fürst and David Lillis until Brendan O'Brien arrived in 1966, before becoming leader of the Bournemouth Symphony. Fürst was a Hungarian refugee or '1956-er'[49] who had lost both his parents in a concentration camp during world war 2. At the time, RÉ had been obliged to make the standard case to justify the appointment of yet another foreigner, and Doherty's statement to the authorities on this occasion is a classic example which also reflects the problems affecting orchestras throughout Europe:

> A considerable percentage of the personnel of the Radio Éireann orchestras consists of Continental musicians and because of the unavailability of suitable Irish players most of the vacancies have to be filled by musicians from abroad. Even on the Continent it is not always possible to get suitable people owing to competition and because of a reluctance among first-class players towards coming to a country that is regarded as without tradition or reputation for the performance of classical music ... Mr Fürst would be offered employment here for 12 months in the first instance ... but having regard to the scarcity of qualified musicians in Ireland, employment would undoubtedly be available for him indefinitely.[50]

He had initially joined the RÉSO at the end of 1958 as rank-and-file in the second violins, and by this stage was temporary sub-leader. In 1963, in relation to Fürst's application for naturalisation as an Irish citizen, Victory had said of him 'Mr Fürst is one of the most useful players in the RÉSO. He has in fact acted as Leader on occasions both for opera performances and for concerts ... I have no hesitation in stating that Mr Fürst's services are highly valuable'.[51] In 1962 he had played the Goldmark concerto, earning praise from Charles

---

48 McCourt to Ó Faracháin, 12 July 1963. **49** The brutal suppression of the Hungarian uprising against the Soviet regime in 1956 caused the emigration of thousands of Hungarians, among whom were many musicians. Fürst had fled to Paris, where he studied at the Conservatoire, before going on to Brussels, where he studied with his compatriot André Gertler (a former pupil of Hubay and Kodály). **50** RÉ to Department of Justice, n.d. [1958]. **51** Victory to Dan Lucey (Personnel), 1 November 1963.

Acton for his 'admirable technique (about the best of our younger players)' and attributing much of the success of the performance to the 'apparently close co-operation' between soloist and conductor (Tibor Paul).[52] Later, he would be the subject of serious disputes within the orchestra and between himself and Tibor Paul.

David Lillis was another example at this time of an Irish player of distinction and promise who could not settle in Ireland with any degree of comfort or satisfaction, and whose relationship with RTÉ would be difficult. Born in 1930, and trained first at the RIAM by Grossi (who, in successive years persuaded the Governors to grant free tuition to the none-too-well-off student), he then studied on a scholarship at the RCM with Henry Holst and Albert Sammons. He had deputised in the RÉSO from 1950, and was appointed rank-and-file the following year, resigning in 1954 to return to London. In 1958 he was back in Dublin, teaching (as was his wife, the New Zealand cellist Coral Bognuda) at the RIAM, and deputising in the RÉLO, where Dermot O'Hara wanted to appoint him leader of the second violins.

A year later (in 1959) he successfully applied for the position of deputy leader of the RÉLO but after less than six months he was asking if he could lead the RÉSO,[53] since that post was now open. (Fachtna Ó hAnnracháin wrote to Matt Doherty: 'Mr Lillis finds that the music played by the Light Orchestra does not present him with a sufficient challenge'.)[54] At this point a plea was advanced by Eimear Ó Broin in respect of a training facility which might help to achieve the desired all-Irish orchestra:

> The RÉSO at the moment is going through a phase in which there is room for some experimentation and improvement. Our aim in Radio Éireann is and should be to make it essentially an Irish Radio Symphony Orchestra in the fullest sense of the meaning of that word. There is now an opportunity to encourage those up and coming native musicians of the younger generation, who are striving hard to achieve the standards we all wish for, and I feel we would be neglecting our duty as conductors if we did not do all in our power to help them. Mr Lillis is, I am sure, only the first of several Irishmen of the younger generation who will make such a request as this in the coming years. He is particularly anxious to get this specialized experience and honest enough to realise the implications of such a request. He does not intend to be leader of the RÉSO, but he feels that the experience gained in leading it occasionally would stand him good, later on, as eventual leader of an RÉ

52 *Irish Times* 9 June 1962. 53 Eimear Ó Broin to Music Department, 30 January 1960. 54 Ó hAnnracháin to Doherty, 5 February 1960.

Light Concert Orchestra and equally so to the benefit of Radio Éire-ann itself. Mr Lillis is a most assiduous worker with plenty of grit and the intelligence to tackle problems with a sense of assurance. He possesses a highly cultivated mind on music matters and has a real sense of earnestness in his desire to see a properly organised musical life flourish in our country. Although of Anglo-Irish background, he is much more keen in such matters than many of us who profess loyalty to Irish ideals and the growth of our cultural life, but who are really cynical and lacking in any real enthusiasm to see the really important issue of making this country absolutely self-supporting in its personnel an effective reality ... I am prepared to give Mr Lillis his well-deserved chance by inviting him to lead the RÉSO on an occasional concert ... if you would kindly consent to let us try this experiment not only with Mr Lillis but with any other Irish musician a conductor may think fit to recommend ... It is often held that we are essentially antagonistic in Radio Éireann to our fellow citizens. I personally don't believe this but we have to prove, now that the opportunities are there, that we really mean to assist our own young people in making the best facilities available. This holds too, for opera as well as symphonic and light music.[55]

Eimear Ó Broin has been quoted at length because not only does his note sum up Lillis's musical and personal qualities, but it also acknowledges, with pathos and clarity, the realities of the situation both musically and administratively within an organisation still finding its way after three-and-a-half decades, of which Ó Broin, from personal and family experience, was particularly aware. As a summing up of the cultural context in mid-century Ireland, and the expectations of those hoping to live and work within it, it could hardly be bettered.

However, the plea, although it did not fall on deaf ears, was insufficient in Lillis's case. In 1962 he went back once more to London, playing in the first violins of the LSO and Liverpool Philharmonic, and on the European tour of the Philharmonia. On the basis of that experience, he applied to RÉ in terms reminiscent of John Ronayne:

> I feel that the tremendous experience I have gained in playing with world-class orchestras and working with conductors like Monteux, Kempe, Dorati, Schmidt-Isserstedt and others would be of great benefit to me in a principal position in the RÉSO. My family and all my connections are in Dublin and I have no wish to settle in London no matter how attractive and lucrative the position ... I do not want to bring my children up in London for many reasons.[56]

55 E. Ó Broin, ms. note to Ó hAnnracháin, 30 January 1960. 56 Lillis to RÉ, 23 May 1962.

On foot of auditions held in London in July 1962 he was offered, and declined, a position as sub-principal of the second violins, although he did some work as a rank-and-file player, until, having again been refused a leading position, he approached Tibor Paul directly in July 1963 in terms which were, to say the least, undiplomatic when addressed to someone as sensitive and self-opinionated as Paul:

> My reaction is one of amazement … This is an orchestra which has no musical standing outside Ireland … I admire the work you are doing in Dublin with unsatisfactory material and it is my dearest wish to live in Dublin. My family, my home, and my roots are in Ireland, and I want my children to grow up as Irishmen which is their right, but I certainly will not live in Ireland if I cannot educate them and this certainly is not possible on the money offered.[57]

To which Paul replied:

> Judging from the tone of your letter, I think it is a waste of paper for us to have any further correspondence because I have to doubt very much your sincerity of intention to join our orchestra at all … I also have to reject your remarks about the orchestra, that it has no musical standing outside Ireland. If your opinion about the orchestra is such, I do not think you will ever be happy playing in this orchestra. I was expecting you as an Irishman to understand the situation and to help the country by bringing the orchestra's standards as high as possible with the means which we have.[58]

Two days later, Paul's emotional blackmail had succeeded, as Lillis agreed to take the position: 'As you so rightly point out, it depends on Irishmen abroad to help and develop the standard which you are striving to create'.[59] Two years later, Lillis became acting leader, but the appointment was short-lived, since in April 1966 he, together with Coral Bognuda and the husband-and-wife Audrey Park (violin) and Archie Collins (viola), took up residence in Cork as the RÉ String Quartet. Lillis's subsequent history was sad: persistent ill-health from 1974 led to the suspension of the work of the Quartet[60] and its eventual replacement by the Academica Quartet from Romania (see below, pp. 417–18). Lillis worked intermittently as rank-and-file in the RTÉSO but he was clearly

---

57 Lillis to Paul, 15 July 1963. He had been offered £18 per week, inclusive of £1 merit award. 58 Paul to Lillis, 17 July 1963. 59 Lillis to Paul, 19 July 1963. 60 The RTÉSQ at that stage consisted of Lillis, Bognuda, John Vallery (violin) and Kieran Egan (viola); the latter three attempted for some months to play as a trio.

unhappy working under the then leader, Colin Staveley, who described him as a 'disruptive influence' and with the orchestra manager, Val Keogh, whom he accused of character assassination; he finally left RTÉ in 1977. His depression, medically certified nervous debility, the effects of the break-up of his marriage and his disappointed expectations as a musician drove him into a pathetic decline which was a distressing end to a career which had offered so much and had delivered so little in achievement.

Some degree of stability was achieved at this point (mid-1966) with the appointment of Brendan O'Brien who remained in the position for two years. In mid-1968 Hugh Maguire was again approached, as was John Ronayne, neither of whom could be tempted, and it was then offered to Colin Staveley, a Dubliner who had just become co-leader of the RPO, and who also declined. Unable to find an Irish player capable of taking on the job, Gerard Victory (who had succeeded Tibor Paul as Director of Music) was interested to receive an application in 1968 from a young English player, John Kitchen, who had been in the first violins of the BBCSO and LSO for the past nine years and who came with a glowing endorsement from Hugh Maguire:

> He is a person of integrity, immensely kind & generous & loyal. His musical talent is above average & is coupled with a capacity for hard sustained work. He has all the experience you require & this job is exactly the one to suit both him & RE. He deserves all the success he has had & I recommend him most strongly. His temperament is just right![61]

Victory immediately responded that if RTÉ had not secured an Irish player by June, he would certainly consider Kitchen for the vacancy. With the refusals of Maguire, Ronayne and Staveley, Margaret Hayes was considered for the position, but she was not invited to audition, on the grounds that 'she is married to an English architect and it was considered quite impossible for her to transfer to Dublin'[62] (a statement that was apparently erroneous and may have been deliberately so) and also because 'it is really a man's job',[63] and the position was awarded to Kitchen from September 1968 for two years, with a one-year extension to October 1971, when he left to re-join the LSO.

In 1971 John Ronayne was once more on the scene, becoming guest leader for eighteen concerts in 1972, the remaining RTÉSO concerts being led by either Arthur Nachstern or James Chapman. This seemed to have suited all concerned (no doubt because it gave Ronayne the position he deserved while

61 Maguire to Victory, enclosed with letter from Kitchen to Victory, 11 May 1968. 62 Victory to Controller of Programmes, 5 June 1968. 63 K. Roche to Controller of Programmes, 23 April 1968.

leaving him free for work elsewhere) so that the arrangement was repeated in 1973, while Victory proceeded to assess another young Irish player, Joseph Maher, who had been a rank-and-file member of the RTÉLO from late 1965, becoming deputy leader from late 1966 while still studying with John MacKenzie (who was now directing the Limerick School of Music). When he resigned in 1968 to join the BBC Academy (the training orchestra maintained in Bristol by the BBC), Kevin Roche (who had become Head of Light Music) pointed out to Ó Faracháin that he had commented several times in the previous two or three years on the deterioration of the string sections of the Light Orchestra, which had begun with the transfer of Audrey Park and Archie Collins to the new String Quartet. He had been grooming Maher as eventual successor to Jack Cheatle.

Maher, who was at this point working with the CBSO, was auditioned in 1971 'for a possible appointment as eventual RTÉLO or RTÉSO leader' and was appointed rank-and-file with a provision that he would lead thirty-five concerts or opera performances in 1972, increasing to forty-five in the next year. Victory justified this on the grounds that a young Irish player with potential must be encouraged and assisted towards full leadership, which he considered was achievable. If some extension and inducement to Maher was not offered, it was likely that he would leave, since, to Victory's knowledge, Maher had been tempted to return to Britain where superior violinists were in demand and pay was better than RTÉ could offer. He acknowledged that there were disadvantages in a triple leadership but felt that it was the only course. The disadvantage, however, was that the RTÉSO now had three 'acting leaders' – Nachstern, Chapman and Maher, with Nachstern leading thirty concerts or opera performances per year. IFMAP wrote to RTÉ that

> The proposal to engage three Leaders [during 1972–3] … is, in our view, not in accordance with accepted professional practice nor do we believe it to be in any way helpful in the sustaining of standards and/or morale. We consider that the proposed situation can lead to internal difficulties or should I say to difficulties within the Orchestra. Indeed the proposal has been the subject of much adverse comment within the members of the Orchestra itself.[64]

Although he was considered less than fully satisfactory, and was unpopular with both his colleagues and the critics, he was appointed co-leader in 1973, but resigned in June 1974 to return to Birmingham. At this stage Fanny Feehan, writing in *Hibernia*, alleged that 'It is no secret that Hugh Maguire would have

64 P.J. Malone (IFMAP) to Dan Lucey, 6 March 1972.

considered leading the orchestra *had he been asked*'.[65] It is, however, extremely unlikely that Maguire would have wanted to give up his work with the Allegri Quartet at that time, and it is also questionable whether RTÉ would have pursued him as a candidate in the light of his previous vacillation on the subject.

Victory had also written 'A really fine full-time leader from abroad (and anything less than excellence is useless) would now cost up to £6,000 per annum. This is the sort of rate which even co-leaders of the British orchestras are getting and this is obviously beyond our scope'.[66] It was also obvious to Victory himself that the 'triple leadership' was insupportable, and it now became possible for him to carry out a recruitment that would solve the problem and pave the way for a succession of leaders who would stabilise the orchestra and see its re-establishment as the National Symphony Orchestra in 1990. 'We must look for a permanent Leader' Victory wrote:

> I would propose to approach Colin Staveley ... who I think might be interested. He is an excellent leader of great experience but his salary ... could now be in the region of £6000. I fear that in present circumstances we cannot obtain a leader of this quality for less ... If these proposals fail, we must look abroad, I am afraid. All our efforts two years ago to interest European players proved entirely unavailing because of the grave shortage now of really fine violinists of experience. The only country which seems to have a surplus of such talent is Japan and Japanese leaders are quite common in Europe. This could involve sending someone to Japan to audition and I would not embark on this course except as a last resort.[67]

Fortunately for Victory and RTÉ, Colin Staveley was now interested: a member of a Dublin musical family (born 1942), and a former leader of the National Youth Orchestra in the UK in 1959, who had moved on from the co-leadership of the RPO in 1971 to lead the BBC Welsh Orchestra – the youngest player ever to hold that position with a British orchestra. At thirty-two, Staveley already possessed wide experience which, combined with a no-nonsense approach to his work and his colleagues, made him extremely effective in his post.

65 *Hibernia*, 13 July 1973. 66 Victory to Personnel, 2 November 1972. 67 Victory to Controller of Programmes, 22 October 1973.

CHAPTER 4

Composers at work

'THE FUTURE OF IRISH MUSIC'

As discussed in chapter 1, two difficulties have beset the majority of Irish composers in Ireland, which have, by extension, affected the nature of Irish music broadcast by RTÉ. This chapter investigates these difficulties, insofar as they have influenced the mutual engagement of RTÉ and Irish composers. After considering Denis Donoghue's essay of 1955, 'The Future of Irish Music', it concentrates on two RTÉ radio series featuring Irish composers spanning a thirty-year period (1958–88), and takes two composers, A.J. Potter and Seán Ó Riada, as examples of their relationships with, and relevance to, RTÉ.

The first difficulty, which is both explicit and subliminal, is that of *anxiety*: the question of whether one acknowledges the pre-emptive burden of tradition, and, if so, how one accommodates that tradition to one's musical horizons (or, more problematically, how one accommodates one's musical horizons to that sense of tradition). This problem has diminished significantly in recent decades: as Kenneth Loveland noted from the 1972 Dublin Festival of Twentieth-Century Music, 'nationalism has few attractions for the young today, and though they may respect their folk heritage, there are not many opportunities to exploit it in their chosen idioms. Bartók, Kodály and Vaughan Williams were just in time, but only just. Much of the music heard from young composers in Dublin this year could have been written by their contemporaries in Warsaw or Hamburg.'[1]

The second difficulty is of a practical nature: how to obtain performances of one's work. In 1970 Brian Boydell said that 'we have the wonderful advantage in this country that anything which is written by anybody reasonably competent is guaranteed immediate first performance. That is something which not many composers in other countries have.'[2] Yet, even if that were entirely accurate of its time, it was by no means certain that a new work would enjoy a *second* performance, which is a general criterion of whether it is capable of tak-

---

1 K. Loveland, 'Composers in search of a national identity' (1972). For several perspectives on the persistence or absence of nationalism as an ideological force in modern composition, see T. Mäkelä (ed.), *Music and nationalism* (1997). 2 C. Acton, 'Interview with Brian Boydell'.

ing its place in the repertoire. The accessibility of the RTÉ airwaves was in any case not as assured as Boydell implied, since it depended on the view taken of any particular composer by the decision-makers – most usually the incumbent Director of Music.

Both types of difficulty contributed to the fact that, as Joseph Ryan pointed out (above, p. 25), most compositions in the period under review have been small in scale and written for forces other than the symphony orchestra – that is, they were written for the Light Orchestra, for a chamber orchestra, or for a smaller chamber ensemble. This inhibition has remained within the consciousness of most Irish composers to this day, for example Jane O'Leary who, with few exceptions,[3] has written mainly for chamber groups such as Concorde. It has also contributed to an eschewing of the symphonic format and the conventional concert platform by composers such as Roger Doyle, who has led the exploration of electro-acoustic composition in Ireland (and was the subject of an RTÉ television documentary by Bob Quinn). Many of these non-symphonic works, especially if commissioned by RTÉ for the RTÉLO, did enter the orchestral repertoire, while others, played by groups such as Herbert Pöche's Dublin Chamber Orchestra, the Prieur Ensemble or Les Amis de la Musique, were recorded in studio for radio transmission – a practice which has been almost completely discontinued in recent years, but to a certain extent replaced by outside broadcasts from Lyric fm, such as concerts by the Limerick-based Irish Chamber Orchestra.

In 1955, Denis Donoghue published his essay 'The Future of Irish Music', the main thesis of which was that a country's musical reputation and international status depend on the number and quality of the composers it produces. Since, in his opinion, Ireland had few composers of any stature (he singled out Boydell as perhaps the only one at that time, with, potentially, Gerard Victory, Potter and Seóirse Bodley in the younger generation), he was able in his opening sentence to state starkly: 'It is quite possible that Irish music may have *no* future existence, and this possibility should be examined ruthlessly and urgently'.[4] Ruthlessly, he proceeded to state that 'internationally, contemporary Irish music does not exist'.

Professionally, Donoghue always works to the highest standards and, as Charles Acton (a successor as music critic of the *Irish Times*) frequently observed, he would review the RÉSO as if it were the Berlin Philharmonic.

3 For example, 'Islands of Discovery' performed by the NSO under Marco Guidarini in 1992, 'Mirror Imaginings', by the RTÉCO and Proinnsías Ó Duinn in 1995, and 'Here, There (and Everywhere)' performed by the RIAM SO under James Cavanagh in 2002 (as part of her work as composer-in-residence at the RIAM). 4 D. Donoghue, 'The future of Irish music'.

Donoghue's eminence as one of the most distinguished literary critics in the world, permits us to place significant emphasis on his musical perceptions; it is quite likely that his judgement in this essay has received attention in proportion to the severity of its strictures, and the intensity of the views expressed therein, rather than its basis in fact. Donoghue dismissed the statement in Aloys Fleischmann's *Music in Ireland* (1952) that Ireland had twenty-nine composers: in his opinion, that just wasn't so. He implicitly contradicted Boydell's statement about access to performance by saying that 'if this statistical fragment means anything, it indicates that ... anybody who had any opus lying around had it performed in public regardless of merit'. The critical distance between Boydell's 'reasonable competence' and Donoghue's 'regardless of merit' may be small, but the standard of work transmitted by RÉ, which concerns us here, was such that most of it continues to be of transmittable standard and has, thus, entered the broadcasting repertoire. Difference of opinion would emerge as to the occasion, or type of concert, to which it might be suitable, but acceptance of 'light' music of an Irish flavour was general.

By a process of elimination, which saw Frederick May dismissed as a working composer (because his 'best work was written fifteen years ago'), not even Boydell merited international attention, because, in Donoghue's view, 'there is in Ireland to-day no composer whose works an intelligent European musician *must* know, in the sense in which that musician must be familiar with the work of Walton, Hindemith, Vaughan Williams, Sibelius'. Donoghue had already given evidence of this prejudice in 1951 when, reviewing a concert conducted by J.M. Doyle, which included two movements from Harty's 'Irish' symphony he had written: 'the difficulty about [the work] is that this sort of thing was done a hundred times more efficiently by Messrs. Delius and Vaughan Williams. Only two movements were done, but I can't honestly say I wanted any more.'[5] If Irish composition was not of the top rank, it was therefore beneath consideration. The same could be said, of course, of countries such as Greece or Sweden, and one is even reminded of the apocryphal story that, when the young Ravel introduced himself to Brahms as 'a French composer' Brahms's retort was: 'There *are* no French composers.' If Donoghue's argument (as opposed to Brahms's) was dispassionate – as many of his subsequent literary judgements have proved to be – then one must seriously follow him in its implications.

Donoghue's reason for reaching this viewpoint was simple, and it goes to the heart of the debate not only about the direction which should, or might, be taken by Irish composers, but also about what attitude RÉ should take to the genres of music that it broadcasts: 'many Irish composers have fallen into

5 *Irish Times*, undated cutting [1951] (Acton Archive).

the trap of folk-music'. This (as Boydell would agree three years later in 'Composers at Work') was perhaps because 'composers have seized on Irish folk-music to conceal the absence of genuine creative gifts', but it also revealed that, whatever the quality of Irish folk-music, Donoghue ruled it out as a source or template: 'as the formal or expressive basis of composition ... folk-music does not answer any of the problems of a composer'. It could enable a composer to produce 'only clever pastiche', whereas top-class music spoke 'an international language ... a creative Esperanto'. Irish composers, with the exception of Boydell and May, on the other hand, could only earn a living 'by arranging Irish folk-songs in versions suitable for small orchestras. Hence the number of available Fantasias, Suites and what-not'. This made such Irish composition 'insular and irrelevant', with 'a low-brow appeal for sentimental reasons as a reminder of our glorious past' which, if it *were* known abroad 'would be regarded as a rather silly joke'. 'I should therefore hope that Radio Éireann would come to see that we now have more Suites of Irish Airs than we can reasonably use, and that the best way to encourage Irish composers is ... to commission them to write quartets, symphonies, songs and operas.' He believed that the presence in Ireland of Vaughan Williams or Hindemith would provide a practical example which Irish composers could emulate, and this was not an unreasonable prospect: 'if two of the finest conductors in contemporary music (Hans Schmidt-Isserstedt and Jean Martinon) could be persuaded to work in this country, I see no reason why a first-rate composer might not similarly be attracted'.

Donoghue's argument can be seen as a living force within Irish composition for the next three decades. As we have seen, Aloys Fleischmann's anxiety expressed itself as a fear of being regarded as 'anti-Irish' if he did not, in Bax's words, 'write Irishly'. Harry White has taken this to mean that the 'recurring problem for Irish composers generally in the new Free State [was] how to circumvent the ethnic repertory, in order to liberate art music in Ireland from the dutiful arrangement of traditional melodies'.[6] Yet the case of A.J. Potter demonstrates not only that it was possible to write modern music that 'arranged', and provided 'variations' on, traditional melodies, but that it was artistically acceptable to those in RÉ responsible for commissioning and broadcasting it, and presumably to the listening public. Potter and, later, Seóirse Bodley were capable of solving that basic problem which had seemed so insoluble to Esposito and which, from quite different perspectives, Éamonn Ó

6 White, 'Nationalism, colonialism ...'. White's other writings on this theme, on which, at the risk of monotony, he has wrought very few variations, include: 'Music and the literary imagination' (1995); 'The conceptual failure of musical education in Ireland' (1997); *The keeper's recital: music and cultural history in Ireland, 1770–1970* (1998) ; 'The divided imagination: music in Ireland after Ó Riada' (2003).

Gallchobhair and Seán Ó Riada on one side, and Denis Donoghue on another, would insist did not require a solution: that of the circularity rather than linearity of Irish melodies, which appeared to deprive them of development, in the sense understood by the mainstream European schools of composition.

White says

> those vital structures of European music, so long neglected in Ireland and so necessary to the reception and development of music ... were all but impossible to attain in a country struggling with economic, cultural and of course political problems which all but occluded the claims of a peripheral art.[7]

While this may have been true of the 1920s and 30s (as Frederick May's comment from 1936 attests), and even possibly the 1940s, it is manifestly invalid as a judgement of modern Irish composition since 1950, and is contradicted by those most ambivalent and controversial figures, Ó Gallchobhair and Ó Riada themselves, both of whom, in their professional embrace of the techniques of harmonic writing which they derived from their 'classical' training, ran parallel to their affirmations of the superiority of Gaelic musical culture. Ó Gallchobhair's reference to *concerted* music encapsulates this ambivalence, which we shall shortly see A.J. Potter embracing as a liberating factor in his work.

Moreover, it is also White's view that the genre of 'variations on an Irish air' is representative of 'the long history of failure which attended its [Irish music's] integration into the orchestral repertory'.[8] At issue here is the question of whether or not Irish music is capable of such integration, if by 'integration' we mean, and expect to have delivered to us, works in the symphonic genre which absorb 'Irish' material into their fabric, rather than exude 'Irishness' implicitly. If, by definition, Irish folk music is incapable of such accommodation, then it is pointless to speak of a 'history of failure'. The genre of 'variations on an Irish air' has produced many fine works, including Harty's and Esposito's 'Irish' symphonies, and, in the period under review in this book, many suites by writers such as John F. Larchet, Arthur Duff, Aloys Fleischmann, Frederick May, Elizabeth Maconchy and Joan Trimble, all of whom, with the exception of Maconchy, were actively encouraged by Radio Éireann. But in addition, and more significantly perhaps, 'Irish' motifs have continued to appear in non-variational works for symphony orchestra and other ensembles. Even more to the point, an increasingly large number of works have emerged from Irish composers in the past three decades which have no discernible 'Irish' con-

7 Ibid. 8 White, 'The divided imagination', p. 18.

tent but which are nevertheless unmistakably 'Irish' in character. As Axel Klein has remarked,

> from Boydell's *Megalithic Ritual Dances* (1956), via Buckley's *Taller than Roman Spears* (1976) to Corcoran's *Mad Sweeney* (1998) and beyond, there is an aesthetically remarkable attempt in Irish music to embrace an indigenous culture long gone, a culture in which Irishness was not defined by its degree of popularity but by mythical art forms which required education and therefore a deeper understanding of music, and so parallels much of today's 'classical' music.[9]

The appeal of and to a *mythos*, which continues to exercise some affect of imaginative memory, is perhaps stronger in Ireland than in most western European countries, not least because that affect was sought by, and fuelled, the imagination of the war of independence. The image of Sweeney 'astray' or 'in frenzy', which in Irish literature has oscillated between the poles of orality and literacy, is an apt icon for the dilemma of many Irish composers caught between the unwritten (because unwritable) and the tabulated (but to them illegible) modes of music.

Issues such as these were seldom explicitly evident in RÉ's music department or its broadcast output, but they certainly featured in speech programmes such as Ó Riada's *Our Musical Heritage*, in 'Éamonn Ó Gallchobhair Remembers', and in the speech segments of the remarkable series 'Composers At Work'.

'COMPOSERS AT WORK' – 1958

In that latter series, in 1958, selected works by seventeen Irish composers were included in a short programme of choral and chamber music, and each composer was invited to contribute a short (2–3 minute) statement, entitled 'Composer's Viewpoint', describing his (all seventeen were men) individual compositional interests and commenting on the problems facing Irish composers at that time. The contributions were remarkably disparate, some of them addressing with considerable seriousness the status of the composer in mid-century Ireland, others concentrating more on the technical challenges to the incorporation of Irish ethnic material into an orchestral infrastructure. Unfortunately, the scope of the series, as far as the works chosen to illustrate each composer were concerned, was limited by its format and its origination

9 A. Klein, 'Roots and directions in twentieth-century Irish art music' (2003), p. 180.

within the choral department: each contribution was commissioned by Hans Waldemar Rosen, who asked for half the items to be sung by the RÉ Singers and half to be suitable for piano or small chamber group.[10]

The most senior composer to contribute was the seventy-four-year-old John F. Larchet, who set the tone for others:

> It is probable that many of you who are listening to me have given thought at some time or another to the possibility of the creation of a National School of Irish composers. It is a curious fact that there has never been a National School of Composition anywhere. The great composers in every period made their own schools. That is why they are called great composers. It is wrong to think of a School of Composition as a group of composers or as a group of buildings called conservatoires. Take for example the great music of Germany. The great German Schools of Composition are found in the scores of the great German composers. There are the Bach, the Beethoven and the Wagnerian schools, but the word 'school' really stands for the word 'style'. When you attempt to write in the manner of Beethoven you are a student of the Beethoven School. And so it will be with the great Irish composer for whom we are all[11] waiting, who will create his own school or style which will influence his contemporaries and the composers who will follow him.
>
> Let us endeavour to visualise our great Composer in such a way that he will agree with our national ideas and ideals. It may be supposed at the outset that it will be accepted as a 'sine qua non' that he is born in Ireland. (In fact this question of birth-place does not always follow for though the great Handel was born in Germany, his music was pure Italian in style and feeling.) It is more important that he should have a thorough knowledge and a keen appreciation of the folk-music and the literature of Ireland, Gaelic and English, and a deep love of his native land. To quote the late Dr Norman Hay, 'it is from the spirit, and not the letter, of our national songs, that a School of Irish composers shall come into being'.[12] All this will be essential to form our great Irish composer's background. His knowledge of great music should be wide and profound. He should possess unusual technical skill in Harmony,

10 H.W. Rosen to A.J. Potter, 10 January 1957 [*recte* 1958] (Potter Archive). 11 In the typescript, the word 'all' has been substituted for the word 'still': script enclosed with RTÉ Sound Archive tape 105MD. 12 Norman Hay (1889–1943) was a northern Irish composer and critic, of whom it has been said 'his critical writings were too honest for a public which does not like its idols revealed with feet of clay; his music spoke with a contemporary voice, unusual enough in Ireland, and in most cases too modern for those who had to play it, let alone those who had to listen to it; his personality was all that being an Ulsterman might imply': David Byers, 'Norman Hay', 1982.

Counterpoint, and Orchestration, and a natural sense of formal structure. To obtain this knowledge he must begin his studies of composition as every other great composer without exception began, by being
a conscious plagiarist. He must plagiarise in particular the works of one
or two great Masters which appeal to him. (Every great Master had one
or more composers upon whom his early tastes were fed.) After years
of incessant and conscientious study, and experience of original composition, he will speak with his own voice, if he is endowed with a God-
given talent, and from the depths of his Irish soul will be born the music
that to us, Irish people, will seem evocative of the spirit of our country.
To other countries this music will sound different from their music.

Probably when this great composer arrives the majority will not
recognise him as such but if he lives long enough he may achieve some
recognition. If a high value is set on his work by musical people outside
this country the enjoyment of fame and the appreciation of his own people will come earlier. The life-story of many great original musical composers tells how often they failed to achieve recognition in their lifetime. It behoves us to be on the look-out for such a one, meanwhile let
us give all the encouragement we can to any worthy young composer.[13]

This messianic and prescriptive declaration is noteworthy for several reasons, not least the tone of address of an elder statesman who nevertheless
embodies a sense of doubt as to his own capacity which borders on cynicism:
as the teacher of most of the practising composers in Ireland at the time,
Larchet was in a position to know – or at least surmise – whether or not the
'great' composer was among them. He certainly seems to have judged that that
time was yet to come. In 1958, on the threshold of a new social and economic
scenario,[14] he carried forward the presumption that there endured a cadre of
people involved in the arts who subscribed to 'our national ideas and ideals'
and that a 'great' composer could write music 'evocative of the spirit of our
country'. While the latter would remain a feature of the writing of many Irish
composers up to the present day, the adoption of an artistic credo consonant
with 'national ideas and ideals' would become increasingly arguable and prob-

---

13 RTÉ Sound Archive tape 105MD; Larchet's works in this programme consisted of: songs for
chamber choir (the Radio Éireann Singers, conducted by Hans Waldemar Rosen, accompanist
Rhoda Coghill) and for baritone solo (Austin Gaffney) and Irish airs arranged for string quartet
– Margaret Hayes and William Shanahan (violins), Máire Larchet (viola) and Maurice Meulien
(cello). All choral or vocal works listed subsequently as part of the 'Composers at Work' series
were performed by members of the RÉ Singers with Hans Waldemar Rosen. 14 The 'First
Programme for Economic Expansion' of 1958 heralded the economic transformation of Ireland
from a predominantly rural, agrarian economy into an urban, industrial and entrepreneurial society during the 1960s and 1970s.

lematic, as social and cultural change, and changes in social and cultural awareness, brought revisionism in their wake, questioning the myths and legends of
Irish identity and the sources and bases of musical inspiration for composers
in the second part of the twentieth century. These changes would inevitably
affect the style and content of music presented to RTÉ by Irish composers.

In the final programme of the series, Aloys Fleischmann (then forty-eight)
took the opportunity to return to arguments that he had first rehearsed as early
as 1936, in particular the choice – or lack of it – open to an Irish composer,
between traditionalism and cosmopolitanism:

> When I started writing music thirty years ago the folk song revival was
> in full swing. Some of the most active composers could indeed do little
> more than add three fraternal parts beneath a tune, and even this harm-
> less activity led to much controversy and mutual slating. But new ideas
> were in the air and it seemed vital at that time to delve into the Hidden
> Ireland, and out of the folk song, out of the heroic tales and romances,
> of Diarmuid and Grainne and of Suibhne Geilt [Sweeney Astray or Mad
> Sweeney], out of the panegyrics and caoine [laments] of Aodhogan Ó
> Raithille, to create an idiom which would express in music some of the
> essence of this rich, untapped literary tradition.
>
> It must be confessed that the public did not take very kindly to the
> results. Even if the performances at that time were often a travesty, this
> was hardly a decisive factor, for only a small minority is at any time inter-
> ested in new music. And the problems which beset the Irish composer
> then beset him still. If he is a traditionalist and deals extensively in folk
> song, he knows that he is working against the stream of European music,
> which is these days largely international and cosmopolitan. I don't wish
> to suggest for a minute that folk song's day is done – it will come again
> as it has done all through history, and we here are still a generation behind
> and for our local purposes need a far fuller and finer supply of folk song
> arrangements. But it is on the whole unwise to work against the general
> pattern of the times. If, on the other hand, the Irish composer flings tra-
> dition aside and rides in the whirlwind of contemporary techniques, he
> must realise that he will have practically no listening audience in this
> country, and like many of our best writers he will have to make his name,
> if he is to count at all, in open competition on the international market.[15]

15 RTÉ Sound Archive tape 121MD; Fleischmann's programme included his 'Three Songs for
Tenor' (Dermot Troy), the finale from his piano quintet, and works for chamber choir, with instru-
mental accompaniment; the instrumentalists were Audrey Park and Elias Maguire (violins), William
Hallett (viola), Maurice Meulien (cello), André Prieur (flute), Sheila Larchet-Cuthbert (harp),
Valentine Keogh (percussion) and Rhoda Coghill (piano).

Fleischmann repeated Larchet's opinion that such a composer would most likely not be recognised in his native land, and added, wistfully, that 'It is indeed a matter of statistics, as Hindemith has pointed out, that about fifty million inhabitants are needed to produce a composer of major rank; but there is always the freak chance of one being produced by a community of any size' – he might have pointed to Sibelius and Finland, a country with a population similar to that of Ireland.

A different note was introduced by Brian Boydell, whose contribution was dismissive of any form of Irishness for the sake of Irishness.

> There has been a great deal of talk about what attitude a composer should take to his work – he should write for the masses – he should seek inspiration in his country's folk-song – he should write in the twelve-tone system ... and so on. I think a great deal of the bad music being written today is a direct result of composers self-consciously adopting some such philosophical ideal which is contrary to their own true nature – even though they may logically have come to the conclusion that it is a good means of expression. I am thinking particularly of the hordes of note-spinners, without an idea in their heads, who have scampered to the bosom of Papa Schoenberg and sought refuge in a 'system' to disguise their lack of anything individual to say. Another haven for characterless technicians is Nationalism – for as long as the fiddling with folksongs is done with reasonable technical assurance, the result is assured of acclaim on a basis of obvious and superficial local flavour.
>
> Now please don't misunderstand me – there is nothing intrinsically wrong with nationalism, or most of the other 'isms' and systems; they are merely means of expression. The important thing is that whoever makes use of them, must have something to say, and moreover, must have a genuine natural inclination towards the particular means of expression which he chooses to convey what he has to say. I could summarise all this with the rather banal statement, which is nevertheless often forgotten, that the artist must be true to himself.
>
> The character of an artist is built up through the influence of his surroundings and the knowledge which his own enthusiasm has led him to seek out for himself. This is the individual, and the interpretation of his rich experience – his enthusiasms and dislikes – and the changing colour of his emotions are what interest me. The fact that he may be French, a Communist, a Mormon or a twelve-tone-ite is of quite secondary importance: nationality, political beliefs, and religion are among the influences which form the character, and the style of music he favours should be an indication of his natural inclination.

For myself, my enthusiasm for music has always tended towards the sophisticated and intellectual, and the expression of the more profound emotions. Music which demands no effort to seek its message, music which lacks subtlety, or which is concerned with regurgitating popular sentimentality holds little interest for me. Thus, among the giants of the past, Bach is my king; and amongst the moderns I have worshipped at the thrones of Sibelius, and Bartók, and owe a great deal to many smaller figures such as Bloch, Prokofiev, Hindemith and Alban Berg.

Perhaps it is my misfortune – but I must accept with honesty the fact that I have never managed to work up any real enthusiasm about folksong – though I am aware that many 'turns of phrase' in Irish folksong have captivated me, and come from time to time from my musical pores. I'm afraid I positively dislike jigs and reels. Now, that is a finger-nail sketch of my musical inclinations; and it will indicate that it would be highly dishonest of me to sit down and emulate Stanford with an 'Irish' Symphony. Nevertheless, my music does, I hope, reflect in a less obvious way the profound effect which a country is bound to have on the character of an individual who is aware of his surroundings.[16]

As an uncompromising personality throughout his career, Boydell represented the antithesis to the thesis that a composer owed some form of allegiance to any particular mode of expression or artistic goal; in this 'Viewpoint' he made it clear that, as an Irishman, he would not bow before any sacred cow, even disavowing Stanford's status as the author of the 'Irish' Symphony to the extent that he himself could not have acknowledged his 'Irishness' in such a way, even though Irish 'turns of phrase' might enter his music subliminally.

Boydell's views are cognate with those of Frederick May, whose strength as a composer was belied by the paucity of his output due to severe and persistent illness.

Composers are sometimes asked by those who like their music how they come by their ideas, but this is a question that cannot be answered because the composer himself is just as much in the dark as his questioner. The source of his inspiration is a mystery, just as life itself is a mystery, and I suppose there are almost as many different ways of going about the actual business of composition as there are composers. It must be wonderful to be able to write music as naturally as one breathes, like the divine Schubert, for example, or Mozart, two composers who were able to gen-

---

16 RTÉ Sound Archive tape 110MD; Boydell's choice of works consisted of the Easter Carol 'Mary Moder' and two part-songs for choir, accompanist Rhoda Coghill, and 'Divertimento' for violin (Jaroslav Vaneček), viola (Máire Larchet) and cello (Maurice Meulien).

erate masterpieces by a process of spontaneous combustion and who could and did write work after work as flawless in construction as they are beautiful in content, with apparently no effort. But unluckily the great majority of us are by no means so fortunate, and I have often felt myself to be like a rock on the sea shore that is covered over by the incoming tide every so often, but when the tide withdraws again it is left once more desolate and forsaken. Sometimes one may ask oneself, in moments of depression, whether it would not be better never to have been given any creative gift at all than only to have been granted an unserviceable kind of half-gift, so variable, so uncertain and so capricious. But to think like that, even if understandable, is also silly; after all, a bridge has its uses even if it is not an end in itself, and John the Baptist is not without honour, for to him it was given to prepare the way for a greater and more resplendent Personality. For a composer of this day and age to be born in Vienna, and to walk the streets once trodden by Beethoven, Schubert, Brahms and the rest of the giants, with monuments in marble and stone to the memory of the immortals all around him, might well breed despair, but here in Ireland the soil is still virgin, and we have it in our power to make the future an exciting adventure. We have a great tradition of folk-song, but no tradition at all of composition, although there are several very interesting composers living and working at the present time, in spite of what is sometimes written against us as a body by certain critics.[17]

How to retain and expand one's creative gifts into old age, supposing one lives that long, ensuring the triumph of mind and spirit over a slowly decaying body, is a problem that was not solved by Wordsworth, or by Ravel, although Yeats, Verdi and to some extent Vaughan Williams held the magic secret. Maybe the best thing is to try to be brave, adventurous and never to refuse new experiences. Maybe you think this is a rather vague and unsatisfactory kind of Credo, but Walt Whitman has summed it all up for me far better than I myself could ever hope to do in the following lines:

'Sail forth, steer for the deep waters only,
Reckless, o soul, exploring, I with thee and thou with me,
For we are bound where mariner has not yet dared to go,
And we will risk the ship ourselves and all,
O my brave soul!
O farther, farther sail
O daring joy, but safe! are they not all the seas of God?
O farther, farther, farther sail!'[18]

17 May had originally written 'by disgruntled correspondents of the *Evening Mail*' – RTÉ Sound Archive tape 118MD. 18 Ibid.; May's programme included three Irish folksongs and two settings

Although by 1958 serious illness had rendered May almost completely defunct as a composer, it was not only this impediment that made him speak of 'depression' and 'despair' – his own pre-war experiences, including his disappointment at the death of Berg, with whom he had intended to study, had produced his string quartet and the 'Songs from Prison', setting words by Ernst Toller. The 'Songs', in addition to embodying a cry for human dignity in general, may well have had the additional, more specific, focus of May's own homosexuality in the homophobic society of Ireland in the 1940s and after. Certainly, as a musicologist, May in this statement took the brave course of stating openly that 'we have ... no tradition at all of composition', thus making it clear that 'an exciting future', even if it came from within the race-consciousness of an Irish composer, would depend on external sources of technical and musical expertise. However much Larchet represented an iconic figure as an instructor and as a link with the Ireland of the late nineteenth century, May's own studies with Gordon Jacob and Vaughan Williams in London and with Egon Wellesz in Vienna were indicative of a general trend among young Irish composers towards study abroad, which included Fleischmann, Boydell, Bodley, Corcoran, Barry and Deane.[19] But above all, listeners in Ireland and elsewhere in 1958 may have experienced a profound *frisson* of intellectual and cultural excitement in witnessing May reciting the challenging words of Whitman, a poet also espoused in the compositions of Rhoda Coghill[20] and Victory.

Daniel McNulty (1920–96), a composer of sacred choral works and of instrumental works (including two concertinos for piano and orchestra which were recorded by Charles Lynch for RTÉ) also bore an affliction with fortitude:

> I suppose I get inspiration much in the same way as other composers. I like reading poetry, and when a poem particularly appeals to me I get the urge to express it in music, and the nucleus of a new song is born.
>
> I enjoy walking in the countryside, listening to the sounds of nature – singing birds, running streams, whispering trees or the peaceful lapping of wavelets by the lakeside. Such pastoral delights create in me moods conducive to musical composition.
>
> Even though I am blind, and cannot see the grandeur of scenic beauty, or visually appreciate ancient ruins, I can always sense a wonderful intangible atmosphere about such places which I feel I must translate into music.[21]

of Thomas Moore, two songs and 'Dialogue' for baritone (Tomás Ó Suilleabháin) and 'Idylle' for violin (William Shanahan) with the composer as the piano accompanist. **19** Cf. A. Klein, 'Irish composers and foreign education: a study of influences' (1996), pp. 271–84. **20** Coghill's cantata 'Out of the Cradle Endlessly Rocking' is a setting of words by Whitman. **21** RTÉ Sound Archive tape 111MD; McNulty presented his 'Lucht Deirce' and two Irish marching songs for unaccom-

Whether or not it was attributable to his blindness, McNulty's source of inspiration – nature – seems to have brought him more closely into the company of composers such as Bax and Moeran than that of those engaged with the major debate over what a composer should 'be'.

For Éamonn Ó Gallchobhair, 'tradition' was never a problem until it came into contact, and conflict, with the type of music education that had the mainstream European aesthetic as its mindset.

> To make clear my own viewpoint in artistic matters, maybe the best approach would lie in the consideration of certain psychological and technical problems that beset a composer who could be called a 'traditionalist'. Many of these problems are peculiar to Ireland, where musical education has not a vestige of connection with the nationalist tradition.
>
> The only academic music education here belongs to this kind and so even the 'traditionalist' composer by education and early practice belongs to the academies: indeed the whole formidable apparatus of modern music-pedagogy must needs have his youthful respect. But any intimate contact with Irish music and its aesthetic principles must force the student to question and examine the very basis of his acquired academic knowledge. He finds that Irish music contradicts quite flatly much of the fundamental dicta of the textbooks – from this it is but a short step to the questioning of the aesthetic validity of academic judgements. These various aesthetic and psychological problems ultimately lead him to see with startling clarity that the Gael belongs to the Mediterranean and not to the north German civilisation. At the same time he will see how little this fact and its implications are understood in the general professional and academic music world in Ireland.
>
> All of which is to say that Irish traditional music is a formidable instrument for conditioning aesthetic judgements. It conditions taste: leaves the composer unwilling to accept the 'bash and bang' methods of many modern European composers. Its lyrical intensity leaves much 19th century music, by comparison, unbearably long-winded and boring: even modern geometries will be preferable to this dreadful tautology.
>
> The traditionalist therefore, leaving his student days behind, finds himself equipped with an excellent academic technique that is of no help to solve the problems of his musical utterance. He is alone: there are no text books for him. He must slowly and painfully build his own technique, in trial and error testing each foot of the way. Could the acade-

panied choir, and three poems by Séamus Ó hAodha for ladies' choir; 'Four Kerry Miniatures' – suite for piano (Julian Dawson) and two songs by Liam Brophy for soprano solo (Minnie Clancy).

mies help him, if they tried? It is doubtful. Maybe like Eugene O'Neill's 'Hairy Ape', 'he doesn't belong'.[22]

This contribution to 'Composers at Work' was, like Fleischmann's, a reprise of propaganda which Ó Gallchobhair had published in the 1930s: in 1937 he wrote 'Academies and Professors' which advocated bringing traditional music into academe, not as an adjunct but so that it would redirect music education, and the approach to 'the great European tradition ... would be governed by a set of values specifically Irish'.[23] Clearly by 1958 Ó Gallchobhair had abandoned that proposal.

Instead, he made the question of musical choice a political question, since the matter of 'conditioning aesthetic judgements' is not merely one of perceiving a work of art but also of perceiving, and organising, one's world. In suggesting that 'the traditionalist ... doesn't belong', Ó Gallchobhair was predicting Raymond Deane's painful point, that there is little if any place for any composer in contemporary Ireland.[24] This rejection of academe was more than a turning of one's back on classical music: it was a painful rehearsal of the fact that the composer in this case was uttering a *cri de coeur* – academe had equipped him for a career that he did not wish to follow, and had *not* equipped him for the career that summoned him.

Havelock Nelson (1917–96), a native of Cork, educated in Dublin and, in 1958, already eleven years into a long and distinguished career with BBCNI, referred to this issue of whether or not to introduce one genre to another, in terms that would be echoed by other contributors to the series:

> A deep affection for our folk music and an association with it both inside and outside the concert hall have naturally imbued my personal idiom with an Irish flavour. I like to incorporate our national melodies and dances in my work – you will find some in the Violin Suite you are to hear. The purist may complain that melodies so created lose their essential simplicity – granted that may be so but I can't help feeling they gain a larger audience in their new setting and are sometimes preserved for posterity when they might otherwise have been lost.

---

22 RTÉ Sound Archive tape 109MD; Ó Gallchobhair's programme consisted of arrangements of Irish folksongs, two songs for tenor solo and piano (Richard Cooper) and two works for flute and piano, played by the composer's wife, Mollie Flynn; the piano accompaniment was by the composer. 23 *Ireland To-day* 2 (March 1937). Despite his antagonism towards academe, Ó Gallchobhair was proposed as a Vice-President of the RIAM in 1951, one of the other candidates being Sir Arnold Bax: neither was elected; cf. Pine and Acton, op. cit., pp. 343–4. A similar distinction is evident in Ó Gallchobhair's contribution to Fleischmann's symposium *Music in Ireland*, 'The cultural value of festival and feis', pp. 210–13. 24 Cf. Deane, 'The honour of non-existence'.

Though to my mind one can overstress Nationalism in music I do feel that one's own country should have some influence on a composer's music. Think of such great names as Haydn, Schubert and Dvořák – surely they are none the less great for their use of their native melodies. So too, I hope we Irish composers may build on our musical inheritance which can scarcely be surpassed anywhere in the world.[25]

Joseph Groocock (1913–97), who had lived in Ireland since 1937, as a teacher at the RIAM and as conductor of the TCD Choral Society, and was a minor composer and arranger, concurred:

I have been asked to say what I think about some of the problems of music in Ireland today. I start with the vexed question of the arrangement of Irish traditional tunes. Now it seems to me that there is a world of difference between the tasteful arrangements made by a small handful of skilled workers in this field, and the ugly monstrosities that so often parade themselves as arrangements of Irish tunes. Certainly in the field of song, I can't help thinking that the unaccompanied melody is generally far more beautiful than any so-called arrangements that can be made of it. As for instrumental music, I am quite certain that for any large-scale composition the direct use of traditional material in any quantity can prove more of a hindrance than a help. I believe that Béla Bartók so steeped himself in Hungarian traditional music, that almost all his compositions have an unmistakeable Hungarian flavour. And yet I am assured that only in a very small proportion of his instrumental music did Bartók make direct use of a traditional tune. Probably we have still to wait for an Irish Béla Bartók.

There are other problems confronting a composer: whether to be in the van of progress and use twelve-note row technique, applauded by a few and misunderstood by the majority of listeners: or to keep to older paths of tonality, more easily understood by the many, and of course labelled old-fashioned by the progressive party. I am willing to own that in style I am several generations behind the times, and I doubt if I shall ever catch up: perhaps my example can be an encouragement to other part-time composers.[26]

---

25 RTÉ Sound Archive tape 115MD; Nelson's programme was: 'The Course of the Year' – a cycle of part-songs for chamber choir, two settings of Irish airs for soprano (Minnie Clancy), and two movements from the Suite for violin and piano (Jaroslav Vaneček), with the composer as piano accompanist. 26 RTÉ Sound Archive tape 119MD; Groocock's programme consisted of two of his six nursery rhymes for unaccompanied choir and six poems by R.L. Stevenson ('A Child's Garden') for ladies' choir and two songs for baritone (Martin Dempsey) with David Lee (organ).

Edgar Deale took up this argument:[27]

> Quite a controversy exists among musical folk in this country, and a great deal of twaddle is talked about the setting and arranging of Irish folk song. Some, if they had their way, would have these traditional tunes performed only as a single thread of melody without any supporting accompaniment or harmonies, and probably indeed without any words, and others on the other hand regard them as good tunes which should be capable of being bawled out in taverns and which the world would be the better for hearing ...
>
> I think we should avoid allowing our thoughts to become too complicated on this subject of folk-song. Let us be thankful for all that Bunting, Petrie and Company have done, and let us give their tunes, which they have collected with such love and labour, to the world, keeping before us of course such matters as style, but bearing in mind the fact that with modern resources musical style must undergo some changes and modifications. I am all for a liberal outlook in this matter as the purists, if they had their way, would never allow these folk tunes of ours to leave the petrified pages of Petrie.[28]

Proinsías Ó Ceallaigh (1908–76), a former member of the RÉLO (which he also conducted) and whose chief occupation was as an Inspector of Music with the Department of Education, presented quite the opposite view:

> In my student days at the Royal Irish Academy of Music in Dublin I knew next to nothing about genuine Irish music. Occasionally I selected tunes from the well-known collections and in my efforts to set them I had the expert guidance of Dr J.F. Larchet who was my professor of harmony.
>
> It was when I was invited by Diarmuid Ó hAlmhain to form an orchestra and later to take over the choir in the Keating Branch of the Gaelic League that I first heard living Irish music. This was real and vital music – completely different from the dead bare bones of the music found in the collections of Bunting, Petrie and others.
>
> To understand Irish music thoroughly I realised I would have to learn the language and as much as possible of its poetry. Also I endeavoured to hear as much as possible of this living Irish music in the Gaeltacht – its natural environment.

27 For a biographical note on Deale, see above, p. 179. 28 RTÉ Sound Archive tape 108MD; Deale's programme consisted entirely of songs: three by Walter de la Mare and three Irish folk-songs for *a cappella* choir; Yeats's 'The Cloths of Heaven' for men's choir; and four songs for baritone (Tomás Ó Suilleabháin with Rhoda Coghill, piano).

In arranging Irish music I think every tune poses its own problem. Traditional Irish music is melismatic and linear, like plainsong, and my view is that the harmonic scheme is implicit in each melody – whether modal or not. And here it is necessary to experiment and to break away from academic text-book training. The rhythmic scheme depends largely on an understanding of Gaelic prosody. Most Irish melodies have been shaped by generations of singers and players and are complete in themselves. Our modern ears, however, require vertical (or harmonic) embellishment but this should be done with taste and discretion – allowing the tune to speak for itself as much as possible …

I think it is vitally necessary for young Irish musicians to absorb as much as possible of our living music, dances and customs – in their own environment. It follows then that the essence of our cultural heritage would appear in whatever they wrote, whether labelled 'Irish' or not. In that event their music would be truly 'national' and, being unconsciously so, all the more convincing.[29]

T.C. Kelly (1917–85), a teacher at Clongowes Wood College and a composer of a large body of orchestral music, was somewhat ambivalent:

There is an aspect of the life and work of Irish composers which is often overlooked.

At the present time we have a number of composers who actually live in Ireland. Before we had a radio station, Irish composers usually lived abroad in the bigger musical centres, as we have such a small musical public. Even though it is growing, it still isn't enough to support a national opera or ballet; apart from Dublin and Belfast, we haven't professional symphony orchestras in our cities and towns.

We have no large scale choral festivals commissioning new oratorios,[30] no film studios demanding scores for films. Apart from Radio Éireann, government publications[31] and the Oireachtas come to the rescue but apart from these the life and living of a serious Irish composer is rather grim. With many of them it is a matter of composing in the leisure hours which are few and far between.

---

29 RTÉ Sound Archive tape 107MD; Ó Ceallaigh's programme was: three part-songs for ladies' choir, two songs for soli and choir and the narrative song 'An Trucaillin Donn' for soli and choir, the scherzo 'Cor Castaidh' for two violins (Audrey Park and Elias Maguire), cello (Erich Eisenbrand) and piano (Rhoda Coghill), and a movement from his string quartet (Park, Maguire, William Hallett and Eisenbrand). 30 The Cork International Choral and Folk Dance Festival had been established in 1954, but its commissioning policy was restricted to small-scale works. 31 Kelly was referring to An Gúm, the official Government publications agency, which published several scores during this period.

We have a very rich heritage of folk music which is very popular, but due to our historical background the more highly organised forms of music have not had much chance to develop. Whether national music[32] should or should not influence a modern Irish composer, and to what extent, are matters which are frequently discussed. There are many theories about it, but in the final analysis it is a matter for the composer to decide. If folk music is in his blood, he will find it impossible to get away from it, and the problem of uniting national characteristics with up-to-date technique will be solved by the genius of the composer. Berg managed to introduce an ordinary chorale into a twelve-tone work. Bartók collected and arranged Hungarian folk music and its influence is felt in most of his major works.

This question is not so very acute in my own case as I am purely a lyric composer. My music seems to be rather bilingual (if I may use such a term in connection with music). If I am setting words of an Irish or Anglo-Irish poet I seem to fall naturally into an Irish idiom, but I have experimented occasionally in different styles.[33]

Kelly's 'bilingualism' is probably the most useful expression to describe the ambivalent approach to composition of all those who attempted to address their work through the medium of both musical languages, whether or not they also tried to invent a third.

Redmond Friel [Réamon Ó Frighil] (1907–79), who was principally an arranger and music teacher, but who also had a 'Symphonic Movement' and a concert suite (based on the Children of Lir) to his credit, admitted this ambivalence since, as a professional arranger of Irish material for Radio Éireann, he depended on such work for his livelihood:

First of all few of us – composers and arrangers [Friel was the only contributor to employ the term 'arranger' as a self-description] – can afford to give 100% of our working day to composition. Time has to be taken off for the earning of one's living usually by teaching, performing, by church choir work and so on. One result of this is that the expenditure of time and of energy on these activities leaves so much less time for composing – and a scarcity of those necessary periods for recollecting in tranquillity.

32 Kelly had originally written 'this folk music' and replaced it with 'national music'. 33 RTÉ Sound Archive tape 113MD; Kelly's works were: Yeats's 'The everlasting voices' and two Irish folksongs; two songs for mezzo soprano (Mary Sheridan) and three interludes for piano and the *lento patetico* from piano sonata in D, played by Julian Dawson.

... About Irish music: my own interest in folk song was stimulated by its modal background, and its obvious affinities with plainchant and sixteenth- century choral music. It has been a never ending pleasure to listen to these airs of ours, played or sung by the traditional performer, and at a later stage perhaps, to make transcriptions of them for concert use. One must face the fact, of course, that in making these transcriptions and arrangements and so on, something of the original is lost. Once a folk song has been dressed up with pianoforte or orchestral accompaniment it ceases to be a folk song, it becomes a concert piece, an art song. Something of the folk quality, as I say, has been lost, the note of freshness, freedom, simplicity, or whatever it is; on the credit side, there is a gain in musical interest, an intensifying of emotion, a better balanced outline. The most successful settings are those which combine the qualities of heightened musical interest with something of the out-of-doors freshness of the original.

The musician will please himself of course in the methods he employs in making arrangements of folk tunes. The problem here is to preserve the modal background of the melody in a 20th century setting. There are fascinating possibilities in the use of what I may call the tonal ambiguities which occur when modern scales and medieval modes confront each other in a folk melody. I am pleased to find so many settings by contemporary Irish composers which exploit this feature in a delightful way. It is gratifying also to find a larger and more appreciative public; and especially among younger listeners – schools and radio, as well as Feiseanna and amateur concert groups have helped enormously. There is also a noticeable broadening of the individual taste – the céilí band addict will appreciate other forms of dance music, and may even take time off to listen to a Mozart quartet or a Stravinsky ballet suite. This is a healthy outlook and to be encouraged.34

Dr J.J. O'Reilly (1905–83), a piano teacher and future Principal of the Municipal College of Music, two of whose orchestral works had recently been played by the RÉSO, captured the irony of whether or not, by 'arranging' or orchestrating a tune, one diminished or eradicated its 'simplicity' or authenticity:

---

34 RTÉ Sound archive tape 112MD; Friel's programme consisted of the Sanctus and Benedictus from his Mass of St Anne, two Donegal songs, two songs by Moore, and 'Lilliburlero' with William Watson, organ; the lullaby from 'The Children of Lir' and the finale from 'Sreath d'Fhonnaibh Gaelacha', both for string quartet and piano (Audrey Park and Elias Maguire [violins], Willam Hallett [viola] and Erich Eisenbrand [cello]), and two songs for tenor solo (Richard Cooper) with Rhoda Coghill, piano.

Preservation of simplicity is probably the composer's greatest difficulty in making choral arrangements of our lovely Irish folk tunes.

To give the tune and words a chance of coming through [is] the major problem ... To capture that quasi-modal flavour, so characteristic of Irish music is, perhaps, the composer's main task in writing original music if it is to sound national in character ...

From time to time the question is often asked: Why do so few Irish musicians devote so little of their time to composition[?]

The answer is that they are so busy earning a living that there is little or no time for this important aspect of our country's work.

Composing and arranging takes a great deal of time. The cost of printing is very high and the opportunities of having one's works performed are so few that there is a lack of incentive for the Irish composer.

Were it not for the great work done by Radio Éireann, the Oireachtas, Feis Ceoil and a few other organisations there would be no incentive at all.[35]

Seóirse Bodley, one of the younger participants in the series (he was twenty-five at the time), set out an artistic credo that would colour all of his later career:

One of the main problems facing the contemporary Irish composer is that of musical nationalism, in particular the relation between traditional Irish music and contemporary European art-music. Since I feel a great deal of sympathy with both types of music, I have attempted to come to grips with the problem of combining them.

As I see it, the type of melodic curve which forms the basis of our best folk-songs is the essence of our traditional music, and is, perhaps, the one element of our folk-music which could be successfully grafted onto the European tradition. I believe that this type of basic curve can form the basis of new, modern, melodic lines, which retain a certain typically Irish quality but are, none the less, original and within the contemporary idiom. These lines form the basis of a fundamentally contrapuntal type of material which is finally moulded into a formal structure.

This is the manner in which I have approached the problem. Sometimes my approach has been conscious, sometimes not. Naturally the manner of composition which I have described could only be used

---

35 RTÉ Sound Archive tape 116MD; O'Reilly's choice of works was: three Irish folksongs for unaccompanied choir, two for ladies' choir and one for two baritone soli, accompanist Rhoda Coghill; Ceól do Bheidlín agus Pianó [two pieces for violin (Sheila O'Grady) and piano (Veronica McSwiney)]; and two numbers from his first Suite of Irish Airs for violin (O'Grady), cello (Brighid Mooney) and piano (McSwiney).

where the composer feels a sufficient degree of sympathy with our folk-music to enable him to absorb the folk-song element completely. It would also be legitimate to ignore our folk-song altogether, or to find other methods of combining the Irish folk-tradition and contemporary art-music. I would be most interested, for instance, to hear an Irish folk-song combined with electronic sounds in the manner employed by Stockhausen in his 'Gesang der Jünglinge'.[36]

The greatest danger which faces the Irish composer is that of false nationalism. In other words, he must not write music in an Irish style out of a sense of duty. On the other hand, the composer living in contemporary Germany, as I am at the moment,[37] has a rather similar problem to face. Serial and pointillistic music are now the fashion in Central Europe, and many composers have fallen into the error of using these two techniques in a purely mechanical manner, and not as an expression of their personality and experience. I do not wish to suggest that a composer should use music to express his feelings about any particular emotional experiences after the fashion of 19th century Romanticism. A piece of music must, however, reflect the composer's personality and life-experience in a general way if it is to have any value at all. Purely mathematical manipulation of tones has never been the object of any musical composition which could be called a work of art. Unfortunately a considerable amount of worthless music receives approval in Central Europe at the moment, purely because it is written in the style of Anton Webern. The Irish composer who wishes to avoid false nationalism must be careful that he does not substitute another false ideal for it.

Since I have discussed the musical pitfalls that I have had to face both at home and abroad, perhaps I should also describe the sort of music that I would like to write. I should like to compose music that would be well constructed, reflect my own experience and background, and be written in the contemporary idiom without regard for passing fashions. This is the ideal against which I would wish the value of my music to be estimated.[38]

Gerard Victory, although an employee of Radio Éireann since 1948, had not yet assumed the senior role that he was to occupy as assistant director and later Director of Music, yet he was alive to Radio Éireann's policy of commis-

36 Stockhausen's work, no. 8 in his catalogue, was composed in 1955–6 and has been described as 'the first work to establish fully the aesthetic viability of the electro-acoustic medium' – Richard Toop, *NG2*, 24/401. 37 Bodley was studying in Stuttgart with Johann Nepomuk David and Hans Müller-Kray 1957–59. 38 RTÉ Sound Archive tape A530; Bodley's programme consisted of Capriccio no. 1 for violin and piano (Margaret Hayes and Rhoda Coghill), two settings of songs for baritone (Tomás Ó Suilleabháin) and one for solo tenor with choir with soloist Richard Cooper and four pieces for piano (Rhoda Coghill).

sioning and accepting music – so much so that, almost alone among the contributors to this series, he omitted any reference to the debate on the status and treatment of Irish music.

> Serious music requires large resources very often for its performance and in the case of orchestral music it is indeed remarkable that so many works by native composers do find a hearing at all.
>
> We are, it must be remembered, a small community and the resources which could be mustered to support the composer – even were our prosperity much greater than it is – would always have to be relatively small. It is perhaps, then, rather remarkable that well over a dozen Irish musicians are consistently engaged in writing serious music and that over the past twenty years or so quite a few works of significance have been written.
>
> The sad thing, I think, is that these achievements are so little known by the outside world. This is an especially great pity at a time when international communication is becoming more and more progressive with scientific advancement. The fault for this must lie, I fear, with the lack of publication. It is, perhaps, strange that while the opportunities for performance have been gradually improving, publication of music has lagged far behind. Now, of course, music publication is a costly business, but the returns in prestige alone in making Irish-composed music better known abroad would be considerable.
>
> There is no doubt that the very large amount of orchestral music written during recent years must be attributed to the foundation of the permanent Symphony Orchestra in Radio Éireann and the helpful policy pursued in assisting composers to write for the Orchestra. This development, while excellent, of course, has perhaps deflected the interest of our leading composers too much away from the small forms, such as choral works, [and] chamber music of various kinds. It is in these fields that nowadays often the best experimental work can be done. Furthermore, it is much more practicable to print and publish this kind of music and to get it known abroad ...
>
> Like many other composers in Ireland, I have frankly tried my hand at a very wide, perhaps too wide, variety of styles. I think that is not too easy to avoid nowadays. The avenues of expression are constantly changing as science advances; the film, for instance, offered a new and startling field to the composer in the matter of background music. The fantastic advances in electronics and tape engineering may eventually[39]

39 At this point Victory deleted the words 'whether we like it or not' – script enclosed with RTÉ

make the well loved instruments of the concert hall obsolete. We are in a transition period and we must make our way as best we can.[40]

Victory's recognition of the possibilities of what would become 'electro-acoustic' music was prescient – he had himself already become the first Irish composer to employ the technique,[41] paving the way for a trend led by Roger Doyle which has effectively kept Doyle, and others working in the genre, out of the concert hall as far as the conception and performance of their work is concerned.[42]

Seán Ó Riada was billed for this programme under his then name of John Reidy. Although he too steered away from direct reference to this debate, the tone of his contribution, echoing in part Boydell's rejection of 'isms', led inexorably towards that of his series *Our Musical Heritage* four years later, while his imagery and syntax underlined that laid down by Frederick May in his references to depression and despair.

> In his essay on Urn Burial, Sir Thomas Browne writes: 'The iniquity of oblivion blindly scattereth her poppy, and deals with the memory of men without distinction of merit to perpetuity'. Now, total oblivion's blank face is our constant companion, haunting our days with anguish, and our nights with dreams of terror. The future seems like a mirror about to shatter, and the god of progress unmasks himself as a demon of folly. Escape from anguish lies only in seclusion, barring the door not to the wolf, but to the death's head.
>
> Music partakes of the common condition, and the common condition has infected music with its insanity of conflicting ideologies. Partisans squabble over the dubious merits of their various faiths, serialism, constructivism, neo-romanticism, neo-classicism, pointillism,

Sound Archive tape 114MD. **40** Ibid. Victory's programme was: Five Joyce Songs for choir and orchestra (in piano arrangement), and two songs for chamber choir; suite for clarinet and piano (Michele Incenzo); and Whitman's 'An Army Corps on the March' for tenor and piano (Richard Cooper), all of which were receiving their first performances. No credit was given for the piano accompaniment, which is presumed to have been by Rhoda Coghill. It is of note, since Victory had stressed the need for foreign recognition of Irish works, that Kenneth Loveland would write fourteen years later 'Of all the composers working in the republic, he is perhaps the one most decisively for export': *Counterpoint* (October 1972); while David Wright has said 'Probably Gerard Victory has done more than anyone else towards making Ireland a partner in the European serious music cadre and in dispelling the curious notion that Ireland has produced only traditional music': 'Gerard Victory', *Classical Music on the Web* http://www.musicweb.uk.net/victory/index.htm. **41** With his work 'The Orphans', a dramatic work which won a special commendation at the Prix Italia in 1957 and 'employed sound as a contextual design feature': cf. Paschall de Paor, 'The development of electroacoustic music in Ireland'(2003), p. 30. **42** For works by Michael Alcorn, Paul Hayes, Michael Holohan and others, cf. ibid.

concretism, folklorism, electronicism, and so forth, a veritable bedlam of 'isms' and 'ists', while around them civilisation totters. One is reminded of the palmy days of Byzantium, with its hundreds of heresies being discussed by thousands of councils, and the roads so full of bishops galloping to them, says Gibbon, that 'the public establishment of the posts was almost ruined by their hasty and repeated journeys'.

A certain amount of security, of quiet and retirement, is needed for the practice of any art, but especially for the art of music. Such is not to be found today in turning one's face outward on the world, but inward on the self, not in the alarms of the present or the future, but in the still waters of the past. The past of music also has its lessons, many of which have been forgotten, and more which were never learnt. Side by side with the advance of techniques has gone the abandonment of the first principles of music, which made Gregorian and Byzantine chant, and our own traditional artsong, and the music of Monteverdi, Vivaldi and Bach.

It is to these first principles, to these basic elements of the art of music, that composers must now return, to a rediscovery of the purity of line, and the rhythmic tension between one note and the next. It is not a change in techniques which is required, but a change of attitude. Music must cease to be a noise in the marketplace, a plaything for critics. The poet Horace, in the second epistle of the second book, has this line: 'I nunc et versus tecum meditare canoros' – 'Abstract yourself from outward appearances – listen awhile to the song the spirit inwardly is singing'.[43]

By complete contrast, A.J. Potter took a thoroughly workaday approach to his already steady output; we should not be completely led astray by his jovial, tongue-in-cheek façade, which masked a completely professional concern for the presentation and reception of his work:

> There are three basic problems which beset a composer. First to get his work written at all; then to get it performed when it is written; then to get people to listen to it when it is performed.
>
> The physical business of getting the work written isn't too bad. All you need is the patience of Job, the manual endurance of a Boswell and the concentration of an Einstein, and, provided the ideas come all right the thing's as good as done before you start. The real difficulty is to

---

43 RTÉ Sound Archive tape 117MD; Ó Riada's programme was an enigmatic 'Piano Piece' (played by the composer); three of his Epigrams from the Greek Anthology (André Prieur [flute], Ó Riada [harpsichord]), receiving their first performance; two Irish folksongs for baritone (Tomás Ó Suilleabháin) and chamber choir; and two Irish folkdances for piano solo (played by the composer).

maintain your integrity whilst you are writing it, and by that I mean write the kind of work you yourself think you ought to write – not the kind of work the gentlemen in the quarterly magazine think you ought to write, however fashionable it may be at the time.

As to the job of getting work performed – well it is true that with a couple of worthy exceptions, our choral societies and such like regard the approach of a contemporary Irish composer with rather less favour than they would a case of bubonic plague. Between you and me I can sympathise in some cases. But we have always RÉ. They will commission works, they will pay for them and they will play them. In fact, if there's no Tschaikovsky on the same programme, they may even rehearse them and what more can you ask than that?

No, the real difficulty that we experience is in getting people to listen to the works. Please note that I say 'listen' to the works. I did not say listen to themselves talking about what they think of the work afterwards. But I'm not quite right in saying 'people'. I don't find much difficulty with ordinary folk – which is a consolation seeing that they're the ones who pay for their tickets – by and large they usually get what I'm driving at. It's the musicians or would-be musicians that I find the difficulty with, because one must have intelligent technical criticism and that is precisely what seems impossible to get. By intelligent technical criticism I means someone who can hear what I'm doing and then write me down whatever of the chords and tunes have struck them afterwards: because if they can't, and can only waffle something about 'neo-modal' influences or some such balderdash, then I'm not interested in their technical opinion although I have the same respect for it as I have for the man who says 'I may not know much about it, but I do know what I like'. Well, not quite the same perhaps. That gentleman is at least honest.

But, perhaps I'm doing you an injustice. Perhaps there are plenty of intelligent musicians listening and you would be only too happy to let me have just the kind of intelligent criticism I have been asking for. If there are, I wonder if you would give me your opinion on the 'Ode to Dives' that you will be hearing shortly … Does it come off I wonder? I would really like your opinion.[44]

Given that the series featured the Radio Éireann Singers in every programme, one could be forgiven, from a glance at the musical content, for deducing that the output of Irish composers in 1958 was largely choral. As a

---

44 RTÉ Sound Archive tape 106MD; Potter's choice of programme was: 'Phantasy for clarinet and piano' (Michele Incenzo [clarinet], Rhoda Coghill [piano]); three part-songs by Belloc and two settings of Moore and 'Ode to Dives' for bass-baritone (William Young).

showcase for work commissioned by Radio Éireann this was certainly a fair deduction: the drawing out of the heritage material available for such arrangement was a major plank in Fachtna Ó hAnnracháin's programming policy at this time, and the fact that so many 'purists' were willing to accede to his requests for work of this kind indicates not merely a financial need but also a desire to become known as a participant in this process of revealing the 'hidden Ireland' to a wider world. Yet, with few exceptions – such as Fleischmann's 'Three Songs for Tenor' and his piano quintet which had already been greeted as major works – the series did help to conceal the range of work being undertaken at that time. The programme of Boydell's works, for example, gave no indication that the listener was hearing music by the author of 'In Memoriam Mahatma Gandhi' or the violin concerto, nor did May's half-hour tell its audience that he had composed significant orchestral works that had been in the RÉSO's repertoire since the 1930s. In the year of transmission alone, RÉ broadcast Beckett's 'Falaingin Dances', Kelly's first 'Fantasia' for harp and orchestra, McNulty's Sinfonietta, Ó Riada's 'Nomos no. 4' and Victory's 'The Enchanted Garden'.[45] The previous year had witnessed even more: Beckett's first Irish Rhapsody, Bodley's 'Salve Maria Virgo', Boydell's second string quartet, McNulty's 'Divertimento', O'Reilly's 'Remembrance: Nocturne for Milan Horvat', the first two 'nomoi' by Ó Riada, and Potter's 'Finnegan's Wake' and 'Gaelic Fantasy no. 5'.

As a leveller, however, it could be claimed that the series presented a mid-century snapshot of Irish composition which did not in fact distinguish between 'major' and 'minor' figures, either in the musical content of the programmes or in what the composers had to say about their work or their attitude to composition: on the contrary, as far as the debate on authenticity is concerned, scrutiny of the texts presented above would not of itself indicate which of the writers was to develop and become a more eminent composer in later decades. Yet on Denis Donoghue's terms, the series would have suggested to the outsider that there was no music of any major significance being written, not least because, of those composers featured, none whatsoever earned his income entirely by composition, and most were, at best, occasional composers or were limited to arranging. From the point of view of their attitudes to composition, however, the suggested 'bilingualism' was, with the exception of Victory, at least partially evident in those who continued to compose 'serious' music.

The preoccupations of the seventeen composers featured in 'Composers at Work', however brief their spoken contributions, fall into two main categories: the first, as discussed, was the major issue of whether or not it was legitimate

45 'The Enchanted Garden' was submitted for the Carolan Prize in 1950, but was placed second behind the only other entry, Nelson's Sinfonietta.

to take away the pristine authenticity of the folk material by introducing it to another, and potentially hostile, genre, which involved the major, and of course extra-musical, question of nationalism. It is striking how many of the contributions implicitly acknowledged the 1905 view of Esposito (above, p. 18) as to how Irish composers were to become 'Irish' in their music, and it is equally astonishing (to younger ears) to note that the vast majority of the speakers were so concerned to address the issue of the Irishness of Irish music.

The second set of preoccupations revolved around questions of recognition and prosperity: how were Irish composers to become known outside Ireland? Would international recognition increase one's chances of being acknowledged at home? How could the musical and social infrastructure be enlarged so as to increase the audience and its level of awareness of serious music? And, above all – and drawing these preoccupations together with those in the first category – how was one to decide between the call of traditionalism and that of cosmopolitanism, each with its rewards and drawbacks?

Of these composers, there could be no greater ostensible contrast between any two – their musical characters, their approach to their work, and the extent of their output – than that between Potter and Seán Ó Riada, who arrived almost simultaneously in the RÉ corridors in 1952–3. From different ends of the country and from different educational and cultural backgrounds, they approached the Irish tradition from benchmarks as disparate as Vaughan Williams and Fleischmann. Yet both became, in the 1950s, prolific arrangers of traditional material, each, according to his own style, achieving a form of fusion of gaelic and European music.

We have been educated to believe that for Ó Riada this was a painful process of attempting to reconcile two polarised traditions. This was partly what Seán Mac Réamoinn had in mind when he wrote that 'Ó Riada ... knew that as an artist there was, in the long run, no place for him in our social structure'.[46] Mac Réamoinn clearly saw that Ó Riada's dilemma – one that he shared with his teacher, Aloys Fleischmann – placed him outside both traditions. In musical terms, Ó Riada expressed this as regarding himself as 'a citizen of the Gaelic nation, not as a citizen of the Anglo-Irish state that we have at the moment, to which other composers belong and I do not'.[47] Yet both Potter and Ó Riada had a place in the 'social structure' of Radio Éireann, one as a prolific supplier of broadcasting material in many forms, the other as an inmate of the institution (as assistant music director 1953–5) and as an *eminence grise* in both mind and voice in the radio series *Our Musical Heritage* (1962). Thus, RÉ was the house – the *ceol-áras* – within which their musics could be given expression by the RÉLO and the RÉSO.

---

46 S. Mac Réamoinn, 'Foreword' in Harris and Freyer, op. cit., p. 10.   47 *Irish Times*, 7 December 1970.

A.J. POTTER

A.J. (Archie) Potter's *entrée* to Radio Éireann, which was to have a significant effect on its broadcast output of Irish music, in fact occurred through the medium of singing rather than composition. Born in Belfast in 1918, he had been a boy chorister in London and had studied composition at the RCM with Vaughan Williams, winning the Cobbett Prize for chamber music. In the second world war he had served in the London Irish Rifles and the Indian Army, in Norway in 1940 (the commando raid on Narvik) and in Burma and Java-Sumatra 1943–6. Writing to the Music Department in January 1952, Potter, who had been appointed a bass-baritone Vicar-Choral in St Patrick's Cathedral, Dublin, asked for an audition, pointing out that he had won the Northern Ireland section of the Festival of Britain with his 'Missa Brevis: Sancti Patricii Thorax'.[48] 'I mention it so that I may avoid any possible misunderstanding by stressing that I am asking to be heard, not as a composer who can sing (?) at a pinch, but as a trained and qualified professional singer who also, and incidentally, happens to compose!'[49]

Potter offered works by Purcell, Bach, Handel, Haydn, Mozart, Beethoven, Schubert, Schumann, Mendelssohn, Bellini, Wagner, Verdi, Brahms, Wolf, Mussorgsky, Borodin and Vaughan Williams. 'You will probably comment that the above all seems a bit on the heavy side. I agree. But the fact of the matter is that my voice is just not suited to the lighter style of singing, and being perfectly aware of my limitations in this direction, I prefer to be judged on the merits of my performance of the style of music to which I am best suited.'[50] This resulted in a trial broadcast in which he sang 'Furibondo spira il vento' from Handel's opera *Partenope*, 'In questa tomba oscura' from Beethoven's *Fidelio*, 'Cinta di fiori' from Bellini's *I puritani*, Prince Igor's song by Borodin and 'A te l'estreme addio' and 'Il lacerato spirito' from Verdi's *Simon Bocccanegra*. However, the monitor's report read: 'Mr Potter is a good musician & therefore his programme was well prepared & correct – but the voice is not pleasing in the upper register & the range of his items brought him up rather too high.'[51]

Having made a not very impressive attempted début as a singer, Potter then asked if Cór Radio Éireann would perform his 'Missa Brevis'. With characteristic openness he told Fachtna Ó hAnnracháin that a performance by the Ormiston Choir of Belfast had been cancelled:

> To be perfectly candid with you, more than somewhat to my relief … For, try as I might, I could never entirely convince myself that a Saturday

---

48 This work was later officially titled 'Missa Brevis: Lorica Sancti Patricii' (Saint Patrick's Breastplate). **49** A.J. Potter to Music Department, 7 January 1952, Music Department file 'A.J. Potter (1) to 5 October 1955'. **50** Potter to Music Department, 10 January 1952, ibid. **51** Ibid. (signature illegible).

night's entertainment in the Presbyterian Assembly Hall in Belfast was the best possible milieu for the introduction of an a cappella setting of the Roman liturgy. The work was rejected by the Studio Singers, the QUB choir, the OUP and the BBC in Belfast … here are a few samples of objections raised from different quarters: It is too 'modern'. It is too old-fashioned. The spirit is too 'Catholic'. The spirit is too 'Protestant'. The counterpoint is too harsh and the harmony too sugary. The harmony is too 'fierce' and the counterpoint commonplace. The work requires too big a choir. The work is only suitable for a small, select, choir. The style is too reminiscent of Vaughan Williams. The style is too reminiscent of Rachmaninoff – and so on and so forth, until, in spite of my natural modesty, I was coming to be almost convinced that I must have produced something quite unique in the annals of art.[52]

It had been praised by composers Julius Harrison and Howard Ferguson (a fellow Belfastman) who had adjudicated the competition. The latter in particular liked 'the vocal writing, the rhythmic flexibility and the justness of the verbal accentuation … admirable'.

Arthur Duff, when asked for an opinion, said 'I find it excessively discordant and I should think most ungrateful to sing, and difficult. I cannot think it is worth accepting for performance',[53] whereas Hans Waldemar Rosen's view was quite the opposite: 'I consider the work well worth a performance on account of its imagenative [*sic*] power as well as its formal qualities. The composer excels in writing a flowing vocal line, which, together with a natural declamation as well as the comparatively simple harmonic structure … should make a performance easier for the singer than it looks at first sight'.[54] The 'Missa Brevis' would have several performances by, and broadcasts from, RTÉ. Potter would continue to elude definition throughout his career as a composer, chiefly because his eclecticism was always tempered by his consummate skills as an orchestrator and arranger, which were to be quickly recognised by Ó hAnnracháin and others and to be utilised extensively by Radio Éireann.

Meanwhile, at the request of Dermot O'Hara, Ó hAnnracháin had invited Potter to make arrangements of folk songs for use by the RÉLO, and he was paid five guineas each for arranging 'The Ninepenny Fidil', 'Dear Little Shamrock' and 'Ballynure Ballad'. This, too, was the beginning of a long relationship between Potter and RÉ. A couple of months later, Potter was writing to Ó hAnnracháin about his 'Fantasy on Irish Airs': 'I have spent a good deal of thought upon it and feel that it should prove an interesting setting and treat-

---

ment of two themes which, to my way of thinking, have always in the past suffered from arrangements notoriously lacking in initiative'.[55] This time, Duff was in favour: 'These scores of A J Potter's are good. The tunes are nicely treated and the orchestration good'.[56] So RÉ bought the first of a series of 'Fantasia Gaelach' and 'Three Irish Airs from Thomas Moore' for £25 and gave Potter *carte blanche* to send in other arrangements for SATB for Cór Radio Éireann and anything else he had available. As Ó hAnnracháin put it, 'Owing to the limited amount of Irish music available, there is little danger of our having too much of it in our library for quite a long time yet!'[57] Duff agreed: 'I really think Mr Potter is a considerable acquisition to us here, and I should be glad to see such work as this find a publisher so that it would be generally available to choirs'.[58]

Ó hAnnracháin next suggested to Potter that he should work on his projected 'Variations on a Popular Tune [the 'Wild Colonial Boy']' for inclusion in the next series of Winter Proms,[59] and a little over a month later, sending in the completed score, Potter wrote: 'I have just had the idea for a good time that it would respond very well to a particular kind of variational treatment: it's such a well known tune that you've got a head start in getting it across to your audience. Incidentally, the version I've used is the simplest of all the ones I've ever heard: it may not be the best, but it is the handiest for the purpose'[60] – again, a typical honesty in explaining how his craftsmanship was brought to bear, in this case, on the raw material, in a work which Axel Klein states to have been 'the first Irish composition using a twelve-note row'.[61]

Potter's own note on the work does not mention the note row, but does draw our attention to the core of the argument about the status, and indeed purpose, of folk-music:

> Folk-music today is studied and explored as never before, but to those, like this composer, who believe in it as the primary source in music, it is menaced by two great dangers. First that the very research and study expended on it, welcome though it may be, will lead to its becoming a purely academic subject of interest only to professors and diploma seekers. Secondly, that being so regarded as a purely academic subject, it may lose its interest for the serious go-ahead composer ... In his variations on this folktune, the composer has tried in the first place to bring it out of the class-room and back among the ordinary folk where it

55 Potter to Ó hAnnracháin, 8 September 1952, ibid. **56** Duff to Ó hAnnracháin, 10 September 1952, ibid. **57** Ó hAnnracháin, internal memo, 15 September 1952, ibid. **58** Duff to Ó hAnnracháin, 6 November 1954, ibid. **59** Ó hAnnracháin to Potter, 24 November 1954, ibid. **60** Potter to Ó hAnnracháin, 2 January 1955, ibid. **61** Klein, 'Roots and directions in twentieth-century Irish art music', p. 180.

belongs by treating it as a popular number in varying orchestral make-ups. Then, to shew that even a well-worn tune can mean more than this to a serious musician these 'popular' variations are alternated with others more intellectual in kind exploring the less familiar aspects of variation technique.[62]

Charles Acton, who was the first to mention publicly the serialist ingredient,[63] reported that 'carefree listening … did not reveal a glimmer of a note-row, which (if it exists) must be so well concealed as to exculpate us from some blame. It must be said also that it is very hard to listen to the work with straight-faced earnestness. Apologies to the distinguished composer, but once more I enjoyed it enormously as a frabjous piece of magnificent comedy and first class music'.[64]

When, later in the 1960s, Potter started to present broadcasts, he introduced himself endearingly to his audiences by saying

> I'd better explain why you're hearing my gravelly tones instead of the honeyed and cultured accents of RÉ's usual announcers. My name is Archie James Potter (Séamus Mac an Photaire in the Gaelic) and, since you've been hearing my arrangements and disarrangements of our traditional heritage of music during the past decade or so Radio Éireann felt it was high time that I should be here in person to exculpate myself and explain exactly what I was doing about it all.[65]

By 1958, Potter reckoned that he had made approximately 700 arrangements 'rang[ing] all the way from orchestra-choir-and-organ down to three part female choir or even harp solo'.[66] The chief point of interest, he concluded, was that they were

> not really an end in themselves, but only a means to one. Even so, they can be used to help set up *some* kind of an indigenous tradition. You can't do much in the way of form, naturally, but you can certainly do a lot in the way of colour experimentation and … I have also tried (and I think this is one of the most important aspects) to bring the melodic idiom of

62 Potter Archive. 63 *Irish Times* 2 July 1960. 64 Ibid., 28 February 1962. 65 Potter script, n.d. (Potter Archive). The programme presented by Potter also included his Rhapsody for Violin and Orchestra ('Rapsoid Eireannaighthe') played by Mary Gallagher, and 'Finnegan's Wake': 'when that piece was first played in Dublin the critics blasted RÉ for wasting their time on trivialities. Later, when it was done in the US the intellectual gents there said what a penetrating psychological study of the mind of James Joyce it was. You wouldn't know, would you?' 66 Potter to Walter Piston, Harvard University, 30 December 1958 (Potter Archive).

folk tune into some kind of relationship with modern harmonic thought – or perhaps better say to evolve from the particular nuances of folk idiom an harmonic structure both appropriate to it and derived from it which can then be applied to original composition.[67]

By 1962, his estimated total had risen to 1500,[68] for which he earned the express gratitude of Erskine Childers, who wrote: 'Your musical work was absolutely splendid and you were of invaluable assistance to me in my campaign to popularise Irish traditional music and to have many airs that were lying on dusty shelves brought to life again'.[69] Childers' 'campaign' is remarkable for its political import: a minister for P&T of Anglo-Irish background was commissioning arrangements of Irish traditional music from a northern Presbyterian in a project dedicated to restoring to Irish people a sense of the indigenous tradition in folk-song. The fact that the work in hand was specifically Irish underlines the 'other' fact – that Potter, at Childers' behest – was undertaking work that appears to have caused him little or no *angst*, whereas it gave others significant cause for concern.

It was also profitable for Potter: it became a standing joke that, because arrangers were paid per bar of music, 'no one arranges a jig in 12/8 time but only in 3/8',[70] so much so that, when he heard Michele Incenzo playing Potter's 'Elegy for Clarinet and Strings' under Franco Patanè, Charles Acton, commenting on Incenzo's 'assured and beautiful performance' said 'we are so used to Dr Potter's rich vein of light-hearted works, whether original or arrangements, that a work of real emotion and personal sincerity is a welcome change'.[71]

A balanced assessment of Potter's ability came in the case of his 'Fantasia Gaelach III' of which Eimear Ó Broin would say:

> This work is very ably scored. Dr Potter shows that he knows what he wants and can get from the RÉLO (for which it is scored) and in this respect he is at his best. The chief drawback is that the Fantasia is based on only two tunes. After the second one ('The Maids of the Mountain Shore') I frankly expected (and I am sure the listeners would expect) to hear a reel-like section. Instead there is a modified recapitulation of the 'Men of the West' and a noisy coda to end the work. There are good points in the recapitulation but it comes too soon and the noisy firework clichés that one associates with Dr Potter's style could have been kept in reserve a little longer, perhaps. Dr Potter ought to be told to

67 Ibid. **68** Potter to Erskine Childers, 14 June 1962 (Potter Archive). **69** Childers to Potter, 15 June 1962 (Potter Archive). **70** As reported by Charles Acton, *Irish Times*, 7 July 1980. **71** *Irish Times*, 19 September 1959.

give us (the performers and listeners) more value in a greater variety of tunes and concentrate less on his admittedly very gifted displays [of] dazzling orchestra tricks.[72]

Duff and O'Hara concurred. This would be the regular verdict on new arrangements by Potter: thus O'Hara would write of 'Finnegan's Wake':

> I have studied the score of 'Finnegan's Wake' by Dr A J Potter and find it full of humour and original ideas. This type of work makes a very welcome change in a programme of Irish music. I would advice [*sic*] that scores like this should be also written for the Symphony Orchestra and used in the lighter types of Tuesday programmes at the Phoenix Hall. I would also remind you that Dr Potter has rescored No 1 Fantasia for symphony orchestra. I have played this in Germany and it is most effective.[73]

And when RÉ received 'Fantasia Gaelach V' in 1958, it would be Ó Broin's turn to comment: 'Dr Potter doesn't give us anything new in this work but what he says is expressed well and with the sound knowledge of an experienced craftsman. The work is, I feel, more sincere and less boisterous than some we have had in the past from Dr Potter.'[74] With wry and dry humour, Ó Broin would say of another piece: 'Yet another arrangement from the Potter factory and turned out with all the usual knick-knacks and tricks of the same firm. The piece has wit and charm as well as the usual moments of gusto and the occasional spicy harmonies'.[75] And on another work, 'Carrigdhoun', 'This is a very effective and sensitive arrangement for the RÉLO. Dr Potter's technique in building up atmosphere and colour with limited resources is shown at its best.'[76] Meanwhile, the motivation expressed by Éamonn Ó Gallchobhair in producing concert versions of folk music is well attested by O'Hara's comment on 'Carrigdhoun': 'the treatment is very varied and extremely well orchestrated. The harmonies are interesting and in keeping with the folk tune idiom.'[77]

Potter's own attitude to what could be achieved with the forces available is summed up in his accompanying note for his 'Fantasie concertante for violin, cello and orchestra': 'The solo parts are written with a view to the maximum of display compatible with a minimum of technical ability and the orchestral parts are also designed to require as little rehearsal as possible. I would stress ... that the piece is intended for the light music audience.'[78] Eimear Ó Broin,

---

72 Eimear Ó Broin, ms. note, 21 September 1955, RTÉ Potter file (1). 73 O'Hara to Ó hAnnracháin, 8 February 1957, ibid. 74 Eimear Ó Broin, official report form, 18 June 1958, ibid. 75 Eimear Ó Broin, official report form on 'Caravat Jig', 9 September 1958, ibid. 76 Eimear Ó Broin, ms note, ibid. 77 O'Hara ms. note, ibid. 78 Potter to Ó hAnnracháin, 21 March 1959, ibid.

who presumed it had been written with husband-and-wife David Lillis and Coral Bognuda in mind, considered it 'Extremely well written throughout and despite the rather heavy scoring for the RÉLO, the solo parts should come through clearly even in a public performance ... I welcome its appearance as something new in the repertoire of the RÉLO's Irish music field. It can be done in "Concert Hall" [a current RÉLO radio series] or at RÉLO concerts in the provinces. There are many details that catch the eye and no doubt will please the ear.'[79] Potter also composed (at the instigation of producer Jane Carty) a work for another husband-and-wife team, John Ronayne and Elgin Strub, with the RÉLO in 1966,[80] and, the following year (again commissioned by Carty),[81] the 'Concertino Benino' for the RÉLO's principal trumpet, Benny McNeill, a practice he adopted for other section leaders.[82]

Shortly after he made his first contact with RÉ, Potter submitted a two-part work which won the station's Carolan Prize for composition. The two parts, known individually as 'Rhapsody under a High Sky' and 'Overture to a Kitchen Comedy', were intended to be heard as one, but subsequent history has shown that each of them traditionally serves as an opening work in a symphony concert. They won praise from the adjudicator, Sir Arnold Bax who wrote to Potter: 'You are not afraid of allowing a figure to continue for several pages, and so you avoid the extreme restlessness of so much present day music.'[83] The former, as evocative in music as Paul Henry's paintings of the west of Ireland are in visual art,[84] was performed in Munich at the International Festival of Light Music in 1966 (as was his 'Nocturne in Bansha' in 1969) and was included in the programme for the RTÉSO's European Tour in 1980, just before the composer's death. The following year, Potter won the Carolan Prize again with his piano concerto, 'Concerto da Chiesa', which was premièred that year by Anthony Hughes. Critic Joseph O'Neill considered that it showed Potter 'to be a composer with considerable technical resource and musical imagination'.[85]

In late 1955 Roibéard Ó Faracháin and Ó hAnnracháin suggested to Gorham 'that we might consider some sort of commission or prize for a Tostal

---

79 Eimear Ó Broin, official report form, 15 April 1959, ibid.   **80** Carty to Potter, 8 July 1966 (Potter Archive).   **81** Jane Carty also commissioned song cycles and other works from Potter, Seóirse Bodley, Brian Boydell, Gerard Victory and T.C. Kelly.   **82** Carty to Potter, 14 April 1967 (Potter Archive). Potter wrote concerto works for almost all wind and brass instruments: 'Hunter's Holiday' for horn (1964), 'Trumpet Concertino' (1964), 'Rapsóid Éireannaighe' for flute (1966), 'Tubaistí Cánach' for tuba (1976), 'Madra Liath na Mara' for cor anglais (1977), 'Lasc and Feadóg' for piccolo (1977) 'Ar Trumpa Mór' for trombone (1977) for Seán Cahill, principal trombonist of the RTÉSO; there is evidence that in 1977 he was writing a clarinet concerto. He also wrote concerto works for viola (1963), guitar (1965), harmonica (1967) and cello (1968).   **83** Bax to Potter, 18 February 1952 (Potter Archive).   **84** It had been suggested that the Rhapsody would make good background music to a Bord Fáilte travelogue (Charles Acton, *Irish Times*, 6 November 1961) and in fact was used by Bill Skinner in his television documentary on Paul Henry (1979).   **85** *Irish Independent*, 26 September 1953.

competition e.g. an orchestral work to be known as Tostal Suite, Tostal Overture or some such title. Frankly', Ó Faracháin told Ó hAnnracháin, 'I have no great enthusiasm for the Tostal part of it, but there is no reason why we shouldn't make the Tostal the occasion for a musical competition which might at the same time give us a new work and put well-earned money into the pocket of a good composer.'[86] A week later, Ó hAnnracháin recommended that Potter be commissioned to write the overture for the Tostal of the following year. 'Having regard to our experience with the Carolan Prize, a competition for an orchestral work is not likely to bring forth anything spectacular ... A serious concert devoted entirely to Irish music is not likely to prove very popular.'[87] The Carolan Prize had been awarded to Boydell for his violin concerto in 1954, when it was the only entry, and the prize itself petered out due to the small number of contestants.[88]

Ó hAnnracháin suggested that the RÉSO should give a concert including the commissioned work and 'perhaps some other Irish composition of distinction ... We have a fairly good idea of public taste from our Proms and An Tostal is not the time to put on a show that might interest a few hundred visitors but not the hundreds of "natives" who alone can assure us of a full house.'[89] When Potter sent the resulting 'Overture to an Occasion', Duff commented 'This overture has the expected bustle and excitement of a noisey [*sic*] festival occasion. Plenty of variety in rhythm and much to do in the woodwind. The slow section ... is effective. I should have expected this tune to return towards the end in a really broad impressive Elgarian manner, but no sign of it. I find the final section ... rather cheap stuff rather reminiscent of "Carmen". However, on the whole certainly accept. Perhaps rather too long. Very difficult.'[90]

The various opinions on Potter's craftsmanship thus tend to converge on three main aspects: his skill in orchestration, including his intimate knowledge of the musicians for whom he was writing; his ability to evoke 'atmosphere' in both original works and arrangements of Irish airs; and his capacity to switch the mood of a piece from sensitive and reflective to sparkling and witty, to outright raucousness. Potter's own tongue-in-cheek – but nevertheless instruc-

86 Ó Faracháin to Ó hAnnracháin, 21 September 1955, RTÉ Music Department file 'A.J. Potter (2) from 19 September 1955'. **87** Ó hAnnracháin to Ó Faracháin, 27 September 1955, ibid. **88** In 1963, when the Prize was revived, the set theme was 'Amhran Dochais' and attracted two entries: the winner was John Purser, and the runner-up was Bernard Geary. **89** Ibid. **90** Duff ms. note 15 February 1956, ibid. Potter told Frederick May that, at RÉ's request, the overture was renamed 'Tostal Overture': Potter to Frederick May, 9 October 1956 (Potter Archive). The work was premièred by the RÉSO with Sydney Bryans in May 1956 as part of An Tostal and received its first broadcast in November that year. Potter (ibid.) informed May (who was writing the programme note) that 'the form of the piece is that of the old "Italian Overture", as opposed to the French one. 3 movements (all joining) ... To this I have added an extensive coda ... I was always taught in my young day[s] that the Italian overture was the real ancestor of the Symphony. This work itself is intended as a very condensed symphonic sketch which is why I chose the form.'

tively realistic – verdict on his work, delivered in 1965, was that 'My own compositions are respectably mediocre: modern enough not to be stigmatised as "academic" but not too avant-garde for the performers to know whether they are on the right note or not.'[91]

Later in 1956 Potter asked if Ó hAnnracháin would be interested in a symphony, and this was readily agreed at a fee of £100. It was expected that he would deliver it the following year.[92] It would prove to be one of his most difficult and original works, and would not in fact be completed until 1969.

In the meantime, Potter was working prolifically in producing original works and arrangements for RÉ, in addition to radio scripts, all of which went relatively smoothly. When television arrived in 1961–2, he was commissioned to write a television opera, *Patrick* (libretto by Donagh MacDonagh), which was conceived by the DG, the American Edward Roth, as a prestigious overture to Irish televisual culture, since he had been involved in a previous project with Menotti's *Amahl and the Night Visitors*. (Charles Acton somewhat unfairly called this 'an uncharacteristically imaginative gesture' on Roth's part.)[93] After several delays, both technical and tragic – the latter due to the sudden death of Dermot Troy, who was to have sung the title role – the opera was eventually screened on St Patrick's Day 1965.[94] Acton called it 'the most important television project to emanate from Donnybrook … A major landmark in Irish music … A major contribution to our culture', commenting that it was 'An act of courage and national maturity to offer for such a prestige venture the idea of the national apostle as a modern Irishman with a vocation to pacify racial fights between Irish and West Indian labouring men in the English Midlands.'[95]

This in fact was a successor to an earlier idea for an opera, originally conceived as 'The Emigrants' and which had to wait many years for a production (which occurred posthumously in 1981) under the title *The Wedding*, produced by Irish National Opera with the RTÉCO and Proinnsías O'Duinn.[96] In the opinion of the present writer, *The Wedding* and 'Sinfonia de Profundis' and, to a much slighter extent, the 'Rhapsody under a High Sky' are not only Potter's most significant works, but works of outstanding achievement on an international scale.

---

91 Potter to an unknown correspondent, 26 September 1965 (Potter Archive). **92** Ó hAnnracháin to Potter, 25 October 1956 (Potter Archive). **93** *Irish Times*, 7 July 1980. **94** The cast included Otmar Remy Arthur, Martin Dempsey, Michael McCann, Patrick Ring, Edwin Fitzgibbon (in the title role) and Bernadette Greevy; Anne Makower directed for television. **95** *Irish Times*, 19 March 1965; Donnybrook, a Dublin suburb, is the location of RTÉ's headquarters. **96** In 1958 Potter wrote to Roibéard Ó Faracháin asking for suggestions for a librettist, as he did not feel competent to write his own libretto; Ó Faracháin suggested Norris Davidson, and although the two began to exchange ideas, Potter eventually wrote his own text (under the nom-de-plume 'Lee McMaster'): Potter to Ó Faracháin, 4 March 1958; Ó Faracháin to Potter, 7 March 1958; Davidson to Potter, 7 May 1958 (Potter Archive).

On occasion, Potter's characteristic sense of mischief could raise eyebrows. On one such, scripts he had submitted were returned by Éamonn Ó Gallchobhair with the wry comment: 'Since we desire a quiet life in Radio Éireann I would be glad if you would reconsider some of the matter in both scripts. In the margin I have pencilled the matters that we think need a more diplomatic approach.'[97]

In the course of a long association with RTÉ, Potter was in fact to make many broadcasts, as well as presenting weekly series by the RÉLO with Dermot O'Hara or Eimear Ó Broin such as 'Light and Alive' from late 1959.[98] One of his most extensive contributions was in the field of educational programmes, in which he scripted and presented two series of 'Listening to Music' (1969 and 1970), 'Talking about Music' (1969), 'The Consumer's Guide to Music' (1970) and 'The Young Student's Guide to Music' (1978), most of which were commissioned by Jane Carty.

The delay in producing the symphony, which eventually became 'Sinfonia de Profundis', was due somewhat to the constant call on Potter's prolific capacity to produce smaller works, but principally to his deepening alcoholism and his recovery from it. As he said in interview with Charles Acton, it was 'meant to tell you the story of what it's like to be an alcoholic and to have DTs and to recover'.[99] As a work which reveals the depths to which the human spirit can sink ('*de profundis ad te clamavi Domine*') and the humble expression of the capacity to return from those depths, the symphony is a signal for those who have experienced that kind of despair (had Frederick May heard it, and if so, what did he feel?) and holds a message for those who wonder about the profundity of such emotions. After its première (by the RTÉSO under Albert Rosen) Acton regarded it as Potter's

> outstanding composition ... a true symphony. It [is] also a work of enormous musical and emotional appeal. To very many people (far more than just those calculated to know its significance) the 'story' which Dr Potter describes was vividly clear, as significant and as clear almost as Beethoven's convalescence in the slow movement of the A minor quartet. And at the end, the audience responded to it with an ovation such as I have not heard any other Irish work receive.[1]

97 Ó Gallchobhair to Potter, 10 February 1959, RTÉ file 'Potter'. The scripts in question are probably those entitled 'The Gap', a two-part interval talk broadcast later in 1959. **98** Potter's other suggested potential titles for the series were: 'Light but/and Living', 'Light but/and Learned', 'Lightly Learned', 'Learning Lightly', 'Sweet Consort' and 'Light, Learned and Living': Potter to Ó hAnnracháin, 26 September 1959, RÉ file 'Potter (2)'. **99** C. Acton, 'Interview with A.J. Potter' (1970). **1** Ibid.

Writing immediately after the performance he described it as 'an overwhelming musical experience [after which] words seem even more inadequate and harder to find than usual … I am seething with thoughts and feelings and the conviction that this was a major national event.'[2]

Potter himself went home that night and wrote to Albert Rosen: 'I feel I must sit down at once and put in writing my gratitude and appreciation … It has been a privilege and an education for me to watch you at work.'[3] It was a mark of Potter's humility (as well as natural courtesy) as a composer that he habitually thanked his performers for their work: on this occasion he also wrote to the RTÉSO leader, John Kitchen to say 'thank you' – 'fortissimo, ben marcato, e molto con espressione'.[4] Similarly when the RTÉ Singers gave his 'Ten Epigrams' (text by Hilaire Belloc) at the composition seminar at the Cork Choral Festival, he wrote 'Ladies and Gentlemen: thank you for that lovely job you did on Ten Epigrams … I hope there will be future occasions on which I have the privilege of having a work premiered by you people: I know they'll be good, but it will take something very special to surpass this one in my memory.'[5]

Gerard Victory's letter of congratulation to Potter referred to the symphony as 'a most compelling personal document as well as being music of a very significant stature … I certainly foresee it as becoming a standard work in our repertoire, and I hope in a much wider field in due course'.[6] When he heard the 'Sinfonia' a second time, after Potter's death, Acton wrote:

> The biographical content of the work is clear and moving. It is also …
> a metamorphosis of the main theme 'Remember God's Mercy' into the
> 'Nisi Dominum' hymn tune, and it is a comment perhaps on Dr Potter's
> work and musical personality that his triumphant harmonising of this
> tune should be so dissonant, and presumably so strange to the
> Presbyterians of his upbringing … Now that we are not hearing his light
> music arrangements week by week, we can hear his fingerprints, such
> as the brass glissandos, for what they really are[7]

– by which Acton meant that certain 'fingerprints' might have only a temporary life in small-scale and ephemeral work but could live more extensively and more effectively in their own right in a work such as this symphony, where the *glissandi* and other effects are suggestive of a haunting *danse macabre* which gives the work its (literally) dreadful undertow.

Profound though the 'Sinfonia de Profundis' literally is, it harbours, and is tempered by, Potter's characteristic humour which many found to be too cyn-

2 *Irish Times*, 24 March 1969. 3 Potter to A. Rosen, 23 March 1969 (Potter Archive). 4 Potter to Kitchen, 23 March 1969 (Potter Archive). 5 Potter to Gerald Duffy, 4 May 1969 (Potter Archive). 6 Victory to Potter, 24 March 1969 (Potter Archive). 7 *Irish Times* 2 July 1981.

ical or vulgar – and yet, if the scoring for brass in that work has a vulgarity, it is a necessary element in its overall emotional impact. 'If you are trying to get a message across ... or if you are trying to project something to an audience, you can't project sermons all the time.'[8] Potter saw this as something inextricably connected with being Irish, 'and I do happen to come from the most Irish part of Ireland'.[9] Potter addressed this in 1970 far more succinctly and directly than he had in 'Composers at Work' over a decade earlier:

> Being Irish does not consist of arranging folk tunes or doing music that happens to have bits and pieces of folk tunes in it or even giving it Irish-sounding titles or anything else. In other words being Irish does not mean doing what Dvořák did, or what Smetana did in 'My Land' or that sort of thing. Being Irish and writing Irish music means doing what J.S. Bach did in the St Matthew Passion or what Verdi did in *Il trovatore* ... Being Irish means you produce Irish music, just as being Irish means you produce Irish literature ... You [i.e. Charles Acton] are pointing out that there is a lot of humour in my music. But I hope you notice that it's always completely side by side with very serious things. That is what makes it such very Irish music.[10]

It was a matter of some concern as well as pride to Potter that he was commissioned by Eoin McKiernan, President of the Irish-American Cultural Institute, to write a second symphony, to commemorate Éamon de Valera: pride to have been chosen as the composer and concern because, athough written in 1976, numerous delays prevented its performance during his lifetime; the symphony had to wait until 1981 for a performance (by the Springfield [Massachusetts] Symphony) and had its Irish première in 1983, with the RTÉSO conducted by Robert Gutter, who had directed the US première.[11]

Potter's last word in that interview with Charles Acton was that he would like to be remembered as a composer for a 'slightly minor work' – perhaps the 'Variations on a Popular Tune' or the ballet 'Careless Love', and that it would be said of him 'He was a real professional'. The measure of his professionalism is the extent to which his dealings with RTÉ show him to have been thorough, assiduous, intelligent and courteous in every detail, even when he was

8 C. Acton 'Interview'. 9 In fact, Acton stressed this in his account of his interview with Potter: 'A Presbyterian born on the Falls Road, with Protestant Republican relations in Co. Tyrone and Catholic Imperialist relations in Co. Cork, with an intimate knowledge and love of Ireland in all 32 counties, A.J. Potter is probably a more truly Irish composer in a basic, historical, realistic way than if he had been born and bred in the Gaeltacht', ibid. 10 Ibid. 11 The première was attended by Gerard Victory, Aloys Fleischmann, Seóirse Bodley and Colm Ó Briain, Director of the Arts Council.

cajoling the organisation to perform his works more frequently, or to pay higher rates for the arranging and copying work which was his bread-and-butter. Whether it was a minor but urgent request for an arrangement at two days' notice, or a major commission, or some intermediate level of composition, such as the opening music sequence for the television News (in 1969) or incidental music for a prize-winning television documentary such as 'Behind the Closed Eye' (on Francis Ledwidge, 1973); whether it was writing programme notes for concerts (a function in which he succeeded Frederick May), a script for the many radio broadcasts that he made (both singly and in series, which included Thomas Davis lectures on international folk-music), sitting on the adjudication panel for the National Song Contest, or an audition for an orchestral appointment, Potter's professionalism was absolute.

SEÁN Ó RIADA

Louis Marcus states that Ó Riada 'was dismissive about his arrangements of reels, jigs and hornpipes for the [RÉLO], deft and all as they were'.[12] Yet these arrangements were milestones along Ó Riada's evolutionary path as a composer, as they were in Potter's; where Potter's comments on his own arrangements reveal the need for self-assertion and justification (in dealing with material that was not part of his early musical experience or education), they also suggest an anxiety lest the work be misconstrued. There is a strong resemblance between Potter's and Ó Riada's arrangements of Irish music, similar also to those of Aloys Fleischmann, Arthur Duff and Frederick May, in that they demonstrate a craftsmanlike concern, and respect, for the fragility of the original material, as we noted in the case of many contributors to 'Composers at Work'.

Seán Mac Réamoinn points out that most of those with whom Ó Riada associated were writers: 'that a talent like Ó Riada's, exploding into genius, should express itself in music, was without social or artistic precedent. He had not alone to teach the Irish a new alphabet, he had first to invent it' (the same is true of Arnold Bax before him).[13] To which Louis Marcus added that, because he 'lacked a language', Ó Riada 'found a world in which there was chaos between the incongruous poles of serialism and Gaelic *sean-nós*'.[14] There is also a profound sense in which the 'language' that Ó Riada lacked was – or might have been – the same 'language' that eluded all twentieth-century Irish composers due to their lack of tradition. To be successfully 'bilingual' (to repeat

---

12 L. Marcus, 'Seán Ó Riada and the Ireland of the Sixties' (1981), p. 21. 13 S. Mac Réamoinn, 'Foreword', ibid., p. 10. 14 L. Marcus, ibid. p. 19; although, conversely, a case can be made for a stylistic *congruence* of serialism and *sean-nós*.

T.C. Kelly's expression) was perhaps to make it impossible to establish that third – or middle – language. To fill that 'chaos', or *gap* – in the Miltonic sense of a formless void – was therefore perhaps a project which Ó Riada shared with fellow composers such as May. It is thus apposite that Gerard Victory should have seen Ó Riada as 'a *translator* of Irish music into the symphonic realm with a voice that was unprecedented and yet utterly "right"',[15] and for Marcus to speak of his score for *Mise Eire* as 'written in the idiom of an Irish symphonic period that had never happened'.[16] This form of irredentism was one of the main reasons for the misplaced admiration of Ó Riada which masked the more profound grounds for crediting him with an advance in Irish music-making.

In Gerard Victory's view, Ó Riada was central to the way in which, in the early 1950s, the RÉLO and the RÉSO 'found their way slowly towards an Irish dimension [of symphonic music]'.[17] Victory refers (in relation to Ó Riada) to 'the ferment of Irish minds and lives in the critical twenty years from 1950 to 1970',[18] and while it is undeniably true that the staff of the Music Department did not agonise daily over the question of identity and Irishness, it is also evident that Ó Riada's presence – and absence – generated at least a curiosity about the role that music might play as a means of translation between these two supposed 'poles'.

It was therefore valid for Victory to say that 'in 1976 we commemorated the fiftieth anniversary of the beginnings of Irish broadcasting, and the more we examined its progress the more we realised that its critical development was inextricably bound up with Seán Ó Riada. Its later history would have been different had he not lived, and he too would have been a very different person in life and career had Irish radio and television not crossed his path so closely'.[19] Thus pupil supplanted teacher in the sense that Fleischmann, who has been called '*the* intellectual force in Irish music in this century',[20] was, over a fifty-year period, not nearly as central to the development of music on radio as was Ó Riada during his much more brief association with the medium. Victory's statement is akin to the view of Ó Riada as a national icon whose early death (at the age of forty in 1971) amounted to a national tragedy. Yet what was true of Ó Riada was also true of Potter, in the sense that his work, albeit largely in a different genre, was also central to the development of RÉ.

The phenomenon of Seán Ó Riada is paradoxical. As David Wright has put it:

> When Seán Ó Riada died ... public grief reached proportions unprecedented for a non-political figure ...[21] This seems extravagant for a mere

---

15 Victory, 'Ó Riada on radio', ibid. p. 49; my emphasis. 16 Ibid., p. 22. 17 Victory, ibid. p. 49. 18 Ibid., p. 42. 19 Ibid., p. 43. 20 Eimear Ó Broin, in R. Fleischmann (ed.), op. cit., p. 261. 21 This is an unacknowledged quotation from the opening of Aloys Fleischmann, 'Appreciation: Seán Ó Riada's *Nomos II*', first delivered at the Gaiety Theatre, Dublin, 13 January 1972; Fleischmann

composer whose output was too slight to justify such a reaction. In simple terms, he portrayed in his music a vision of Ireland and of an Irish mode of life in line with the country's oldest and finest traditions, striking a vibrant chord not only in the Irish but also in the wider cosmopolitan world.[22]

In 1967 Charles Acton had written of Larchet's expression 'the great Irish composer for whom we are all waiting', that 'a strong potential candidate for this position is Seán Ó Riada … one of the few musicians well known and respected by just about every sort of musician in Ireland' – a respect which, he said, was 'argumentative, personal – and real'.[23] His death served to focus people's minds on the fact that, as Acton put it, he was 'the first modern composer essentially of modern Ireland to be taken from us'.[24]

Yet at the time of his death, it was necessary for his former teacher, Aloys Fleischmann, to remind the audience at a memorial concert that 'there was another, lesser-known side' to the Ó Riada of Ceoltóirí Chualann, the group he formed for the authentic performance of Irish music: 'he wrote a small number of works having no relation to his country in either subject-matter or idiom' – and he mentioned the 'Hölderlin Songs', 'Five Epigrams from the Greek Anthology', 'Hercules Dux Ferrariae [Nomos 1]', and 'Nomos 2': 'he had this breadth and this depth, and the ability to tackle with imagination and technical skill broad philosophical themes which go beyond the regional and the finite, and reach into questions of time, of the ultimate, of the hereafter'.[25] In *that* sense, Ó Riada does deserve our attention, but the fact that his output was limited almost entirely to these works severely restricts his claim to a breadth of attention, however deep it might be.

It seems that the 'centrality' of Ó Riada in the consciousness of Irish musicians and musicologists is unquestioned, yet to what was Ó Riada central? – to the course of traditional music? – to that of classical music? – or even to the evolution of RTÉ as a channel or conduit of musical transmission? To view Ó Riada as *the* central figure is absurd. There is no central figure. If one takes prolific output as a determining criterion, then Potter and Victory share the honours; if meticulous and ascetic preparation and presentation, then James Wilson and John Kinsella; if international recognition, then Wilson and Gerald Barry. It is wrong to place Ó Riada himself at the centre of the debate, although many of the questions he asked of himself and caused others to ask *were* and *are* central to that debate.

also said: 'No chieftain ever came to rest among his people amidst a greater manifestation of general sorrow': *Counterpoint* (November 1971). **22** David Wright, 'Seán Ó Riada', *Classical Music on the Web* http://www.musicweb.uk.net/oriada/index.htm. **23** C. Acton, 'Seán Ó Riada: The Next Phase'. **24** *Irish Times*, 4 October 1971. **25** Fleischmann, 'Appreciation', loc. cit.

It is fundamental to our understanding of Ó Riada, as it is of Potter, that both the original and the derivative strands of his work were supported by Radio Éireann, although in Ó Riada's case the encouragement to produce 'original' work declined, whereas it increased in the case of Potter.

David Wright continues: 'the music ... is flawed but rather special. His film score *Mise Eire* (I am Ireland) brought him an acclaim that no other composer has received in Ireland. Indeed he *was* Ireland – for a while'.[26] This was echoed by Douglas Sealy: 'the popularity of the film ... gave the tune the status of a second national anthem, and Ó Riada the status of a national composer'.[27] Such a judgement is fair in that it identifies the *persona* of the composer in the public imagination, with which the critic Charles Acton concurred:

> Not only was this a new voice in the ... Irish cinema, but it showed to the urban viewer a new and tingling aspect of Irish traditional music. Up to then (as a gross simplification) Irish melodies were Moore's, come-all-ye's, or the possession of cliques of pipers, gaelgoiri, small farmers in western pubs, and so on. 'Mise Eire' brought 'Róisín Dubh' with a wallop into the consciousness of city viewers as something of eternal greatness.[28]

By so doing, it referred those viewers to the 'mythic' character of Ireland and thus established its affective claim on their attention.

Ó Riada's musical output came almost entirely after the brief period he spent as an administrator in Radio Éireann (1953–5). In 1955 he produced his first major work, the 'Olynthiac Overture', followed in 1956 by 'The Banks of Sullane'. Hearing the 'Olynthiac Overture' three years after it was written, conducted by Vilem Tausky, Charles Acton wrote: 'Mr Reidy has since left its tonalism for the fetters of serialism. If he eventually breaks loose from them he may become a very significant composer'.[29] 'Nomos 1' ('Hercules') came in 1957, and, in successive years, he wrote the 'Nomos 4' for piano concertante (1957–8), the choral 'Five Epigrams' (1958), a festival overture 'Seoladh na nGamhna' (1959, for the Cork Orchestral Society), the incidental music for Roibéard Ó Faracháin's 'The Lords and the Bards' (1959), the orchestral 'Triptyque' (1960), and the music for the films *Mise Eire* (1959) and *Saoirse?* (1960).

Of 'Nomos 4' Acton wrote (when it was premièred at a studio concert by Eimear Ó Broin with Charles Lynch): 'It says a great deal for John Reidy that his new "Nomos" can follow Hindemith and completely hold its own ... Like pre-classical polyphony, serialism can be a safe refuge for the dry-as-dust with

---

26 D. Wright, loc. cit. 27 D. Sealy, 'Seán Ó Riada: man or mask?'; Sealy summed up his survey by asserting 'this country still awaits a composer who will stand head and shoulders above the ruck of minor figures'. 28 C. Acton, *Irish Times*, 3 October 1981. 29 *Irish Times*, 9 February 1959.

nothing to say. John Reidy has plenty to say and says it interestingly an ingly ... a composer of achievement and originality'.[30] When it had its performance, nine months later, at a Public Concert conducted by Maurice Miles, again with Lynch, he added: 'There is no sense of aridity, of "formalism", or even of cleverness. And, while it is an absorbing essay in strange timbres, these are obviously inherent necessities of the music and not just superficial ingenuities ... about the best work we have had from an Irish pen'.[31]

In 1961 Ó Riada formed Ceoltóirí Chualann and in 1962 he broadcast *Our Musical Heritage*, the fourteen-part series in which he analysed and promulgated the essence of Irish traditional music. This marked a *caesura* in his output, although it did not herald a complete break with his 'classical' compositions, since he wrote, in the choral or vocal vein, the four Hölderlin Songs in 1964, the very large 'Nomos 2' in 1965, 'Sekundezeiger' (1966) and, in 1968, a Requiem (commissioned by RTÉ for Éamon de Valera, then aged 86, who did not in fact die until 1975). A third film score, for *An Tine Bheo*, was written in 1966.

Acton wrote of 'Nomos 2', premièred by Tibor Paul with tenor Herbert Moulton, the RÉ Singers and the RÉ Choral Society in April 1965, 'It seemed to me that ... we were in the presence of a masterpiece; ... one of the most important pieces of music to have been written in Ireland so far',[32] and added, in a retrospective summary a year after Ó Riada's death, that the three quotations in the score represented 'at the same time a valedictory to western European art music and an assertion that the path of Irish music should in the future be different'[33] – as telling an epiphany as the poet Michael Hartnett's *Farewell to English*.

In 1969 Ó Riada precipitately dissolved Ceoltóirí Chualann, many of whose members were already playing as The Chieftains. His last years, up to his death in 1971, were occupied with his lectureship in music at UCC (where he had been teaching since 1963), the people of Cuil Aodha [Coolea] for whom he wrote a Mass (and another for the community at Glenstal) and with the harp music of Carolan, which he attempted to complement on the harpsichord, which Louis Marcus called 'a longing to touch the hand of the last Irishman for whom the Gaelic and European traditions of music were not irreconcilable'.[34]

Ó Riada's restless fascination with musical forms was recognised by Charles Acton during Ó Riada's lifetime, when he wrote, shortly after the composition of 'Nomos 4' and while the career of Ceoltoirí Chualann was in full swing:

> Seán Ó Riada is one of the most interesting figures in our musical life. His first and fourth 'Nomoi' deserve international fame; his recent set-

30 *Irish Times*, 21 February 1959. **31** *Irish Times*, 2 November 1959. **32** *Irish Times*, 26 April 1965. **33** *Irish Times*, 3 October 1972; the quotations are from Mozart's G minor symphony, Beethoven's seventh symphony and Brahms's 'St Anthony Chorale'. **34** L. Marcus, op. cit., p. 20.

tings of Hölderlin songs ... are very highly regarded by those who know
them ... His 'Mise Eire' music is a uniquely successful combination of
folk, art and film ... He has an almost infinite capacity for development
and fame, but also (I suspect) an equal talent for living for the present
and taking the line of musical least resistance. He remains a question
mark, coloured with equal measures of confident hope and exasperation
to his admirers.[35]

Acton was of the opinion that

> Seán was not the first or last Irish writer in various media who needed
> the stimulus of a deadline. RTÉ offered him neither deadlines nor the
> encouragement of repeats. I have become firmly convinced that, tricky
> and difficult as he undoubtedly was ... RTÉ's music department during
> his last decade is primarily responsible for his pitifully small output.[36]

As Acton told Harry White:

> The third, fifth and sixth Nomoi do not exist,[37] because RTÉ never
> sought them out, although everyone knew that he had them sketched.
> But it is clear that Victory had no clue whatever to Seán's convoluted
> personality and music. G[erard] V[ictory] was not only highly profes-
> sional but a superb technician. He could write (and did) anything from
> R[alph] V[aughan] W[illiams] to Boulez to Cage ... But Seán's per-
> sonality and music were clearly beyond his comprehension. He cannot
> be altogether blamed. Gerry did commission from Seán a Requiem for
> the State occasion of Dev's death ... In the Gaiety Theatre one night
> I asked GV that he should use more of Seán's music. For instance, I
> said, when did Radio Éireann last broadcast any of his songs, particu-
> larly the Hölderlin songs? Gerry, who was never short of words,
> hummed a bit and said 'Yes, you know I submitted them last year to the
> UNESCO Rostrum of Composers in Paris and they all seemed bewil-
> dered and did not know what to make of them. They didn't really think
> they were even competent'.[38]

---

35 *Irish Times*, 30 December 1964. **36** *Irish Times*, 3 October 1981. **37** This was a slip of the
pen, since Acton was well aware that Nomos no. 6 had been performed in 1967 at the Belfast
Festival; he most likely meant to indicate the *seventh* projected *nomos* – see below, note 68, p. 271.
38 Acton to White, 15 August 1996 (Acton Archive). Acton's letter was written after he had read
the draft of the latter's chapter on Ó Riada in *The keeper's recital*. Acton also wrote (ibid.) 'Grattan
[Freyer] should not have invited Victory [to contribute to *The achievement of Seán Ó Riada*] any
more than someone should ask Hanslick to contribute a chapter to a book about Wagner'.

Yet Tomás Ó Canainn gives us some indication that, when Ó Riada had gone to live in Coolea, RTÉ continued, as it did with Potter, to send material for urgent arrangement, which provided Ó Riada with essential income. (The Hölderlin songs, in a recording by Bernadette Greevy, were in fact transmitted by RTÉ Radio 1 on the evening of Ó Riada's death.)

This coincides with what Victory himself wrote, making the point that Carlo Franci, who incorporated 'Hercules' into his repertoire and recorded it with the LPO, was the exception to the rule:

> As often as not these eminent [visiting] conductors regarded the simple arrangement of an 'Irish air', stripped of its native decorative complexity and harmonised in very 'correct' textbook classical harmony as what they might most reasonably expect of the Irish composer. As often as not this was what the Irish composer, trained in rather orthodox schools, felt himself he could best provide. When, as sometimes happened, a composer decided to write in a more adventurous way, it seemed at best to such eminent conductors strange and even bewildering.[39]

But, as Acton recalled, the advent of Ceoltóirí Chualann was welcomed by Radio Éireann and incorporated into the schedules:

> Kevin Roche, head of light music in the station, immediately saw the potential of the Ceoltóirí and gave them a weekly slot … But, even with them, he [Ó Riada] was frustrated. When he was forming the group, he told me about his plans. He knew that I knew of his dissatisfaction with the Hellenic, Hegelian process of development, and felt committed to the sean-nós or Schönbergian idea of continuous variation … He would make a group of traditional musicians who would, under his guidance, and composition, follow a new path of the Irish traditional way of repetition with continuous variation and work out their own form of counterpoint … the rediscovery of medieval counterpoint/polyphony … After a few years he was *artistically* dissatisfied, for two reasons. Artistically, that only a minority of his Ceoltóirí could read music … so that he had to work *writing* material for those who could read and relying on rote teaching and conducting for the rest. So the idea of carefully drafted new polyphony/counterpoint had to go by the board. And the immense listenership success, both RÉ and Gael-Linn records, got him onto a commercial treadmill that he could not afford to get off.[40]

39 G. Victory, op. cit., p. 47.   **40** Acton to White, loc. cit.

But Ó Riada's contribution to Irish music on Irish radio by this means had been far-reaching. His revolutionary creation of Ceóltoirí Chualann provided RÉ with a new form of Irish music-making that has subsequently become a worldwide phenomenon. Writing that 'without him … [performances of Irish music] could easily have submerged the whole thing in a welter of céilí bands' Acton observed that

> Light Orchestra arrangements, synthetic 'folk' from America, banjos, electric guitars … all of those things descend at various removes from Anglo-German harmony and form. Ó Riada cut through them. He had the clarity to eliminate harmony as such; to see the importance of melodic variation; to reinstate the vital principal [*sic*] of ornament; and to reach for an art music based on the development of folk-music with these principles. And the impact of Webern on Ó Riada was an important contributing factor.[41]

'OUR MUSICAL HERITAGE' – 1962

If Ó Riada's musical productions did not find their fullest outlet on RTÉ, *Our Musical Heritage* by contrast constituted a major radiophonic essay on the nature, status and future of Irish music, in stark contrast to, and polarity from, the view of Denis Donoghue. In *Our Musical Heritage* Seán Ó Riada set out to startle Irish ears by speaking of, and illustrating in depth, the music to which they were theoretically accustomed, but to the themes and nuances of which they had become deaf. He began with the unequivocal statement that

> Irish music is not merely not European, it is quite remote from it. It is, indeed, closer to some forms of Oriental music. The first thing we must do, if we are to understand it, is to forget about European music. Its standards are not Irish standards; its style is not Irish style; its forms are not Irish forms.[42]

Harry White comments that 'the very rhetoric it employs could come straight from Éamonn Ó Gallochobair [*sic*] and the worst traditions of defensive, jingoistic insularity … The ideology … is a virulent strain of nationalism which sanctifies a degree of musical stasis.'[43] I, on the other hand, find the rhetoric aggres-

41 *Irish Times*, 22 April 1965. 42 S. Ó Riada, *Our Musical Heritage*: programme 1, broadcast 7 July 1962, RTÉ Sound Archives tape 00604; the extant tapes in the RTÉ Sound Archives differ in significant detail from the text of the programmes as published. 43 H. White, *The keeper's recital*, p. 141.

sive rather than defensive, and expansionist rather than insular. White believes
that the explanation for this 'overheated propaganda ... protesting too much',
is that 'some great hurt lies beneath'. By giving Seán Ó Riada access to the microphone to explore in such depth not merely the richness of Irish music but, more
importantly, its very nature, Radio Éireann was assisting him simultaneously to
explore the nature of the hurt, to reposition Irish music as a force which is far
from static, and to reorient listeners' attention and understanding. By the end
of the series, Ó Riada had given expression very explicitly to the 'great hurt':

> It is clear that the vast majority of Irish people think of Irish music as
> being of the greatest importance. This is as it should be; it is one of the
> few things left which we can call our own. There are some who sneer at
> it; they are the ignorant and the stupid, slavish lackeys of foreign tradi-
> tions, servile lapdogs who lick up the crumbs which fall from the stranger's
> table. Let nobody say that our traditions are inferior to those of any other
> country. They are our traditions, and as such they suit us best. If they had
> not suited us, they could not have become traditions in the first place. It
> is precisely because of their suitability that they have survived so long, in
> the face of so much opposition, from our own people and also from our
> oppressors. What of our traditions do, in fact, survive? Our way of life,
> and our customs, are being thrown out in favour of an alien materialism.
> Our hospitality, at least in the urban areas, is long-forgotten, a joke. Our
> language is made the excuse for cynical hypocrisy. Our literature is given
> over mainly to aping foreign models. Our nation, that was bought with
> blood, is being sold, spiritually as well as physically, before our own eyes,
> a great madness. The strongest surviving tradition we have is our music.
> We must not let it go. And it is up to ourselves to keep it. We have too
> long been looking for help from elsewhere.[44]

One wonders what impression such a *coda*, with clear overtones of both the
béal bocht [poor mouth] and what would later be called the 'Brussels begging
bowl', would have made on listeners in 1962. While the recorded voice of
Éamonn Ó Gallchobhair in his own broadcasts displays a laconic cynicism bordering on despondency, and a suggestion that in his case the 'hurt' was a personal one which fuelled that cynicism, Ó Riada's voice, in the extant tapes of
Our Musical Heritage, is vibrant, pursuing, with a lapidary urgency, the need to
win his audience to the essentials of his argument and to excite them as to the
protection and development of their heritage. Of course there is ambivalence
in his discussion of 'our innate conservatism' – which both impedes (or inhibits)

44 Ibid., p. 80.

the development of musical tradition and empowers the conservation of that tradition, and it is likely that at this time he was at his most undecided about the relationship of these two different types of music, the Irish traditional and the European post-Renaissance.

Ó Riada expressed the Irish-Ireland belief that 'it is the gael that absorbs' – in the sense that Ireland could assimilate non-Irish influences (as he himself had done in the course of his own education), but that the gaelic influence was stronger than whatever it encountered. He could thus be a very European Irishman, yet at the same time could reject Ireland's contemporary movement towards Europe.

> By 'traditional' I mean the untouched, unarranged, undiluted, unEuropeanised, unWesternised, un-dressed up, native, orally trans-mitted music which is still, to the best of my knowledge, the most pop-ular type of music in this country … Irish music is not European music, but the fact that this is an obvious statement has previously clouded some of its implications … Our innate conservatism is responsible for this: it is this conservatism which has maintained the basic characteris-tics of the Irish language for well over two thousand years, at least; it is this conservatism which has maintained the basic characteristics of the Irish literary tradition; it has maintained the basic characteristics of the Irish people and it has kept Irish music alive for us, its basic character-istics unchanged, with very little outside influence. European music, as we know it today, is by our standards comparatively young. It began to take shape during the early Renaissance, compounded in a mould con-taining Dutch, French, German and Italian ingredients. Since then, and until fairly recently, it developed along predominantly German and Italian lines. The Renaissance, on the other hand, passed us by, and the best of our classical poetry was in full flower before it. Its effect on Irish poetry was minimal, if any, and it certainly did not affect Irish music at all. Therefore, when I said Irish music is not European music, I was making not quite so obvious a statement after all, perhaps.[45]

45 Seán Ó Riada, 'Our Musical Heritage' – first programme, loc. cit. In fact the fascination with Ó Riada's career – and therefore with his place in Irish cultural history – lies as much in his per-sonality as in his musical output. In his letter to Harry White, Charles Acton made some telling comments on both the personality and the music: although an exchange between the two, pub-lished as 'A correspondence with Charles Acton' in *The achievement of Seán Ó Riada*, appears to have polarised their viewpoints, they had enjoyed much deeper exchanges in earlier years, when Ó Riada had shared many of his musical insights and ambitions with Charles and Carol Acton. Acton recorded that 'I grew up (as did most others) with an idea of Irish folk music being Moore's Melodies and ceilidhe dancing'. However, he had lived in Palestine in the 1930s, and 'little though I knew of Arab music … I could hear that this Beduin music was different. They were singing long

What *were* the characteristics of this 'conservative' tradition as Ó Riada saw it, and in what way were they incompatible with, or fundamentally different from, European art music?

> Traditional Irish art has never adopted the Graeco-Roman forms spawned by the Renaissance, which have indeed become the basis of European art. I refer specifically to the European notion of development – a development which moves in a rising crescendo of tension, with its end being a crisis the resolution of which produces catharsis. Let me give you an example of what I mean. Take any Beethoven symphony – a movement will start off with two contrasting musical ideas, these are developed, played off against one another, given new significance by being led through a series of different keys. This creates a gradually mounting tension, until a climax is reached. At the climax a tension is resolved, producing a feeling of release, or catharsis, and the original musical ideas appear transfigured, as a result of what has happened to them ... It is the basis of European art and it is quite foreign to traditional Irish art. The simplest picture of traditional Irish art is the ancient symbol of the serpent with its tail in its mouth – my end is my beginning. It is essentially a cyclic form ... This is the idea that has lain at the root of all the traditional art of this country since pre-Christian times.[46]

Ó Riada introduced an element of excitement into these lectures by suggesting that this introduction to the heritage was a form of adventure, a learning experience of extreme novelty:

> In approaching our vocal music, that style of singing traditional songs which is called in Irish the '*sean-nós*' – the 'old style' – it is best to listen as if we were listening to music for the first time, with a child's new mind; or to think of Indian music rather than European.

ballads (perhaps equivalent of our aislings) – the words, I was told, were by 10th or 9th century poets of the Bagdad caliphate ... When I was back living in Ireland, sometime in the 1940s I heard on RÉ Tom Collins, the then white-haired leader of the violas of the RÉ orchestra, play (quite solo) what must have been a sean-nós tune with all its pulseless rhythm and full, differing decoration each time, and knew immediately that I was hearing not only something totally different from 'folk' and dance music of the Irish urban world, but the same *sort* of music that I had heard in the desert. Shortly after that I heard my first flamenco and read ... that flamenco was but a debased form of cante jondo which dated back to the Moorish times in Iberia ... I put it to Seán that the legends were right ... and that the music had travelled from the Arab lands, and across North Africa and Galicia. Bless his heart, Seán took the idea up enthusiastically – though he took it too far claiming to have found artefacts in Morocco cognate with Irish early medieval art': C. Acton to H. White, loc. cit. Acton had previously claimed this contribution to Ó Riada's ideas in a letter to the Editor of the *Irish Times*, 29 July 1981. **46** S. Ó Riada, 'Our Musical Heritage', second programme, transmitted 13 April 1963; RTÉ Sound Archives tape 00605.

Sean-nós singing cannot be appreciated except on its own terms. The *sean-nós* singer is unaccompanied. *Sean-nós* singing demands great skill and technique, and an artistic understanding beyond the demands made on the average European singer. This is because a good deal of *sean-nós* singing is improvised, and the singer must know how to improvise in the proper style ...

Perhaps the most important aspect of *sean-nós* singing is what I call the 'Variation Principle'. It is not permissible for a *sean-nós* singer to sing any two verses of a song in the same way. There must be a variation of the actual notes in each verse, as well as a variation of rhythm ... Since the ability to make artistic variations is creative, we actually demand the talents of a composer in the *sean-nós* singer.

In stressing the purity of the old style, Ó Riada also found it necessary to puncture the pretentiousness, or simply the mistakenness, of traditional music-making as it prevailed at that time:

The use of piano to accompany traditional fiddle-playing is unfortunately prevalent. This is a scar, a blight, on the face of Irish music, and displays ignorance on the part of those who allow or encourage it. The reason for it is easy to see. It is a truism to say that we suffer in this country from a national inferiority complex. To combat it we have developed a number of tricks which we hope will fool others into thinking we are better than we are – while we are only fooling ourselves. The piano is such a 'trick'. It has become a symbol of respectability. The house that has a piano looks down on the house that hasn't, even if the piano is never played. The piano is an excellent instrument, of course, for playing serious European music, but it is not suitable for Irish music ... The traditional fiddle-player who insists on a piano accompaniment is falling into the same trap of 'respectability'. He has a suspicion that classical music ... is somehow more respectable than Irish music and he must have a piano accompaniment too. Someone might even call him a 'violinist' ... Fritz Kreisler and Michael Coleman were both fiddle-players, or if you like, violinists. Kreisler was not better than Coleman, nor was Coleman better than Kreisler. They were different.

This brought him to the disingenuous discussion of the dichotomy between the purism of solo activity and the prevailing tendency towards group playing, of which the céilí band was his *bête-noir* – disingenuous because it ignored the fact that he had in fact formed Ceoltóirí Chualann the previous year:

Irish music is entirely a matter of solo expression and not of group activity. It is a direct expression by an individual musician or singer. It is a matter of personality – of musical personality. Everything that comes in the way of that direct expression beclouds and confuses it ... However, for one reason or another, group activity in Irish music has come to stay. It is a common thing to hear two or three players playing together. In such small numbers, however, with a piper and a fiddle-player playing together, it is still possible for each to preserve his individuality.

In 1926, Seamus Clandillon, the first Director of Irish Broadcasting, conceived the idea of the céilí band:[47] eight or nine musicians playing together ... One might expect that, after a certain time, the céilí bands would have managed to work out some kind of compromise between the solo traditional idea and group activity. But instead of developing this kind of compromise, the céilí band leaders took the easy and wrong way out, tending more and more to imitate swing or jazz bands which play an entirely different type of music and are organised on a different principle ... The result is a rhythmic but meaningless noise with as much relation to music as the buzzing of a bluebottle in an upturned jamjar ...

I have given a fair amount of thought to the idea of playing Irish music as a group activity. It seems to me that this is one of the most important ways in which Irish music could develop. Let us postulate, therefore, an ideal type of Céilí Band or orchestra. The first thing it must have is variety – which, expressed through variation, is a keystone of traditional music ... The more variation the better, so long as it has its roots in the tradition, and serves to extend that tradition rather than destroy it by running counter to it.

As to the instrumentation of this imaginary idea band: I think that all the instruments most suited for playing traditional music should be represented. The uilleann pipes, the flute and the whistle would make up a reasonable wind section. Fiddles there should be, of course, and also accordions to help fill out the passages where the whole band is playing. As for drums, the modern notion of using a jazz drum-kit is entirely out of tune with Irish music. Their sound is coarse and without subtlety. But I think that our native drum, the bodhrán, whose history goes back well into pre-Christian times, would be very suitable ... I think also that a harp played in the traditional fashion would lend an edge, and occasional touches of harmony, to this ideal band.

47 It is surprising that Ó Riada should have perpetuated this myth; céilí bands long pre-dated the foundation of 2RN: see below, chapter 5.

And, as it appeared in the printed version of *Our Musical Heritage*, this was followed by Ó Riada's peroration on the centrality and essentiality of Irish music as one of the few remaining features inhering in the Irish personality ('The strongest surviving tradition we have is our music. We must not let it go'). If there is a sense in which Ó Riada 'was Ireland', and deserved a kingly funeral, it lies in a synthesis of the 'Mise Eire' music, the passion of this *coda* to *Our Musical Heritage* and in his fascination with Carolan, explored through the medium of the harpsichord, which was issued posthumously as *Ó Riada's Farewell*. To these elements, the majority of the small number of 'classical' works are not incidental, but they certainly run parallel to, and reinforce, Ó Riada's original claim to any lasting significance in Irish musical history.

There is, however, a profoundly political connotation to Ó Riada's Irishness. If his insistence on the core values of Irish society and culture were at odds with the general direction being taken by Ireland in the 1960s, and if his exegesis of 'our musical heritage' was so fraught with the contradictions that he faced in practical daily life with Ceoltóirí Chualann, it explains why he told Orla Murphy in 1970 that he was 'a citizen of the Gaelic nation, not ... a citizen of the Anglo-Irish state that we have at the moment, to which other composers belong and I do not'.[48] For Ó Riada, therefore, there were two Irelands, irreconcilable, with that unbridgeable 'gap' between them. For quite different reasons from those of Raymond Deane, Ó Riada as a composer did not 'belong' to the Ireland that was, in his view, moving away from gaelic culture. Séamus Heaney captured this in a blinding one-line image in his poem 'In Memoriam Seán Ó Riada': 'he was our jacobite': the definition neatly marches alongside Yeats's lapidary statement that 'Ireland, until the Battle of the Boyne, belonged to Asia'[49] – that is, an Ireland which pre-dated the polity of western Europe in its imaginative curriculum, and which was overcome when the battle, between the Jacobite and Orange claims to the British throne, had settled so many questions about the direction of that polity, leaving old Ireland, like Ó Riada himself, in a time-warp or psychic gap.

Tomás Ó Canainn tells us that 'he didn't seem to go along with normal metaphysics, but claimed that the absurd was at the heart of everything'.[50] Such a belief would allow him to tolerate that gap – which for him was, probably, 'at the heart of everything' – only as long as he could find relief in its absurdity. When Charles Acton referred to 'the inherent schizophrenia'[51] of 'The Banks of Sullane', he was not merely identifying the problem of giving symphonic treatment to folk material but was also suggesting that its author was putting himself into the gap which was a potentially fatal – even if inevitable – place for a creative spirit to explore.

48 *Irish Times*, 7 December 1970. 49 Quoted by Séamus Deane, 'Remembering the Irish Future' 1984. 50 Ó Canainn, op. cit., p. 14. 51 *Irish Times*, 13 July 1957.

Ó Riada's insistence on the necessity of composition (which he gave as his reason for resignation from his administrative post in RÉ) was perhaps more deeply anti-social than the way in which many others might express it – 'It is my composition which gives meaning to my existence'.[52] It is essential to realise that all of Ó Riada's musical output was at the mercy of his personality and of his intellectual restlessness. Harry White affirms (if that is not too ironic a term) that 'he meditated on the question of voice and style in Irish music to the extent that each overlapping phase of his compositional development undermined its predecessor'.[53] Yet there is a misfit between this view (a harsh one in my opinion) and that which follows it: 'The difficulties which he confronted have continued to affect Irish music to the present day'.[54] It suggests, if only by association, that the difficulties of style and content encountered by Ó Riada are the same difficulties encountered by contemporary Irish composers. While it is certainly true, as I have demonstrated in chapter 1, that there is a sense – whether explicit or subliminal – of 'indenture' of Irish composers to the idea of 'Ireland', and while it is also arguable that this is commensurate and cognate with explorations of 'Irishness' in other media, the figure of Seán Ó Riada is by no means the dominant point of reference at the turn of the twenty-first century. The fact that he could find some meaning, literally, on the banks of the Sullan(e) river, from where he believed he drew most of his cultural inspiration, is of little interest to today's Irish composers, whose work may derive in some cases from their own sense of locality or of history, but who are increasingly free of Ó Riada's type of difficulty.

White is nevertheless correct in identifying Ó Riada as 'the crucial recipient of Ireland's musical progress in the decades immediately prior to his emergence as a composer',[55] pointing out that he was the pupil of Fleischmann, the successor of May as Musical Director at the Abbey Theatre, and, if only briefly, of Éamonn Ó Gallchobhair as a key member of the administrative staff at Radio Éireann.[56] An outsider by inclination, he was nevertheless a part, however unwilling or ambivalent, of the fabric of Irish musical society. Fachtna Ó hAnnracháin has recorded that Ó Riada (or John Reidy as he referred to him) was not suited to the administrative tasks that were assigned to him.[57] The fact that his personal temperament and interests led him away from a career that would concentrate solely on that particular form of musical progress is not

52 I am indebted to Fachtna Ó hAnnracháin for showing me a copy of Ó Riada's letter of resignation (undated) and his previous memorandum of 25 February 1955 which includes the statement relating to composition.   53 H. White, entry on Ó Riada, *NG2* 18/698.   54 *NG2* 18/699. 55 White, *The keeper's recital*, p. 137.   56 H. White, 'The Divided Imagination', p. 13. It is significant that neither Ó Gallchobhair nor Ó Riada could reconcile their creative work with their administrative duties at RÉ for which both acknowledged that they were unsuited.   57 'Seán Ó Riada (John Reidy) as Assistant Music Director, Radio Éireann', memorandum by Fachtna Ó hAnnracháin, Nollaig 1996, communicated by Ó hAnnracháin to the author.

something for which he should be rebuked (as if he had failed to fulfil some preordained promise) nor should it be a problem for composers who were contemporaneous with him or who came after him. In the more than thirty years since his death, his almost exact contemporaries Seóirse Bodley and John Kinsella have pursued careers as symphonic composers in quite different styles, while slightly older figures such as Gerard Victory and James Wilson have also contributed to the orchestral, operatic and chamber music repertoires without any discernible obeisance in the direction of Ó Riada. Thus, Ó Riada's own difficulties and his position as the 'crucial recipient' of musical progress do not necessarily make him a crucial *influence* or even, in White's words, 'the crucial figure in Irish music of the twentieth century'.[58] I am not at all sure that he 'forced the abiding difficulty of art music in Ireland to its crisis'[59] if, by that, White means to insist that that difficulty, in Ó Riada's own case, continues to be a crisis for later composers. (The situation would be tantamount to suggesting that the dissensions among the harpers at the end of the eighteenth century were the principal cause of the erosion of Irish music in the nineteenth.)

It is nevertheless true, as White states, that Ó Riada 'found a voice that gave to traditional Irish music a cultural centrality which it had never before enjoyed',[60] an ironic situation given that Irish music had dominated the consciousness of Irish composers for at least the past sixty years. By this, White in fact means that by articulating the claim of Irish music to cultural superiority (as well as centrality) he made it clear that it should be considered and exercised as a genre in its own right. Thereby, he brought his own (and Ó Gallchobhair's) argument for that superiority into conflict with Denis Donoghue's view that 'folk-music does not answer any of the problems of a composer' – that is, if one allows that folk music should necessarily occupy the attention of a composer. Ó Gallchobhair's arrangements – even of the 'con̆certed' type – and the orchestrations and vocal arrangements by Potter and Ó Riada of traditional airs, may not have brought them anywhere near the level of achievement of Grieg or Sibelius (the latter in fact succeeded in creating music that is indubitably and unmistakably 'Finnish' without once using an actual Finnish folk tune) but they existed within the 'music-house' of RTÉ alongside compositions – in the case of the RTÉ Singers – by Matyas Seiber and Goffredo Petrassi and in that of the RTÉLO and RTÉSO by Grieg, Sibelius, Borodin and more recently Andrzej Panufnik.

Because I am unable to subscribe to the polarisation of Irish 'traditional' music and the 'classical' mainstream of Europe, on any grounds other than the distinction between circularity and linearity, I am equally unable to view the change in Ó Riada's musical direction as a 'decline' of his 'original' composi-

---

58 *The keeper's recital* p. 125. **59** Ibid., p. 128. **60** Ibid.

tions in favour of a vigorous embrace of traditional music with Ceoltóirí Chualann. That there was a change in direction, and indeed of emphasis, is obvious, but in his intensified exploration of the music of such as Carolan, there is a refraction of that 'original' work.

This became clear in an interview between Ó Riada and Acton in 1970 (published in 1971) when the latter asked 'have you given up writing art music entirely?' to which Ó Riada retorted: 'When you say art music you mean art music as understood in the very narrow scope of western European art music.'[61] Ó Riada went on to make the distinction between

> the rational man and ... the instinctive man. The instinctive man in me is getting dug in ... to the Irish tradition ... The rational side of me can ... cope with European music. The instinctive side of me is involved in traditional music because I am first and foremost, more than most Irish composers, involved in traditional music from my early youth ... But there is a third side and that is, no matter what I say to you now today, I do not know what my instinct is going to make me do next week, or even tomorrow, I can't prophesy to you.[62]

As Acton would later comment, 'Seán's greatest artistic creation was himself and his biography.'[63] Ten years after Ó Riada's death, Acton would write of his paradox and enigma, his use of conceptualism to project mythical *personae* which defied the facts of his biography, in order to protect his inner privacy.[64] In this interview of 1970, Acton went on to challenge Ó Riada:

> CA: Is it right that you should be doing merely what you want to do, while a person of your talents or genius could be writing music of greater and longer-lasting merit for your country or for the world?
> SÓR: I can see you are aiming at the words 'What I *should* do'?
> CA: I am indeed. In other words, we have got a potential Sibelius who is mucking around in a boat on the Kenmare River because he wants to do it, instead?

The idea that somehow Ó Riada owed anything to Ireland at this stage of his career, and was therefore acting irresponsibly, did not find favour with the composer:

> Well, what you've got is somebody who is going to do what he wants to do and who believes that what he wants to do is what he should do. But

---

61 C. Acton, 'An interview with Seán Ó Riada'. 62 Ibid. 63 Acton to White, loc. cit. 64 C. Acton, *Irish Times*, 3 October 1981.

let me put it in this way, Charles. I think I have changed the face of Irish music already. I have changed it in terms of orchestral groups and I have changed it in terms of traditional music. And I feel that I am entitled to do what I want to do … And at the moment what I should do is my involvement with my people in Coolea, developing the idea of liturgical music along purely Irish traditional melodic lines, which is an extension of my work with Ceoltóirí Chualann. That work is now finished and I feel that the European tradition can struggle along without me for the time being.[65]

Despite the arrogant tone of the riposte, Ó Riada's claim to have influenced the profile of Irish music-making – perhaps the only well-documented instance of such self-regard – was justified in that he had attracted attention to the relative status of both traditions and had persuasively suggested that they could be introduced to each other. But there was a limit to that possibility, because the 'third side' – where such an accommodation might be found – eluded him as it has eluded most others who have attempted it. At the end of the interview Ó Riada acknowledged this:

SÓR: I'd like to see professional orchestras in the country playing my music or playing music which derives from the kind of thing I've been trying to do. Both traditional groups and ordinary international symphony orchestras.
CA: Then you think there can be a fusion between the two?
SÓR: They are different aspects of the same thing. I don't think it is a matter of fusion, though of course there can be, but you are going to have to get a very tenacious sheepdog to do it.

The nub of our misunderstanding of Ó Riada may be in Victory's assertion that Ó Riada's 'startling voice … was to reconcile the old and the new as no one had done before'.[66] If by 'the old' Victory intended 'Irish traditional (or folk) music', and if by 'the new' he intended western 'classical' music since the Renaissance, then he was making the cardinal mistake of believing that Ó Riada wished for such a reconciliation. Ó Riada's express interest in western music stopped at the Renaissance. His intention was to reconcile 'old' with 'old' in the sense that he wished to restore Ireland, as a world culture, to the position it had occupied when it was a major contributor to scholasticism and culture generally, in a quite different Europe. This is clear from his repudiation of post-Renaissance music and it is also clear from his interest in the music of

---

65 'An interview with Seán Ó Riada'.   66 *The achievement of Seán Ó Riada*, p. 44.

Carolan. In fact, it had been clear since Ó Riada's undergraduate days, .. he had written a thesis on serialism: 'The Schoenberg method, as he himself has formulated it, cannot survive. Over-complexity is the rope with which it strangles itself. What is needed in music today is a return to simplicity and innocence ... The medieval spirit in art must be re-born'.[67]

'Hercules Dux Ferrariae' (the first of a projected series of seven *nomoi* of which only three were eventually completed)[68] is perhaps Ó Riada's most significant work in this context, because it aligned itself in inspirational terms with the era of Josquin des Prez (*c*.1450–1521), itself a transitional period on the cusp between the late middle ages and the Renaissance. Gerard Victory observed that neither 'Hercules' nor the 'Five Epigrams' could have been written 'had Radio Éireann's musical development not reached the point it had arrived at around the year 1957 ... Without his close knowledge of the rising string standard of the RÉ Symphony Orchestra Ó Riada would hardly have attempted such a work [as 'Hercules'].' And Victory went on to affirm that the work was thoroughly 'Irish': 'Although 'Hercules' betrays little evidence of the melodic contours we associate with Irish music, it was unmistakably the work of a great Irishman and could have been written by no one else. The type of imagination which informs it with its peculiar blend of real scholarship ... with irony, even cynicism and almost perverse gaiety is unmistakably Irish.'[69]

The restlessness of the composer masked a much more deep-seated anxiety which was concerned not only with the nature of composition but also, as Seán Mac Réamoinn noticed, the place of the composer in society. This puts Ó Riada in the same company as Boydell and May, as a thinker whose horizons could not be limited by accepted social or cultural thinking, and whose own eclectic culture gave him both the capacity to absorb and transform external musical and literary influences, and the ability to reject them in favour of his own brand of Irishness.

In *Our Musical Heritage* Ó Riada did not, in fact, reveal to Irish listeners the Irishness of Irish music, but that version of Irishness which his persuasive voice and passionate manner were capable of advocating, and which came from his own intense, dynamic and subtle perceptions, which in turn became his idiosyncratic beliefs about Irishness. That he insisted on its non-European nature (as did Éamonn Ó Gallchobhair) was as much due to his personal chem-

---

67 Quoted in Tomás Ó Canainn, *Seán Ó Riada: his life and work* pp. 93–4. In a letter to Ó Riada's sister, Charles Acton refers to Messiaen having 'rejected the post-Renaissance idea of development in music' and wishing that, when he had lived in Paris (1955) Ó Riada had actually met Messiaen (as he allowed it to be supposed that he had): 'it could have been an immensely fertile exchange for both. But "if only" does not get one anywhere': Acton to Louise Verling, 2 October 1985 (Acton Archive).   **68** In addition to the six *nomoi* commonly listed in works of reference, a seventh – a violin concerto – was also planned: C. Acton to H. White, 15 August 1996.   **69** G. Victory, op. cit., pp. 52–3.

istry as it was to any received wisdom on the subject. It says much for Ó Riada's charismatic personality that in 1962 he could persuade Radio Éireann to transmit programmes of such import and such extent, at a time when the station was in the throes of an identity crisis brought on by the advent of television, and when its output of music of all genres was to be challenged under the directorship of Tibor Paul.

Since Ó Riada wrote incidental music for the BBC's transmission of Thomas Kinsella's version of *The Táin*, it is significant that Kinsella should have commemorated Ó Riada in his poem 'A Selected Life', and even more so that Kinsella's brother, John, should have produced a choral/symphonic setting of the poem which was premièred by RTÉ in 1975. Despite Gerard Victory's view of the significance of Ó Riada to RTÉ, it was not, however, until 1987 that a major retrospective of his work was presented on RTÉ Television, with three programmes featuring his film music, with the RTÉCO conducted by Elmer Bernstein; his traditional music, with original members of Ceoltóirí Chualann and Cór Cuil Aodha; and the RTÉSO in 'Nomos 2', 'Nomos 4' (with John O'Conor) and the 'Olynthiac Overture'.

COMPOSITIONAL STYLES

Although the series 'Composers at Work' as a whole had little continuing impact, Larchet's phrase 'the great composer for whom we are all/still waiting' has continued to resonate within the acoustic of Irish music-making in the almost half-century since it was spoken. Subliminally it suggested to many participants and spectators in the 1960s and 70s that Irish music had a destiny which would be fulfilled when a 'Sibelius' or a 'Dvořák' or a 'Bartók' would emerge, capable of reconciling 'national ideas and ideals' with the techniques of classical composition. (In 1974, sending to Charles Acton a copy of *Irish Folk Music Studies* which contained his essay which proposed a notation system for *sean-nós* singing, Bodley wrote 'all I have to do now is use this to write the "great Irish music" that everybody keeps talking about, and I will have filled another gap in Irish life!!!').[70] Yet behind this aspiration lies Frederick May's truer identification of the obstacle: 'we have a great tradition of folk-song, but no tradition at all of composition'. The lack of any continuity from Philip Cogan and the Roseingraves or from the harpers in the eighteenth century, the huge lacuna of music in the nineteenth, the Anglicisation of Stanford and the internationalisation of Harty, meant that whatever composition might come from people of Irish descent was almost certainly achieved outside Ireland and

70 Bodley to Acton, 21 June 1974 (Acton Archive).

in milieux that were largely anathema to the purists of the indigenous tradition. The most celebrated occasion of this torsion between the two traditions was G.B. Shaw's condemnation of Stanford's 'Irish' symphony as 'a record of fearful conflict between the aboriginal Celt and the Professor'[71] – a meeting of native and academe of which we have seen Ó Gallchobhair so dismissive.

Barra Ó Séaghda has suggested that 'in the absence of a nourishing tradition, those who wish to create have to generate their own musical worlds', and quotes Gerald Barry to the effect that 'coming from nowhere' gave him an advantage over fellow-composers in Britain: 'free of expectations, he was free to follow his own direction without impediment',[72] or, as Joseph Ryan has put it, 'caught between two antipodal contours which effectively deprived him of a tradition, the Irish composer was forced to create outside of any supporting context'.[73]

Two parallel questions therefore relate to the practice of composition. If the relationship of music to literature (for which 'rhetoric' might be a more appropriate term) has inhibited the creation of a body of 'art-music', this would accord with May's observation of the complete absence of a tradition of composition. Yet it has also been vigorously argued that there has been a significant corpus of work which – with the obvious exception of song-writing – is separate from anything written within the literary ambit. The trove of the RTÉ Sound Archive is living evidence of this (see Appendix).

Thus, as far as the relationship of Irish composers with RTÉ is concerned, the works written for, or commissioned by, the RTÉ Singers between 1958 and 1983 belong, predictably, to the first category: original works or arrangements of Irish folk-songs which are text-based and which were intended principally as a foundational indigenous repertoire to complement the wide range of music for chamber choir from the mediaeval and Renaissance periods to the contemporary, which the Singers developed mainly under the creative direction of Hans Waldemar Rosen. In addition, we should count the equally extensive body of arrangements by Friel, Potter, Ó Riada, and Ó Gallchobhair, which fuelled the output of the RÉLO at least up to 1961–2, and thereby provided a reasonably generous income to several composers.

To take further Boydell's and Potter's points about the ease of obtaining a first performance, one might say that, with a relatively small number of composers, most of whom relied on some source other than composition for their livelihood, the rarity of large- or even small-scale orchestral works (other than arrangements commissioned for the RÉLO) meant that Radio Éireann was almost bound to accept submissions, provided that they were, in Boydell's words, 'reasonably competent'.

71 *The World*, 10 May 1893. **72** B. Ó Séaghda, 'Harping on'. **73** J. Ryan, 'Nationalism and music' p. 127.

In addition to the fact that composers have felt constrained to write for smaller forces, they have also been affected (quite apart from the question of adherence or non-adherence to indigenous material or themes) by the lack of a 'school' of composition. The concomitant fact that individual composers have adopted whatever style has seemed most appropriate, has resulted in a plethora of persuasions as far as the 'isms' are concerned. Although Larchet taught most of the composers working in Ireland in the mid- to late twentieth century, by his own definition his class could hardly be said to have established a 'school of Irish composition', since he himself was not a 'great' composer in the same sense as Stanford and Vaughan Williams who, at the RCM, had taught the majority of English composers and thereby founded a 'school'.

Without a stable base which would ground them technically and aesthetically in an understanding of where Irish music might be going, budding composers were left to their own devices to find their stylistic direction and, perhaps more importantly, their sense of artistic identity. Thus, Axel Klein has identified 'impressionism' in the work of Bax, Herbert Hughes, Trimble, Coghill, Ina Boyle and Norman Hay; 'romanticism' in the pursuit of the folkloric in Stanford, Harty, Larchet, May, Fleischmann, Moeran and Maconchy; nineteenth-century 'conservatism' in Ó Gallchobhair, Friel, T.C. Kelly and McNulty; a subconscious or subliminal 'traditionalism' in May, Fleischmann, Boydell, Buckley and Bodley; 'serialism' in Potter, Ó Riada, Bodley, Victory, James Wilson, Kinsella, de Bromhead and Sweeney; and 'post-neo-classicism' in Bodley, Kinsella, Jane O'Leary, Philip Martin and John Gibson.[74]

The generic groupings of titles for Irish-oriented works such as 'Rhapsody', or those incorporating place-names, or those 'Suite(s) of Irish Airs/Irish Suite(s)' receive a late typification in RTÉ's 1996 commercial recording by members of the RTÉCO[75] under Proinnsías Ó Duinn. The choice of Victory's 'Three Irish Pictures', Potter's 'Rhapsody Under a High Sky', Larchet's 'By the Waters of Moyle', Duff's 'Echoes of Georgian Dublin', Ó Riada's 'Banks of Sullane' and Pádraig O'Connor's 'Introspect' – employing the overall title of 'Romantic Ireland'[76] – may have been dictated by market forces, but it makes a corporate statement about the readiness of RTÉ to present its music-making – regardless of the innate musical quality of the individual works – in such a format.

'COMPOSERS IN CONVERSATION' – 1988

In 1988, Dermot Rattigan interviewed sixteen composers for the series 'Composers in Conversation' on RTÉ Radio 1. Of the seventeen who had taken

74 Klein, 'Roots and directions in twentieth-century Irish art-music', pp. 172–81. **75** Billed as 'RTÉ Sinfonietta'. **76** Marco Polo 8.223804.

part thirty years previously in 'Composers at Work', ten had died, and only four – Bodley, Boydell, Fleischmann and Victory – were included in Rattigan's series; the remaining three (Deale, Nelson and Groocock) were excluded because the participants in the series were all members of Aosdána – the self-elected parliament of artists established under the aegis of the Arts Council in 1982 – and were considered, as a peer group, to be nationally recognised and to have international status.[77]

It is an immediately noticeable feature of 'Composers in Conversation' that Rattigan did not deem it necessary to question his subjects on the issue of Irishness. Where, in 1958, the composers had, almost all, specifically responded to their brief by making explicit reference to the 'problems' confronting an Irish composer, in 1988 that option was not available to them, and as a result the 'snapshot' of composition from that period is free of any immediate anxiety concerning influence or responsibility: when an individual chose to speak about Irishness, either in his background or in his music,[78] the statement came from a context apparently untroubled by questions of national identity or its modes of expression – this, in a period when in other arenas and other art forms, the nature and formation of Irish identity were being hotly debated. The contrast with the 'viewpoints' of Irish composers thirty years earlier could not be more pointed: in the Ireland of 1958 anxieties about Irishness were of a different order; in the Ireland of 1988, while several composers were anxious to discuss what Ireland, or Irish influences, meant to their music, the discussion was almost subliminal and the issue of how to treat a traditional tune was no longer on the agenda.

In 1988 Bodley, following the largely autobiographical format of 'Composers in Conversation', told Rattigan that, like many other listeners in the late 1940s and the 1950s, he was introduced to twelve-note music by visiting conductors at the RÉSO concerts such as the Schönberg specialist Winfried Zillig (above, p. 138). Bodley's early work, such as 'Music for Strings' (1952) – an assured work for a nineteen-year-old which was written for the Dublin Orchestral Players and soon recorded by the RÉSO under Horvat – indicated, in the composer's words, 'influences from Irish music but nothing very overt … a "wrong-note" treatment applied to Irish music'.[79] Earlier, he

---

77 Author's conversation with Dermot Rattigan, 3 September 2003. In addition to those mentioned above, the interviewees were: Gerald Barry, Walter Beckett, John Buckley, Frank Corcoran, Raymond Deane, Jerome de Bromhead, Roger Doyle, John Kinsella, Philip Martin, Jane O'Leary, Eric Sweeney and James Wilson. **78** The only female composer, Jane O'Leary, is American by birth and education. **79** S. Bodley, interview with Dermot Rattigan, 'Composers in Conversation', 1988, RTÉ Sound Archive tape A4346. 'Music for Strings' was recorded on the Decca label in an album entitled 'New Music from Old Erin'.

had referred to the fact that his approach in 'Music for Strings' had been 'not so much the ornamentation ... which is so much bound up with the actual method of performance, but with the basic line. It's a technical problem ... [while in his Chamber Symphony] I was trying to expand the Irish idiom by the use of notes foreign to the modes'.[80]

Bodley then engaged in protracted study in Germany, where he pursued 'the question of approach to larger forms', which we may interpret as an indication that he wanted to explore a movement away from the 'smaller' forms that constitute the Irish musical heritage. Some of his time was spent at Darmstadt where, in the 1960s, avant-garde figures such as Luigi Nono, Bruno Maderna, Karl-Heinz Stockhausen and Pierre Boulez lectured and conferred: Bodley, in the words of Michael Dervan, 'became the first Irish composer with an unalloyed allegiance to serial techniques'.[81] Nevertheless, he 'gradually developed an interest in traditional music',[82] and subsequently introduced to these techniques an Irishness to be found in 'A Small White Cloud Drifts Over Ireland' which was premièred by the RTÉSO under Proinnsías Ó Duinn at the 1976 Festival of Twentieth-Century Music, and repeated under Pierre-Michel le Conte the following year. Bodley's note on the piece refers to an approach to 'Irish traditional music from the viewpoint of irregular musical structure, derived from my experiences in avant-garde music ... In all this is a musical picture of the ethos of Ireland formed at a viewpoint from which a new synthesis can be discerned'.[83] Bodley stressed that this interest in Irish music is evident in his early and later work, but not in that of his middle years. His Chamber Symphony of 1964, for example, which he recorded with the RÉSO, shows him 'moving away from tonal to twelve-note music', and in 'Configurations' (1967) and 'Meditations on Lines from Patrick Kavanagh' (1971) serial technique is predominant. Bodley was conscious at this time of 'a very dangerous and very forbidding psychological split ... between the conscious and the unconscious mind ... Total serialism is an attempt to compose music entirely with the conscious mind ruling out the unconscious whose filtering-through was with us in all traditional music.'[84]

In 2002, in the context of a presentation by Seóirse Bodley in the 'Composer's Choice' series at the NCH, Michael Dervan wrote:

> If Seán Ó Riada had lived an average lifespan, he would be in his early seventies now. It's probably idle to speculate what Ó Riada might or might not have done on the classical side of his output during the three

---

80 C. Acton, 'Interview with Seóirse Bodley'. 81 *Irish Times*, 25 March 2002. 82 S. Bodley, 'Conversation' 1988, loc. cit. 83 *Counterpoint* (January 1976). 84 C. Acton, 'Interview with Seóirse Bodley'.

decades since he died in 1971. It's interesting, however, to see wh.
the other major Irish composers born in the 1930s explored in the yea.
since Ó Riada's passing. Thirty years ago or so, both John Kinsella (born
1932) and Seóirse Bodley (born 1933) wrote pieces which were aligned
with the output of the European avant-garde. The whole notion of the
avant-garde as it prevailed in musical circles in the 1950s and 1960s has
since disintegrated, and both Bodley and Kinsella have come to write
music in a manner that, I suspect, neither of them would have predicted
at a time when Ó Riada was alive. It was Bodley who took the most
unexpected turn, taking his European modernism into a head-on
encounter with the sound-world of traditional Irish music.[85]

Reviewing the première of 'A Small White Cloud', Charles Acton had written that Bodley

> comes back from his *avant garde* and Oriental experiences to consider
> Irish traditional music from [Bodley's words] the 'viewpoint of irregu-
> lar musical structure' … I felt that here may be a synthesis that I have
> been desiring for 30 years, the thing that Ó Riada ought to have reached
> from 'Hercules' and the Ceoltóirí, but did not; the creation of an Irish
> music that was far from those foreign-sounding and derivative Irish
> rhapsodies of decades ago … I suspect that it may turn out to be a pio-
> neering exploration rather than the full discovery, but if so it should lead
> Dr Bodley in a very significant direction.[86]

The significance of the work is underlined by musicologist Axel Klein, who
observes that

> In a long history of exchanges between traditionally inherited and
> imported composed music in Ireland, this extended period in the work
> of Bodley represents the only instance of a cultural encounter of the two
> musical traditions in which both remained uncompromisingly intact.[87]

In the light of this judgement, Bodley's works from those years, which also
include 'Never to Have Lived is Best' (1965), his first string quartet (1968),
'The Narrow Road to the Deep North' (1972) and 'CeathrIunti Mhaire ni
Óghain' (1973), merit closer attention, since it is possible that in them the long-
debated capacity to make those 'exchanges' resulted in an 'encounter' of importance to the history of music-making in Ireland.[88]

---

85 *Irish Times*, 25 March 2002. **86** *Irish Times*, 6 January 1976. **87** Klein, 'Roots and directions',
op. cit., p. 179. **88** The composer's programme note for 'The Narrow Road to the Deep North'

However, not every commentator has been so generous: fellow-composer Raymond Deane has said that Bodley's 'attempts to wed traditional Irish music to an "avant-garde" idiom can only lead to a kind of Bord Fáilte aesthetic ... Such music as Bodley's does a grave disservice to the tradition to which it purports to pay homage'.[89] Such a judgement of course returns us to the initial point of anxiety: whether it is ever possible to 'pay homage' to the indigenous tradition by any means other than those available from within the techniques of that tradition.

In a largely unsympathetic survey of Bodley's music up to 1983, 'Examining the Great Divide', Malcolm Barry exposed the 'tensions' in Bodley's output arising from the competing claims of Irish material and his studies in serialism. He asked whether 'the unsuspecting listener', hearing 'Configurations' and 'The Narrow Road to the Deep North', would realise that they were by the same composer.[90] In Bodley's Chamber Symphony (1964) he noted that 'the language of the work is twelve-note although, retrospectively, traces of inflections from Irish traditional music may be heard'. As Bodley's work continued in the 1960s, Barry saw this feature as a 'clash' between serialism (twelve-note or 'dodecaphonic') and 'his own natural lyricism'. It has been a persistent characteristic of Irish composers speaking of their work that they have referred to their natural inclination towards lyricism as the factor that drew them away from, or made them less tolerant of, the serial formula – a factor that was either explicitly or implicitly attributed to their Irish background.

Bodley's difficulty thus emerged – as it did in the case of Ó Riada – when he attempted a reconciliation of the technical demands and limitations of Irish and European musical genres. As Malcolm Barry opined in 1983:

> Bodley seems to be trying to obliterate the familiar associations of each type of musical material. Both Irish traditional music and 'avant-gardism' have preconceptions built into them ... and Bodley's deliberate attempts to break these down, while laudable in this age of eclecticism, remain oddly unsatisfactory. The material remains ultimately intractable.[91]

In the commissioned work to commemorate Patrick Pearse, 'I Have Loved the Lands of Ireland' (his second symphony), Bodley, in Barry's opinion, demonstrated that 'the idea of lands, of space, whether real or psychological,

---

states that it 'is not only a description of a place or events – it also represents a psychological journey through a territory of the mind. The wanderer in this land is suggested by the newly-composed melody in the Irish style. The tune is original but composed "to an echo" from "A Spailpin, a Ruin" ... Constructional principles of Irish music were applied to an "atonal" basis for some of the material'. **89** R. Deane, *Soundpost* 13 (April/May 1983) and 14 (June/July 1983). **90** *Soundpost* 16 (October–November 1983). **91** Ibid.

is clearly vital'; this concurs with what was suggested in chapter 1, that *land* as a *persona* can be both a concrete and an abstract presence in Irish composition: in his original programme note Bodley stated that 'I have considered the "lands" of the title in the sense of territories of the Irish mind and spirit ... Actual expressions of Irish reality ... Myth ... in the form of Aislingí (visions) or pieces expressing an Irish vision of some psychological reality ... Irish experience – Exile ... Love.'[92] Although Bodley has said more recently that 'no influence was ever exerted on me to write in an Irish style', he has also acknowledged that in his second symphony 'the idea was to go back to the sources of Pearse's inspiration in Irish myth'.[93] It is unclear, in saying that 'no influence' was exerted on him, whether Bodley meant a specific attempt on anyone's part to influence the course of a particular composition, or a more general sense of 'influence' as a presence within the Irish tradition.[94] But his distinct reference to the sources of myth makes it clear that a consciousness of such myth – even in the context of the specific commission to commemorate Pearse – informed Bodley's compositional sensibility.[95]

Previewing this second symphony, Charles Acton referred to the fact that Bodley 'has started forging a new personal language. This is a fusion of the languages of traditional music and all that he has assimilated in the international field. In "The Narrow Road" ... there was little or no fusion – the elements were as oil and water unemulsified.'[96] Having heard the composer play through the symphony on the piano, Acton was convinced that 'we have here a major advance in Irish symphony' which (quoting Bodley) 'sets out to delineate the essence and psychological history of the Irish people ... evoking three aspects of Ireland – reality, experience and myth'.

Commenting on this prescriptive intention, Acton said: 'The composer's ambition would have a breathtaking arrogance were it not that the creative artist has a duty (if he is willing to assume it) to express the visions of his people.' (Acton's natural chauvinism – the inclination to hyperbolise the significance of any Irish achievement that he thought worthy of promotion – is evi-

---

92 *Counterpoint* (December 1980–January 1981). **93** Quoted by Patrick Zuk in 'Music and nationalism' (2003). **94** He was responding to a query by Patrick Zuk as to whether or not he 'experienced constraints to compose "Irishly"': ibid. **95** In reply to a question in the Dáil, Charles Haughey (Taoiseach) stated that, in respect of the Pearse commemoration, 'The Arts Council ... were invited to take part with Dr Gerard Victory, Director of Music of RTE, with Professor Anthony Hughes, UCD, and Miss Dinah Mulloy [*sic*] of the Arts Council in advising on a composer for a major orchestral work, for the smaller competitions, for example, compositions for a brass and reed band, for the New Irish Chamber Orchestra and for a suitable work for the Irish Ballet Company. So far as the major orchestral work is concerned I do not know whether it is the practice or whether it is feasible to commission a number of people to submit contributions but in this case the four people whom I regard as being well qualified for the purpose suggested that Mr Seoirse Bodley be commissioned to write an orchestral work': DD. 313, 3 April 1979, cols. 966–7. **96** *Irish Times*, 9 January 1981.

dent here, as is his insistence, which we have already seen in his interviews with Seán Ó Riada, that an artist has a 'duty' to his country.)

However, having heard the work's première by the RTÉSO under Colman Pearce, Acton was troubled by influences on the work and by its lack of development. 'At the time of any new work audible ancestry poses a problem … I could hear some sound of Mahler's and even what Ó Riada disseminated … [In the first two movements] the material did not develop, seemed rather a continuum of visual images.'[97] Whether or not this could be termed, as Malcolm Barry calls it, an 'extra-musical impulse' is debatable, but it makes clear that, in moving away from serialism in what Bodley calls (in respect of his second symphony) 'a post-modern Irish symphony', the composer is once again encountering symbols which demand his attention through some form of recognition or representation in his writing.

Michael Dervan's description of Bodley as 'the most chameleon-like of Irish composers'[98] sums up *in parvo* the changing relationship of a composer with the two strands which have both energised and enervated the works of those who encountered, espoused and in many cases rejected or amended the demands of, on one side, serialism in favour of, or in deference to, Irish material or themes on another. Bodley himself has both borne out the aspiration he expressed in 1958 – to write 'in the contemporary idiom without regard for passing fashions' – and typified the dilemma identified by Wordsworth: 'every great and original writer … must himself create the taste by which he is to be relished'.[99] For the Irish composer, without tradition, without technical foundations, writing *ex nihilo* for an uncertain audience, and never quite sure what expectations might be harboured by his or her most obvious patron – RTÉ – the challenge to initiate standards of both style and taste was, in most cases, almost insuperable.

Of the three other composers who featured in both the 1958 and 1988 series, Boydell merely reiterated what he had held as a lifelong *credo*: 'I would be the last person to impose my views on other people.' He remained 'suspicious of gimmicks which are in any way contrived in order to trick an audience into thinking "this is very peculiar and fascinating and very modern".'[1]

Elsewhere, however, Boydell stated, 'I would like to be remembered as an Irish composer first, rather than any of the other achievements that I might have'.[2] Thus, a public figure who, like his counterpart in Cork, Aloys

97 *Irish Times*, 10 January 1981. **98** *Irish Times*, 25 March 2002. **99** Quoted in E. de Selincourt (ed.), *Letters of William and Dorothy Wordsworth* (Oxford: Clarendon Press, 1969), vol. 2. Eimear Ó Broin (interview with the author, 8 February 2004) considered that Bodley's 'Movement for Orchestra' (1956), is 'a short masterpiece, beautifully wrought, which accepts the manner and techniques of Hindemith'. **1** RTÉ Sound Archives tape no. AA4342. Boydell's works featured in the programme were: Five Joyce Songs (1946), his first string quartet (1949), and 'Mouth Music' (1974). **2** C. Acton, 'Interview with Brian Boydell' (1970) 97–111.

Fleischmann, was responsible for transforming the third-level teaching of music, and who eschewed any deliberate Irishness in his compositions, wanted to be recalled as an 'Irish composer'. Moreover, Boydell went on say that he was very gratified at receiving the commission from RTÉ to write a work ('A Terrible Beauty is Born') commemorating the 1916 Rising: it was

> a particular challenge … I was so much excited by the fact that I was offered the commission at all, being Protestant Anglo-Irish and a pacifist to boot … [The challenge was] to try and get over a point of view, though this is quite extra-musical if you like. That is a point of view that what we should be doing in the 50th anniversary of 1916 is not waving flags about the past but thinking about what we should do for our country in the future.

A further challenge was that of writing for an occasion 'which would appeal on that particular occasion without playing down … I think it was honestly written but in an idiom which I feel could communicate with the ordinary person on that particular occasion'.

In the case of Fleischmann, Dermot Rattigan chose to introduce the recording of the composer's 'Viewpoint' from 1958, and Fleischmann affirmed that he 'felt the same way' thirty years later:

> There is far more being produced today than there was then. There is still a great deal of performances of works by Irish composers, possibly not of the same proportion. When there were far fewer of us thirty years ago, everybody was well represented on the air. Nowadays there are so many composers there probably isn't room for them.[3]

Fleischmann also stated quite clearly that 'In my early days the strongest influences were those of Irish folk song and dance, Irish language and literature and the Irish scene generally'.[4] Four years later, in a broadcast obituary tribute to Fleischmann (23 July 1992), Gerard Victory spoke of Fleischmann's work as others have of Bodley's:

> His work perhaps uniquely combined both an intense and recognisable Irishness and a totally cosmopolitan musical mind … He brought [his

---

3 A. Fleischmann, 'Composers in Conversation', 1988, RTÉ Sound Archive tape A4340; the works performed were: three extracts from 'Sinfonia Votiva' (1977); the song cycle 'The Fountain of Magic' (1946); the 'Four Masters' overture (1948); the choral dance suite 'The Planting Stick' (1957) and 'Cornucopia' (1970) for horn, played by the RTÉSO with Victor Malíř, the composer conducting. 4 Ibid.

background in Irish music] into many of his own works, but never in the form of a routine arrangement or a folksy style. In so many works it remained as a kind of foundation to his own imaginative voice, which transformed it into something very new and yet faithful to the spirit of its origins.[5]

Having greater faith – or perhaps hope – than Frederick May, Fleischmann had at least believed that, in addition to the treasure-house of folk material, 'we have ... a half developed art-music which is for the most part alien' and that between the two there might be 'a Gaelic art-music which will embody all the technique that contemporary music can boast ... and be rooted in the folk-music spirit'.[6] But as Philip Graydon has argued, the two styles and traditions were largely kept apart in Fleischmann's own output,[7] although Séamus de Barra and Graydon himself have, respectively, put forward the 'Trí hAmhráin' and the Piano Suite as works that successfully achieved Fleischmann's aims.[8] Graydon has drawn attention to an apparent dichotomy between Fleischmann's narrow pursuit of 'the hidden Ireland' (and even, capitalised, to give increased significance, 'the Hidden Ireland') and his 'avowed pluralist approach to music'.[9]

De Barra also draws attention to Fleischmann's increasing sense of the conservatism of his output, in an era when 'nationalism itself was made to seem questionable, and indeed for Irish intellectuals any overt expression of nationalist sentiment became something of an embarrassment'.[10] If, as de Barra states, 'the whole of Fleischmann's compositional imagination ... was bound up with the idea of cultural nationalism', and to accompany Bax on his journey of discovery of 'the hidden Ireland', then, in de Barra's words, 'such a project, so acceptable earlier, could only seem faintly ludicrous in the Ireland of the 1970s'.

Why then did RTÉ continue not only to accept work which Fleischmann admitted to being 'conservative' (such as the 1963 'Song of the Provinces')[11] but also to commission such work – for example the 'Ómós don Phiarsach' [Homage to Pearse, commissioned for the Pearse centenary]? Was it considered that 'occasional' pieces, because they were referential, were bound to be backward-looking and therefore might be justifiably 'backward' in style, even if they commemorated a revolutionary such as Pearse? If so, it indicates an ambivalent policy on the part of RTÉ, on one hand wishing to perform and broadcast retrospective discourses on the nature of Irish history and, on another, expecting a younger

5 In R. Fleischmann (ed.) op. cit., p. 293. 6 Fleischmann, 'The outlook of music in Ireland', p. 124. 7 In R. Fleischmann (ed.) op. cit., pp. 303–4. 8 de Barra, 'The music of Aloys Fleischmann', p. 328; Graydon, 'Modernism in Ireland' (2003), p. 69. 9 Graydon, 'Modernism in Ireland', ibid. 10 'The music of Aloys Fleischmann', p. 339. 11 In a letter to Gerard Victory, quoted by de Barra, ibid. For 'conservative' one might, in the circumstances, read 'provincial'.

generation to be more introspective, concerned not so much with the past, icons and affects, as with their own musical vocabularies and mindsets.

Gerard Victory, who in 1958 was yet to join the Music Department, spoke to Dermot Rattigan in 1988 from the position of the recently retired Director of Music, and most of his contribution as a professional administrator was concerned with his role as deputy to Tibor Paul. Speaking as a composer, he acknowledged his eclecticism, pointing to his early experience of variety theatre in Dublin and its 'magical world' as a model for the entertaining nature of much of his music. Eclecticism – which in his own work reached its acme in 'Ultima Rerum' (1981) – was also 'a desire not to be labelled in any one direction and to some extent to try to pull a number of things together – to draw ideas from a wide range of things – not to specialise, or to have "pan-Irish" music".[12] Victory believed that eclecticism was 'an Irish characteristic common to all of us'.

In the 1950s, Victory reflected, Irish composers were writing 'in the mould of a neo-classicism, a sentimental pastoral style as far as serious music was concerned', and in his own case 'I had to compromise on what would conceivably be accepted'. Trying to 'break through it', from 1960 onwards

> I went into a very atonal period … for about six or seven years most of the works were either very strictly serial or atonal with a modified serial structure. From the seventies on, I moved into a returned tonal music, but with the tonalities related not by logical sonata relationships but by a type of serial relationship … so that the hierarchical classical structure was to some extent replaced by a more modern concept of the equality of pitches which I think is something germane to the modern ear.[13]

In his 'Prelude and Toccata' for piano (1962), premièred by Veronica McSwiney and subsequently recorded by Charles Lynch, he tried to demonstrate that he 'became more aware of the need to try to shake off for a time a too easy style of writing which smacked of light music, smacked of traditional elements, perhaps, that were not too exciting to a lot of people, a bit "old hat"'. Mentioning the visit of Stravinsky the following year during the RTÉ festival, Victory recalled 'There was also in the air the first onrush of modernism in Ireland – a very dramatic period, a lot of optimism … a lot of international connections, a lot of important overseas musical people – not only the then Director of Music [Tibor Paul] but a lot of others. [In] this whole climate I think I was drawn towards a more Schönbergian language which I had studied'.[14]

---

12 G. Victory, 'Composers in Conversation' 1988, RTÉ Sound Archive tape A4343; his chosen works for inclusion were: 'The Enchanted Garden' (1950); 'Prelude and Toccata' for piano (1962); and excerpts from 'Ultima Rerum' (1981). **13** Ibid. **14** Ibid.

If it can be argued that *some* composers working in Ireland from the 1920s were working in a vacuum – that is, without overt reference to, or connection with, folk music – then there is a narrative which has only been partly explored by musicology to date.[15] With extremely few exceptions, however, Irish composition in the later twentieth century continued to display what Harry White has called 'the divided imagination', but not necessarily for the reasons that White might put forward. But with the notable exceptions of Gerald Barry and Raymond Deane, most composers working in Ireland have consciously worked in both the 'indigenous' and the 'cosmopolitan' traditions, commuting between them but seldom attempting the type of fusion rejected by Ó Riada but still sought by Bodley.

Naturally 'occasional' music – commissioned and written for a specific event, such as Boydell's 'Jubilee Music' (1976, for the 50th anniversary of RTÉ), the Pearse centenary or the State Opening of the NCH (as in the case of Bodley's second and third symphonies respectively), or Fleischmann's 'Ómós don Phiarsach' – will reflect the context of that occasion and will almost inevitably incorporate or acknowledge 'extra-musical impulses'. (Fleischmann's 'Four Masters' overture and 'Clare's Dragoons' from the 1940s would be comparable works in this vein.) But, in addition, many works which have no specific point of historical reference have been inspired by events, characters, ideas or themes in Irish history, the Irish landscape or the Irish imagination and thus are referential to those 'extra-musical impulses' to some degree.

It may surprise those who consider Frank Corcoran – a student of Boris Blacher – to be an unapologetic and resolute avant-gardist that in 1988 in 'Composers in Conversation' he referred to the landscape of his childhood in Tipperary as inherent in his musical imagination: 'I'm not a Séamus Heaney of music in any sense, but I have a deep longing for the soil, for the roots – the sounds and the soundscape of animals, of nature, went very deep … Very potent – not to be underestimated'. He spoke of 'a yen for the rhythm of country life' and said that 'the skirl of the [uilleann] pipes went very deep … In my music I recognise that – the microtone in those bagpipe yelps.' In addition, the nineteenth-century ballads to be heard at 'come-all-ye's' had a 'power of expression with the ABBA structure of a Schubert lied' which influenced his musical evolution. Corcoran believes that 'a lot of composition is exorcism – getting it up from the tap-roots'.[16] Corcoran's own pursuit of roots that are psychological as much as personal and local can be traced in his 'Mad Sweeney' with textual inspiration from *Sweeney Astray*, the version of 'Buile Suibhne' by Séamus Heaney.

15 Cox and Klein (eds.), *Irish musical studies 7: Irish music in the twentieth century* includes articles on electroacoustic music, analysis of works by May, Boydell, Fleischmann, Bodley, Ian Wilson and Corcoran, and an extensive bibliography; Benjamin Dwyer (*Journal of Music in Ireland* 3/6, September–October 2003) points out that the essays are far from comprehensive and that the editors might have 'include[d] in the title the subheading "Part 1"'. 16 F. Corcoran, 'Composers in

The idea that 'the way forward is the way back to deepest human experience' is explored in an essay by John Page on Corcoran's second symphony: 'what does it mean for a composer of the late twentieth century to write a work entitled "Symphony" … what, if anything, does it mean to be an Irish composer writing such a work?'[17] The answers to such questions are inextricably connected with the lack of a symphonic tradition in Ireland (or the lack of an Irish symphonic tradition) and as such are at least as problematic and complex as the relationship of 'symphonic' writing to other genres. Page points out that Victory, Bodley, Kinsella and Corcoran who had, respectively, completed four, five, eight and four symphonies by 2000 (most of which had been performed by the RTÉSO/NSO), had pursued that route, whereas Raymond Deane and Kevin O'Connell regarded the term as 'an archaic and somewhat anachronistic construct that remains the symbol of a tradition that has no place in their musical imaginations and creative processes', and Gerald Barry's music is 'a radical distancing from the traditional symphonic ideal'. Given that, with the exceptions of May, Fleischmann and Boydell, Irish composition had little contact with, or exposure to, contemporary European composition until after the second world war, the wider debate as to the relevance of the 'post-war symphony' becomes even more difficult to conduct in Ireland, and the availability to RTÉ of the work of the leading composers of the middle and younger generations for public performance (as distinct from broadcast) becomes more problematic, and brings Irish composers into areas of discussion common to practitioners in other art forms, such as the role and status of an artist in a post-colonial society.

Page identifies Bodley's second and third symphonies and Kinsella's fourth ('Four Provinces') and fifth ('The 1916 Poets') as examples of 'the engagement of nationalist thought through symphonic form … [which] is an aspect of the nineteenth-century symphonic tradition that seems to reinvent itself in the imaginations of certain Irish symphonists throughout the twentieth century'. In the case of Corcoran, Page finds an example of a composer who has accepted that 'the idea of a generic category entitled post-war "Irish" symphony is … an impossible one' but relies 'upon the traditional abstract definitions whilst remaining open to the possibility of using Irish material for inspiration'.[18] In Corcoran's second symphony (1981) – first performed by the NSO in 1998 and recorded for the Marco Polo label in 1999 – Page detects the composer's 'vital' need to manifest 'a pre-historical Irish psyche', and refers to the work as 'Corcoran's attempt to deal with the past … the undeterred obsession with

Conversation' 1988, RTÉ Sound Archive tape A4347; Corcoran's similar remarks on landscape and history in 1995 are quoted above, p. 31. Corcoran's choice of works in 'Composers in Conversation' were: 'Medieval Irish Epigrams' (1973), Piano Trio (1978), 'Balthazar's Dream' (1980) and 'Symphonies of Symphonies of Wind Instruments' (1981). **17** J. Page, 'A post-war symphony: Frank Corcoran's Symphony no. 2' (2003), pp. 134–49. **18** Ibid., pp. 138–9.

time and our past'. Elsewhere, Corcoran has addressed the question 'what's Irish music?' with another question: 'what was the music of Knowth, what was going on in neolithic Ireland, what was the music of the Ceide Fields? And then later, medieval, late-medieval, polyphonic Irish music, what was the music that Hugh O'Neill listened to in Dungannon? ... Very early on, people who made music ... were trying to get beyond the grave, a bit like building the dolmen, building a dolmen in sound. I'm still at that. The very act of making music is a leap into the tomb, to try and get beyond.'[19]

That Corcoran can say 'it's almost a pity that we haven't had our Auschwitz experience' and that 'we're seeing ... the twilight of art music'[20] has a Wagnerian resonance that also suggests Adorno's much quoted dictum that after Auschwitz there can be no excuse for poetry. But at the time of the 150th anniversary of the 'great' Irish Famine (1845–9) attention was focussed dramatically on the enduring psychic wound that that catastrophe had caused, not least perhaps because of the way it arrested social and cultural development in Ireland, and may have inhibited the admission of classical music into a wider national consciousness. When we see this in the wider context of Corcoran's statement that 'It's been only short, 100 or 150 years, the institution of concerts, of orchestras, of ensembles and of a whole way of approach to a certain kind of music ... what we recognise as music which is argument, which needs plenty of retention faculty in the listener, which uses musical logic, musical concentration ... the end is coming very soon'[21] – we encounter a problem that concerns the custodians of the NSO (as of any other ensemble of its kind) in that they are the facilitators of a changing musical landscape and environment. This will be considered in chapter 7, particularly since it is becoming increasingly evident that Irish composers can present their work in forums other than RTÉ and can in fact obtain commissions from outside Ireland – including Corcoran himself, Gerald Barry, John Buckley, Eric Sweeney and Raymond Deane.

As Corcoran told Dermot Rattigan for RTÉ in 1988, he has learned that 'any large dogma about composition is dangerous' and that the dogmatism of the serial composers has had its day. 'I'm very thankful that now, after a lot of experimentation, a lot of Cage-like experiences, we've come out the other side, we have a lot behind us, and now a lot of the old sacred cows are dead, a lot of those bitter battles in theory, in ideology, are thankfully past and I think now is time to get on with the job which as always is a difficult one, of making new forms, of making strong new music, a composer finding a style and a voice using this immense mound of possibilities from the past'.

There is detectable here a suggestion that, having dispensed with the question of *form* in music, the distinction between Irish and non-Irish musical tra-

19 Michael Dervan, 'A very worried man', *Irish Times*, 22 September 1995. 20 Ibid. 21 Ibid.

ditions is no longer relevant, since tradition itself is open to question. In that case, it can only be observed that it was particularly unfortunate for the evolution of composition in Ireland that it coincided with the advent of serialism and modernism.

The fact that RTÉ's near-monopoly in music meant that, willingly or not, it carried a concomitant *responsibility* for music, has been especially acute in the case of composition. The remit of the Arts Council (established 1951–2) had at its back de Valera's aspiration 'to restore [the] primacy … once held by things of the spirit … to give our people an abiding interest in the intellectual life and to stimulate them to aspire to win for our nation a worthy place in the realm of culture',[22] but he had conceived it as being principally concerned with the visual arts, music being a matter for RÉ and the Department of Education.[23] De Valera's apparent wish to exclude music from the Arts Council's functions and to corral it elsewhere may have been due to a belief that music, as distinct from broadcast music, did not require support from the Arts Council but – leaving aside the matter of music education – it served to reinforce the view of R(T)É as the sole institutional provider and supporter of music activity in the public sector. The point made in the Dáil at that time by Maurice Dockrell (Fine Gael, Dublin South-Central) underlines this: that to include musical experts among the members of the Arts Council would facilitate the encouragement of musicians who would thus find it easier to 'feed' the RÉ orchestras.[24]

It also gives us cause for concern in considering RTÉ's past and present relationship with composers, insofar as the connection of Irish composers with Irish cultural history and practice and cultural life in general has been, arguably, restricted. In the sense, therefore, that in the 1950s and 60s, and to a lesser extent subsequently, a composer's focus or horizon was limited to the doorway of R(T)É, for the acceptance and performance of orchestral or choral works, R(T)É has had a somewhat stifling relationship with that composer. The fact that, as a member of the EBU and other international bodies, RTÉ has been the organisation almost exclusively responsible for nominating Irish works to the International Rostrum of Composers (the largest and most prestigious annual forum for new work, since 1954),[25] to the EBU 'Let Us Know the Names' exchange scheme, the Prix Italia, or the Queen Elisabeth of the Belgians Competition,[26] has also meant that RTÉ has been the chief conduit for the reputation of Irish music internationally. R(T)É continued to commission – or accept – 'suites of Irish airs' rather than following Denis

22 Cf. B. Kennedy, op. cit., p. 100. 23 Quoted in ibid., p. 104. 24 DD. 125, 24 April 1951, col. 1323. 25 The Rostrum is organised by the International Music Council under the aegis of UNESCO; Gerard Victory, as RTÉ's Director of Music, was president 1981–84. 26 In 1964 Tibor Paul, as RTÉ's Director of Music, invited A.J. Potter to put forward a work as the Irish representative at the biennial composers' section of this event: Paul to Potter, 14 July 1964 (Potter Archive).

Donoghue's suggestion of commissioning quartets, symphonies and operas, principally because the performance and production opportunities for large-scale works such as operas, in particular, were few and the challenges were more than daunting; secondarily, because concert audiences began, with the phasing out of 'free' or 'invitation' concerts, to indicate resistance to much contemporary music, especially in the serialist idiom.

There is no 'school of Irish composition'; instead, there has been a preoccupation with the 'Irishness' of composition that has been more instructive than it has been productive. The post-1988 direction of Irish composition – increasingly cosmopolitan, increasingly European and alert to the phenomenon of 'world music' – suggests that some at least are able to follow Esposito's direction in 'how to become an Irish composer' and that a *personal* rather than a *communal* awareness of Irishness (as we have seen it expressed by Corcoran) is evident in much of their work. Recent RTÉ commissions such as Deane's oboe concerto and Marian Ingoldsby's 'Overture' (both 1995) and Deane's violin concerto (2003), in addition to Kinsella's series of symphonies, seem to confirm this.

Perhaps the preoccupation of Irish composers – and of their media channels – should focus not on identity but on a sense of purpose. The anxieties evident in 'Composers at Work' in 1958 had largely given way in 1988 to a more comfortable and less stressful attitude to the business of writing. In order to present a schedule balancing all genres and shades of composition, RTÉ, like any public service broadcasting organisation, must reflect the country's symphonic writing, its chamber music, its light music, those works which can expect a long life in the repertoire, and the ephemeral. It must therefore seek to establish a relationship with the writers of these kinds of music, commissioning where necessary or appropriate. It will find few composers capable of writing, or willing to write, operas or large-scale symphonic works, and even if it had an unlimited supply of these, it would encounter a limited interest on the part of both concert-goers and radio audience. It *has* found a large body of writers capable of producing smaller-scale works for both orchestra and chamber groups, and it is increasingly finding composers whose musical interests extend beyond – and perhaps have left behind – the symphonic or orchestral genre.

In such circumstances, RTÉ has a responsibility to consider the gamut of musical tastes, musical expression and musical ambitions present in the world of Irish composition. Just as Irish television drama runs from the austere works of Samuel Beckett to the frivolous or light-hearted, such as *The Irish RM* by Somerville and Ross, and just as it reflects, in its soap operas, a cross-section of urban or rural life (in *Fair City* [1989–] and *Glenroe* [1983–2001]),[27] so too

---

27 RTÉ screened the complete plays of Beckett in 2001; cf. Helena Sheehan, *Irish Television drama: a society and its stories* (1987), and its sequel *The continuing story of Irish television drama* (2004), in

the music broadcast on RTÉ radio and television and played to live audiences by its performing groups will range from a 'difficult' work such as Corcoran's 'Symphonies of Symphonies of Wind Instruments' (1981) or the large-scale requiem by Victory ('Ultima Rerum' [performed 1984]) to serious but more accessible works such as the symphonies of John Kinsella, to the 'easy listening' of Potter's 'Overture to a Kitchen Comedy' (1952). To regard the latter as in any way inferior would be utterly out of place.[28] If Ó Riada was 'dismissive' of his work as an arranger, it was only in the context of his striving for success and meaning in other genres, rather than a disenchantment with the professional business of arranging.

There will naturally always be composers who regard their craft as being an unremitting search for perfection of expression at the highest level (even though that may not necessarily be for the largest forces), just as there will be those who revel in – and excel at – the creation of entertaining 'light' music. The questions an Irish composer should ask him- or her-self, in whatever genre he or she is working, are primarily those of any composer anywhere: does the music he or she produces reflect, or relate to, the society (narrow or wide) in which he or she lives? Does it have its own integrity? Is it authentic, do its rhythms connect with the rhythms of the world beyond the writing room? Does it respect, or reject, tradition? Does it express a new consciousness, exploring new artistic or social horizons?

It is not necessary that any of these questions be answered in the affirmative for the music to be entertaining, enlightening or acceptable to its auditors. But it is essential, for the work to gain currency, that it should 'speak' in a 'language' that is accessible – if not a language already familiar to the listener, then one which the listener is ready, willing and able to learn. We have had the examples, expressed through the medium of R(T)É, of composers seeking such a language: T.C. Kelly's 'bilingual' approach; Ó Riada's search for a new language and Bodley's commuting between the languages of traditional music and serialism. We have also seen the same composers assessing the structural problems of assimilating one tradition to the other: Bodley speaking of 'grafting on' Irish elements to European forms; Potter wondering if, by arranging Irish airs, he could 'evolve' a harmonic structure adequate to the nature and needs of traditional music; Ó Riada moving towards, and away from, the idea of 'fusion'. The notion that there might be a 'third way', an included middle that would take the characteristics of

this series, 'Broadcasting and Irish Society'. 28 Potter described the title as meaning drama that was 'hopelessly provincial, hence the slight sense of disparagement in which the term is usually used ... You know what is going to happen before the curtain even rises, but you don't go there for the sake of the plot – any more than you go to Shakespeare for the sake of the scenery. You go to hear the accents – the infinity of variety discernible to the connoisseur': Potter to RÉ, 14 June 1952 (Potter Archive).

both traditions and make a new entity, has been the desired, but admittedly unattainable, end. In the view of other composers who have moved musical horizons in the same direction as Ó Riada, there is a possibility of 'synthesis' (as it has been said of Shaun Davey),[29] or, again, fusion or a 'hybrid' with the composer as 'mediator' (as used in the context of Micheál Ó Suilleabháin).[30]

The question of 'writing "Irishly"' was argued by Joseph Ryan in an RTÉ Radio programme in 1996, in which he conducted the original Bax quotation through the course of subsequent Irish composition to examine its influence or at least its presence in the works of Irish composers.[31] As 'Composers in Conversation' made clear, even if implicitly, the basic question which must be either answered or discarded is: why do many listeners, crtitics and musicologists, and some composers, continue to argue the topic of 'Irishness' in composition, while others in each of these categories appear unaffected by it? In a country which is now well past the phase of rebellion and independence, and whose capacity for self-determination is now intimately implicated with the fate of Europe as a collectivity of interdependent states, has the time come when a nationalist agenda is certainly *passé* in the political sphere but remains, in the minds of many, a major issue and cause of anxiety in the cultural sphere? And what role should be played by a 'national' broadcaster, or by a 'national' symphony orchestra, in relation to that artistic debate? Even in the work of Bill Whelan, whose *Brendan Voyage* and *Seville Suite* (the latter commissioned by RTÉ for performance by the RTÉCO at Expo 1992) are ostensibly dissociated from contemporary politics, the historical dimension continues to draw the imagination of listeners into the deeper histories of Irish international activity.

There can be no doubt that the *political* dimension of composition by Irish people remains powerful: from Boydell's 'In Memoriam Mahatma Gandhi' to the current work of Raymond Deane, an anxiety about the condition of politics itself, and the people affected by politics, is present in work performed by an Irish orchestra for Irish audiences. Deane has moved significantly, from the position of a composer consumed only by the centrality of composition in his life, to that of a composer who is deeply concerned with political and humanitarian matters and who at certain points reflects those concerns in his work.[32] In doing so, he is part of an Irish tradition – in so far as that word can be used in an intellectual (rather than a musical) sense – that has produced, in addition to Boydell's 'In Memoriam', the 'Songs from Prison' of May, and Shaun Davey's 'Relief of Derry Symphony'.

---

29 Piper Liam O'Flynn quoted by Michael Cunningham, 'Shaun Davey: making history into music', *Irish Times*, 30 May 1987.   **30** Robert O'Byrne, 'Creating a new hybrid', *Music Ireland* 4/6 (June 1989).   **31** The composers under discussion were Bax, Stanford, Sullivan, Harty, Esposito, Larchet, Duff, May, Bodley and Ó Riada. 'Writing Irishly' was transmitted 17 March 1996, and was awarded a prize at the 1999 Shanghai Radio Festival; RTÉ Sound Archives tape no. AA11316. **32** Cf. Arminta Wallace, 'The man behind the music', *Irish Times*, 22 October 2003.

radio éireann

festival of music 1963

concerts programme

17 Programme for the RÉ Music Festival, 1963.

18 Seán MacRéamoinn with the RÉ mobile recording unit, 1950s.

19 Fachtna Ó hAnnracháin, Terry O'Connor and Nancie Lord.

20 Arthur Nachstern, for many years deputy leader of the RTÉSO.

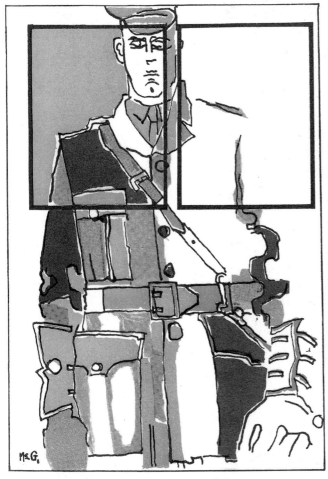

the
irish
national
anthem
a soldier's song
o donnell abú

our lady's choral soc.
r.e.s.o.

2 1 Sleeve of the RÉSO's recording of the National Anthem.

22 The RÉ Singers with Hans Waldemar Rosen, 1955.

23 The RÉ Singers with Hans Waldemar Rosen, 1965.

24 Seán Ó Riada.

25 Ciarán MacMathuna behind a radio microphone, *c.* 1974.

26 The RÉLO with conductor Dermot O'Hara, 1955.

27 A.J. Potter.

```
                              3 Bethel Terrace,
                                Greystones,
                                  Co. Wicklow.
                                    21st October,1955.

The Music Director,
Radio Eireann,
Dublin.


    Dear Mr. Ó hAnnracháin,

            In pursuit of my letter of the 11th, I can now
offer you some concrete suggestions which I hope may be something
after the lines of what you are wanting. I say 'concrete',but
I don't mean that just too literally ; you know how the material
you start with is apt to get changed in the course of writing
it down.

            What I have sketched in my mind is a concert
overture of the straight-forward 'Italian' type,only in one
continuous movement,or rather series of movements. Something
roughly on the following lines :-

            Fanfareish type of opening ::::::::
```

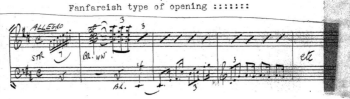

```
leading to an 'exposition' and 'development',more or less, of
various themes beginning with :::::::::
```

```
and continueing with ( among others ) :::::::::::::
```

28 Sketch by A.J. Potter for his 'Tostal overture'.

29 The Rowsome family of pipers in their home, *c.*1964
(Leo Rowsome is second from the left).

30 The RTÉLO 25th anniversary concert, with leader Jack Cheatle
and conductor Robert Murphy, 1973.

31 Leaders of the RTÉSO/NSO: (a) Geraldine O'Grady.
(b) Colin Staveley.

31 Leaders of the RTÉSO/NSO: (c) Audrey Park
(d) Alan Smale.

Backbone

INTRODUCTION

It has become a commonplace for RTÉ to state in its corporate literature that 'RTÉ, since its inception, has been the backbone of music-making in Ireland' – a formula for which the author must take a major share of responsibility.[1] We have seen that, in the early years of the 2RN Station Orchestra, and for most of the 1930s, orchestral concerts were provided by the Dublin Philharmonic Society in addition to those mounted by Vincent O'Brien with his augmented band, so that it is not entirely valid to claim that 2RN was the sole provider of such events. And in chapter 7 we shall explore the extent to which many other 'players' in the Irish music world have become more active and more prominent since 1926, and shall ask whether RTÉ continues to be the 'backbone' in the sense in which it has been understood over the past seventy-five years.

But in this chapter we shall examine the various areas in which 2RN, Radio Éireann and RTÉ unquestionably (even if debatably) led developments in both the geographical and the conceptual dimensions, and thus earned that recognition of an indispensable presence in Irish musical life: the growing sense of responsibility for nationwide provision of music facilities, especially live concert-giving; the involvement of musicians from all genres, and from all parts of the country, in its broadcasts; and the understanding of what a public service broadcaster can achieve by way of commitment of resources, in stimulating an awareness and appreciation of music in all its forms and in encouraging the practice of music-making.

In these areas, we shall see RTÉ as the provider of: orchestral support for what were termed, originally, 'outside bodies', particularly the opera seasons in Dublin and, later, Wexford; of educational programming and ancillary activities such as concerts for schoolchildren; of ensembles such as the RTÉ Singers

---

1 As Arts Promotions Officer within the RTÉ Public Affairs Division 1983–1999, I wrote and produced numerous brochures, press releases and fact sheets for RTÉ Music, in addition to the RTÉ Annual Report, with the purpose of presenting a corporate profile of RTÉ's music-making within the general contexts of broadcasting and of the nationwide spectrum of music activity, the chief aim of which was to establish the indispensability of RTÉ as a provider of music-making facilities, which in turn would assist in justifying RTÉ's claim to provide 'value-for-money' as a public service institution.

and the four successive string quartets resident in Cork; and as the agent of recording and transmitting the vast repertoire of traditional music throughout the country. It will also indicate the pressures that can be put upon a public service organisation from private individuals, arts interests and public representatives in the pursuit of goals that are not always altruistically motivated or in the public interest.

As will be seen in the case of the orchestras, the question can be asked: whether they would have existed if RTÉ itself had not existed. Given that RTÉ *has* been in existence since 1926, and *has* been a provider of live and broadcast music of all kinds since that time, the question can also be asked: if RTÉ had not created a professional chamber choir or a full-time string quartet, and had not made its orchestras available for various opera seasons and choral societies, would these activities, which are essentially extraneous to broadcasting, have taken place? The question may be academic, but it is worth bearing in mind: at the beginning of the twenty-first century there is every likelihood that Ireland would have an opera season in at least Dublin, maintained by arts councils or local authorities or commercial sponsors; but it is extremely unlikely, in the culturally restricted society of Ireland through at least the second and third quarters of the twentieth century, that provision would have been made other than by an agency such as R(T)É, which was already fulfilling a self-prescribed role as the major provider of classical, traditional and popular music. And it is arguable, given that RÉ was the first such organisation to instal a quartet-in-residence, whether, without that example, any other body would be supporting one today.

In 1961 G.J. Willoughby, Concerts and Orchestral Manager of the BBCSO, was invited to survey all RÉ's performing groups, as part of a general review by the Director-General, Edward Roth. Willoughby's recommendations regarding the RÉSO and RÉLO are considered at the start of chapter 6, but here we should note that Willoughby was surprised by the level of non-broadcasting use of the groups in the service of the wider music community. 'The position is exceptional in that the RÉSO and the RÉLO make a number of contributions to the musical life of Dublin which are only remotely connected with broadcasting and in some cases, i.e. accompanying the National Ballet, completely dissassociated from broadcasting ... The educational programmes performed in schools are considered to be of the utmost importance ... As to the answer to the question "why should Radio Éireann provide an orchestra for activities not directly connected with their own service[?]" I feel it would be quite improper of me to provide one'. Willoughby 'assumed', however, 'that a moral obligation for it to function in this way exists'.[2]

2 G.J. Willoughby, 'Report on Radio Éireann Symphony Orchestra etcetera', 10pp. Typescript, TCD Ms Moody papers, 10048/RTÉ/Box 25.

'I HEARD IT ON THE RADIO'

In 1950 George Bernard Shaw was asked 'Has the radio had an important influence, one way or the other, on musical appreciation?' and replied: 'It has worked
both ways. It has corrupted musical taste, and degraded musical instruments
by the most obscene sort of jazz as well as reviving Haydn's vogue and making
Bach a popular composer.'³ He might well have been commenting, or even
repeating, the tone of debate in Ireland on the subject of what kind of music
was, or was not, appropriate for Radio Éireann, as reflected, most importantly
of all, in the debates of Dáil Éireann.

As I have written elsewhere, 'I heard it on the radio' was, and perhaps continues to be, a catchphrase acknowledging the centrality of Radio Éireann in
Irish communication:⁴ the fact that almost every Irish home has a radio and,
nowadays, a television, has meant that R(T)É's broadcast output has permeated the country, in many cases (especially those regions which were traditionally called 'single channel areas')⁵ providing a unique cultural and informational service. To provide a *balanced* service, transmitting what might be
cultural lifeblood to one listener and anathema to another, was a precarious
task, and successive ministers at P&T were frequently subjected to questions
and remonstrations from all parts of the House. In particular, the debate, led
by the Gaelic League, over the propriety of jazz (which the first Secretary of
P&T, P.S. O'Hegarty, had denounced as leading to 'fatty degeneration of the
morals, of the character, to inefficiency and extinction') was hotly contested.⁶
In this, O'Hegarty was supported by one minister for P&T, Gerald Boland,
who candidly but realistically told the Dáil 'I do not like jazz and I would like
to see it eliminated altogether, but I am afraid we will not be able to do that'.⁷
Later, however, under P.J. Little, a brake was applied to the broadcasting of
dance music, by which P&T intended 'swing', 'jive', 'hot' music and 'crooning' (which E.J. Moeran had described as 'flaccid, emasculate and positively
indecent – makes me want to go to the lavatory and vomit').⁸ In 1948 Seán
Collins (Fine Gael, Cork West) would make a broad-minded appeal when he
said: 'I do not care very much for jazz music or light swing but at the same time
I think the Minister might consider the desirability of giving those of our people who like that kind of music an hour's programme two or three times per
week. I think the programme needs balance'.⁹ Looking back from 1959,
Thaddeus Lynch (Fine Gael, Waterford) reminded the house that

---

3 *The Stage*, 20 April 1950. 4 Pine, *2RN*, p. xi. 5 I.e. those areas which, before the advent of the
second RTÉ television channel, were able to receive only RTÉ1. 6 Cf. Pine, *2RN*, pp. 164–6.
7 DD, 61, 26 March 1936, col. 400. 8 E.J. Moeran, interview with Éamonn Andrews, 1947, loc.
cit. 9 DD, 112, 20 July 1948, cols. 848–9.

> I come from a constituency where, in the last generation, if we went jazzing we were lost and, when the Charleston came in, we were supposed to be without either faith or nationality. Our generation survived and I notice that a lot of the people who took part in the modern dances of those days did all right for themselves nationally and did all right for themselves in the vocations which they followed.[10]

And in 1943 James Dillon, at that time an independent TD for Monaghan (and later leader of Fine Gael), put the choices most clearly when he asked 'Why should I not be allowed to listen to "swing" music, if I wish to do so, or why should I not be allowed to listen to céilidhe band music, if I wish to do so? I think it is just ignorant narrow-minded bigotry on the part of those who want to hear one type of music, to deny the opportunity to others to hear a different type of music which, admittedly, may not have a very wide appeal.'[11] Providing every kind of music, from the Eurovision Song Contest to *Die Meistersinger von Nürnberg* was, and is, no simple matter and, as we shall see in chapter 7, musical politics within the station continued up until at least the 1980s.

The issue, at all times, was similar to that which preoccupied many Irish composers in the earlier part of the twentieth century: what was the special element that constituted Irishness, and what were the elements that affected Irish people adversely, or prevented them from being Irish? In cultural matters, identity was not achieved at the same speed as independence, and therefore what Radio Éireann transmitted could, in the view of some, build up a sense of identity and cohesion, while in the views of others it could undermine this elusive quality of Irishness which was so important to copperfasten the capacity for self-determination. Some deputies felt this more deeply than others, but on occasions debates about RÉ's output could become explicit: in 1955 Erskine Childers, then in opposition, referred to its schedule as being 'not only a professional entertainment programme, it is a programme devoted to the resurrection of a nation'.[12] However, this was a point on which views could be less than clear: twenty years later, when the expansion of RTÉ was being hotly contested, Frank Carter (Fianna Fáil, Longford-Westmeath) could point out that he did not entirely understand what the Minister (Conor Cruise O'Brien) had meant when he said that 'the notion of national culture as traditionally used in the broadcasting context did not altogether coincide with the concept of national identity which was commonplace in the political context'.[13]

The position of both politicians and civil servants could thus become invidious, as cultural values and political motives became engaged with one another

---

10 DD, 176, 22 July 1959, col. 1666. 11 DD, 91, 9 November 1943, col. 1792. 12 DD, 152, 6 July 1955, col. 283. 13 DD, 285, 30 October 1975, col. 684.

when unpopular or controversial decisions were taken. Deputy Roderick Connolly (Labour, Louth) told the Dáil in 1949

> It is a very important thing ... that the Minister [James Everett] ... should act as the patron of the musical arts. He himself may suffer from the same disability as I do. He may be as non-musical as I am, but still he has a duty to the country to foster musical art and to encourage the young aspirants to develop their talent and make it possible for them to continue the high repute Irish singers and musicians have throughout the world.[14]

But the previous year Seán Collins had been perhaps more forward-looking when he advised:

> On the subject of radio generally, I think that with the best will in the world the wrong people to run radio are civil servants. I feel that the Minister should contemplate the possibility of a different type of directorship and managementship of radio altogether – one that would be virtually independent so far as it would be possible within a general statement of policy to make any director of radio independent.[15]

In these years, after the first coalition government had taken office, the debate concerning the short-wave radio station, capable of broadcasting to Irish people and others abroad, was continued, and raised the question of the image that might be presented of Ireland: Bernard Butler (Fianna Fáil, Dublin South-West) announced 'I want to try to get our people not to give way to this pressure for cheap and rubbishy music ... Céilí music as a rule is not popular in this country, but our people abroad love it. I have been talking to missionary priests and they assured me that our people simply love céilí and traditional music'.[16] In the same debate, Peadar Cowan (Clann na Poblachta, Dublin North-East) asserted that it was pointless to employ the radio as a medium for inculcating a love of, or interest in, any particular form of music or culture:

> There is no sense in that approach to the radio because, although you may put these things on the radio, you cannot make the people listen to them. The younger people, as I have seen them growing up, want to hear jazz, they want to hear modern dance music. They listen to it and they sing to it ... I may like on a Saturday night when I am out motor-

14 DD, 117, 12 July 1949, col. 585.   15 DD, 112, 20 July 1948, col. 847.   16 DD, 117, 12 July 1949, col. 610.

ing to tune in and be told how to mend a fork or how to take a stain out of a mahogany table. That may suit me but it may not suit the people who are travelling with me and they may want to switch on to some other station. Radio Éireann being the one station we have at the moment, we must endeavour as best we can to cater for all tastes. In the last resort Radio Éireann is not an instrument for culture; it is an instrument for spreading information and for giving entertainment.[17]

Seán Collins had been critical of the employment of foreign musicians, and had pursued the question of balance:

> If Radio Éireann is to be anything I say that it must be symbolic of Ireland and her tradition. That symbolism and that tradition of Ireland can be best transmitted to the world through the medium of people born and reared in this country and steeped in the tradition of this country who have proved their efficiency either as musicians, singers or various other types of artistes ... I think great improvement could be made in the radio programmes if less highbrow music was used. I am not a devotee of highbrow music. I want to see programmes of characteristic Irish music ... When the Minister reconvenes the advisory council I want him to consider seriously the question of balance as far as Radio Éireann programmes are concerned.[18]

Three years later, Irish society was in a state of even faster change, which Erskine Childers, as Minister for P&T, had to acknowledge: 'there is undoubtedly a demand for our own music, instrumental and vocal, and we do our utmost to satisfy it. Let no one, however, have any illusions. A great number of the young people in this country have adopted light variety, operatic and Anglo-American dance music as their folk music, along with our own melodies, in the same way as other European countries'.[19] But the following day his Fianna Fáil colleague from Cork, Seán MacCarthy, put across a point which was central to nationalist feeling and probably reflected the views of most deputies:

> The first thing which I think we ought to consider, without being exclusively or too strictly obviously so, is that our radio should be national and recognisable as such when anybody tunes in to the station to listen

17 Ibid., cols. 611–2. **18** Ibid., cols. 847–9. **19** DD, 134, 5 November 1952, col. 926. Childers was correct in identifying 'pop' music as young people's 'folk': as Christian de Quincey wrote in 1970: 'the essential characteristics of pop and folk music are spontaneity and immediacy ... in today's world, pop music serves the same purpose as folk music did in the past: it serves the expression of feeling': *Irish Times*, 31 December 1970.

to its music or its general features. It should not be merely a case of wait-ing for the tinkling dulcet notes of *O'Donnell Abú* to know that we are tuned into Radio Éireann. It is most important that in its national fea-tures we should have the language in its various aspects, our national pastimes, our traditional and dance music, historical features and past and present-day dramatic presentations ... We could have gramophone records of some of our best singers as, for instance, the late John McCormack, Miss Margaret Burke Sheridan and others. We could have musical presentations by our pianists and our best musicians.[20]

MacCarthy returned to this point in 1958:

Generally speaking, our broadcasting service should be such that any-body listening to it would know he is listening to a broadcast from a dis-tinctive nation, with its own culture and language, and even though music is international and even though many things broadcast are of advantage, educationally and otherwise, I hope our radio will never lose its character of being a good standard national broadcasting station.[21]

Douglas Hyde could not have asked for a better apologist. On the same occa-sion former minister James Everett, objecting to the presence of 'rock'n'roll' on RÉ, said 'We should devote some of our time to our fine national songs instead of propagating foreign music which is not music at all.'[22] When, in 1979, RTÉ launched 'Radio 2' (later 2FM), as a response to the domination of the pop airwaves by 'pirate' broadcasters, many thought that transmission of pop by the 'national' broadcaster was a travesty of its mission.[23]

When the early performance of the television service was being debated, these issues naturally arose again, in almost the same terms. Already in 1960 Patrick Cummins (Fianna Fáil, Dublin South-Central) had spotted the poten-tial permeation of domestic life by television when he stated:

The service, I submit, will present a challenge to all those men and women to play their part in creating and sustaining a new tradition in Irish music, drama and entertainment generally. The Radio Éireann Symphony Orchestra and the Light Orchestra have done great work in

20 DD, 134, 6 November 1952, cols. 1156–7. In 1951 Margaret Burke Sheridan recorded her life-story – 'Vissi d'arte' – for RÉ and had given a series of illustrated talks; much of her recording was incorporated into Norris Davidson's documentary, 'A Silenced Voice' (25 December, 1962): RTÉ Sound Archives tape no. AA12194. 'O'Donnell Abú' [O'Donnell for ever] was for many years the 'call signal' of Radio Éireann. 21 DD, 167, 17 April 1958, col. 335. 22 Ibid. cols. 359–60. 23 Cf. John Boland, 'The bland leading the bland?', *Hibernia*, 31 May 1979.

their journeys through the provinces and, in particular, by their concerts for school children. Inevitably there was a large number of children throughout the country who could not take advantage of the opportunity to hear these concerts. The television service, I submit, would
remedy that. It would bring the orchestras into every home and thus
help to foster in our children an appreciation of good Éireann [*sic*] in
the name of Gaelic culture. Music, music that is civilised, permanent
and immortal and, at the same time, light and entertaining. That, in my
opinion, would help to counteract the unhealthy effects of the neurotic,
hysterical effusions which are sometimes described as modern.[24]

Brendan Corish referred to the lack of music on television, and recalled:

I am sure the Minister [Michael Hilliard] was a jazz fiend in the Twenties
… We were Bing Crosby men and Frank Sinatra men. There was an
attempt by Radio Éireann then and by our parents to introduce us to
reasonably good music. Telefís Éireann are doing little or nothing in
that respect. It may be said that sound is the next best medium for giving this better type of music, whether Irish, continental, operatic or
symphonic. But Telefís Éireann could contribute something and certainly could continue using the symphony orchestra.[25]

Just as deputies had argued for more music, of one sort or another, on radio,
so they now asked for more symphony concerts and more céilí music on television. In 1967, at a time when RTÉ was trying to divest itself of the responsibility – financial at least – for the RTÉSO, Childers, during his second period
as Minister for P&T, put the case that, as with the BBC, there were few symphony concerts on television, because 'it is a question of having to consider the
number of people listening and viewing in relation to the total programes. I
am always encouraging RTÉ to go a little in advance if they can in order that
more and more people will take an interest in everything – our culture, our
economic and social problems'.[26] And in 1973, at the start of the debate on the
nature of the second television channel, which stimulated further discussion
on national identity, John Wilson (Fianna Fáil, Cavan, a future minister for
both P&T and education) wanted to see RTÉ 'used in the context of a university of the air … The television service and the radio service should act as
mirrors to the nation',[27] while John Kelly (Fine Gael, Dublin South-Central;
Parliamentary Secretary to the Taoiseach) warned that 'To treat television

---

24 DD, 180, 16 March 1960, cols. 629–30. 25 DD, 209, 13 May 1964, col. 1439. 26 DD, 228,
23 May 1967, col. 1390. 27 DD, 266, 20 June 1973, col. 812.

purely as an entertainment and a mode of relaxation ... is a luxury people in a community like ours cannot afford. We have got here a very powerful weapon for mobilising people's minds and influencing their actions'.[28]

The very limited screen time allotted to the RTÉSO would, in fact, become a point of contention both within and outside RTÉ over the next four decades, one difficulty being a lack of policy as to whether or not televised symphony concerts, without any specific televisual treatment, were worthwhile. But the presence of the RTÉLO/CO on screen has become familiar to many viewers, with a broad range of programming such as, in 1974, 'The Bright New Moon', produced by Bill Skinner and introduced by Ian Fox, which featured five one-hour programmes of contemporary Irish composition performed by both the RTÉLO and RTÉSO with the RTÉ Singers and String Quartet, including fifty-six works by twenty-eight composers, of whom all but three were living. 1974 also featured Bernadette Greevy with guest artists such as James Galway and the New Irish Chamber Orchestra (conducted by Havelock Nelson) in 'For Your Pleasure' followed by 'Colman Pearce Presents'. In more recent decades, the studio-based series 'Simply Music' in 1980 and 1981, 'Invitation to Music', 'Encore' (1981), 'The Music Show' (a 26-part series hosted by tenor Niall Murray in 1983), 'Concert Hour' and 'Concerto Time' (1987) provided a regular diet of light and light-classical music for 'middlebrows'. In fact, the 1980s was a comparatively fruitful decade for music on television. John O'Conor's three series of 'Piano Plus' in the late 1980s (followed, in the 90s, by 'Hands Across the Keys'), Geraldine O'Grady's invitation series 'Strings in the Air' (1988), and documentaries on personalities such as Margaret Burke Sheridan, Bryden Thomson, János Fürst, Hugh Maguire, Charles Lynch, Brian Boydell, E.J. Moeran, Audrey Park and violin-maker and -restorer William Hofmann. Short, late-night, series such as Micheál O'Rourke playing Chopin's nocturnes (a series that RTÉ sold to French television) also gave classical music a regular presence in viewers' consciousness, while 'Music for Me', presented in 1986 by Ingrid Miley, brought a series of young musicians to the screen. The 'I Live Here' series featured conductor Ethna Tinney's orchestra for the unemployed, 'Classical Graffiti', an iconoclastic venture supported by the Social Employment Scheme (1989).

Outside broadcasts, apart from televising orchestral concerts, were much more rare, but the 1982 series of Beethoven sonatas for piano and violin, played by Jan Čap and Mariana Sirbu (then leader of the RTÉ Academica String Quartet) in Carton House was a major exception, and the concert performances, mostly with Irish casts (directed by Anne Makower), of costumed operas over five years of the 'Proms' – *Rigoletto*, *La bohème*, *La traviata*, *Don Pasquale*

---

28 DD, 285, 30 October 1975, col. 659.

and *Madama Butterfly* – brought into people's homes the type of in-house enter-tainment normally available only from opera houses such as Covent Garden and the New York 'Met' which they could see regularly on Network2. Irish-born opera also made a brief appearance with James Wilson's *Letters to Theo* in 1986 (also directed by Makower), while Louis Lentin's dramatised version of *Messiah* (1986) raised eyebrows and went on to gain attention at the 'Prague d'Or' television festival.

But radio continues not only to provide the lion's share of broadcast music – especially since the limited availability of FM3 was superseded in 1999 by the establishment of the 24-hour Lyric fm – but also to maintain its attraction for listeners, with Tommy O'Brien's long-running operatic 'Your Choice and Mine' (1952–83) and Des Keogh's 'Music for Middlebrows' (beginning in 1968 and still running under a new title) which has made occasional forays into the concert hall.

OUTREACH

One enduring facet of Radio Éireann's preoccupation with ensuring that it ful-fils its public service remit was its anxiety to provide a nationwide service: if listeners paid a licence fee in order to receive a radio service, they were not only entitled to a clear radio signal but, because they also supported the exis-tence, in the form of the RÉ Orchestra, of a performing group which appeared before Dublin concert audiences, then those nationwide audiences also deserved to witness live music-making as far as resources would permit it.

Apart from the inescapable conclusion that J.J. Walsh, as Minister for P&T and a TD for Cork, would have wanted a second station in the country's sec-ond city, this thinking may also have been partly responsible for the short-lived establishment of 6CK (the Cork station) 1927–30, which provided not only programming to the Munster region (which the Dublin transmitter might not have reached) but, more importantly in this context, musical fare from local players.

Touring the orchestra was, however, an expensive item for which there was no sanction from the Department of Finance, and, by way of a compromise, 'Concert Tours' were organised. Séamus Ó Braonáin recalled that

> It was strongly felt that too much of the music-making emanated from Dublin, and in order to remedy this to some extent the programme called 'Concert Tour' was established. The idea was to encourage musi-cal organisations in places outside Dublin to arrange series of concerts of good music, employing the best artists available. To help towards

meeting the expenses of such concerts, Radio Éireann arranged to relay a portion of each concert at a specially increased fee.[29]

One of the first was from Waterford City Hall on 16 September 1942, and another, featuring local tenor William Watt, with Adolphe Gébler (clarinet) and Ida [Starkie] O'Reilly (cello) on 22 October that year. These usually consisted of a small number of musicians being employed by RÉ to visit a regional centre (others took place in Cork, Sligo, Limerick, Wexford and Galway), with live transmission of the concert fulfilling at least part of the station's self-imposed remit to reflect music-making around the country.

On one occasion, a technical hitch was reported by Music Director, Michael Bowles, who wrote: 'a nice atmosphere came over. There was a little misunderstanding in the announcements due to their being made from here [i.e. Dublin]'.[30] Charles Kelly sent this on to Séamus Brennan with advice: 'I think personally in all our concert tours it would be preferable if announcements were made on the spot ... It is impossible for our [Dublin] announcer to know what is going on locally. Last night a group of songs was announced and the listeners heard an encore by Charles Lynch! It leaves our man "in the air", not "on it".'[31]

Such technical problems having been ironed out, Waterford, due to the activity of its Music Club in promoting recitals, became a favourite venue for OBs by Radio Éireann: in April 1943, the amateur orchestra of the Waterford Orchestra Society broadcast a concert including the overture to Hérold's *Zampa*, a selection from *Rigoletto*, cello solos by Ida O'Reilly and concluding with the overture from *Maritana*.

There were many broadcasts from Waterford of live recitals: in August 1945, for example, RÉ relayed the recital by Renée Flynn, accompanied by Kitty O'Callaghan; in February 1946, the Lang Quartet;[32] in November 1948, Oda Slobodskaya; in September 1949, Francis Engel (piano) with Máire ní Scolai (soprano); three months later, Jaroslav and Kveta Vaneček; in October 1950, Franz Reizenstein; the following February, André Prieur (the new principal flute with the RÉSO) with the Dublin String Quartet;[33] in April 1952, Leon Goossens (oboe) with Kitty O'Callaghan, and a year later, the Benthien String Quartet.[34] These provided the template for later series of collaborations by R(T)É, most notably the recording of recitals for the members of the RDS,

---

29 S. Ó Braonáin, in A. Fleischmann, *Music in Ireland*, p. 201. 30 Bowles departmental memo 17 September 1942. 31 Kelly to Brennan, ibid. 32 Carmel Lang and Hazel de Courcy, violins; Charles Maguire, viola; Betty Sullivan, cello. 33 François d'Albert and William Shanahan, violins; Máire Larchet, viola; Maurice Meulien, cello. 34 Ulrich Benthien and Rudolph Maria Mueller, violins; Hans Georg von Bargen, viola; and Wolfram Hentschel, cello – the latter had been a member of the RÉSO.

and many Dublin concerts presented by the Limerick Music Association, which were undertaken during the 1960s, 70s and 80s.

The first concert by the RÉSO outside Dublin was given in Cork on 18 September 1949, and attended by León Ó Broin.[35] Six months later, Ó Broin was cautiously making a case to Finance for continuation of such concerts, and for making the RÉSO into a national orchestra:

> These visits of the orchestra are already bearing fruit. A keen interest has been created among music lovers throughout the country by the possibility of having symphony concerts in their cities and towns and what is even more welcome, the concerts at Cork and Waterford were attended by a large number of people who had never previously seen a symphony orchestra in action.[36]

Finance, in the person of Ó Broin's opposite number, Seán Ó Muimhneacháin, took a less altruistic view:

> The financial results of the two concerts already given ... have been uninspiring. In Cork £31 was lost despite, it is understood, a full house but the concert might have been self-supporting if you had increased the admission charges slightly. Waterford would have been a financial flop if you had not been given such generous assistance locally. With this experience we are not too enthusiastic about other ventures, particularly in smaller centres, but we are prepared to consider the matter further. We should like to make it clear, however ... that if, say, Limerick or Galway want to hear the orchestra, the bill should be footed locally and there should be no question of public funds coming to the rescue.[37]

The Department of Finance remained in the same mindset that we have seen in relation to the orchestral budget generally, in that it refused – or was constitutionally unable – to recognise a musical need that, in its opinion, could be solved, or eliminated, by a financial measure. Thus, Ó Muimhneacháin continued:

> In considering the cost of a concert, it occurs to us that if a soloist were dispensed with the saving would be material, and there would be a better chance of making ends meet. Is a soloist absolutely necessary in

35 The programme was: Wagner, overture to *Die Meistersinger*, Rachmaninov's 'Rhapsody on a theme of Paganini' (soloist Charles Lynch) and Beethoven, 'Eroica' symphony (no. 3), conducted by Hans Schmidt-Isserstedt. 36 Ó Broin to Secretary, Dept. of Finance, 22 March 1950, P&T file 63/59, 'Symphony Concerts – provincial – Correspondence with Finance 22.3.50–19.6.52'. 37 Ó Muimhneacháin to Ó Broin, 14 April, ibid.

these cases? Why do you propose a separate performance for school children?[38]

To which Ó Broin responded:

> The concerts for children we consider the most important aspect of this work as it is on them our chief reliance is for the future of symphony music. The pieces are played over to the children beforehand and the instruments as well as the music explained to them.[39]

Ó Broin and his department thus found themselves in the same position as we have noted in the 1930s and 40s, when a case had to be made that made no sense at all to those whose sole responsibility was to balance the nation's books, at a time of serious economic stringency. Even had the concept of cost-benefit analysis been available at that time, it is unlikely that it would have carried much weight. Ó Broin persevered:

> I suggest that we take a realistic view of this matter. All of us know that the arts, which have to depend for practice and advancement on the minority, cannot pay financial dividends and symphony music is not expected to pay for itself as a business matter no more than an art gallery is. It is subsidised heavily in every country that has any pretensions to culture … No adjustment of admission charges can make concerts by these orchestras pay; the attendance is limited and higher prices may only mean reduced income … Due to a great extent I suppose to historical causes we have only one Symphony Orchestra built up by great effort primarily for broadcasting purposes. Outside this the State and the Municipalities have contributed absolutely nothing to help the performance of symphony music and four-fifths of our population have never had an opportunity of hearing a symphony concert played. The broadcasting orchestra is the only combination that can do something in a small way to remedy that deficiency. I suggest that the State should eagerly avail of the chance to do it and it will at least be saving its face for a trifling sum.[40]

He appended a statement of 'Annual Subsidies to Symphony Orchestras in Britain' which showed that the CBSO received £5000 from the state and £7000 from the local authority in Birmingham; the Hallé (Manchester) had £9000 from each source; the RLPO had £9000 and £8000 respectively; and the LPO had £10k and £20k.

---

38 Ibid.   **39** Ó Broin to Finance, 5 May 1950, ibid.   **40** Ó Broin to Finance, 5 May 1950, ibid.

In response, Ó Muimhneacháin granted a total of £100 for the losses on provincial concerts, with a maximum of six concerts per year.[41] A year later an internal P&T memo indicates that the department was undertaking some advanced thinking on the subject of concert promotion:

> The Department would like to send the Orchestra to every town with a reasonable population in the country and even across the Channel as a national propaganda but the question of expense is a difficult one ... We are considering asking business organisations if they would be prepared to sponsor concerts.[42]

An out-of-Dublin concert could be expected to incur a deficit in the region of £40-£50. It was thus clear that the subsidy authorised by Finance, even if a tour eliminated some of the repetitive transport costs, would not allow P&T to contemplate more than four concerts per year by both orchestras.

If the mandarins in Finance decried expenditure of this order, members of the Dáil were vociferous in calling for visits to their constituencies by the orchestras. In 1952, for example, Brendan Corish put the case for their educational deployment:

> I do not believe that I could listen to the symphony orchestra for any more than half an hour. I would certainly go up the walls or close my ears to it after that. I know that it is good music, but I cannot appreciate it yet, and I would go so far as to say that 80 per cent. of our people cannot appreciate that type of music yet. We know that it is good music, but the only way the people can get an appreciation of it is by being gradually trained or educated into a love of that type of music. The Minister should do a little more with regard to getting these two orchestras around the country. I know he has done it and that it is being done at present. So long as he keeps that up and so long as he sends the light orchestra, in particular, around the country, so long will the people have a greater appreciation of him and of Radio Éireann.[43]

As Minister for P&T 1951–4 (and again 1966–9), Childers shared this concern for countrywide appearances. A file dated February 1954 refers to his request (and in Childers' terms, a 'request' was tantamount to an instruction) that RÉ 'take a more positive part in arranging for concerts by the orchestras' in co-operation with existing local organisations.[44] If R(T)É has been the 'back-

---

41 Ó Muimhneacháin to Ó Broin, 20 May 1950, ibid. 42 Ibid., 29 June 1951. 43 DD, 134, 6 November 1952, cols. 1150–1. 44 Matt Doherty to F. Ó hAnnracháin, 28 May 1953, P&T file

bone' of music in Ireland, the organisations in towns and cities which have hosted the RTÉSO and RTÉCO over the decades have in their turn been pillars of that activity: beside the major bodies such as the Cork Orchestral Society, the Limerick Symphony Concerts Society and later the Limerick Music Association, the Waterford Music Club and Music for Galway, local community groups such as arts festivals, and local branches of national organisations such as Muintir na Tíre, have provided expert knowledge and commitment which have been indispensable in making local arrangements and ensuring a worthwhile attendance. It is incontrovertible that without such back-up, regardless of the nationwide advertising of which RTÉ is capable through its national radio and television channels, the regional outreach of the performing groups could not be undertaken with any degree of reliability or with any assurance of engaging with that local population.

As Ó Broin had told Finance three years previously:

> To help in this work of encouraging symphony music we are trying to enlist the support of a cultural minority of people throughout the country. The number is small, perhaps three or four enthusiasts in each place. Not alone have they to overcome the mediocre tastes fostered by the cinema and the dance hall but even the simple matter of the provision or enlargement of a stage in a hall designed for other purposes may cost them £20 or £30. To treat these few enthusiasts who are doing an immense amount of work which should really belong to the State and the municipalities on a business basis is, I suggest, an impossible outlook … It is quite clear that nobody can make money on these concerts but the offer [of a subsidy] helps to urge the organisers to try to do a little better than avoid loss.[45]

Thus in 1954, with Childers' encouragement, the RÉSO toured in March to Cork, Limerick, Waterford and Galway, and in September to Sligo, Derry, Belfast and Dundalk – the latter with the outstanding Hungarian violinist Joseph Szigeti as soloist – while the RÉLO was to visit at least two venues outside Dublin.[46] The RÉSO plan would become the model on which the current twice-yearly national tours by the NSO are based, although visits to venues in Northern Ireland, which were firmly on the itinerary in those days, became less frequent with the onset of overt political disturbances from the late 1960s onwards. The visit of the RTÉSO to Belfast in 1976 was the first since 1965.[47]

838/53/1: 'RÉ Orchestra – Provincial Concerts Feb 1954 – Cork, Limerick, Waterford – arrangements with local organising committees'. **45** Ó Broin to Finance, 5 May 1950, file 63/59. **46** Ó hAnnracháin to Director, 1 June 1953, file 838/53/1. **47** In 1972 Michael Bowles revealed that in 1943, when British army bands were no longer available, players from the Army bands in the south

Nevertheless, the rewards of bringing live music to a town or city where, otherwise, the experience of hearing it would be confined to radio listening were to be weighed against financial costs. As an unidentified newspaper clipping states:

> It was an interesting experience to hear the work of this orchestra without having to submit to the vagaries of transmission, which usually destroy tonal quality when we listen to performances from Radio Éireann. That such a difference could be possible makes us realise that it is time that something should be done to improve matters at 2RN. If it is true that new studios and new apparatus will soon be available, this would be good news indeed.

When the RÉSO visited St Patrick's College, Maynooth, in April 1950, the reaction was rewarding:

> The reaction of the students could be reported only in superlatives; they were thrilled, stunned and delighted beyond measure ... You have by your visit accomplished a very great thing for music in Ireland. This sounds rhetorical and declamatory, but from what I can learn it is no more than the truth ... Many of the students feared the worst from a symphony performance, the type that is frightened by bogeys of 'highbrow' but they surprised themselves by liking it.[48]

An undated cutting from the *Munster Express* (almost certainly relating to the 1954 visit by the RÉSO to Waterford) conveys the excitement – even allowing for local hyperbole – that such an event could evoke:

MUSIC AT ITS BEST

SCINTILLATING SUCCESS SCORED

ADULTS AND CHILDREN ENTHRALLED

> They came, they played, they enthralled – and they fascinated. Thus might be epitomised the scintillating success which crowned the bril-

---

went, unofficially, to augment the concerts of the Belfast Philharmonic Society, together with members of the RÉ orchestra: 'Looking back on it all now, the conspiracy and secrecy and anxious circumspection surrounding the affair was just plain bloody silly, the material for a comic-opera sequence in any other country in the world. But the notion of a Dublin orchestra helping a Belfast orchestra had to be treated seriously, not, as God knows, from a fear that anyone in the diplomatic corps was likely to holler about a breach of Irish neutrality but simply because of that hysteria still very much in evidence 25 years later, when the temeritous Captain O'Neill invited the broadminded Seán Lemass to lunch': 'Hands across the musical border', *Irish Times*, 15 February 1972. **48** J.G. McGarry (St Patrick's College, Maynooth) to Ó hAnnracháin, 20 April 1950; critics Robert Johnson (*Irish Press*) and Joseph O'Neill (*Irish Independent*) commented that the acoustics were preferable to those of the Phoenix Hall. The RÉSO returned to Maynooth the following year, 24 March 1951, with conductor Albert van Raalte and soloist François d'Albert in the Mendelssohn violin concerto.

liant performances given last week for adults (on Thursday night) and for children (on Friday morning) at the Olympia Ballroom by the RÉSO. Both occasions … were memorable milestones in the further happy progress of this form of culture in an ancient city whose love for music has given it a place of prominence in the provinces.

As the Minister, James Everett, said in his official voice,

> Leaving aside the chief aim – that of stimulating the appreciation of classical or serious music – one has always the hope that, seated in one or more of these audiences, is a handful of boys and girls, or of young men and women, in whom the gift for musical accomplishment is dormant. Should our symphony orchestra be the means of awakening such gifts, it will more than have justified its existence.[49]

The RÉLO gave its first concert outside Dublin on 31 May 1950, in the Gaiety Cinema, Ballyhaunis, County Mayo, 'under the auspices of the Ballyhaunis Town Improvements Committee', when Dermot O'Hara conducted a programme including 'The Dream of Olwyn', 'Clair de Lune', a Brahms Hungarian Dance, Strauss's 'Blue Danube' and a selection of Irish music. The soloists were the leader, Jack Cheatle, and tenor Joseph McNally. The hall was not full, and a loss of £43 was incurred by the organisers. Roibéard Ó Faracháin had written to Ó Broin that

> There is general agreement in principle here that it would be a good thing to send out the RÉLO to some of the smaller towns. As a matter of fact we had discussed the possibility of sending it with 'Beginners Please' … There is, however, in my opinion, a good case for sending the RÉLO for concerts as distinct from variety shows and the Ballyhaunis invitation will enable us to investigate what is entailed. We think here we should not be part of a miscellaneous local show, though one local artist, where good ones were available, would be an addition. Without going into too much detail I should indicate that it will be rather more difficult to free the RÉLO from station duties than it is to free the RÉSO which works independently and makes fewer appearances on the air.[50]

Laurence Freeley of the Ballyhaunis committee wrote subsequently to Ó hAnnracháin: 'Leaving the financial question completely aside, I should like to say the concert was a tremendous social and cultural success, and will long

49 DD, 121, 25 May 1950, col. 613. **50** Ó Faracháin to Ó Broin, 6 April 1950, P&T file 555/53/1, 'Applications from outside organisations for services of Radio Éireann Orchestras, Ballyhaunis'.

live in the memory of all who had the good fortune to be present ... Making profit out of the concert was our least worry, and I can assure you, we all felt it a great privilege to have the members of the Orchestra and other Concert Artistes as our guests, especially so when it was their first public appearance outside the studios, and whilst not even attempting to throw bouquets at ourselves, I think we made their stay in Ballyhaunis as comfortable and pleasant as we possibly could.'[51]

Dermot O'Hara appended a manuscript note to this file, reading: 'The members of the orchestra and myself were treated with the utmost courtesy and the arrangements for both the presentation of the broadcast and accommodation of the orchestra were carried out in a most satisfactory manner'. But he added 'The introduction of some local variety turns which were introduced during the interval lasted for over an hour, and had a most exhausting and boring effect on the audience. This type of padding is rather unnecessary and should be avoided on future occasions'.[52] Further outreach by the RÉLO followed quickly, with concerts in towns such as Tralee, Fermoy, Mallow, Kilkenny, Carlow, Ballinasloe, Clonmel, Drogheda and Ballyshannon.

Quite apart from acoustics, the variable quality of venues in cities such as Limerick and Waterford has at times placed a question-mark over the viability of concerts in those venues. For the Concert Orchestra, the problem is not so acute, and its tradition of undertaking at least one regional tour each year (and mostly two) has been less subject to interruption than that of the Symphony Orchestra. The Savoy Cinema in Limerick was probably the least favourable venue, and there was no guarantee that the hall would be in a suitable condition on any particular evening; on one occasion, a mystery beat on one of the timpani – quite unconnected with any action of the timpanist – was found to be due to raindrops falling from a hole in the roof. Only the City Hall in Cork, which has an acceptable acoustic and is a large and comfortable venue, has been a constant in such tours, and almost without exception, until the 1990s, four of the NSO's concerts each year were repeated in Cork. Thereafter, they became part of the one-week national tour which the NSO gives, in association with the *Irish Times*, twice each year, the other venues being the new University Concert Hall in Limerick, Leisureland in Galway (which continues to be severely problematic) and the Institute of Technology in Waterford. 'Music for Fun', pioneered by Gareth Hudson and myself in 1982, a long-running series of family concerts by the RTÉCO which 'stripped away the mystique of classical music', also took on a national dimension in 1985 when it went on tour to Wexford, Clonmel, Tralee, Limerick, Mullingar, Galway, Westport and Sligo, as part of 'European Music Year'.

---

51 Freeley to Ó hAnnracháin, 23 August 1950, ibid. 52 Ibid., 6 June 1950.

'An Tóstal', the festival dating from 1953 (for which, as we have seen, RÉ commissioned an overture from A.J. Potter), gave rise to several other festival manifestations, of which the longest running has been the Dublin Theatre Festival.

Apart from its regular appearances in Dublin and regional centres, RTÉ has pursued a policy of supporting arts ventures such as festivals, by ensuring that a symphony concert acts as a magnet for a hinterland such as Kilkenny where, for several years, the RTÉSO appeared during the annual Arts Week, with St Canice's Cathedral as its hub. Waterford, which has hosted an annual International Festival of Light Opera since 1960, had the RTÉ Light Orchestra in residence for many years, as did the Castlebar International Song Contest (from 1973), while in 1990–2 the NSO and the RTÉCO appeared at the Adare Festival at Adare Manor, County Limerick, which had Cathal MacCabe, RTÉ's Head of Music, as its Director.

In 1983, the RTÉCO, conducted by Proinnsías Ó Duinn and Robin Stapleton, took part in a fresh opera venture, Cork City Opera, designed to originate opera productions in Cork, in addition to shows that might be brought there by the DGOS. The operas, in what was a modestly successful first year (and were recorded for television transmission – the first Irish productions to receive this treatment), were *Madama Butterfly* and *Il trovatore*; in 1984, *Carmen* and *La bohème* and in its third and final year, *Rigoletto* and the double bill of Mascagni's *Cavalleria rusticana* and Leoncavallo's *I pagliacci*.

In 1995 the RTÉCO was again in Limerick for 'Summerfest', a series of light concerts conducted by Gareth Hudson, and three years later, celebrating its fiftieth anniversary, it took the 'Bank of Ireland/RTÉ Proms' on a national two-week tour, visiting Limerick, Waterford, Cork, Sligo, Galway, Clifden, and Dundalk.

One successor to An Tóstal was the Dublin International Festival of Music and the Arts which took place in June 1959 at the Theatre Royal and the Gaiety Theatre, under the patronage of the (Catholic) Archbishop of Dublin, and with the backing of Bord Fáilte and the Taoiseach. Initial plans included the choir of the Sistine Chapel and baritone Dietrich Fischer-Dieskau. Its committee (chair, Louis Elliman, artistic director John F. Larchet, treasurer Bill O'Kelly and secretary Fr Andrew Griffith) met Maurice Gorham and Fachtna Ó hAnnracháin in July 1958 to discuss the participation of the RÉSO.[53] It was to prove one of the most bizarre, as well as somewhat amusing, episodes in the history of such involvement, and if there is a 'backbone' to the story, it is one of misplaced identity and political, rather than musical, sensitivities.

The proposal was for the RÉSO to take part in Vaughan Williams' opera *Riders to the Sea* at the Gaiety, for a concert under Barbirolli, and for a joint

53P&T File 188/58: 'Dublin International Festival of Music and the Arts June 1959 – Appl. for services of RESO'.

concert by the RÉSO and the Hallé Orchestra, with the relatively young Our Lady's Choral Society, in Mahler's second symphony. The RÉLO was requested for a series of ballet performances.[54] Gorham would give no firm commitment, but then a letter from the Taoiseach's private secretary to the Minister's private secretary amounted (as we shall see in the case of the DGOS) to a directive to make such a commitment.[55]

The first RÉSO concert was to consist of Glinka's overture to *Russlan and Ludmilla*; Arthur Duff's Suite or two short works by Larchet; Brahms' second piano concerto with Gina Bachauer; Mozart's 'Haffner' symphony and Stravinsky's 'Firebird'. (Barbirolli stated that he preferred the Larchet pieces to the Duff suite and Berlioz' 'Carnival romain' to the Glinka.)[56] An additional second concert was to consist of either Rossini's overture *La gazza ladra* or that to *L'italiana in Algeri*; Haydn's oboe concerto with Evelyn Rothwell (Barbirolli's wife); Harty's 'With the Wild Geese'; and Schubert's 'great' C major symphony.

Problems arose when it was proposed to add Handel's coronation anthem 'Zadok the Priest' (1727) to the Mahler symphony in the joint concert with the Hallé. 'Zadok', which has been sung at every subsequent British coronation, contains the lines 'And all the people rejoiced and said: "God save the king! Long live the king! May the king live for ever."' It fell to Fachtna Ó hAnnracháin to inform the committee that Radio Éireann could not be party to this performance: to participate, only a decade after the Republic had come into existence, in a performance in which Irish musicians would accompany Irish singers in singing 'God save the king!' was politically incorrect. Griffith responded that the objection was 'fatuous'.[57]

Thus, a confrontation took place between RÉ (Gorham and Ó hAnnracháin) and the Festival committee. 'The Director explained again why it would embarrass Radio Éireann to take part in a performance of "Zadok" or to be associated with a concert in which it was included. Lt. Col. O'Kelly made reference to his own efforts in the cause of Irish freedom … and at one stage became so excited that the Director invited him to leave the room if he wished to do so … After much discussion it was finally agreed that the RÉSO would not take part in "Zadok" and that the work would be performed by the Hallé and Our Lady's Choral Society only. The RÉSO will come on stage after the performance of "Zadok".'[58]

---

54 The RÉLO's ballet programmes, with the troupe of 'Antonio and his Spanish Ballet', conducted by Benito Lauret, were, firstly: 'Albaicin' (Albeniz), 'Fantasia Galaici' (Hallfter), The 'Three-cornered Hat' (Falla); secondly, 'Pas de Quatre' (Pablo Sorozabal), 'Sortilegio de los Collares' (Granados), 'El Llanto a Manuel de Falla' (Vicente Asencio), 'Viva Navarra' (Joaquin Larregla), 'Zapateado' (Sarasate), and 'Los Serranos de Vejer' (Soler). 55 Letter of 5 August 1958, ibid. Other features of the Festival were 'I Virtuosi di Roma', opera from Venice and Naples, and a céilí with the Gallowglass Céilí Band (from Naas, County Kildare). 56 E. Edwards (Hallé Orchestra) to Griffith, 11 March 1959, ibid. 57 Ó hAnnracháin departmental memo, 4 May 1959, ibid. 58 Ó hAnnracháin departmental minute, 14 May 1959 of meeting of 13 May, ibid.

Gorham's minute of the same meeting records:

> Just to give an indication of the circumstances under which negotiations with amateur music impresarios are sometimes carried on, I am reporting these incidents ... At one point Colonel O'Kelly burst into an account of his own service to the cause of national independence, introducing also the fact that his brother was shot. This was apparently intended to show that if he did not object to the singing of the words 'God save the king' which was the point at issue, none of us should. Colonel O'Kelly has before now made violent assertions of his patriotism at meetings in connection with the DGOS, but this is the first time he has invoked his brother. Fortunately nobody entered into competition with him and the discussion proceeded on more normal lines. A little later, Colonel O'Kelly flung himself sideways in his chair, clasped his head in his hand, and said audibly 'Will we never get out of this?' I told him that he was free to leave the meeting if he wanted to, but as it was held in my office, I was not. Later again, Dr Larchet, speaking of our reasons for not wanting the item including 'God Save the King', said 'That can't be the real reason'. I admit that this imputation on my veracity made me very angry ... I told the meeting that whatever Dr Larchet thought, the reason I had given was the real one, and unless we all agreed to believe that the others were telling the truth, there was no point in continuing the discussion. All ended amicably, as usual, but it is a queer way to have to arrange for Radio Éireann to co-operate in artistic activities.[59]

The picture of a veteran of the war of independence, vigorously demanding a performance involving 'God save the king', while an RÉ official of Anglo-Irish background (and a former BBC employee) refused to countenance such a demand, is a strange reflection on the kind of role-reversals which followed the cause of Irish freedom. It is hardly surprising that, after the Festival, Gorham told the committee that in 1960 the most RÉ was likely to be able to undertake would be a single symphony concert.

In addition to the regular excursions by RTÉ's performing groups, many special occasions have been marked by a unique concert. The NSO inaugurated the University Concert Hall in Limerick on 18 and 19 September 1993, giving the première of John Buckley's 'Rivers of Paradise',[60] and in 1994 the

59 Gorham, departmental minute 15 May 1959, ibid. Jack O'Kelly, also an army officer, had been killed during the civil war.   60 The speakers in Buckley's work were Bill Golding and Bernadette

RTÉCO and Proinnsías Ó Duinn at Our Lady of Lourdes Church, Drogheda, gave the première of Michael Holohan's 'Cromwell', commissioned by Drogheda Federation of Residents and Tenants Association to mark the town's 800th anniversary in 1994. Both orchestras participated in 2001 in the formal opening of Farmleigh House in Dublin's Phoenix Park, to which the RTÉCO has returned for popular concerts in successive summer seasons.

Support for choral societies such as the Culwick (founded 1898), Our Lady's (1945), the Guinness Choir (1951), the St James's Choir (1965) or the Limerick Choral Union (which Hans Waldemar Rosen was instrumental in establishing in 1967) has been forthcoming from RTÉ for the traditional Christmas-time performances of Handel's *Messiah*, and many other choral works, such as requiems, have been performed by the NSO with one or more of these choirs, in addition to its work with the RTÉ Philharmonic Choir. The largest such occasion was a performance in 1992 by the NSO and RTÉCO (under Owain Arwel Hughes) of Mahler's 'symphony of a thousand' (the eighth) in Dublin's Point Theatre to mark the quatercentenary of TCD, which involved ten choirs (including the RTÉ Philharmonic and Cór na nÓg RTÉ) and was the biggest assembly of such forces in Ireland since 1847. The RTÉCO returned to the Point later that year with the Irish Chamber Orchestra for a performance of *Messiah* conducted by James Cavanagh, with the Tallaght, Culwick and Our Lady's choral societies, and the choirs of Christ Church and St Patrick's cathedrals, under the aegis of the Gay Byrne Show on RTÉ Radio 1, in aid of relief work in Somalia. The NSO has also given many concerts at the Point with international stars such as José Carreras, Kiri te Kanawa and Luciano Pavarotti.

Other significant one-off events which have either involved RTÉ's performing groups or have been organised by RTÉ include the US Bicentennial (1976), the Patrick Pearse centenary and the 250th anniversary of the RDS (both in 1981),[61] the performance of the 'Irish Ring' in 1982 by the Glasnevin Musical Society and the RTÉCO, the James Joyce centenary (also 1982),[62] a concert to mark the end of Patrick Hillery's term of office as President in 1990 (the NSO conducted by Proinnsías O'Duinn, including Gerard Victory's 'Ómós don Uachtarán'), the official opening of the O'Reilly Hall in UCD by the RTÉCO in 1994 and – a sad and even traumatic event for those taking part – the 1995 Daffodil Day of the Irish Cancer Society to celebrate the life of Audrey Park Collins who had recently died from cancer, commemorated by Bill Whelan's

Comerford; the programme also included Beethoven's 'Emperor' piano concerto (no. 5), with soloist Barry Douglas, and Dvořák's symphony no. 9 ('from the new world'), conducted by Colman Pearce. 61 Pearse was born in 1879, but it was not possible to stage the commemorative concert, with Seóirse Bodley's commissioned symphony no. 2, until January 1981. 62 The RTÉSO's concert included Humphrey Searle's 'The Riverrun' and Gerard Victory's 'Six Epiphanies of the Author'.

'Pictures of Audrey', and also marking the recent cancer deaths of other members of the orchestras: Audrey's husband Archie Collins, violinists Carlos Assa-Munt, Ray Cavanagh and Jack Leydier, violist Charles Maguire and bassist Herbert Nowak, as well as former principal conductor Bryden Thomson.

Ballet has been served by the RTÉ orchestras, with the RÉLO working with Patricia Ryan's Dublin-based National Ballet in A.J. Potter's 'Careless Love' (1960) and 'Gamble, No Gamble' (1961)[63] and, more recently, with Irish National Ballet (Cork) in its final production, 'Oscar', with music from the *oeuvre* of Arnold Bax and choreographed by Domy Reiter-Soffer (1989).

When an event such as 'European Music Year' (1985) takes place, it is, ironically, difficult for an organisation such as RTÉ to know how to make any exceptional contribution, since its performing groups will, in any case, be giving their usual annual quota of concerts and broadcasts. However, since that year was the tercentenary of the births of Bach, Handel and Scarlatti, RTÉ presented performances of Bach's B minor Mass and his Easter and Christmas Oratorios, and Handel's *Judas Maccabeus* and his organ concerti, and, looking to the future, premières of Irish composers including three new symphonies, Raymond Deane's 'Enchainement' and James Wilson's cello concerto. Many other special broadcasts and chamber music events were included in the RTÉ schedules for 1985, including a documentary on the life and work of János Fürst ('The Making of a Conductor') and another on a European tour by Comhaltas Ceoltóirí Éireann. Another international event that drew on RTÉ's resources was the concert in 1992 to mark the United Nations Conference on the Environment and Fresh Water, which featured John Buckley's 'A Thin Halo of Blue' (originally RTÉ's entry to the 1990 Prix Italia).

A different aspect of outreach to the Irish musical community at large has been the appearance of an RTÉ orchestra as part of a special musical event such as the Dublin Festival of Twentieth-Century Music which took place from 1969 until 1984, and was a joint venture between the MAI and RTÉ.[64] With invited guests such as Messiaen (1976, 'Turangalîla-symphonie'), Peter Maxwell Davies (1978, with his group 'The Fires of London'), Andrzej Panufnik (1978), Witold Lutosławski (1978: first symphony and cello concerto), Elliott Carter (1980), Karlheinz Stockhausen (1982, with 'Inori') and Arne Nordheim and Mauricio Kagel (1984), it was unique among festivals of its kind for its exclu-

---

63 'Careless Love' was to a libretto by Donagh MacDonagh; 'Gamble, No Gamble' was to Patrick Kavanagh's 'The Gambler: A Ballet': for an account of its gestation and production, cf. A. Quinn, op. cit., pp. 401–2. 64 The prime movers in the establishment of the Festival were Gerard Schurmann and Gerard Victory, soon joined by Brian Boydell, who effected the administrative support from the MAI. A subsequent festival was presented by RTÉ alone in 1986, and featured the première of Jerome de Bromhead's first symphony. Schurmann (b. 1924), a Dutch composer now living in the USA, attracted considerable early attention from the 1940s, and had visited Ireland frequently before proposing the idea of the Festival to Victory.

sive attention to twentieth-century work, and was responsible for the increased toleration of, and interest in, contemporary music among Irish audiences. Lothar Faber, as soloist in Bruno Maderna's oboe concerto, A.J. Potter's 'Missa Brevis' and Mogens Ellegaard performing the accordion concerto by fellow countryman Ole Schmidt, were the orchestral highlights of the 1971 festival;[65] Raymond Warren's second symphony, Gerard Victory's 'Jonathan Swift: a symphonic portrait' and Brian Boydell's cantata 'Mors et Vita' came in 1972; and in 1974, the performance of the Berg violin concerto by Kyung-Wha Chung (who had previously recorded the Tchaikovsky and Beethoven concertos for RTÉ television).

The Festival was originally conceived as an annual event, but quickly became biennial, with RTÉ providing a 'mini-festival' in most of the fallow years. Its importance was underlined by the presence of many foreign critics, such as Felix Aprahamian (*Sunday Times*), William Mann (*The Times*) and Robert Henderson (*Sunday Telegraph*) who thus became acquainted with the work of the RTÉSO, and the RTÉ Singers and String Quartet. The Festival did much to foster an awareness and appreciation of contemporary music which had been largely missing from concert programmes in recent years, and it became possible for RTÉ thereafter to introduce more new works to the repertoire, although not as extensively as we have noted in the 1940s and 50s.

Since 1980, Ireland has hosted an international organ competition, to which the RTÉ orchestras have contributed, but perhaps the most prestigious (because most highly publicised) international event to which the NSO is party is the triennial Dublin International Piano Competition since 1988, for which it plays on the two final nights in the concerto round, and guarantees a future engagement for the first prizewinner.

This brief survey of outreach by RTÉ performing groups would not be complete without the observation that, since very early days, many of its musicians have formed freelance groups. At first, with the encouragement of Michael Bowles, members of the studio orchestra gave late-night broadcasts under the name 'Studio Players'. Zola Cirulli, Jack Cheatle and others were encouraged to supplement their income with *ad hoc* groups of various 'combinations', and were succeeded in later years by such as the André Prieur Ensemble,[66] Les Amis de la Musique (of which the prime mover was bassoonist Gilbert Berg), Heinz Rittweger's 'Czardas Orchestra' and 'Alpine Band', Herbert Pöche's Dublin Chamber Orchestra (which visited Denmark, with RTÉ's encouragement in 1969), Colman Pearce's 'Ulysses Ensemble' which was the backbone

---

65 The 'highlights' listed include only those concerts involving RTÉ personnel. 66 The members of the Prieur Ensemble varied on occasion, but the core players (in the 1950s) were Jaroslav Vaneček (violin), Máire Larchet (viola), Maurice Meulien (cello), Albert Solivérès (oboe) and André Prieur (flute), with (occasionally) Síle Larchet (harp) and Anthony Hughes (piano).

of 'Summer Music at Carrolls', the contemporary music group 'Concorde' (founded by Jane O'Leary)[67] and the successive Irish Chamber Orchestra(s), the first of which (1963–6) sparked off a major crisis in the RTÉSO; the second (1970–94) gained international status, touring to the USA (1972, '78 and '85), France (1974, '75 and '77), Italy (1975), Russia (1979) and China (1980), besides touring in Ireland to almost every major town.

These groups have, with RTÉ's permission,[68] provided much of the non-broadcasting musical life of Ireland. Some of these, for example Dublin Concert Brass and the Georgian Brass Ensemble, were composed entirely of RTÉ players,[69] and occasionally performed with other RTÉ groups, and even used the RTÉ name (for example 'the Brass Ensemble of the RTÉSO').[70] Audrey Park, as leader of, first, the RTÉCO and then the NSO, also had a number of chamber groups named after the maker of her violin – the Testore String Quartet and the Testore Chamber Orchestra – but also led 'The Audrey Park Ensemble' in her own right.

Members of the RTÉ Singers – especially Patrick Ring, Peter McBrien and Gerald Duffy – were the core of Irish National Opera, founded in 1965, which toured small-scale opera performances to over eighty venues in twenty-nine counties which might not otherwise have the opportunity of seeing live opera performances. The company utilised a piano accompaniment – the instrument and trailer having been provided by Lady Mayer – but it gave James Wilson's *Twelfth Night* in Wexford and Dublin in 1969–70, and its apogee was reached in 1981 when, backed by the RTÉCO under Proinnsías Ó Duinn, it gave the première of A.J. Potter's *The Wedding* at the Abbey Theatre. Lauding that event, INO's Patron, George Colley, Tánaiste and Minister for Energy, said that 'it is undoubtedly largely due to INO's doughty persistence ... that there is now a re-awakening of interest in opera all across the country'.[71] It was therefore a matter of public regret that, in establishing Opera Theatre Company on a professional basis in 1986, to tour with an orchestra to smaller venues, the Arts Council considered it necessary to withhold funding from INO, as if there was a conflict of interests between the two organisations.

---

67 Concorde's regular members are: Alan Smale (violin), David James (cello), Madeleine Staunton (flute), Paul Roe (clarinet) and Richard O'Donnell (percussion) with Jane O'Leary (piano). **68** Traditionally RTÉ's musicians had been contractually obliged to seek permission from line management to undertake paid freelance work, and the acknowledgement that they appear 'by permission of the RTÉ Authority' was printed in the relevant concert programme. On occasions RTÉ withheld permission, particularly when the event was sponsored by a competitor such as Century Radio or 98FM, but in 1992 this requirement was rescinded. **69** Dublin Concert Brass: Victor Malíř, Patrick McElwee, Tom Briggs and Colin Block (horns), Joszef Csibi and Charles Parkes (trumpets), Carey Donaldson (trombone) and Hartmut Pritzel (tuba). **70** The Georgian Brass Ensemble were Patrick McElwee (horn, leader), Seán Cahill (trombone), Hartmut Pritzel (tuba), and Eric Dunlea and Szabolcs Vedres (trumpets). **71** 'Address by the Tánaiste and Minister for Energy', 27 May 1981, Government Information Services.

TRADITIONAL MUSIC

It would be absurd to attempt to encapsulate in such an abbreviated form such a major topic as RTÉ's attention to Irish traditional music since 1926: so much has already been written on the subject and documented by way of radio and television series. Much more so than a standard concert programme of 'classical' music, a broadcast of 'traditional' music, played in, literally, an inimitable style from a unique recording, is a form of documentary that establishes its own *raison d'être* by virtue of the broadcast itself. Here, we shall consider the main strands of that music on the airwaves, particularly in the early years of RÉ. But equally, it is impossible to evade the question of 'Irishness' in describing the collection and transmission of traditional Irish music by the agents of R(T)É from the late 1940s onwards. While, therefore, this chapter cannot provide a *catalogue raisonnée* of the music broadcast on radio and television (any more than it can detail all the highways and byways of 'classical' music that have been explored by its performing groups) it is possible, even with brevity, to outline the phases through which this collection and transmission have moved; this in itself will indicate both the elements in Irish music-making which have become icons of authenticity, and those which have become serious points of contention.

The five-part television series *Bringing It All Back Home* in 1991 did much to draw attention to the macaronic nature of modern Irish music-making by emphasising its mixture of styles and musical languages. A significant element in this compounding of musical styles has been the repatriation of some of the musical genres of Irish traditional music which had been driven into exile through enforced emigration to the USA, due to poverty, famine and disease, and had encountered and embraced cognate musical expressions – in particular, in the Appalachian mountains. Exile, as an experience of absence (and thus of longing for what has been lost or forsaken), often operates as a focus on identity and helps to preserve a particular sense, and even practice, of that identity. Much Irish music could be said to have been waiting for rediscovery and, as *Bringing It All Back Home* indicated, the visits of Ciarán MacMathúna to the USA in 1962 and 1966, to record programmes for his radio series 'A Job of Journeywork', acted as a catalyst in bringing to Irish listeners a strand that was, at least, unfamiliar.[72] The re-introduction of the music of Michael Coleman, which had been so popular in commercial recordings in the 1920s, was another epiphany of Irish music-making which had been almost hermetically encapsulated in a time-warp for many decades.

72 The US version of the programme was entitled 'American Journeywork'. One of the performers recorded by MacMathúna was Larry Redican (1908–75) who had been a student of Arthur Darley.

Perhaps the issue as it faced 2RN at the outset is best exemplified by the context of 1927, the year after its inauguration, when Frank Roche wrote in his 'Notes on Irish Dancing', 'our policy and ambition for the future should be to make full use of the great store [of dance music] already in our possession'[73] which is precisely what 2RN/RÉ, following the lead set by the Irish Folklore Commission since 1935, aimed to achieve, once recording equipment became available in the 1940s. Before that time, however, the mixed blessings of the céilí band were the most evident example of a form of music-making that, rather than representing continuity of form, had been invented to serve an evolving social need of Irish people in London in the 1890s.[74] Its emergence thus reflected the fact that Irishness in music had already become an internationally active affair (as it had in literary and linguistic matters with the foundation of the Irish Literary Society in London in 1891–2 and branches of the Gaelic League after its establishment in 1893).

The 'Irishness' of Irish music – and consequently the politicisation of musical representations of Ireland – has produced its own ambivalence: firstly, the 'céilí band' or the 'céilí house' as a social phenomenon, emphatically reproducing what are believed to be basic and inherent characteristics of Irish people in the rhythms of their dances, and, secondly, the nationalism presumed to be underlying those characteristics and which can be mobilised when music is required to express an inalienable Irishness in unmistakably Irish forms.

It may seem unnecessary to raise points such as these in a description of R(T)É's musical output, but as the more recent television productions have shown – especially the fall-out from Micheál Ó Suilleabháin's *River of Sound* – the debate which we have already noted between 'purists' and adulterers in so-called 'classical' arrangements and treatments continues to fuel discussions of Irishness in 'traditional' circles. The sentiments expressed by Henebry, as evident in the attempted ban on radio transmission of jazz and other foreign forms of dance in the 1930s and 40s, found support among the more articulate members of society such as TDs – including, as we have seen, at least one minister responsible for broadcasting – and, in the period of debated and negotiated nationalism that saw the introduction of censorship of films and publications, the advent of Fianna Fáil as a one-party government, the economic (and cultural) war with Britain and the depression of the 1950s, a deep division among Irish composers as to what 'Irishness' in music might, or might not, be.

---

73 Quoted in F. Vallely, *The companion to Irish traditional music*, p. 320. Roche (1866–1961) was a friend of Hardebeck, Séamus Clandillon and Mairéad ní Annagáin; his life spanned a period of Irish history that saw the land wars, the creation of the GAA and the Gaelic League, the war of independence, the civil war, the creation of Radio Éireann, the economic war, the 'Emergency', the founding of CCÉ and the debate leading to the creation of Telefís Éireann. Within these social, cultural and political developments he looked for the creation of a 'national school' that would nurture the music brought to light by the collectors.   74 Cf. F. Vallely, op. cit., p. 60.

The fact that on the opening night of 2RN (1 January 1926) violinist Arthur Darley was chosen to play three Irish airs in the earlier part of the programme and, later, a romance by Hugo Wolf and a bourrée by Alfred Moffat, is indicative of the new station's intention of bridging the two prevalent musical traditions, at a time when it was by no means certain that either would have a viable future. Darley, as an accomplished and highly respected practitioner in both the classical and traditional genres, had played at the Abbey Theatre (symbol, for many, of the renaissance of Ireland's literary fortunes) in the days before Larchet had formed the theatre's resident orchestra, came from a family which counted Dion Boucicault as a member, had been violin professor at the RIAM, became the first Director of the Municipal School of Music, and was noted as a collector of traditional music, of whom Annie Patterson said 'he identified himself with the culling and preservation of what music the country still possessed in a somewhat fluctuating and unrecorded condition'.[75] That the balance achieved in the inaugural programme (which, if anything, leaned towards the 'national' in its emphasis on content, and 'international' in its choice of performers)[76] was followed by a 'clatter' of céilí music of unchecked standard, is indication, in its turn, of a poor understanding of how Irish music might be transmitted. The notion of 'céilí' as sociability, however much it may have served the purpose of community-building both at home and among Irish emigrants, was an insufficient basis for the representation of those values for which Irish music is prized today, and which would remain largely undiscovered for the first twenty, or perhaps even thirty, years of RÉ's existence.

The inherently unsatisfactory nature of the céilí band, as argued by Seán Ó Riada, was identified by an anonymous internal RÉ report from 1942 on the Silver Star Céilí Band:

> Not at all first class, nor to my ear up to broadcasting standards. The 'arrangements' were so miscalled, for divil an arrangement at all could I detect, and the various players just blew away to their maximum volume output, as though each one were contracted to drown his neighbour, while at the same time outpacing him.[77]

This shows how unstable was the attempt by RÉ to represent Irish music-making in the area of ensemble playing. It has long been an international joke that one of the earliest genres of broadcasting on Irish radio was *dancing*, yet the imperative to re-introduce Irish listeners by means of radio to one of the two main constituents of Irish music, as evidenced in social life, was obviously very

75 *Irish Statesman*, 4 January 1930; Darley's son, also Arthur, was a violinist and a medical doctor who became a friend of Samuel Beckett.   **76** Cf. Pine, *2RN*, pp. 148–53.   **77** RTÉ Music Department file, 'Silver Star Céilí Band'.

strong in the minds of Clandillon and Vincent O'Brien, and it was one of the main reasons for the maintenance of the céilí band on the airwaves. For example 'Dancing on the Radio' was presented by the Kincora Céilí Band for twelve years from their formation in 1937,[78] by means of which the rhythms of step-dancing were made familiar by Rory O'Connor to audiences who might otherwise not have been acquainted with the genre – such was the move against dancing in all forms in the wake of the 1935 Public Dance Halls Act (which institutionalised what had been a spontaneous and unregulated activity up to that point). 1938 also saw the establishment of An Coimisiún an Rinnce or Irish Dancing Commission (parallel to the Coimisiún le Rincí Gaelacha set up by the Gaelic League in 1929–30), which sought to re-establish the primacy of authentic dancing, in an area in which cultural politics were very noticeable in the decisions as to which dances were 'Irish' and which were 'non-Irish' or 'un-Irish'. The fact that these are, today, still hotly contested issues, and that RTÉ's hosting of the 1995 Eurovision Song Contest saw the inception of the *Riverdance* phenomenon, which has both challenged and stimulated the notion of what Irish dancing is, and what contribution it can make to, and derive from, international dance genres, is evidence of how strong people's feelings can become on a subject that may not affect their lives directly, but which nonetheless causes them to ask continuing questions about their cultural identity.

The common belief, fostered or at least repeated by authorities such as Seán Ó Riada himself, that Séamus Clandillon 'invented' the céilí band, is completely erroneous, since the céilí band had existed long before the advent of 2RN. However, it is fair to say that, with Clandillon's encouragement by way of providing access to the airwaves, the concept of the céilí band gained common acceptance and credence, and its future as a medium of transmitting a form of Irish musical culture became assured.

It is also more than fair to say that, due partly to Clandillon's desperate need to find live performers from all walks of life and all genres of musical performance, and also partly to a laxity of style – which Ó Riada would attribute to the inherent weakness of the structure of the céilí band itself – the quality of performances deteriorated during the 1940s and 1950s to the point where they were less than acceptable.

One of the first bands to broadcast was the Austin Stack Céilí Band, which continued into the 1950s, appearing at that later stage in the programme sponsored by Mitchelstown Creameries.[79] Another was the Mayglass Céilí Band,

---

78 Its members were Kathleen Harrington and Pat O'Brien (fiddles), Tom Liddy (accordion), John Egan (flute), Benny Carey (drums) and Kathleen O'Connor (piano). Kathleen Harrington and her brother, John-Joe Gardiner, also gave several concerts on 2RN. 79 The members of the Austin Stack band were Edith Cross Moore, Seán Fitzpatrick and Pat Maguire (fiddles), Pat Greene (drums), Tommy Breen (piccolo) and Leo Redmond, the band's founder (piano).

formed in 1927, which continued in existence up to the 1960s. Perhaps the best-known was the Aughrim Slopes Trio (fiddlers Paddy Kelly and Jack Mulcaire, with accordionist Joe Mills) which had established a radio presence and a huge audience, especially in its own locality, since 1927, and made a commercial record in 1928. Joined by Jim Drury and Paddy Fahy (fiddles), Josie Halloran (piano), and others, they were reconstituted as the Aughrim Slopes Céilí Band from Ballinasloe, County Galway, and appeared frequently on 2RN from 1933 onwards, with a regular weekly slot on RÉ and a very extensive calendar of live engagements, including a British tour in 1945. The radio appearances were, in fact, a major plank in the band's strategy of securing live engagements, but they also helped its members individually: Mulcaire (as Secretary), wrote to T.J. Kiernan, 'as I am the only teacher of Irish music in the County of Galway it would help me a good deal if our Band was called to broadcast a few times each year'.[80] The following year he wrote to supplement that appeal: 'I give lessons on traditional Irish music on the violin and in that way help to earn a living and that's one of the reasons why I would like to broadcast occasionally'.[81]

Mulcaire was part of an old tradition with tenuous connections to the days of Carolan, in that he had played traditional music in the 'big house': living 'just beside the late Lady Gregory Coole Park and Tyllyra [*sic*] Castle the residence of the late Mr Edward Martyn', he told Vincent O'Brien (who of course had known Martyn well) 'I often played and sang Irish songs in days gone by at parties given at Coole Park for the people I have mentioned & also for Dr Douglas Hyde. If those people were here to-day I could count on good friends to help me in the musical world'.[82] What Mulcaire can have meant by assuming that Hyde (who became President of Ireland that year) was not 'here to-day' can only be imagined. But the appeal to a bygone era, populated by the dead, and with links to *illo tempore*, is a significant reminder that the era of mass communications arrived on the cusp of another that was already part of folk memory and reminiscence, and which Lady Gregory's 'Kiltartan' plays, and Hyde's collections of 'Love Songs' and 'Religious Songs' of Connacht had put into the public domain.

The Aughrim Slopes (so named from the village of Aughrim near Ballinasloe, which gave the band its signature tune of 'Lament after the Battle of Aughrim') in fact utilised every means available to secure its broadcasting, recording and performing future. In March 1937 (when the band was already well established), the Minister for P&T, Oscar Traynor, received what can only be described as a 'representation' from Senator T.V. Honan of Ennis:

> Seán O'Grady and myself had a F[ianna]F[áil] conference at Kinvara ...
> After the conference I was approached by the leader of a local ceilidhe

80 Mulcaire (writing as 'Seán Mulkere') to Kiernan, 1 January 1936, RTÉ Music Department file, 'Aughrim Slopes Céilí Band'. 81 Mulcaire to Vincent O'Brien, 17 January 1937, ibid. 82 Ibid.

band titled 'The Aughrim Slopes Ceilidhe Band'. This is a really high class band travelling far & wide to unearth really high class traditional Irish music. They have broadcasted with great success – Dublin – Athlone – for which they were allowed £8.8.0 to cover all expenses for 5. Altho' a small allowance, they were satisfied to carry on. But now they have been notified that their allowance for a band of 5 Gort-Dublin 130 miles and back, has been reduced to £4.4.0 which would scarcely pay their bus fares. Now is this the way to encourage Irish music and Irish culture? I am aware it is not of your doing, but I thought that you may be able to do something about it, because this really high class Irish music band are told in other words No Irish need apply.[83]

A week later, the band broadcast from UCG at a fee of £4.4.0, and, as they were making a record in Dublin the following month, asked if they could broadcast at the same time, which was declined. The band broadcast regularly on RÉ up to 1941, but their subsequent disappearance from the airwaves may be attributable partly to the growing demand on their time both nationally and internationally and partly to the fact that these low fees and travelling expenses operated in favour of Dublin-based bands and soloists. Whatever the 'political' situation prevailing within RÉ at the time, there was definitely a problem insofar as the regulations (imposed on RÉ by the civil service) were unhelpful to long-distance travellers. As Joe Mills wrote to RÉ:

> The broadcast is usually arranged for a Sunday night between 10pm and 12pm. This means that if we travel by rail we have to go on Saturday and return on Monday. This costs at the very least £2.10.0 per man. Now to travel by car it will cost £7.10.0 for the car and about £1.5.0 for refreshments. Then there is the danger of failure at the last moment to get a car owing to petrol shortage. You will see from above how far £6 will go to defray expenses. City bands can easily play for £6 and still make money. I respectfully suggest you increase the £6 to a sum that will leave it a bit easier on our pockets.[84]

By 1949, this was being seriously argued in the Dáil, where Roderick Connolly urged that favouring Dublin-based groups was affecting the livelihood of others: 'The only way many of these musicians, entertainers and singers down the country can establish their position in reasonable time and without

---

83 Honan to Traynor, 2 March 1937, ibid. Honan (1878–1954) was a Fianna Fáil Senator 1922–54; O'Grady (1889–1966) was a Fianna Fáil TD for Clare 1932–51 and in March 1937 was Parliamentary Secretary to the Minister for Defence. 84 Mills to RÉ 2 January 1941, ibid.

the great labours involved for some of their predecessors in the arts is to obtain engagements in Radio Éireann.'[85]

It appears that thereafter the fees and expenses offered were insufficient to induce the Aughrim Slopes to broadcast on anything other than a sporadic basis, but there was also a question of quality: in December 1951 RÉ received another representation, from Gerald Bartley TD, asking for a mobile unit to travel to Ballinasloe to audition the band, but it seems that this was declined.[86] Four months later, a note was put on the file, and copied to the Minister's private secretary, 'This is very bad indeed. They all play the tune in a noisy raucous way'.[87] Fintan Vallely records that 'different personnel joined and left over the years, emigration broke the band up, but its hallmark sound remains a nostalgic, but vivid, landmark in the music'.[88]

London-born Frank Lee, who has been credited with the creation (in 1918) of the term 'céilí band', was the founder of the Tara Céilí Band, which appeared frequently in Britain for the English Folk Dance and Song Society, and which recorded on acetate discs for 2RN in 1932. The Belhavel Trio, founded by Joe Liddy, a member of the Garda Céilí Band, also recorded for 2RN at this time.[89] A later band of note on radio was the McCusker Brothers from County Armagh, who were frequent performers in the 1940s on 'Céilí House', a series which had many manifestations, continuing into the 1960s with stalwarts such as the Dysart Céilí Band, named after the birthplace of its founder, fiddler Frank Custy.

The quality of sound, which was one of the main factors determining Ó Riada's attitude in his condemnation of the céilí band as a genre, was also a serious issue in the case of the Silver Star Céilí Band from Kells, County Meath. This band, which had broadcast from RÉ on approximately twenty occasions, beginning in 1941, had demonstrated a variable quality from the start. Nevertheless, the band was adept at provoking favourable comment in the press: the *Meath Chronicle* of 29 November 1941 observed that

> Mr J J Carr's 'Silver Star' Ceilidhe Band, Kells, was on the air from Radio Éireann on Sunday night with a programme of Irish dance music. The band, which is well known at ceilidhes and feiseanna in County Meath, gave delightful renderings of Ireland's old dance tunes with that splendidly marked rhythm and wonderful co-ordination between the instruments which characterises all its performances.

85 DD, 117, 12 July 1949, cols. 586–7. 86 Bartley to RÉ 5 December 1951; Bartley (1898–1974) was Fianna Fáil TD for Galway/Galway West 1932–51, and at this time was Parliamentary Secretary to the Minister for Agriculture. 87 Ibid., 23 April 1952. 88 Vallely, op. cit., p. 10. 89 The members of the Belhavel Trio were also part of the Kincora band and were closely associated with the Harrington and Gardiner families.

And the following year a letter-writer to the Dublin *Evening Mail* said:

> On Sunday night I had the pleasure of listening to a fine ceilidhe band
> from Radio Éireann. What impressed me most was the almost perfect
> blending of the various instruments, which gave each particular air a
> sweetness which seems to be lacking in other bands. Special praise is
> due to the very finished playing of the clarinet and accordeon [*sic*], whose
> tempo throughout was perfect.[90]

These were not points on which the judges in RÉ would agree with the music
critic of the *Meath Chronicle*, since a note on the broadcast report for their
appearance on 18 November 1942 was extremely critical.

The band continued to obtain broadcasts up to 1945 or 1946, after which
the Assistant Music Director wrote to the band's secretary, John Carr, 'in view
of the fact that the question of céilí bands has been completely re-examined
recently, it will be necessary for your céilí combination to have a further audition before another engagement can be considered'.[91] Thereafter, successive
attempts by the band to get an engagement were rebuffed, Carr being told that
it had failed an audition on 11 January 1950,[92] and again in mid-1951: 'The
standard of performance of your band is not sufficiently high to warrant a broadcast, as we found wrong chords in the piano part and the tone of the strings
very harsh'.[93] When subsequent auditions also failed, Carr wrote to the Minister
– at that time Erskine Childers – claiming that he was unfit for other work, and
that the band was his only source of livelihood. Pointing out that his son was
the local secretary of Fianna Fáil, he stated 'my other two sons look after transport at election times, I myself do impersonation agent we are all staunch members of your party all our lives ... Please do your best and try to get us on the
radio ... but no matter what the result we are still going to keep you there where
you should be all the time'.[94] Childers refused to rise to the political bait, and
simply referred the correspondence to the department. Another, unsuccessful,
audition was given in May 1953, after which the file is silent.

Quality and performance styles were also issues in the Dáil: in 1949 Éamon
Ó Ciosáin [Kissane; Fianna Fáil, Kerry North] complained:

> Sometimes ... we hear musicians rendering Irish traditional airs and
> Irish dance music and they do not seem to be up to the mark. I do not

90 'Basil', *Evening Mail*, 12 February 1942. 91 A. Duff to Carr, 19 December 1947: RTÉ Music
Department file, 'Silver Star Céilí Band (Kells)'. 92 RÉ to Carr, 18 May 1951, ibid. 93 Ibid.,
31 July 1951. 94 Carr to Childers, 12 January 1953; the letter mentions Michael Hilliard TD
(Fianna Fáil, Meath, 1943–73, and later Minister for P&T) and Senator Patrick Fitzsimons (senator 1948–73) as contacts.

know whether there is a stiff test applied nowadays or not. There used to be a fairly stiff test. But, if we are to have Irish traditional music, we should have the very best, if we can. We should be all-out to popularise and spread our native Irish music and the only way to do that it to get the best Irish musicians that we can find. It would be a good thing if somebody from the Minister's Department would go down the country and search for talent as regards Irish traditional music. The talent must be there. The best place to find it is where the language is still spoken or in places adjacent to the Gaeltacht. It is very important that we should hear our own traditional music often on the wireless and that what we hear of it is the very best ... A short time ago I listened in to a céilí band and was not at all pleased with the performance. It was supposed to have some harmonisation of Irish traditional music and, so far as my opinion goes, that so-called harmonisation destroyed the music. The Minister and his Department should see to it that no céilí bands of that description come into the studio or, if they do, they should be thrown out on the top of their heads with their fiddles and bows. I hate to hear any musician or any band destroy good Irish traditional music. The way to play Irish traditional music is the way in which our forefathers played it, without any unnatural frills.[95]

Traditional music has been presented in a variety of styles, ranging from the informal and popular, such as 'Newcomers' Hour' in the 1940s, and 'Balladmakers' Saturday Night' in the 1950s (with Albert Healy and singers such as Joe Lynch and Seán Ó Síocháin) to 'Ceolta Tíre' (1955–70) which introduced Ciarán MacMathúna to Irish listeners and in which he presented his recordings of Elizabeth Crotty, fiddlers Martin ('Junior') Crehan, Fred Finn and John Doherty and flautist Peter Horan. All these subsequently appeared in MacMathúna's own programme, 'A Job of Journeywork' (1957–70: the title being derived from the set-dance of the same name), which was marked by an RTÉ publication in 1989, and was succeeded by 'Mo Cheol Thú'. 'Fleadh Cheoil an Raidió' and 'Reachaireacht an Riadaigh' were outlets for the revolutionary style devised by Seán Ó Riada for Ceoltóirí Chualann in 1961–2, which went on to reach its peak with the concert recorded as 'Ó Riada sa Gaiety' in 1969. Following Ó Riada's death, Bill Meek wrote that 'Fleadh Cheoil an Raidío' (which also featured *seannchaí* [storyteller] Éamon Kelly and singers Seán Ó Sé and Seán Ó Siocháin) 'was more than a programme for traditional enthusiasts. All over the country thousands of homes would tune in to what was one of the *social* highlights of the week'.[96] 'The Long Note' (1974–90),

95 DD, 117, 12 July 1949, cols. 583–4. 96 *Irish Times*, 11 October 1971.

'Reels of Memory' and 'The Heather Breeze' (both 1979–81), 'Sunday Folk' (1981–5), 'Sounds Traditional' (1996–8), besides a programme sponsored by CCÉ in the 1970s, have continued the regular marking of the history, and developments, of Irish traditional music.

To give some brief examples of well-known individual musicians who broadcast from RÉ: from Millstreet, County Cork, fiddler Liam Ó Murchadha gave at least thirteen broadcasts from RÉ between early 1944 and mid-1953; the Belfast fiddler Seán Maguire (1924–2005), winner of the Belfast and Lisburn feiseanna in 1946–7 and of the Oireachtas in 1949, who described himself as 'progressive traditional',[97] played on BBC Belfast and RÉ with the Malachy Sweeney Céilí Band before making his first solo appearance on 6 March 1948, in a ten-minute recital in which he played (with guitar accompaniment) three reels ('The Dairy Maid', 'Bonnie Kate' and 'Jenny Chickens'), three jigs ('Brennan's Favourite', 'The Boys of the Town', and 'Wheels of the World') and three hornpipes ('The Bashful Bachelor', 'The Fiddler's Contest' and 'The Sunshine'). Nine months later he was on the air again, and over the next decade he appeared on average twice per year, although an altercation with John Reidy led to a hiccup in his contributions in 1954. He also formed the Seán Maguire Céilí Band 'of Radio Fame' which broadcast on the BBC Home Service. Fintan Vallely remarks that Maguire's habit of playing with accompaniment is 'something frowned upon by traditional music aesthetics yet he remains respected as a grand virtuoso'.[98]

Another fiddler who made appearances on RÉ in the 1940s and 1950s described himself in his publicity brochure as 'Irish Radio Violinist'. This player, despite having impressive credentials, did not impress RÉ as much as he should, and appears to have been lucky to secure engagements, since Fachtna Ó hAnnracháin wrote of his 1948 audition: 'very amateurish performance … the general effect was like a student performance of mediocre quality. I fear [he] does not really feel the music he plays, or, if he does, he fails to impress his audience of the fact'.[99] The instance is one of many, illustrative of the legendary fact that the demand for broadcasters, singly and in groups, was far greater than the supply of players of acceptable standards, and that this had been the case since the inception of 2RN. Nevertheless, it was necessary for RÉ to continue to seek new and better players, while it continued to tolerate those whose standard only barely reached a broadcastable level.

One example of a player who met all the criteria, and whose work was so exemplary as to enable RÉ to establish standards for others to emulate, was piper Leo Rowsome, who made his first broadcast from RÉ on 28 April 1940,

---

97 F. Vallely, op. cit., p. 223. 98 Ibid., p. 224. 99 Ó hAnnracháin, note on RÉ Music Department file, name withheld, 1948.

and continued to perform regularly for at least the next decade. During an eleven-year period, with a significant break of almost a year in 1943–4, Rowsome made at least forty-one solo broadcasts, and seventy-four broadcasts with the 'Leo Rowsome Pipe Quartet'; his only appearances in 1945 were with 'Leo Rowsome's Uilleann Pipe Band', and in 1950 the 'Juvenile Pipe Quartet' made what seems to have been its only appearance.[1]

It may not be readily appreciated by those today to whom Rowsome has become not only synonymous with the piping tradition but also one of the most renowned and respected figures in twentieth-century Irish music, that when he began his broadcasting career at the age of thirty-seven he was almost unknown, and the uilleann pipes themselves, as an instrument, had very little public profile and were regarded by most as outlandish. Born into a Huguenot family of pipe-makers, Rowsome succeeded his brother Thomas as a teacher of pipes at the Municipal School of Music (1920–70) and was in turn succeeded by his own son Leon.[2] He was a co-founder of the revived Dublin Pipers' Club in 1936, and of CCÉ in 1950–1.

Fintan Valley remarks that 'living in the age before recognition of traditional music as an art, Leo's economy of concerts and teaching was precarious … [He] practised both his art and his craft in the difficult years of Irish music's transition from necessity of life through practical redundancy into revival. He has been one of the architects of that comeback'.[3] Although the extant file covers only the years up to 1951, it is clear that it was RÉ's intention to retain Rowsome as a broadcaster thereafter: when he wrote to Ó hAnnracháin that his teaching job at the Municipal School meant that he was unpaid for the summer months, Ó hAnnracháin replied 'we shall endeavour to arrange as many broadcasts as possible for you during that period'.[4]

The establishment in 1947 of a mobile recording unit in one sense brought broadcasting into the company of the legendary collectors of folk material since 1792, and, in another, created a new, technological future for that tradition of collecting. The essential tool stipulated by Bartók was at last available: Séamus Ennis (1919–82), himself best known today as a piper, was its first recordist, moving four years later into the service of the BBC for its own series 'As I Roved Out'.[5] The recording equipment, loaded into the back of Ennis's car,

---

1 RÉ Music Department file, 'Leo Rowsome'. Rowsome's quartet, in addition to Rowsome himself, included, at various times, Seán Seery, Willie Clancy, Séamus Ennis and Jack Wade. 2 For a letter from Thomas Rowsome concerning the making of pipes in the early twentieth century, *vide* Pine and Acton, *To talent alone*, p. 346. 3 Valley, op. cit., p. 323. 4 Rowsome to Ó hAnnracháin 1 May 1951; Ó hAnnracháin to Rowsome 2 May 1951, RÉ file 'Leo Rowsome'. 5 Séamus Ennis was the son of James Ennis, an early broadcaster on 2RN with 'The Fingal Trio': Fintan Valley (op. cit., p. 118) describes him as 'one of the country's most important traditional music figures this century';

consisted of a disc-cutting machine on which sound was recorded directly onto fragile acetate discs; tape-recorders came into use a few years later. Ennis was shortly joined by Seán MacRéamoinn, later a journalist, broadcaster and Controller of Radio at RTÉ, and Proinsías Ó Conluain (a former student of Seán O'Boyle), who went on to make such radio series as 'The Ballad Tree', 'The Singer and the Song' and 'Between the Jigs and the Reels' and documentary programmes on collectors including Hardebeck, Sam Henry and Capt. Francis O'Neill. One of their earliest recordings was with 75-years-old storyteller Peig Sayers, and another, recently issued by RTÉ as a CD, was made on Arranmore Island in 1953 with the 74-year-old singer Róise Bean Mhic Ghrianna (Róise na nAmhrán).[6] To entitle the resultant series 'Ceolta Tíre' was to attempt an identification of music with land, with territory, with an idea of space, and of course with Ireland itself.

Ciarán MacMathúna joined this unit in 1954 from the Placenames Commission, and in itself his career as a collector and broadcaster, spanning over fifty years of dedication to Irish folk song and folk lore, and embodied in long-running series such as *A Job of Journeywork* (1957–70) and its successor *Mo Cheol Thú* (1970-), constitutes a form of ongoing documentary of Irish music-making in all its forms. Mac Mathúna has become synonymous with both the presentation and representation of Irish music, and listeners to his programmes soon become aware that he has spent a lifetime not only in listening to, and recording, music in all kinds of venues, but also in reaching an understanding of what it is, and how it relates to other areas of Irish civilisation. In this pursuit, MacMathúna has a place in the genealogy of Irish folklorism, the first modern figures of which were Bunting and Petrie. With the advent of portable recording equipment, the creation of a radio archive became possible. Some of MacMathúna's earliest recordings, in 1955, with concertina player Elizabeth Crotty (1885–1960), created a template for his style of 'house sessions' which brought the listener to the fireside of some of the great players and singers, and thus brought the past into the future. As Mac Mathúna said himself, 'It was a whole new concept. Public broadcasting was going to the people for the first time'.[7] Fintan Vallely notes MacMathúna's 'relaxed microphone style' as a component in 'the key period of revival of interest in traditional music' as it 'became the voice of [that] revival, the link between all parts of the country and with emigrants, a source of comparison and inspiration' and 'developed by education the listening audiences which re-patterned the music community'.[8] The copying and transfer from RTÉ to the Irish

his daughter, Catherine, is an organist. **6** *Róise na nAmhrán: songs of a Donegal woman*' RTE CD 178. **7** 'People in Business' by 'Mercator', *Irish Times*, 27 January 1986. **8** F. Vallely, op. cit., pp. 221–2.

Traditional Music Archive of re-mastered recordings dating from the 1940s, for which RTÉ producer and presenter Harry Bradshaw has largely been responsible, is the final phase in its custodianship of this unique national store-house and the opening of yet another future as this material, including over 10,000 hours of recordings, becomes available to a wider public.

Documentary programmes have also been a major feature of radio output from the earlier period of RÉ up to the present day. From the 1940s, the poly-mathic scholar Donal O'Sullivan (1893–1973) made several ground-breaking series, most notably 'Songs of the Irish' (1948 and 1959–60), and 'Songs of the Harpers' (1956), the former appearing in book form in 1960.[9] 'Songs of the Harpers' was a remarkable series, eliciting the following response from a radio-listening group in Dublin: writing to Veronica Kennedy, who sang the songs with harp accompaniment by Síle Larchet, Michael Walshe said 'This – and you are too young to know it – was the flame that fired the Gaelic movement more than fifty years ago, this passionate ecstasy of true Gaelic, that led to the Language Movement, and to the Irish resurgence. This performance ... was the living spirit of the Gael. It has almost been commercialised and too often subjected to political opportunism in modern days'.[10] A third major series by O'Sullivan described the 'Great Collectors' (1958): Bunting, Petrie, Forde, Hudson, Pigot, Goodman, Joyce and O'Neill.

This rediscovery of areas of the Irish heritage by means of such program-ming (which in itself represented only a summary of painstaking scholarship by such as O'Sullivan) is one of the most valuable activities undertaken by the enlightened 'talks officers' or 'general features officers' at RÉ who included the writers Roibéard Ó Faracháin (1939–47) and Francis McManus (1947–65). It has continued under the aegis of the music department with researcher-pre-senters such as Harry Bradshaw, who incorporated much documentary mate-rial in the series 'The Long Note' and 'The Dance Music of Ireland', and the series in which he retrieved much Irish material of the 1920s and 1930s, 'The Irish Phonograph', presented by Nicholas Carolan 1983–6 (which in turn gave the impetus to the establishment of the Irish Traditional Music Archive).

9 O'Sullivan, a barrister by training, was Clerk of the Senate, in 1940 publishing the controver-sial *The Irish Free State and its Senate*; he edited the *Journal of the Irish Folklore Society* and provoked a *cause célèbre* in legal, musical and radio circles when he published a scathing review of Séamus Clandillon's *Songs of the Irish Gaels* in the *Irish Statesman*, for which Clandillon sued unsuccessfully for libel. O'Sullivan was subsequently a lecturer at both TCD and UCD, and the acknowledged expert on Carolan, his *Carolan: life and times of an Irish harper* (1958, reissued 2002) being the stan-dard work on the subject. His second series on Songs dealt with historical, drinking, patriotic and religious songs, love songs, lullabies, laments, songs of occupation and songs of the harpers. His scripts were illustrated by singers James Cuthbert (husband of Síle Larchet-Cuthbert), Richard Cooper, Cáit Lanigan (Cooper's wife), Veronica Kennedy, Tomás Ó Suilleabháin, Liam Devally, Bernadette Greevy and Mary Tinney with harp accompaniment by Síle Larchet-Cuthbert.
10 M. Walshe to V. Kennedy, 6 October 1956.

Bradshaw has also been responsible for re-mastering the 1947 acetates of piper Johnny Doran in 'Bunch of Keys' (1988) and for 'repatriating' the reputation of Sligo-born fiddler Michael Coleman (1891–1946) who began his recording career in the USA in 1921 and whose records have been described by Bradshaw as 'classics of their kind … among the finest examples of recorded folk music in the early twentieth century'.[11]

Peter Browne has also presented and produced series such as 'The Long Note', 'Ulster Folk' and 'Airneán', as well as working beside MacMathúna on 'Mo Cheol Thú', and has produced documentaries on such classic figures as Pádraig O'Keeffe ('the Sliabh Luchra fiddle master') and his pupil Denis Murphy, and Séamus Ennis, all of which have given rise to commercial CDs published by RTÉ.

Traditional music has been served far better by television since 1962 than has 'classical' music. Tony MacMahon, who has presented many television programmes (and initiated 'The Long Note' for radio) was responsible for 'Aisling Geal' in 1969, followed by 'Ag Déanamh Ceoil', which ran for eighty editions, focusing on regional variations. He has also made the evocatively titled series 'My Own Place' (1980) and 'The Pure Drop' (1989–96, with, among its presenters, singers Dolores Keane and Iarla Ó Lionaird) and, most recently, the archival series 'Come West Along the Road'. A stimulating studio encounter in 1977 between traditional flute player and Chieftains member Matt Molloy and 'classical' populist James Galway revealed hidden gifts in both the wooden and golden instruments and did much to quash the prejudicial idea that players from two 'traditions' cannot work together. In 1984 an idiosyncratic series, 'Atlantean', produced and presented by former RTÉ producer Bob Quinn, explored an idea first promulgated by Charles Acton and Seán Ó Riada, that the roots of Celtic culture (for example, *sean-nós*) were to be found in the Islamic periphery of the Mediterranean; Quinn returned to this theme with 'Navigatio – Atlantean 2' in 1998.[12] Micheál Ó hEidhin, a schools inspector and CCÉ activist, whose parents broadcast on 2RN, has worked on programmes such as 'Guth na nÓg', 'Bring Down the Lamp' and 'In Song and in Story', in addition to appearing on 'A Man and His Music'. The turn of the 1990s saw 'Cur agus Cúiteamh' (1990), produced by Cathal Goan (later Ceannasaí of Teilifís na Gaeilge and now Director-General of RTÉ), and 'Up Sráid Eoin – the story of the Dingle Wren' (1991) produced by Ríonach Uí Ógáin. 1991 also saw the screening of 'Bringing it all Back Home', a co-commission by RTÉ and the BBC, produced by Nuala O'Connor and Philip King, which explored the for-

---

11 In Vallely, op. cit., p. 75. 12 The 1984 series was also published in book form, as *Atlantean: Ireland's North African and maritime heritage* and republished as *The Irish Atlantean: Ireland's oriental and maritime heritage*, (2004).

tunes of Irish music in the context of emigration and its encounters with other musical genres; its suggestive juxtaposition of performers such as Mary Black and Dolores Keane with Emmylou Harris, of Irish fiddler Paddy Glackin with Appalachian fiddler Ricky Skaggs, or piper Davey Spillane with the Everly Brothers, and an interview with composer John Cage on the subject of his work 'Roaratorio' (1961), based on Joyce's *Finnegans Wake*, which employed Irish traditional players and which he described as 'a circus of live Irish music [with] sounds recorded in places mentioned in the *Wake*',[13] was, perhaps, less contentious than, and could even be seen as a prelude to, 'River of Sound' (1995), a seven-part series also co-commissioned by RTÉ and the BBC, presented by Micheál Ó Suilleabháin (and also produced by Philip King) and featuring many varieties of Irish music including a chamber orchestra. 'River of Sound' provoked a 'Late, Late Show' programme in which Tony MacMahon challenged the authenticity of Ó Suilleabháin's work in the context of change and/or continuity. This in its turn was responsible, in part, for a debate during the first 'Crossroads' conference the following year, which was also partly provoked by the advent in 1995 of 'Riverdance', with seduction of land by river at the centre of a modern dance spectacular which has gone on from its original incarnation as the seven-minute 'interval act' of that year's 'Eurovision Song Contest' hosted by RTÉ, to become a worldwide phenomenon as a ninety-minute stage show running concurrently on at least two continents at any one time.[14]

Teilifís na Gaeilge/TG4, the Irish-language television channel established under the aegis of RTÉ in 1996, has also contributed to viewers' knowledge of the traditional genre, with series (directed by Philip King and produced by Nuala O'Connor) such as 'Sult', presented by Donal Lunny, with guests Van Morrison, Sharon Shannon and Elvis Costello; 'Geantraí', originally a series of thirty 20-minute programmes from Cork and Tuam which ran to seven seasons; and 'Ar Bhruach Dhún Réimhe', featuring the music of Oriel (south-east Ulster), and documentaries 'Bláth gach Géag dá dTig' (on Lillis Ó Laoire, featuring music from Donegal), 'Meitheal' (on the musical partnership of Séamus Begley and Steve Cooney), and 'Laoi na Píbe' on piper Liam O'Flynn. Tony McCarthy of Forefront Productions has directed seven series of 'Geantraí' and two series of 'Abair Amhrán'.

YOUTH AND MUSIC

From its earliest years, Radio Éireann was perceived as a powerful medium of education. Music had a part in that area of the schedules concerned with intro-

---

13 *Irish Times*, 2 August 1983.   **14** 'Riverdance' was partly anticipated by Dublin City Ballet's 'Time Dance' for the interval act of the 1981 Eurovision Song Contest.

ducing listeners to the cultures of other countries, with illustrated lectures by Walter Starkie, an expert on gypsy culture and an accomplished violinist. Today, by means of 'Music in the Classroom' and the illustrated concerts which were given for schoolchildren in association with Ceol-Chumann na nÓg 1952–91, RTÉ has reached a wide range of young people whose appreciation of live music enhances their school studies.

In her important study *Passing It On: the transmission of music in Irish culture*, Marie McCarthy reminds us that in 1926 the Irish National Teachers' Organisation recommended the gramophone 'for the purpose of developing the pupils' musical taste', and that in 1927 Professor John F. Larchet advocated that every school should have a 'cheap gramophone ... as an aid to the collective development of musical skill, taste and culture'.[15] In 1930 a combination of broadcasting and the gramophone – the two most powerful mass media of the day – was being recognised as the agent of an improvement in musical taste, and advocated as a means of developing critical listening skills.[16] Marie McCarthy does not hesitate to emphasise that the *transmission* of musical skills was a highly motivated concern, with heavy political overtones, and we would do well to reflect that, at that stage in the life of the Free State, access to the microphone, especially in the case of broadcasts reaching and affecting the young, was a matter for mature reflection on the part of the gatekeepers. However, while it is valid to speculate that 'cultural leaders seeking to build a national identity were aware of the power of radio to shape musical taste' (especially when she points to the campaign against the broadcasting of jazz), one might demur at her notion that 'a policy for music in the national radio service was developed',[17] if she means to indicate an *explicit* policy. As we have seen in chapter 2, there is no evidence whatsoever to indicate that Vincent O'Brien as music director, or Séamus Clandillon and Séamus Brennan as directors of the radio service, had any such policy. Nevertheless, indiscriminate though the broadcasts of some forms of music might become, in the earliest years a serious concern was evident in what was transmitted and who transmitted it. Without any overt policy regarding indoctrination of the nation's young, there was an implicit consciousness of the significance of the medium in serving the interests of all sections of the fledgling community.

From 1936, a series of weekly broadcasts relating to music teaching in primary schools was initiated, featuring the Army bands and produced in consultation with the departments of education and defence.[18] In addition to the

---

15 INTO 'Report and Programme of the Second National Programme Conference' 1926, and the *Irish Times* 6 October 1927, both quoted in McCarthy, p. 247. 16 Ibid., p. 122. 17 Ibid. p. 110. 18 For the information contained in this paragraph, I am indebted to Dr Marie McCarthy's pioneering study *Passing it on*, and to her 'Music education in the emergent nation state' in Pine (ed.), *Music in Ireland*.

bands themselves, the programmes described the music and instruments to be played, and the lives of the composers. Marie McCarthy tells us that the series as a whole addressed a 'comprehensive treatment of Irish music', and also included the Garda Céilí Band, ballads, Irish language songs introduced and performed by Pilib Ó Laoghaire (the Cork-based founder of Cór Cois Laoi), children's percussion bands, and plainchant, the latter involving, among others, Fr John Burke, dean of UCD, who had been organising a summer school in the subject since 1926. Each programme ended with the playing of the national anthem. The series continued until 1941, when wartime conditions brought restrictions to all areas of radio activity. The Department of Education supported the broadcasts, in the expectation that they would 'help considerably towards the development of musical culture in the schools and the creation of a taste for music'. In 1937, 400 schools listened to the broadcasts; two years later this had risen to 750, but had declined to merely 76 when they concluded in 1941. Marie McCarthy comments that 'these series were highly successful in promoting a variety of Irish musical traditions, and in serving to mediate between official nationalist policy and the music education of the nation's youth ... In effect, the programmes were a direct manifesto of Irish identity, emphasis being placed on Irish music and musicians and the musical traditions of the Catholic Church'.[19]

A special series of schools broadcasts on the work of collector Edward Bunting was given in 1943 to mark the centenary of his death, and another, of fifteen programmes, illustrated by the RÉ Orchestra and by gramophone records, was designed to encourage 'the appreciation of good music'. In 1948 the incoming minister for education, General Mulcahy, considered that the cost of restoring the schools programmes outweighed their educational benefit. The limited number of schools taking advantage of the broadcasts was, of course, due to the availability, or non-availability, of suitable receiving equipment which was still costly, and for which the Department of Education provided no financial aid. However, at that early stage (1945–6) Brian Boydell was already giving 'Children's Broadcasts' such as 'Pianoforte Music for the Young Student', 'Stories in Music' and 'Music in the Making'. For the latter, broadcast in 1947–8, he intended 'to talk about Musical Form in such a way as not to terrify young listeners – pointing out the structural shapes of the sort of music they come across in singing and playing the piano or violin'.[20]

One of the most noteworthy innovations in education was the introduction by the Department of Education in 1946 of a Summer School of Music, which

19 McCarthy, *Passing it on*, pp. 122–3. 20 B. Boydell to Kathleen Roddy, n.d. [August 1947], Music Department file 372/53 'Brian Boydell'.

was held in conjunction with Radio Éireann.[21] There were no fees, and participants' travelling expenses were reimbursed. Courses in orchestral and choral conducting were open to conductors of school or adult choirs and orchestras, and courses in piano and violin were available to advanced players. So popular was the scheme that 120 attended the course in choral conducting, and over sixty enrolled for the course on the training of school orchestras. As already noted, orchestral conducting was in the hands of Jean Martinon, with a class of thirty-five; Henry Holst, whom we have already encountered as a soloist with the RÉ orchestra, took the violin and viola class (among the members of which were Hugh Maguire and John Ronayne), which not only included tuition in chamber music but also gave participants the opportunity of hearing the complete Beethoven quartets broadcast live by Holst's Philharmonia Quartet.[22] In addition, fifteen budding composers received advice, encouragement and criticism from Sir Arnold Bax.

So successful was the summer school that it was repeated the following year, with additional courses in cello, wind and voice production, and again Holst and Martinon participated, the latter also taking over the composition class. In 1948 Martinon (who by this time was regularly conducting the fledgling RÉSO) again taught both conducting and composition, with Kendall Taylor (who was to appear several times with the RÉSO in the 1950s and 1960s)[23] in charge of piano, while violin and chamber music were taught by another soloist with the orchestra, André de Ribaudpierre. In 1949, Martinon was succeeded by Hans Schmidt-Isserstedt in the conducting course, while Alan Rawsthorne took over the composition class, with Jean Fournier teaching violin and chamber music. The following year this course was provided by the RÉLO, with the French conductor Louis Martin. In later years, pianists who worked with the Summer School included Ginette Doyen and Carlo Zecchi.

Summing up the success of the second School, 'G. O'B.' in the *Irish Times* referred to the fact that 'Martinon's viewpoint was broadly cosmopolitan but he did not lose sight of the national angle. He told the students that they had in Irish folk-music a practically unexplored field of infinite possibilities. He warned them that there was little use in "quoting" complete folk tunes in their original works. They should rather, like modern composers in other European countries, delve down into the rich national deposit of folk-music "in which their sub-conscious self has its roots" and find there the inspiration for a modern Irish art.'[24]

---

21 Eimear Ó Broin (interview with the author 4 August 2003) believes that this was effected at the behest of P.J. Little. 22 It was reported that in the course of the 'very thorough tuition' given by Holst, 'he had to take many students back to the elementary principles of violin playing, the bed-rock of technique': 'G. O'B', *Irish Times* undated cutting [1948] (Acton Archive). 23 Taylor, who was professor of piano at the RCM 1929–93, played the Beethoven third concerto in November 1954 and the fifth in October 1961, and Rawsthorne's first concerto [1939/42] in 1969. 24 'G. O'B', *Irish Times*, loc. cit.

With teachers of this calibre, it is little wonder that this summer school is still recalled with awe and affection by those who took part, and it is all the more regrettable that it was discontinued in 1956, especially when, in 1951, P.J. Little spoke of the Fianna Fáil government's policy ('adopted ... on the advice of men like Hamilton Harty and Adrian Boult and poor Moeran, God rest him') 'to develop the orchestra and the summer school of music. When both of these are developed the people should be encouraged then to improve and we would pass on to a national school of music, a conservatoire, which is a teaching academy for the purpose of taking those who have reached a very high standard of proficiency a little further'.[25]

From 1932 onwards, Col. Brase had provided live concerts by the army bands, aimed at primary schools, and similar ventures had been started by bodies such as Cork Orchestral Society and Waterford Orchestral Society, which in 1950 hosted the first schools' concert by the newly established RÉSO. But in 1951, Ceol-Chumann na nÓg had been founded as a result of teachers attending the summer school.[26]

The first concert given for Ceol-Chumann na nÓg by Radio Éireann was on 5 February 1952, and in the next four years a total of fifty-six concerts was given, attended by almost 28,000 children from 285 schools. Most of these were given in the RÉSO's home, the Phoenix Hall, and by 1956 it was being announced that 'due to small numbers to be admitted to the Phoenix Hall [with seating for 300], one school can only be invited every two years. We have a long waiting list of those schools who have not yet been to a concert'. The success of the scheme was gauged by the number of children collecting second-hand records, or attending the Public Concerts, which in both cases was judged to be appreciable. One Dublin school, CBS Baggot Street, had begun a small string orchestra and, after attendance at a RÉ schools concert, membership doubled. A letter from the organiser of Ceol-Chumann na nÓg, James Blanc, read: 'We need more concerts or else the present number, given in a large hall capable of holding 1000 children. In view of the difficulties, Ceol-Chumann hopes to organise gramophone concerts to be given in schools but it can well be understood that it is the live performance that counts. I am amazed at the enthusiasm of the children & the attention they give during the orchestral concerts'.[27]

---

25 DD, 125, 24 April 1951, cols. 1324–5. 26 McCarthy, *Passing it on*, p. 124, states that a previous organisation with the same name had been founded in 1937. 27 RTÉ file, 'Ceol-Cumann na nÓg', no date but *circa* 1954; James Blanc (1917–2001), of a Huguenot family, was a church organist by vocation, working in Dundalk 1944–47, Dún Laoghaire 1948–79 and Blackrock 1979–99. (I am indebted to Mr Patrick Blanc for biographical information.) James Blanc devoted much of his life to the service of Ceol-Chumann na nÓg, which had been set up with the encouragement and financial assistance of Dorothy, Lady Mayer, wife of the naturalised British philanthropist Sir Robert Mayer who initiated the Robert Mayer Concerts for young people in 1923 and the 'Youth and Music' organisation in Britain (itself modelled on Belgium's Jeunesses Musicales) at the same

In addition, and separately, the RÉSO gave schools concerts in regional centres such as Cork, Limerick, Galway, Sligo, Wexford and Tuam, and the RÉLO in Wicklow, Fermoy, Athlone, Galway, Carlow, Sligo, Ballyshannon, Kilkenny, Ballinasloe and Drogheda. These were organised by local committees, and usually took place on the morning following a formal evening concert. The venues for the RÉSO concerts were those which could accommodate the larger orchestra; those for the RÉLO were indicative of the smaller, far more numerous, halls throughout Ireland which hosted visits by the RÉLO on its regular regional tours.[28] In the cases of Limerick, Wexford and Cork an inspector from the Department of Education attended 'to help in the organisation of the concerts and in the vital work of preparing the children' (by way of a preparatory talk).[29] It rapidly became clear, however, that the availability of inspectors was limited, and was restricted to the role of giving the preparatory talk, rather than a wider responsibility for organising the concerts themselves.[30]

In fact, during the 1955–6 year alone, eleven schools' concerts were given for Ceol-Chumann na nÓg, attended by 4435 children from 75 schools,[31] all of which were given by the RÉSO (with guest conductors Brian Boydell, Col. J.M. Doyle and Sydney Bryans), with the exception of one by the (new) London String Quartet. Well over half the children had attended the preparatory talks. Two of the concerts had taken place through the medium of Irish (conductor, Eimear Ó Broin) in pursuit of Ceol-Chumann's policy of giving one third of the concerts in Irish. Concerts began with an invitation by the conductor to the audience to participate by singing the National Anthem.

The following year, the much sought increase in numbers was partially achieved with the use of Dublin's Metropolitan Hall (now demolished) where the 12 concerts permitted 6000 children to attend, with, again, over half attending the preparatory talk. By that stage, a total of 73 concerts had been given, with over 36,000 children attending, with an average of almost four preparatory talks per concert. Eventually, a plateau was reached, with a 700 capacity attendance at the SFX in the 1960s and 70s, increasing again in the 1980s at the NCH which holds over 1100 people.

The measures taken to interest groups of schoolchildren (many of whom may have no musical knowledge and are principally in a state of excitement on a day trip from school) include individual members of the orchestra demonstrating their instruments (the bassoon, tuba and piccolo are especially popular) and well-known pieces such as Rossini's overture *William Tell* which imme-

period as the inception of Ceol-Chumann na nÓg. **28** The term 'regional' was adopted by the author, when Concerts Manager, in favour of 'provincial' since the latter suggested a condescending or patronising attitude on the part of RTÉ. **29** F. Ó hAnnracháin to P&T, 20 January 1955, RTÉ file 'Ceol-Chumann na nÓg'. **30** Ibid. **31** 22 primary schools, 43 secondary, 8 vocational and 2 private: source, Ceol-Chumann na nÓg Annual Report, 1956, ibid.

diately excites attention with its 'theme from The Lone Ranger'. Works with a strong visual potential such as Mendelssohn's 'Hebrides Overture', with its storm sequence, or a humourous work including speech, such as Saint-Saëns' 'Carnival of the Animals' with accompanying poems by Ogden Nash, or Prokofiev's 'Peter and the Wolf' (narrated, on some occasions, by Brian Boydell) are both informative and entertaining, and give children a valuable introduction to the orchestra.

In 1955 (after it had been in existence a mere four years) a serious division appeared within the committee of Ceol-Chumann na nÓg, as to the use of gramophones to provide in-school concerts for schools which could not attend the live concerts. Those arguing against such a project included two inspectors from the Department of Education, P.J. Killian and Thomas Kindlon.[32] It almost resulted in the resignation of James Blanc, who, on the day following the committee meeting, wrote that he found that 'the work was no longer just music and children but had got too complicated and full of red tape'[33] – a diplomatic way of saying that he found it difficult to reconcile his own vision of the organisation's function with that represented by officialdom. Fortunately for the interests of Ceol-Chumann na nÓg, Blanc was prevailed upon to remain in office for a further thirty-five years, until 1991. In that year RTÉ entered into a sponsorship arrangement with the *Irish Times* to present 'Music in the Classroom',[34] as a result of which the Arts Council decided that the association's work had become superseded, its funding was withdrawn and Ceol-Chumann na nÓg devoted itself to giving the preliminary illustrated lectures for a further three years, until it was wound up in 1994.

In its forty-three years of existence, Ceol-Chumann na nÓg and James Blanc, with assistance from Lady Mayer and the Arts Council, and with the full co-operation of RTÉ, had organised 500 concerts, which had been attended by 319,000 children, and 1,345 lectures, attended by over one-third of those children.

In 1982 family concerts called 'Music for Fun' were started, the brainchild of Gareth Hudson, an English timpanist and percussionist who had been working with the orchestra for some time and was interested in developing his career as a conductor: this immensely popular series aimed not only at attracting a young audience but also at thereby bringing into the concert hall parents who would thus become 'hooked' on light classical and popular classics. Items such as Suppé's 'Light Cavalry' overture and Vaughan Williams' Fantasia on 'Greensleeves' rubbed shoulders with 'Classical Gas' and the theme from *Dallas*.

---

32 Minute of Ceol-Cumann na nÓg committee, 9 February 1955, ibid.   33 J. Blanc to Ó hAnnracháin, 10 February 1955, ibid.   34 'Music in the Classroom' was issued by RTÉ/*Irish Times* on audio cassette and, in 1991 and '92, was televised from the 'Pavilion' in the RTÉ grounds which was the venue for the 'Bank of Ireland Proms'.

These were sellout successes which ran until 1991, with national tours, followed briefly by a scaled-down model called 'The Music People'.

More recently, the NSO has undertaken a one-week 'residence' with schools in Kerry in 2001 and in Donegal in 2003 – the first occasions that the NSO had appeared in these counties: these have featured formal concerts and informal workshops conducted by David Brophy (NSO Assistant Conductor),[35] James Cavanagh (a former member of the RTÉSO and director of the conducting course at the RIAM) and Robert Houlihan, a freelance conductor who lived in France for many years, working with orchestras in France, Romania and Hungary, and who has conducted extensively with both the NSO and RTÉCO.

Perhaps the most stimulating contribution made by broadcasting to the development of young musicians has been the competition originated by Jane Carty in 1976 as the 'Young Musician of the Year', and which subsequently became 'Musician of the Future'. The competition has moved through several formats, growing in the number and type of sections. The earliest exposure of young musicians to the airwaves was 'Children at the Microphone', a 'talent-spotting' series from the late 1940s into the 1950s, produced by Kathleen Roddy. Carty, who joined RTÉ in 1964 as a programme assistant on 'Céilí House' and 'Reachaireacht an Riadaigh' and as presenter of 'Music of the Nation', had been working as a producer on a later weekly programme 'The Young Entertainers', presented by Proinsías Ó Ceallaigh since 1968, and 'Voice of Promise', consisting, as Mary Leland recorded, 'of comments on young singers from around the country which are essentially thoughtful assessments of the voices heard'[36] – which Carty, as a singer herself, was well qualified to offer.[37] She had realised that there was room in Ireland for a competition of this kind, and enough talented youngsters to make it worthwhile. (A similar venture on television in 1986 was 'Music for Me', presented by Ingrid Miley, in which young performers, including Hugh Tinney and Jimmy Vaughan, played and spoke about their musical interests, thus giving other young hopefuls an insight into the possible routes that their own musicianship might take.) The fact that most prizewinners in 'Musician of the Future' have gone on to careers in music, both in Ireland and abroad, and in many cases have become pre-eminent in their field, is indicative of the high level of musical achievement and of RTÉ's ability to recognise it.

In the first competition there was no provision for an overall winner: the sectional winners were Hugh Tinney (piano), now an international prizewin-

35 A position in which he was succeeded in 2004 by Gavin Maloney. **36** *Irish Times*, 11 August 1975. **37** Concurrent with 'Voice of Promise' was another 'commentary' series, 'Young People in Concert'.

ner and artistic director of the Festival in Great Irish Houses; Deirdre Brady (flute), now a member of the NSO; Frank Schaeffer (cello); and Fergus O'Carroll (horn), co-principal in the NSO. Subsequent winners have included pianists Finghin Collins (later winner of the Clara Haskil competition), Peter Tuite, Rebecca Čap and Dearbhaile O'Donnell (who chose to pursue a career in medicine); violinists Maighread MacCrann (who became leader of the Vienna Radio Symphony Orchestra), Cora Venus Lunny and Michael d'Arcy (later leader of the RTÉCO); cellist Gerald Peregrine; flautist Gareth Costello (today a member of the RTÉ Music Department); brass players Donal Bannister (trombone), Cormac Ó hAodáin (horn) and Mark O'Keeffe (trumpet); saxophonists Gerard McChrystal and Kenneth Edge (a leading participant in *Riverdance*); accordionist Dermot Dunne, organist Michael Quinn and singers Andrew Murphy and Cara O'Sullivan. The category for singers was discontinued from 1991, when the Veronica Dunne Bursary (later an international competition) began, honouring one of Ireland's foremost singers, but categories were added for composition (won by Rob Canning, Gráinne Mulvey and Elaine Agnew) and chamber music. From 1986 the best competitor under the age of nineteen also went on to compete in an EBU international competition, the first being violinist Seamus Conroy. Due to financial constraints in 2000 the 'Musician of the Future' was suspended, but plans for its revival were announced in 2003.

OPERA (1): DUBLIN

It is an obvious, but seldom fully appreciated, fact of opera that the orchestra's role in any production is vital. On the concert platform, a poor performance may result from bad relations with the conductor or lack of sympathy with the music, quite apart from tiredness towards the end of a demanding season or lack of togetherness at the beginning of a new one. Such poorness will be immediately apparent to most audiences, but during an opera performance the singing, the visual attraction of sets and costumes, and the near invisibility of the orchestra itself, will diminish one's awareness of infelicities or defects in the orchestral part of the work. Similarly, excellent playing, because, in a fully integrated production, it blends into a total *mise-en-scène*, will often be taken for granted. Thus, an orchestra seldom receives the plaudits it would automatically attract for a comparable performance on the concert stage. For a professional opera orchestra, such as that of the Royal Opera House Covent Garden, this is taken for granted; for the RÉSO, during the years when it was the house orchestra for the Dublin Grand Opera Society (DGOS) and Wexford seasons, to be virtually ignored by the critics could be a disappointment. A review which stated, in a common cliché, that a conductor 'coaxed some polished playing from the Radio Éireann Symphony Orchestra', could be regarded not merely as a last-minute inclusion of the orchestra in a review understandably dominated by a consideration of the singing and acting on stage, but also as a put-down of an ensemble which would only require 'coaxing' if it were in some way dispirited by extra-musical matters. Why that should feature frequently in reviews of opera, when it hardly ever occurs in relation to concerts, is impossible to explain, although most likely it arises from the perceived difficulty in holding together what is happening on stage – singing and movement – with the performance of the orchestral music, but it also suggests that often the players (most of whom cannot see the action on stage) can become bored, alienated or indifferent, especially in the case of a production which they feel to be sub-standard.

An orchestra will be perceived to shine in an opera's overture – especially the more lively, such as *The Marriage of Figaro*, or the more dramatic, such as *The Flying Dutchman* – and in certain key places where it seems that suddenly the attention is drawn simply because no other activity is taking place, such as the *intermezzo* of Mascagni's *Cavalleria rusticana*, the prelude to the last act of *La traviata* or the '*méditation*' of Massenet's *Thaïs* (also an *intermezzo* but played *solo*, usually by the leader). The fact that (with the obvious exception of recitative, or spoken dialogue as in German *Singspiel*) the orchestra plays throughout, may strike the reader of the average opera review as a point that has escaped the critic.

Although the Radio Éireann orchestra was not officially involved with opera until 1948, when it began to play under its new name for the DGOS, the engagement of its members by and with opera companies in Dublin dates from November 1937, when the Dublin Operatic Society (DOS) had hired members of the orchestra for its winter season of four operas, followed by another season in spring 1938.[38] The significance of this exercise lies primarily in the fact that it was considered necessary for the DOS to have the services of the most professional orchestra in the country, rather than seek to form an *ad hoc* orchestra utilising players accustomed to the pit of the theatre, or from cafés and other cinemas and theatres. The same assumption on the part of 'outside bodies' would shortly manifest itself in the case of the DGOS and, later, in that

---

38 P&T File 61/59/3: 'Further requests from musical bodies for the loan of the studio orchestra for outside productions 27.7.38–7.9.38' (files 61/59/1 and /2 appear to be no longer extant); includes a Department of Finance minute S. 104/4/37 dated 12.4.38. The Dublin Operatic Society was founded in 1928, with John McCormack as its Patron, Dermod O'Brien PRHA as its President and, among its vice-presidents, Hugh Kennedy (the Chief Justice), T.S.C. Dagg (a senior civil servant) and Walter Starkie. Its conductors were Vincent O'Brien, Arthur Hammond and Lieut. J.M. Doyle. In November 1938 its productions were *Der Freischütz* (Weber), *Maritana* (Wallace), *La bohème* (Puccini) and *Il trovatore* (Verdi).

of the Wexford opera festival. The irregular and at times chaotic nature of the arrangements in the years 1937–48 laid the foundation for an inefficient and unstable use of RÉ's resources for half a century. In this chapter it is possible, from the evidence of surviving files, to describe the early years of RÉ's association with both of the Dublin opera societies and with the festival in Wexford.

In 1938, the DOS asked for the provision of the RÉ orchestra for its season in November – a week of four operas, but, 'as they are in debt £200 they ask for a fee for relays of 2 of the 4 operas'.[39] Almost simultaneously, one of the organisers of a charity concert in aid of St Vincent de Paul, to take place in the Capitol cinema in October 1938, also requested the orchestra's services. Dr T.J. Kiernan, Director of Broadcasting, advised the Secretary of P&T, P.S. O'Hegarty, that

> There is no other orchestra on which these organisations can call, and it is not a serious inconvenience to us to lend the Orchestra. In view, however, of the growth in the number of applications for the loan of the Orchestra, the matter was put before the Broadcasting Standing Committee … [which said]: 'The Committee recommended that the Station Orchestra should not in future be lent to outside bodies'.[40]

It was a difficult and an unpopular decision to take, which would recur throughout subsequent decades, until agreements were reached with the opera companies and, later, a regulation was introduced controlling the acceptance, by members of the orchestras, of freelance engagements with outside bodies. As we have seen, RÉ players had been engaged for work with Ceol Cumann (not to be confused with Ceol-Chumann na nÓg) and at this point Kiernan put the situation to the Standing Committee: 'As between An Ceol Cumann and the Dublin Operatic Society, I cannot draw a line. The former is doing good pioneer work in developing modern Irish music and from a Gaelic point of view is very important. We are really being asked to give a form of hidden subsidy to certain musical organisations'.[41]

As will become evident, the degree of influence that any particular organisation was able to exert on a person in authority would be a significant factor in swaying a decision as to whether it would receive the 'hidden subsidy'. At stake for Radio Éireann was, at first, not so much the use of influence to secure the release of the orchestra as the interruption which this caused in the regular schedule of rehearsals and broadcasts. As the assistant secretary, Joseph Cremins, told the Minister, 'So far as the proposed St Vincent de Paul concert is concerned, there is no more reason for lending the orchestra in connection

39 Ibid. 40 Ibid. 41 Ibid.

with it than in connection with any other public concert. The concert would be purely a money-making venture and, however laudable the object, it would not be in the same category as the [other] contemplated productions'.[42] (Later, a criterion would be established that an event at which admission charges were made would not qualify for the 'hidden subsidy'.) The department at this stage was aware that a case could be made for helping a body that was trying to develop musical appreciation: 'The Standing Committee felt some concern lest a refusal to co-operate in the matter with outside musical associations should have any detrimental effect upon musical activities and musical development' and it therefore asked the Director of Music, Vincent O'Brien, to adjudicate; O'Brien 'does not consider that any great impediment to musical activity would be likely to accrue as the result of a refusal' to lend the players for the charity concert.

Once the Standing Committee had placed a blanket obstacle to outside engagements, the DOS lost no time in appealing to Seán MacEntee, Minister for Finance, who, besides having huge fiscal responsibility, was a cultured man and, like his future counterpart in P&T, P.J. Little, wrote occasional poetry. Adopting what would become a familiar pattern in succeeding years, MacEntee contacted his opposite number in P&T, at that time Oscar Traynor, suggesting that

> the arrangement seems to have a good deal to recommend it. It does not give any official benediction to the Society while, at the same time, it releases them from a very serious predicament ... I think the Society which is performing a very useful function in the cultural life of the city, deserves at least the measure of official accommodation which the arrangement involves.[43]

Not content with this coup, the DOS then asked that the orchestra's nightly broadcast should be given earlier, so that the players could arrive at the Gaiety Theatre in time for the opera performance, in return for which co-operation it would give RÉ one free broadcast. Kiernan passed on this request to O'Hegarty, and it was agreed by O'Hegarty and the Minister.[44] Both Kiernan and O'Hegarty must have harboured serious reservations about the degree to which the DOS was being accommodated, as it quickly became clear (and

42 Cremins to Traynor, 25 August 1938, ibid. Oscar Traynor (1886–1963), a participant in the 1916 Easter Rising, was a Fianna Fáil TD for North Dublin 1925–27 and 1932–61, and Minister for P&T 1936–39; subsequently Minister for Defence 1939–48 and 1951–54 and for Justice 1957–61. **43** MacEntee to Traynor, 8 September 1938, P&T File 61/59/4: 'Request from Dublin Operatic Society that broadcasting programmes be arranged so that certain individual members of Broadcasting Orchestra may be engaged for the Society's operatic performance (Samhain 1938 and Abran 1939)–12.9.38–7.5.40'. **44** Kiernan to O'Hegarty, 14 September 1938, ibid.

would subsequently in the case of the DGOS) that the tail was about to start wagging the dog.

Kiernan told O'Hegarty two weeks later that he had informed the DOS 'that they should only engage RÉ players where no other could be found elsewhere',[45] but here an extra, internal, complication raised its head in that the members of the orchestra insisted they should all be engaged without exception. As the Chairman (and, in effect, the chief agent) of the DOS, George Sleator, wrote to Kiernan:

> It is very definite from an interview with Miss Terry O'Connor and other members of the Orchestra that my Company will not be permitted to select only certain instrumentalists, with reasons as follows:- To play with musicians that they are not acquainted [with] must effect [*sic*] their status. It is a slight to the reputations of the members not engaged by the bringing in of outsiders. To have to play with strangers, mindful of the limited rehearsals must seriously effect [*sic*] the balance of the Orchestra. Whether engaged privately or otherwise they remain members of the Radio Orchestra and have a reputation to uphold as Ireland's instrumentalists hence anxiety to play as a unit or not at all … Remember, Chamberlain and Hitler representing mere nations have met, can we representing the classics not settle to the mutual benefit of all?[46]

Sleator, a jeweller by profession, was an extremely adroit agent, who had succeeded (so far) in keeping the DOS afloat by dint of clever manoeuvres of this sort as well as investing very large sums of his own money in the Society. In this letter he reveals his diplomacy, firstly by throwing onto the orchestra themselves the responsibility for the problem, and then taking their side as far as quality was concerned: once RÉ had been inveigled into acceding to the DOS's political manoeuvres, it could hardly deny the validity of the argument regarding the players' 'reputation … as Ireland's instrumentalists'.

The DOS spring season consisted of *La traviata* (Verdi), *Lurline* (Wallace) and *La favorita* (Donizetti); RÉ paid £10 in respect of two relays and took the third free of charge in lieu of a fee for the orchestra.[47] However, Vincent O'Brien who, as a conductor of the DOS, was wearing two hats, wrote to Kiernan after the season that it was necessary to resolve this unsatisfactory situation before the next season, mainly because it was considered inadvisable for either the orchestra or leader to be named in the DOS publicity or programme.[48] At this stage, two-thirds of the orchestra agreed to the arrange-

45 Kiernan to O'Hegarty, 27 September 1938, ibid. **46** Sleator to Kiernan, n.d., ibid. **47** Kiernan to O'Hegarty, 4 March 1939, ibid. **48** O'Brien to Kiernan 25 May 1939, ibid.

ment with the DOS, and the remainder did not. 'My own personal view' O'Brien said,

> is that it would be a pity if the excellent musical work which has been achieved through co-operation were not to be continued in the future, and I feel that it would be practically impossible for the Society to carry on in an adequate way without the services of the Irish Radio Orchestra. The continued co-operation would also be of advantage to the Station for the following reasons:
>
> 1. The occasional appearance of our Orchestra in public, tends to combat the tendency to become mechanical in their work – an aspect which is the bane of even the finest broadcasting orchestras.
>
> 2. The favourable opinion of many thousands of listeners who recognise that the artistic work achieved would not be possible, were it not for the help given by the Broadcasting Service, would be gained.
>
> 3. One free relay.
>
> 4. Judging by the interest taken from the point of view of attendances at the theatre, it seems to be one of the few departments in which our public takes a real live interest.[49]

Bearing in mind O'Brien's possibly divided loyalties, we should appreciate that his own difficulties in bravely producing studio performances of opera would have weighed heavily in favour of making some acceptable arrangement with the DOS which would be mutually beneficial, especially, as far as RÉ was concerned, in enabling it to broadcast two seasons of opera each year with almost no administrative or artistic effort required – as Kiernan said in support of O'Brien's memo, the alternative was to produce the operas in-house.[50] This was consolidated by an agreement whereby, in order to prevent any misunderstanding, RÉ would pay the DOS an increased fee of £10 per relay per opera.[51] O'Hegarty was deeply worried by the strain that the demands of the DOS were placing on the organisation:

> These increasing demands of the DOS must be definitely resisted. It is quite out of the question for the Department to allow itself to become involved in the difficulties which apparently exist between the Society and various artists whom they are desirous of engaging. The Society should be informed with an expression of regret that the proposal ...

49 Ibid. 50 Kiernan to O'Hegarty, 26 May 1939, ibid. 51 Kiernan to O'Hegarty, 4 May 1940, ibid.

cannot be entertained; nor is it possible for the Department to contemplate any extension of the special arrangements in relation to the
Station Orchestra which have hitherto been made for the purpose of
facilitating the Society's operations.[52]

O'Hegarty could see quite clearly that, while the situation remained one
of a freelance engagement of individual players, rather than an official accred-
itation of the orchestra as a whole, the department could do no more than bend
over backwards to facilitate a request, not least due to political pressure. But
to become further involved in such an unclear operation, without being in control of it, would result in RÉ and its orchestra being the victim of any organisation with sufficient credentials to make a case for such an accommodation.
It would, in fact, lead to the extensive involvement of RÉ in the artistic affairs
of the DGOS without being able to exercise any appreciable control over them.

O'Hegarty's prescience was well-founded: by 1941 the number of players
who declined to work for the opera seasons had risen to a large majority: also,
there were now two rival opera companies, with the establishment of the
DGOS, and, although the days of the DOS seemed to be numbered, unpeace-
ful co-existence would occupy the next couple of years, during which both
opera companies recruited their own orchestras with, apparently, satisfactory
results. As the new Director of Broadcasting, Séamus Brennan, reported to
O'Hegarty, 'The interests of musical development in the city and county would
appear to be best served by our keeping aloof and forcing the operatic societies to develop their own orchestras'.[53] In fact it suited RÉ that its players
would not take part in opera, since during the opera season the remaining
members of the orchestra were not required to work, thus causing a severe disruption to its own schedules, usually solved unsatisfactorily by a temporary
merger (in later years) of the RÉLO and 'Symphony Residual Group' – referred
to cynically within the station as 'Light and Dregs'. In addition, the public concerts under Michael Bowles were due to start, with five in the winter of 1942,
and five in the spring of 1943.

The DGOS was founded in 1941, a public meeting having been convened
by a member of the DOS chorus, Captain (as he then was) William O'Kelly,
who believed that 'the DOS was falling apart at that time'.[54] He was quickly
joined by one of the DOS conductors, J.M. Doyle, and the producer Sydney
Russell. With rival companies seeking favours from RÉ, the situation intensi-

---

52 O'Hegarty to Kiernan, 7 May 1940, ibid. 53 Brennan to O'Hegarty, 4 November 1941, P&T
File 61/59/5: 'Question of facilitating outside musical societies in regard to the engagement of
members of the orchestra for the purpose of operatic etc productions 4.12.41–6.2.43'. 54 Quoted
in G. Smith, *Love and music: the glorious history of the Dublin Grand Opera Society, 1941–1998* (1998),
p. 1.

fied and, following fresh representations, as a compromise Matt Doherty (RE's Establishment – or chief administrative – Officer) told Brennan that the Minister for Finance had requested that the orchestra be offered to one society in the winter, and to the other in the spring, provided that the engagements were outside the new Public Concert season.[55] This was rigorously rejected, the new Minister, P.J. Little, deciding that all requests should be refused: his manuscript note on the file reads: 'Present stringent conditions of broadcasting arrangements will not permit of facilities being granted'.[56] The situation was further complicated, however, by the fact that the members of the orchestra, who had become disinterested in taking freelance work from the opera companies, reversed their position and asked to be allowed to play for the DGOS: 'owing to war-time conditions we are now quite unanimous in wishing to avail of this opportunity to augment our incomes'.[57] The problem was acknowledged by Brennan, who pointed out to O'Hegarty that 'the Symphony Concerts even have worsened their position – extra laundry, perms &c'.[58]

By spring 1942, Radio Éireann was in a quandary: Brennan admitted to O'Hegarty that 'the present arrangement with the DGOS ... is a very profitable one for us. To put it in a nut-shell we are getting, as far as time is concerned, ordinary studio value from our Orchestra and, in addition, 15 hours of opera for nothing – the equivalent, at a very modest estimate, of £180 worth of live time'.[59] But the disruption to the schedule was unsupportable in the long term, especially with the Public Concerts during the same period, the extra work burden of which was severely felt by the players. The DOS winter season in 1941 consisted of *Martha* (Flotow), *Les Contes d'Hoffman* (Offenbach), *Ernani* (Verdi) and, again, *Maritana*; in September 1942 the operas were *The Magic Flute* (Mozart), *Faust* (Gounod), *Manon Lescaut* (Puccini) and a revival of *Ernani*; this was followed immediately in December by the DGOS's massive season of *Aida* (Verdi), *La favorita*, *La bohème*, *La traviata* and, surprisingly, both *Il barbiere di Siviglia* (Rossini) and *The Marriage of Figaro* (Mozart).[60] The Easter 1943 season at the DGOS presented *Tannhäuser* (Wagner), *Don Giovanni* (Mozart), *Rigoletto* (Verdi), *Faust* (Gounod), *Carmen* (Bizet) and *Madama Butterfly* (Puccini). By any standards, and allowing for the revival of some productions, this was a very serious amount of largely unfamiliar music for the players to bring to anything like an acceptable professional standard. Moreover,

---

55 Doherty to Brennan, 22 December 1941, file 61/59/5.   56 Ibid., 9 February 1942.   57 Ibid. 23 February 1942. The opera societies paid £3.10s.0d. per week plus five shillings per rehearsal: Brennan to O'Hegarty, ibid., 17 June 1942.   58 Brennan to O'Hegarty, 24 February 1942, ibid. The extra costs incurred by the musicians in respect of public concerts would eventually be offset by a 'dress allowance' built into their tax-free allowances.   59 Brennan to O'Hegarty, 14 April 1942, ibid. 60 Both these operas are based on works by the same writer, Beaumarchais: *Le barbier de Séville* and *Le mariage de Figaro*, and feature similar plots and the same cast of principal characters.

with the DOS moving to the Olympia Theatre, RÉ received a letter from five of the more senior members of the orchestra, stating that 'we find ourselves unable to accept the engagement owing to the unhealthy condition of this theatre. We were lucky last year to have escaped typhoid fever.'[61]

Levels of professional standards were also a point of contention, since while Radio Éireann may have had some control over the competence of its own players, it seemed to have none over the capacity of the opera societies to present their productions in an acceptable manner, a situation which would continue at least into the 1980s. The chief areas of concern were timekeeping, stage management, stage design and the quality of the chorus. As these societies were largely amateur in status and, therefore, reliant on voluntary effort, it was extremely difficult to secure any assurance that artistic standards would be achieved and maintained, and it became necessary for R(T)É to insist, as time went on, and as public expectations of artistic standards were raised, that it should be involved in the artistic process.

On 2 March 1943, the RÉ announcer, Séamus Heavey, reported on the DOS performance of *Maritana*:

> The first Act was a poor and scrappy performance. The orchestra was nicely placed and balanced, but the singing was representative only of the mediocre and the bad. In the spoken parts the performances were really appalling. In the whole Act, Leo Maguire was bad, and none of the others were good. The second Act started quite differently: it was lively and coherent. In the first aria Cecily Keary gave a most beautiful piece of solo singing: everything about it was memorable. I do not recall a more appealing mezzo performance of any kind. Francis Russell here made a fine job of the 'Let me like a soldier fall' but with this exception he did not distinguish himself during the relay. His singing to me was thin and he appeared to be forcing a lot. Leo Maguire almost redeemed himself in 'Happy moments day by day' of which he gave a very adequate rendering, though he was inclined to 'scoop' and I think he went out of tune twice. Lina Mernora did not at any time excel. Anything I have not mentioned specifically was only middling. A most unpleasant gap occurred during the change of scene in Act 2. For seven minutes 8.49–56 the curtain was down, and nothing was to be heard save house noises. As I had been informed the interval would only be for a moment, I made no announcement, but it lasted just half as long as the inter-Act interval. The first Act ran 11 mins. over scheduled time; the first inter-

61 Nancie Lord, Rosalind Dowse, Terry O'Connor, Chrissie Fagan, and Madeleine Mooney, 5 February 1943, ibid.

val was 4 mins overtime; the whole pgm. ran wildly over time & had to be cut at 9.17, i.e., 12 mins after programme time.

Summary: a prairie of sound, relieved by one mountain & one or two hills.[62]

A further note on this report from Doherty to Brennan states: 'As an example of mistiming, we have on the file a statement from DGOS that the first act of La Bohème takes 25 mins, and from the DOS that it takes 50 mins. Actually the timing, we found, was 38–40 mins'.[63]

Within Radio Éireann there were mixed feelings about the broadcasting of opera, similar to those prevailing in RTÉ in the 1990s regarding the televising of orchestral concerts. Charles Kelly (the deputy director) told Brennan:

> My own view … is that most operas make bad broadcasting. Divorced from the visual advantage of the theatre, they sound complicated, disjointed and, frequently, silly, particularly in the recitative portions of the book. I do not believe, for instance, that listeners can be made familiar with operas through broadcasting unless the operas are specially adapted for broadcasting. This is what the BBC do, and it is an extremely expensive business. They can spend hundreds on one opera broadcast, adapting and recording the work with interpolated commentary, or interpolating a recorded commentary into a live performance, or using live commentary with live performance. These things are possible only where the production is under the control of the broadcasting authority and certainly can never be satisfactorily worked out in connection with productions by amateur companies, whose timing is invariably erratic. My suggestion would be to relay only those operas which are 'old favourites' and can be followed reasonably well. Who cares, for instance, about the plot of 'Maritana'? All the opera followers want to hear are the solos. For lesser known operatic works, I think we should confine broadcasts to recordings with interpolated commentary to keep the listeners in touch and to direct their attention to the points of special musical interest.[64]

It was a viewpoint which would gain much currency as RÉ did, in fact, exercise more control over DGOS productions as far as broadcasting standards were concerned. Furthermore, RTÉ's own presentation on radio of a series of studio-based Irish operas, edited, produced and introduced for listeners by Jane Carty in the 1960s, and conducted for radio broadcast by Colman Pearce, with

62 P&T File 61/59/6: 'Relays of operas staged by Dublin Operatic Society and Dublin Grand Opera Society. Programme difficulties arising from faulty timing of Acts, etc. 5.3.43 –28.7.43'. 63 Doherty to Brennan, 3 March 1943, ibid. 64 Kelly to Brennan, 2 April 1943, ibid.

members of the RÉ Singers, performed exactly the function foreseen by Kelly twenty years previously: Stanford's *Shamus O'Brien* and *The Travelling Companion* (the latter with a memorable duo performance by Austin Gaffney and Tomás Ó Suilleabháin), Balfe's *The Siege of Rochelle* and *The Bohemian Girl*, and Wallace's *Maritana, Lurline* and *The Amber Witch*.[65]

Commentary on the DOS and DGOS productions was undertaken up to 1938 by the Rev. Savell Hicks, minister of the Unitarian Church in Dublin's St Stephen's Green, and thereafter by the music critic, musicologist and composer H.R. White, until Norris Davidson, a member of the RÉ staff, took over the function as part of his official duties, in the late 1940s. Davidson's introduction brought a greater degree of professionalism to the presentation of the operas and his voice, informed by his thorough knowledge of the operas, continued to be the chief agent of RTÉ's entrée to the performances from Dublin and Wexford until his retirement in 1994, when he was succeeded by Ray Lynott. Presentation of the operas, however, remained dependent on factors within and outside RTÉ: the R(T)É engineering staff was responsible for the sound quality of the transmissions, which in early years often fell below acceptable standards, usually due to the insufficiency, and poor positioning, of microphones; a production, taken overall, might be unsuitable for broadcast due to its length or its subject-matter, or a particular evening's performance might have too many defects to justify its transmission.

By the end of 1943, the demand on the time and concentration of the orchestra was so great that, as Brennan reported to O'Hegarty, each season meant that orchestra broadcasts were disrupted:

> the orchestra endeavouring to do two jobs – and some of them with other irons in the fire – is worn out towards the end and is doing its work mechanically. To put the matter in a nutshell, the orchestra will not be fulfilling its function properly for Radio Éireann during 12 important broadcasting weeks. The public cannot or will not understand this, but in justice to the orchestra and its conductors, I wish to make the position clear to the Minister and the Dept.[66]

A season of opera required, in the first week, rehearsals totalling 21 hours, plus 24 hours of performances, in addition to the orchestra's 28 hours of duty in

65 Opera magazine programmes were a noticeable presence on Radio 1 and later on FM3, with Venetia O'Sullivan (under the name 'Carey Kent') presenting 'Opera Box', and later 'Monday Night at the Opera' presented by Jane Carty in 1983. Carty also travelled to opera houses in Europe to compile such programmes, often accompanied by O'Sullivan and Ray Lynott.
66 Brennan to O'Hegarty, 9 November 1943, P&T File 61/59/7: 'Proposal to discontinue granting permission to members of the Orchestra to accept engagements with operatic societies for operatic productions, 9.11.43–13.10.45' (originally W 10973.37 Part VIIIA).

RÉ – a total working week of 73 hours – and, in the second week, 27 hours of opera commitment on top of the regular 28 hours. As Joseph Cremins wrote to the Minister (now P.J. Little),

> This obviously is not merely intolerable but impossible. In fact, the members of the Orchestra do not give the prescribed minimum atten- dance with Radio Éireann while they are engaged with the Operatic Society. On occasion their attendance for a week has been as little as five hours, i.e. five programmes without any rehearsal. Apart altogether from the effects on the performance by the Orchestra, this is something which we cannot possibly defend.[67]

As a result, orchestral broadcasts were tending towards 'easy music', repeated at frequent intervals.

> These unsatisfactory conditions obtain for 12 weeks of the year, but the ill effects on the Orchestra must persist for an even longer period ... It has always been at least open to doubt whether the better interests of music in Dublin might not be served by refusing to lend members of the Radio Éireann Orchestra for operatic productions and forcing the Societies to engage other musicians. There seems to be no doubt that they would be able to get together satisfactory combinations. Apart from the Gaiety and Capitol orchestras, orchestras in existence at the moment include the Dublin Musical Arts Society, Dublin Orchestral Society and the Municipal String Orchestra. At present there is a tendency to give the Radio Éireann Orchestra a monopoly of engagements which might equally be carried out by other musicians. This is bad for music in the city, causes less employment, and will ultimately react on ourselves in the recruitment of musicians for Radio Éireann.[68]

Little's reply was to acknowledge that 'the members of the Orchestra, being part-time, cannot be prohibited from accepting outside engagements. But any such engagements can, in no circumstances, be allowed to interfere with the service ... which the artistes are obliged to give to broadcasting under their con- tracts'.[69] It was a crisis similar to that which RTÉ and Tibor Paul would face in 1966 with the extensive freelance activity of the Irish Chamber Orchestra.

Immediately after Christmas 1943, Brennan informed the orchestra mem- bers of this ruling, but George Sleator, now desperate to secure the survival of his society, appealed for a reversal of the decision:

67 Cremins to Little, 6 December 1943, ibid. **68** Ibid. **69** Little to O'Hegarty, 15 December 1943, ibid.

> Ever striving to maintain the highest tradition and to combat as far as possible the mad craze of popularity enjoyed by the film – a source of entertainment that is daily reducing the moral outlook of our people to that of mere slaves,

he contested the idea that the existing other orchestras were acceptable.

> The Capitol Theatre management [to which the DOS had transferred its seasons] is not yet in the happy position enjoyed by their rivals the Jewish controlled theatres (Royal, Gaiety, Queens) of having sufficient instrumentalists with experience to do our work. If we present the operas with the orchestra presently at the Capitol Theatre, the standard of our productions must suffer irreparable loss.[70]

Refusal 'would ... mean the closing down of our Society and the end of any real attempt at restoring Grand Opera to its proper place in the cultural and entertainment pursuits of our people ... I cannot believe the Minister for Posts and Telegraphs, Mr P J Little and yourself shall ever be a party to this tragedy'. It was the kind of brinksmanship of which Lt. Col. O'Kelly of the DGOS would prove himself more than capable in the decades of negotiations with RTÉ with which his organisation was involved.

In response, Brennan gave O'Hegarty a list of 'Available, Good-Class Musicians' (which included several players who would soon join the RÉSO), such as violinists Dora Hall, John MacKenzie,[71] Bessie O'Harte Bourke, Carmel Lang, Fanny Feehan, May Lord and Edith Coplin; cellists Ida O'Reilly, Kathleen Pollaky, Una Lord, and Betty Sullivan; and flute, Doris Cleary (*postea* Keogh).[72]

However, Little was prevailed upon to bend with the wind, and instructed O'Hegarty that, given the problem of the DOS, 'I have decided to grant the facilities sought on the strict understanding that this will be definitely the last season in which we can upset our programmes and our Orchestra for the sake of the Operatic Societies ... The Societies will have to consider their future arrangements for operatic performances without any reference to the Radio Éireann Orchestra'.

Within twenty-four hours, a letter was received from the DGOS, asking for the same facilities; Brennan suggested that the Minister's decision relating to the DOS should also apply to the DGOS on this occasion, with the warning that this was the last time that such an accommodation would be made.[73]

---

70 Sleator to Brennan, 29 December 1943, ibid. The xenophobic reference to 'Jewish controlled theatres' refers to the fact that the three theatres mentioned were owned by the Jewish family of Louis Elliman.   71 Who, in 1961, would found the Limerick School of Music.   72 The list also included 'Mrs N Kiernan (ex leader Philharmonic)' and 'Constance Harding (Musical Arts Leader)'. 73 Brennan to O'Hegarty, 10 January 1944, ibid.

History was to prove very shortly that a fascination with the spectacle of opera, coupled with strong links to government, would ensure the survival of this particular art form, where others were to languish for want of political will and administrative resources.

Within a few weeks, not content with this temporary concession, both societies had gone on the offensive: the *Irish Press* at the end of February carried a report that

> Dublin Operatic Society may have to close down, said Mr Geo W Sleator, Director, at the annual meeting last night, as they cannot secure the services of the Radio Éireann Orchestra. He stated that the many intricacies of advanced orchestral playing could not be entrusted to amateurs ... It was decided to appeal to An Taoiseach to intervene.[74]

Three days later, the *Evening Mail* told its readers that

> the loss of the Radio Éireann orchestra, while serious, will not end the presentation of first-class grand opera in Dublin, said Mr A E Timlin, Hon Secretary of the DGOS, discussing with an *Evening Mail* reporter the subject of the proposed withdrawal of the Radio Orchestra from operatic performances in the city ... There are schools of music and instrumentalists in Dublin turning out pupils of high merit, not to mention the professional musicians outside the Radio Éireann Orchestra – sources waiting to be tapped ... If one were to accept the principle that opera cannot go on without Radio Éireann, the holding of the Feis Ceoil and other national competitions would be a waste of time ... The policies of the DGOS and the DOS are irreconcilable in so far as the former depends mainly on Irish artists in filling the principal roles ... It recognises, of course, that music is international and will include guest artists other than Irish ...Heretofore young Irish artists had to establish themselves in foreign lands before being accepted here, and it is part of the policy of this Society to give promising young artists an opportunity of finding their feet in their own country before proceeding abroad.[75]

An undated and unsigned departmental comment on this statement, that 'this is the first piece of sensible talking on this matter that I have seen, and ... confirms the views already expressed by us to An tAire [the minister]',[76] was self-deluding: the DGOS, as it rapidly transpired, had no intention of recruiting its own orchestra, and was merely playing politics with its rival – a fact which

---

74 *Irish Press*, 26 February 1944. **75** *Evening Mail*, 1 March 1944. **76** File 61/59/7.

was presumably evident to the editor of the *Evening Herald*, who opined that the two societies should unite and co-operate with RÉ in presenting studio opera – 'a form of broadcasting almost neglected here'.[77]

The extant files are silent on the situation during the rest of 1944 and most of 1945, by which time Sleator had left the ailing DOS and formed another company, National Operatic Society of Ireland, and the DGOS had made representations directly to the Taoiseach.[78] Fresh support came at a high level, when the former Patron of the DOS, John McCormack, spoke from the stage of the Gaiety at the close of a DGOS performance, appealing 'To the Radio Authorities to let out the Orchestra if opera was to be successful'.[79] As Brennan wrote to the new secretary of the department, Joseph Cremins,

> This unfortunate speech of Count McCormack is having repercussions in all directions. It had the effect of belittling the work of the orchestra which had just completed a fortnight's hard work in the DGOS productions, and the general feeling was that the orchestra and its conductor – Commdt Doyle – had done very well. An answering speech by Ml O'Higgins on the same night repudiating what Count McCormack said and suggesting that the Radio Orchestra had been 'hogging' all the plums for years and that it was time the principle of 'one man one job' was adhered to raised further trouble, and made matters rather uncomfortable in Dublin musical circles generally.[80]

Sleator appealed again to Little and was refused,[81] while the DGOS went to the Taoiseach once more, only to be rebuffed when de Valera referred the matter to P&T.[82]

Nevertheless, Little did receive a deputation from the DGOS,[83] asking – as had Sleator – for the availability of some key players whom they were unable to secure elsewhere. (RÉ had refused similar requests not only from Sleator's new society, but – perhaps surprisingly – from the CEMA orchestra in Northern Ireland and the Belfast Philharmonic.)[84] On this occasion, Little refused the request from the DGOS also,[85] eliciting the predictable response from William (Bill) O'Kelly, 'There seems to be nothing for it now but to import Cross-Channel instrumentalists, a step which my Society only agreed to take in the last resort'.[86]

---

77 *Evening Herald* 28 February 1944. 78 P&T file 61/59/8. 79 Sleator to Brennan, 7 December 1944, ibid. 80 Ibid. 81 Sleator to Little, 14 December 1944; Little's ms. note on file, 16 December 1944, ibid. 82 Ibid. 83 Consisting of Commdt. William O'Kelly, Col. J.M. Doyle, Victor Waddington (a prominent art dealer) and Joseph Groome (owner of Groome's Hotel in Dublin's Cavendish Row, and a Fianna Fáil activist): memo by León Ó Broin, 3 October 1945, File 61/59/7. 84 Ibid. and P&T file 61/59/8. 85 P&T to William O'Kelly, 6 October 1945, ibid. 86 O'Kelly

The next episode in this saga came in February 1946, when the DGOS again used the media to exploit the situation. The *Evening Herald* and the *Irish Times* both carried reports of the DGOS agm, stating that its President, Dr Larchet, 'announced that the ban which [prevented players from the Army School of Music, the Garda Band and the Radio Éireann Orchestra] from taking part in operatic productions has been lifted ... Permission had been given this week for RÉ players to perform at the National Operatic Society's productions at the Olympia, and Dr Larchet said he was sure the Minister would not differentiate between societies'.[87] Larchet claimed to have been misquoted, saying that his statement should have been preceded by the words 'It seems'. Michael Bowles, as Director of Music, thought that Larchet had said 'the opinion was widely held that Mr Sleator had been given special concessions', and Brennan told Ó Broin, 'I doubt very much that Dr Larchet has been misquoted.'[88] Brennan remonstrated with Larchet: 'A public pronouncement from you carries a great deal of weight in musical circles.'[89]

If this was a deliberate attempt to embarrass Radio Éireann, it failed, but it did not deter the DGOS (Sleator's endeavours having come to an end by this stage, although the DOS itself continued in existence until the early 1950s and was still applying – unsuccessfully – for assistance from RÉ as late as 1949). In 1947, the DGOS and the French *chargé d'affaires* in Dublin, Baron de Juniac, had joined forces to ask for twenty-five players for Debussy's *Pelléas et Mélisande*. They returned to the issue the following year, when the orchestra had been re-established as a full-time body, the RÉSO. Given that administrative personnel in RÉ had also changed, and Roibéard Ó Faracháin – unsympathetic to musical development at the best of times – was now Deputy Director of Broadcasting, the result could hardly be expected to be any more favourable: 'I believe we all agree that having been delivered by providence from complete immersion in *Pelléas et Mélisande* we should not now get our feet wet. I strongly recommend a determined "No!"'[90] – to which Charles Kelly added: 'It is a wholetime orchestra for the purposes of broadcasting solely and to lend it, or 25 members of it, leaving the rest of it useless, is outside our authority.'[91]

One can readily see, in Kelly's reiteration of his view of the RÉSO as a purely broadcasting entity, a restrictive argument that accorded with the fact that, for the first five years of its existence, the orchestra was denied a public *persona* in the form of the popular public concerts, and maintained its profile

to Little, 13 October 1945, ibid. **87** *Evening Herald*, 28 February 1946. **88** Bowles to Brennan, 1 March 1946; Brennan to Ó Broin, ms. note (n.d.): P&T File 61/59/9: 'Statement made by Dr Larchet that ban which prevented members of Broadcasting Orchestra taking part in outside operatic productions had been lifted. 1.3.46–12.4.48.' **89** Brennan to Larchet, 5 March 1946, ibid. **90** Ó Faracháin memo, 24 March 1948, ibid. **91** The DGOS presented the production of *Pelléas et Mélisande* by the Opéra Comique, Paris, in its spring season, 1948.

almost entirely by means of its 'invitation' concerts at the small Phoenix Hall. In such circumstances, lending the orchestra to outside bodies, however worthwhile, might seem an inconsistent use of resources, especially at a time when efforts were being concentrated in building up the RÉSO's (by definition) symphonic activities, and when RÉ, like the rest of the public service, was suffering the effects of the government's 'Economy Campaign' which, in the case of P&T, threatened to halt the planned expansion of the Symphony Orchestra.

Nevertheless, the DGOS was hardly likely to share that perspective, and it is therefore little surprise to learn that the next step was a representation from Senator Michael Hayes to the Minister on the same day that Ó Faracháin had penned his 'No!' Hayes simply mentioned that 'The President of the Society [DGOS] is my colleague, Professor Larchet of University College, and the Chairman Commandant O'Kelly was on duty with me from 1927 to 1932 and has always remained a close friend of mine'.[92] To cite a military connection with a veteran of the war of independence (as we have seen O'Kelly to have been), even though the connection had occurred in peacetime, seems to have been sufficient to at least provoke a conference between P&T and the DGOS (represented by Larchet, O'Kelly and J.M. Doyle) the following day, and another two days later, at which Larchet said, quite reasonably, that the situation was different since now RÉ 'had absorbed all the available players of standing and they [DGOS] could no longer obtain the players they wanted outside'. Ó Broin said that RÉ would try to facilitate the DGOS if Larchet would put this point in writing, but that this was a one-off situation only because of the opera in question, and the DGOS was not to make any further applications. As far as the departmental note of these meetings reveals, the DGOS agreed to this.[93]

History, of course, repeated itself, although one could be forgiven for believing that the next phase of the relations between RÉ and the DGOS saw them moving onto a new footing. Nevertheless, the RÉSO undertook its first formal engagement with the DGOS for the production of *Pelléas et Mélisande*, under the baton of the conductor regarded as the definitive interpreter of the opera, Roger Désormière. As J.M. Doyle recalled, 'the availability of the RÉSO was essential if the society's musical standards were to be raised to an international level and in order to accompany visiting operatic companies'.[94] It was regrettable that such a worthwhile and understandable musical ambition on Doyle's part had been pursued by O'Kelly with such undiplomatic ferocity, but the exercise, however frustrating for Radio Éireann, at the outset of its administration of the new orchestra, did result, as O'Kelly himself acknowledged, in the fact that the association with RÉ enabled the DGOS to undertake more

92 Ibid., 24 March 1948. Michael Hayes (1889–1976) was a Sinn Féin senator 1922–65. Part of O'Kelly's duties as an army officer was the protection of public figures. 93 Ibid. 94 Quoted in Smith, op. cit., p. 52.

ambitious and more challenging projects, such as the presentation of unusual operas, with greater confidence.[95]

Meanwhile, following the change of government in 1948, and on the basis of fresh representations *via* General Richard Mulcahy (leader of Fine Gael and Minister for Education) to the incoming Minister for P&T, James Everett, it was noted that Mulcahy urged 'It would be most desirable that there would be formal and systematic co-operation between Radio Éireann authorities and the principal opera and musical companies'.[96] Everett agreed to see J.M. Doyle and Bill O'Kelly [whom the departmental minutes consistently referred to as 'Kelly'].[97] In preparation for this meeting, Ó Broin prepared a detailed memo, stating the department's position as strongly as befits a senior civil servant making an administrative case to a political figure (and one who had no interest whatsoever in the matter in hand).

> They [the RÉSO] are now full time and that makes the position even less easy for granting facilities ... We also have two Symphony Concerts a week (as against one a fortnight in 1944) and it would seem out of the question for the Orchestra to do the rehearsals for these concerts and rehearse for opera as well ... The Orchestra could not be permitted to be handed over entirely to an outside body during these weeks while at the same time employed and paid by the State. Running the operas as joint undertakings by Broadcasting and the Operatic Societies would be equally difficult. An instance of that was the recent performance with St Mary's Choral Society of Verdi's Requiem which involved us virtually in a strike of the orchestra.[98]

Referring to the undertaking by the DGOS not to request fresh favours, Ó Broin had to ruefully tell the Minister:

> notwithstanding the undertaking the society has now come forward again with a request for facilities ... the society has pushed very hard

---

95 Cf. Smith, op. cit., p. 64. Up to that point, RÉ had made the orchestra available in two ways: one category of performance, which acknowledged the official participation of the RÉ Orchestra, was undertaken by the players as part of their regular RÉ duties, and RÉ received free relays from the DGOS; the other category, when RÉ did not wish to take a relay, was undertaken by the players on a freelance basis. Thereafter, all performances were played officially by the RÉSO, although it would be some years before the players received an extra payment for such work. **96** Mulcahy to Everett, 15 October 1948: P&T file File 61/59/10: 'DGOS – Reps through Minister for Education that Broadcasting Concerts should be arranged to allow Society to engage members of Orchestra for Dec. 1948 Season of Opera. 15.10.48–25.11.49'. **97** Everett to Mulcahy 18 October 1948, ibid.; the meeting with the DGOS took place on 28 October. **98** Ó Broin to Everett, 28 October 1948, ibid.

from time to time to break the ban on giving facilities and they perhaps think they may have a chance if they begin again with the present Government. We would like very much to help them in their musical endeavours and we should also like to be able to get the additional fees for the Orchestra as they are not too well paid. We have found, however, after exhaustive experience that to try to arrange our orchestral programmes to suit some body outside instead of our own requirements would involve us in a very compromising position in Broadcasting.

At the meeting it was explained that the situation was complicated by the fact that Francesco Mander, one of the more interesting visiting conductors, had been contracted for four concerts at the specific period for which the DGOS wanted the orchestra.[99] The meeting was adjourned until the following day, when a decision had been promised. Matt Doherty recorded that 'Comdt Kelly professed not to be able to see how Radio Éireann could be upset by putting back the time of its concerts and changing the time of its other programmes if necessary and apparently nothing would convince him that the [Department was] influenced by anything but a lack of desire to co-operate'.[1] It was argued that the DGOS would lose £2000 if it could not engage the orchestra, and Ó Broin 'finally agreed to the concert times being put back during the two weeks – only if the musical difficulties could be overcome'.

One might easily argue that, with the apparent lack of resolve on the part of the Department, P&T was digging its own grave as far as its future relations with outside bodies were concerned. But if a civil servant, with as much acumen and foresight as Ó Broin had already proved himself to be, could be induced to grant concessions time after time, one must also acknowledge that, at least in the 1940s, political persuasion, on both sides of the political divide, could make it impossible for him to hold a firm line, and could oblige him to enter into untenable positions.[2]

The DGOS was nothing but audacious. Two days later, General Mulcahy was writing to Everett 'I find that while certain definite concessions have been offered to the Company they don't go far enough'.[3] He suggested a 'long distance' view and a 'short distance' view: 'The long distance considerations would, I think, result in an agreement that for six weeks in the year the normal work of the Symphony Orchestra would be interrupted somewhat in order to provide encouragement and assistance to our Operatic Societies doing high-class

---

99 Mander conducted four concerts in December 1948.   **1** O'Doherty minute, 2 November 1948, ibid.   **2** Although political support for, and in some prominent cases membership of, the DGOS has been evident from the ranks of Fianna Fáil, it is instructive that, during this period, the officers of the DGOS were equally adept at securing the support of Fine Gael.   **3** Mulcahy to Everett, 4 November 1948, ibid.

work'. The 'short distance', as always, was of course the surrender of the orchestra to meet the immediate demands of the DGOS. This was strenuously resisted by Ó Broin, who wrote to Everett

> In the first instance, you have laid it down as your policy not to interfere with the internal arrangements, programmes, etc., of the Broadcasting Service. The Broadcasting people have already noted the great benefits that this change has introduced and the liberty of action it promises. The pressure that is being exercised by the DGOS to compel the Broadcasting people to do something they dislike involves a complete reversal of your policy and I cannot too strongly impress upon you the importance of rejecting this pressure ... Notwithstanding this solemn assurance the DGOS does nothing whatever in the meantime to provide an alternative orchestra but calmly and coolly enters into arrangements with singers and the Theatre and when everything is settled presents us with an ultimatum and backs it up with Ministerial pressure. You are already aware of how far I have personally gone to induce the Broadcasting people to do something they dislike and which I know is not good for broadcasting. I agreed that the starting time of our symphony concerts – which are the highlights of the week's programmes ... should be pushed back so as to enable the opera to begin at 9 o'clock. This arrangement was stated to be entirely acceptable to the DGOS but the very next day they came along asking that the starting time should be half an hour earlier still and that moreover a morning rehearsal of ours should be foregone in order to enable the orchestra to rehearse opera ... We know that opera cannot be properly done without a good orchestra but it is too simple to say that because that is so our orchestra should be made available. If the Minister for Education wants to help opera his best line is to insist that something is done now other than by Radio Éireann to provide the necessary players.[4]

This is probably the nearest that a department secretary, with responsibility for the operation of such a large and complex administration, which included such a sensitive area as music and broadcasting, could go in admonishing his political master and in accusing him of countenancing political interference in that administration. It was a situation demanding diplomacy, since no one denied the legitimacy of the claim of opera, in principle, to secure the best resources available for its purposes; yet when, as in this case, that claim presented an obstacle to the pursuit of the goals for which the RÉSO had been established, and

4 Ó Broin to Everett, 5 November 1948, ibid.

was backed up by representations which were almost always unseen and unheard by those whom they most closely affected, a point was arrived at when Ó Broin had to speak as plainly as the language of the civil service permitted. If the DGOS had not been an amateur body (which remained its chief systemic problem for the next fifty years), if Radio Éireann had not had grave and legitimate doubts about the artistic and management expertise and judgement of the DGOS hierarchy, and if there had been an organic relationship with opera, built into the RÉSO's schedule, then the centrality of RTÉ to the development of opera in Ireland would have been far more effective and far freer of acrimony. The fact that, throughout the next half-century, the RTÉSO/NSO concert schedules were suspended to accommodate the DGOS winter and spring seasons, and, from the 1960s, that of the Wexford festival, is the legacy of those politicians in the 1940s who permitted themselves to become the messengers of this unseen influence. In itself, it constituted an excellent argument for the removal of RÉ/RTÉ from the sphere of direct political influence and its establishment as a quasi-autonomous semi-state body.

In what must seem like desperation Ó Broin, knowing that the Taoiseach, John A. Costello, was about to receive another deputation from the DGOS, appealed to Patrick Lynch, at that time private secretary to the Taoiseach:[5]

> Our orchestras are asked to become the plaything of the DGOS ... We are to adjust ourselves to their requirements. The Taoiseach will recognise that this would produce an intolerable position for us and one we could not possibly stand over ... What this country needs in music, as in many other things, is more specialisation and that aim of ours will be defeated if our symphony group is to be at the beck and call of outside organisations no matter how well intentioned.[6]

One of the ironies of the situation is the fact that, with the sole exception of León Ó Broin, few if any of those involved – Everett, Mulcahy, Lynch, Costello – had any interest in, or understanding of, classical music or opera whatsoever.

One can gauge the seriousness of the entire scenario by the fact that, five days after the Taoiseach had met the DGOS, Charles Kelly and Ó Broin were summoned to meet the Taoiseach and the Minister for Education (Mulcahy) – significantly, without their own minister being present. Kelly's minute recorded that

---

5 Patrick Lynch (1918–2001) was one of the most influential figures in the political economy of modern Ireland; beginning his career as a civil servant, he exercised considerable power in persuading the Taoiseach, John A. Costello, to introduce a Keynesian approach to economic policy; he became Professor of Political Economy at UCD 1975–80, and held many positions of authority and influence including the chairmanship of Aer Lingus 1954–75. 6 Ó Broin to Lynch, 11 November 1948, ibid.

An Taoiseach made it clear that he had no wish to press the Broadcasting Service to do anything which would be unreasonable from its own point of view and he recognised the magnitude of the difficulties. He asked that we should arrange to see the representatives of the Operatic Society and tell them that he and the Minister for Education had discussed the position fully with us and that no way could be seen out of the difficulties connected with the forthcoming operatic season ... An Taoiseach and the Minister for Education both agreed that it should be made clear to the Society that they should consult us before making any definite arrangements.[7]

This was of extra importance, since the DGOS had planned to import productions from the Hamburg State Opera the following year. As we shall see, the DGOS's cavalier attitude, the chief cause of Ó Broin's grievance (as expressed to Patrick Lynch), would become practically uncontainable as time went on.

On foot of this meeting at the highest level, Charles Kelly met Professor Larchet and Denis McCullough of the DGOS:[8]

Dr Larchet again pressed very hard for a further alteration of the time of our concerts but I stood firm. I told him we were satisfied that one concession led to another, with the result that the Broadcasting Service lost all control of its affairs and was at the mercy of the very uncertain workings of an outside body ... Dr Larchet said that the theatre would have to be closed on the four nights of our concerts and that this would mean bankrupting the Society, which would go out of existence. I told him that it was extremely foolish of the Society to be planning their seasons as if they had no difficulty about an orchestra. They might as well face the fact that they were counting on our help without the slightest regard for the effect on our arrangements, and that it was hardly fair, in present circumstances, for them to be making ambitious plans without consulting us and then making us appear to be ill-disposed when we found it impossible to meet their demands.[9]

Despite the new note of confidence detectable in Kelly's minute, due no doubt to his own reading of the meeting with the Taoiseach, there was in fact

7 C. Kelly minute, 18 November 1948, ibid. 8 Denis McCullough (1883–1968), a native of Belfast, had, with Bulmer Hobson, been an organiser of the IRB and a member of its supreme council. At the instigation of Michael Collins, he was one of the founders of New Ireland Assurance. A piano tuner by trade, he set up his own music shop in Dublin which eventually became McCullough-Pigott Ltd; his son, Mairtín, succeeded him in the business and was chairman of the Arts Council 1984–89. 9 C. Kelly, 20 November 1948, minute of a meeting on 19 November 1948, ibid.

no real cause for satisfaction, since, a week later (on 25 November), P&T received a letter from the Taoiseach's office stating that RÉ must advance the time of its concerts in order to make the orchestra available for rehearsal with the eminent Australian soprano Joan Hammond, who would not be available at any other time.[10] Hammond was then reaching the peak of her powers, had just made her Covent Garden début as Leonora in *Il trovatore*, and had been booked to sing the title role in Puccini's *Tosca* in Dublin on 9 and 11 December. The shortness of the notice – barely a fortnight – given to P&T in this round-about way is a prime example of both the perfunctory nature of the DGOS's own schedule planning and its methods of conveying it.

An undated memo by Charles Kelly makes it clear how seriously the incident was regarded by those whose day-to-day responsibility was the administration of the orchestra and the implementation of policy that emanated from above:

> The Government's decision regarding the facilities required by the DGOS places the Broadcasting Service in the worst position it has ever been in vis-a-vis any outside body. The position is particularly bad for the Director of Broadcasting because he gave a 'final' decision to the … Society at the express wish of An Taoiseach and this decision has been reversed without any consultation … The Director and his staff were heartened by the Minister's declaration to the Dáil that the Broadcasting Service was not, and would not be, interfered with in the discharge of its functions, in other words, that it would have freedom to do the work it was there to do. The Government's decision makes it clear that freedom for the Service is a matter for interpretation according to the amount of pressure which can be brought to bear on the Government.[11]

---

10 Department of Taoiseach to P&T, 25 November 1948, ibid. 11 Ibid. Everett had told the Dáil on 20 July 1948: 'I should say here that within the present broadcasting organisation a most competent staff has been collected and I am satisfied that no alternative type of organisation, such as a semi-independent corporation, would be able to secure more highly qualified people. I am quite certain they are capable of doing everything that broadcasting requires of them if they can be made to feel that they are free to do so without all the inhibitions associated with the more normal type of Civil Service department. To give an adequate trial to the present broadcasting set-up I feel that one desirable step is the creation for these people of an atmosphere in which they can give of their best. A form of encouragement I believe in is to tell the staffs responsible for the programmes, as I do now, that I have every confidence in them and that apart from laying down policy for them in general terms I propose to give them the widest measure of freedom possible to do their job. This will help towards the provision of better programmes and will give us the opportunity of judging, at our leisure, under the better conditions created, whether a Civil Service organisation is capable of catering adequately for this most unusual type of State service. I am sure that in this task the Broadcasting Service will continue to benefit from the advice tendered by the advisory committee which is being reconstituted with an enlarged membership': DD 112, col. 823.

Ó Broin, using a different language, but one which went over the edge as far as diplomacy was concerned, once more attempted to impress on his minister the gravity of the situation:

> Dear Minister
> I presume you were a party to the Government decision recorded in the attached minute but if you were I make bold to suggest you were not fully aware of the implications of that decision. On the face of it it turns down the Radio Éireann authorities on a matter affecting the internal arrangements of the Station and, in effect, hands over the Orchestra to the DGOS. The decision will demonstrate to the DGOS and to others that if they want anything done in Radio Éireann which the officials best qualified to judge consider undesirable the way to get it done is by approaching Ministers. However, the decision cuts deeper than that. It turns the Department down as well as Radio Éireann and leaves us wondering where we stand having regard to the undertaking given by you regarding the freedom of the Station so far as day to day administration is concerned ... The result of the new policy has been a marked improvement in the broadcasting service ... A good, lively, independent job is being done so far as news and talks features are concerned. I quite sincerely fear that the Government decision regarding the use of the Orchestra will cause everybody concerned to believe that that freedom is now being withdrawn and that interference in other directions may be anticipated.[12]

Everett, however, told Mulcahy that P&T would comply with the government decision but, pointing out 'I am anxious to put the position on a proper basis for the future', insisted that in future the DGOS must consult RÉ before entering into arrangements, since the RÉSO's first obligation was to RÉ:

> If these things are recognised Radio Éireann can get down to discussing the possibility of future co-operation. Radio Éireann is naturally reluctant to begin discussions until some set of principles ... is accepted. Without them we can only have a recurrence of the recent unpleasantness ... There can be no real music development here until Radio Éireann can concentrate on doing its own job and until an alternative orchestra, either permanent or recruited ad hoc, is available.[13]

It was a weak response, and reflected a compromise between the claims of P&T to run its own affairs and the reality of the political situation.

12 Ó Broin to Everett, 25 November 1948, ibid. **13** Everett to Mulcahy, 3 December 1948 and 11 December 1948, ibid.

In fact, with its newly boosted confidence, the DGOS felt capable of invit-ing the Hamburg State Opera to bring its productions of *Don Giovanni* and *Così fan tutte* to Dublin for the spring season of 1950 – a coup which is still treasured for its artistic resonance among those who attended the perform-ances. With soloists of the calibre of Martha Mödl, Annaliese Rothenberger and Matthieu Ahlesmeyer, production by the intendant of the Hamburg Staatsoper, Günther Rennert and, as we have seen, Arthur Grüber conduct-ing, it was not only a 'first' for Ireland but also for Germany, as it was the first time since the second world war that the complete cast of a German opera house had visited another country. As Síle Larchet recalled, Grüber 'knew what he wanted from the orchestra, and he got it … Everything blended so beauti-fully, the singing, the music, the whole atmosphere around each opera was realised and came across'.[14] The telling word is 'realised', since the Rennert-Grüber production, with an orchestra led by Nancie Lord, had conceived and made real the integrity of the works.

The Hamburg company repeated its visit in 1951, with *Il barbiere di Siviglia* and, in winter 1953, with *Don Giovanni* and *Die Entführung aus dem Serail* (Mozart), the same year that saw the Munich State Opera coming in the spring with *La bohème*, *The Marriage of Figaro*, *La traviata* and *Tristan und Isolde*. Munich returned in spring 1954 with Beethoven's *Fidelio* and Humperdinck's *Hänsel und Gretel*, while in 1956 the Essen Municipal Opera brought Wagner's *Die Walküre* and Mozart's *Idomeneo* and in 1964 Wiesbaden State Opera with *Die Entführung* and Wagner's *The Flying Dutchman*. In *Tristan* the Munich com-pany was conducted by Robert Heger (1886–1978), conductor at the Staatsoper and President of the Hochschule für Musik, who had previously held posts at the Vienna, Munich and Berlin Staatsoper. He had also made numerous appear-ances at Covent Garden, and was himself a composer of five successful operas. He was noted as one of the last survivors of his generation as a Wagner inter-preter, and in Dublin Gerald Larchet, a young horn player (and son of John F.), recalled 'I remember thinking how privileged I was as a young musician to be performing Wagner's music under a conductor of Robert Heger's stature … It was his skill in shaping the music that made you admire him, his use of tempos and the way he coped with the great dramatic climaxes in the music … I remember one newspaper critic asking why the orchestra couldn't play up to this standard more often and of course the answer was that professor Heger wasn't always the man with the baton'.[15] Meanwhile his harpist sister, Síle, recounted that 'when he was conducting *Tristan* I got this feeling that it was Richard Wagner himself who was up there, for he had this incredible insight into the composer's music and created a mood that merged stage and pit in

14 Quoted in Smith, op. cit., p. 71. **15** Ibid., p. 97.

one unit. He was able to shape the music to convey every nuance. It reminded me so much of Roger Désormière's conducting of *Pélleas et Mélisande*, though of course Debussy and Wagner's music is entirely different.'[16]

Fachtna Ó hAnnracháin was part of the DGOS party that travelled to Munich to negotiate the contract for the 1953 season, for which the German authorities required assurances as to the quality and conditions of the Dublin presentation, a difficulty which the success of the Hamburg company's visit did much to smooth. Ó hAnnracháin was able to observe Bill O'Kelly in action: 'they respected his determination and enthusiasm. He was a realist and knew what was needed and how to achieve it. He impressed people by his sincerity and obvious organising skills ... Behind his somewhat abrasive exterior there was a good-natured man.' Ó hAnnracháin formed the view that O'Kelly 'was running the Society his way ... He was able to inspire and cajole people and though they might argue he was autocratic few could deny his leadership skills which undoubtedly helped to hold the DGOS together.'[17] While the DGOS recollected (as far as is recounted in Gus Smith's history of the organisation) that RÉ's Music Director was required to travel to Munich to allay any doubts that the Staatsoper might have about the quality of the RÉSO, RÉ's own files suggest that its principal motive in sending Ó hAnnracháin on this and subsequent visits to Munich was to ensure that the DGOS did not enter into any agreement to which RÉ itself could not be a party.[18]

Ó hAnnracháin, as Director of Music, had the general responsibility of deciding which operas would be broadcast, and factors which were weighed in his consideration included the fact that 'small parts were not always well filled and ... the society was more concerned about the singing than about improving the staging of the operas. More rehearsal time was needed, especially with the orchestra'.[19] On occasions, performances broke down and had to be stopped, as when Charles Mackerras halted a performance of *Faust* in the winter season, 1961, when a cue from the electronic organ, which had lost its power supply, failed to bring in Ane-Raquel Satre, singing Marguerite, and silence ensued. In such circumstances a broadcast could be fatally flawed, with more criticism being directed at the medium than the source, and so R(T)É adopted the precaution of recording each performance and editing the results into one acceptable version for transmission; the thrill for listeners of witnessing a live broadcast was thus sacrificed for the possibly higher value of ensuring that the end product was as near to a high professional standard, in all aspects, as was possible.

16 Ibid. **17** Ibid., p. 84. **18** Ó Broin to Secretary, Department of Finance, 30 September 1952, P&T file 61/59/13, 'DGOS – visit of Music Director and Representative of DGOS to Munich and Hamburg to arrange for operas for 1953 and subsequent years'. **19** Quoted in Smith, op. cit., pp. 99–100.

Ó hAnnracháin later recalled that 'I saw it [the DGOS] very much as an amateur society, working on an inadequate budget which militated against achieving higher production standards ... As it was, they were doing a good job in the circumstances and the seasons were hugely popular with all sections of the community. We were happy to be part of that scene, though a few people in Radio Éireann didn't share my enthusiasm.'[20] From the late 1940s up to the late 1950s, Ó hAnnracháin would maintain that the involvement was worthwhile, writing in 1957:

> All my recommendations in regard to the DGOS in recent years have been based ... on the assumption that we must collaborate with the Society. Over the years there has been a definite raising of standards and any return or partial return to previous practices would most likely have deplorable results ... In brief, I submit that we get more from the Society than they get from us. After all, the Orchestra is working for us as well as for the DGOS during the opera seasons and it helps to provide programme material which is probably far more acceptable to the general body of listeners than our studio symphony concerts.[21]

However, the perceived need, on the part of R(T)É, to maintain and improve standards, as a move towards the professionalisation of the DGOS, would remain a major point of contention between the two organisations. In 1983, Patricia Quinn (later the Director of the Arts Council) opined that, while RTÉ enjoyed an excellent working relationship with the DGOS, this 'hardly disguises the fact that [it] broadcasts what are ... fourth-rate productions of nineteenth-century warhorses' and that 'their quality is often such as to encourage sensitive opera lovers actually to stay away', and suggested that Jane Carty, RTÉ's opera producer for radio, was limited in the range of programming available to her, with 'no say whatsoever in the choice of performers or repertoire' at the DGOS.[22]

The chief arguments concerned, firstly, the *locus* of decision-making on artistic matters, which an Arts Council investigation in the late 1970s failed to penetrate. RTÉ's position as the provider of the orchestra was invidious, since it had no part in the selection of repertoire, singers, conductors or producers. It had, however, met with some success on the second problem – the quality of the chorus, which, up to the 1980s, was composed mainly of subscribing members of the society. During one of the DGOS's perennial financial crises

---

20 Ibid. 21 Ó hAnnracháin to Controller, 5 March 1957, P&T file 39/57: 'DGOS – Financial position of Society following Winter 1956 season and question of terms on which RÉ will participate in future occasions. Agreement etc for Spring 1957 season and later seasons'. 22 'Opera in the Home', *Soundpost* 12, February–March 1983.

in 1957, Maurice Gorham (Director of Broadcasting) suggested a fiscal measure by which the DGOS would be saved a cost of £400 per season, on condition that the saving be applied to the engagement of 'a suitable Chorus Master' and at least some paid choristers or small-part soloists.[23]

At the same time, Ó hAnnracháin advised Gorham that the excuse proferred by the DGOS – that poor performances were caused by unforeseen illness – was hollow:

> illness is something which is completely unpredictable but whereas the Society was generally able to overcome these crises caused by illness, the real fundamental weaknesses had nothing to do with illnesses. If a situation like that of 'Faust' occurs again I really think that Radio Éireann would be fully justified in refusing to collaborate in the performances. 'The Tales of Hoffmann' was almost as bad as 'Faust' but the really annoying thing is that both of these shows could be transformed by two really good stage rehearsals.[24]

Roibéard Ó Faracháin's manuscript note on this memo read: 'We should certainly avoid at all costs ... compromising the reputation of RÉ by continuing collaboration through any given production which is likely to fall well below reasonable standards. I suggest that any repetition of the "Faust" situation should call for immediate consultation here, with the possibility of withdrawing the RÉSO from the particular production.'[25] The difficulty was that, having entered into an agreement with the DGOS, it would have been perceived as irresponsible and unfair on RÉ's part if it were seen to withdraw, once a production was under way.

The following year, Leo Donnelly – a former treasurer and chorus member of the DGOS, who had become assistant to the Director of Music in RÉ and was Concerts Manager 1962–74 – wrote to Ó hAnnracháin (apparently at the latter's request):

> Chorus: I am afraid they show no improvement ... Some of the ladies are getting a bit long in the tooth and could, with grace, begin to withdraw in favour of the younger members who, I understand, are eager to take over ... It was lamentable at one performance of *La traviata* to see only one tenor on stage and for the 'Matador' chorus to see one of the men in the front of the stage just 'mouthing' the words. It was obvious he knew neither words nor music and was just on stage to fill a vacancy ... It seems strange to me that so much expense and effort is spent on

---

23 Gorham to Ó'Kelly, 16 November 1957, P&T file 39/57. 24 Ó hAnnracháin to Gorham and Ó Faracháin, 17 December 1957, ibid. 25 Ibid.

the principals and orchestra and so little on the chorus. Apparently there is no check on make-up, wigs, shoes, etc. The attitude seems to be 'It's good enough'. It's hard to blame the chorus members as they appear to lack guidance or control on these matters, indeed they attend or not as they please. Certainly there is no check on who goes on or remains off.[26]

As a result of this report, Ó hAnnracháin, despite his internal memorandum setting out the advantages to RÉ of maintaining the link with the DGOS, proposed as a condition of RÉ's co-operation that paid choristers should be engaged.[27] This was necessary not merely to effect a weeding out of the older singers in favour of the younger, but also to provide paid employment for the up-and-coming younger would-be professionals, who had been encouraged by the existence of a professional chamber choir, such as the Radio Éireann Singers, to envisage a career in singing. It would remain a stumbling block for the DGOS up to the formation of the National Chamber Choir in 1991, when young, versatile singers at the start of their careers, would be available.

Ó hAnnracháin's proposals also included a recommendation that the season be limited to five performances per week, that no more than two new operas be produced in each week, that there should be a minimum of six hours' stage dress rehearsals for each opera, and – predictably – that conductors and soloists must have experience of the work they were engaged to perform. These may seem obvious today, to the point of being quite unnecessary, but the fact that it *was* necessary to express them in 1958, ten years after the beginning of RÉ's formal association with the DGOS, and seventeen years after the inception of the DGOS, indicates how slowly improvements were introduced in all but the area of programming. It also indicates that, as a result of ambitious programming, standards of stage presentation were being jeopardised, thus emphasising the amateurishness of the venture. Ó hAnnracháin's upbeat enthusiasm for the linkage with the DGOS *en principe* was thus tempered by his actual experience of its shortcomings, resulting in an ambivalence that continued to characterise the attitude of his successors up to the 1990s.

The earlier German visits also paved the way for the DGOS to forge a relationship with a number of Italian agents and impresarios and to achieve an annual subvention from the Italian government for a spring season of operas which was initiated by Cardenio Botti in 1955 and continued until 1966/7, when Dublin began to see a troupe of Romanian singers from the Bucharest opera dominating productions.

26 Donnelly to Ó hAnnracháin, 18 December 1958, ibid. The same point was made by Hans Waldemar Rosen: cf. G. Smith, op. cit., pp. 69–70. 27 Ó hAnnracháin internal memo, 18 December 1958, ibid.

During the early 1960s, a more stable relationship existed between RTÉ and the DGOS, not least due to the continuing presence of the Italian conductor Napoleone Annovazzi, with whose name the DGOS's twice-yearly seasons became almost synonymous.[28] Geraldine O'Grady (guest leader of the RÉSO 1961–3, and therefore extra-sensitive to the advantages and disadvantages of the conductor of the day) recalled that Annovazzi was 'an outstanding conductor. He breathed and lived the music ... During an actual performance he sang every word and note and so was a superb guide to the singers'.[29]

Behind the scenes, however, relations between RTÉ and the DGOS were turbulent. Throughout the 1950s, as far as the extant records reveal, the financial position had been difficult and gave rise to acrimony. The DGOS, ever looking over its shoulder at its bank manager, naturally attempted to secure every penny of its income from box-office, grant-aid and other fund-raising exercises, to meet its production expenses; RTÉ, for its part, as a public body, naturally wished to obtain value for money, as far as its investment of human and technical resources in DGOS productions was concerned. Complaints were frequently voiced from the echelons above the music department – levels which in any case were not necessarily sympathetic to opera *per se* – that the DGOS did not adhere to its undertakings in financial matters any more than it had earlier on questions of scheduling.[30]

O'Grady expressed the experience of most members of a pit orchestra whose main work is on the concert platform, when she mentioned just a few performances that she had found moving, such as Gian Giacomo Guelfi in the title role of Verdi's *Nabucco* and Piero Cappuccilli as Giorgio in *La traviata* or Count di Luna in *Il trovatore* in the spring 1962 season. And she expressed a professional point of view when she spoke of working conditions: 'the pit itself could be freezing'. Even though, as Gus Smith suggests, 'musicians hadn't the same rights then as they enjoy nowadays and often [O'Grady] felt they were being exploited',[31] the onward momentum, even when the artistic reward was dubious, was a professional imperative, unless conditions were absolutely prohibitive. 'A Mozart opera was the most difficult to accompany and one could

---

28 Annovazzi (1907–84) had been a prodigiously talented musical youngster, making his first triumphs with productions of Wagner operas; at 20 he had been appointed to the State Opera in Riga; he had conducted Max Reinhardt's production of *Die Fledermaus*, had worked with Chaliapin, Gigli, Tito Schipa, Gino Bechi, and Carlo Tagliabue, before being appointed principal conductor at the Gran Teatro del Liceo in Barcelona where he conducted *Turandot* with Laura Volpi. From 1945 he headed the San Carlo Opera in Lisbon for five years, working with Victoria de los Angeles, Monserrat Caballe, Giuseppe di Stefano and Mario del Monaco before making his first appearance in Dublin in 1961 with *Aida*, *Manon Lescaut*, and Cimarosa's *Il matrimonio segreto*. **29** Quoted in G. Smith, op. cit. p. 167. **30** P&T file 39/57 *passim*; to quote financial details from this file would be to reveal sensitive information which, even at this chronological remove, might prejudice ongoing relations between RTÉ and the DGOS/Opera Ireland. **31** G. Smith, op. cit. p. 167.

never relax one's concentration for a moment. The appeal of the Italian repertoire was contained in the lovely melodies and the opportunity it afforded artists
to show off their voices. There were times when the atmosphere in the Gaiety
could be electric and the audience on a high.'[32]

Moments of doubt might be caused not only by the physical conditions in
the pit but, more importantly, by the quality of the music itself, the singers
and, as far as the orchestra was concerned, the conductor. Other, younger,
singers who later went on to outstanding worldwide reputations were Anna
Moffo, Edith Mathis, Giuseppe di Stefano, Raimund Herincx and Luciano
Pavarotti: to work with musicians of such calibre was no less a challenge or a
rewarding experience than to do so with the soloist in a concerto, but the physical distance between pit and stage made the collaboration less obvious to the
audience. Under *maestri* like Franco Patanè, Charles Mackerras, Annovazzi
and Albert Rosen, the orchestra could usually look forward to rewarding work.
Mackerras, who conducted in Dublin from 1956 to 1962 (a total of seven productions), recalled that the RÉSO 'was quite good, although very variable. It
did not have a homogenous style because so many of the players were of different foreign origin. For example, the four horns led by a Frenchman [Leopold
Laurent] were all of different nationalities and all played in different styles.'[33]
It is also recalled that on one occasion 'the rehearsal ... was going badly ...
Mackerras seemed to be getting frustrated. Worse, the musicians in the pit
were doing crosswords and throwing paper aeroplanes. Mackerras put down
his baton and said to them "Gentlemen, those people up there have no music,
you have music before you, just take it easy".'[34]

Two illustrations of such difficult situations are Charles Acton's reviews of,
respectively, *Der Rosenkavalier* in 1975 and *La bohème* in 1981, both conducted
by Annovazzi. Of the former, when the singer in the role of the Marschallin
had withdrawn at the last minute, he wrote:

> It must be very unsettling for everyone for the first night curtain to go
> up with the leading character totally unrehearsed in the production and
> all praise to everyone for not showing their anxieties. The most obvi-
> ous sufferers were the RTÉSO, who gave the sort of performance that
> would have passed in a Verdi opera but not in this intricate, wholly inter-
> connected and beautiful score. Inevitably Napoleone Annovazzi had to
> give an extremely high proportion of his attention to helping and will-
> ing and easing his singers.[35]

Of the latter, on the other hand, he gave evidence of just how thrilling a fully
integrated performance can be:

32 Ibid., pp. 167–8. **33** Ibid., p. 117. **34** Ibid., p. 118. **35** *Irish Times*, 3 December 1975.

It was the sort of performance during which one was not aware of the conductor as such, or the orchestra as such, but, when he leaves the theatre, the critic realises that he has had a first-class evening because of the conductor – and the RTÉSO will know from that the height of my praise for them.[36]

If Annovazzi's connections with Italian and Romanian opera houses brought DGOS productions to a new level, Albert Rosen's début in 1969 with *Die Fledermaus* (which was hardly central to his repertoire), ushered in another new era. His first real triumph, one of those occasions when all elements of the production fused into an artistic unity, was in 1971 with Smetana's *The Bartered Bride*, directed by his compatriot Jaroslav Horáček, sung in Czech with principals of the Czech National Theatre, to whom of course Rosen was a familiar colleague. The partnership of Rosen and Horáček repeated its triumph the following year with Tchaikovsky's *The Queen of Spades*, sung in Russian, and returned to the Czech repertoire in 1973, again with Czech principals, in Janáček's *Jenůfa*. This and the earlier *Bartered Bride* are still regarded as among the high points of DGOS production history.

As the provider of the orchestra, and with complex contractual arrangements with the DGOS, R(T)É was anxious to ensure that adequate artistic arrangements were put in place, since the reputation of its orchestra was vulnerable to those conditions. Not only were there regular discussions between RÉ and the DGOS, but Fachtna Ó hAnnracháin continued to attend auditions which, with the Italian connection, were now held principally in Rome. Ó hAnnracháin, from a broadcasting perspective, tried to ensure that, in both Dublin and Wexford, performances would be intelligible to the radio listener. In his words, 'it was not an unfruitful collaboration'.[37] But although the timetable for rehearsals improved enormously over the decades, it was still possible in the 1980s for a production to open after only six rehearsals, with predictable artistic consequences, and it was necessary for a member of RTÉ's music department to attend every performance in case any accusation might be levelled at members of the orchestra.

A series of artistic, financial and organisational problems, to which RTÉ was not a party, and which therefore concern us only peripherally here, brought about a professionalisation of the DGOS (including a succession of name changes to, eventually, 'Opera Ireland') which saw a management structure and the elimination of the amateur choir in favour of the National Chamber Choir. These changes coincided with the long overdue withdrawal of the RTÉSO and its replacement by the RTÉCO as the pit ochestra: as with

36 *Irish Times*, 4 April 1981. 37 Interview with the author, 11 February 2004.

Wexford, it had long been considered a nonsense that members of the larger orchestra, who could not all be accommodated in the pit, should be either unused during opera seasons or amalgamated temporarily with the smaller orchestra which was, in fact, of the appropriate size. Additionally, RTÉ had had to insist that rising costs made it necessary for the DGOS to meet at least part of the expense of supplying an orchestra, for which, up to 1970, no charge had been made. The disruption of the NSO's season by both the DGOS (spring and winter) and Wexford (autumn) was seen to be totally unnecessary and to deprive concertgoers of continuity of performances, and in 1994 the complete substitution of the Concert Orchestra for the NSO was effected.[38]

OPERA (2): WEXFORD

In 1951 a new challenge – or the possibility of one – presented itself to Radio Éireann. An appeal was received from Wexford, at that time a small town in the south-east with a limited reputation as a fishing port and with important historical associations with the 1798 rising. Wexford was, musically speaking, however, negligible compared with the neighbouring Waterford where, as we have seen, RÉ had established long-lasting relations with an active musical population. When, therefore, a group proposing to establish an opera festival in this small town put forward a request to RÉ for the use of its Light Orchestra, it could only be the warmth of the personal conviction and advocacy of its co-founder, Dr Tom Walsh, that gave it any chance of a successful reception, and only the positive personal response of Fachtna Ó hAnnracháin that gave it any chance of being heard beyond the confines of the music department.

Rapidly, 'Wexford' came to be synonymous with an opera festival of international repute and status; 'Wexford' meant, for Dubliners, an out-of-town excursion of previously unknown proportions as far as operatic repertoire and standards were concerned, and one which, they quickly discovered, was shared by opera 'buffs' around the world (and especially from the United Kingdom) for whom the choice of works and artists, and the unusual excitement of the venue, created an atmosphere and an experience unlike anything else in the opera calendar.

Gus Smith, in his history of the Wexford opera festival – or Wexford Festival Opera to name the organisation correctly – states that in early April 1951 Dr Tom Walsh travelled to Dublin for a crucial meeting with Fachtna Ó hAnnracháin to put the case for the loan of the RÉLO for its inaugural pro-

---

38 The RTÉCO had in fact been playing for the Winter season of the DGOS since 1988, but from 1994 it played for both the Winter and Spring seasons.

duction. He records Ó hAnnracháin's recollection that 'I pointed out to him that there would be numerous difficulties', not least the fact that other 'outside bodies' were also applying for similar facilities – and that following that meeting the then Director of Broadcasting, Maurice Gorham, had expressed a disinclination to favour such applications.[39]

In fact, Ó hAnnracháin had received a letter from Walsh's sister Nellie (who was to become a key figure in the opera festival) in mid-February 1951, stating that, on foot of a conversation with Seán Mac Réamoinn, she hoped that Ó Annracháin would agree to meet her brother: 'I am writing to you as my brother doesn't know you & was shy of writing to you'.[40] Dr Walsh's 'shyness' must have come as a complete contrast to the forward nature of Bill O'Kelly, and Ó hAnnracháin was to encounter, emanating from Wexford, a tactfulness and sincere effort to please, unlike the assertiveness and insistence of its Dublin counterparts.

In advance of his meeting, Dr Walsh sent Ó hAnnracháin a handwritten letter setting out the objectives of his committee, which had grown out of a Wexford Opera Study Circle:

> Since Balfe lived in Wexford for a time, the raison d'etre of our festival is a revival of his forgotten operas; – which I consider really do deserve to be revived. We have consequently booked the Theatre Royal here for four days, November 1st to November 4th next, and for these four evenings we hope to present 'The Rose of Castille'. The principal artists for this will come from London and Dublin; (If we can get her Gwen Catley is our choice for Elvira), the chorus will be local, and most important of all, for orchestra we were intending to ask next Tuesday if you could let us have the Radio Éireann Light Orchestra. The producer, I expect, will come from London, scenery and costumes will be specially designed; in fact as far as lies within our power, neither expense [n]or trouble will be spared to make this an artistic venture of national importance. Now although opera will be the principal item of the festival programme, we also intend, during the mornings and afternoons to have a number of instrumental recitals, and lectures, by first class lecturers and recitalists. We have also planned an exhibition of paintings and an exhibition of objects connected with old operas and singers ... and with Balfe. Finally if we had your orchestra at our disposal, if it were possible, I should like to have a morning concert for schoolchildren.[41]

39 G. Smith, *Dr Tom's festival legacy* (2001), pp. 1–2. **40** Nellie Walsh to Ó hAnnracháin, 19 February 1951: P&T file 640/53/1: 'The Wexford Festival of Music Nov. 1st–4th 1951. Participation of RÉLO'. **41** T.J. Walsh to Ó hAnnracháin, 23 February 1951, ibid.

He asked for the orchestra for a total of six days, to facilitate rehearsals, but, realising that the orchestra might have restricted availability, 'If six days is too long, what is the maximum period we could have it for[?] … Would the dates I have mentioned be suitable for you, or failing this what dates about this period would be suitable[?].'

Moving on, he wrote 'Next concerning finance. We have calculated that the venture must lose something between £250 and £500, which will have to be recouped by local subscription' and asking if the opera might be broadcast in exchange for a fee to reduce this deficit. 'I should be very grateful if you could find time to answer these troublous questions and let me have your opinion on any further point you may consider advisable.'

Ó hAnnracháin's immediate response was in fact very positive: 'In principle, we could possibly arrange for the absence of the RÉLO from Dublin for some days', but a fee for a broadcast was out of the question. 'The dates you have suggested for the Festival would appear at this stage at any rate to be suitable'.[42] Even given the untried quality of the Wexford organisers and their proposed festival (which was originally titled 'Wexford Festival of Music and the Arts') it was no doubt attractive to RÉ to consider the opportunity of presenting the Light Orchestra outside its studio base, and it also probably struck Ó hAnnracháin as very realistic that the application concerned the Light, rather than the Symphony, Orchestra. It would not only give the RÉLO exposure outside its studio *and* outside Dublin, but it would also introduce it – and its conductor, Dermot O'Hara – to the genre of opera.

Their meeting actually took place on 23 April, as a result of which Ó hAnnracháin supported the application, having been told by Walsh in the meanwhile that the organisers had already secured £350 by way of guarantees. He told Charles Kelly (then Deputy Director of Broadcasting) that 'the organisers seem to be determined to leave no stone unturned to make the Festival a great artistic success'.[43] It seems extraordinary, with hindsight, that at that stage no principal singers had been engaged, and this remained the case right up to late June and early July, when London agents started to reply, belatedly, to enquiries which had been sent out for suitable singers for the roles of Elvira, Manuel and Don Pedro. It rapidly transpired that the fees being quoted were far beyond what the committee could afford: Ibbs and Tillett (one of the leading London artists' agencies) were quoting 150 guineas for the Dublin-born Laelia Fineberg,[44] Heddle Nash and Dennis Noble, and 125 guineas for Victoria Sladen.[45] Nor had any producer been engaged, which RÉ found disturbing as

---

42 Ó hAnnracháin to Walsh, 3 March 1951, ibid. 43 Ó hAnnracháin to Kelly, 9 May 1951, ibid.
44 Singer, pianist and cousin of Samuel Beckett; educated at the RIAM. 45 Ibbs and Tillett to
Ó hAnnracháin, 27 June 1951, ibid.

the time for rehearsals came close, but Wexford succeeded in pulling off a coup in securing Ria Mooney as producer and Michael O'Herlihy as designer. 'To my knowledge no operatic production in this country has had scenery and costumes specially designed for it by an artist of Mr O'Herlihy's calibre for well over a hundred years'.[46] Ria Mooney, at that time 'resident director' (in today's terms, artistic director) of the Abbey Theatre, was, with the exception of Hilton Edwards at the Gate, Ireland's leading theatre director, but with the fire that destroyed the Abbey on 17 July, her participation at Wexford was cancelled, and the job was taken up by Powell Lloyd, a former producer at Sadler's Wells who had been working with the DGOS in recent years.

On 13 July, Walsh wrote to Ó hAnnracháin:

> That a suitable tenor should be engaged without delay presents the immediate problem of discovering one. You will no doubt remember your own experience when after two months Messrs Ibbs & Tillett, with one or two exceptions, sent you a roster of most unsuitable singers who <u>might</u> undertake to sing the roles. Of these, Heddle Nash was the only suitable tenor by any standards listed, and he, I am reliably informed will not learn a new role, and certainly not an unprofitable one in 'The Rose of Castile' [*sic*].[47]

There had been some discussion of which Irish singers might be available, and Walsh wryly added:

> It [is] better policy to engage let us say second rate Irish artists than third raters and 'has beens' from England ... When applied to an opera singer, 'suitable' is a term which I think needs to be defined. For example I have seen many arm-flailing Italians with enormous voices and even more enormous figures who were considered suitable for La Scala or Covent Garden, but who in one small four hundred seating Wexford Theatre would be laughed off the stage. Your contemporary provincial Irish opera audience bases its standards, not on the operatic stage, which it knows nothing about, but on the operatic film, with Dorothy Kirsten and Gladys Swarthout as its models. No Elvira – even though she possessed the finest voice England ever produced – if she weighs sixteen stones will appear credible in peasant boys' costume when she is within six yards

---

46 Walsh to Ó hAnnracháin, 13 July 1951, ibid. O'Herlihy had designed three shows at Dublin's Gate Theatre and was shortly to design *Tolka Row* by Maura Laverty, and went on to become the director of the US television series *Hawaii 5-0*. Walsh was probably unwise, however, to describe O'Herlihy as 'Ireland's leading theatre designer', a description best applied to Micheál MacLiammóir, who was to design Verdi's *Aroldo* for Wexford in 1959. 47 Ibid.

of the audience. Suitability to the small Wexford Theatre means, in my opinion, good, well produced, young fresh voices and a good appearance and these are the type of singers we are searching for'.[48]

Walsh was clearly aware of his potential audience and, perhaps more importantly, of what the small stage and the peculiar acoustics of the tiny Theatre Royal would bear; and he demonstrated his already prodigious knowledge of the world of international opera which it was essential for any artistic director of an opera season, however modest, to possess:

> You are I am sure aware that English singers have been known to arrive in Dublin on the morning of their performance, and with a very imperfect knowledge of their role when this was not previously in their repertoire. You are also I am sure aware that artists will break their contracts at almost the last moment. A crisis not insurmountable when the opera is 'Faust' or 'La Traviata' but a very serious matter when the opera is 'The Rose of Castile' [*sic*].

And he was under no illusions about what they were setting out to achieve:

> The difficulties of this production, which you must have visualised from the beginning, as we did in Wexford, are in fact twofold. From a first class artist's point of view Wexford, to use an Americanism, is 'out in the sticks', and singing an unknown Balfe opera there is consequently hardly worth the trouble ... All this I think should assure you that we are fully cognisant of the enterprise we have undertaken and that we have no intention of mounting any production that will not alone bring credit to Radio Éireann and to Wexford, but honour to Ireland.

Eventually, Maureen Springer was cast as Elvira, with Murray Dickie as Manuel and James Cuthbert as Don Pedro.[49] Not only was there difficulty in attracting 'suitable' singers, but also RÉ had some problems in augmenting the RÉLO to the necessary strength of thirty players, since most of the freelance players approached were unwilling to make the trip to Wexford.

In addition to the four nights of opera and a concert by the RÉLO, the full festival ran for a fortnight, and featured a piano recital by Josef Weingarten, a

---

48 Ibid. Dorothy Kirsten (1910–92) was an American soprano who sang mostly at the Metropolitan, New York, as Violetta (*La traviata*) and Marguerite (*Faust*) and in the title roles of *Manon Lescaut* and *Louise* (which she had studied with the composer, Charpentier); Gladys Swarthout (1900–69) was an American contralto, also at the Met, where she made her début in 1929; retired 1954.
49 Others who had been approached unsuccessfully to sing the role of Don Pedro were Martin Dempsey and Dermot Troy.

violin recital by Jaroslav Vaneček (accompanist, Kitty O'Callaghan), a performance by the Dublin Marionette Group, three exhibitions, one including pictures
from the National Gallery of Ireland (the first time that any had been lent outside Dublin) which was opened by the Earl of Longford, and several lectures.

Given the circumstances of its late start, hesitancy in engagement and ambi-
tiousness for a first-try programme, the inaugural Wexford festival was a most
impressive début, which clearly gave Radio Éireann a considerable confidence
in its new-found partner, which was to persist until the withdrawal of the NSO
in 2000.

Today, the familiarity of the international opera world with Wexford perhaps masks the fact that in 1951–2 this was a remarkably ambitious project for
such a small town. Even in 1956, when Charles Acton began to cover the festival for the *Irish Times*, he could write that it was 'an unusual venture in a small
market town and port, equivalent perhaps to Barnstaple ... The kernel of the
festival is its two opera performances in the curious little early-nineteenth-cen-
tury Theatre Royal. This has a stage barely twenty feet square and holds only
385 people. These limitations, and the fact that the whole festival ... is entirely
a matter of unremitting voluntary effort, give the festival a quite extraordinary
intimate atmosphere of friendliness which envelops the visitor.'[50]

In its second year, 1952, the Wexford festival became even more ambitious,
asking for, and securing, an orchestral concert by the RÉSO in addition to the
services of the RÉLO in the pit. Relations with RÉ appear to have been
extremely smooth: although there were more 'teething' difficulties in the second year than there were in the first, Ó hAnnracháin's relations with Walsh
were notably better than those with Bill O'Kelly in Dublin, and as a result
responses to difficult requests were that much easier.

Wexford originally planned to produce *The Barber of Seville* in 1952 but,
discovering that the DOS was to do so, transferred its attention to Donizetti's
L'elisir d'amore. Given that Wexford has built its reputation on the discovery
and production of lesser known items from the repertoire, this may seem a
strange choice, but at that time *L'elisir d'amore* was not the favourite feature of
the operatic diet which, along with works such as *La traviata* and *Madama
Butterfly*, it is today. Wexford achieved its first coup, as far as engaging outstanding international singers was concerned, by securing tenor Nicola Monti
'who earlier this month created such a furore in Rossini's "Le Comte Ory" at
the Florence Festival'[51] and it followed this by engaging as producer Peter

50 C. Acton, *Musical Times* (December 1956). 51 Walsh to Ó hAnnracháin, 20 May 1952, P&T
file 640/53/2: 'The Wexford Festival of Music 29.10.1952–2.11.1952. Participation of RÉLO'.
Monti, who sang Nemorino, had made his début in 1951 at the Teatro San Carlo, Naples, in
Bellini's *La sonnambula*, closely followed by Nemorino at La Scala. He returned to Wexford
throughout the 1950s.

Ebert (son of Glyndebourne artistic director Carl Ebert) who would direct many productions in the 1950s and 60s.

The RÉSO made its first appearance with a concert conducted by Milan Horvat, which included T.C. Kelly's 'Three Pieces for Strings' and a return to Wexford by Josef Weingarten as soloist in the Grieg concerto. The RÉLO also gave a 'popular' concert of Offenbach, Gilbert and Sullivan, Tchaikovsky, Strauss and Rodgers and Hammerstein, with soprano Patricia O'Keeffe (who would make many appearances at Wexford) singing (among other items) arrangements by Walter Beckett of Moore's 'Oh breathe not his name', by Ó Gallchobhair of 'Danny Boy' and by Potter of 'The Ninepenny Fiddil'. Once again, the festival also featured exhibitions (including a special feature on Stanford in his centenary year), lectures, historical tours and opera films, and 'Festival Forum', a panel discussion which became a lively feature of succeeding years, with (in 1952) the Festival President, Sir Compton Mackenzie, Erskine Childers (Minister for P&T), Seán MacBride, TD and Eoin ('Pope') O'Mahony.

After the 1952 festival, Charles Kelly wrote to Tom Walsh 'I hardly need to say that all of us in Radio Éireann were very happy to collaborate in the Festival and to know that it was such a success. We should like to feel that it was as great a success financially as it was artistically, but I suppose one could hardly expect that; the arts have to be subsidised everywhere and Wexford will owe a big debt to those who shouldered the heavy responsibility of putting the Festival on its feet, where it now definitely is.'[52]

Perhaps the only major dispute between RÉ and the Wexford committee occurred in 1953 (Donizetti's *Don Pasquale*), when Fachtna Ó hAnnracháin discovered that, in the previous years, the public had been admitted to the dress rehearsal, on foot of Wexford's policy of charging a small attendance fee, 'which enables the poorer people of the town to hear first class opera'.[53] Ó hAnnracháin insisted that 'we never allow members of the public into our rehearsals ... and we would certainly never think of asking people to pay for admission to a rehearsal. For a presentation like an opera it is nearly always necessary to stop during the course of a rehearsal and re-do certain sections which are not quite satisfactory. The Conductor or Producer often finds it necessary to say things to performers which cannot be said in the presence of members of the public without causing embarrassment.'[54] To which Walsh retorted: 'My point about the poorer people of the town hearing first class opera is ... insurmountable, in fact, so important is it that if the dress rehearsal is not open to them at these nominal prices so great would be the ill-feeling in the town

---

52 Kelly to Walsh, 12 November 1952, file 640/53/2.   53 Walsh to Ó hAnnracháin, 28 April 1953, P&T file 640/53/3: 'Wexford Festival of Music 1953. Participation of RÉLO & RÉSO'.   54 Ó hAnnracháin to Walsh, 1 May 1953, ibid.

that it would mean the end of the Wexford Festival. As one who saved pennies to hear opera in Wexford I would think it a most despicable business that people in the town who could never have the opportunity of hearing a great tenor such as Monti should be precluded from doing so.'[55] A compromise was reached whereby an extra 'dress rehearsal' was staged once the rehearsals necessary for achieving a performing standard had taken place, and this may well be the first instance in Ireland of today's practice of 'low-price previews' in theatres.

Nineteen-fifty-three was also the year when Dermot O'Hara stepped down as conductor of the opera performances (apparently as a result of objectionable behaviour the previous year)[56] and Bryan Balkwill began a long association both with opera in Ireland and as an orchestral conductor.[57] The RÉLO continued as the resident orchestra up to 1959, when the theatre was closed for a year for reconstruction. Carina Daly suggests that the decision not to re-engage the RÉLO was prompted by Sir Alfred Beit, who regarded the orchestra as 'of exceptionally low quality', and would have preferred a selection from the RÉSO or an English chamber orchestra such as the Boyd Neel.[58] After one season (1961) with the RLPO, at a cost of £2,500, the RÉSO took up this task at a cost of £1,700, remaining in place until 2000, after which it became impossible for RTÉ and Wexford to agree on the level of expense that the festival should bear, resulting in the withdrawal of the (now) NSO and its replacement by the National Philharmonic Orchestra of Belarus, a development which has provoked criticism of the festival – for employing foreign rather than Irish players (similar to that experienced by P&T in the 1940s and 50s) and has fuelled the argument that an opera orchestra should be established to service Opera Theatre Company and Wexford, if not also Opera Ireland.[59] The replacement of the NSO did nothing to solve a problem in the mind of the then artistic director of Wexford, Luigi Ferrari, who was of the opinion that the NSO 'was essentially a symphony orchestra, not an operatic one, and as such was used to performing *on* stage rather than *under* it'.[60]

A proposal, similar to the new arrangement with the DGOS, that the Concert Orchestra should also take on Wexford, foundered on financial grounds. A recent report on opera, commissioned by the Arts Council, pointed out that the Council had benefited from the Irish opera companies' relationship with RTÉ 'in that the real costs of providing orchestral accompaniment … have borne for them',[61] meaning that in other circumstances the

55 Walsh to Ó hAnnracháin, 4 May 1953, ibid. **56** Cf. C. Daly, *Tom Walsh's opera* (2004), pp. 29, 31. **57** He conducted nine concerts with the RÉSO between 1958 and 1961. **58** C. Daly, op. cit., pp. 62–3. **59** Cf. M. Dervan, 'Wexford Opera's Minor Miracle', *Irish Times*, 7 November 2001. The Wexford Festival paid 50% of the costs of the RTÉSO up to 1981, following which RTÉ sought, and obtained, a higher proportion of the ever-increasing costs: C. Daly, op. cit. p. 127. **60** C. Daly, op. cit, p. 157. **61** Pamela Smith, *Towards a policy and action plan for opera* (2002), p. 45.

Council would have been obliged to increase its financial aid to Wexford and the DGOS (the cost of such provision having been calculated at €400k for the RTÉCO at the DGOS and €1m. for the NSO at Wexford).

Nineteen-sixty-five saw the début of Albert Rosen, conducting Massenet's *Don Quichotte* (produced by the veteran Carl Ebert) – Rosen had been conducting it in Prague – which opened the door to his appointment as Principal Conductor of the RTÉSO three years later, and to many further engagements at both Wexford and with the DGOS. As in Dublin, his arrival introduced a new level of both expectation and achievement, and his work invariably won praise which often eluded other visitors. Wexford became a much more contentious opera house than Dublin, chiefly because of the choice of operas. The current reputation of Wexford for producing relatively unknown operas is based on its original *schema* in staging Balfe's *Rose of Castille* – to introduce work that was unfamiliar and at the same time worthy of revival. With debate and dissension among audience and critics as to the relative merits of the artistic directors' choices, the possibility of equal disagreement as to a producer's and conductor's abilities increases.

Some operas chosen by Wexford have been minor works by well-known composers, or by composers whose names are hardly known; others have been 'alternative' operas to other, better-known works on the same theme (for example Paisiello's *Il barbiere di Siviglia* or Leoncavallo's *La bohème*), others have been simply neglected masterpieces which might never have left the repertoire had circumstances been different. This certainly proved to be the case with Rosen's direction of Janáček's *Kátya Kabanová*, Prokofiev's *The Gambler* and Britten's *The Turn of the Screw*. In the latter, local boy James Maguire was cast as Miles (he subsequently wrote music criticism for some years) and recalled that Rosen 'was an old-fashioned maestro in his words and gestures, yet after a performance he could be friendly in his own way and even helpful. I do remember he once said earnestly to me "Boy, don't ever go into opera; open a restaurant and make some money" … On another occasion … I found him sitting at the piano. He called me over and asked me to pick out any three notes … then he played the notes and began to do a sparkling jazz improvisation which was magical to listen to'.[62] Colin Staveley, working with Rosen as leader of the orchestra, found that the conductor was frustrated by the space available for the orchestra, which inevitably reduced the volume it could create: 'Albert would demand more sound at all times and would even change dynamics to achieve this result. He was one of those conductors who demanded sustained intensity, and this could be tiring on the players.'[63]

62 G. Smith, *Dr Tom's festival legacy*, pp. 168–9. 63 Ibid., p. 194.

As has already been remarked, critical notice of the orchestra's work in opera is infrequent, but both the national and international press referred to the RTÉSO's work in some detail – the intimacy of the theatre, as opposed to the large space of the Victorian Gaiety, may have drawn more attention to its work. Alan Smale, as leader, remarked that consistently good notices were 'a morale booster', but he also went on to say that 'some producers and designers were using Wexford to further their own careers and … this was noticeable in their attitudes to the orchestra. It is of course important that a good working balance is achieved in these things, and the right working climate provided, otherwise the orchestra, for instance, can feel ignored … Albert Rosen always strove to have proper recognition given to the orchestra in Wexford – and proper respect. He saw it as "his" orchestra.'[64] Another conductor whom Smale admired was Robin Stapleton, whom he saw as 'a big personality who tended to bring musicians along with him, thus ensuring a closely integrated performance',[65] and it was almost inevitable that Alexander Anissimov, when he joined the NSO as Principal Conductor, should pull off a triumphant *Demon* by Anton Rubinstein (1994).

Rosen also had a temper which, although not quick, could become fiery and cutting. Several witnesses of his outburst to Sergei Leiferkus (connected to the latter's poor pronunciation of German) during the 1986 rehearsals for Humperdinck's *Königskinder* were shocked by the force and manner of his remarks but, given Rosen's pre-eminence in the opera house and his passion for his work, it is easy to appreciate that he strove for perfection that sometimes was unattainable. I myself recall a rehearsal by the chorus of the DGOS when Rosen, frustrated by their lack of volume, stopped conducting and, staring like a ship's lookout into the far horizons of the stage, shouted 'Who iz zere? Vair zey are?' 'Here, maestro' said a brave chorus member. 'I don't see anyvun, vy don't I hear anyvun?' 'We *are* singing, maestro'. 'No, zere iz novun zere; if zere's somevun zere, vy zey don't sing?'

CHORAL MUSIC

One of the least visible of RTÉ's contributions to Irish musical life has been in the area of choral music. At the end of 1942, P.J. Little announced the establishment of a 24-member part-time 'radio chorus', intended to improve the resources for studio opera productions 'as well as for part-singing and general choir work'.[66] This led to the formation of Cór Radio Éireann, which remained in existence for nine years, giving a monthly concert, usually in association

64 Ibid., p. 195. 65 Ibid., p. 228. 66 DD, 88, 26 November 1942, col. 2575.

with the orchestra. Among the choir's members were Mary MacGoris (later music critic of the *Irish Independent*), and future agricultural consultant and EU official Tomás Roseingrave. Crucial to the recruitment of the choir was Sir Hugh Roberton (1874–1952), composer, and founder and conductor for forty-five years of the Glasgow Orpheus Choir, who conducted Cór Radio Éireann's inaugural concert on 25 June 1943, with the Taoiseach, Éamon de Valera, in attendance. An example of its work is the concert given on 20 January 1948, with the RÉ Orchestra, conducted by Edmond Appia, in a contemporary chorale by Templeton Strong, followed by 'Dixit Dominus Domino Meo' by Michel Richard de Lalande (1652–1726).[67] Fachtna Ó hAnnracháin, who was conductor of the Cór (until he handed over to Hans Waldemar Rosen), wrote in 1952 (when it was near the end of its life) that its formation had been 'welcomed by all who had the future of choral music in this country at heart';[68] as the forerunner of the R(T)É Singers, it provided a benchmark for the professionalisation of singing as a career rather than a social pastime, which continued to be a feature of RTÉ's musical life until 1995.

In 1952 an eighty-strong voluntary Choral Society was formed, which made more feasible the performance of large-scale choral works, such as the Bruckner Mass which it gave in 1955 (and his 'Te Deum' in 1964) and a Mozart Mass the following year. Its first concert, conducted by Hans Waldemar Rosen, included Schumann's 'Paradise and the Péri' (based on Thomas Moore), with soloists Clothilde Johnson and Dermot Troy. It was to combine forces with the R(T)É Singers on many occasions and gave the premières of Brian Boydell's 'Mors et Vita', Gerard Victory's 'The Rivers of Heaven' and many other works. The Choral Society continued in existence until 1976, although Fachtna Ó hAnnracháin recalled that, from its inception, it had been thought to run counter to the interests of established choirs such as Our Lady's Choral Society, which had enjoyed extensive broadcasts on RÉ, and it therefore concentrated on works which those choirs were unlikely to undertake, such as Orff's 'Carmina Burana'.[69]

At the same time, it was decided to replace the Cór with a full-time professional chamber choir of ten voices, the Radio Éireann Singers, which was largely the brainchild of Erskine Childers. The existence of the R(T)É Singers, from 1953 until their disbanding in 1984, gave for the first time in Ireland a public profile to a professional chamber choir. Gerard Victory wrote that 'If anything, the Singers ... were perhaps even more influential [than the RÉSO]

67 The Cór was joined on this occasion by soloists Rita Lynch (soprano), Violet Burne (mezzo-soprano), Eva Tomsohn (contralto), Donald Murray (tenor – later a member of the RÉ Singers), Frank Keyte (baritone) and Peter Morgan (bass). 68 F. Ó hAnnracháin, 'Choral singing in Ireland', in A. Fleischmann, *Music in Ireland*, p. 237. 69 F. Ó hAnnracháin, interview with the author, 11 September 2002.

in changing the course of Irish musical thought and, in particular, that of composition.'[70] It was unique among R(T)É's performing groups in that it could, with no musical difficulty, give performances of vocal music from the Irish tradition and folk-song from many other countries, as well as 'art-music' in highly crafted compositions, both sacred and secular.

Much of the credit for this must be attributed to the Choral Director of the Singers from their inception until his retirement in 1974: Hans Waldemar Rosen (1904–1994) was born in Leipzig and studied there at the State Music Academy and at the Universities of Leipzig and Innsbruck. In Leipzig he had studied composition with Karg-Elert and voice production with Reinecke. His early career was as an opera and choral conductor and music critic, in which capacity he had written over 2000 articles in the *Leipziger Neueste Nachrichten*, the *Deutsche Allgemeine Zeitung* and the *Berliner Tageblatt*. He had also worked as programme editor of the Gewandhaus concerts 1935–9, and had been decorated by the Finnish and Italian governments for musicological work.

Conscripted in 1939, he became a war correspondent and, when he was captured by the British, he was sent to Wales as a prisoner of war, allegedly being one of the very first to be released; he came to Ireland as chorus master of the DGOS (1948–51) for whom, in 1950, he was invaluable in mediating between the Dublin organisation and the visiting company from Hamburg.[71] In his early years in Dublin, despite his eminence as a conductor and trainer of voices (his close personal contact in former years with Richard Strauss was one of his chief claims to international significance) he was forced, due to a lack of sufficient income, to live for some time in the Salvation Army hostel in Dublin's York Street.

Rosen set up as a vocal teacher, producing such pupils who became household names as soprano Cáit Lanigan (for many years the director of the Goethe Choir) and her husband Richard Cooper (tenor), Frank Patterson (tenor), Tomás Ó Súilleabháin (baritone), Charles Mitchel (the inaugural newsreader on RTÉ Television), and the American tenor Herbert Moulton.

However, in 1948 he was appointed director of Cór Radio Éireann, and in 1953 of the RTÉ Singers, with whom he gained national and international renown. He had founded a male Octet in 1949 which was eventually recognised as the 'Radio Éireann Men's Octet'. Seventeen applications were received by RÉ for the position of Choral Conductor, Joseph Groocock coming second to Rosen. It was Rosen's remarkable achievement to blend a group of ten highly individual voices (four sopranos, two contraltos, two tenors, a baritone and a bass), many of whom played an extra role as soloists in opera and oratorio and therefore had their own idiosyncratic vocal identity, into a unique choral character; even more

70 G. Victory, 'Ó Riada on radio', p. 54.   71 Cf. Smith, *Love and music* p. 69.

so, that his extraordinarily creative programming, based on an extensive knowledge of, and empathy with, most areas of the repertoire, made this choir an integral part of R(T)É's music schedules, with both themed and eclectic programmes
that never betrayed his own personal predilection for the baroque era, and in
fact led him enthusiastically towards contemporary music, making the Singers
such an important part of the seminar on the subject held each year in UCC in
connection with the Cork International Choral Festival.[72]

As has already been shown in the case of the RTÉLO/CO, the work of such
a close-knit group of musicians is difficult to demonstrate or discuss except in
terms of its repertoire, and therefore the following illustrations of the Singers'
output in their first decade must serve as an indication of the enormous breadth
of that repertoire, as well as Rosen's adroitness in building programmes that
would intrigue the newcomer to this kind of singing, as much as it would satisfy the aficionado.

In 1955, in opposition, Erskine Childers touched – whether deliberately or
accidentally is unclear – on a serious musical issue, when he commented that
'this choir is very pleasant in many ways, and their renderings of folk music of
different countries are really delightful to hear, but I do not know yet whether
the choir of Radio Éireann understands yet how to present Irish songs in a way
which, so to speak, relates to the traditional manner of singing and at the same
time is tuneful to the modern ear'.[73] He urged his successor as minister at P&T,
Michael Keyes, to speed up the business of arranging Irish folk material for the
Singers, a matter to which he had given considerable attention when in office.

An inspection of the RÉ Singers' programmes from 1955 to 1960 reveals
them at the peak of their achievement, while at the same time it gives a graphic
indication of the extent to which arrangers such as Seóirse Bodley, Redmond
Friel, T.C. Kelly, Daniel McNulty, Éamonn Ó Gallchobhair, A.J. Potter, and
John Reidy/Seán Ó Riada were busily involved, in mining the wealth of folk
song in order to translate it into 'art-music', in addition to extant arrangements
by Herbert Hughes and Hardebeck.

One of the first services which the Singers performed in order to demon-
strate the geographical diversity of such song was the series 'Round the
Counties', broadcast from mid-1955 to mid-1956, which, in addition to the
Singers themselves, featured singers such as Mary O'Hara (soprano: soon to
make an international career singing to her own harp accompaniment), Nellie
Walsh (soprano: sister of Wexford chairman T.J. Walsh), Joseph MacNally,
Charles Kennedy and Richard Cooper (tenors), Tomás Ó Suilleabháin and

---

72 Although the Festival, founded in 1954, was a competitive event, the R(T)É Singers for many
years gave what might be described as 'demonstration' recitals in addition to their participation
at the contemporary music seminar. 73 DD, 152, 6 July 1955, col. 277.

Austin Gaffney (baritones), Martin Dempsey (bass), with traditional instrumentalists such as fiddler Denis Murphy, uilleann pipers Leo Rowsome, Micheál Ó Riabhaigh and Tomás Riabhach, harpists Síle Larchet, Máirín ní Sheaghda, Blaithín Desmond and Mercedes Bolger, and Albert Healy (accordion), with prose readings by poet and playwright Donagh MacDonagh.[74]

'Round the Counties' enabled the Singers to do justice, for example, to Derry, with 'The Maiden City', 'The Gates of Derry', 'The Pride of Londonderry', 'The Banks of Claudy', 'The Derry Hornpipe', 'Kitty of Coleraine', 'Song for the Anniversary of the Shutting of the Gates of Derry' and (predictably) the 'Derry Air' in their programme. County Down featured 'John McAnanty's Courtship', 'The Flower of Magherally', 'The Defence of Crossgar', 'Grá Geal Mo Chroí' and 'The South Down Militia'. Cavan was represented by 'Sweet Cootehill Town', 'Lough Sheelin Side', 'Flower of Finea' among others, while Enniskillen had 'The Enniskillen Dragoon', 'The Buachaill Rua', 'Lough Erne Shore' and 'Buachaill o'n Eirne'. Tyrone was celebrated with 'The Sash my Father Wore', 'The Hat me Father Wore' and 'Flower of Sweet Strabane'. Meath found Tomás Riabhach rendering 'O'Carolan's Farewell' and for Carlow he played 'Eileen Aroon'. Celebrity of a rare order was introduced when, in one of three programmes devoted to Dublin, Brendan Behan rendered a solo of 'The Zoological Gardens', 'The Old Triangle' and 'Whack Fol the Diddle'.

A regular slot in the schedule enabled the Singers to call their next series 'Music at Eleven' (from mid-1956 to mid-1957), which featured a wide range of classical songs from Germany, Britain, Czechoslovakia, Austria and France which were arranged thematically, and also introduced programmes devoted to the works of Stanford and Reger and another to Jewish culture. These broadcasts were intelligently structured in the realisation that an entire programme of *a cappella* singing or even accompanied choir would not sustain listeners' interest, and therefore was interspersed with solo items from performers like Charles Lynch (piano: one of Schumann's 'Waldscenen' and Brahms' first ballade), David Lillis (violin: Vaughan Williams' 'Lark Ascending'), Egon Jauch (cello: Bruch's 'Kol Nidrei'), Jaroslav Vaneček (violin: Dvořák's 'Romantic Pieces') or Michele Incenzo (clarinet: the *adagio* from Mozart's concerto and the 'Introduction, theme and variations' by Weber).

Parallel with this series (also mid-1956 to mid-1957) was 'On Wings of Song', an eclectic concoction of favourites in which a single programme might include (as did the first, on 13 August 1956) L.J. White's 'There is Sweet Music

---

74 Donagh MacDonagh (1912–68), in addition to his literary interests, was a barrister and became a District Justice in 1941, parallel to a career as a popular broadcaster on RÉ, which allowed him to express his interest in folk ballads.

Here', Bizet's 'Serenade' (from *The Fair Maid of Perth*), Schubert's 'Hark! the Lark', 'The Maid of Bunclody' arranged by Bodley, Robinson's 'The Snowy Breasted Pearl' (a tenor solo for Dermot Troy), with instrumental solos by William Shanahan (violin: Kreisler's 'Caprice Viennois' and Debussy's 'Girl with Golden Hair') and Tommy Dando (organ: Elgar's 'Salut d'amour'); Dando (well known as a Dublin theatre organist) featured as the resident soloist throughout the series, as did accompanist Rhoda Coghill. The series signature tune was Potter's arrangement of Mendelssohn's 'On Wings of Song'.

Later programmes continued this exploitation of the popular vein, with items such as Esposito's version of 'The Lark in the Clear Air' (for tenor solo: Richard Cooper), Jerome Kern's 'Make Believe', Schumann's 'Träumerei' for cello solo (Erich Eisenbrand), Cole Porter's 'In the Still of the Night', Ketelby's 'Sanctuary of the Heart', Noel Coward's 'Dearest Love' (soprano solo, Louise Studley), or Henry Hall's 'It's Time to Say Goodnight'.

If these programmes were unashamedly popular, they were also successful in showing off Ireland's only professional choir in a wide variety of work, with some of the country's leading instrumentalists (almost all drawn from the ranks of RÉ's two orchestras), both as accompanists and soloists, which gave them an opportunity to broadcast in a genre which might otherwise be denied to them.

By contrast, 'Soirées musicales', broadcast from July to November 1957, was structured to feature music that would have been performed in one of Europe's major cities during a chosen year. Thus 'Vienna 1810' included works by Haydn, Mozart, Beethoven, Weber, Martini and the now forgotten Johann Rudolf Zumsteeg (1760–1802). 'London 1870' also re-introduced rarely heard works by Ciro Pinsuti (1829–88), Stephen Heller (1813–88) and Sydney Smith (1839–89) among others. 'Berlin 1940' was perhaps a brave choice on Hans Waldemar Rosen's part, with two works by the Nazi-banned Hindemith, and others by Helmut Bräutigam (1914–42, killed in action), Hugo Distler (1908–42, died of exhaustion) and Wolfgang Fortner (1907–87) who was one of the instigators of the Darmstadt 'school' in 1946. 'Zurich 1874' was an all-Brahms affair, marking the composer's holiday that year at Ruschlikon, while 'Weimar 1861' celebrated Wagner's visit to Liszt after the scandal of *Tannhäuser* in Paris, which included his meeting with Cornelius, composer of *The Barber of Baghdad*. 'Leipzig 1730' was almost completely given to the work of J.S.Bach. The exception to the city-based format of 'Soirées musicales' was 'Hengrave Hall 1620', which visited (in musical spirit at least) the English country house of the Kytson family which was home from 1595 to 1628 (at the height of the Jacobean Renaissance) to madrigalist John Wilbye (1574–1638), with music (including harpsichord solos by Sydney Bryans) by Wilbye himself, Thomas Morley (1557–1602), Giles Farnaby (1563–1640), John Bull (1562–1628) and Thomas Weelkes (1576–1623) whose name Dr Rosen invariably pronounced as 'Vale-kesh'.

'A Musical Bouquet', which ran weekly from mid-1957 to mid-1958, was, like 'On Wings of Song', an extended medley with Potter's arrangement of Stanford's 'There's a Bower of Roses' as its signature tune. Again, guest soloists were drawn from the orchestras (Max Thöner, Margaret Hayes and Geraldine O'Grady, violins; Maurice Meulien, Brighid Mooney and Otto Pacholke, cellos; Helmut Seeber, oboe; Hans Kohlmann and André Prieur, flutes; Gilbert Berg, bassoon; Mercedes Bolger, harp) pianists Anthony Hughes, Patricia Herbert and Veronica McSwiney, and from the now familiar cadre of freelance singers in the country such as Troy, Gaffney and Ó Suilleabháin. Joseph Dalton, distinguishing himself as an operatic bass, was in evidence, as was James Cuthbert (bass), Veronica Dunne and Mary Tinney (soprano, who subsequently became Irish ambassador to Sweden, Belgium and Kenya). The range of vocal items was less popular in this series, and one could find, cheek-by-jowl, Constant Lambert's 'Lines from Four Poems by Li-Po', Friel's arrangement of Moore's 'When Love is Kind', Moeran's 'An Irish Love-Song', Peter Warlock's 'Captain Stratton's Fancy', Gaetano Braga's 'La serenata' (well-known at the time), 'Cill Cais' by Mairéad Pigóid of RÉ's music department, Vincent O'Brien's 'The Fairy Tree' and one of Larchet's best-loved, 'Pádraic the fiddler', together with works by d'Indy, Mozart, Ravel, Brahms, Gounod and Schubert.

An occasional series which succeeded 'A Musical Bouquet' was, under the general title of 'Concert of Irish Music', a collaboration between the Singers and, on some occasions, the RÉLO, conducted by Dermot O'Hara and in most programmes 'An Triréad Gaelach' (The Gaelic Trio: Mollie Flynn, flute; Elias Maguire, violin; Kitty O'Callaghan, piano), with guests Leo Rowsome, accordionist Dermot O'Brien, harpist Deirdre O'Callaghan, and Austin Gaffney. Once again, the majority of pieces were short, and arranged by Bodley, Edgar Deale, Friel, Hughes, Kelly, Larchet, May, McNulty, Ó Gallchobhair, Ó hAnnracháin, Potter, Reidy/O'Riada, and Walter Beckett. Naturally, these were exclusively Irish programmes, demonstrating not only the volume of material available but also the different applications to which it might be put, with the variable timbres of orchestra, choir-plus-orchestra, instrumental trio, solo voice with orchestra, and *a cappella* choir.

Another thematic series which ran parallel to these concerts (mid-1958 to January 1959) was 'Music in Profile' which, like 'Soirées musicales', took specific musical circumstances as a frame for each programme. Thus 'Theater an der Wien' (with Vaneček as soloist) featured music by Haydn and Mozart; 'In an American University' (soloist, Charles Lynch) presented Samuel Barber, Aaron Copland and George Gershwin. 'In a Portuguese Village Club' (soloist, Julian Dawson, piano) had works by Ivo Cruz (who had conducted the RÉ orchestra five years previously), Claudio Carneiro (1895–1963) and José Vianna da Motta (1868–1948); across the border, 'In a Spanish Cathedral' (soloist

George Minne, organ) presented works by Vittoria, Francisco Correa de Arauxo, Tomás de Santa María and Miguel Lopez from the sixteenth and seventeenth centuries. 'The Palazzo Gesualdo in Venosa' (soloist David Lee, organ and harpsichord) featured Gesualdo himself, Merulo, Frescobaldi and Trabaci in music from the Italian sixteenth century; while 'A Little Square in Naples' (with Richard Cooper, Gary Moore [mandoline] and Jack Gregory, a guitarist who appeared frequently with the RÉLO) contained Rossini, and (again, predictably) Luigi Denza's 'Funiculì funiculà'. Other programmes in the series visited Carinthia (Kremser, Benatzky, Koschat and Jurek); the Leipzig Gewandhaus (Brahms); St Paul's Cathedral, London (Bull, Tomkins, Gibbons, Byrd and Peerson);[75] Versailles (Costeley, Couperin, le Jeune and Lully); El teatro de la Zarzuela (Morera, Granados, Arrieta, Albeniz, Morena Torroba, Caballero and Barbaieri); the Hofburg, Vienna (Bartók, Suk and Kodály: with the programme note 'Austrian aristocrats at a chamber music recital in the Castle of the Emperor in Vienna during World War I deplore the growing independence and cultural influence of Czechs and Hungarians, foreshadowing the downfall of the Austrian Empire'). Perhaps the most curious programme in the series was '"Erin": the strange fate of an opera' which offered excerpts from a one-act opera, *Erin*, by Leopold Hassenkamp, on the theme of the last hours of Robert Emmet, which was staged on 28 September 1918 at the Theater des Westens in Berlin, but which was suspended due to the flight from Germany of the Kaiser and Crown Prince at the end of the world war.[76]

'Music All Inviting' was the name of the Singers' next 'catch-all' series, running 1958–9, featuring the 'Concert Trio' consisting of Audrey Park (violin), Maurice Meulien or Aileen Cheatle (cello)[77] and Kitty O'Callaghan (piano), and introducing new younger talent such as the nineteen-year-old Bernadette Greevy (contralto) and soprano Maria Viani, daughter of the RIAM professor of singing, Adelio Viani. Schubert's 'Tender Music' provided the signature tune, again arranged by Potter. The programme-mix was similar to that in previous series, but succeeded in introducing Irish items such as 'The Shepherdess' by 'Dermot McMorrough', and 'Hush Song' by Geoffrey Molyneux-Palmer, together with Bax's 'I heard a piper playing', rarely heard work by English composers such as John Ireland's 'Spring Sorrow', Elizabeth Lehmann's 'Myself When Young', 'Five Eyes' by Cecil Armstrong Gibbs, the

75 A later programme was devoted to the 'Ayres' (1620) by Martin Peerson (1571?–1651). **76** Cáit Lanigan sang the role of Sarah Curran, Richard Cooper was Emmet, Austin Gaffney sang the prologue (from Thomas Moore) and the cast also included Gerald Duffy: *Radio and TV Review* 3 April 1959; I am indebted to Ita Beausang for drawing my attention to the information regarding Hassenkamp (b. 1881), a student of Humperdinck and Philipp Scherweka, who was Kappelmeister at the Berlin operetta theatre and, in addition to *Erin*, also wrote *Der Militärfalter* and *Das Tanzverbot*. **77** Aileen Cheatle was the wife of Jack Cheatle (leader of the RÉLO) and was, at various times, a member of the cello sections of the RÉLO and RÉSO.

'Shepherd's Cradle Song' by Sir Arthur Somervell, Landon Ronald's 'Down in the Forest', and Sir Edward German's 'Who'll Buy my Lavender?'; these would be sung alongside numbers by Reynaldo Hahn, Jerome Kern, Franz Lehár and Cole Porter, older Irish material from Balfe and Moore (and Irish-based material such as Benedict's *Lily of Killarney*), and the more recent arrangements from the almost resident stable of Ó Gallchobhair et al. (Ó Gallchobhair's 'Crúibíní Muice', which first appeared in this year, was to become a standard feature of the Singers' more light-hearted programmes in later years.) Rarely were works repeated, such was the extent of the material available, and to which new work was continually being introduced, such as that of the British-based Hungarian Matyas Seiber (1905–60), who was to become a pillar of the Singers' later repertoire.[78]

'Pro Musica' (1959) was a structured series, featuring in one programme 'modern madrigals' by Hugo Distler, Debussy, Hans Bergese and Sir William Harris (1883–1973); in others, 'part-songs and poems about summer birds'; 'drinking songs from various lands'; songs to lyrics by Shakespeare (including 'O mistress mine' set by Molyneux-Palmer); 'evening songs by German Romantics' (including, of course, Brahms' 'Abendlied'); 'on the sea' with Weber, Milhaud, Delius and Moore; 'open air songs' including Edgar Deale's 'Tom's Angel'; 'songs about wells and fountains' including Tippett's 'The Source' and 'O fons bandusiae, splendidior vitro' by the American Randall Thompson (1899–1984);[79] and, finally, a programme of 'farewell songs' opening with Molyneux-Palmer's 'On Song'.[80]

In late 1959 the Singers' main series was 'Sentimental Journey', many programmes in which featured young emergent talent from Viani's class at the RIAM such as Georgina O'Carroll, Marie Gilbert and Claire Kelleher (sopranos), Máire Frewen (mezzo), Edwin Fitzgibbon (tenor – later to have a career as a diplomat), Michael O'Connell (baritone) and Hubert O'Connor (bass baritone). The series was followed by 'Dreams of Other Days' (1960) which allowed Moore to shine frequently, not least in the series' signature tune (arranged by Potter) 'How dear to me the hour'. The series, always evocative of atmospheric musical ambience, was well served by 'Rusalka's Song to the Moon' (Dvořák), 'When I grow too old to dream' from Sigmund Romberg's film *The Night Is Young*, Smetana's 'In the Twilight', 'Wien, du Stadt meiner Träume' from

---

78 On 16 October 1959 the Singers gave a complete programme of new music by Seiber: 'Sirmio' (words by Catullus), 'Zwei madrigale' (Christian Morgenstern) and 'Three Nonsense Songs' (Edward Lear). **79** A complete programme was devoted to Thompson's settings of Horace's Odes on 1 September 1959: 'O Venus, regina Cnidi Paphique'; 'Montium custos nemorumque, virgo' and 'O fons bandusiae'. **80** The Irish composer Geoffrey Molyneux-Palmer (1882–1957) is largely neglected today; six of his part-songs, 'Roses', 'The Robin', 'O mistress mine', 'Hush song', 'On Music' and 'The fields in May' were the subject of a single programme by the RÉ Singers in November 1959.

Wienerlieder op.1 by the Austrian Rudolf Sieczyński (1879–1952), and 'All in the April Evening' by Sir Hugh Roberton.

In addition to these regular series, the RÉ Singers would undertake special concerts for seasonal occasions such as Christmas (with Rosen's German background evident in 'Heilige Nacht' for Christmas 1957) or Purcell's 'Ode for St Cecilia's Day 1692', when the Singers were joined by the RÉ Choral Society and RÉSO.[81] Other concerts displaying Rosen's affinity with, and profound knowledge of, the German repertoire were the 'Neue Deutsche Lieder' (1577) of Leonhard Lechner; Schumann's 'Spanisches Liederspiel'; vocal quartets by Brahms; settings of Heine by Mendelssohn, Robert Franz and Liszt; 'The Wondrous Horn of Plenty' from the 'Deutsches Volkslied-Spiel' by Hermann Zilcher (1881–1948); an all-Hindemith programme;[82] contemporary German madrigals by Bergese and Bräutigam; and the première of 'Drei Madrigale' by Hermann Reutter (1900–85), together with the first public performance of Bodley's 'An Bhliain Lán' which the Singers had given its première broadcast the previous year.[83] With the RÉSO the Singers undertook a major choral work in 1959 with Handel's 'L'Allegro, il Penseroso ed il Moderato' to mark the bicentenary of his death.[84] Another collaboration with the RÉSO (and the RÉ Choral Society) was Mozart's music for 'Thamos, König in Ägypten' by T.P. Gebler (1773), a precursor of Mozart's *The Magic Flute*, for which an early Mozart *sinfonia* (no. 26 in B flat, K.184) was employed as an overture.

Besides his natural orientation towards German music, Rosen also introduced a wide range of European music, all of it in the genre of 'art-music', but from many sources: folk songs from Brittany, part-songs by Vaughan Williams, Poulenc and Milhaud, two programmes of music from the Scottish highlands (one of them marking St Andrew's Day 1959), 'Carillons for choir' featuring 'bell songs' (including Sir Robert Stewart's 'The Bells of St Michael's Tower'), negro spirituals and sea shanties, 'choruses from forgotten plays' by Bizet (*L'arlesienne*) and Schubert (*Rosamunde*), while, in contrasting moods, the Singers gave an all-Moore concert in March 1960 (in the same vein as 'Dreams of Other Days'), conducted by Sydney Bryans, entitled 'Nostalgic Exile', and John Reidy/Seán Ó Riada arranged a programme 'Where the fuschias grow' celebrating the music of Kerry and West Cork.

The most instructive aspects of all this programming are, firstly, the versatility of the Singers in the scope and mastery of their work – a distinguishing feature right up to the date of their last engagements; and, secondly, the remark-

81 The broadcast was 10 November 1959, although St Cecilia's day is 22 November. **82** 'Wahre Liebe'; 'Frauenklage'; 'Vom Hausregiment'; 'Landsknechtstrinklied'; 'Art Lässt nicht von Art'; 'O Herr, gib jedem seinen eignen Tod'. **83** Reutter was the Director of the Musikhochschule in Stuttgart where Bodley was studying at the time. **84** The soloists were Patricia O'Keeffe, Richard Cooper and Gerald Duffy, with Julian Dawson (organ and harpsichord).

ably entertaining way in which Hans Waldemar Rosen (known affectionately to and by the Singers – for no ascertainable reason – as 'Jack') built up short programmes both singly and in series that were effectively educational.

The Singers were also noteworthy for having undertaken foreign tours – the first performing group from RÉ to do so. In their tenth anniversary year (1963) they visited broadcasting stations in Hamburg, Munich, Frankfurt, Cologne, Brussels and Hilversum. Their programme was remarkable in that it was all-Irish, with arrangements by John Reidy, Hardebeck, Ó Gallchobhair, Ó hAnnracháin, Friel, T.C. Kelly and Bodley. The tour was supported by a grant of £400 from the Department of External Affairs, and, after broadcasting fees were deducted from costs, it incurred a net loss of £336.[85] In describing this tour, Tibor Paul was at pains to impress his superiors, by stressing that it was *'the first ever undertaken by a body of performers from the Radio Éireann staff'* and that it included performances of eighty-one different pieces which the six stations would broadcast in forty programmes: 'the propaganda value of this for Ireland and Radio Éireann is beyond measure … It was quite obvious that, after their performances, the Singers were acknowledged at the Continental Stations as a vocal ensemble of international standing'.[86]

In 1965, they sang at the 18th International Heinrich Schütz Festival in Berlin, singing works by Schütz, Bodley, Killmayer, Poulenc and Kokkonen in the Kirche aum Heilsbronnen, and, on the same tour, performing for radio in most of the same broadcasting stations, substituting Stuttgart for Brussels. In 1969 they were at the Schwetzingen Festival, where they gave Victory's 'Kriegslieder' and three madrigals by Boydell; also taking in broadcasts in Munich, Basel, Cologne, Berlin, Herford, Hilversum and at the BBC; the cost of their excursion had risen to £1,500.[87] In 1972 they visited Paris, Nürnberg, Tutzing (as part of the cultural programme of the Munich Olympics) and the BBC. Music critics in these centres commented consistently on Rosen's ability to blend the individual voices into an integrated sound that several compared to a finely tuned musical instrument.

The Singers' final overseas tour was to Britain in 1977, when, under Proinnsías Ó Duinn, Rosen's successor as Conductor/Vocal Adviser, they appeared at Oxford, Cambridge, Bangor and the Purcell Room on London's South Bank, with a programme including Eric Sweeney's 'Gloria', Victory's 'The Poor Old Flea' and arrangements of Irish folk-song by Edgar Deale, Bodley, Stanford, Ó Gallchobhair, T.C. Kelly, and Redmond Friel; instru-

85 The Singers' personnel in 1963 were: Mabel McGrath, Patricia Hanley, Mary Sheridan, Bene MacAteer and Eithne Troy (sopranos); Ruth Maher and Angela Carroll (contraltos); Richard Cooper and Donald (Danny) Murray (tenors); Peter McBrien (baritone) and Gerald Duffy (bass). **86** T. Paul, 'Music Department Report for the Year 1962–63'. **87** By 1969 Minnie Clancy and Cáit Lanigan had replaced Mary Sheridan and Eithne Troy among the sopranos.

mentalists taking part were Una O'Donovan and Nuala Herbert (harps), Philip Martin (piano) and Martin Metrustry, the RTÉSO's percussionist.[88] A single concert in London's Wigmore Hall followed under Ó Duinn's successor, Eric Sweeney, as part of the 'Sense of Ireland' festival in 1980, which included John Buckley's 'Pulvis et Umbra' (with Veronica McSwiney, piano), Potter's 'Belloc Songs' and Boydell's three madrigals.

As a result of their German tours, the Singers were one of the first of RTÉ's performing groups to make an international commercial recording: in 1965 the German label Harmonia Mundi recorded works by Bodley, Deale, Friel, Hardebeck, Kelly, Larchet, Ó Gallchobhair, Ó Riada, Stanford and Victory, billing the songs as 'Irische Volkslieder' by the 'Kammerchor von Radio Eireann'.[89]

Most of the Singers' appearances before an audience were studio concerts in the Phoenix Hall and later the SFX, with a mindset in RÉ that still regarded audiences as ancillary to the recorded performance. In 1965, at a poorly-publicised and -attended concert, which Charles Acton regarded as their first 'serious' Dublin concert, he noted that 'they sing as an extremely polished group, showing their long experience of professional full-time work. Their sense of pitch is excellent. Their blend and balance are extremely good. Their diction and participation in what they are singing are enviable'.[90] Given Acton's consistency in promoting worthwhile musical endeavours, and his assiduous noticing of programme content, it is astonishing that he was not aware of previous 'serious' work in Dublin by the Singers, such as a performance of Lully's 'Te Deum' in 1960 or a concert of rarely heard psalms (Schütz, Goldberg, Handel) in 1962. Now, he praised the Singers' excellent sense of pitch, their blend and balance, diction and 'participation in what they are singing'.[91]

But with the decision by James White, Director of the National Gallery, to make the gallery a venue for performance, the Singers' work took on a new dimension, with their first concert there in February 1973, as Dr Rosen's career with them was nearing its close. It was in this environment that the architecture of the Singers' programmes became evident to non-radio audiences to a marked degree, with a regular season of monthly concerts. This continued after Proinnsías Ó Duinn had succeeded Rosen, with dresses for the ladies commissioned from couturier Ib Jorgensen adding a definitive public identity,

---

88 The Singers on this tour included Minnie Clancy, Mabel McGrath, Patricia Hanley and Mary Sheridan (standing in for Bene MacAteer), sopranos; Ruth Maher and June Croker, contraltos; Patrick Ring and Paul Deegan, tenors; Peter McBrien, baritone; and Gerald Duffy, bass. **89** HMS 30691. The RÉSO had previously made two records for Decca for distribution in the USA (see below, p. 566). **90** *Irish Times*, 13 November 1965; he was overlooking what he had called 'an extraordinarily interesting concert of unusual choral music' which they had given (Schütz, Gottlieb Goldberg and Handel) in 1962: *Irish Times*, 26 October 1962. **91** *Irish Times*, 13 November 1965.

which also saw them visiting many parts of the country, including offshore concerts on Cape Clear and Inishmore.

In addition to their regular public appearances, the Singers also gained national and international attention by their participation in the seminar on contemporary choral music which had been part of the Cork International Choral Festival since 1962. The Seminar features commissioned works whose composers nominate a choir to perform the work(s), followed by a discussion, or analysis, of the music. The Singers' appearances in Cork included seminar performances of Herman Reutter's 'Tres Laudes' (1964); Potter's 'Ten Epigrams' (1969, when they also sang Boris Blacher's 'Anacaona'); and Boydell's 'Mouth Music' (1974) which Charles Acton reported the composer as describing as 'avowedly quasi-instrumental music written for human voices as instruments'.[92] Recalling the occasion of the Reutter performance in 1964 Charles Acton had written: 'They virtually stopped the show by their accomplishment and their breathtakingly moving interpretation of their music.'[93] After the disbanding of the Singers, the role of artists-in-residence would be fulfilled by their successors, the RTÉ Chamber Choir.

The Singers in fact excelled in contemporary music and were an important feature of the Dublin Twentieth-Century Festival, but they also gave many separate concerts with well-designed programmes of unusual repertoire, such as the three concerts of modern church music that they gave in St Bartholomew's Church, in Dublin's Clyde Road in June 1976, with works by Michel Ciry, George Manos, Knut Nystedt, Panufnik, Krzysztof Penderecki, Ernst Pepping, Poulenc, Reutter and Victory. A major row – not at all typical of the Singers' normally pacific work schedule – arose in 1982 when they refused to sing Anthony Burgess's 'Blooms of Dublin'.

On occasions, however, lapses were to be noted. While Acton praised Ó Duinn for having restored their 'dynamic nuances', he complained that their diction had disimproved.[94] But Acton's general verdict was laudatory of 'the vigour to which we are for so long accustomed from this group and for a lot of really delicate phrasing'.[95] In 1982 he found himself agreeing with the Singers, who had vigorously objected to the content of 'Blooms of Dublin', commissioned by RTÉ for the Joyce centenary, writing that the musical 'which has probably received more publicity [than Seán Ó Mordha's documentary, 'Is There One Who Understands Me?'] because of the utterly unJoycelike crudity of words which the RTÉ Singers have been compelled to sing, in spite of their being very repugnant (very properly) to the Singers and very many listeners'.[96]

92 *Irish Times*, 1 May 1974. **93** *Irish Times*, 6 April 1966. **94** *Irish Times*, 2 June 1976. **95** *Irish Times*, 24 September 1980. **96** *Irish Times*, 29 January 1982.

The activities of most of these ten singers in extra-curricular engagements such as opera and oratorio meant that choral societies, as well as the DGOS (and to a much lesser extent Wexford), could find solo performers whose daily work enabled them to maintain a standard of performance previously unavailable on a regular basis. This, too, was part of the invisible spine that helped, subliminally, to hold together Ireland's musical tree during the 1960s and 70s. Peter McBrien, for example, made his DGOS début as El Dancairo in *Carmen* in 1967, with his colleague Patrick Ring as fellow-smuggler El Remendado (Ring had already appeared as Roderigo in *Otello* in 1964, in a season which also featured the young Luciano Pavarotti as Rodolfo in *La bohème* and Alfredo in *La traviata*). Both Ring and McBrien went on to give many performances at the DGOS, as did Mary Sheridan and Ruth Maher, the latter singing, in one season, Flora in *La traviata*, Giovanna in *Rigoletto* and the roles of Madelon and the Contessa in *Andrea Chénier*. Maher made the important point regarding the availability of Irish singers for the smaller roles: criticising those who were dismissive of these roles, she said, 'They believe that anybody can sing them which of course is not true; musically they can be extremely difficult,'[97] as she herself went on to prove in Wexford in Luigi Ricci's *La serva e l'ussero* opposite the legendary Sesto Bruscantini in 1977, working with him again two years later as La comare in Ricci's *Crispino e la comare*. McBrien, however, had to wait until 1984 for *his* first part on the Wexford stage, when he sang as the Painter in Massenet's *Le jongleur de Notre-Dame*.[98] Sheridan made her DGOS début in 1962 as the Shepherd Boy in *Tannhäuser* and went on to sing in *Aida* (1962), *Carmen*, *Die Fledermaus* and *Le nozze di Figaro* (1963), *La traviata*, *Andrea Chénier* and *Nabucco* (1964).

When Rosen reached the age of seventy, it was thought impossible to continue his employment, even though his work was as vigorous and as satisfying as ever. At this stage he wrote to Gerard Victory: 'The RTÉ Singers, as you know, are a very precious instrument, and, as all precious things, also very vulnerable, how much, I am afraid, nobody knows but myself after 20 years of working with them. I am most anxious that we find the best possible way to ensure that this work will be continued successfully by a young Irish musician for a long time to come'.[99]

In Victory's mind, Proinnsías Ó Duinn was best qualified to succeed Rosen, and Ó Duinn was appointed in 1973–4, remaining with the Singers until his appointment to the RTÉCO in 1978. Then, the Singers were joined for a year by Eric Sweeney, after which the appointment of Colin Mawby ushered in a

97 Quoted in G. Smith, *Love and music, p. 234*. **98** He had been unavailable when invited to sing in 1963 in Balfe's *The Siege of Rochelle* and in the touring production of Massenet's *Grisélidis* in 1982; he did, however sing in James's Wilson's *Twelfth Night* in 1969 but this was not staged in the Theatre Royal. **99** Rosen to Victory, 6 September 1973.

completely new approach to, and course in, choral activity in Ireland. Mawby had been Master of Music at Westminster Cathedral from 1961 until 1978 (when he left as a result of a disagreement on policy), and also held a part-time professorship at Trinity College, London and had worked with the BBC Singers where he was associated with Pierre Boulez. He had worked with the London Mozart Players, the Nash Ensemble and the Wren Orchestra, and as an organist had recorded on the Oiseau Lyre and Enigma labels. A prolific composer of mainly sacred music, he had a reputation in London at the end of the 1970s as an extremely energetic and successful musician.[1] The fact that he was available to RTÉ impressed Gerard Victory considerably, and it was clear from the outset that major changes were about to take place in RTÉ's choral department.[2]

The quality of the Singers' performances had been less satisfactory in recent years, (with Acton complaining in the *Irish Times* of their 'staid, inflexible way of singing which has somewhat antagonised audiences except for very special occasions')[3] and it is likely that Victory pursued the recruitment of Mawby as a catalytic agent in bringing about their retirement. Certainly he had discussed this with Mawby in advance of the latter's taking up his post, making Mawby aware that a wholesale standing-down of the Singers would not be welcomed at that stage. 'I understand that there is no objection to gradually renewing the membership through re-auditioning' he wrote to Victory. 'This would obviously have to be done slowly and with considerable discretion.'[4] Victory replied:

> There has been since inception an acceptance by both Union and Management that re-auditioning of the Singers would have to take place at some interval, given the nature of the work, the high standard required and the limited span of any singing voice. There have, however, been different views on how this should take place. For some years there was a regular annual mass audition. It was agreed that this imposed, perhaps, a needless strain and worry on all members and for some years it was accepted that the Director would, primarily, initiate individual audition after warning the Singer concerned if he felt that standards had fallen ... It would be one of the tasks, certainly, for the new Director to

1 Mawby's career as a composer continued to burgeon during his period at RTÉ, and by 2003 he had written twenty-four masses, several of them commissioned by Westminster Cathedral, Liverpool Cathedral, and the Royal School of Church Music as well as several shorter pieces of sacred music and a fanfare for the opening of DCU's concert hall. His setting of Psalm 23 was included on Charlotte Church's CD 'Voice of an Angel'. 2 Victory remarked to the author that Mawby had conducted at London venues such as the Albert Hall, which he considered a hallmark of success; Mawby subsequently told the author that he had hired the hall for self-promotion. Later, as Mawby's plans for choral activity became more far-reaching, Victory also said 'We'll soon cut him down to size' – which appears to contradict his earlier impression and the reason for Mawby's appointment. 3 *Irish Times* 7 October 1981. 4 Mawby to Victory, 9 October 1980.

consider standards and his recommendations would be followed by an official Board to audition and make final decisions.[5]

This question of re-auditoning had a bearing on contracts: from the beginning of 1964, contracts had been for a five-year period; from the beginning of 1969 their duration was three years, at which point the deputy DG allayed fears expressed by IFMAP that this was leading to a phasing out of the Singers, by stating 'this preference for a shorter contract ... should not be interpreted as an indication of a decision, intention or leaning towards the possibility of disbanding the group at the end of 1971 or later'.[6]

Ironically, the Singers' success in the contemporary field was a major cause of the increasing dissatisfaction with their work in the early 1970s. As Gerard Victory saw it:

> Over the past 20 years indeed, and particularly since 1969, the Singers have tended to specialise more and more in contemporary music. This was partly because of a rise in their ability to perform such music, partly to an increasing interest in such music, but more particularly because of the fact that a much more satisfactory repertoire for a very small chamber choir exists in the modern field. Much of the romantic and classical repertoire is wholly suitable only for a larger ensemble: when we attempt this music now it is often with the Choral Society or a specially augmented choir ... This has produced very good results in that we have a choir with a wide repertoire of suitable music, but this has also imposed greater strain in reading and interpretation. In 1970 28% of their music was modern, and in 1973 44%.[7]

At the time of Mawby's arrival, two of the Singers had signalled their desire to retire, and, although Mawby had in his mind the complete cessation of the Singers as a group, he settled down to work with them, so much so that at the end of his probationary period Victory was able to report: 'I have found Mr Mawby's quality ... has been of the very highest level. The standard of the Singers (who were indeed beset hitherto by many handicaps resulting from a higher average age than would be ideal and lack of stability in direction for some years) has risen most decidedly since his arrival. The concerts Mr Mawby has given in the National Concert Hall in recent months were extremely impressive.'[8] Certainly Charles Acton agreed, opining that Mawby had brought 'a flexibility and a light and shade in their work that was a most welcome surprise'.[9] However, Mawby

---

5 Victory to Mawby, 14 October 1980. 6 John Irvine to Ó Faracháin, 7 June 1969. 7 Victory to Staff Relations, 23 January 1974. 8 Victory, Probabtion Report on Colin Mawby, 7 April 1982. 9 *Irish Times*, 7 October 1981.

was determined that a new chamber choir of seventeen, with younger voices, should replace the existing ten-voice choir and he persisted with this proposal with Victory's, and then John Kinsella's, support. After protracted negotiations between union and management, and of course the Singers themselves, for whom this was an exceedingly traumatic process, agreement was reached in 1984. Several of the Singers took early retirement while others accepted re-deployment within the organisation – for example, Bene MacAteer became assistant librarian to the RTÉSO, Patrick Ring became librarian for the new RTÉ Chamber Choir and Gerald Duffy became assistant to Mawby in relation to the RTÉ Chorus.

In 1984, the RTÉ Authority enunciated its 'New Choral Policy', 'based on wide community involvement'. It announced the establishment of a seventeen-strong 'specialised choir' of 'potential professional singers who will be engaged on fixed-term part-time contracts', of 'a large amateur choir entitled the RTÉ Philharmonic Choir', of a children's choir (Cór na nÓg) and envisaged a development of the Chorus, as well as a new initiative in educational broadcasting.

The Authority acknowledged the work of the Singers over the past twenty-five years, a 'dedicated group' which had had 'a vital influence on the formation of contemporary Irish choral music' but stated firmly that, 'as a result of radically changing circumstances within the choral profession, their work is now complete'. One of the circumstances put forward in support of this statement was that 'thirty years ago singers were, of necessity, prepared to commit themselves to one choir; to-day's singers do not think in these terms.' In addition, 'certain facts have to be faced about the present RTÉ Singers. The shortest serving member has been with the group for nineteen years, the longest for thirty-one. The average age of the group is fifty-one and it has to be stressed that at this age most singers have either retired or are thinking seriously of retiring … The effects of ageing can already be detected in the RTÉ Singers' work both individually and as a group. This can only get worse'.[10] The further point was made that it was musically almost impossible for a younger voice, replacing an older singer, to blend in with the rest of the choir. The choir of ten voices was too small (as Victory had outlined above) and enlargement was impossible financially, whereas the student bursaries payable to the new Chamber Choir would not exceed the present salary costs of the Singers. The policy document concluded: 'The RTÉ Authority has a responsibility not only to ten Singers, but also to the hundreds of thousands who form the listening and viewing public. The Authority is convinced that a new and dynamic policy is essential for the well-being of choral broadcasting.'

Yet again, irony puts in an appearance at this juncture. In 1976, Charles Acton noted the proliferation of choirs and choral societies in Ireland, and

10 'RTÉ's new Choral Policy', 6 pp. typescript.

there can be no doubt that the example of the RTÉ Choral Society was an impetus in this direction, as was RTÉ's willingness to collaborate with promising, as well as established, choirs in presenting choral works. At this point, somewhat unfairly, Acton said that RTÉ was celebrating its golden jubilee 'by disbanding their own Choral Society'.[11] As a full-blooded journalistic strategy this was clever, but, although RTÉ probably mis-handled the affair, it was not in any way a true reflection of the situation. One of the reasons given by Gerard Victory in justifying the disbanding was that it was taking work away from other choirs, which Acton dismissed as a weak reason. But Victory argued forcefully that these choirs were in fact able and willing to undertake 'modern and less usual works in conjunction with RTÉ'.[12] The Choral Society was succeeded by the RTÉ Chorus which, like the original Cór Radio Éireann, was composed of professionals paid per engagement.

With the RTÉ Chamber Choir, which gave its inaugural concert in March 1986, Mawby made huge strides: the fact that seventeen young singers could secure subsistence (in the form of student bursaries) as a launching pad for their professional careers was a quantum leap in Irish choral conditions. If it had not been for the financial cutbacks imposed on RTÉ by the government in 1990, it is possible that the furore that occurred three years later might have been averted. There were, however, certain built-in administrative problems with the Chamber Choir which lent a structural imbalance to the situation. In my Introduction I mentioned physical disposition of an organisation's buildings: in the case of the Singers and their successor the Chamber Choir, the Portobello Studios were always unsatisfactory, both in their facilities and in their distance from headquarters in Donnybrook. It was perhaps inevitable that a sense of isolation should develop, a sense that they were a self-enclosed unit that had been largely ignored by the higher echelons of the music department.

A Chorus of twenty-four semi-professional singers had made its début under Eric Sweeney in early 1980 but, after the arrival of Mawby, its progress was reviewed and it was re-constituted in 1986, giving its inaugural concert in its new format under Geoffrey Spratt with the RTÉCO at the Royal Hospital, Kilmainham, in January 1987. Kilmainham would be the venue for a focussed series of orchestral chamber and choral concerts in the first six months of 1988, which found the RTÉCO and Chorus working with the renowned British choral conductor Harry Christophers, and, under Proinnsías Ó Duinn, performing Mozart's 'Thamos, King of Egypt' which we saw as a feature of a concert by the RÉ Singers and Choral Society thirty years previously. The season also saw the début of Cór na nÓg RTÉ, conducted by Mawby, with the première of Gerard Victory's 'The Land of Lilliput'.

---

11 *Irish Times*, 18 October 1976. 12 *Irish Times*, 23 October 1976.

In 1990 the Minister for Communications, Ray Burke, introduced a Broadcasting Act which imposed a 'cap' or limit on the amount that RTÉ was permitted to earn by means of on-air commercial advertising. The financial consequences were very severe, since by that time revenue from advertising had far outstripped that from licence fees – the traditional source of income for public service broadcasters. RTÉ had been increasingly conscious of the precarious nature of its income base, since the need to earn a greater and greater proportion of its total income from advertising was seen as incompatible with, and potentially damaging to, its function as a public service. Nevertheless, without a real increase in the licence fee (which the Minister had not granted since 1986),[13] it was in fact necessary to seek as much income as possible from other sources, and therefore this legislation, seen by many as a deliberate wounding of the organisation by Fianna Fáil, and by Ray Burke in particular, was especially, and ironically, disturbing. The 'cap' remained in place until it was rescinded by Michael D. Higgins, the incoming minister with responsibility for broadcasting in the coalition government in 1994.

The consequence for the Music Department was that it was required to identify its share of the budgetary 'cuts' to be made across the organisation. It is likely that within the organisation itself, and within the music community in Ireland, none of the possible options would have been either popular or acceptable, and it is equally clear that there was very little sympathy for the critical condition of RTÉ's finances, within which some extremely difficult and painful decisions had to be made. Chapter 7 describes the position in which the Music Department found itself. Put very briefly, the view was taken that the least damaging option was the disbanding of the Chamber Choir and the standing down of the String Quartet (although after negotiations, and representations from powerful interests in Cork, the Quartet reached an agreement by which it continued to receive 40% of its contracted salaries).

The decision to disband (or to put a more favourable slant on it, to discontinue) the Chamber Choir had two effects: it caused a furore in the world of choral music which painted RTÉ in an extremely unfavourable light, and it led to a rapidly worsening relationship between Mawby and the rest of the RTÉ music department and between RTÉ and the members of the Chamber Choir, who immediately took steps to re-establish themselves as the National Chamber Choir, with Karina Lundström as their administrator. Mawby's dismay at hearing the news, not from any official in RTÉ but on a radio news broadcast, can be easily understood: to him, it meant that no one in the music department cared enough, or had sufficient tact, to inform the Choral Director, or the members of the choir, that the group was being stood down.

---

13 The licence fee remained at £62 from 1986 until 1996, when it was increased to £70, to allow RTÉ to finance the production of one-hour-per-day programming for Teilifís na Gaeilge.

It is no wonder that, during this crisis and afterwards in 1993, when the financial position permitted the re-instatement of the Chamber Choir, Mawby acted as if he had lost all sympathy with the music department in the same way that he perceived that the department had abandoned *him*. Music Department records indicate that senior management regarded him as a trouble-maker who was disloyal to his employers insofar as he seemed unwilling or unable to carry out the managerial parts of his job. In the author's opinion, Mawby's wilful pursuit of what he regarded as the legitimate artistic goals of the choir entirely superseded the performance of any managerial function; this may have been compounded by the fact that there may well have been a a lack of clarity, at the time of his appointment, as to the extent of that function.

Mawby was first and foremost a passionate musician and, secondly, a reluctant administrator/manager. His sympathies would always lie with the artists in his charge and the musical goals which they were trying to achieve. Within RTÉ it would be clear that, provided there is no conflict between a performing group and the organisation, an administrative and an artistic post might be merged, and throughout the tenures of Hans Waldemar Rosen, Proinnsías Ó Duinn and Eric Sweeney there was hardly any occasion for such conflict. But in the case of the Chamber Choir it was equally clear that a close artistic collaboration such as that between the choir and its conductor would be untenable, if that conductor was also obliged to issue administrative directives. A situation analogous to that of Michael Bowles or Tibor Paul would arise, in which a systemic fault, which had gone undetected and unchallenged, was suddenly revealed. The situation was not helped by the fact that, after the Choir was re-instated in 1993, *two* choirs existed which were identical in all but name: the National Chamber Choir and the RTÉ Chamber Choir, each with Mawby as its director, and each, allegedly, having a separate and discrete existence.

The exchanges between Mawby and his superiors, Cathal MacCabe as Head of Music and Simon Taylor as General Manager of the performing groups, became so acrimonious and personalised that it would be unfair to any party to quote from them to any great extent. It is, however, important to reveal that, personalities apart, RTÉ, as a monolithic structure, regarded Mawby as an unacceptable 'fifth columnist' to the extent that, at the time of the cuts, as MacCabe wrote to Taylor, 'Colin was a particular embarrassment to the organisation in his public utterances and general behaviour ... It must be made perfectly clear to Colin Mawby that his function is to fit in with your general masterplan for the Performing Groups area, providing choral music as is required for FM3 Music.'[14] The point would be reached when Taylor would inform Mawby that his contract would only be renewed if he gave an undertaking that

14 MacCabe to Taylor, 13 December 1993.

'you can co-operate effectively in all the areas of activity that are appropriate to the part of Choral Director'.[15] On the other hand, Mawby could complain to the Director-General in June 1995 that Taylor had not visited Portobello once in the previous year, and that when he did speak to the members of the choir 'he was uninformed, contradictory and unable to answer the choir's questions ... His replies were largely incomprehensible and choir members are now totally confused about their position.'[16]

Similar difficulties arose in connection with the running of the RTÉ Philharmonic Choir, a voluntary body which succeeded the RTÉ Choral Society and came into existence during a hiatus in the life of the RTÉ Chorus. With approximately 80–100 singers, it made its début under Mawby, with the RTÉCO, in June 1985, with a programme including the Bruckner 'Te Deum' of which Charles Acton wrote: 'what was really exciting ... throughout the evening was the vigorous, joyous excitement of these young and enthusiastic voices'.[17]

In January 1993, RTÉ reached agreement with the Naxos record company for a recording of Verdi's *Aida* which would involve the Philharmonic Choir in addition to several other groups. Mawby was not informed of this decision until July, when he expressed his reservations and asked, unsuccessfully, that they be conveyed to Naxos. He felt that 'the over-riding of my professional opinion and the lack of concern for my reputation' were serious grounds for resignation.[18] His objection to the inclusion of the Philharmonic was based on the fact, as he wrote directly to Naxos, that 'the RTÉ Philharmonic Choir is a fine amateur group; it is not, however, a large professional opera chorus and because of this, the proposed CD will in no way equal the superb professional recordings [of *Aida*] that already exist. I would not, for example, ask the chorus of La Scala to record Stanford's Requiem, or a cathedral choir to record Wagner'.[19]

As a result of the deteriorating situation (which became public and explicit as a result of Mawby's participation in the PIANO forum – below, pp. 569–94), Mawby resigned his position in RTÉ, but retained his conductorship of the *National* Chamber Choir, a situation which led to even greater confusion and an increasing suspicion of the NCC during a period of negotiations in which Cathal MacCabe proved intransigent in his opposition to any linkage with the NCC while it had Mawby at the helm.[20] He was succeeded by Mark Duley as director of the RTÉ Philharmonic and by Blánaid Murphy as director of Cór

---

15 Taylor to Mawby, 25 March 1994. **16** Mawby to Director-General, 28 June 1995. **17** *Irish Times*, 20 June 1985. **18** Mawby to Taylor, 26 January 1994. **19** Mawby to David Denton (Naxos), 26 January 1994. **20** MacCabe to Assistant DG and Director of Radio Programmes, 16 February 1996. These negotiations, which fall outside the scope of this book, involved the possibility of the establishment of the NCC as an opera chorus in addition to its role as a chamber choir; provision of accommodation at Dublin City University; and the financial arrangement whereby RTÉ would purchase recorded programming.

na nÓg. As of 2003, RTÉ maintains its relationship with the National Chamber Choir by means of a payment of €150k per year in respect of recorded programmes, and full access to the library of the former RTÉ Singers.

AN ORCHESTRA FOR CORK?

It is generally known that the presence in Cork of a string quartet associated with RTÉ, dating from 1958/9, is due to a compromise having been reached whereby the members of the quartet, in addition to their function as recording and performing artists in RTÉ's employment, would also be available within the music community of Cork to act as tutors and teachers; and that – according to the 'received wisdom' – this was achieved almost single-handedly by Aloys Fleischmann, Professor of Music at UCC, in part satisfaction of Cork's expressed wish for an orchestra resident in the city. It is not known, however, that while Fleischmann was the chief protagonist in the campaign for an orchestra in Cork, this came about largely as a result of negotiations of an intimate nature centering on the personality and career of Fleischmann himself.

In 1954, RÉ was anticipating the opening of its new studios in Cork in two years' time, which would be accommodated in a premises recently built by Cork VEC for the School of Music, and was endeavouring – as Maurice Gorham, Director of Broadcasting, wrote to his Minister, Erskine Childers – to 'ensure that Cork and the South generally make a fitting contribution to our programmes in the way of talks, discussions, plays, variety, Irish dance music, outside events, and recorded features, both in English and in Irish'.[21] As part of this, it had already been decided that 'from the point of view of Radio Éireann' the provision of an orchestra 'is neither necessary nor economic'.

> We would have little room in our programmes for a new orchestra that would merely do less well what is being done now by the RÉSO and the RÉLO ... However, pressure from Cork to date has been mainly for a resident orchestra, and Professor Fleischmann's demands for a 24-piece orchestra, to be recruited abroad in the absence of qualified players in Cork, already resulted in semi-acceptance of the idea that Cork should have at least a resident Octet. A station Octet is of little use for broadcasting except by contributing music for features, and there will not be a very constant demand for this in Cork. However, station Octets have a habit of growing into Symphony Orchestras, and a Cork Octet would

21 Maurice Gorham to Childers, 16 January 1954, P&T file 286/54/1: 'Proposals that a new Radio Orchestra should be established at Cork or that Light Orchestra should be transferred to Cork'.

presumably follow the same pattern, although it would be necessary at every stage to recruit players from abroad.[22]

In the absence of other records it is clear, therefore, that a view was forming that a nucleus of eight players – which might conceivably constitute a small chamber orchestra – could be put in place as part of RÉ's commitment to Cork. Equally clearly, however, Gorham (no doubt against his own better judgement) decided that he should also rehearse the larger question:

> A new orchestra playing the classical repertoire, within the limits of its capacity, might well promote orchestral music in Cork and its neighbourhood as Professor Fleischmann desires, but so far as broadcasting is concerned it would be a waste of money and players. If it is considered politically desirable to station Radio Éireann musicians in Cork, we should take the opportunity to create a new kind of orchestra that would be of real value to our programmes and so serve listeners all over the country. The Radio Éireann Light Orchestra is one of our greatest assets; it plays in a wide range of programmes, from opera to music-hall, is most popular with listeners, and has been consistently neglected by comparison with the Symphony Orchestra. If we are to add another orchestral combination, the thing to do is to free the Light Orchestra of its variety commitments; make it a real light orchestra playing popular classics, music from opera, operettas, and musical comedies, which have an assured public; and form a Variety Orchestra of 15 or 16 pieces to do accompanying work. This new orchestra would have to be recruited, but there is more likelihood of finding players for it in Ireland than of finding players for the present orchestras.

At this point, Gorham reached the kernel of the argument, as far as it affected the RÉLO:

> The Variety Orchestra would have to be stationed in Dublin, but the Light Orchestra could equally well be stationed in Cork, and use the new studio there.[23]

By putting down markers about the size of a possible Variety Orchestra, Gorham had rebutted Fleischmann's reported demand for twenty-four players; he had pointed out that no useful broadcasting purpose would be served by stationing

---

22 Gorham was repeating his own, much-quoted, view that 'string quartets have a habit of becoming symphony orchestras'. 23 File 286/54/1.

a new orchestra in Cork; he had insisted that the envisaged Variety Orchestra could only be based in Dublin; and he had therefore raised the prospect of relocating the RÉLO to Cork. This was a bold gamble on his part, since clearly he hoped to contain the expansion of music within RÉ. But the following day Childers, on perhaps the only occasion on which he did so, pre-empted a decision in relation to Cork, by publicly announcing that 'an orchestra stationed in Cork was inevitable [and] a variety orchestra was also possible'.[24]

Three months previously, Childers had given his department officials substantial warning of his thoughts, when he wrote, in respect of the anticipated foreign intake from Germany, that

> The foreign players coming in should be loaned occasionally to the Cork String Orchestra and any others available ... Broadcasting must touch significantly the regional areas and an orchestra of 70 is far more suitable for purposes of giving local help. The Cork people will want to hear their orchestra when it is strengthened.[25]

This public embarrassment meant that RÉ officials were plunged into negotiations with Cork where, on three consecutive days in March 1954, Gorham and Ó Faracháin met with the deputy Lord Mayor (Albert Healy), Bernard Curtis (Head of the School of Music), sculptor Séamus Murphy (with his wife Mairéad, a leading activist in artistic circles in Cork), the chairman and secretary of the VEC (respectively Dean Joseph Scannell and P.F. Parfrey), and four representatives of UCC: Prof. Denis Gwynn (H. St. John), Atkins (Registrar and 'considered likely to be the next President'),[26] G.T. Pyne and Fleishmann himself. 'Our explanation that this would be of no value to the broadcasting service did not cut much ice as the interest of these people seemed to be entirely in concert-going and some of them admitted that they would rather watch a bad performance than listen to a good one'.[27] (One quickly forms the view that the single-mindedness with which the matter of a resident orchestra in Cork was pursued by Corkonians was cognate with that of the DGOS personnel in obtaining the RÉ orchestra for its own purposes – in other words, regardless of the core purpose for which the performing groups of the broadcasting service existed.)

The RÉ officers were informed that

> This demand for an orchestra has been brought to a head by the possibility that Professor Fleischmann will apply for the job in Dublin that Dr Larchet is shortly to vacate.[28] The Registrar [of UCC] was particu-

---

24 *Irish Times*, 17 January 1954. **25** Childers to Gorham and Brennan, 23 October 1953, file 286/54/1. **26** Gorham, departmental memo, 13 March 1954, ibid. **27** Ibid. **28** Larchet was then approaching his 70th birthday, but did not in fact retire from the professorship of music in

larly candid about this, saying that he was concerned only with keeping Professor Fleischmann in Cork, that he hoped to arrange for his academic salary to be raised to the full professorial level, and that he was merely interested in enquiring whether we could help by providing an orchestra that Professor Fleischmann could conduct ... Professor Fleischmann himself asked whether, as a last resort, we would consider stationing the Light Orchestra in Cork. I told him confidentially that we had already considered this but I did not want it talked about until I had the views of the orchestra and of course the conductor himself.

While it is clear that this memo conflated the results of separate meetings, and that therefore Fleischmann was not present at the meeting with Atkins that so greatly concerned his future position, there is nevertheless something bizarre in the spectacle of a university registrar asking the director of a broadcasting station to provide an orchestra so as to secure the retention at that university of its professor of music: such was the local stature of Fleischmann in the mid-1950s.

Three months later Fleischmann himself informed Gorham that Cork Corporation was likely to provide £1000 per annum for the support of public concerts, if a professional orchestra was available to form 'a nucleus' for them. Gorham undertook to enquire whether the new Minister, Michael Keyes, was prepared to receive a deputation from Cork for this purpose.[29] For Keyes, he rehearsed the current scenario, explaining that Fleischmann was the key figure, who would be 'the most likely conductor of the public concerts' if they materialised, but argued that it was not certain that Cork Corporation would in fact provide the rumoured level of support, also stressing that 'if Cork wants public concerts, Cork should itself provide a professional orchestra'.[30]

Cork meanwhile was practising some clever sleight of hand. An undated and unsigned cyclostyled document (in fact written by Fleischmann) entitled 'Scheme for the Provision of a Small Professional Radio Orchestra in Cork, and for a Series of Public Orchestral Concerts' had been distributed, arguing that 'with the opening of the new broadcasting station in Cork in the autumn of 1955, it seems desirable that a small professional orchestra be stationed here, such as is to be found in every regional station in England and on the Continent'. The argument then proceeded: 'a studio orchestra was actually employed in Cork from 1927 to 1930, when the Cork station provided the Sunday night programmes for Radio Éireann. Not only was this orchestra of

UCD until 1958. **29** Michael Keyes, a Labour TD for Limerick East, had been Minister for Local Government 1949–51 and was Minister for P&T in the second inter-party (coalition) government 1954–57. Gorham's note of a conversation with Fleischmann, 11 June 1954, ibid. **30** Gorham to Keyes, 19 June 1954, ibid.

the same size as the Dublin studio orchestra, but every six weeks or so a full orchestra of about forty players was engaged for the broadcast of a symphony concert from Cork at a time when no studio orchestral concerts were broadcast from the Dublin station'. The sleight of hand consisted in the fact that, at the time in question, the Dublin 'orchestra' consisted of a sextet, which could hardly provide the basis in 1954 for parity with the current RÉLO. Furthermore, the sextet in Cork was not a permanent feature of the Cork station's complement, and its augmentation for larger concerts was entirely a matter of the initiative of Seán Neeson, the station director. It was untrue to state that Cork at that time was filling a gap that Dublin was unable to provide, since, as we have seen, Vincent O'Brien was constantly devising ways of increasing his basic orchestra to provide larger studio (as well as public) concerts.

Cork was determined to emphasise that 'amends are to be made for the long period of neglect' since the closure of the local station in 1930, part of which should include 'a just distribution of the orchestras as between Dublin and Cork'. The argument, which had its obvious extra-broadcasting merits, was that a series of six symphony and six 'popular' concerts 'would transform music in Cork, would give the public the chance of first-hand acquaintance with music which it now can only hear over the radio, and would give our local musicians both incentive and employment'. The orchestra could also provide concerts for opera, for the nascent International Choral Festival, for schools, and 'for factory workers, so that the enjoyment of good music, hitherto quite wrongly regarded as the privilege of the wealthier classes, could be extended to all sections of the community'. No mention was made of the largely amateur Cork Symphony Orchestra which Fleischmann had founded in 1934 and had conducted thereafter, and which was about to hold a celebratory twentieth anniversary concert, although when a deputation from Cork met the Minister for P&T on 10 November it was stated that the orchestra was 'on the point of disbanding' owing to the absence of an influx of professional musicians.[31]

The Cork manifesto which, it emerged, was written by Fleischmann, argued for the provision by RÉ of an orchestra of twenty-five players (the RÉLO) which would be augmented 'by the inclusion of the best local players available' for the symphony concerts. It pointed out that, while 'the municipality could not shoulder such a responsibility' it might support it, just as Belfast Corporation paid £2000 per year for the augmentation of the BBCNI orchestra into the 'Belfast Municipal Orchestra'. It also stated that if 'the scheme' should be adopted, Lady Mayer '(wife of the founder of the scheme for children's concerts in England)' was willing to pay the salary of a lecturer who would give preparatory schools talks. A budget was included, indicating that the anticipated loss on each con-

---

31 Notes of a meeting of Cork delegation with Minister, 11 November, ibid.

cert would amount to £75, and it was added that, if the RÉLO were transferred to Cork, £12k of the £450k paid in licence-fees 'and hitherto almost exclusively spent in Dublin' would 'in future be spent in Cork'.

Fleischmann now wrote again to Gorham, mentioning that 'a number of Cork deputies have been actively engaged in furthering the proposal', which included speaking to the Minister. He reported that Cork Corporation had agreed to a subsidy of £500 per annum, provided this was matched by the Arts Council. More to the point, he asked why, if the RÉSO was available to the opera season in Dublin, and the RÉLO to that in Wexford, the latter could not be sent to Cork for the season of the Cork Grand Opera Society.[32]

Later, Fleischmann would put forward the view that 'the main objections to the Cork proposal are not financial, but psychological – the reluctance to break up the existing programme pattern, to face the many modifications necessary if any appreciable part of the broadcasting machine is to extend to the second city of the State.'[33] But this argument, valid though it might have been – given the institutional resistance to change and the provision of extra facilities – came only after part of the case had been won, a major concession had been made by RÉ, and there was little left for which to fight.

León Ó Broin then entered the picture, advising the Minister to meet a Cork delegation and telling him that he had met Fleischmann and had insisted that it was necessary to look at the context of 'Cork and its hinterland' in terms of programming as a whole 'and not by considering primarily the musical needs of the city, which was a mixed question in the sense that it involved other factors and institutions'. Ó Broin also 'stressed that finance was very much in the picture and that the present time, with a major economy campaign in progress, was not the very best time to consider a proposal for creating a third orchestra'. He stated that a transfer of the RÉLO to Cork was most unlikely since it was always necessary to effect transfers between it and the RÉSO, but that 'Cork should show a greater interest than they had hitherto in the matter of a local contribution'.[34] This latter point was taken up by a leader-writer in the *Evening Mail* who suggested 'It would be better for Cork's morale and better for all in the long run if the orchestra that is considered essential to its cultural future should be formed by the initiative and enterprise of the local people'.[35]

Meanwhile, Gorham had accepted an invitation to speak at the University Art Society in UCC, and had been at pains to stress that the Radio Éireann service was nationwide, subject to competition in English from the BBC, and that it existed to serve both the majority and a series of minorities. It had a

32 Fleischmann to Gorham, 5 August 1954, ibid.   33 'Cork's Case for a Radio Orchestra', *Irish Times*, 24 June 1955.   34 Ó Broin to Keyes, 9 September 1954, file 286/54/1.   35 *Evening Mail*, 24 June 1955.

new-found freedom to be more adventurous in its programming, and, in relation to Cork, it must have special regard to what might become available when the new studios came on stream. 'We want more programmes that could only come from Cork'. The call for a station orchestra did not emanate from a broadcasting motive, and 'concerts from Cork would sound the same as concerts from Dublin or Belfast'. Taking his cue from his earlier meetings in Cork, he repeated: 'Some say they'd rather *see* a bad performance than listen to a good one. But it is not broadcasting's job to provide for one'.[36]

When Keyes met the Cork deputation on 10 November,[37] he told them firstly that there was no question of the RÉLO being relocated in Cork. Developments in Cork had to be seen in the overall context of the new studios and the programming that might or might not follow on from that: the new staff 'should be allowed to feel its way and … the policy of drawing upon the South of Ireland should be promoted in advance of any decision being taken to impose something on Cork in the way of an orchestral combination'.[38] Radio Éireann would look favourably on any request for assistance in connection with an opera production or for more frequent appearances of both orchestras in Cork. But 'Cork, orchestrally speaking, should creep before it walks. Speaking quite theoretically, it would seem reasonable if Cork started with a small local combination of high quality, a group of players of high reputation who, in addition to making a regular contribution to the Radio Éireann programmes, would be available in the city as teachers and who would participate in local orchestral efforts'. The Minister repudiated any suggestion that his predecessor had 'promised', or committed RÉ to the provision of, a third orchestra either in Cork or elsewhere, although Childers would state quite unequivocally in the Dáil that he had done so.[39] Keyes did not, however, close the door on the delegation completely, undertaking to refer the whole matter to Comhairle Radio Éireann and to have the Comhairle meet with Fleischmann and Curtis.

The mention of 'a small … combination of high quality' with a teaching remit must have come as a shock to the Cork contingent, but it is evident that, without any documented discussion, P&T had already come to the conclusion that the compromise to be reached was a *string quartet*: the terms in which the Minister introduced it at this juncture admit of no other possible development, and this is borne out by a note from Gorham to Ó Broin the following week, when he referred to an article in that month's bulletin of the MAI stating 'the

36 Gorham's typescript notes, file 286/54/1. 37 The delegation consisted of all the public representatives (TDs and senators) of Cork City (including a future taoiseach, Jack Lynch) plus Aloys Fleischmann and Bernard Curtis. 38 Speaking notes 'Cork deputation regarding provision of a Light Orchestra for Cork, 10th November 1954' ibid. 39 DD, 152, 6 July 1955, col. 282: 'I must admit that, from the very outset, in so far as I could, I committed Radio Éireann to establish a Cork orchestra.'

need for a permanent string quartet in Ireland – one which is not tied to the Radio Station, but which is free to tour the country'. This, Gorham thought, 'seems to fit in well with your suggestion for a string quartet in Cork which would receive regular but not too frequent broadcasting engagements'.[40]

Whether it was clear or not, that the Minister was 'between the lines' telling the delegation from Cork that they should expect no more than a string quartet, cannot be established. Most likely the politicians did realise what was afoot; Fleischmann, however, was not prepared to yield, and went to extraordinary lengths to strengthen his case, even when it must have seemed that it was hopeless. It is small wonder, therefore, that Cork expressed dismay at what was self-evidently a rejection of its larger demands, and support for Fleischmann continued.

Two weeks went by, and Gorham had a further meeting with Albert Healy (deputy Lord Mayor) who 'is himself an occasional impresario and has brought some celebrity concerts to Cork', and who applauded Gorham's contention that RÉ had no obligation to provide Cork with an orchestra. 'He himself is outside the Fleischmann group and says that Fleischmann is apt to prepare projects very thoroughly in his own mind and then try to impose them on other people without due time for reflection'.[41]

This was adverted to in a departmental minute of January 1955, which had clearly been commissioned in order to establish definitively, for the benefit of Comhairle Radio Éireann, the position regarding the costs involved, as well as an early attempt at cost-benefit analysis. It not only reiterated that 'there is no *broadcasting* need for an additional orchestra' (which was adequately met by the existing orchestras) but that the cost of providing an orchestra of twenty-three players would be £20k and, for twenty-seven players, £25k. An octet would cost £7k and a quartet £3,500. The finances of RÉ prohibited any such development. 'The demand for the provision of a radio orchestra in Cork may not be so widespread as the representative character of the deputation ... would seem to suggest'. Quoting Healy's comment to Gorham, the minute continued 'Fleischmann is, of course, the moving spirit in the demand for a radio orchestra at Cork and while his enthusiastic interest in music generally is admitted it is felt there is a personal touch in this present demand. As a conductor his reputation would be enhanced by having an orchestra to conduct regularly in public performances. Hence the demand is for an orchestra for public performances and the requirements or absence of requirements by broadcasting apparently do not enter into it ... In brief it would seem that this pressure from Cork ... is being inspired largely by Professor Fleischmann for purposes which

40 Gorham to Ó Broin, 22 November 1954, ibid. 41 Gorham's minutes of meeting with Healy, 29 November 1954, in memo to Ó Broin, ibid.

have little if anything to do with broadcasting. Radio Éireann should not be forced into considerable expenditure for something which it does not need and which it cannot afford.'[42] The minute went on to suggest that the RÉLO might be sent to Cork for, say, a three-week residency once a year.

Three members of the Comhairle, Charles Brennan (the chairman), Patrick MacNamee and Patrick Lynch (the former private secretary to the taoiseach and now a lecturer in economics at UCD), met Fleischmann and Curtis, at which a considerable amount of the hyperbole contained in the former's circular was withdrawn, but at which, when the provision of a string quartet was mooted, the need for an orchestra was reiterated. Fleischmann pointed out that there were 'six full-scale regional radio symphony orchestras in Australia ... and three in Norway (a country comparable to ours).'[43] 'Professor Fleischmann said that chamber music which would be provided by a quartet would have only an infinitesimal public ... Teachers of all the instruments required could be got from a small group ... [The Comhairle's decision] would be taken as a "test" case of the State's interest in devolution of activities to areas outside Dublin'.[44] That decision, taken at its meeting of 19 February, and reconsidered on 12 March, ruled out 'either an orchestra or smaller musical combination', and said that no steps should be taken until the new studios were operational and staff had had the opportunity of 'looking-out' for sources of programming. The Comhairle did not dismiss the possibility of assisting a 'small combination' in Cork when circumstances might be more favourable.[45]

Fleischmann continued to mobilise public representatives, prevailing on Anthony Barry (Fine Gael TD for Cork Borough) to write to the Minister in protest at this decision. Keyes, in reply, pointed out that all suitable Irish players had been recruited to the two existing orchestras, with the remaining vacancies being filled by foreigners, so that a new orchestra 'would have to be composed of practically 100% foreign players. That is a development which I think none of us would look upon with ease'.[46] Whether by coincidence or design, Sir Adrian Boult penned a letter to the *Irish Times* urging 'the authorities concerned to hasten on this very healthy form of decentralisation and give musi-

---

42 Minute 'Claim for Radio Orchestra at Cork', 11 January 1955, ibid.   43 Fleischmann to Matt Doherty, 21 February 1955, ibid. Fleischmann subsequently added that in addition to maintaining the radio orchestras in Oslo, Bergen and Stavanger, the radio service also part-paid the salaries of the Oslo, Bergen and Trondheim Philharmonic Orchestras, and that in Denmark a similar arrangement was in place in respect of the orchestras in Aarhus, Aalborg, Odense and Randers: 'Cork's Case for a Radio Orchestra', *Irish Times*, 24 June 1955.   44 Minute: 'Claim for radio orchestra in Cork – deputation to Comhairle' undated, ibid., to which corrections by A. Fleischmann have been appended.   45 Minutes of Comhairle Radio Éireann, 19 February 1955, ibid.   46 Keyes to Barry, 3 June 1955, ibid. Barry, a tea merchant by trade, was the father of Peter Barry (deputy leader of Fine Gael, government minister and Tánaiste) and grandfather of Myra Barry TD.

cians and music lovers of Cork what they obviously so richly deserve'– on which he received a tart response from his former BBC colleague Maurice Gorham, referring to the lack of local commitment; Boult replied suitably chastened, drawing attention to the situation of the 'National Orchestra of Wales' twenty-five years previously.[47] The exchange was apposite, since the following month the London *Times* reported that a key regional orchestra of seventy-two players in Yorkshire, which had been supported by Leeds and other local towns, had been disbanded, with £15,000 being provided by Leeds City Council to bring in outside orchestras in its place.[48]

Boult's letter had referred to a public meeting in Cork, which took place on Monday 6 June in Cork's City Hall, and which received prominent coverage in *The Cork Examiner*, a photograph appearing of a 'platform party' including Senators Jennie Dowdall and R. S. Anthony, the Protestant bishop George Otto Simms, the Lord Mayor of Cork (Alderman Patrick McGrath, TD) and his deputy (Albert Healy), the Chairman of the VEC (Monsignor Scannell), TDs Anthony Barry and Stephen D. Barrett, Eoin Ó Mahony and a representative of the Catholic bishop of Cork. In a defiant speech, Fleischmann claimed 'Radio Diffusion Française was doing more for its Arab population in Algiers and Tunis than Radio Éireann would think of doing for Cork', and that 'Radio Éireann is a misnomer. It should be "Radio Atha Cliath"'.[49] Other speakers supported him to a greater or lesser extent, and a message was read from the Catholic bishop. Dr Lucey, 'stating that the concentration of its orchestras in Dublin by Radio Éireann was socially and culturally indefensible'.[50]

Fleischmann, in his lengthy speech, drew attention to the provision of regional radio orchestras throughout Europe: eight operated by the BBC outside London; seven networks in Germany outside Berlin; three in Italy; two in Austria, outside Vienna; one in each of the principal cantons of Switzerland; and arrangements in Norway, Sweden, Holland, Belgium, Denmark and Portugal, whereby the national radio service had a relationship with regional professional orchestras. Fleischmann's peroration was emotionally calculated to stir his audience:

> We are a cynical city. Our legendary reputation for being a musical city is, I think, largely based on the type of devastating criticism which is so general here, and I think it is true that where activity or productivity is lowest, there the critical faculty is most highly developed, as a sort of inverted inferiority complex. I think it would be important for our morale, for our self-respect, for our confidence in ourselves and in our

47 *Irish Times*, 7 June 1955; Gorham to Boult 7 June 1955 and Boult to Gorham 14 June 1955, file 286/54/1.   **48** *The Times*, 30 July 1955.   **49** *Cork Examiner*, 7 June 1955.   **50** Aloys Fleischmann, 'Cork's Case for a Radio Orchestra', *Irish Times*, 24 June 1955.

city to have here a professional orchestra such as the second city of every other state in Western Europe regards as its privilege, its ornament and its right.[51]

The meeting drew the satiric wrath of 'Myles na Gopaleen' in the *Irish Times*, who asked of Fleischmann 'By what magic wand (or baton) did he manage to assemble on the one stage such a constellation of dignitaries of Church and State ... all uniformly swearing that Cork was finished unless it had a "radio orchestra"? ... I aver that I know two of them personally and reasonably well, and I know that neither has any interest whatsoever in music, therefore no knowledge of it, and that their presence on Dr Fleischmann's platform was another of those acts of public humbug so dear to the Irish heart'.[52]

As a result of the public meeting, a petition was signed by approximately 3000 Cork citizens, in addition to all public representatives and 'church dignitaries', with explicit support from Cork Corporation, Cork Harbour Board, the Governing Body and Academic Council of UCC, Cork Chamber of Commerce, the Cork Branch of ICTU, Cork Workers' Council, Cork Public Library Committee, City of Cork VEC, the music department of UCC and the Municipal School of Music. Among the more notable signatories were former director of 6CK, Seán Neeson and his wife Geraldine (representing the Music Teachers' Association), Séamus Murphy, Joan Denise Moriarty (Cork Ballet Company) and James N. Healy (impresario).[53]

Faced with such a petition, which the Lord Mayor of Cork presented to the Minister on 5 July, action (or compliance) of some kind was inevitable. Speaking on the Estimates on 6 July, Keyes said:

> I have some trepidation about mentioning Cork in connection with broadcasting because I know that before this Estimate is through the House I shall be hearing a renewed demand from the Deputies from Cork, united as one man, for the provision of a Radio Éireann Orchestra in Cork City. I may as well, therefore, anticipate their demands and explain the broadcasting side of the picture ... Radio Éireann has ... a light orchestra which, although not as expensive as the symphony orchestra, is still a relatively costly affair. It has been suggested that this orchestra should be transferred holus-bolus to Cork. I want to show that that is impossible. The light orchestra is one of the props of the broadcasting service. It contributes a great deal of music on its own to the programmes of Radio Éireann and performs in conjunction with

51 A Fleischmann, 'Cork's Plea for a Radio Orchestra', cyclostyled, 14pp., on file 286/54/1.
52 *Irish Times*, 29 June 1955.   53 The petition is contained in P&T file 286/54/1A 'Signed Petitions for a RÉ Orchestra in Cork'.

the Radio Éireann Singers and other vocalists and variety artistes in a multiplicity of shows that can only effectively be organised in Dublin. The light orchestra could not be taken out of Dublin without detriment to the whole structure of the Radio Éireann programmes. Apart from that, it would not be a job to my liking to uproot a whole combination of people who have their houses and families in Dublin and transfer them elsewhere *en bloc* ... I am not opposed to Cork having an orchestra. I want to make that very clear. Like my predecessor, I believe that with the progress of broadcasting, especially when we reach the point of having a second programme, this will be a natural development. I would not be averse, if the money could be found, to an arrangement whereby Radio Éireann and the Cork vocational authorities would jointly finance and benefit from the presence in the city of a number of players of distinction. Between the school of music and the broadcasting studios, musical activities could grow in Cork and, as local material became available and Radio Éireann's own programme possibilities expanded, the enlargement of this group could be undertaken more rapidly. I may mention here that since I have prepared this statement I have had a development in the form of the presentation of a petition from the citizens of Cork, presented through the medium of their Deputies and the Lord Mayor, Deputy McGrath. I have read the grounds to be put forward by this petition and I may say that they have opened up new possibilities. There are certain proposals contained in it which are well worthy of consideration and I will bring the matter before the Government for their close as possible consideration before I reply to Deputy McGrath.[54]

What these 'new possibilities' are is unclear, since the petition merely called upon the Minister to 'assign a radio orchestra to Cork'. However, the remarkable fact about the public meeting and the petition is that it represented at best a pyrrhic victory for Fleischmann and Cork. Knowing that it would be impossible to reverse the decision already taken (and announced), that RÉ would not provide Cork with an orchestra, and that a smaller group might be contemplated in the near future, Fleischmann nevertheless went ahead with a protest which might more purposefully have been organised a year previously when, with a more sympathetic minister in place, public opinion might have been more effectively mobilised.

As it was, in the same week that the petition was brought to Dublin, Fleischmann was admitting that, following a meeting with the Taoiseach, 'it is

---

54 DD 152, 6 July 1955, cols. 269–72.

now agreed that we should not pursue our request that the Light Orchestra be transferred to Cork, and that – in deference to An Taoiseach's suggestion – we should seek a compromise solution'. He thought that a string orchestra would not be practical, since it 'is not a popular medium and the literature for it is exceedingly limited' and because it would 'rule out our scheme for public con-certs here'; but 'we think that a *Chamber Orchestra* would be a most suitable medium from every point of view' and would be 'an asset to the broadcasting programmes'. He asked for an orchestra of twelve strings, four woodwind and five brass and percussion (a total of twenty-one), which he said was 'seven or eight players less than the Light Orchestra' (which actually numbered 22–25).[55]

THE RTÉ STRING QUARTET

Maurice Gorham recalled that the inaugural recital by the new Radio Éireann String Quartet, on 7 August 1959, was used by the new Minister for P&T, Michael Hilliard, to announce the setting up of a semi-State board to admin-ister the combined radio and television service which would come into being the following year. Thus a major development in Irish broadcasting was linked to a major development – however unexpected by Corkonians – in the musi-cal life of Ireland's second city. By negotiation, Cork would be provided with four string players who, in addition to rehearsing and performing for RÉ, would reside in Cork as members of its musical community and would teach at the Cork School of Music. The continued presence of successive quartets in Cork (allowing for lapses during changes in personnel) would prove to be the germ of its burgeoning musical life.

The quartet appointed was the English-based Raphael Quartet (Roger Raphael and Brendan O'Reilly, violins; Peter Sermon, viola; and Sermon's wife, Gwenda Milbourn, cello – she would later be replaced by Radoslav Vocadlo) who were interested in moving their base to southern Ireland. They were in their twenties, and O'Reilly had only recently given his MAI 'coming-out' recital, having been praised by Charles Acton as 'a most musical player, an innate interpreter and the possessor of almost the loveliest tone of any Irish violinist of his age'.[56] Their inaugural recital in Cork was greeted by Geraldine Neeson: 'the impact of this ensemble was exhilarating and the influence exerted by it on musical thought in Cork must be exceedingly great when time has welded the different parts more firmly together'.[57] In Dublin, Charles Acton observed the quartet's steady improvement as it grew together as a unit, and in June 1963, when it appeared as part of the RTÉ Festival, he wrote:

55 Fleischmann to Ó Broin, 4 July 1955, file 286/54/1. 56 *Irish Times*, 29 April 1958. 57 *Irish Times*, 10 August 1959.

They understood the works ... and shared them with the audience. And they had a great deal of guts and passionate forcefulness, with less sense of cautious restraint than they have ever had before. As far as all these good qualities go, they can (on last night's performance) hold their own with the quartets of any city of Europe, outside Prague.58

By the end of that year, he would be saying:

I will not pretend that they are the equals of the Busch [quartet] or that Mr Raphael's tone [with which Acton had consistently found fault] is quite lovely enough, but they proved that they are a group of maturity, of full stature, able now to put Ireland on the international chamber music map. This was a really important day for Irish music.59

A condition of their employment required them to travel as widely as possible, continuing and extending the outreach undertaken by the orchestras. By 1962 they had visited musical clubs (mainly gramophone societies) in Carlow, Galway, Listowel, Loughrea, Birr, Gorey, Portarlington, Athlone, Nenagh and Millstreet, and twice each in Ballina, Wicklow and Tullamore. They had outstanding invitations from twenty-two other centres, including the Gramophone Society of the Curragh Camp Cadet School.

They appear to have fitted in to life in Cork very satisfactorily, but inevitably there is a time when all such groups either lose, or shed, a member, especially in a quartet where the intimacy of the daily work, and the nature of that work, places heavy strains on the members both individually and collectively. In the case of the Raphael Quartet, the leader himself moved on in 1964, and the remaining three players asked for the appointment of a Czech violinist who was not acceptable to the Director of Music, Tibor Paul. Paul made strenuous efforts to secure Hugh Maguire as leader, but Maguire, just as we saw in the attempt to attract him to the appointment with the Symphony Orchestra, was at first willing and then reluctant to accept.60 Knowing that Paul wanted an Irish leader, Fleischmann had pushed forward Brendan O'Reilly,61 but Paul insisted on the appointment of Brendan O'Brien, whom in turn the quartet members resisted. Personal differences intensified as Paul imposed O'Brien on them and they then resigned with effect from mid-1966. Even though the imposition of the new leader was rescinded (O'Brien was then appointed leader of the RTÉSO), the depleted quartet went ahead with their joint resignation, and the search for a new quartet commenced.62

---

58 *Irish Times*, 20 June 1963. 59 *Irish Times*, 18 November 1963. 60 Tibor Paul to A. Fleischmann, 20 January and 4 February 1964, RTÉ Music Department file, 'String Quartet'. 61 Fleischmann to Paul, 11 January 1964, ibid. 62 RTÉ Authority minutes, 16 February 1966.

Paul had in fact started off his tenure as Director of Music on a bad footing with the Raphael Quartet: in late 1962 he had told them that he was disappointed with their standard: 'I thought that ... there were faults in intonation, a generally unsatisfactory tonal blend particularly in the upper strings,
and a lack of the general design and purpose which quartet playing at its highest level must possess'.[63] As the quartet was preparing for a European tour in
early 1963, his suggestion that it was not of sufficient standard to present to
continental audiences must have been alarming. Paul's tone was nothing less
than a basic criticism of the leader, and may well have caused Raphael's eventual departure. On this occasion, however, Raphael replied in strong terms: if
a top standard was required, top conditions should be provided. 'I have talked
to a number of leaders of well-known ensembles and a group such as the
renowned Janáček Quartet spend no less than five weeks preparing one of the
less difficult Haydn quartets ... Such a quartet would present not more than a
dozen works annually and it would take their entire career to build up a repertoire of forty to sixty quartets – the Smetana Quartet repertoire is 40 works.
Please contrast this with our output of well over a hundred different works
during a period of less than three years ... We decided to live under the same
roof in order to be able to work together any time of the day or night. We cannot see any other way of substantially improving the quality of the recordings
than by drastically reducing the quantity of the different works required from
us'.[64] The quartet was required to provide a 45-minute programme, three weeks
in every four; for this, they rehearsed separately every morning, and for five
hours together, for three days each week, recording on Saturday nights in a
three-hour session, and teaching at the School of Music one afternoon and
evening. Sunday was free.

A week later Raphael was telling Gerard Victory, Paul's more sympathetic
deputy, that 'we are capable of performing ... up to a standard comparable and
even superior to that of a number of touring quartets which are considered
worthy of representing their countries abroad, such as the Benthien, Parrenin,
Wuehrer, Glazunov, to name just a few'.[65] Victory, however, had to follow Paul's
line, and retorted that 'his opinion as Director of Music must prevail on any
matter regarding the standard of playing at any particular time' and that 'an
international standard has not been achieved'.[66] It seems, however, that Paul's

It was rumoured at the time that Paul's preferred candidate to succeed Raphael was Hugh Maguire:
Charles Acton, interview with Hugh Maguire, *Irish Times*, 5 June 1976.   **63** Paul to Raphael, 3
December 1962, RTÉ Music Department file, 'String Quartet'.   **64** Raphael to Paul, 5 December
1962, ibid.   **65** Raphael to Victory, 12 December 1962, ibid. The Benthien Quartet played several times in Ireland and recorded Boydell's first quartet. The Parrenin Quartet was founded in
1944 by Jacques Parrenin and continues in existence with successors to the other original players;
it enjoyed a high reputation in the 1950s and 1960s, performing more than 150 premières.
66 Victory to Raphael, 14 December 1962, ibid.

objections were overcome, as the Quartet undertook its tour, playing quartets by Mozart (K.387), Beethoven (op. 95), Janáček (no. 2, 'Intimate Letters'), Haydn (op. 20 no. 2), Vranicky,[67] and two Irish works which had been requested by the host organisation in Stuttgart, Proinnsías Ó Duinn's op. 10 and Boydell's first quartet.[68]

Although it was not intended to take any action immediately in relation to forming a new quartet[69] (and it was rumoured that RTÉ wished to appoint the Dublin String Quartet, three of whose members were playing in the RTÉ orchestras),[70] the appointment of Brendan O'Brien to the symphony orchestra had had the effect of displacing the acting leader, David Lillis, and this coincided with further strong representations from Cork, making it possible to form an all-Irish quartet.[71] RTÉ did not in fact have to look far for its next quartet, and had it in place before the Raphaels' notice had expired. The husband-and-wife teams of David Lillis (violin) and Coral Bognuda (cello), and Audrey Park (violin) and Archie Collins (viola), all of whom were at that stage playing in the orchestras, were brought together and settled, initially, in Dublin for six months before transferring to Cork, on the understanding that half their working year would be spent on tour.[72] Their appointment coincided with the decision by James White, recently appointed Director of the National Gallery, to open the Gallery for concerts, so that from late 1966 the Quartet (like the Singers) had a public platform for its recitals other than RTÉ's own studios.

The hallmark of this quartet's music-making was, in Acton's words, 'fidelity to the composers', on which he remarked at its performance at the inaugural Twentieth-Century Festival in 1969, when it played works by Marek Kopelent, Webern, Boydell and a new quartet by Bodley.[73] The new quartet had some significant successes, including visits to the Wexford festival and to Belfast, and playing new music (such as Raymond Warren's first quartet [1965], Boydell's second and third, and Kinsella's second) and giving three performances of Frederick May's quartet within a year in 1967. Overseas visits took in Newcastle-upon-Tyne in 1969 and Bergen in 1970.

In the absence of detailed correspondence, it appears that all went smoothly with the new group until 1971, when, somewhat surprisingly for a group which had been together for five years, Archie Collins wrote to John Kinsella 'we have found through experience in the quartet medium that the nature of such a closely knit group is incompatible to us, particularly in Mrs. Collins's case.

---

67 It is not clear whether the composer was the Czech, Paul Vranitcky (1756–1808) or his brother Anton (1761–1820). **68** A letter from the DG, Edward Roth, to the Lord Mayor of Cork (Alderman Seán Casey) dated 13 August 1962 suggests that the RTÉ Authority had decided to change the name of the quartet to 'Cork String Quartet', but the reply (16 August 1962) appears to reject this proposal. **69** RTÉ Authority minutes, 16 February 1966. **70** Cf. *Irish Times*, 25 February 1966. **71** Ibid., 9 March 1966. **72** Ibid., 25 May 1966. **73** *Irish Times*, 7 January 1969.

She has now fully realised that her particular interest is in playing light music, and she is most happy in this medium'.74 Given that Audrey Park-Collins was a very fine quartet player, who would form the Testore Quartet75 and would later be approached by RTÉ with an offer of appointment for her quartet to go to Cork, this is somewhat disingenuous. Collins seems to be telling Kinsella that his wife was unhappy as second violin to Lillis's leadership, and it is also likely that Lillis's personal mannerisms were afflicting the quartet as a group. In addition, Audrey Park had been offered the post of sub-principal in the BBC Light Orchestra, but was holding out for a better post back in Dublin, where she was regarded as a natural successor to Jack Cheatle as leader of the RTÉLO. Both Collins and Park were offered positions in the orchestras at this point, but declined this move and resigned from RTÉ, rejoining a year later, Park as leader of the RÉLO and Collins as principal viola of the RÉSO, transferring to the Light Orchestra six months later. As discussed above, membership of this quartet was unstable, with Collins and Park being replaced by two younger players and their work being suspended due to Lillis's persistent ill-health.

Out of deference to Lillis's condition, it was agreed that the quartet (now constituted by Lillis, Bognuda, John Vallery [viola] and Kieran Egan [violin]) should move to Dublin, and, for the same reason, Aloys Fleischmann 'refrained from making the issue a public one'.76 After two years, in the course of which it became evident that the quartet was now completely dysfunctional,77 it was stated (in a surviving fragment of a memorandum signed by both Gerard Victory and John Kinsella in 1975) that the recomposition of the quartet could be justified because, among other reasons, ten works had been written by Irish composers for the quartet; its visits to Belfast 'and other Northern centres played quite a role ... in helping to further a cultural unity in the country'; and that its teaching commitment, though onerous, was valuable.78

At the same time Fanny Feehan, writing in *Hibernia*, suggested that the Testore Quartet become a quartet-in-residence in a number of Irish universities in rotation. Charles Acton further suggested to Aloys Fleischmann that he should ascertain whether the Testore would be interested in living in Cork, as a prelude to a campaign to have that quartet appointed by RTÉ. Acton's concern was that 'some practical means [should] be found whereby this very fine group can continue and grow as a first-class, permanent, professional Irish quartet who, given the encouragement, would soon be able to take their places

74 Collins to Kinsella, 24 April 1971. 75 Audrey Park and Clodagh McSwiney, violins; Archie Collins, viola; Aisling Drury-Byrne, cello. 76 Fleischmann to Charles Acton, 10 March 1976 (Acton Archive). 77 In any case, Egan was due to go abroad for further study in 1975, so that the quartet had no long-term expectation with that complement. 78 Victory and Kinsella to an unknown RTÉ recipient (probably Controller of Radio), 2 January 1975 – page 2 only.

among the major quartets of the world'.[79] When the members of the Testore signalled that they were not interested in moving to Cork,[80] Fleischmann began what must have seemed to him to be the 1955 campaign all over again, writing to the *Irish Times* 'we cannot afford to lose the relatively small concession we succeeded in wringing from RTÉ. Let there be no doubt but that the city will resist to the utmost any question of a new quartet being housed anywhere but in Cork'.[81]

Eventually, RTÉ appointed a young Romanian quartet, the 'Academica', who had been formed while at the Conservatoire Ciprian Porumbescu in Bucharest in 1967, and had subsequently won awards at international competitions at Liège, Munich, Geneva and Belgrade. They were Mariana Sirbu (leader) and her husband Mihai Dancila (cello), Ruxandra Colan (second violin) and Constantin Zanidache (viola). After several protracted difficulties with exit visas, they arrived in Cork in mid-1978 and gave their inaugural concert in May. In their wake, over a two-year period, came Ruxandra's husband Adrian Petcu (now lecturing at the Cork School of Music) and her brother-in-law Mircea Petcu (now a member of the RTÉCO) and others, marking an astonishing importation to Cork of eastern European string players.

Unlike the first and second quartets, the Academica had been working together for over ten years at this stage, so that musically and personally its members had already achieved a plateau of togetherness which marked their playing to such an extent that audiences realised that, for the first time, there was a resident quartet in Ireland of world stature.

As Gerard Victory said in introducing the Quartet before its inaugural recital in Cork in March 1978, 'the Romanians have combined their folk tradition with the great classical central European tradition in a way we have not yet quite achieved. This superb blend of folk imagination and freedom with the discipline and elegance of the classical school has produced a race of fine string players to which the Academica Quartet must surely belong'.[82]

When the Quartet made its Dublin début two months later, Acton remarked that 'They all have a remarkable strength, but this extraordinary power is not at the expense of beauty of tone. They can make an electrifying attack and yet the tone still sings'.[83] Later that year, he was writing of their 'enormous commitment, power, dedication and seriousness',[84] and six months after that he wrote of a performance of the Debussy quartet, 'The rare satisfaction of this performance came perhaps from a combination of their playing "what is there" as Toscanini used to say, and a perfect and always caring balancing of each chord,

79 *Irish Times*, 8 March 1976. **80** Audrey Park, interview with *Sunday Press* undated cutting [1980] (Acton Archive). **81** *Irish Times*, 21 February 1976. **82** Quoted in the *Irish Times*, 6 March 1978. **83** *Irish Times*, 25 May 1978. **84** *Irish Times*, 20 September 1978.

and also perhaps an unusually conscientious tempering of all the chords so that they spoke with particular character and emphasis'.[85] After a performance of Beethoven's final quartet (including the *grosse fuge*) he said 'One could sense that the RTÉAQ are always striving to get closer to perfection ... The increasing intensity of their totally unified view of the work was remarkable'.[86] Acton, who had heard all the world's great quartets at the RDS and other venues in the course of his career, opined: 'If the Smetana are still the world's greatest quartet, and the Amadeus is the most polished, what we may now call ours have an equal technique and the excitement and questing seriousness of youth'.[87]

The appointment of the Academica Quartet was probably the high point of the career of John Kinsella as RTÉ's chamber music specialist, as its break-up was the lowest. Unfortunately for RTÉ, Cork and music-making generally in Ireland, the Academica was not as 'totally unified' as Acton believed. It came as a bombshell to discover that three of its members wished to part company with the fourth, violist Constantin Zanidache, in favour of an American player, James Creitz.[88] When faced with a request from the three players, voiced by Mihai Dancila, that RTÉ dispense with the services of Zanidache, Kinsella was at pains to point out that the contracts of employment of each member protected them from this kind of eventuality, and that unless something untoward occurred to prevent them from playing as a quartet, no change in the current situation could be envisaged, especially since there was no dissatisfaction with Zanidache's conduct or performance. In this situation, Sirbu, Colan and Dancila resigned from RTÉ, re-grouping with Creitz as the 'Academica Quartet' and continued to give recitals, while Zanidache remained as the sole member of the 'RTÉ Academica Quartet' until his departure became inevitable. A certain amount of 'disinformation' was published in the national press, indicating that Creitz's appointment had resulted from the resignation of Zanidache, which was emphatically not the case. As far as the present writer is concerned, the break-up of the Academica was tragic in that an ensemble of such excellence could dissolve. The new Academica, having a far smaller income base (once its salaries from RTÉ had ceased), moved away from Cork for considerable periods and the quartet itself ceased to function in 1994 when Sirbu and Dancila, with their daughter Cristina and violist Massimo Paris, formed the Quartetto Stradivari.

RTÉ was now in the position of auditioning for a successor to the Academica, the fourth resident quartet (to date). After a delay of a year, advertisements appeared and Kinsella recommended the appointment of the Vanbrugh Quartet, ahead of fifteen other applicants. The Vanbrugh had already competed at the Banff and Portsmouth international competitions for quar-

85 *Irish Times*, 7 March 1979.   **86** *Irish Times*, 27 October 1981.   **87** *Irish Times*, 27 September 1979.   **88** What follows is based on the author's personal observation of developments within the RTÉ Music Department in 1983–5.

tets, and after taking up appointment in Cork returned to Portsmouth where a jury, including Yehudi Menuhin, awarded it first prize, thus boosting its international prestige and confirming Kinsella's judgement. Its inaugural recitals were given in Cork and Dublin in mid- and late-1986 and its members rapidly settled into a routine of six concerts per year in Dublin and Cork, plus ten in other centres. The original members, all from the RAM, were Gregory Ellis and Elizabeth Charleson (violins), Simon Aspell (viola) and Christopher Marwood (cello), but in 1998 Charleson, suffering from recurent shoulder problems, was replaced by Keith Pascoe.

The Vanbrugh has undertaken a very extensive touring programme in Ireland, in addition to its international career and its recording commitments, which includes much modern and new work such as quartets by May, Tavener, Moeran, Robert Simpson, Ian Wilson and John McCabe, besides the complete Beethoven cycle which it gave in its Irish concerts. It has premièred quartets by Kinsella, Jane O'Leary, Ian Wilson, Raymond Deane, Donncha Dennehy, Eric Sweeney and Deirdre Gribbin. Its most imaginative and adventurous project was the establishment, in 1996, of the West Cork Chamber Music Festival, held in Bantry House, which rapidly became recognised as one of the leading festivals of Europe, supported by Lyric fm and broadcast widely by the EBU.

It can confidently be said that RTÉ, as the first radio station in the world to establish a quartet-in-residence, led the concept internationally and stimulated the appreciation of chamber music in Ireland over the past forty-five years. The establishment of quartets-in-residence in Sligo (Vogler, 1999) and Galway (Con Tempo, 2003) can be traced to this initiative. With quartets of the calibre of the Academica and Vanbrugh, it has hosted music-making at a level not yet reached with any consistency by its other performing groups, while contributing significantly to the musical life of the city of Cork and, more recently, to the Munster region in general.

CHAPTER 6

A modern orchestra, 1962–82

The period during which Tibor Paul was both Director of Music and Principal Conductor of the RTÉSO (1961–7) is characterised by two factors: first, the tensions between Paul himself, the RTÉ organisation as a whole and the orchestral personnel, and second, Paul's ambition to build the RTÉSO into an international entity which would in turn reflect well on his own freelance career. During the first years of his tenure, he made extensive efforts to attract world-class soloists and visiting conductors to Dublin in order to enhance the concert programmes and increase the confidence of his players. Unfortunately, but perhaps predictably, his ambitions led him to behave in a high-handed fashion, causing friction and character clashes with many of the players and unease among his superiors as to his decision-making. The high points of Paul's achievements in musical terms were the 'Radio Éireann Festival of Music' of 1963 featuring Igor Stravinsky, the RTÉSO's first foray overseas with concerts in London in 1966, and his concluding Beethoven cycle in the following year. The low points, in organisational and personal terms, were the exodus of players from Dublin with the formation of the Ulster Orchestra in 1966, and the decision by RTÉ not to renew his contract when it expired in July 1967.

The fifteen years following the departure of Tibor Paul were marked, in orchestral terms, by five main factors: firstly, the rising visibility of the RTÉ Light Orchestra (repositioned in 1978 as the RTÉ Concert Orchestra), as it gave an increasing number of public concerts both in Dublin and nationally; secondly, international tours by both the RTÉCO and the RTÉSO which brought them worldwide recognition as exemplars of their individual performing characters; thirdly, and concomitantly, a new understanding of the role of music and musicians on the part of RTÉ itself, as it acknowledged the status of its orchestras by accepting independent assessments which awarded the musicians not only improved salaries but also improved conditions of employment and a degree of parity with other skilled employees of RTÉ; fourthly, a concern for what RTÉ expects of the RTÉSO's Principal Conductor; and fifthly a debate, which still continues, as to the role of orchestras which were inaugurated with a primarily broadcasting function but which have subsequently grown into performing groups whose public appearances are at least as important as their broadcasts, and whose custody may not necessarily be most thoroughly, or most effectively, served by their current employer. Most of these factors continued to operate in the period after 1982, and will be re-examined in chapter 7.

THE TIBOR PAUL ERA

Tibor Paul (1909–73) was a graduate of the Royal Academy of Music in Budapest, where he had been a pupil of Kodály and, for conducting, Felix Weingartner. He had been appointed a conductor of the Hungarian Broadcasting Commission in 1940, and had also been music director of the Hungarian film industry, before leaving Hungary in 1948. Since 1953 he had lived in Australia, where he had been appointed conductor of the National Opera in Sydney and professor of conducting at the New South Wales Conservatory. He had an impressive catalogue of recordings with the Vienna Symphony Orchestra on the Philips label, including Brahms' Hungarian Dances, Bartók's 'Two Images', Kodály's 'Háry János' and Liszt's Hungarian Rhapsodies and 'Les Préludes'. He had first come to Ireland on the recommendation of Sir Charles Moses[1] and, like many visiting conductors, had initially conducted five concerts in 1958–9, and subsequently a series of seven concerts in September-October 1959 (his first 'Prom' was on 18 October) and was re-engaged for a further six concerts in January 1960. The success of these led to another series of nine concerts in late 1960 and, by the time he was appointed Principal Conductor (from September 1961), he had had charge of a further four RTÉ concerts plus a Beethoven Festival at the Olympia Theatre in aid of the MAI's 'Concert Hall Fund'.[2]

Paul's first engagement with the RÉSO had been on 14 November 1958, with Verdi's overture to *La forza del destino*, Richard Strauss's 'Don Juan', Delius' prelude 'Irmelin', Blacher's 'Variations on a theme of Paganini' and Beethoven's seventh symphony. Charles Acton liked the overture and the Blacher, and immediately recognised Paul's special affinity for Beethoven which was to be a hallmark of his conductorship in Ireland.[3] When Paul started to appear more frequently, Acton noticed 'an impression of an improvement all round, already; and of the beginning of a real orchestra-conductor relationship'.[4] In fact, after Paul's first five concerts in 1958–9, Acton considered that 'the RÉSO is continuing to show a startling improvement under Tibor Paul. After these five concerts of his, may I ask RÉ or the Government to induce Mr Paul to become

1 Managing Director of the Australian Broadcasting Corporation 1935–65. 2 His Beethoven festival featured the nine symphonies, the piano concertos played by Fou Ts'ong (no. 1), Anthony Hughes (no. 2), Charles Lynch (no. 3) and Shura Cherkassky (nos. 4 and 5) and the violin concerto (Tibor Varga). 3 *Irish Times*, 15 November 1958. 4 *Irish Times*, 3 October 1959.

our permanent conductor? On the evidence so far, he could make the RÉSO into one of the orchestras of Europe'.[5] After that appointment, he regarded Paul's 'outstanding quality as a conductor' to be the ability 'to feel and communicate the musical structure and shape of a work that suits him, as a whole and in detail ...He is at his best in the largescale work, especially the romantic one. With his architectural sense goes a feeling for the literary or pictorial ingredients in music and an emphasis on personal connections between composers and music ... Tibor Paul is a powerful force in musical life and when eventually he moves on to wherever his proper ambitions take him the effect he is having on our musical life will be felt for a long time afterwards'.[6]

However, a residual problem – which would also manifest itself in the case of Albert Rosen – was the fact that Paul's career took him away from Ireland for substantial parts of the year, with the result that standards in the RÉSO fluctuated. Acton was to observe that 'It is remarkable how much polish the RÉSO seems to lose during Tibor Paul's absences ...[7] Let us hope he will not, like Sisyphus, have to start at the bottom of the hill when he returns in a couple of months' time ...[8] [The orchestra are] playing well, as if Tibor Paul has by now brought them back to the standard at which he left them in October. One of the many important tasks awaiting the new musical director of RÉ is to prevent this decline during the principal conductor's absences'.[9] This latter remark was, of course, based on the assumption that Paul would *not* become Director of Music.

Coinciding with Paul's appointment, the RTÉ Authority had been asked by Director-General Edward Roth to make decisions on the future of both orchestras. RTÉ had commissioned a report from George Willoughby, the BBCSO's Concerts and Orchestral Manager.[10] Roth had written to a selection of people in Irish musical life, asking them 'to assist Mr Willoughby in making this completely objective analysis', which he regarded as 'an event of vital importance'.[11] Willoughby spent two weeks in Ireland in late May and early June 1961, interviewing a large number of people, among them Eimear Ó Broin (to whom he complained that he had hoped to meet representatives of organisations such as trades unions, rather than a series of individuals).[12] He submitted a report at the end of June, which Roth circulated to Authority members three months later.

5 *Irish Times*, 10 October 1959. 6 *Irish Times*, February 1963 and 16 October 1964. 7 *Irish Times*, 30 December 1961. 8 *Irish Times*, 2 January 1962. 9 *Irish Times*, 6 January 1962. 10 In which capacity he had brought the BBCSO to Ireland in 1958, with concerts in Derry, Belfast (three concerts), Cork, Limerick and Dublin. 2000 people attended the Dublin concert, and Willoughby reported that 'the tremendous enthusiasm shown for the conductor and Orchestra after Sibelius No. 5 and Schubert's C Major gave a tremendous uplift to all concerned': Nicholas Kenyon, *The BBC Symphony Orchestra 1930–1980* (1981), p. 284. Willoughby retired in 1963. 11 A copy of Roth's circular was sent to A.J. Potter (Potter Archive). 12 E. Ó Broin, interview with the author, 3 May 2002.

Very few, apart from the members of the Authority, saw Willoughby's report, and the fact that no copy of it survives in any location within RTÉ is an indication of the sensitivity of its contents. That an American, still feeling his way into Irish culture and society, should entrust an Englishman (even one from a broadcasting and orchestral background) with research, the result of which would have such consequences for the organisation as a whole, and for the Light Orchestra in particular, is remarkable.

Willoughby found a dichotomy in the status of the RÉSO: because it was 'the only existing orchestra of that type it has tended to be regarded as a "National" acquisition, and since there is only one channel for sound broadcasting to cover all the legitimate listening interests of the country, it has had sufficient time to behave as such'.[13] Thus, not only had the orchestra been regarded as a national institution, but its employer had, by default, allowed it to be regarded as such. Since it was perceived as a national orchestra, it should appear more frequently in regional venues. Its position was already anomalous, since it was 'a very expensive proposition, although if live orchestral music is to be a feature of Sound Programmes in Ireland it is an essential part of the organisation'. It was on this basis that Roth would argue for the retention of the orchestra, but it was on the same basis that the Authority would ask for government support in maintaining it.

Willoughby found that 'the relationship between the orchestra and the management ... generally is deplorable', and a closer relationship should be developed between the orchestra committee and management. Tibor Paul 'can be a bit tyrannical' – 'good choice for a Resident Conductor but it might be dangerous to leave him the sole responsibility of "hiring and firing"' – and 'there would need to be an amicable association between [him] and a firm and tactful Music Director'. If the RÉSO were to be of 'international standard', the string sections must be increased to balance the wind and brass.[14] A 'Resident Conductor' must be appointed, 'who can be responsible for the orchestra and actually "reside"' – at the BBCSO such a person conducted sixty concerts each year. Finally, Willoughby recommended that the orchestra be re-named 'The National Orchestra of Ireland' or 'The Irish National Orchestra'. 'Despite the large proportion of time that is spent on work not directly concerned with broadcasting which might even increase, control of the Symphony Orchestra should remain firmly with Radio Éireann and neither be shared nor delegated, whatever its official title'.

On the subject of the RÉLO, Willoughby was aware of the preceding debate as to whether or not it should be based in Cork, and decided that if this

---

13 G.J. Willoughby, 'Report', loc. cit.   **14** 16 first violins, 14 seconds, 12 violas, 10 celli and 8 basses.

move had been effected at the time, it would have been beneficial, but that it was not advisable now, in view of the needs of television. His main recommendation was that its 'style is old fashioned and a "shot in the arm" is called for': its development should be monitored in the light of its television work. Willoughby also supported H.W. Rosen's 'plea' that the Singers should be increased in strength from ten to sixteen, and that the string quartet, the existence of which 'shows imagination and courage', should not be so closely monitored from Dublin as to its hours of work.

As far as the future of the two orchestras was concerned, and specifically with regard to their work for television, Willoughby recommended that 'serious' music should be separated from 'light' music, with a specialist Head for each.

On the basis of Willoughby's report, Roth argued that 'with a threefold combination of a reorganisation of the Music Department, a re-evaluation of each member of the Symphony and Light Orchestras, and an increase in money, the Radio Éireann Orchestras could, within a brief period, assume a position equal to the great orchestras of Europe. This is important to Ireland'.[15] It is noteworthy that the slimness of Willoughby's report (ten pages in total) did not deter Roth from reading into its findings significances which the report was scarcely capable of bearing. Addressing the position of the RÉSO, Roth continued:

> The third consideration, that of money, while immeshed in all our radio and television activities, is absolutely vital to any consideration of the Symphony Orchestra. The Willoughby Report will demonstrate just how serious and complex a problem this is. The Authority remembers the unsuccessful attempts of the past to gain financial assistance for the orchestras and how every effort made was turned down. The dilemma still exists and it must be solved. What the Radio Éireann Symphony Orchestra needs is an increase of money and a specific and clear-cut direction or plan. Both are lacking at present. It is traditional that symphony orchestras are never financially stable. There is perhaps no symphony orchestra in the world that does not rely almost completely on some form of subsidy. One might argue that classical music has only minority appeal. Although this might be statistically true, it is equally true that our mass radio and television audience is made up of many minorities each of whom should and must be catered to. If proof were needed, I am of the opinion that the Willoughby Report has proven the need for the RÉSO despite its acknowledged minority interest. Although I am personally in agreement with those who maintain that to disband the RÉSO would be to create a cultural vacuum of serious proportions,

15 Director-General to RTÉ Authority members, 7 October 1961.

I must point out to the Authority the relevant sections of the Broadcasting Authority Act, 1960, i.e. Sections 22, 23, 24, and 25, in particular … If the Authority quite justifiably maintains that the radio and television service should not carry the entire burden of the RÉSO then the Authority must agree upon a firm policy with respect to alternative financing and adhere to it. That is to say, the Authority should seriously consider advising the Dublin Corporation, the State Government and any other interested group that unless a more sympathetic, and one might add realistic, attitude toward orchestral financing is taken immediately the Authority cannot continue to support the symphony orchestra and fulfil its legal obligations under the [Act] … If this new policy is again rejected it would then follow that the immediate dismissal of the Symphony staff would take place. What this catastrophe would mean to Ireland is described in the Willoughby Report and needs no further comment from me.[16]

Roth's memorandum is the third milestone in the evolution of RTÉ's orchestras in administrative terms. Kiernan's analysis of 1935 had pointed to the need for both efficiency and guidance; Ó hAnnracháin's implementation of P.J. Little's decision in 1947–8 had made possible an ambitious political project with enormous unresolved consequences; and now the implication in Roth's memorandum was that that same political project, with financial repercussions, demanded to be placed on a new footing. Even the suggestion that all existing players should be re-auditioned or 're-evaluated' (which was definitely *not* one of Willoughby's recommendations) implied that whatever problems had been inherited from the past were to be eliminated from the new equation by a totally fresh start on a different financial basis.

It is instructive that Roth displayed an ambivalent behaviour towards the Symphony Orchestra, similar to the difference in attitude of James Everett when in government and out of it: while here he was arguing the importance of the orchestra, both organisationally and nationally, in private he would tell Charles Acton that 'it was not worth while keeping the RÉSO in being because "only" 30,000 people listened to its broadcasts'.[17]

From 1962, and the advent of television, RTÉ was to argue, for the rest of the decade, that the maintenance of the RTÉSO was an unwarranted financial burden, even though Roth himself appears to have seen the merits of televising the RÉSO concerts: in 1963 he told a newspaper interviewer

Most nations and communities are composed of a collection of minorities, and the broadcaster recognises that the great majority of people

16 Ibid. 17 Acton published his recollection of this conversation: *Irish Times*, 21 March 1974.

seek in their television viewing – and in this order – entertainment, information and culture. To provide acceptable entertainment, and simultaneously to encourage the general improvement of standards, is a difficult and complex task. Telefís Éireann, despite its shortcomings, has made significant contributions in this area. The Symphony Broadcasts have, for example, brought classical music into the homes of many thousands of people who previously had no knowledge of, or interest in, symphonic music.[18]

But during Tibor Paul's tenure as principal conductor his personality and his conduct as musical *maestro* dominated the decade; he carried the fortunes of the RÉSO on his own personal tide, while at the same time the orchestra's employers would seek to divest themselves of the very asset which it was his purpose to enhance.

There can hardly have been a less propitious start to a principal conductorship, although the fact that, together with the Willoughby Report, Roth also circulated a report by Paul himself, suggests that the 're-organisation of the Music Department' already envisaged the combining of the posts of Principal Conductor and Director of Music, a measure that would have severe repercussions for Paul's retention of both positions. As early as May 1962, the Minister for P&T (Michael Hilliard) was being asked whether he would relieve the Authority of this burden,[19] and two days later whether the Authority was empowered to disband the RÉSO.[20]

The position of Director of Music was advertised, and the post was offered to Havelock Nelson by a panel which included William Glock of the BBC; Nelson, after some soul-searching, declined it.[21] It was therefore by no means predictable that Paul, would be appointed, however much he had impressed by the vigour of his personality and the artistic success of his concerts to date. But, in the absence of any other candidate considered sufficiently strong to take up the post, Roth offered it to Paul, and in mid-1962 he combined the two positions. Gerard Victory became his deputy and Kevin Roche, former orchestra manager and assistant Music Director, became Head of Light Music, with a remit for both RÉ and Telefís Éireann. Fachtna Ó hAnnracháin saw that Roth did not appreciate the difficulties that might arise if Paul occupied both positions, but as he himself had relinquished the post of Music Director he did not wish to intervene.[22] The schizophrenic nature of the dual mandate was expressed by Charles Acton, writing at the end of Paul's tenure, when he stated,

---

18 *Evening Press*, 22 January 1963. **19** Patrick Cummins (Fianna Fáil, Dublin South-Central) DD. 195, 15 May 1962, cols. 759–60. **20** Seán Treacy (Labour, Tipperary South) ibid., 17 May 1962, col. 1122. **21** A.J. Potter was one of the unsuccessful applicants. **22** F. Ó hAnnracháin to author, 30 October 2003. Ó hAnnracháin then became RTÉ's Legal and Contracts Officer.

idiosyncratically, 'There is much evidence that the great improvement made by the conductor was very greatly retarded by the music director.'[23] It will also be noted that the combination of the two positions was implicitly rejected in the Willoughby report, which argued against Paul as Music Director.

By the end of 1965, when Paul had announced that he had secured a concert for the RÉSO in London, it had become clear that his dual mandate was problematic, and an *Irish Times* leader observed that

> From every point of view it is highly undesirable to appoint the same man to be principal conductor of the RÉSO and Director of Music of the broadcasting service. Apart from the principles of effective administration, the two positions demand more time than one man can give; there is a certain conflict of interest between the two; the qualities of personality needed for the two posts are very different and unlikely to be found in the same man, especially if the conductor is a master of high romantic music and of the great occasion, as Mr Paul undoubtedly is.[24]

Paul was determined to make the RTÉSO a world-class orchestra, an ambition which harmonised well with the much-vaunted and much-voiced expectation of politicians such as Erskine Childers, civil servants such as León Ó Broin and – to a much lesser extent – the top echelon of RTÉ. In 1965 Paul told an interviewer that he saw a major function as building an audience for the anticipated Kennedy Hall: firstly, to make symphonic music more widely acceptable; then to improve the conditions for chamber music; and thirdly to concentrate on soloists and vocalists: 'always I'm trying to enlarge the audience, by appealing to the young, as well as to the society audience that have tended to put opera higher in their minds than orchestral music'.[25] To do so, he knew that he must not only recruit the best available players, but also spread the word on the worldwide musical grapevine by means of visiting soloists and conductors. Paul was in fact to be the architect, in musical and administrative terms, of the new fortunes of the orchestras. As Pierre Boulez would say in 1984 at an EBU symposium on the future of radio orchestras, 'In general – and I say this in no disparagement of radio, since I was myself an employee – radio orchestras lack the glamour of the great orchestras, and do not seem to attract star conductors. Everyone is more or less aware that broadcasting is not the vehicle for an individual wishing to increase his prestige.'[26] But Paul's own enormous ego and ambition would fuel the transformation of the RÉSO, in

23 *Irish Times*, 30 November 1966. **24** *Irish Times*, 30 December 1965. The tone of this editorial suggests that it had been at least influenced, if not actually written, by Charles Acton. **25** *RTV Guide*, 29 October 1965. **26** In Lionel Salter (rapporteur), *EBU: Symposium on the Future of Radio Orchestras*, p. 41. Boulez was Principal Conductor of the BBCSO 1971–5.

particular, into an international ensemble, at the expense of the RÉLO which would be relegated to studio work far below the standard and status of its previous variegated output.

He was successful in attracting some of the world's top-class soloists to work with the RTÉSO (the orchestra added 'Telefís' to its title in 1966). When Howard Hartog, of the London agency Ingpen and Williams, sent a list of suggested soloists for the 1962–3 season, Paul replied: 'The names you suggest are not suitable for our coming season as they are pretty unknown in Ireland. You will no doubt understand that as television started in this country in January we have now to compete with this very new attraction.'[27] When Hartog then offered pianists Monique Haas and Alexis Weissenberg, and violinist Manoug Parikian, Paul still found them insufficiently attractive.[28] He wanted, but could not obtain, the services of pianists Claudio Arrau, Wilhelm Backhaus and Vladimir Ashkenazy, guitarists Julian Bream and Andrés Segovia, singers Elizabeth Schwartzkopf and Leontyne Price, violinist Ruggiero Ricci, and of Paul Sacher, the Swiss conductor and music patron. Others who eluded him were conductors Antal Dorati and Pierre Monteux and composer Paul Hindemith. Otto Klemperer was quite frank about the proposition: his daughter replied to Paul's enquiry 'Thank you for your letter regarding Dublin, which – however – does not interest my Father.'[29] In some cases they were simply unavailable; in others, the fees they demanded were excessive – Segovia, for example, asked for 500 guineas merely for a television recording, and Schwartzkopf quoted 1000 guineas to sing in the Beethoven 'Missa Solemnis'.[30] But in his early years Paul did succeed in hiring, among others, pianists John Ogdon (twice) and Paul Badura-Skoda, with cellist Tortelier making a return visit to Dublin. And he was able to decline the services of conductors Edgar Cosma and Serge Commissiona when they were offered by the Finzi agency in 1963, although the former had conducted two concerts at the Phoenix Hall in February and March 1962.[31]

Despite recognising the power and competition of television, however, Paul did little or nothing to meet its challenges, or to harness its potential. In the drama department, after the departure in 1964 of the first Head of Drama, Hilton Edwards, there was a distinct realisation that conventional stage techniques must give way to the new possibilities of the camera, and thus to transform the reception of drama *via* the medium of television. But, with the sole

27 Tibor Paul to Howard Hartog, 13 June 1962, RTÉ Music Department file 'Ingpen and Williams'. 28 Hartog to Paul, 28 August 1962, ibid. 29 Klemperer quoted by Ibbs and Tillett to Tibor Paul, 1 November 1962 in RTÉ Music Department file 'Ibbs and Tillett'. 30 Information from ibid., correspondence file 1962–65. 31 T. Paul to Finzi, 1 August 1963, RTÉ Music Department file, 'Finzi agency'. Cosma's concert on 23 February 1962 included Enescu's symphony no. 1.

exception of Potter's opera *Patrick*, the presentation of music on television evaded Paul's imagination. Although he succeeded in organising symphony concerts and chamber music from the television studio, his relations with the television administration (primarily the first Controller, Michael Barry, and his successor, Gunnar Rugheimer) were frosty, and with individual producers ranged from the tentative to the offensive. He rightly criticised problems with sound quality in television recordings – which was a persistent complaint throughout the 1970s – and also early learning difficulties with vision mixing, but the basic lack of sympathy and understanding between 'Television' and 'Music' led to mutual opposition and, in Charles Acton's view, 'resulted in a determination by everyone concerned with the practicalities of tv to have nothing to do with the orchestra if they could help it'.[32]

With Television as the new wonder, able to assume immediate superiority to the 'senior service' of Radio, it was unfortunate, to say the least, that it had not proved systemically possible to integrate the role of music broadcasting into television *ab initio*. Neverthless, Paul did succeed in setting up a series of orchestral concerts, 'Music in View', and a fortnightly chamber music recital, 'Music Room', from the autumn of Telefís Éireann's inaugural year, while the RÉLO appeared in 'Music from Montrose' on a monthly basis. Paul congratulated Anne Makower (the producer with whom he seemed to establish the best rapport) on her visual achievement: 'for the first time the Orchestra looked like a large symphony orchestra and not a chamber orchestra'.[33] Despite his difficulties with the medium, Paul had ambitious but conservative plans for television which were largely frustrated. In addition to regular symphonic fare, he intended to record works by Irish composers including Boydell's 'Megalithic Ritual Dances', May's 'Songs from Prison', Harty's 'With the Wild Geese', his 'Irish' symphony and 'The Children of Lir', McNulty's 'Four Provinces', Victory's 'Enchanted Garden' and Potter's 'Overture to a Kitchen Comedy'.

But when Paul pulled off a coup in engaging top-flight artists, such as José Iturbi, Pierre Fournier and Hephzibah Menuhin, to appear as soloists in televised concerts, Michael Barry pointed out that 'it is of the essence that these programmes be designed in such a way as to appeal to the largest public audience. This is the *only* reason why I have sanctioned the high cost involved in procuring big name soloists. From the point of view of television there can be no other approach to this matter, and both the programme selection and the presentation must have only one purpose in mind, namely, to appeal to a popular audience'.[34] When Paul objected to a series of television decisions on which

32 Acton to Hugh Corr, 9 March 1981 (Acton Archive). 33 Paul to Makower, 20 March 1963, RTÉ Music Department file 'Correspondence with Controller of Programmes Television up to December 1964'. 34 Barry to Paul, 23 May 1964, ibid.

he had not been consulted, including the engagement of artists, and the quality of some performers, asserting 'the fundamental issue that Music Department is responsible for the musical standard of television as well as on sound' which was 'in practice, being constantly overlooked',[35] he was politely ignored. Although Rugheimer sought to establish 'an effective working liaison' between television producers and the Music Department, with Gerard Victory as the liaison from Music,[36] it was clear from the tone of the memo that, in the event of a dispute over a decision, the television producer's, or Controller's, decision would be final.

It is arguable that if, with his forceful personality, Paul had succeeded in pushing the door to television more effectively open for the music department, there could have evolved a genre of televisual treatment of orchestral concerts, opera and chamber music, at the vital formative stage of RTÉ's understanding of what could be achieved through the new medium. Yet the few instances when television was attempted proved that Paul's personality was an obstacle and an irritant to the pursuit of sensible programming. It remained for individual producers such as Makower, Bill Skinner and, later, Louis Lentin, to demonstrate enthusiasm and initiative in regard to televising music, and usually with insufficient collaboration between Television and Music to effect an integrated production.

In 1963, at the end of his first full year as Director of Music, Paul reported on his progress. He claimed (although there must have been sleight of hand in the accounting) that for the first time the 'Proms' had broken even; and he drew attention to the concert soloists including Hephzibah Menuhin,[37] Badura-Skoda, Tortelier, Hugh Maguire, Bernadette Greevy and Mary Gallagher. Overall, 'the majority of the RÉSO conserts were conducted by Tibor Paul, but arrangements were made to ensure that local conductors [including Ó Broin, Boydell, Groocock, Doyle, Ó Duinn and Michael Murtagh] were represented'. He reported that he hoped to expand public concert activity because, in its monopoly situation, RÉ 'has a strong obligation to provide the orchestra in public concerts as far as possible', and also because 'programmes of the quality and calibre obtained from these concerts *could not be obtained* from the ordinary studio performances'. He also claimed that he had given, or facilitated, the Irish premières of Mahler's 'Das Lied von der Erde', Stravinsky's 'Rite of Spring', Kodály's 'Psalmus Hungaricus', Bartók's 'Miraculous Mandarin'

35 Paul to Rugheimer, 28 October 1963, RTÉ Music Department file 'Sundry Internal Correspondence 1963–66'. 36 Rugheimer to Television staff, 13 January 1964, 'Correspondence ...' 37 Hephzibah Menuhin performed three times in concert with the RÉSO: Mozart's concerto K.414 on 30 September (Dublin) and 1 October (Cork) 1962 and Bartók's second on 2 February 1964.

and Blacher's 'Concertante Musik', and new works by Irish composers: Boydell's 'Mors et Vita', Bodley's 'Divertimento for strings', Victory's 'Short symphony' and Ó Duinn's string quartet. Nevertheless, shortage of new Irish works had led to the re-introduction of the Carolan Prize (Paul phrased this to suggest that he himself had introduced it, whereas in fact it long pre-dated his appointment) and that the prize in 1963 would be awarded for a work on the theme 'Amhrán Dochais' – which would be won by John Purser, with Bernard Geary placed second.

Paul then moved to address chamber music, disingenuously suggesting that his relations with the String Quartet were successful, and praising it for its European tour. On the subject of Vocal Music, he advised that the Singers had appeared in Derry ('the first time outside the Republic') and that they had performed Raymond Warren's chamber oratorio 'The Passion'. As we have seen, he took great pride in asserting the importance of the Singers' first foreign tour. But his assertion that 'a major change in policy was the concentration on serious music and folksongs, with a weekly series, "Nocturne"' makes one wonder how short were the memories of those to whom this was addressed, since there had in fact been no such change in policy.

Paul was also adept at stating the opposite of the truth: in this report, he said 'We are the only department in Radio Éireann, apart from the Sports Department, which handles programmes on both sound and television. [It should be recalled that RÉ and Telefís Eireann were, technically, separate organisations.] The Music Department used this facility to make the television a complementary service to the sound programmes … The same programmes were used jointly on sound and television on different dates, and were designed to introduce serious music on the new medium in such a way as to reach the homes of people who had never before attended concerts'.[38]

RTÉ's Festival of Music in June 1963 was a major international event for Ireland, with Igor Stravinsky and his assistant Robert Craft conducting Stravinsky's own works, and another concert featuring the legendary American pianist Van Cliburn with Rachmaninov's third concerto; both concerts took place in Dublin's Adelphi Cinema in the absence of any other suitable venue of sufficient size. Craft conducted Stravinsky's 'Le baiser de la fée' and Stravinsky himself directed his Variations on Bach's 'Von Himmel-Hoch' and the 'Symphony of Psalms', with the RÉ Choral Society and RÉ Singers.[39] A

38 T. Paul, 'Music Department Report for the Year 1962–63', 6 May 1963, 12pp. typescript.
39 Stravinsky's fee was $3000. He declined to receive an honorary degree from the NUI on the grounds that he had also chosen not to accept one from either Oxford or Cambridge university: Paul to Séamus Wilmot (Registrar of NUI) 3 May 1963.

third Dublin concert, featuring violinist Nathan Milstein and conductor Anatole Fistoulari, was cancelled due to Milstein suffering from bursitis.[40] The Munich Philharmonic Piano Quartet and the RÉ String Quartet performed in the ballroom of the Shelbourne Hotel, the former featuring a contemporary work (piano quartet, 1935) by Kurt Hessenberg (1908–94), at that time professor of composition at the Frankfurt Musikhochschule, and the latter Brian Boydell's first quartet (1949). Paul's and RTÉ's commitment to Cork, as part of the Festival, was demonstrated in a concert there dedicated to the 150th anniversary of Wagner's birth, with Wagner specialist soprano Astrid Varnay, then at the peak of her career (although it was not the first target for an out-of-Dublin dimension to the Festival, which had been planned for a performance of Verdi's Requiem with Our Lady's Choral Society in Mullingar Cathedral, which was refused by the church authorities, much to Paul's chagrin).

It seems that Paul was not even content with having secured Stravinsky – arguably the greatest living composer at that time – and as late as December 1962 he had written to the London agents Ibbs and Tillett: 'An urgent matter! Dublin Festival 1963. Would it be possible to have Peter Pears and Benjamin Britten?'[41] Neither was available. But to have succeeded in putting together such a programme, with such eminent artists, was a major achievement on Paul's part. Not alone was the level of musical accomplishment one of the most distinguished to which Irish audiences had ever been exposed, but the imagination of the event, reflected even in the design and typography of the festival programme book, was a mark of where Paul's artistic vision might lead in Irish music-making. RTÉ could justifiably state, in the words of its Director-General, Kevin McCourt, that the Festival would bring Ireland

> into line with the practice of most European nations ... Never before in Ireland has a programme of concerts by such distinguished artists been presented in so short a space of time ... I think I can assure all the overseas visitors to the festival that they will be well rewarded for their journeys ... They will be warmly welcomed by a country long famous for its scenery, its hospitality, its wealth of folk-song and tradition – and now rapidly establishing itself in the international field as a notable centre of concert and operatic activity.[42]

For future Festivals Paul tried, without success, to engage singer Dietrich Fischer-Dieskau and conductor Antal Dorati (he almost succeeded in the latter case) and to commission Paul Hindemith to write a work – Hindemith was

40 Wilfrid van Wyck to Tibor Paul, 4 June 1964, Music Department file 'Wilfrid van Wyck'.
41 Paul to Ibbs and Tillett, 7 December 1962, RTÉ Music Department file, 'Ibbs and Tillett'.
42 In an advertising brochure prior to the Festival.

interested but too busy. His attempts, and the artists' demurrals, are typical of the ambitions and frustrations attendant on any effort to mount artistic events of the highest standard.

Behind the scenes of the 1963 Festival, moreover, there had been serious complications which demonstrate the difficulties of artistic personalities which are frequently to be encountered in the engagement and presentation of musicians. Ironically, the complications in this instance relate to the concert which never was – featuring Nathan Milstein, the Ukrainian-born violin virtuoso, now a US citizen. The initial difficulty was the size of Milstein's fee: his agent, Wilfrid van Wyck, had told Paul 'there is no hope whatever that he would agree to make two appearances for an inclusive fee of £400',[43] to which Paul replied 'Many thanks for your letter. How much?'[44] and was told 'not less than 500 guineas'.[45] Paul's reply read: 'I must congratulate him on having such a marvellous impressario [*sic*] to put his fees up to such a high level',[46] to which van Wyck, who was well-known for being a very hard bargainer on behalf of his clients, testily retorted 'Milstein sets his own fees and, as you know, is not an easy man to deal with at the best of times!'[47] The fee was for a single concert, whereas Paul had wanted Milstein to repeat the Dublin concert in Cork. 'There is no hope of Milstein giving two concerts for 500 guineas. You must face the fact that he will want this for one appearance in Dublin, otherwise you had better abandon the idea' was van Wyck's characteristic comment.[48]

A second difficulty was Milstein's choosiness about the conductors with whom he would agree to play. Paul had already tried, and failed, to engage either Rudolf Kempe or Igor Markevich, and Milstein vetoed Eugene Ormandy; in the outcome Milstein agreed to work with Anatole Fistoulari. This in turn caused further problems, since Paul was anxious for Fistoulari to perform an Irish work, suggesting Fleischmann's 'Four Masters' overture. As Paul wrote to van Wyck,

> It is customary … We have had several guest conductors in the last seasons, e.g. Hans Schmidt-Isserstedt, Enrique Jorda, Sir John Barbirolli, Jean Fournet, Maurice le Roux, Louis Fremaux, etc., and not one ever refused to honour the country in this way. As you know, Mr Fistoulari was not our choice but we were pressed to take him by Mr Milstein. I am sorry to say that neither of Mr Fistoulari's programme suggestions would suit in our Fesival. If he does not wish to conduct the Fleischmann overture, we can perhaps supply him with some other Irish scores, but

43 Van Wyck to Paul, 16 November 1962, RTÉ Music Department file, 'Milstein'. 44 Paul to van Wyck, 22 November 1962, ibid. 45 Van Wyck to Paul, 24 November 1962, ibid. 46 Paul to van Wyck, 26 November 1962, ibid. 47 Van Wyck to Paul, 28 November 1962, ibid. 48 Van Wyck to Paul, 31 November 1962, RTÉ Music Department file 'Wilfrid van Wyck'.

I am afraid that if he is reluctant to do so my Directors will insist on asking Mr Milstein to agree to another conductor.[49]

Fistoulari considered that the work by Fleischmann 'is not a work with which he is in sympathy'.[50] Paul persisted, and one can detect genuine concern on his part that the principle of reciprocity, and a courteous gesture to the host country, should underpin a highly visible support by RTÉ for Irish composers:

> I am perfectly aware as a conductor that these Irish composers are neither Beethoven nor Mozart ... When I conducted two years ago a Festival concert in Scheveningen in Holland I was also asked at the last minute to start the programme ... [with] a Dutch work of which I also didn't think very much. Still, as it was a Holland Festival, I would not have dreamt of refusing ...
>
> You can still tell him that the Fleischmann score which he sent back would be, in my opinion, the best choice, and as it is an overture it does not matter very much.[51]

Paul then asked his new assistant (and eventual successor) Gerard Victory, to send Fistoulari the scores of May's 'Spring Nocturne', Potter's 'Rhapsody under a High Sky' and 'Overture to a Kitchen Comedy', Havelock Nelson's Sinfonietta and Ó Riada's 'Hercules Dux Ferrariae'. Victory put forward his personal view of the Ó Riada piece as having been 'performed with success on the Continent and is most unusual and striking in effect'.[52] None of this was of any avail: the concert which they would have played – had Milstein not cancelled – consisted of Tchaikovsky's 'Romeo and Juliet' and Brahms' first symphony framing the Tchaikovsky violin concerto.

It was not the only occasion on which Paul encountered resistance from visiting artists to performing Irish works. At about the same time, the Basque harpist Nicanor Zabaleta (1907–93), then at the peak of his powers and acknowledged as the greatest harpist in the world, was envisaged for a Dublin concert. 'As you probably know', Paul told van Wyck, 'this artiste has taken an interest in a work by Dr Walter Beckett, an Irish composer, and we would like to know when he will be able to spare the time to learn this work, in which

---

49 Paul to van Wyck, 1 January 1963, ibid. Fistoulari had suggested Tchaikovsky's fantasy overture 'Romeo and Juliet', the overture to Wagner's *Tannhäuser*, Berlioz' 'Roman Carnival', Borodin's 'In the Steppes of Central Asia', Weber's overture to *Oberon* and Liadov's overture 'The Enchanted Lake', which, as a collection of small-scale pieces, did not amount to a substantial programme. 50 Van Wyck to Paul, 1 January 1963, ibid. 51 Paul to van Wyck, 6 April 1963, ibid. 52 Victory to Fistoulari, 8 April 1963, ibid. The work had appealed to Carlo Franci, who had conducted it several times and recorded it with the LPO.

case we would be glad to incorporate him into our season.'[53] The work was most likely a version of Beckett's 'A Suite of Planxties'. Van Wyck's tart reply was: 'he has been too busy to learn it. You will, I feel sure, understand that an artist of Mr Zabaleta's age and distinction cannot allow an engagement for him to be dependent on whether or not he agreed to learn a particular work'.[54] Another opportunity to introduce an Irish work to the international repertoire was lost, and Dublin would not hear Zabaleta until 1969.[55]

These exchanges help to negate the commonly held idea that Paul had no interest in Irish composers, which is also contradicted by Table M (pp. 456–9), which shows that, contrary to popular belief, there was little diminution in the works by Irish composers performed during his 'reign'. It should also be remarked that, while Paul was anxious to secure world-name performers, he also paid special attention to Irish soloists of merit. Possibly the most outstanding of these was soprano Veronica Dunne, of whom he wrote after a performance of Verdi's Requiem: 'We had an impressive performance ... at which the two Irish soloists [Dunne and Bernadette Greevy] for the first time outclassed the visitors ... After the excellent singing of Veronica Dunne ... we all agreed that she [should be engaged] as the Countess in "Figaro"'.[56]

In following years, Paul was once again unsuccessful in obtaining either Ricci or Arrau, and failed to attract pianist Emil Gilels and violinist Wolfgang Schneiderhan.[57] But in 1964 Yehudi Meuhin played the Beethoven violin concerto and Geza Anda played the second Brahms piano concerto (Dublin and Cork), while Julius Katchen returned to Ireland for another Beethoven cycle at the National Stadium, playing all five piano concertos in a series of three concerts which also included the third, fourth and eighth symphonies. In 1966 Henryk Szeryng played the Mendelssohn violin concerto (which he would repeat in Dublin and Galway in 1975). In 1965, in a departure from the normal concert schedule, Wilhelm Kempff, with whom Paul had worked in Bordeaux two years previously, came for a 'Prom' at the Gaiety (Beethoven, 'Emperor') and, the following day, played the Schumann piano concerto at the Saint Francis Xavier Hall (SFX) in Dublin's Upper Sherrard Street, which had become the RTÉSO's studio in 1962 and in which it remained until its transfer to the National Concert Hall. Kempff had previously refused to travel to Ireland because he could not trust weather conditions for his onward journey

---

53 Paul to van Wyck, 4 October 1962, ibid. 54 Van Wyck to Paul, 8 October 1962, ibid. 55 On 23 March 1969 he played the Ginastera concerto with Albert Rosen conducting. 56 Paul to Michael Rainer (Organisation Artistique Internationale, Paris) 30 September 1963. Dunne had sung opera since her earliest days as a student in Rome: for the DGOS she sang Micaela in *Carmen* (1950), Nedda in *I pagliacci* (1955), Antonia in *Tales of Hoffman* (1957), Mimi in *La bohème* and Elvira in *Don Giovanni* (1965) as well as singing opposite Kathleen Ferrier and Joan Sutherland at Covent Garden. 57 Information from RTÉ Music Department file, 'Harold Holt'.

to his next engagement; Paul's reply to Kempff's agent indicates his anxious-
ness to dispel the obvious assumptions:

> Je serais très reconnaissant si vous pourriez approcher Monsieur Kempff
> un fois de plus pour lui dire que maintenant Aer Lingus Irish
> International Airlines a un très grand nombre de vols que travers le
> monde entière. En effet, en fevrier il peut aller direct de Dublin à
> Amsterdam … Aussi vous pouvez lui assurer que je fais pas mal de voy-
> ages par avion entre Dublin et Europe et quoique on trouve London
> Airport en panne au cause de brouillard, il y a jamais du brouillard a
> Dublin – nous n'avons pas du brouillard dans ce pays.[58]

At the conclusion of the 1963 Music Festival Paul had reported that one of
his aims had been 'to fill the gap of non-activity between the winter and autumn
concert seasons' – a strategy that would be ultimately achieved by RTÉ when
the NSO transferred to the NCH and withdrew from the Dublin opera seasons, thus allowing an almost unbroken annual concert season. Paul justified
the expense and the administrative headaches, but blamed RÉ's publicity
department for lack of exposure, which he believed had contributed to disappointing box-office returns. 'Concert promotion is a highly specialised and
technical business and we would, it appears, need better planning and liaison
as regards publicity on future occasions. This applies, of course, not only to
the Festival but to all public concerts throughout the year'.[59]

Paul's own repertoire inclined towards the classical, but in his first two seasons
as a guest conductor he had also been responsible for introducing some more
unusual and contemporary works to Ireland, as he did as Principal Conductor.
From his native Hungary he brought Kodály's 'Háry János' suite in September
1959, which he would repeat at his second concert as Principal (on 22
September 1961), and Bartók's 'Divertimento'. Also in 1959, the contemporary 'Symphonic Music' (1957) by Marius Flothuis, Barraud's third symphony
(1957), Hartmann's third symphony (1948–9); in 1960, Egk's 'French Suite',
Willem van Otterloo's Sinfonietta for Wind (1943), Clive Douglas' 'Essay for
strings' (1952), Theodore Karyotakis' 'Suite for orchestra' (1946) and, in 1961,
John Antill's ballet suite 'Corroboree' (1946). Among the modern classics which

---

58 T. Paul to Kiesgen agency, 10 March 1964, RTÉ Music Department file, 'Kiesgen'. [I would
be very grateful if you would contact Mr Kempff again to tell him that Aer Lingus has a large
number of flights throughout the world. In fact, in February he can fly direct from Dublin to
Amsterdam. Also you could assure him that I have no trouble with planes between Dublin and
Europe – although London Airport can be closed due to fog, there is never fog in Dublin – we
don't have fog in his country.] **59** T. Paul, 'Festival Appraisal', 9 July 1963, 5pp. typescript.

were as yet almost unheard in Ireland, he performed Richard Strauss' 'Also Sprach Zarathustra', Stravinsky's 'Capriccio' (with Margaret Kitchin as piano soloist), Hindemith's 'Sinfonia Serena', Prokofiev's 'Peter and the Wolf' (narrated by Brian Boydell), Martinů's oboe concerto (with Evelyn Rothwell), Liszt's 'Totentanz' (Charles Lynch) and 'Les Préludes'.

Irish works included Potter's ballet suite 'Careless Love' (in both 1960 and '62) and his version of the 'Bouquet pour la fête de Son Excellence Monsignor le Cardinal de Fleury' of 1741 by the Irish-Frenchman, Henri Madden; Duff's 'Irish Suite' and 'Echoes of Georgian Dublin', Stanford's first Irish Rhapsody, Fleischmann's 'Lament for Elizabeth McDermott Roe', Boydell's 'Shielmartin suite',[60] and the première of Victory's 'Rapparee' overture.

Paul's first concert as Principal Conductor, on 15 September 1961, featured Bach's Brandenburg Concerto no. 4 (soloists Geraldine O'Grady, violin and André Prieur and Hans Kohlmann, flutes), Dittersdorf's symphony and Haydn's symphony no. 82. After his appointment came into effect, he continued the introduction of Hungarian works, with Kodály's symphony and his 'Psalmus Hungaricus' and Bartók's third piano concerto with Paul Badura-Skoda as soloist. Other contemporary works were Barraud's String Symphony (1955–6), Rivier's flute concerto (1956; soloist, André Prieur), Egk's 'Temptation of St Anthony' (1947; alto solo Ruth Maher), and Lex van Delden's concerto for two string orchestras, performed the year after its composition. Paul signalled his 1963 Festival, featuring Stravinsky, with the Irish première of the 'Rite of Spring'. Other large-scale works in his first year were Berlioz' 'Harold in Italy' (with Máire Larchet in the solo viola part), and Richard Strauss's 'Ein Heldenleben', of which he gave two performances, in 1961 and '62. His connection with Irish composition continued with the 'Short Symphony' (no. 1) by Victory and the première of Seóirse Bodley's 'Divertimento'.

ORCHESTRAL MANOEUVRES

Despite the artistic successes being notched up by Tibor Paul, a serious question-mark was hanging over the existence of the Symphony Orchestra, quite apart from that hanging over Paul himself. In early 1966 the DG (Kevin McCourt) was asking the Authority to take a policy decision along the same lines as that requested by Roth less than five years previously. Pointing out that the proportion of Irish to foreign players in both orchestras had diminished

---

60 Commissioned by the BBC for performance in its 1960 Festival of Light Music by the BBC Concert Orchestra, and the only work in which Boydell ever consciously employed an Irish folk melody.

from 59:40 in 1959 to 70:33, he neverthless observed that it was unrealistic to have expected that an all-Irish orchestra could ever be achieved, and went on to pose the question:

> I am not sure at this stage as to what is the purpose of our orchestras – is it to provide the best possible standards of music in the interest of cultural development of the nation or is it to have an all-Irish orchestra knowing that this could only be achieved by a reduction in musical standards? ... A clear definition of Authority policy will have to be given, namely, do we go for a prestige orchestra capable of the highest possible performance within our financial resources or do we deliberately set out to find young Irish musicians, train them and gradually dispense with imported musicians with whatever may be the consequential drop in musical standards[?][61]

Clearly, the intervening five years had not produced an answer to Roth's implied questions, and it cannot therefore be presumed that the events of 1966–7 were entirely due to Paul's overweening behaviour towards either his superiors or members of the Symphony Orchestra.

McCourt's own questions had been brought to a head by the revival of the debate on music education and the desirability or otherwise of having a fully Irish orchestra. IFMAP had submitted a lengthy document to RTÉ in October 1965, which referred to the failure of the policy of importing foreign musicians to the orchestra with the further purpose of teaching Irish students. It made the contrary point that 'continued importation retards cultural development in Ireland ... RÉ has a central role in determining Irish musical standards and its policies are of national concern ... Irish musical prestige cannot be raised with an orchestra more than half of whom are foreign. The use of foreigners should be restricted to teaching in a Conservatoire'. It made the further point that, with the increase in record sales and the gradual extinction of the theatre orchestras, there was an even greater focus on RTÉ as a provider of jobs.[62]

> We are not actuated [*sic*] by any spirit of narrow nationalism but rather with the object of encouraging cultural development in Ireland. To raise standards at the expense of practising and potential Irish musicians by the recruitment of foreign players will do nothing for the musical health of the nation at large ... It is scarcely necessary to emphasise the impor-

61 McCourt to Éamonn Andrews, Chairman of the RTÉ Authority, 20 January 1966. 62 IFMAP memorandum 7 October 1965.

tance of Radio Éireann, both in view of the control which it exercises over the survival and quality of the music profession in Ireland, its influence on musical standards, the education and musical taste of the population and because of the part it plays in establishing the prestige of Ireland and of Irish culture in other countries.[63]

Quoting a Dáil speech of Erskine Childers from 1953, to the effect that 'the future of this country depends much upon the abandonment of the avoidably mediocre' and that standards must be raised in the variety and quality of RÉ performances 'since broadcasting affects all music',[64] IFMAP continued:

The mistake has been made in the past, and is still being made, of attempting to raise standards not by providing better facilities for native practising musicians but by a decision not to employ them ... Indeed, the higher standards required were erected upon the privations of those who, very often, for unspectacular earnings, had kept music alive in the dark days. Standards should not be set at the expense of fundamentals. If musical opinion does not come out strongly on our side it is because musical opinion tends to be articulated by people who are drawn from the more leisured classes – classes to whom the sheer question of bread and butter has never starkly manifested itself. There can be little doubt that the treatment meted out to Irish musicians would provoke violent conflict if it were attempted in an industrial context. The truth is that there is little honour in 'avoiding the mediocre' in one sphere by employing methods which are regarded as being decidedly below the mediocre in another ...

Permanent standards cannot be imposed. They grow up from the soil of a country – they are achieved by providing the musically gifted members of the community with expert tuition and suitable employment opportunity ... There is a dogged pursuit of standards when the general musical condition of the country cries out for the simple rudiments of education ... If we want to establish ourselves as a musical nation, the way lies through the education of our people and the affording of opportunities to young and promising musicians to advancement ... The process will be slow and unspectacular, but in the long run other countries might be more impressed by a nation in its shirt sleeves rather than by imported expertise ... [Young Irish musicians] should not have to wait until the struggle for existence has dulled their sensibility and vitality.[65]

63 Ibid. 64 Childers had been speaking on the Estimates for broadcasting, DD. 142, 10 November 1953, col. 1766. 65 Ibid.

Based on this emotive memorandum, in January 1966 Tibor Paul convened a meeting representative of the music teaching profession, including the directors of the Dublin and Cork colleges of music, the secretary and professor of composition of the RIAM, the professors of music from UCD, TCD, UCC and Maynooth, and two inspectors from the Department of Education. By way of greeting, Paul stated that the reasons for the meeting were 'very urgent and critical'. He put it to the meeting that RÉ's twin responsibilities were not always compatible: 'the first is to maintain and improve the artistic standards expected of us as a national organisation in a world where such standards are continually rising. The second duty is ... to employ at all costs, the maximum number of Irish performers consonant with the maintenance of these standards'. Paul went on to say that 'recognition of Irish musical acievement abroad has never been so high ... Irish serious composers are obtaining wider recognition and world name musicians have become aware of our standing and are anxious more and more to come here and perform for us'. However, he warned, 'There are signs that unless something is done urgently, this progress may be impeded and indeed reversed by the growing shortage of young players available ... This shortage – especially in the strings sections – is of course symptomatic of a world shortage of string players and a sharply growing competition everywhere for players of talent.'[66] He asked for all parties to co-operate in resolving this difficulty, and it was agreed by the RIAM and the Dublin College that their senior students would amalgamate to form 'the nucleus of a National Youth Orchestra or Training Orchestra which could tour and fill many of the gaps in provincial performances ... Such an undertaking would, however, have to become a professional one with some form of suitable salary (say £10 per week)'.[67] As no such action resulted from this meeting, it is assumed that the schools of music eventually resisted this proposal – it would be 1996 before the orchestral forces of the RIAM and the DIT would amalgamate for a single concert.[68]

On the same day, and also in direct response to the IFMAP document, the Director of Personnel advised the DG that

> The Federation would presumably argue that our standards are too high and that we should drop them to take Irish players in preference to importing foreigners. They would further argue that these Irish play-

---

[66] Minutes of meeting of 19 January 1966 (Potter Archive). [67] Ibid. [68] On that occasion, Charles Acton wrote to James Cavanagh, the RIAM conductor, that if he were still writing reviews 'I would have praised you for ... getting such sensitive and unanimous playing from *one* student orchestra, let alone from two separate ones together, and for such a rewarding performance ... I also found myself thinking back to the late 1940s and realising that the then RÉSO could not have been relied on to give such a performance': Acton postcard to Cavanagh, 1 February 1996 (Acton Archive).

ers will, in time, reach the standard or, if not, that at least we will have a truly Irish orchestra, emanating from an Irish culture. This culture, in turn, will be stimulated because of the openings we provide. Herein lies the nub of the issue … We have an eminent foreign conductor who appears to have a mandate to recruit and train the finest orchestras possible within certain financial, but not national, constraints. [If the policy were changed in favour of Irish musicians] would a conductor of international repute allow himself to be associated with a 'sub-standard' orchestra? Would the present 'high standard' Irish players stay with the orchestra or would they feel the need to move to another where they would be playing with people of their own calibre?[69]

He also reported to the Controller of Radio that he had attended a meeting with the DG and deputy DG:

We discussed in general terms the feasibility of ever having an orchestra of high standard, how this might be brought about, including the formation of a junior orchestra, and the total effort which we might have to make in RTÉ in the development of particular talents. Clearly anything which we might be inclined to do for musicians would have to be considered in the general context of developing many necessary talents throughout the organisation.[70]

Once again, we have to realise that RTÉ, as a complex broadcasting system, could not be seen to give priority to specialised training in one area without taking an overall view of its training needs, especially given that in television, which was only four years old, skills were still being acquired and honed as new technologies came onstream, not only in Ireland but worldwide.

Our discussions tended to suggest that the line of reproach [*sic*] which might give us the best return for any money which we would spend, would be to concentrate on helping selected promising students with the aim of bringing them to the standard required … including if necessary a period of training abroad … Do we know … the approximate numbers of really promising students in the Academy and elsewhere who might, with help, develop to the standard required[?] … Do we know … which instruments they are studying? What amounts of training would need to be provided …? What kind of help would be necessary and what would it cost us?

---

69 MacNeill to DG 19 January 1966, file H/E/1: 'Employment of non-nationals in the orchestra, 23.7.63–16.9.70'. **70** MacNeill to Ó Faracháin, 1 March 1966, ibid.

> Could we attempt a projection for a few years ahead in which we would estimate the cost of the help ... and the extent to which there would be an increase in Irish membership in the orchestras?[71]

Whether or not the Personnel Director was aware that Paul had held such a meeting on that same day is unclear, but the fact that the issue was being addressed simultaneously both within the Music Department and by senior management is indicative of the extent to which it was being recognised – even though, as we have seen, that recognition had been voiced, but insufficiently addressed, as much as thirty years previously.

The Personnel memo, and perhaps some communication from Paul, prompted the DG to contact the Chairman, pointing out

> If we got rid of all foreigners from the orchestras tomorrow, particularly from the Symphony Orchestra, we could not replace them within the country; if we set ourselves a target of getting rid of foreigners, say, within a three or a five-year period, a costly and troublesome training scheme for musicians capable of playing different types of instruments would have to be inaugurated, and I think that any musician would say that, even then, it would have to be accepted that standards would appreciably reduce. The complications, contentions, and contradictory subjective judgements in this whole issue of standards of music and the training of Irish musicians because we wanted all Irish are, to say the least, deterring.[72]

The concept of RTÉ becoming involved in music education, if only for its own purposes, was once more – but not for the last time – dropped, but would resurface as a fundamental issue at the time of the PIANO review and today continues to vex the question of employment opportunities for would-be Irish orchestral musicians.[73]

However, the composition of the RTÉ orchestras was perhaps of less significance than their very existence, which was threatened at the same stage as this debate was taking place, by the financial position of the organisation as a whole. As early as January 1966, John Irvine (deputy DG) had written to McCourt

> It is not inappropriate to observe that Radio Éireann's own attitude in the last few years towards the orchestra has been one of reluctant own-

---

71 Ibid.   72 DG to Chairman, 20 January 1966, ibid.   73 As will be evident from discussion of the PIANO report, the author was – and is – personally involved in the initiative of establishing a national training orchestra.

ership and responsibility. It has been finding it hard to shoulder the big unavoidable cost increases that have taken place and it has been directing its energies along the lines of ultimately getting itself relieved of the major responsibility for the orchestra.[74]

Only six weeks previously, the RTÉ Authority, discussing the Broadcasting Authority (Amendment) Bill, 1965, had come to the conclusion that radio and television could not continue to operate independently, and that advertising revenue from television was essential to sustain extended radio hours; furthermore, the Government must relieve RTÉ of most of the annual costs of the RÉSO.[75]

In its Annual Report for 1966 RTÉ specifically stated that in view of its ongoing losses, it had to consider whether it could afford to sustain the RTÉSO: the cost of £170k 'is naturally militating against a better utilisation of radio income for the expanding needs of the radio service. It is the Authority's view that the future arrangements in relation to the Kennedy Memorial Hall should provide for the association of the symphony orchestra with that undertaking.'[76] A year later, it was sounding even more urgent: 'While the orchestra is an important part of the musical life of the nation … it is clear that the Authority, while bearing the full cost of the orchestra, is, nevertheless, being called upon to subsidise non-broadcasting musical activities at a high rate.'[77]

It might be asked, if Tibor Paul, as both Director of Music and Principal Conductor, was the person responsible for setting and achieving orchestral standards, why he had not been consulted on these matters. In the absence of any personal file relating to Paul, we can only surmise that his exclusion from these discussions was due to the fact that, in parallel, serious objections were being raised not only to Paul's dual mandate but also to his personal and professional manner towards the players. At the annual general meeting of the RTÉ branch of IFMAP (as communicated by them to the DG)[78] it was resolved (echoing the *Irish Times* editorial of four months previously) 'that this meeting considers that the position of Director of Music in Radio Éireann should be separate and distinct from that of Conductor since each of these posts is in itself a whole-time occupation and the qualities required for each are not identical'. In January 1966 (at the exact time that the detailed discussions were being held about the training of musicians) Olive Smith, on behalf of the MAI, had written to the DG supporting IFMAP.[79]

It was not only a question of double-jobbing, or even that each job required distinct skills, but that the power exercised by one person in the two functions

74 Irvine to DG, 19 January 1966, file H/E/1. 75 RTÉ Authority minutes, 1 December 1965. 76 RTÉ Annual Report 1966, p. 8. 77 RTÉ Annual Report 1967, p. 2. 78 IFMAP to DG 29 April 1966, RTÉ file H/E/1: 'Employment of Non-Nationals in the Orchestra 23.7.63–16.9.70'. 79 O. Smith to DG, 25 January 1966.

placed him above scrutiny and beyond appeal. This came to the fore in particular in the case of Thomas Lisenbee, an American trumpeter who had come to Ireland on the recommendation of conductor Eugen Jochum, having spent time with the Concertgebouw as principal trumpet. He had worked with the Israel Philharmonic but 'I am not at all happy with living in the Levant under the guns of 60 million Arabs, nor am I entirely satisfied egotistically and artistically with being an alternate first trumpet.'[80] He had started a two-year contract on 1 September 1964 and resigned at its expiry because, as he wrote in an unprecedented personal letter to the DG:

> I cannot tolerate a system whereby musical and non-musical facets of my employment are decided and considered by the same person; because I cannot remain an artist of integrity within an organization whose attitude seems to be that all solo fees, chamber music fees, and additional weekly allowances are no more than bribes or rewards for 'loyalty' to the Director of Music. In addition I find the Principal Conductor of the RÉSO an ill-mannered person who does not respect the dignity of the individuals with whom he is working. It is a personal principle with me that no man has the right to deliberately inflict misery on his fellows. I therefore accept each insult to a colleague as one to myself. I am so hurt and saddened by the daily spectacle of conductor insulting musicians (who by the way are helpless to pursue the normal avenues of redress, the Principal Conductor being the Director of Music) that I can tolerate it no longer. You cannot expect anyone who has even a modicum of sensitivity and compassion to be able to watch some of his fellow musicians being berated and browbeaten before his eyes … The Radio Éireann Symphony Orchestra is a very unhappy group of individuals. Some of them destroyed as sensitive artists, others are being tortured for retaining artistic sensitivity.[81]

It was equally unprecedented that Kevin McCourt asked to see Lisenbee, ironically offering him extra inducements to stay, but Lisenbee was resolved that only radical administrative change would satisfy him. Another key player, percussionist Freddie Lembens, also resigned in 1966, stating that his decision was attributable solely to Tibor Paul's attitude towards him, and that he would only remain with RTÉ if Paul were to leave. Other players with whom Paul had bad relations were the bassist Jacques Lavaud, whose method of playing in the French style was not to Paul's liking, and Michele Incenzo, since Paul

80 Lisenbee to DG, n.d.. His 'thrilling trumpet playing' had been noted by Charles Acton: *Irish Times* 15 February 1965. **81** Lisenbee to DG, 15 May 1966.

himself had been a clarinettist and 'made life impossible' for the section leader.[82]
Leo Donnelly, newly appointed as Concerts Manager, found it necessary 'to
lodge a strong complaint against Mr Paul's behaviour towards me in the presence of the full Symphony Orchestra … yesterday morning. I was scarcely in
the Theatre when I was bitterly attacked about the seating arrangements for
the American Ambassador for the Van Cliburn concert and when I attempted
to explain the situation, I was shouted down in a storm of abuse … I have gone
a long way in accepting unjustified strictures from Mr Paul … but now I have
reached the limit.'[83] Donnelly's dilemma illustrates perfectly the 'double bind'
in which Paul's underlings found themselves, since the only course of action
open to Gerard Victory, recipient of the memo, was to pen a note: 'Dir. Music:
As discussed. I now forward Mr Donnelly's memo for your consideration' – on
which, of course, Paul would not act.

The loss of key players made replacement difficult, since there was severe
competition for them from bigger, better and more prosperous orchestras, and
one RTÉ administrator told his colleagues 'I have the feeling that the difficulties which Mr Paul is experiencing are, to a fair extent, of his own making.'

Another player with whom Paul had bad relations was János Fürst, who
had been with the Symphony Orchestra since 1958, at the age of twenty-three,
and had been acting leader, in rotation with David Lillis, since late 1965,
although almost at the same time he had been suspended for insubordination,
having been absent without notice. By early 1966 (now aged thirty-one) his
absences – with and without medical certificates – were causing concern, and
it was widely believed that they were due to his freelance work as founder-con-
ductor of the Irish Chamber Orchestra.[84] Fürst, for his part, had alleged that
Tibor Paul was personally prejudiced against him, Paul having requested the

---

82 Fachtna Ó hAnnracháin, interview with the author, 27 May 2003. The two styles of bowing
for the bass – French and German – have invariably caused friction within the section, and
Victory commented on Lavaud (the only player in the RÉSO in the French style) that he never
fully integrated with the rest of the section. **83** Donnelly to Victory, 17 June 1963. Donnelly
(who was succeeded as Concerts Manager by the author in 1974) was one of the first examples
of professionalisation which Tibor Paul introduced to the Music Department (even though his
background was as a clerical officer), a similar appointment being that of Val Keogh as RÉSO
Manager. Donnelly recorded that 'As part of my duties I am obliged to meet all visiting artists
on their arrival in this country, irrespective of time of day or night, or of day of week, take them
to and from place of rehearsal and performance and finally escort them to place of departure.
Occasionally also, if the artists are of high standing in their profession, I take them on local scenic drives. I must also visit the various provincial centres from time to time, to examine and
report on suggested venues for concerts, and for discussion with local music organisations':
Donnelly to Personnel, 10 July 1967. Although the duties of the post were more extensive and
onerous than Donnelly's note suggests, it does give a reasonable sense of the continuous nature
of the work and the call on energies and commitment. **84** MacNeill to Redmond Walsh, 1
April 1966.

termination of a special allowance to Fürst after what he termed his disloyalty to the orchestra and the organisation.

The seventeen-strong ICO, led and conducted by its co-founders, respectively David Lillis and János Fürst, gave its first independent concert in March 1965, including in its programme John Kinsella's new 'Two pieces for string orchestra'. Charles Acton called it 'one of the outstanding events in Dublin's musical history' and suggested that 'If János Fürst and his players can retain this enormous vitality and excitement and their ability to communicate thus the core and soul of the music, there is no reason why they should not be internationally famous. It was not only a joy to be at this event: it may turn out to have been a historical privilege'.[85] When ICO had given further concerts, some in association with the Guinness Choir and Irish Opera Group, Acton was told by Fürst that ICO had had the encouragement of Tibor Paul and RÉ and had been given rehearsal facilities – in return, the standard of ensemble playing in the RÉSO was rising.[86]

Fürst was, of course, window-dressing: not only were the personnel authorities in RÉ becoming increasingly disturbed by his own absences, which they attributed to his freelance conducting, but Paul was anything but pleased by the new departure and, following the ICO's appearance at the RIAM with the Irish Opera Group, RÉ restricted its members' permission to undertake outside work to one concert per month.[87]

Twenty years later, Fürst would admit that the urgency of getting the ICO established (which also gave its members a *frisson* lacking in their relationship with Paul) had contributed to problems with their employer, RTÉ. 'We were getting too big for our boots. It was as simple as that. We were caring too little about our jobs, which was Radio Éireann. They were paying us a full salary and we wanted to play concerts elsewhere and Paul was very irritable ... One of the reasons I left was him. One day ... he said to me, you have a lot of talent but as long as I'm here you won't conduct. And I said, thank you very much for your honesty. One of us will have to leave. So I did.'[88]

Whatever the truth may be about the relationship between the two Hungarians – conductor and leading violinist – there is substantial circumstantial evidence, firstly, that Fürst was representative of a growing dissatisfaction within the orchestra with Paul's behaviour on the podium, and secondly that increasing freelance work with the ICO was impairing the daytime work of a number of players in the RÉSO. Thirdly, however, this was connected with a fresh development which was to have serious complications for RTÉ: the formation, in Northern Ireland, of the 35-strong Ulster Orchestra. Charles

85 *Irish Times*, 22 March 1965. 86 *Irish Times*, 12 October 1965. 87 RTÉ Personnel memo, 31 March 1966. 88 *Music Ireland*, 2/1 (December 1986–January 1987).

Acton, who was later to disclose that Paul 'had consistently opposed' the ICO,[89] was writing with his tongue firmly in hs cheek when, reporting plans for the formation of the Ulster Orchestra, he said 'Belfast is most unlikely to entice RÉSO players away for purely financial reasons'.[90]

At an RTÉ Authority meeting in February 1966, reference was made to the advertisements for the new northern orchestra, and the Chairman, Éamonn Andrews, said that the Minister, Joseph Brennan, had suggested to him that RTÉ might propose the formation of a joint orchestra. The Authority as a whole thought that this was an unlikely proposal.[91]

However, while RTÉ was seeking to discipline Fürst for his apparent unauthorised absences from work, and while he was on sick leave in April 1966, he appeared on BBC television in a feature announcing the formation of the Ulster Orchestra. On 16 April, the *Irish Times* carried a report by Charles Acton with the headline 'János Fürst Appointed as Leader of New Orchestra'.

> János Fürst's first duty will, in fact, be to sit with Maurice Miles [the orchestra's inaugural conductor] and the rest of the audition board ... in Belfast today and Dublin tomorrow ... In an interview Mr Fürst spoke with enthusiasm of having the opportunity of helping, as leader, to build up a new orchestra of quality from the start. A year ago he applied for the then advertised position of leader of the RÉSO. He was glad now that he had not been offered the engagement since the scope of his new appointment would be much wider. He particularly welcomed the North's policy of encouraging the members of the orchestra to form chamber music groups ... This policy, followed by most of the world's leading orchestras, was in marked contrast to Radio Éireann's negative attitude to the Irish Chamber Orchestra ... He was certainly not severing his ties with Dublin. Indeed, he would go on considering himself a Dubliner, and he looked forward to the Irish Chamber Orchestra having a vigorous future before it.[92]

Fürst submitted his resignation to RTÉ two days later. He was followed by several members of the orchestras, including his compatriots János Keszei (timpanist) and Joszef Racz (double bass), by Yvonne McGuinness and Thomas Kelly (violins), Brian Mack (viola) and Maurice Meulien and Brighid Mooney (celli). In mid-June he wrote to the DG asking for a meeting, stating that the motives of himself and of others who were leaving the orchestra had been misunderstood – 'a long line of misunderstandings, misinterpretations, allegations

89 *Irish Times*, 3 June 1976. **90** *Irish Times*, 14 February 1966. **91** RTÉ Authority minutes, 6 February 1966. **92** *Irish Times*, 16 April 1966.

and indeed lies' was responsible for the bad feeling occasioned by his departure: 'there are a lot of aspects of the difficulties and disappointments of the last two years that are not disclosed'[93] – by which he signified the still hidden history of discontent at the iron rule of Tibor Paul. McCourt, though sympathetic, declined to meet him. 'All indications are that he is a good professional and it is a pity that personality problems broke up his relationship with us.'[94]

It was a very serious situation for Paul. Within a few weeks he had lost several key players, many of them as a result of their frustration or dissatisfaction with his direction of the concerts and of the orchestra itself. While, in public, he had been building up the profile of the orchestra by working with international soloists and, eventually, bringing it on its first overseas visit to one of the meccas of classical music, behind the scenes there was confusion on the part of his employers as to whether or not the orchestra should be maintained, and manifest opposition both to his dual function and to the manner of his conduct as *maestro*. In these circumstances, it was inevitable that the Authority should discuss the matter, and, although 'it was difficult to assess the conflicting and emotional evidence which was alleged inside and outside of the organisation of the orchestra's problems', it was faced with the likelihood of further resignations. The Authority backed Kevin McCourt in his view 'that the problems experienced with the Symphony Orchestra significantly arose out of the duality of the appointment held by Tibor Paul' and it was decided to split the positions and to advertise that of Director of Music.[95] A fortnight later, at the end of May, with eight losses from the orchestra (which the Director of Personnel was unsuccessfully attempting to repair by offering higher pay to those who were leaving), McCourt told the Authority 'that Tibor Paul's personality and temperament had contributed to an exacerbation of unrest in the orchestra' but that he would defer giving notice to Paul of the Authority's decision until later in the year, when as a matter of course his contract would come up for discussion.[96]

McCourt in fact told Paul at a meeting in late September that his contract would not be renewed, stating that it was time for a change. Paul then wrote to the DG refusing to accept this, especially since eighteen months' notice was normal in the event of non-renewal, and asking the Authority to re-open the discussion on the matter. On 7 October the Authority meeting was told that Paul had been offered a contract to conduct 50% of the concerts 'as principal non-resident conductor' and that it was proposed to appoint Gerard Victory as Director of Music.[97] That evening, just before a concert at the RDS, Paul received a letter from McCourt – the letter was marked 'Private, confidential

93 Fürst to DG, 13 June 1966. **94** DG to MacNeill, 14 June 1966. **95** RTÉ Authority minutes, 11 May 1966. **96** Ibid., 25 May 1966. **97** Ibid., 7 October 1966.

and urgent' but Paul did not open it until he had returned home from the concert. Although, contrary to popular belief, it did not state that his contract would not be renewed, it asked for his immediate resignation as Director of Music and offered him a three-months-per-year guest conductorship.[98] A heart attack – and hospitalisation – followed, giving Colman Pearce his first major break with the RTÉSO the next week at a Gaiety Concert, standing in for Paul. The London foray was still to come in November, after Paul's recovery, and Paul was still to stage his own last bow with his third Beethoven cycle at the end of his term.[99]

Not only did Paul, from his hospital bed, blame McCourt for his effective dismissal, but he revealed that a planned six-week, thirty-six concert tour of the USA in 1968, organised by Columbia Artists, had fallen through due to his inability to get a meeting with McCourt to discuss it. Paul believed that McCourt's action – or inaction – was 'sabotage – there is no other word for it'.[1] Paul had seen a recent concert in Belfast, the London concert and the USA tour as three stages of 'a big achievement in our cultural expansion ... Ireland is such a cultural country. The trouble is nobody knows.'

In the Dáil, the Minister, Joseph Brennan, found it necessary to rebut some of the adverse publicity that RTÉ had received, even though he said that the Authority had its own responsibilities and the matter was, strictly speaking, outside his remit. An *Irish Times* editorial, for example, had said that Paul's dismissal 'appears to be one more piece of insensitive, thoughtless mishandling of personal relationships to add to a series that is as old as RÉ itself'.[2] Without quoting from McCourt's letter, Brennan divulged its essential details, pointing out that it was not a curt note of dismissal, but an offer of guest conductorship consequent on Paul's acceding to the request that he stand down as Director of Music – 'which', the Minister said, 'I personally agree with'. He felt that the offer – of concerts in the 1967–8 and 1968–9 seasons – was reasonable, but that, in the light of Paul's subsequent behaviour, he no longer merited the offer. On the question of the proposed US tour, at a cost of £12k, 'That would not be a lot if it had any great prestige. I am sure it would have prestige for the artists and perhaps it is a pity it is not taking place, but I question the amount of prestige which the orchestra would have with a foreign conductor and a high percentage of the players non-nationals playing classical music in America'.[3]

98 This information is derived from an interview by Paul with Des Mullan, published in the *Evening Herald* on 12 and 16 October and the *Irish Independent* on 13 October 1966; it conflicts with a statement by Paul's wife that the letter from McCourt was one of dismissal (*Irish Times*, 12 October 1966). **99** In 1991, Michael Dervan would inexplicably refer to Bryden Thomson's Beethoven cycle as 'the first in Dublin in living memory': *Irish Times*, 22 November 1991. **1** *Evening Herald*, 16 October 1966. The RTÉ Authority minutes of 7 October 1966 record a decision that the US tour 'be deferred indefinitely'. **2** *Irish Times*, 14 October 1966. **3** DD. 224, 27

Public opinion, expressed in the form of letters to newspaper editors, extended articles in the opinion columns and questions in Dáil Éireann, judged that, even though he had been abrasive and arrogant, Tibor Paul had immeasurably increased the public profile of music and improved the quality of the RÉSO. When Paul spoke to the press, RTÉ withdrew its offer of guest engagements after the termination of his contract.[4]

Much of the support for Paul was fuelled by Maud Aiken, wife of the Minister for External Affairs; the incoming Chair of the RTÉ Authority, C.S. Andrews, recorded in his memoirs that the Paul episode caused a coolness between him and his friend, Frank Aiken.[5] When it was debated in the Dáil, the Minister was taunted with the fact that, rather than the House being divided on party lines, the Fianna Fáil government was embarrassed by Mrs. Aiken's championing of Paul. He insisted: 'There is no political significance whatsoever in this. As Deputy Dockrell said, the music world knows no political boundaries. I am prepared to accept that there is some emotionalism attaching to the musical world because some people seem to have lost their heads completely, judging by the statements made in relation to a matter about which obviously they did not know the facts. It is regrettable that I should have to stand up here and say these things. It ought never to have been necessary' – to which Stephen Coughlan (Labour, Limerick East) retorted 'What was Mrs. External Affairs talking about so?'[6] In fact, Patrick Lindsay (Fine Gael, Mayo North) had commended Maud Aiken for 'the very simple, very honest and very brave expression of opinion': 'It would be a good thing if other Ministerial wives were equally honest and equally brave and thus influence their husbands in the Front Bench of this Government'.[7]

The London concert seems to have come about as a result of prompting by Mrs. Tillett (of the London artists' and concert agency which bears her name): 'at some time in the near future you should consider bringing the orchestra to London for a concert at the Royal Festival Hall. There is such a large Irish population here in London that I cannot help thinking that it would be a very big success, as they would be very proud to have their own orchestra performing here. It is quite possible that ITV might be interested in such an occasion'.[8] Paul may already have had such a project in mind, since he had already per-

---

October 1966, col. 2189. **4** RTÉ Authority minutes, 4 November 1966. **5** C.S. Andrews, *Man of No Property*, p. 283. Cf. Charles Acton (*Irish Times* 29 July 1967): 'Tibor Paul's final series of concerts has been turned into … a display of sensational emotionalism, apparently by the group of people whom musical Dublin has been calling the Fan Club' – many of whose names, including those of Maud Aiken, Hilton Edwards and Micheál MacLiammóir, were published in news items in the *Irish Times*, as donations were solicited for a presentation to Paul, which was made after his final concert. **6** DD. 224, 27 October 1966, col. 2191. **7** Ibid., col. 2152. **8** Ibbs and Tillett to Paul, 1 January 1963, file 'Ibbs and Tillett'.

32 The RTÉ Singers, in Ib Jorgensen couture, with conductor
Proinnsias Ó Duinn, 1977.

33 Albert Rosen, Principal Conductor, RTÉSO.

34 Colman Pearce, Principal Conductor, RTÉSO.

35 Proinnsías Ó Duinn, Principal Conductor, RTÉ Concert Orchestra at the Carrolls RTÉ Proms, Montrose Pavilion, Donnybrook, May 1991.

36 Gerard Victory, Director of Music.

37 RTÉ Academica String Quartet, at the National Gallery of Ireland.

38 Jan Čap and Mariana Sirbu, Carton House.

39 Poster advertising Micheál O'Rourke's series
of Chopin nocturnes, 1983.

40 Principal Conductors of the RTÉSO/NSO: (a) Bryden Thomson
(b) János Fürst.

40 Principal Conductors of the RTÉSO/NSO: (c) George Hurst
(d) Kasper de Roo.

40 Principal Conductors of the RTÉSO/NSO: (e) Alexander Anissimov (f) Gerhard Markson.

41 The RTÉCO at Kilmainham Jail.

42 The RTÉCO, conductor Noel Kelehan, at Eurovision.

43 Sir Michael Tippett acknowledges applause at the NCH.

44 Identity for Lyric fm.

45 'Music in the Classroom' 2004.

suaded RTÉ to bring to Dublin two major London critics, Martin Cooper of the *Daily Telegraph* and William Mann of *The Times*, to review a concert in November the previous year (Haydn's 103rd symphony, Bartók's third piano concerto with Paul Badura-Skoda, and Strauss's 'Ein Heldenleben').

He now rose to Mrs. Tillett's bait, although the concert would not take place until 30 November 1966, as part of the RPO's season of visiting orchestras (the others being the Prague Symphony, the BBCSO, the English Chamber Orchestra and the Hallé). Paul's programme was Bartók's concerto for orchestra, Brahms' first symphony and Mahler's 'Kindertotenlieder' with Bernadette Greevy as soloist.[9] There was some controversy at the time as to whether or not he should have included a work by an Irish composer, and it transpired that he had in fact attempted to commission five works at around this period, possibly with the idea of including one of them in his London or US programmes, but that none of them was available in time. The five were Brian Boydell, who declined because he was fully committed at that time; Seán Ó Riada, A.J. Potter, Gerard Victory and Seóirse Bodley, each of whom accepted the invitation to write a twenty-minute symphonic poem, but none of whom, according to Paul, had completed the work by the agreed date. This was hotly disputed by Potter and Bodley.[10] Why Paul did not include an already extant work is unexplained.

The London venture had been greeted by the *Irish Times* when it had been announced, in December of the previous year:

> Our Symphony Orchestra was founded for broadcasting, but it is also our national orchestra … Every new evidence of our cultural and artistic development … enhances our national reputation in a way that directly assists our exports and industry … Potentially, ours could be among the well-known European orchestras. Many things need to be done administratively to give the orchestra the opportunity to improve, to make its present best performances its normal ones. This forthcoming visit to London may well pave the way for a famous future.[11]

As Gerard Victory remarked with obvious pride after the Festival Hall concert, 'The remarkable ovation announced that London had become aware of a new dimension in Irish life'.[12] In the *Guardian* Edward Greenfield expressed his prejudices and judgements in equal measure: 'You might expect an orchestra

9 Paul had given Greevy much encouragement: she had made her 'Prom' début in 1962 with Mahler's 'Wayfarer' songs, and the following year sang 'Das Lied von der Erde'. 10 The information from Paul was contained in a letter to Peter Haley-Dunne quoted by him in a letter to the Editor, *Irish Times*, 15 November 1966. Letters by Bodley and Potter to the Editor, *Irish Times*, 9 November 1966. 11 *Irish Times*, 30 December 1965. 12 *On the Air: the staff magazine of RTÉ*, 2/11 (January–February 1967).

with the name "Radio Telefís Éireann Symphony Orchestra" … to nurture a race of wild Irish musicians, but in fact as … last night showed very clearly, this is a highly civilised, stylish body well capable of taking virtuoso scores by Bartók and Mahler in its stride'.[13] He found Greevy most expressive in the shading of her tone colour. The critic of the *Financial Times*, David Cairns, commented that 'Mr Paul has built up a strong, predominantly young band, with a good sonority to it … As an interpreter he seems to have somewhat less to offer. The performances lacked some elusive ingredient of character, personality, distinctive, coherent artistic purpose'.[14] He praised Greevy's 'memorable serenity and breadth of soft, finely-spun line' in the fourth of Mahler's songs. Under the headline 'Lovely Bernadette backs musicians from Eire', the *Daily Express*'s Alan Blyth praised 'the warmth of the strings, precision of the woodwind, and mellowness of the brass …[which] merged as a deeply satisfying entity' in the symphony.[15]

The following day the orchestra travelled to the Fairfield Halls, Croydon, for a television recording for BBC-2 which was transmitted on 8 December – this was a mixed programme of Irish songs (Beckett's arrangement of 'Down by the Sally Gardens', Larchet's 'Wee Hughie' and Harty's 'Sea Wrack') sung by Greevy, Chausson's 'Poème' (with Geraldine O'Grady), Strauss's 'Don Juan' and Dukas' 'Sorcerer's Apprentice'.

'Six years ago there was nothing here, but now there a flourishing musical life', Paul had told the *Evening Herald*.[16] The assertion that Ireland had been 'a musical wilderness' before his advent was one that Minister Brennan found necessary to fiercely rebut during the Dáil debate immediately after Paul's 'dismissal': 'That is not fair to the great conductors who preceded him and who did a magnificent job of work … It is not fair to write down the work of these conductors, some of whom have since gone to the top in the music world'.[17]

At the time of Paul's farewell Beethoven cycle, Fanny Feehan, a former orchestral musician and now music critic, wrote 'No musician coming to this country has made such an impact on the man in the street as Tibor Paul … [He] achieved some memorable achievements during his stay here – some of them on the de Mille scale, such as the Berlioz Requiem. He brought Rostropovich, Szeryng, Menuhin, Ricci and other equally big names here …. Nobody could ever say … that Mr Paul did not think big.' But Feehan also pointed out that a succession of one-off, big names did not maintain an orchestra:

> What does an audience expect of a conductor? Dublin audiences don't expect anything; they take what they get and like it. They must be the

13 *Guardian*, 1 December 1966.   **14** *Financial Times*, 1 December 1966.   **15** *Daily Express*, 1 December 1966.   **16** *Evening Herald*, 12 October 1966.   **17** DD. 224, 27 October 1966, col. 2190.

most undiscerning audience in the world. Is it lack of good aural training or just good nature? When Tibor Paul came here first he electri-
fied the whole of us and we thought we were in for a musical renaissance. The audiences soon put paid to that. Even the best conductor in
the world, faced with constant adulation (and Mr Paul must have had
nearly as many standing ovations as Toscanini) relaxes unless he keeps
an iron discipline and listens critically to his own performance. As a
musician Paul undoubtedly has great integrity. He rehearsed the orchestra intelligently and was never boring, but he seldom made any exciting difference to a work and I never came away from a familiar work
having heard a new facet of it ... If he had not been appointed Music
Director things might have been different. This appointment showed
the most disastrous lack of foresight on the part of the Authority ... A
visiting conductor could not possibly have imbibed enough knowledge
of Ireland to guide and encourage a culturally backward population however unpalatable that fact may be, and carry out his duties as conductor
as well.[18]

After the final Beethoven concert, summing up Paul's achievement, Charles
Acton wondered whether there had been any appreciable improvement overall in the quality of the orchestra's performances: 'I have the strong impression
that if the tape of Mr Paul's first performance here of the Seventh [Beethoven]
be compared with that of last week, not all that much difference will be shown:
and I doubt very much if the tape of the "New World" [Dvořák] under Silvestri
... would prove in any way inferior to Mr Paul's most recent performance of
it.' Nevertheless, 'Tibor Paul has more often enabled the RTÉSO to realise
the potentialities which it had before his arrival than other conductors here
have done'. (Visiting conductors during Paul's tenure included Edgar Cosma,
Kurt Woss, José Iturbi and Enrique Jorda.) The duties of Director of Music
had 'caused even him to rely too much on his recollection of scores he knew
intimately, [and] to be unable to expand his repertoire as much as he would
have done otherwise'.[19] There was a strong feeling that RTÉ should continue
to offer Paul guest engagements, and that Paul should accept them – an accommodation that neither side felt able to entertain.

In an interview in the *RTV Guide* in 1965, Paul had acknowledged his personal problems: 'Look, they say I am temperamental, forceful, dynamic. You
know why? The word impossible I don't recognise. Tibor, they say, he never
takes no for an answer. Without taking decisions, you get nowhere ... You
know why I stay here? The challenge'[20] – on which the (anonymous) inter-

18 *Hibernia*, July 1967. **19** *Irish Times*, 29 July 1967. **20** *RTV Guide*, 29 October 1965.

viewer commented 'a man as thrusting as Tibor Paul is bound to be charged with arrogance, even with vanity. Yet, as an outsider, a non-Irishman, he can get, and has got, things done that just weren't done before.'[21]

Leo Donnelly, as RTÉ's first Concerts Manager, saw both sides of the man and was clearly willing to give credit where it was due, despite his own experience of Paul's boorishness: 'Tibor Paul had the worst temperament of the lot. He was a horror – but he tore the cobwebs off music in this country. He got things done in his own way, without consulting either superiors or subordinates. He brought in Stravinsky, for instance – he did magnificent things for Irish music'.[22] Jack Leydier, eventual leader of the second violins in the RTÉSO (in succession to Alfonso Evangelisti) said 'with him you knew you had to watch your step or pack your suitcase'.[23] At the time of his own appointment as principal conductor (1987), Fürst said that Paul 'had as many faults as anybody and he had as many good points as anybody. It was just a very funny mixture. He was ... an authoritarian to the extreme. And a man of extreme vanity who could not take a single tiny word of criticism ... He disciplined the orchestra without question. He built programmes, he opened up doors ... He actually was the first person who truly *cared* what happened to that orchestra. People say that ... it was his ambition. But when *his* ambition and the *orchestra's* ambition were put together it worked for its advantage ... Those years were important years for the orchestra and for the country, musically.'[24] When Paul died suddenly in 1973, Charles Acton wrote 'He was tireless in promoting "his" orchestra, in involving Limerick, Cork, Belfast, Derry in the national music making ... Only a Hungarian could have had his energy. If he used this to further his own power and command, it was because he knew that he was serving music and was sure that, by exercising as much power as he could get, he could bring renown to his orchestra, to the music he conducted and to the community in which he found himself.'[25]

Gerard Victory, who worked more closely with Paul than any other in RÉ, described him as a 'catastrophically brilliant and tempestuous figure' with whom he 'got on well because I understood his temperament'. 'He was at heart an extremely kind person which is not very often recognised because he had a turbulent way of acting and could be strident, could lose his temper easily, could be a bit outrageous in his demands – they were always to a good purpose, they were never just for the sake of doing it – but it appeared very overwhelming to people outside ... It worked very well for some years; I think the biggest advances [in repertoire] were made during that brief period of his early occupancy.'[26]

21 The writer was almost certainly John O'Donovan. 22 *Irish Times*, 'An Irishman's diary' 15 November 1973. 23 Interview with Arminta Wallace, *Irish Times*, 5 January 1990. 24 *Music Ireland*, 2/1 (December 1986–January 1987). 25 *Irish Times* 12 November 1973. 26 'Composers

It is indicative of the successive crises through which RTÉ was moving in these years that it was not prepared to compromise on rules and regulations in order to continue the evident artistic benefit that was accruing as a result of Paul's régime, but it is equally clear that there was a limit to what he could in fact achieve. If the RTÉ management was not equal to the flair of its principal musician, the time was probably not right for such a high flyer, yet if Paul had not made those controversial years so 'important, musically' – not least by concentrating attention, even if unintentionally, on the role of Music Director – it is likely that later phases in the RTÉSO/NSO's history would not have been reached so easily, or with such prescience. Michael Bowles, who had his own axe to grind against RTÉ, told the *Irish Times* that 'The unpleasant row with Mr Tibor Paul ... should not be considered as a single occurrence but rather as part of an undulant fever of dissension afflicting the Radio Éireann music department for more than two decades. Indeed, from what I hear, the orchestra is now rapidly acquiring the reputation of being a sort of conductor's graveyard ... Notwithstanding changes of conductors and of office personnel, a continuous thread of brusquerie has characterised the dealings of Radio Éireann with musicians'.[27]

CHARLES ACTON AND THE 'IRISH TIMES' (1)

In 1961, at the end of Fachtna Ó hAnnracháin's term as Music Director, Charles Acton, music critic of the *Irish Times* from 1955 to 1986, could write, of a performance by Tibor Paul of Bruckner's unfamiliar seventh symphony, with a full house, that 'Radio Éireann and Fachtna Ó hAnnracháin ... have created an audience in Dublin that desires the interesting and not the pot-boilers'.[28] By 1965 he would be disenchanted with Paul's choice of repertoire, and asking if a performance of Walton's violin concerto and Tippett's first symphony 'represent[ed] a return to RÉ's erstwhile adventurousness'.[29] Concurrently, Acton noted a rise in the standard of the orchestra. When the Hallé, under Barbirolli, played Schubert's 'Great' C major symphony in Dublin during the 1959 music festival, he thought that the work would have been 'beyond the present RÉSO'.[30] Ten days later, 'I have to take back those words', having heard Jean Meylan conduct the same work with the RÉSO, reflecting a considerable improvement in both technique and interpretation over recent performances. 'The RÉSO showed itself on a par with the Hallé'.[31]

As Tibor Paul's tenure was drawing to a close, Acton took the opportunity to write three articles on 'RTÉ and Irish Musical Life' in the *Irish Times*.

in Conversation', 1988, loc. cit. **27** *Irish Times*, 2 and 3 January 1967. **28** *Irish Times*, 23 October 1961. **29** *Irish Times*, 2 January 1965. **30** *Irish Times*, 20 June 1959. **31** *Irish Times*, 1 July 1959.

Table M: orchestral works by Irish composers performed by the RTÉSO
and RTÉLO, January 1959–December 1968

	Year of composition	Date(s) of concert(s)		
Arnold Bax (1883–1953)				
In the Faery Hills	1909	16.05.61		
Overture to Adventure	1935	29.06.65		
Tintagel	1919	15.02.59	30.08.60	12.02.63
Walter Beckett (1914–96)				
Falaingin Dances	1958	01.02.59	12.05.59	05.02.61
Suite	1945	09.02.66		
Irish Rhapsody no. 1	1957	15.11.59		
Colin Block (b. 1944)				
Concertino for horn	1965	27.05.66		
Denis Blood (b. 1920)				
Bravade		03.09.65		
Piano concerto		06.09.63		
Seóirse Bodley (b. *1933*)				
An Bas is an Bheatha	1960	22.01.61		
Configurations	1967	29.01.67	02.02.69	
Divertimento	1962	15.06.62	08.10.62	
Movement for orchestra	1955	12.11.61	13.11.61	
Music for strings	1952	01.01.60	11.09.64	19.01.68
Never to have lived is best	1965	11.06.65		
Salve Maria Virgo	1957	30.06.60	29.03.66	
Symphony	1959	23.10.60	10.04.64	15.04.66
Symphony for chamber orchestra	1964	07.02.65		
James Bolger				
Bagatelle for bassoon and orchestra		03.06.66		
Contrasts		16.12.66		
Impromptu		19.03.67		
Brian Boydell (*1916–2000*)				
Megalithic Ritual Dances	1956	14.01.68		
A Terrible Beauty is Born	1965	11.04.66	08.07.66	
Ceol Cas Corach	1958	18.01.59	21.07.59	
Five Joyce Songs	1946	17.11.61		
In Memoriam Mahatma Gandhi	1948	18.10.59	27.10.68	
Meditation and Fugue	1956	22.01.61		
Mors et Vita	1961	27.01.63	17.04.64	
Shielmartin Suite	1959	13.11.60	10.05.63	
Symphonic Inscapes	1968	26.01.69		
Violin concerto	1953/54	08.11.64	14.01.66	
Edgar Deale (1902–99)				
Five poets, seven songs	1961	28.10.66		
Arthur Duff (1899–1956)				
Echoes of Georgian Dublin	1955	15.01.61	15.12.67	11.02.68
Drinking Horn suite	1953	12.06.61		

Irish Suite for Strings	1940	25.10.59	24.01.60	04.11.62
		11.01.63		
Music for strings	1935	29.03.68		
An Old Irish Melody		06.08.65	20.05.66	
John Field (1782–1837)				
Piano concerto no. 6	1819	23.05.61		
Aloys Fleischmann (1910–92)				
Lament for Elizabeth				
McDermott Roe	1941	15.10.61		
The Fountain of Magic	1946	13.09.63		
Songs of Columcille	1964	03.01.64	03.02.67	
Introduction and Funeral March	1960	12.02.60	28.02.61	11.02.62
Overture, The Four Masters	1944	11.09.64		
Clare's Dragoons	1944	03.05.66		
Songs of the Provinces	1965	29.06.65		
Redmond Friel (1907–79)				
Frolic no. 1	1951	06.08.65		
Bernard Geary (b. 1934)				
Provocations	1960	20.06.61		
Variations on Amhrán Dóchais	1963	09.02.64		
Carl Hardebeck (1869–1945)				
Seoithin Seo		04.02.62		
Herbert Hamilton Harty (1879–1941)				
Irish Symphony	1904	15.04.66		
Piano concerto	1922	14.07.61		
Field Suite	1939	28.07.61		
Comedy Overture	1906	17.05.60		
Water Music (Handel)	1920	23.05.61	27.09.66	
The Wake Feast (orch. A.J.Potter)	1914	03.06.66		
With the Wild Geese	1910	09.02.60	30.10.60	
T.C. Kelly (1917–85)				
Rhapsody on Children's Themes		18.02.66	30.09.66	04.08.67
Fantasy for flute and piccolo		18.03.66		
Dance Rhapsody no. 2	1966	12.08.66		
Capriccio for piano & orchestra	1965	10.02.67		
Harp fantasia	1958	23.08.68		
Piano concerto	1960	01.09.61		
The Everlasting Voices	1959	26.06.59		
Three pieces for strings	1949	18.06.61		
Variations on The Dear Irish Boy	1956	29.10.65	07.01.66	
John Kinsella (b.1932)				
Two pieces for strings	1965	06.03.66		
Antoinette Kirkwood (b.1930)				
Symphony no. 1	1960	03.03.61		
J.F. Larchet (1884–1967)				
Dirge of Ossian & Macananty's Reel	1940	03.02.63		
Daniel McNulty (1920–96)				
Divertimento	1957	26.06.59	29.01.61	
Piano concertino	1964	10.04.64	15.04.66	

Sinfonietta no. 1 [4 Provinces]	1958	05.05.61		
Sinfonietta no. 2 [The Shamrock]	1960	27.02.62		
Elizabeth Maconchy (1907–94)				
Dialogue	1940	10.07.59		
Suite on Irish Airs	1954	08.11.59		
Frederick May (1911–85)				
Spring Nocturne	1937	05.03.63	11.02.66	
Suite of Irish airs	1953	08.11.59	28.01.62	22.04.66
Songs from Prison	1941	03.04.64		
Sunlight and Shadow	1955	26.10.59	12.02.61	17.02.67
E.J. Moeran (1894–1950)				
Sinfonietta	1940	13.10.59		
Alicia Needham (d. 1945)				
The Queen of Connemara		29.04.66		
My Dark Rosaleen		27.05.66		
Havelock Nelson (1917–96)				
Sinfonietta	1950	06.07.65		
J.J. O'Reilly (1905–83)				
Nocturne – Remembrance	1958	08.05.59		
Seán Ó Riada (1931–71)				
Festival Overture	1959	26.06.60		
Banks of Sullane	1956	30.06.61		
Hercules Dux Ferrariae	1957	18.11.62	19.11.62	03.05.66
		24.03.68		
Nomos no. 2	1963	23.04.65		
Nomos no. 4	1958	20.02.59	01.11.59	
Olynthiac overture	1955	08.02.59	28.01.66	
A.J. Potter (1918–80)				
Cardinal Fleury	1959	06.11.60		
Careless Love	1959/61	15.01.60	29.10.61	23.01.62
Clarinet Elegy	1956	18.09.59	14.02.60	
Dance Fantasy for piano and				
Orchestra		11.08.67		
Finnegan's Wake	1957	06.08.65		
Concerto for orchestra	1966	12.03.67		
Irish Rhapsody for violin and				
Orchestra	1963	17.03.63		
Rapsóid Deireadh Lae	1966	29.04.66		
The Scatterin'	1961	20.05.66		
Hail Mary	1966	03.09.66		
Piano concerto	1952	22.04.66		
Rhapsody Under a High Sky	1950	15.11.61	01.09.67	
Sinfonia de Profundis	1968	23.03.69		
Variations on a popular tune	1955	27.02.62	25.07.69	
John Purser (b. 1942)				
Variations on Amhrán Duchais	1963	06.10.63		
Epitaph	1966	18.10.68		
C.V. Stanford (1854–1924)				
Irish Rhapsody no. 1	1902	31.01.60		

Joan Trimble (1915–2000)

Suite for Strings	1953	03.11.59	

Gerard Victory (1922–95)

Ballade	1963	02.02.64	
The Enchanted Garden	1958	07.02.60	03.06.60
Favola di notte	1966	26.02.67	
Five Mantras	1963	02.07.65	25.03.66
Homage to Petrarch	1967	02.02.68	
The Music Hath Mischief	1961	20.10.67	
Pariah Music	1965	17.10.65	
The River of Heaven	1964	22.10.65	
Elegy and March	1951	02.01.59	
Esquise		30.09.66	
Mirage		25.08.67	
Rapparee overture	1959	25.07.61	14.01.62
Short symphony	1961	14.09.62	

James Wilson (b. 1922)

Trefoil	1966	25.10.68	

Charles Wood (1866–1926)

A Braid Valley Love Song (orch. T.C. Kelly)		20.05.66	

Summary: 34 composers (of whom, 26 living), 123 works, 175 performances

Although he had been music critic of the paper for eleven years at this stage, and had written hundreds of reviews and feature articles, it was his first major commentary on RTÉ's policy. Acton played a leading role in stimulating public discussion by way of his reviews of individual concerts and his almost weekly opinion column, which was by turns questioning, incisive and polemical. Fiercely idiosyncratic, he was nevertheless devoted to what he saw as the overall matter of the fate of classical music performance and the music profession in Ireland, and to the continual betterment of music through raising awareness, broadening knowledge and the means to appreciation, and above all – in the case of RTÉ and its performing groups – the rational, demonstrable and strategic use of resources. He could often be ruthless in his deployment of information garnered from a variety of sources, and his style – a mixture of coaxing and cajoling, of demanding and diatribe – often exasperated his *Irish Times* readers and the authorities to whom they were directed, but there was no doubting his compassion for the real artist and his/her music-making.

In this he was supported by the more genteel and restrained leadership of the Music Association of Ireland and by colleagues such as Fanny Feehan writing in *Hibernia*, but there had been no widespread discussion of the subject until the specific debate on the status and management of the NSO in the 1990s, occasioned by the PIANO review group, by which time Acton had retired. Acton's methods, which often had the character of personal appeals to, or criticisms of, figures such as Gerard Victory and his successor John Kinsella, or the directorate of the DGOS, focussed the attention of his readers on the issues involved – especially programming policy and engagement of artists – which in turn sparked off exchanges of letters in the *Irish Times* – but they failed to engage the interest of either the politicians and civil servants who might have initiated that debate a decade earlier, or the 'anonymous bureaucrats' who, Acton was convinced, operated within RTÉ at a higher level than that of the Music or Information Departments in stifling or ignoring artistic or managerial initiatives.

The importance of these articles is that there was no other sustained public source of, or forum for, criticism or examination of such issues. Admittedly, the authors of *Sit Down and Be Counted: the cultural evolution of a television station* (1969) confined themselves to television and reported recurring crises in areas such as current affairs, but in the theoretical sections of the book they referred to 'culture' and 'communication' in broad terms which might have addressed the issue of music, both on television and within the overall broadcasting environment. Presumably their agenda was dominated by the political dimension of broadcasting and the personnel who took the leading decisions during the formative years of RTÉ's televisual existence. Nevertheless, their theoretical bases provide us with a series of questions similar to those which Charles Acton asked and attempted to answer, such as: 'Literature and art are ideal principles by which our imaginative experience can be so organised by the intensity, perfection and beauty of the work that the human psyche can *play* with that which it dare not assimilate on the level of reality'.[32] Set against this was the statement of RTÉ's Director-General that 'minority groups … can and must be given a service. But the operation of television is too costly and too complex to be run for the benefit of a handful of people. If a service does not justify itself in terms of the mass audience then it cannot be justified'.[33] That music was ignored by both sides of the argument within RTÉ concerning quality and standards was all the more reason for Acton and the *Irish Times* to take it up in a way that unashamedly sold newspapers.

Acton was concerned that any debate about the status of the RÉSO should not obscure the need to consider the breadth of functions of the Director of Music, which included 'fostering Irish artists (creative and executant) so that they can as nearly earn a decent living in their own country as is possible, without either chauvinism or any lowering of standards'. He believed that 'we have a flowering of musical talent that in after years may be likened to the literary harvest of the early years of this century'. He did not think that the RÉSO

32 Dowling, Doolan and Quinn, op. cit., p. 260. 33 T.P. Hardiman, *Irish Times*, 30 October 1968, quoted in ibid. p. 271.

should be 'hived off' from the music department (although he would come round to that view twenty years later), or that 'gulfs should be fixed between traditional music and light music and "serious" music … There has in the past been far too great a tendency everywhere to think of music as divided up into separate compartments, instead of being (as it is) a continuous field, each part of which shades into each other part'. He wanted Paul's successor to 'make its traditional music programmes of headline interest', including television exposure, 'giving our musical heritage a real shot in the arm'. Commending the RTÉ Singers and String Quartet, looking for an improved RÉLO, fearing 'a constant stream of pop', demanding more jazz, he summed up the incoming Music Director's task as 'to fight the corner of the music department in the allocation of new programme schedules', especially as far as television was concerned; and to improve the music department's communication with the public. He was highly suspicious of RTÉ's reference to the RÉSO in its annual report, and pointed to the low morale caused, among other factors, by the haemorrhaging of a quarter of its members over the past year. He rightly observed that management attitudes could influence performance: 'every time some *bêtise* is committed by the people running the orchestra, there must be a reaction in its performance – but an unconscious one, not any conscious insubordination'. As far as musical direction is concerned, 'an orchestra cannot … play well for a conductor whom they do not respect as musician and man. No conductor ever got good results by slave-driving or fear.' And a principal conductor 'should search for the very best conductors who are complementary to him. When, as now, we have a specialist in the romantics, we need guests who are outstanding with the classical period and with modern music.' Finally, he called for better programme-planning and -building in a return to the achievements of the pre-Paul era, 'where one of the most adventurous audiences of Europe ha[d] been built up by the judicious provision of modern works of various types … For programme planning is more than an overall annual balance: it means retaining your audiences week by week and making events seem part of a continuity.'[34]

When the RTÉ Authority published another annual report, again stating the financial costs of the RTÉSO, Acton took up his pen to write an 'Open Letter' to the Chairman, C.S. Andrews, analysing, and disagreeing with, the figures, suggesting that RTÉ was 'misleading' by exaggerating them, so as to over-state its case for government subvention of the orchestra. The report claimed that concerts such as those for Ceol-Chumann na nÓg were not broadcast, thus making them uneconomic; Acton retorted: 'you should take pride in helping to train your future audiences instead of griping, and … it is high time you did record and broadcast these, and did some little thing to help children

34 *Irish Times*, 21, 22, 23 November 1966.

outside the main cities to appreciate the arts'. He concluded: 'Is it not time you and your colleagues did more to satisfy the cultural needs of the Irish listener instead of trying to find means of betraying them?'[35]

In his reviews, too, he not only gave his opinion of the concert perform-ance but also, where he considered it relevant, addressed longer-term issues. Thus in 1968 he commented:

> For many weeks now I have been worrying about the violins of the RTÉSO. It seemed to me that their excellent work was being spoilt by one or two people unable to be dead on the note in the higher positions ... A visit by the Ulster Orchestra has confirmed ... that the present position is deplorable and that something should be done about it. Fear of being captious is reinforced by anxiety lest any unfavourable com-ment should put a weapon into the hands of the philistines of the [RTÉ] Authority who apparently want to get rid of our orchestra; or should confirm the too numerous snobs who do not think their orchestra could be good enough for them to listen to.[36]

This was an issue to which he returned in 1973: 'Perhaps Albert Rosen is too gentle to rehearse such passages [Dvořák's seventh symphony] desk by desk. Perhaps the weaker sisters do not take their music home to practice such pas-sages. Perhaps RTÉ are taking in players who are not yet ready'.[37] Nevertheless, he always gave praise unstintingly where he felt it was deserved, and through-out 1975 and 1976, and again in 1979–81, his reviews noted a rising standard in concert performance, in which he felt able to acknowledge the successful work of both Rosen and Colman Pearce.

In these articles, Acton set down markers for the contributions he would make to the public debate on the status and future of music and broadcasting which, as we shall see, produced similar series in 1974 and 1979–81: the chief issue being the relationship between artistic policy and financial and person-nel management. His final comment in his 'open letter' to RTÉ may have been unfair ('trying to betray them') and it may have smacked of the tone of voice adopted by the MAI, but it betokened a passionate concern for the wellbeing of music and musicians which permeated everything he would write to, and about, RTÉ and other music promoters who, in his opinion, were either falling short of their responsibilities or failing to do justice to their potential.

35 *Irish Times*, 22 August 1967. **36** *Irish Times*, 25 November 1968. **37** *Irish Times*, 19 November 1973.

THE RTÉ LIGHT ORCHESTRA

Parallel to the development of the RTÉSO under Tibor Paul, and as a result of the advent of television, the Light Orchestra underwent a transformation in the early 1960s. In the same memorandum in which the DG, Edward Roth, had advised the Authority on the future of the Symphony, he had also informed them:

> As the need for a new approach to the modern idiom became more apparent as time passed, Frank Chacksfield was asked to join us, for intermittent periods during the next year, to assist in the overall re-development of the Light Orchestra ... It must be clearly understood that the term 'modern idiom' will not prohibit the RÉLO from playing the type of music which has identified it in the past. It is expected that the all-purpose RÉLO will play a lighter type of music but will also perform Irish traditional and light classical music as it has in the past.[38]

Chacksfield (1914–95) was a very well-known British band-leader and arranger, whose image in the late 1950s and early 60s made it evident in which direction it was thought the RÉLO should go. He had entered – and topped – the UK charts as a composer/arranger of numbers such as Charlie Chaplin's *Limelight* (1953), 'Ebb Tide' (1954), 'Donkey Cart' (1956) and the 'Flirtation Waltz'. The sound of his band, with which he appeared regularly on BBC radio programmes such as 'Friday Night is Music Night', was characterised as a lavish, sweeping style modelled on that of Mantovani. He himself, and conductor-arranger Bobby Murphy (with a background in the Artane Boys' Band and a number of Dublin dance bands), would work with the orchestra in developing both its repertoire and, consequently, the instrumentation (Murphy would in fact work with the orchestra for many years). Meanwhile, Eimear Ó Broin and Dermot O'Hara, who (with Éamonn Ó Gallchobhair) had carried the burden of the LO's conducting responsibilities since its inception, but who had both been criticised in the Willoughby report, were assigned to other duties – Ó Broin referred to this action as 'being cast aside'.[39] Chacksfield's changes introduced saxophone, alto flute and guitar to the group and, since there was no possibility of augmentation, the first clarinettist doubled on alto sax, the second clarinet on baritone sax and the first flautist on piccolo and alto flute.

The RTÉLO was now set on its new path: from its origins as a 'salon' orchestra, conceived as a multi-purpose ensemble incorporating features of a

---

38 E. Roth, loc. cit. Charles Acton recalled that 'Edward Roth once told me that he wanted an RÉLO that would have a recognisable individual sound quality as distinctive as the Melachrino strings or Duke Ellington's band': *Irish Times*, 22 November 1966. 39 E. Ó Broin, interview with the author, 3 May 2002.

'céilí band', it would now gradually introduce lighter classical and 'pop' material while gradually phasing out the arrangements of traditional Irish music which had in fact been the backbone of its repertoire. This change of repertoire was fundamental, rescinding the existing schedule and introducing new musical styles, featuring what Eimear Ó Broin contemptuously referred to as 'glossy three-minute sachets as played in hotel foyers and in planes before take-off'.[40] Certainly, Charles Acton did not like it: 'Perhaps the saddest thing about the new RÉLO was its lack of musical variety. "When the Saints go Marching in" showed that it was further away from jazz than before. "Tonight" from "West Side Story" showed it dulling the edge of a modern American musical. The "Merry Widow" selection was far too jazzy (in a loose sense) for Léhar. I am certain that "An Cailín Dubh" was far removed from the effect A J Potter intended in arranging it. And the accompaniment to Wagner's "Dich, teure Halle" was incongruous.'[41]

Nevertheless, over the next twenty years the RÉLO would become one of the most distinguished radio orchestras in the world, winning the Nordring Prize in three successive years, and would play host to visiting companies in Dublin such as the Bolshoi Ballet (in 1963 and 1965) and to Liberace, Henry Mancini and Elmer Bernstein.

It also saw new premises, leaving the – by now too cramped – studio at Portobello and shortly after taking up residence in the O'Connell Hall, at the rear of what is now the Royal Dublin Hotel in O'Connell Street.

The RÉLO had its first television engagement on the opening night of Telefís Éireann, new year's eve 1961, when it played at the gala ceremony at Dublin's Gresham Hotel. However, with the exception of the 1962 television series 'Music from Montrose', it remained studio- and radio-bound for the greater part of the next ten years, with regular series such as 'Melody for You', 'Music in the Air' and 'Rhythm Roundabout', and a long-running Saturday night show from 1963, 'The RÉLO Show', presented by Val Joyce, which was succeeded in the mid-1960s by 'The Sound of the Light', 'Invitation Concert' and 'Music of the Nation'. Its twenty-first birthday concert in 1969, and its role as the resident orchestra at the 1971 Eurovision Song Contest, brought it to increased public attention. (See Table N for the orchestra personnel in 1969.)

The issue of employing foreign musicians was a problem in the RTÉLO also:

> Since about 1960, the Federation [IFMAP] has tried to put a complete embargo on the employment of foreign musicians in the Light Orchestra. The result is that, while Irish musicians of from adequate to excellent standard are available for most of the woodwind and brass posi-

---

40 Interview with the author, 4 August 2003. 41 *Irish Times*, 13 April 1962.

tions and several of the string positions, Irish <u>violinists</u> of even adequate standard have become more and more difficult to obtain ... The standard of performance in the two violin sections is at its lowest ebb ever. If we cannot get some very good violins in the Light Orchestra soon, the question must arise as to whether we can continue to maintain the orchestra in its present instrumentation and character. In short, the elimination of the string sections, and the conversion of the orchestra into a 'big band' would have to be considered. I think such a change would be a great pity.[42]

In fact, with the RTÉLO's twenty-first anniversary looming, Kevin Roche asked for an increase in size, with two extra first and second violins, an extra viola and cello, and a double bass doubling bass guitar, plus a 'Cordovox' accordion.

The advantages would be that we would have a fine concert orchestra string sound, together with a modern electronic sound from the bass-guitar and Cordovox, and a vast widening of repertoire and style. The bass-guitar is an essential instrument for modern orchestrations. The Cordovox adds a tremendously rich modern sound to the orchestra, can imitate everything from an organ to tubular bells, and can substitute for any of the woodwind instruments in an emergency.[43]

By this time, with the orchestra again working with staff conductors Ó Broin, Noel Kelehan, Colman Pearce, Albert Rosen and Hans Waldemar Rosen, and visitors Bernard Geary, Fred O'Callaghan, Walter Landauer and Vladimir Benič, productivity was so good that output could be increased by reducing rehearsal time. Kevin Roche was hopeful of matching that of the BBC Midland Light Orchestra, which he had just visited, which broadcast seven half-hour programmes each week.[44] An indication of difference in musical styles between the two orchestras arose when the need was perceived for a second oboeist in the RTÉLO, which Victory had to explain to his ever-suspicious superiors:

I have a feeling that when the orchestra was reorganised by Frank Chacksfield ... he did not add an oboeist because he foresaw at that time that the orchestra as was then planned would largely play light rhythm music (and hence he added guitar and increased the strings to provide for divided multiple sound). In fact of course the repertoire had to

42 K. Roche to O. Maloney (Director of Personnel) , n.d. but after 7 November 1968, file H/E/1. 43 Ibid. 44 K. Roche to Controller of Programmes, 11 April 1969, RTÉ Staff Relations file H/R/4/A.

change and in particular Irish concert music has to figure in quantity and in this the oboe has an exacting and all-important role.[45]

This was graphically supported by Eimear Ó Broin, who wrote:

> This post is one which makes a very great demand on the stamina and artistic capability of any player, no matter what the individual standard of technical competence may be ... The RTÉLO repertoire requires the oboe to play a type of repertoire which displays or emphasises the expressive or lyrical aspects of the instrument, whereas the oboes in the RTÉSO are rarely exposed for very long in such a manner and generally play a type of music emphasising the more formal or structural aspects of the orchestra repertoire.[46]

By this time, the RTÉLO was also appearing substantially on television, in 'The Anna McGoldrick Show', 'The Tony Kenny Show' and the 'Jimmy Kennedy' programme, in addition to the National Song Contest and, in 1971, for the first of seven occasions, the Eurovision Song Contest.[47]

In June 1972 the RTÉLO resumed nationwide touring, with concerts in Longford, Sligo and Galway – the Galway concert marking the last appearance of Jack Cheatle as leader. (He would be succeeded in quick succession by Loretta McGrath and Maurice Cavanagh, before Audrey Park took the leader's chair in late 1972.) In November that year, the orchestra visited Birr, Tralee and Fermoy, after which Eimear Ó Broin, who had returned as a guest conductor, gave the following report:

> The concerts ... were supported largely by a middle-aged section of the community. There was little evidence of support from the younger generation. Perhaps the absence of the RTÉLO from the Provincial Tour scene in the decade 1961–71 has had something to do with this. The RTÉSO has maintained its regular visits to its main provincial centres during this period and reinforced them with Childrens' Concerts so that the younger generation in Cork certainly has come to accept concert-going as a civilised social activity. The non-cultural emphasis of the Irish educational system may also be a hindrance to creating the social acceptance of orchestral concerts in provincial towns in Ireland, particularly

---

45 Victory to Controller of Programmes, 17 August 1974, ibid. **46** Ó Broin to K. Roche, 10 September 1974, ibid. **47** The EBU's Eurovision programme organises an annual Song Contest for member organisations, which is conventionally hosted by the country whose representative has won the previous contest. Ireland, represented by 'Dana' (Rosemary Scallon), won the 1970 contest and therefore hosted the 1971 event. Ireland subsequently hosted the contest in 1981, 1988, 1993, 1994, 1995 and 1997.

among young people. Those who did come to hear the Orchestra were enthusiastic and the artists were well received.[48]

Ó Broin's memo went on to paint a clear picture of the conditions under which tours such as this were undertaken, and in which the orchestra was expected to work:

> Of the venues used for the concerts, I much preferred the Marian Hall, Birr, with its reverberant acoustics. The Mt. Brandon Hotel Ballroom in Tralee was a distinct and depressing failure acoustically and I was much surprised that it had, in fact, been chosen as the most satisfactory centre for recording! The school hall in Fermoy was crowded for the final concert, but the stage was too small for the Orchestra and we were all rather cramped and overheated during the performance. Nevertheless, the Fermoy hall did produce, on stage at least, a cohesive orchestral sound even if the acoustics were very dry ... The next Autumn Tour should be held in late-September or October but not in November when the onset of Winter makes touring less agreeable and deters people from coming out of the warmth of their homes, often to drive considerable distances to a concert.[49]

In the experience of the author (who, as Concerts Manager, was responsible with the RTÉLO manager, Frank Murphy, for identifying suitable venues outside the larger cities for these tours in the mid-to-late 1970s) lack of proper staging and lighting, coupled with poor acoustics and bad sight-lines from the auditorium, made these regular appearances an act of faith and often an adventure into the unknown, rather than a musical pleasure. Nevertheless, with Audrey Park as the new leader, soloists of the calibre of baritone Austin Gaffney, and nationally recognised radio personalities such as Liam Devally and Valerie McGovern presenting the concerts, they were the mainstay of RTÉ's regional musical presence in venues which could not accommodate the Symphony Orchestra and would probably have been less receptive to the symphonic repertoire.

GERARD VICTORY AS DIRECTOR OF MUSIC

With the departure of Tibor Paul, his assistant, Gerard Victory (1921–95) became Director of Music, a post he would hold until his retirement in 1982. Frequently described as the most important, or powerful, job in music in

---

48 E. Ó Broin, RTÉ Music Department memorandum, n.d. [1972]. **49** Ibid.

Table N: The RTÉ Light Orchestra, 21st Anniversary Concert, 1969

1st Violins	*2nd Violins*	*Violas*	
Jack Cheatle	Georg Gerike	Charles Maguire	
Maurice Cavanagh	Patricia O'Brien	Noel Merrigan	
Djorge Nikolic	Abraham Cohen		
Michael McKenna	Doris Lawlor		
Donald Roche			
Joseph Maher			
Celli	*Basses*		
Kathleen Behan	Robert Bushnell		
Christina Cooley			
Flutes	*Oboes*	*Clarinets*	*Bassoons*
Thomas Stewart	Catherine O'Callaghan	Daniel O'Reilly	James Bolger
Ann Kinsella	Thomas Cole		
Horns	*Trumpets*	*Trombones*	
Malcolm Willott	Bernard McNeill	Patrick Potts	
Liam McGuinness	Joseph Cassells	John Tate	
Thomas King	Harry Knowles		
Harp	*Timpani and Percussion*	*Guitar*	*Piano*
Anne Jones	Alfred Barry	Jack Gregory	Eileen Braid

Among the strings, Michael (Mick) McKenna, Donal(d) Roche, Abe Cohen, Doris Lawlor, Charles Maguire, Noel Merrigan, Kathleen Behan, Christine Cooley and Robert (Bobby) Bushnell were long-term appointees, and Joseph Maher was to appear as leader of the RTÉSO; the same can be said of Ann Kinsella, Bernard (Benny) McNeill, Joseph Cassells, Patrick Potts, John (Johnny) Tate – also renowned as a highly talented arranger – Harry Knowles and Alfred Barry. The long-term association of these artists contributed significantly to their achieved sound and to their capacity to work together in often difficult circumstances.

Ireland, this post needed stability after the damage that Paul's tenure was perceived to have caused. Writing in *Hibernia* in mid-1967, 'Reginald Shannon' [a pseudonym of Charles Acton] put the case very bluntly:

> This is a position in which *we do not want a foreigner*. Not for any reasons of chauvinism, but simply because at this exact moment the music director must know the Irish musical scene intimately, in Ballinrobe and Bunclody as much as in Dublin and Cork. Nor, similarly, an Irishman long resident abroad. We do not want a civil servant, if only because (to quote Michael Bowles) 'the reticence of the civil servant' is a grave disadvantage in any place that is part of show business, which RTÉ is …

The first quality [in the new Director of Music] is width of musical interest. He has the responsibility for *all* our broadcast music: traditional, folk, céilí, pop, jazz, light, 'musicals', singing, the Singers, recitals, chamber music, opera ... We are now poised to take a great leap ahead. A widely knowledgeable Music Director with vision and deep conviction can make us take this leap.[50]

Victory (whom Acton presumably had in mind) possessed both the vision and the conviction, and was also familiar, and able to deal, with the civil service mind. His knowledge of the corridors of power in RTÉ had been acquired as a talks producer from 1953 and as deputy to Paul since 1962. It is instructive to note that, as deputy Director of Music, he was 'to be responsible for radio programmes and you will advise as required as regards music programmes in television'.[51] Having attended Belvedere College 1931–9, and UCD 1939–43 (gaining a BA in Celtic Studies) he had also studied piano with Louis O'Brien (brother of Vincent, into whose shoes he was about to step) and composition with John F. Larchet. He had been a junior administrative officer in the Department of Industry and Commerce (1943–8) before joining RÉ as one of the first actors in the Radio Éireann Players on their formation in 1948, transferring briefly to television as a producer in 1961. During this time he had had further study in composition with Walter Beckett, 1951–3, who, he said 'cut me down to size usefully in some ways'.[52] Tomás Ó Canainn states that Victory had been offered the post of Music Director at the Abbey Theatre in succession to Éamonn Ó Gallchobhair, but that he declined it and it was secured by Seán Ó Riada.[53]

At the time, it would have been regarded as astonishing that the DG, Kevin McCourt, should have consulted someone outside the organisation on the question of the directorship, but McCourt was a forthright and resourceful figure who came to RTÉ owing nothing to the organisational culture; his decision to ask Brian Boydell, one of the country's most eminent composers and leading music activists, to advise him seems therefore, with hindsight, very sensible (and it is possible that McCourt did not know, or did not care, that Boydell had been a previous applicant for the post). 'I had asked him to give me his ideas as to the best functions of a Director of Music in this organisation', McCourt wrote to his deputy, John Irvine.[54] The job specification written by Boydell read:

50 *Hibernia*, April 1967. The same view had been taken in an *Irish Times* editorial on 14 October 1966, during the debate over Tibor Paul's position: it is likely that Acton also influenced that text, which added 'The challenge of how to present music on television has not been answered yet. RTÉ needs vision and sense in equal proportions'. 51 Redmond Walsh to G. Victory, 25 May 1962. 52 Quoted by David Wright, 'Gerard Victory'. 53 T. Ó Canainn, *Seán Ó Riada*, p. 41. 54 McCourt to Irvine, 25 April 1967. In his autobiography, Boydell had recorded that, prior to

> The Music Director should have those qualities of informed leadership, authority, and personality which are necessary to inspire the coordinated team-work of those Assistant Directors of music sub-departments directly and indirectly under his control. It should be borne in mind that in Ireland, RTÉ not only provides virtually the sole major employment for musicians, but is also responsible for the major part of the performance and dissemination of music. The Music Director therefore carries a direct responsibility for the well-being of the art of music in the <u>country</u>, as well as in the field of radio and television . He must therefore have initiative and imagination, and seek every means of increasing musical interest and activity in Ireland, and of increasing the image of Irish music abroad. He must have the enthusiasm, vision, and determination to endeavour to place Irish musical activity within the over-all European picture. Having under his control the only professional orchestras in the country, he must be ultimately responsible for their standard, well-being and morale. To this end, he should actively show a friendly and authoritative interest in their welfare by keeping in personal contact with their leaders and leading personnel.[55]

Translated by John Irvine into officialese, the specific responsibilities of the post were originally listed as:

- to ensure the most beneficial balance between the various forms of music disseminated by RTÉ, striking the right balance between the demands of the majority, the needs of the minority, and the duty of the Broadcasting Authority to the cultural ideals of the country (the 'balance' being between 'serious', 'intermediate' and 'light and variety');
- to coordinate music on Sound Radio with that on Television, in consultation with the respective Controllers of Programmes;
- to encourage the standard and achievements of Irish instrumental playing and conducting by thoughtful supervision of employment of Irish musicians and by using such influence and facilities that he [*sic*] may have, to encourage provision for the training of young Irish musicians;
- to be responsible for the adequate encouragement of Irish creative activity in music;
- to supervise the maintenance of Archive Tape Recordings of works by Irish composers.[56]

Paul's departure, McCourt had 'invited me to act as his confidential music adviser' – quoted in Cox et al., *The life and music of Brian Boydell*, p. 19. **55** Forwarded by Roibéard Ó Faracháin to Irvine, 2 May 1967. **56** Ibid.

The second responsibility was rewritten the following day, presumably by Irvine: 'His primary responsibility will be in respect of broadcast music … His role as to music in the television service will be in an advisory rather than an executive capacity'.[57]

Victory was also a rising composer and conductor and could therefore be presumed to have an artistic as well as an administrative grasp of this senior position. Two days after his job specification had been finalised, RTÉ announced the appointment:

> Mr Victory has composed many musical works, most of which have been performed by the RTÉ Symphony Orchestra. After leaving school he studied music privately for six years with Hubert Rooney, Walter Beckett and Alan Rowsehome [*sic*]. His compositions include symphonic, vocal and chamber music and have been performed in Britain, Germany, Austria, Australia and other countries. He is also a composer of film music and has composed scores for documentary films both at home and abroad.[58]

The job specification is instructive for several reasons. Firstly, it gave no specific direction as to the management of the Music Department as such; perhaps, after the near dictatorial style of Tibor Paul, it was thought prudent to let Victory set his own guidelines and reporting parameters for his subordinates. Secondly, the emphasis on 'balance', and on the 'duty' of the Authority suggests that the top echelon of RTÉ was still feeling its way in defining its relationship with the administration; the 'demands of the majority' and the 'needs of the minority' were to become a millstone round the necks of all broadcasters – and had already done so in many cases – so that a policy for the appropriate balance was best left to the lieutenant closest to the area of programme output. Thirdly, the obvious restriction on the role of the Director of Music *vis-à-vis* television made it clear that a member of Radio Division had effectively no remit whatsoever outside that division, unless requested. Fourthly, it suggested that RTÉ had a function in respect of music education which, as we have seen, had already been studiously

---

57 Ibid., 3 May 1967. 58 Ibid., press release dated 5 May 1967. Hubert Rooney was a pupil of the Polish singer Jean de Reske, and a noted private teacher in Dublin (Veronica Dunne was one of his pupils) and also taught plainchant at the RIAM 1937–58; Walter Beckett, composer, taught privately in Dublin before living in Italy for an extended period, returning to teach composition at the RIAM 1973–84; the English composer Alan Rawsthorne (1907–71) had taught at the Summer School of Music in Dublin in 1950; it was at his suggestion that Victory had gone on to study with Beckett. Victory's first public performance was of his operetta *Nita* (1944, in an amateur production), and his first professional performance was a revue, *Spring Fever* (1945); his first broadcast had been incidental music to a radio play, *Chinese Lantern Moon*, in 1946, while his own musical play, *Once upon a Moon*, was broadcast in 1949.

and extensively canvassed, and gave both Victory and his successors serious cause for concern. Fifthly, it severely restricted the Music Department as far as archival policy was concerned, by specifically referring to 'works by Irish composers'. As a result of this policy, while performances of works by Irish composers were mandatorily archived, other tapes were consistently re-used, for reasons of expense and restricted storage space, unless specifically archived for musical reasons by the individual producer responsible for that particular programme. The onus of encouraging creativity in Irish composers would be a major challenge for Victory and his successors.

Above all, the opinions expressed by Boydell, and the eventual job specification itself, were aspirational. A prominent figure in contemporary musical life, who might well be regarded as a thorn in the side of RTÉ, Boydell had underlined the national role of the organisation both as broadcaster and as performer, had urged the operation of a European perspective, and had repeated his earlier strictures regarding the well-being of the orchestras by identifying this key position, and more importantly the personality of the post-holder, as the *responsable* whose performance of his functions would determine that well-being. The organisation itself had taken those aspirations and declined to translate them into anything more than a broadly phrased set of duties, some of which were more closely controlled than others: the negativity of the roles in relation to television and archival policy was more than compensated by the near vagueness regarding the actual performance of the job.

Victory was in most respects admirably suited to the performance of these vaguely defined functions. A keen and proficient linguist, with a profound understanding of, and sympathy for, European and indeed world culture, music and literature, he was also an Irish speaker who had explored Irish mythology and legend. His nationalist background[59] had not blinded him to the increasing focus of Ireland on European affairs (Ireland was shortly to accede to what was then the European Economic Community), but had allowed him to remain rooted in things Irish while he maintained a lifelong eclecticism in relation to the wider world. He was deeply sympathetic to the situation of individuals, especially musicians – at times too much so for the general welfare – yet here he encountered the organisational constraints which prevailed in dealing with those individuals and, indeed, with groups such as the RTÉ Singers and the representative committees of the orchestras. Here, Boydell's words about the post-holder are remarkably prescient, although it is more than likely that he knew that Victory was the favourite for the job: 'he should actively show a friendly and authoritative interest in their welfare' – it would prove beyond

---

59 His uncle, James Victory, was a Fianna Fáil TD for Longford-Westmeath (later Athlone-Longford) in the fifth Dáil (1927) and 1933–43.

Victory's skills (or of any other person in his position) to be both friendly and authoritative, since the system almost always militated against anything other than the strict application of procedures, in meetings which were often confrontational – the exceptions being the private consultations in the interstices between official meetings, when a degree of diplomacy and even compassion might alleviate what appeared to be an intractable position.

Victory's flair as a composer, in which his eclecticism stands out, was both a help and a hindrance to his work as an administrator. Accustomed to working with musicians on a professional as well as an amateur level, on appointment as Director of Music he immediately became at least one degree remote from them; yet, as someone who would continue to present his work to them for performance he was still required to maintain a fraternal relationship with them as interpretative artists. At the same time, his creativity as a composer often gave him an insight into, and an ability to solve, problems that others regarded as impossible. His strength as an administrator was to employ his avenues of communication to make the best possible case in whatever circumstance required it – not unlike a kind of plea-bargaining in criminal law – and thus to be able to say, honestly, that the outcome was the best that could be expected. In this he was likely to be suspected by both his administrative superiors and the musicians. His weakness lay in the same area – to take a middle road which might endear him to neither side, and which resulted in a lack of dynamic in the eyes of some of his more progressive colleagues. It was impossible for Victory to succeed, however much he may have wanted to, and as a result an increasingly severe staff relations problem developed, with P.J. Malone of IFMAP becoming a hazardous and entrenched opponent.

Nevertheless, under his direction, some of the most far-reaching decisions were taken in regard to the growth of both orchestras (including their international touring) and the appointment of successive Choral Directors (Proinnsías Ó Duinn, Eric Sweeney and Colin Mawby) and (at the behest of his own deputy, John Kinsella) of the Academica String Quartet. Where Tibor Paul had attempted to take the Music Department by the scruff of the neck and to make it into an international body, Victory, by a far more diplomatic and gradual approach, succeeded in achieving an exponential growth in most areas of activity, even though it left a legacy of frustration in others. When he retired, he would write: 'I hope my contribution has not been too inadequate to an area with a long and honourable history stretching back to the first day of Irish broadcasting and in my own opinion a very important one, which the changes in social climate and public taste have not made, in my opinion, any less important but indeed perhaps more so.'[60]

60 Victory to Director of Radio, 15 February 1982.

In 1979, near the end of his tenure, Victory wrote an article, 'What broadcasting contributes to music in Ireland' for the *Irish Broadcasting Review*. It was both a retrospect and a preview of some of his expectations, although its tenor was tempered by the fact that, as early as 1975, Victory had already signalled his interest in leaving his post, if only on secondment. Victory's headline read 'RTÉ's task is to achieve a balanced integration of all forms of musical achievement, including Irish traditional music. The future development of music in Ireland will be influenced by fostering the interaction of the different native and foreign genres'.[61] He was thus echoing the terms of reference set for him by Brian Boydell and endorsed by the Authority on his appointment over ten years before. Victory was quite unequivocal on the subject of the challenges facing RTÉ which, he acknowledged, were largely radiophonic and only marginally televisual. He stated quite clearly where the credit lay for the status quo:

> The achievement of establishing, in a relatively short time and against considerable odds, a full Symphony Orchestra, a Concert Orchestra, a Staff Quartet and Choir must be given its full credit. The absence up to twenty years ago of any really professional organising of serious music-making, thrust, in a way unknown in other European countries, an exceptional burden on to RÉ in integrating its broadcasting work with the task of providing at least the nucleus of general serious concert-going and similar activities ... The decision to accept this charge ... was a courageous acceptance of an unavoidable responsibility and a realisation that at the time, whether it liked it or not, RÉ was the only body capable of undertaking this task in the absence of any other organisational cadre in the country.

(In this he was, of course, ignoring the remarkable foundations laid by Michael Bowles in the Public Concerts of 1941–7.) But he also anticipated the crisis that would arise in the 1990s, as pressure mounted for the removal of at least some of the performing groups from RTÉ. 'One of the ever-present problems [is] to keep a just balance between the commitments of all these groups to purely radio and television needs as compared with the demands for their usage in non-broadcasting musical events. RTÉ found itself in the somewhat invidious position of holding a near-monopoly of professional music-making.'

Referring to the suggestion (raised by the Authority itself in 1965–7) that RTÉ might divest itself of some of its groups, Victory pointed out the international prestige gained by the groups, the benefit of their existence to the growing number of Irish composers, and the fruitful relationship between RTÉ

61 *Irish Broadcasting Review*, 5 (Summer 1979).

and the NICO, formed in 1970 by players mostly in the RTÉSO. Ironically, one of his arguments for retaining the orchestras was that RTÉ had built up an expertise in concert management – a point which had been strenuously resisted by P&T in 1924–6 when debating how 2RN was to be run.[62]

He also asserted that the Music Department 'is responsible for the development of music policy on television in conjunction with various other departments and in particular in relation to serious music'. Here he was stretching a point, as he was when he said that the RTÉSO had undertaken 'a short German tour' in 1977 – the orchestra had in fact given a single concert in Mainz that year – an example of Victory's ability to be prodigal with the truth.

He ended with an up-beat claim that 'it is difficult to envisage the present highly-organised art-music life of Ireland as it now exists without the RTÉSO … [while] the whole apparatus of instrumental art-music in Ireland clings closely to the appearance in recitals of the RTÉSO's leading players'.

One of Victory's first tasks on appointment had been to take on the musicians' union in response to its continued complaint about the employment of foreign players to the neglect, and detriment, of Irish players. In this sense he was the last *responsable* in RTÉ to encounter the original objections of IFMAP to the employment of foreign musicians. The correspondence with IFMAP is a litany of demurrals at the idea – forcefully asserted by the union – that RTÉ was excluding Irish players who were qualified for the positions advertised:

> We invited applications from percussion players in February of this year and no application was received from any Irish player.[63]

> We have tried to get a competent Irish harpist [for the RTÉLO] but none of the people we have contacted is interested or available.[64]

> Oboe vacancy – RTÉLO: no suitable Irish player is forthcoming for this post.[65]

> As you are probably aware, we did not find any suitable Irish trumpeters at this year's auditions …[66] Their 'dance' or 'bandsman' tone cannot be put right by experience but by study and tuition.[67]

---

62 Cf. Pine, *2RN*, ch. 3 passim.   **63** RTÉ to IFMAP, 23 August 1966, file H/E/1.   **64** RTÉ to IFMAP, 23 May 1967, ibid.   **65** R Walsh, internal memo, 3 October 1967, ibid.   **66** RTÉ to IFMAP, 12 September 1967, ibid.   **67** G. Victory to Personnel 20 August 1968. At a meeting with the Department of Labour on 22 August 1968 Victory repeated that one of the main reasons for the deficiencies of Irish musicians as regards symphonic work was that 'in their early lives [they] tended to play for Dance and Showbands where they made more money and only sought orchestra posts when they were too old to be acceptable for this type of playing' – RTÉ Personnel memo 23 August 1968, file H/E/2.

When the annual auditions were held in April last we had two vacancies for violins in the RTÉSO. The only Irish candidates coming forward were advanced students who did not wish to take full time work
because of study commitments.[68]

No other Irish [cellists] who are willing to take full time appointments
have come forward at any of the recent auditions.[69]

There were no suitably qualified Irish bassoonists available from this
year's orchestral auditions.[70]

Of the nine foreign and seven Irish members of the RTÉSO who had
resigned during 1966 (including nine who went to join the Ulster Orchestra),
at least ten would be replaced by foreigners, the only major appointment of an
Irish player being that of Brian O'Rourke as principal clarinet.[71] (O'Rourke
himself had been playing in a Norwegian orchestra, before returning to the
RAM in order to graduate.)

Following further representations from IFMAP, which was particularly worried at the number of musicians coming to Ireland from eastern Europe (who,
unlike their western counterparts, found the Irish rates of pay very attractive),
Kevin Roche was asked by the Director of Personnel (Oliver Moloney, later DG)

whether, by raising rates of pay, we could compete with the orchestras
of west European countries and therefore attract musicians from these
countries, and/or attract more Irish people to the musical profession.
The answer is, I think, that we could not do this without undertaking a
vastly increased commitment in the subsidisation of music. We must
therefore find musicians where we can, provided that our basic principle is to seek a foreign player only when a suitable Irish player cannot
be found ... We must have imported upwards of a 100 foreign musicians
in the past 20 years and I doubt whether more than half-a-dozen of them
have been sub-standard. There may have been a few errors of judgement,
but in general the standard of performance ... has been extremely high.
For every sub-standard foreign player that Mr Malone could name, I

---

68 RTÉ to IFMAP, 14 July 1969, file H/E/1.   69 RTÉ to IFMAP, 25 July 1969, ibid.   70 RTÉ
to IFMAP, 11 September 1970, ibid.   71 O'Rourke, a brother of pianist Micheál O'Rourke and
husband of orchestra leader Mary Gallagher, remained as principal clarinet until a neuromuscu-
lar condition, *focal dystonia*, dictated his retirement in 1997; in addition to his taxing solos as principal clarinet (such as those in the first movement of Mahler's first symphony or Rachmaninov's
second) he played several concertos [Mozart, Weber (no. 1 and the Concertino), Spohr (no. 1),
Nielsen, Thea Musgrave, the Rossini 'Variations' and Farhat and, with John Finucane, Durkó's
'Hungarian rhapsody for two clarinets and orchestra] and performed the Mozart quintet with the
Academica Quartet.

guarantee that I could name (a) at least one sub-standard Irish player at present in our employment (b) at least six young Irish players to whom we have given encouragement, employment, training and experience, and (c) eight or ten foreign players of excellent standard.

The primary object of employing foreign musicians is to raise the standard of the orchestra, but the secondary object is to attract good teachers to this country. Patricia Dunkerley, Edward Beckett and Patricia Cheatle would not be the flautists they are to-day if we had not brought André Prieur here in 1950. The same applies to oboeists Peter Healy, Muriel Dagg and Catherine O'Callaghan, who studied under Helmut Seeber; and to several cello students of Maurice Meulien.[72]

History then repeated itself, with Victory telling the Controller of Radio:

The establishment of a Youth or training Orchestra would certainly help, but I do not foresee RTÉ being able to undertake this. It is a project which the Arts Council might perhaps subvent. One of the main problems bedevilling the whole matter is the mutual antipathy of the two Dublin schools (Dublin College and RIAM) who have between them the basic material for such an orchestra.[73]

ALBERT ROSEN

The duumvirate of Victory and Albert Rosen, who had both been appointed in 1967/68 in succession to the dual mandate of Tibor Paul, marked another stage of growth in both the RTÉSO's standards and its musical outlook. With hindsight, it was unusual that RTÉ should appoint as Principal Conductor a man who had conducted only five concerts with the orchestra, and even more so a conductor whose reputation, however distinguished and promising, had been achieved in the opera house rather than on the concert platform. Rosen (1924–97), born in Vienna of Czech parentage, had studied there with Hans Swarowsky[74] and then in Prague with Pavel Dĕdeček (the teacher of Rafael Kubelik and Václav Neumann), with the opportunity to conduct the conservatory orchestra, led by Josef Suk. Rosen was at this time Director of the Smetana (opera) Theatre in Prague and resident conductor of the Prague National Opera, positions of immense prestige which he was obliged for polit-

72 K. Roche to O. Moloney, n.d. but after 7 November 1968, file H/E/1. 73 Victory to CP, 11 November 1968, ibid. 74 Swarowsky (1899–1975) was a pupil of Schönberg and Webern (for composition) and Weingartner and Richard Strauss (for conducting); his pupils included Claudio Abbado and Zubin Mehta.

ical reasons to relinquish in 1971. He had made an enormous impact at Wexford, where he first conducted in 1965 and, on the slim basis of these few guest engagements with the RTÉSO, he was appointed in 1968, holding the position until 1981, after which he became Principal Guest Conductor and, on his seventieth birthday, Conductor Laureate; elsewhere, he was principal conductor of the five orchestras of the Australian Broadcasting Corporation. Parallel with his work on the concert platform, he conducted altogether nineteen operas in Wexford and twenty-four for the DGOS, as well as working with opera houses abroad (including English National Opera and the San Diego and San Francisco opera companies).

Charles Acton picked up on the potential problems in Rosen's background (as far as orchestral concerts were concerned): on his first concert with the RTÉSO, during the Wexford festival, he remarked 'Possibly he is primarily an opera conductor (the rarity of any independent movement of his left hand would be evidence for that theory) ... Perhaps he was off form because nowhere did he seem to add any finesse or flexibility or shape to the music'.[75] When he took his first Gaiety concert three months later, however, Acton was impressed: 'I think that this must have been the most careful and conscientious performance that Brian Boydell's [Megalithic Ritual] Dances have yet had'. Of Tchaikovsky's fourth symphony, 'All through Albert Rosen obtained a deliberate and remarkable separation between the three choirs: wind, brass and strings. And within each he made the different strands quite distinct ... Notably well-shaped as a whole, with a most exciting sense of phrase answering phrase and some examples of luxurious lilt'.[76] (Rosen in fact acknowledged to Acton that he was 'learning his scores' through his work with the RTÉSO.)[77] Acton himself was often criticised for making 'invidious' comparisons, and when, a week later, he remarked that Rosen might not yet be getting the best out of the orchestra because 'In recent years they have been driven by tension and fear' but that 'the next month will be extraordinarily interesting to watch',[78] he was vehemently attacked in a letter from Maud Aiken, who rightly inferred that a retrospective judgement was being imposed on Tibor Paul.[79] It was not the last time that Acton would use such a tactic to make a telling point.

By the time Rosen made his first appearance as Principal Conductor in January 1969, he had established a better platform rapport with the orchestra, at least sufficient to please Acton, who wrote 'This was the best performance of the Tchaikovsky [sixth symphony] I have heard here for many years. There

75 *Irish Times*, 26 October 1967.   **76** *Irish Times*, 15 January 1968.   **77** Information to the author from Carol Acton, January 2004.   **78** *Irish Times*, 20 January 1968.   **79** *Irish Times*, 26 January 1968.

have been performances with more subjective drama, emotionalism, hysteria, and so on. To whatever extent all of that may be inherent in Tchaikovsky's symphony as well as in his personality, what we heard now was the music itself ... This was a most beautifully *musical* and, therefore, completely satisfying performance. The playing made me proud of our orchestra and the reading made me feel that Albert Rosen should be the right conductor for us'.[80]

Rosen's concerts were distinguished by the consummate atmosphere of *mittelEurop* with which he invested them. Especially 'at home' in the works of Czech composers such as Dvořák, Smetana, Janáček and Martinů, but also in the entire gamut of the Slavonic repertoire, he was the master of emotions on the orchestral tone-palette, and not at all oblivious of the effect that his demonstrative conducting style would have on his audience. As Charles Acton observed, a performance of Smetana's 'Ma Vlast' 'engulfed us with drama and luxurious sound ... the whole orchestra were caught up in this authoritative and almost exalted performance'.[81] Similarly, of Dvořák's eighth symphony on the eve of departure for the 1980 European tour: 'Mr Rosen's Dvořák always melts one's heart. If, in concert halls where they can be properly heard, the RTÉSO gives as caressing, seductive an account of this infinitely melodious symphony as they gave it last night, their foreign audiences should think very highly of them'.[82] Eimear Ó Broin made a telling contrast between the styles of Rosen and Paul when he recalled that whereas, in conducting Mahler's fifth symphony, Paul's personality cult 'turned it into a type of Nuremburg rally', Rosen, by contrast, showed 'most wonderful insight into a great work at the end of a musical era and the end of a social and political era'.[83] When Rosen conducted the RPO in 1974, Alan Blyth in *The Times* commented that he achieved 'the kind of verve that its players usually reserve for conductors they admire' and that in Schubert's 'Unfinished' symphony Rosen had 'a carefully conceived reading instinct with spontaneity and attention to balance'.[84]

Stylistically, Rosen's tenure added to the European timbre that had been achieved by his predecessors, Horvat and Paul: the intonation and phrasing he evoked made a more impressive and satisfying architecture out of his music than many more pedestrian conductors. His weakness was in accompanying concertos: while he was not at all deaf or unsympathetic to the soloist, especially the inexperienced, he could at times seem impatient, his *tempi* not always agreeing with the soloist's interpretation. This had been noticed by Acton in his first notice of Rosen, when Jean-Rodolphe Kars and Rosen seemed to have 'totally different conceptions' of Mozart's piano concerto K.491: 'it would be a really lovely experience to hear him playing the work with a sympathetic

---

80 *Irish Times*, 27 January 1969. 81 *Irish Times*, 1 July 1974. 82 *Irish Times*, 11 February 1980.
83 Eimear Ó Broin, interview with the author, 3 May 2002. 84 *The Times*, April 1974.

accompaniment'.[85] Part of Rosen's impatience was to do with his major strength: the symphony. His sense of the dramatic, which in the opera house made a completeness out of phrase, gesture and nuance, effected a relationship between orchestra, conductor and audience in which he was, literally, the medium. The impetus of his performances was due in large part to his meticulous preparation of his scores, which often caused him to change dynamics to achieve the desired effect in his conception of *his* interpretation of the composer's intentions. Michael Dervan, Acton's successor, found fault with this in one memorable review of Dvořák's second symphony and Tchaikovsky's 'Romeo and Juliet', when he referred to 'The conductor's propensity for ironing out a host of dynamic distinctions and then making up for the deficiency with exaggerated climaxes'.[86] It was not a particularly erudite judgement, but it gave an insight into the way that Rosen's determination might sometimes drive him to lose sight of the music's subtleties.

After a performance of Verdi's 'Requiem' in 1975, the year before the orchestra's first European tour, Acton wrote: 'Nearly a quarter of a century ago, the then Minister for Posts and Telegraphs, Erskine Childers, gave it as an aim to equal a BBC regional orchestra. It is now a European class orchestra',[87] and Rosen's contribution in reaching that stage of development had been crucial. The verdicts from foreign critics which came during the orchestra's European tours, noting the idiosyncrasies of its performing style, marked his impact on the RTÉSO as an interpreter who allowed certain characteristics in the players (noted by the critics as a form of Irishness) to flourish within the ambience of the repertoire, in a way that combined form and force in a usually successful fashion. Nowhere was this more evident than in the great sweep of an orchestral phrase from Dvořák or Scriabin, nowhere was it more exciting than in his direction of the *ensemble* of operas such as *Jenůfa* or *The Bartered Bride* with which opera performance in Ireland took a quantum leap. This was expressed at a memorial service in 1997 by clarinettist Brian O'Rourke, for many years co-chair of the orchestra committee, who had played under Rosen for many years and who spoke of 'the white heat of *Kátya Kabanová*, the frenzy of *The Gambler*, the malevolence of *The Turn of the Screw* or the comedy of *The Devil and Kate*'.

CHARLES ACTON AND 'THE IRISH TIMES' (2)

Despite Albert Rosen's success since 1968 as Principal Conductor, in March 1974 Acton published a three-part article in the *Irish Times*, 'What Can Be

---

85 *Irish Times*, 26 October 1967. **86** *Irish Times*, 16 February 1990. **87** *Irish Times*, 24 March 1975.

Done With The RTÉSO?', based on interviews with Gerard Victory and Proinnsías Ó Duinn, whose champion he appeared to be: he put forward Ó Duinn (who had made his début with the RTÉSO in 1962) as a conductor with experience of orchestra-building from his four years of 'virtually creating the National Orchestra of Ecuador' or, as Ó Duinn himself put it, 'trying to find out how a successful orchestra works, what makes it work, and how to get the best from an orchestra'.[88] He said that he did not see why his views 'should antagonise anybody', although in fact those same views, expressed in the context of an extensive article in what RTÉ would have regarded as the hostile environment of the *Irish Times*, probably did more than anything else to withhold from Ó Duinn the principal conductorship of the RTÉSO. As Director of Music, Gerard Victory had little time for Ó Duinn's qualities as a symphonic conductor, for example denigrating his adoption of the 'Stokowski seating' by means of which he brought the woodwind from the middle of the orchestra of the Gaiety Theatre to his right side, where they might be better heard with regard to the theatre's proscenium arch.[89] Victory, to the personal knowledge of the author, demeaned Ó Duinn to the advantage of Colman Pearce, in many ways Ó Duinn's rival and his almost exact contemporary, who would eventually obtain the principal conductorship.

Acton, conversely, had been impressed by the young Ó Duinn's début concerts with the RÉSO, whereas he disliked the first impressions made by Pearce. Thus, in June 1962: 'Proinnsías Ó Duinn gave us real grounds for hope that at last we have the material that may become a truly able Irish conductor';[90] in April 1966: 'I do not doubt that Colman Pearce is musical, but I am forced to the opinion that he is unable to communicate to an orchestra any sense of the beauty of the music he conducts, or of any love of music and its flow.'[91] His view of Pearce would, however, undergo a major change after Pearce's study with Hans Swarowsky, but he continued to put Ó Duinn forward as the leading light, especially after the latter had held principal appointments in Iceland and Ecuador.

---

88 *Irish Times*, 19 March 1974. When Ó Duinn returned to Ireland from Ecuador, Acton wrote of his first concert: 'Quite clearly, Mr Ó Duinn had authority. He knew what he was doing and knew what he wanted – and got it with clarity and no fuss. He had the air of being willing to, and knowing that he could, trust his players as artists without unnecessary and annoying detailed gestures': *Irish Times*, 13 January 1971. In 1973, he wrote: 'Proinnsías Ó Duinn has of course a rather special understanding of strings: he can mould phrases so that the speed fits the players' breathing and bow length like a glove; this knack or skill makes it very rewarding and satisfying to play with and for him. Add to that the ability to play a romantic work such as the Sibelius [second symphony] with such musical feeling that one wanted to sing the tune with him': *Irish Times*, 2 July 1973. Acton's successor. Michael Dervan, would also appear to be a champion of Ó Duinn's conducting skills: in 1990 he wrote (*Irish Times*, 16 March 1990) 'he is still one of the most inspirational conductors working regularly with any Irish orchestra'. **89** Ó Duinn had studied privately with Stokowski in New York. **90** *Irish Times*, 2 June 1962. **91** *Irish Times*, 24 April 1966.

Acton's articles, and his interview with Ó Duinn, were based on the asser-tion that 'for some time critics and public have been anxious about the RTÉ Symphony Orchestra, since many of its performances seem to be sub-standard'. Ó Duinn's ideas included changing the orchestra's rehearsal schedule in order to maximise mental and physical energy: acknowledging that musicians' activ-ity and attention were not limited to the time spent in rehearsal and perform-ance, they should be encouraged to teach and play chamber music: 'chamber music playing is not just a matter of nixers [freelance engagements], but it restores and refines musical and ensemble techniques ... Orchestral playing at its best is an extension of chamber music ... A conductor's job is therefore to encourage each member of the orchestra to give more than his best, while at the same time listening to his colleagues and taking pleasure in the sound they are making.'[92] Ó Duinn is an accomplished cellist and chamber music player, and his comments help to explain his artistic success with the close-knit Concert Orchestra.

Ó Duinn then went on to say that there were too many weak players in the orchestra, mainly in the strings sections. This once again raised the question of music education:

> We have such a shortage of violinists that we have to ask the student to go into the orchestra before he is really ready. And with the long rehearsal hours the most he can hope to do is merely to maintain his technique at the level at which it has arrived. It is terribly difficult to improve on it under such conditions. It is almost certain to decline. If you put a student into an orchestra for six hours a day, it's far more tir-ing for him to watch the notes going by than it is to play them, so these students leave after six hours rehearsal completely saturated and weary. So to have a fresh mind to improve themselves is out of the question.[93]

At almost the same time, Albert Rosen was expressing the same reservations to myself, while twenty years later, Alan Smale, leader of the NSO, would say: 'the NSO has a long tradition of giving students and young professionals oppor-tunities to perform, and it is a commitment we take very seriously indeed, *but* as members, the NSO should only take in the "finished" product'.[94]

Moreover, the rehearsal hours (10am–12.30pm, 1.30–3.15pm) prohibited many violinists who were also mothers from working in the orchestras. Ó Duinn was also critical of the fact that, as Principal Conductor, Albert Rosen

92 *Irish Times*, 19 March 1974. A later critic would also comment on the cameral nature of orches-tral playing: '[Benjamin] Zander aspires to a style of conducting which encourages orchestral musi-cians to interact as if they were working on a piece of chamber music': Michael Dervan, *Irish Times* 26 January 2004. **93** Ibid. **94** A. Smale, ms. letter to Geraldine O'Grady, 1 August 1994 (PIANO Archive).

was not resident in Dublin, and thus was not in a position to monitor the standards of the orchestra and of guest conductors and soloists on a year-round basis. Led by Acton, Ó Duinn committed the cardinal sin, in RTÉ-speak, of agreeing that 'the good of the orchestra is being offered up to the organisation mind ... We should get out from under the heels of people with civil service minds and then we will have a chance'.[95]

Ó Duinn then pushed the conversation towards the seminal point: 'the function of an orchestra in society'. Pointing out that there were three types of concert – the public subscription concerts at the Gaiety, the Friday night concerts with audience at the SFX and the Tuesday recording sessions without orchestra – he believed 'that it's a luxury for a country like this to maintain an orchestra solely for the purpose of broadcasting'.[96] 'I don't see any attempt by RTÉ to get the public interested in its orchestra or to get them accorded the dignity and reputation that they should have'.

In response, Gerard Victory put forward numerous factors which 'make it rather difficult to get off the treadmill of time'[97] in relation to the rehearsal schedule, and did not accept the argument that it militated against the inclusion of more experienced married women; his comment 'I think you would be surprised how resilient many of the married women players are' was typical of his ability to turn a point to his – or rather, the organisation's – advantage while ignoring the point at issue, which related to women who, by choice or necessity, were *not* in the orchestra. On the other hand, Victory's argument that the orchestra should perform as often as possible, while maintaining standards by means of sufficient rehearsal time, was a valid counter to the example of municipal and regional orchestras on the continent of Europe which frequently repeated programmes during their extensive touring schedules in their hinterlands.

The difficulty of making anything other than minor changes to the organisation and operation of the orchestra was made clear in Victory's statement that 'RTÉ is not a package of self-contained entities. The orchestra (and all that belongs to it) is a part of quite a large public service organisation, with its grades and privileges and the rules'.[98] Such a statement typifies both the advantages and the disadvantages of the orchestra's – and the Music Department's – position. As a concert-giving organisation, the Music Department was constrained by its sister departments which were not ancillary but superior: Finance, Personnel and of course Radio Programmes, within which it was located and through whose hierarchies any proposed change must be shepherded. Victory himself, while a man of immense creativity, artistry and imagination, was not, as an employee of RTÉ, a 'self-contained entity' but a bureaucrat who had to speak the language of his opposite numbers and to elicit the

95 *Irish Times*, 19 March 1974. 96 Ibid. 97 *Irish Times*, 20 March 1974. 98 Ibid.

sympathy of his superiors for the fortunes not only of the two orchestras and their cadre of conductors, arrangers and administrators, but also the musicians outside RTÉ who depended on the organisation for employment as either orchestral or chamber players or as soloists, and the music-loving public attending their concerts or receiving their broadcasts in their homes.

As far as the prestige of the orchestra was concerned, Victory felt that 'when you use the term national orchestra, this is true in a sense; and I think it is accepted by many people because it is the only outstanding professional body here. But we must also bear in mind that RTÉ must keep its interest in this very much to the fore, and it must not fail to be seen to be the maintainer of the group'.[99] Victory was in fact previewing the difficulty RTÉ would encounter in 1990 by changing the orchestra's title to 'National Symphony Orchestra', which did result in a diminished perception of RTÉ as its 'maintainer' and in an ambiguous second (but never official) change of title to 'RTÉ National Symphony Orchestra'.

The major positive points in Victory's interview were: his acknowledgement that the Symphony Orchestra should undertake more international touring (which would in fact be achieved two years later with its first European tour) but which also faced the fact that 'we are in a fairly difficult geographical position to achieve anything'. He also hoped to see more experimental music 'not only in the contemporary music festival (which has been very successful)', and 'a proper hall which is absolutely essential'.[1]

If Ó Duinn's anxieties were energetic and radical, and Victory's response appears lacklustre and institutional, it can be explained, as Charles Acton put it, as the difference 'between the idealist on the outside who feels he can see what must be done, and the man in the hot seat who has to cope'.[2] That difference, which is essentially an artistic-versus-pragmatic gap, is prototypical of the problem of balancing the management of culture with the culture of management which I discussed in my Introduction: the proposal twenty years later to separate the NSO from RTÉ and establish it as an entity in its own right was the only attempt to set it free of the organisational constraints which have always inhibited the enabling aspects of such a large and powerful parent.

But Acton did not let it rest there: he also characterised Ó Duinn as a practising musician with administrative experience and Victory as 'something of an outsider to an orchestra's problems in spite of being a composer and having done a certain amount of conducting'.[3] He hoped that 'Mr Rosen might now take a stronger line with Dr Victory and demand that more be accorded to the orchestra ... Certainly some of the red tape surrounding all RTÉ's decisions might well be thrown away.'[4] But Rosen was also an arch-pragmatist,

99 Ibid. 1 Ibid. 2 *Irish Times*, 21 March 1974. 3 Ibid. 4 Ibid.

knowing, from his background in dealing with the *apparatchiks* in Prague, exactly what could be achieved by the art of the possible. While he was without doubt one of the finest musicians ever to work with the orchestra over extended periods, he was not one to rock the boat in administrative matters.

Acton also foresaw the 1990s when the influential Naxos label would engage both the NSO and the RTÉCO: 'If RTÉ had a forward-looking policy that did engage the best players for the orchestra and treated the orchestra as artists and not as insurance clerks and understood them as musicians, then I believe that we could have international recording companies here choosing the RTÉSO.'[5]

His conclusion was that 'The National Song Contest is regarded as something of national television importance and the RTÉSO is regarded as the Cinderella of the entire broadcasting organisation. Is it not high time that somebody in the organisation took his responsibility for this fine body of musicians reasonably seriously?'[6]

The question, although ostensibly addressed to Victory himself, also embraced Victory's immediate superior, the Controller of Radio, and, above him, the DG and the Authority.

Acton's interview with Ó Duinn brought praise from composer Malcolm Arnold, at that time living in Dublin. Calling Ó Duinn 'that most excellent musician', Arnold said, 'I have often hoped in my 53 years as a professional musician to see such practical sense in print.'[7] Others, however, did not agree. Patricia Herbert challenged Acton's view that recent performances had been 'sub-standard', asking by what standard they were being judged, and suggesting that he was making comparisons with 'the major symphony orchestras of Europe'. She put forward the BBC Welsh, CBSO, the Oslo Philharmonic and the Helsinki Radio Symphony as comparable and said that the RTÉSO was at least as good, if not superior. She also promoted the view of 'the RTÉSO's particular function as a broadcasting orchestra and its special commitment to the listener'. Rather than increasing or expanding the orchestra's public appearances, Ms Herbert went in the opposite direction, stating that 'the failure to realise the full potential of broadcasting as a means of communicating music lies in the fact that music in this country has been dominated by a concept of communication rooted in a 19th-century social tradition, with a concession to broadcasting as a mere relay function'.[8] Meanwhile Michael Bowles asserted that the orchestra's management was 'in the hands of amateurs'.[9] As we shall see, it was an accusation to be laid against RTÉ's door twenty years later in acerbic measure.

5 Ibid. 6 Ibid. 7 *Irish Times*, 22 March 1974. 8 *Irish Times*, 27 March 1974. 9 *Irish Times*, 8 April 1974.

The professional response to Acton's articles came in the form of a detailed letter from P.J. Malone, Secretary of IFMAP, which highlighted, and categorised, the need for a balance between musical commitment and organisational control: 'regulations are necessary, but they should not blunt the musician's enthusiasm and attachment to his calling'. In particular, he called for some degree of participation by musicians in decision-making, better accommodation for the RTÉSO,[10] and 'societal recognition of the importance of the artist in the community'. As far as RTÉ's Music Department was concerned, the union wanted to see better deployment of the performing groups on radio and television, and greater awareness within the department of the needs, skills, and capabilities of its musicians. The letter amounted, in fact, to a demand for a much more profound understanding of musicians and music-making on the part of the department. Malone warned: 'If the treatment afforded to the orchestra were to be attempted in an industrial context, the resulting upheaval would be most serious. It may yet come to that'.[11]

Shortly after these exchanges, however, Colin Staveley took over the leader's chair for a five-year tenure, which brought stability to many areas of the orchestra, and which Acton was quick to recognise. Reviewing Staveley's first concert as leader, he wrote: 'This is the most important thing that has happened to the orchestra at least since Albert Rosen's appointment as principal conductor'.[12] Two weeks later:

> I would hardly have thought that Colin Staveley had been back long enough to have made the enormous difference to the violins that we experienced ... Last time we heard the 'New World' [symphony by Dvořák] the imprecision, lack of agreement and downright poor playing ... repeatedly made me wince ... This time we heard a real section, unanimous in pitch and ensemble, who consequently gave us a performance ... that stirred and satisfied the senses.[13]

Stability was increased further when Staveley was joined by Alan Smale as co-leader in 1977 and, when Staveley resigned in 1979, both orchestras benefited by the new disposition, which saw Audrey Park rejoining the RTÉSO as leader – a post she would hold until shortly before her death in 1994 – and Smale taking her place as leader of the RTÉCO, where he would remain until returning to the NSO as leader.

---

10 The new Radio Centre at RTÉ headquarters was nearing completion and would – arguably – provide suitable accommodation for the RTÉLO, but the RTÉSO would remain at the SFX for a further six years. 11 *Irish Times*, 5 April 1974. 12 *Irish Times*, 8 July 1974. 13 *Irish Times*, 22 July 1974.

MUSICIANS' STATUS CLAIMS

An important point had already been reached six years previously, when an internal RTÉ personnel memo observed that, by stating in its annual report for 1968 that 'the orchestra is in effect the National Symphony Orchestra of Ireland, serving public purposes far beyond the needs of Broadcasting itself', RTÉ had acknowledged its responsibility to reward its players appropriately for their 'professional skills and qualities'.[14] Once this admission had been made *within* the organisation, rather than as a matter of external public relations, RTÉ was set on a course of granting a claim by the musicians for better pay and working conditions, and increases were awarded in 1969.

RTÉ's dilemma was that the RTÉSO represented 17% of broadcasting costs, yet contributed only 2.5% of the schedule. Of 288 hours of performance, only 130 (or 45%) were broadcast.[15] The net cost had not in fact increased significantly over the mid-sixties, and in 1967 amounted to £180k. Gerard Victory suggested that the orchestra could become more productive if another group (he suggested the Ulster Orchestra) would undertake the Wexford and DGOS seasons,[16] but this was a premature proposal that would not gain a hearing for another two decades. As an editorial in the *Evening Herald* put it at the time of granting the increase,

> it is a very costly operation to keep [the RTÉSO] in being and yet it is seldom heard in public performances or on radio ... A duty therefore devolves on [RTÉ] to state a clear policy and to implement it with vigour in order that our young people will not grow up ignorant of the art of the cultural heritage of Europe which our symphony orchestra is capable of giving them. One has only to look at the age level of the audience at [the SFX] ... to realise that our young people want this kind of music ... Is there somewhere in the background a cold-blooded cost accountant who thinks that X hours performance for Y days per year would put all the clasics on tape and thus enable an expensive orchestra to be disbanded?[17]

By 1974, it was again felt that there was some slippage in the rates of pay, and a claim for an increase of 10% was submitted. The wording of the claim was almost exactly the same as that of the 1968 submission. There was almost no resistance to the claim, Victory acknowledging that the orchestras 'have

14 RTÉ Personnel Department file H/M/3, 'Musicians' Status Claim 1968'. **15** In 1949, Music Department's total output (from both orchestras, records and freelance players) was 38% of total output, amounting to 1,057 hours. **16** Victory, ibid., 11 November 1968. **17** *Evening Herald*, 16 July 1969.

shown real rising standards in the last two years and the sternest critics have conceded this', much of which he attributed to the appointment of Colin Staveley as leader and to Albert Rosen and Colman Pearce as conductors. 'It would be wrong however not to credit the general players with a great share of this – with few exceptions there has been enthusiasm, goodwill and diligence, often under still rather depressing playing conditions'.[18] There was, however, severe resistance to some of the musicians' arguments in regard to the maintenance of instruments and the level of education required for the work involved. Victory gave his opinion that, although an instrument might be costly, it was also likely to appreciate in value, while 'There may be some exaggeration of the theoretical or "intellectual" requirement – a high natural gift for an instrument plus technical skill and continuing experience is much more important than any other studies'.[19] Kevin Roche concurred: 'Bows do not require re-hairing every two to three months; instrument cases of good quality can last for an entire career; lower strings last 5 or 6 times longer than upper strings; woodwind and brass instruments last at least twice as long as stated (a modern flute lasts virtually for ever and I happen to know that Leon Goossens is still playing on an oboe which he bought new in 1907).'[20]

There was less agreement five years later, when a further claim – for increases of 35% – was submitted by IFMAP, and on this occasion Seán Tinney, senior engineer with, and a member of, the Electricity Supply Board, was invited by both sides to adjudicate.[21] The musicians put forward as the basis of their claim the cost of purchasing and maintaining instruments, the unsocial hours of work, inadequate annual leave, and the lack of promotion opportunities. RTÉ, as previously, admitted some slippage in relativity with other categories of employees, and awarded an *interim* pay increase of 10%, but argued that the extra increase sought was far in excess of the national wage agreements and contrary to public pay policy.

Tinney's meticulous and compassionate assessment of the status of the musicians was remarkably fair and realistic. He recognised that those holding 'Principal' positions (section leaders and other key players) 'play a vital role in the communication process which takes place between the conductor and the group' and that consequently 'the position of Principal deserves to command a high rank in the RTÉ staff structure'.[22] Despite the general empathy on the part of the Music Department (and especially of Victory) for the status of

---

18 Victory to Personnel, 22 October 1974: Staff Relations file H/M/4 'Musicians' Salary Claim 74'. **19** Victory to Personnel, 12 August 1974. **20** Roche to Personnel, 19 August 1974. Roche was almost certainly mistaken as to the date of Goossens' purchase, as the latter was only ten years old in 1907. **21** Tinney was also a brother of singer (and diplomat) Mary Tinney, and father of musicians Hugh and Ethna, and later became President of the Royal Dublin Society. **22** 'Claim by RTÉ Musicians and Singers – Assessor's Report', 30 November 1979, 14pp. typescript.

orchestra members, it is doubtful if it had ever been brought so firmly to the attention of the organisation as a whole that such personnel were integral to the 'RTÉ staff structure'. Tinney in fact equated Principals with the rank of Radio Producer as a yardstick of slippage, and found that there was a discrepancy of 20% between their rates.

Furthermore, 'musicians ... are practically unique among professional people in owning and providing the tools of their trade', and 'there is an unsocial aspect to their work conditions in that they do not enjoy freedom on week-ends to the same degree as does the average worker'. Tinney also acknowledged that chances of promotion were restricted for orchestra members, and suggested that where rank-and-file players could not progress to principal positions, a 'service payment' should be awarded to recognise long-term commitment. However, he considered the current leave entitlements satisfactory, and rejected the view, which had been put forward consistently by IFMAP since the advent of television, that television work should attract extra pay: 'I find it difficult to see why an Authority whose broadcasting mandate covers TV as well as Radio should be obliged to make extra payments to its full-time orchestras and singers for their work in one of these media.' Overall, Tinney recommended a further award of, in general terms, 10%, which was accepted by both RTÉ and IFMAP. This was to continue to be the basis of remuneration for the musicians until a major renegotiation of conditions of service in the 1990s.

EUROPEAN TOURS

A major test of Rosen's term as Principal Conductor came in 1976 when, ten years after the RTÉSO's first and only excursion outside Ireland, it undertook an eighteen-day, eleven-concert European Tour; most concerts were in fact in Britain, but the tour also featured concerts in Belgium (Antwerp), Holland (Rotterdam) and Germany (Kleve), and enabled RTÉ thenceforth to regard its principal orchestra as truly international. Under Rosen's baton, the Irish soloists were Bernadette Greevy and John O'Conor, and the featured work by an Irish composer was May's 'Sunlight and Shadow' (see Table P). It is significant that it was necessary, in the opinion of promoters at the concert venues, that pianists Moura Lympany and John Lill, and cellist André Navarra, should be added to the bill in order to attract audiences.

Anxieties were expressed as to the wisdom of an Irish orchestra visiting Britain at that time. As an unsigned news item in the *Irish Times* reported: 'Members of the orchestra have ... expressed concern at the risk to which an Irish orchestra would be exposed during a British tour ... Police forces in the British centres to be visited by the orchestra have indicated that special arrangements would have to be made, but the general feeling was that there was no great security risk. A spokesman at police headquarters in Manchester ... said that there was a very strong anti-IRA feeling, but he could not see that extending to a symphony orchestra. There had been quite a number of Irish concerts and entertainments in the area and no difficulties had been experienced'.[23]

In Bristol, after a poorly attended concert at the opening of the tour, absentees were castigated by the *Bristol Evening Post* for missing 'one of the finest orchestral concerts of the season ... [with] an immensely powerful, strong yet sensitive account of Dvořák's New World Symphony'.[24] In Manchester, the daunting Gerald Larner wrote:

> Certainly it is a good orchestra. It does not have a spectacular sound or a particularly distinctive style, but it is a well balanced ensemble, and clear all through. The brass section is stirringly bright but not domineering. The woodwind is unfortunately apt to fail in intonation. The strings are true, attractive if not voluptuous in sound.[25]

From Croydon came the dismissive opinion of David Squibb: 'The one notable characteristic lacking in the performance was unity, as if they were not used to playing the repertoire with each other'.[26] In Rotterdam, A. van Amerongen of *Niewe Rotterdamse Courant* was impressed by the orchestra's 'musical zest, its warm, nuanced sound and remarkable rhythmic discipline'.[27] As Concerts (and Tour) Manager, I wrote to Charles Acton: 'one of our objectives has certainly been achieved, in that generally the opinion of the orchestra is very high and ... informed people think we are worth inviting again. Also, almost needless to say, the orchestra have a wonderful enthusiasm for their work and a new sense of status as a result'.[28]

A side effect of this tour was the question raised by Michael Bowles:

> Why were Mr Colman Pearce and Mr Proinnsías Ó Duinn not sent, even in some sort of capacity as "associate conductors"? Was it because they were thought to be not yet fit to be presented in the great big world of music outside Ireland, as many tend to assume in the absence of an explanation? ... In my observation of their work, and with what is at least a wide experience of watching conductors in many parts of the world, I believe Mr Pearce and Mr Ó Duinn have in full measure the weight of personality, the technical skill and the extent of experience

23 *Irish Times*, 9 December 1975. 24 Quoted by Charles Acton, 'What reaction to the RTÉSO tour?', *Irish Times*, 24 March 1976. 25 Ibid. 26 Quoted in Charles Acton, 'Summing up on the RTÉSO tour', *Irish Times*, 7 April 1976. 27 Ibid. 28 R. Pine to Acton, 13 April 1976 (Acton Archive).

they need, right now … There is no question whatever of here min-
imising the work of Albert Rosen, an excellent and experienced conductor. But I think our native sons, Mr Pearce and Mr Ó Duinn, have
much to commend them above some of the talent unveiled at Wexford
and elsewhere.[29]

In 1977, the RTÉSO gave a single concert in a visiting orchestra series in
Mainz, the other participants being the Utah, Bamberg and Zagreb sym-
phonies, the Mozarteum of Salzburg and Antal Dorati's 'World Symphony
Orchestra'.

The European Tour of 1980 was a more adventurous undertaking, even
though, with at this stage two co-principal conductors sharing the concerts, it
reflected the fact that the personalities of Colman Pearce and Albert Rosen in
such a two-year arrangement (1979–81) were pulling the orchestra in different directions. This tour was also of eighteen days' duration, with fourteen
concerts, but it went further afield, with five concerts in Britain, two in Antwerp
(as in 1976), three in France (two in Paris, one in Strasbourg), and four in
Germany (see Table Q). Where, in 1976, the 'London' concert had actually
been in Croydon (Fairfield Halls again), in 1980 the venue was the Royal
Festival Hall, as part of the 'Sense of Ireland' festival; Edinburgh, Birmingham
and Paris were substantially more interesting, rewarding and prestigious centres than some of those visited four years previously, although the Strasbourg
concert was almost certainly misjudged. Irish composers were more extensively
featured (Boydell, Potter and Victory) while five Irish soloists were available:
Greevy, O'Conor, Geraldine O'Grady, Philip Martin and Micheál O'Rourke.
The orchestra was also variously billed in Germany as, in addition to its proper
name, *das Irische National-Rundfunk-Sinfonieorchester Dublin* [Irish national
broadcasting symphony orchestra Dublin], or *Irische Nationalsymphonie Dublin*,
since the mere 'RTÉ Symphony Orchestra' would mean little or nothing to
concert-goers outside Ireland.

Reviews were in general favourable, and took the view, as they had in 1966
and 1976, that something spontaneous and spirited in the orchestra's *attacca*,
which might or might not be attributed to its Irishness, made its performances
more interesting, even at points where they were musically adrift: a question
of *style* was raised and answered affirmatively. As Ulrich Bumann put it in *Rhein-
Zeitung* of Koblenz, 'while one should be careful in seeking to identify national
characteristics, this orchestra nevertheless seemed to be reflecting something
of Ireland in its playing. There was a fair share of robust imperturbability, a
full and darkly resonant tone from the strings, a solid and compact sound from

29 *Irish Times*, 27 March 1976.

the wind instruments – in short, the performance seemed less "fussy and mannered" than that of comparable continental ensembles'.[30]

The tour came at a time of cutbacks in the BBC, so it was no surprise to find Ian Robertson in the *Glasgow Herald* saying of the Edinburgh concert 'Unlike some broadcasting companies one could mention, the RTÉ in Dublin clearly believe that a good orchestra should be treated with respect and displayed to the world'. The performance of Mahler's fifth symphony displayed 'real integrity and spirit'.[31] So also Conrad Wilson in *The Scotsman*: 'Radio Telefís Éireann are proud of their Symphony Orchestra which is more than can be said for BBC Scotland ... What the orchestra had to offer ... was not so much finesse or weight of tone in the Mahler as a certain nervous gusto.' Of Boydell's 'In Memoriam Mahatma Gandhi' he thought 'it went through the innocuous motions of the period when Vaughan Williams was Britain's leading composer, but reviving it in 1980 seemed a pointless exercise. Presumably, however, it pleased Dublin's Department of Foreign Affairs, listed among the tour's sponsors'.[32]

Owen Dudley Edwards, reporting from Edinburgh for the *Irish Times*, thought that Rosen's conducting of the Mahler 'with a zeal and fire which rules the emotions of the house as firmly as the orchestra' had opened up the possibility of an engagement for the RTÉSO at the Edinburgh Festival.[33] In Leeds, Ernest Bradbury wrote that, with Audrey Park as leader, 'it must be the envy of every orchestra in Europe with the possible exception of the Hallé'.[34] In Birmingham, Barrie Grayson noted that 'the orchestra has personality, with every department of it, particularly the string section, displaying virtuosity within a sure ensemble framework, and its playing, always colourful, held flexibility as well as artistic finesse'.[35]

The embarrassment of Pearce's position as co-principal was made evident when William Mann, in *The Times*, referred to the apparent fact that Rosen, 'whose work will be familiar to many readers, gave the direction of this London concert to his young assistant, Colman Pearce, not yet so well known but a conductor of whom we expect to hear much in the future'.[36] But where, fourteen years previously, Edward Greenfield had commented on the high proportion of foreign names in the orchestra, now he applauded the fact that 'not only do Irish names predominate ... there is also a higher proportion of women players than I have noticed in any major orchestra ... This time, too, the conductor was no import from central Europe but a genuine Irishman, Colman Pearce' whom he described as 'associate conductor'.[37] Several reviewers thought it important to comment on the high proportion of women.

30 *Rhein-Zeitung*, 24 March 1980. 31 *Glasgow Herald*, 5 March 1980. 32 *The Scotsman*, 5 March 1980. 33 *Irish Times*, 17 March 1980. 34 *Yorkshire Post* 7 March 1980. 35 *Birmingham Post*, 10 March 1980. 36 *The Times*, 11 March 1980. 37 *Guardian*, 11 March 1980.

Table P: RTÉ Symphony Orchestra European Tour, 1976

Bristol – Colston Hall	12 March
Leeds – Town Hall	13 March
Manchester – Free Trade Hall	14 March
Newcastle-upon-Tyne – City Hall	16 March
Cardiff [Barry] – Memorial Hall	18 March
Huddersfield – Town Hall	19 March
Croydon – Fairfield Halls	21 March
Antwerp – Salle Reine Elisabeth	24/25 March
Kleve – Stadthalle	27 March
Rotterdam – De Doelen	28 March

Tour Manager:	Richard Pine	
Works:	Frederick May:	'Sunlight and Shadow'
	Weber:	Overture, *Euryanthe*
	Richard Strauss:	'Don Juan'
	Elgar:	Sea Pictures
	Beethoven:	Piano concerto no. 1
	Beethoven:	Piano concerto no. 3
	Tchaikovsky:	Variations on a rococo theme
	Mahler:	Symphony no. 1
	Berlioz:	Symphonie fantastique
	Dvořák:	Symphony no. 9
Artists:	Bernadette Greevy, *contralto*	
	John O'Conor, *piano*	
	John Lill, *piano*	
	Moura Lympany, *piano*	
	André Navarra, *cello*	
Leader:	Colin Staveley	
Conductor:	Albert Rosen	

Throughout, Bernadette Greevy's performances gained her universal commendation, and reviewers were generally appreciative of the other soloists. Both Rosen and Pearce were given praise for their direction.

COLMAN PEARCE

Colman Pearce (born in 1938), an accomplished pianist, had come to RTÉ as an assistant to Hans Waldemar Rosen with the RTÉ Singers, and in 1964 had secured a contract to work with the RTÉLO. Four years later he was offered, and declined, its principal conductorship. 'I didn't want to specialise solely in

Table Q: RTÉ Symphony Orchestra European Tour, 1980

Edinburgh: Usher Hall	4 March
Leeds – Town Hall	5 March
Hanley [Stoke-on-Trent] – Victoria Hall	7 March
Birmingham – Town Hall	8 March
London – Royal Festival Hall	10 March
Antwerp – Salle Reine Elisabeth	12/13 March
Paris – Salle Pleyel	14 March
Paris – Salle Gaveau	15 March
Strasbourg – Palais des Fêtes	17 March
Neustadt-an-der-Weinstrasse – Stadt Saalban	18 March
Stuttgart [Böblingen] – Kongresshalle	20 March
Koblenz – Rheinmoselhalle	21 March
Bielefeld – Oetkerhalle	22 March

Tour Manager: Richard Pine

Works:

Brian Boydell:	In Memoriam Mahatma Gandhi
A.J. Potter	Rhapsody Under a High Sky
Gerard Victory	Olympic Festival Overture
Janáček:	'Taras Bulba'
Rossini:	Overture, *La gazza ladra*
Barber:	Piano concerto
Beethoven:	Piano concerto no. 3
Beethoven:	Piano concerto no. 4
Chausson:	Poème
Elgar:	Sea Pictures
Gershwin:	Piano concerto
Mahler:	'Lieder eines fahrenden Gesellen'
Rachmaninov	Piano concerto no. 3
Ravel:	Tzigane
Wagner:	'Wesendonck Lieder'
Brahms:	Symphony no. 1
Dvořák:	Symphony no. 8
Dvořák:	Symphony no. 9
Mahler:	Symphony no. 5
Tchaikovsky:	Symphony no. 5
Chabrier:	España
Falla:	Dances *from* 'Three-Cornered Hat'

Artists: Bernadette Greevy, *contralto*
Philip Martin, *piano*
John O'Conor, *piano*
Geraldine O'Grady, *violin*
Micheál O'Rourke, *piano*

Leader: Audrey Park

Conductors: Albert Rosen, Colman Pearce

that area of music' he told Ciaran Carty of the *Sunday Independent*. 'I didn't want to become the Sidney Torch of Dublin'.[38] Instead, he was selected by Tibor Paul to work with the RTÉSO and over the next twelve years, in over eighty concerts, he had a mixed relationship with both orchestra and critics – as we have seen, he had not impressed Charles Acton with his early meetings with the orchestra.

The problem concerning Pearce's future career was exacerbated by the fact that RTÉ, corporately, saw the departure of Albert Rosen from the principal conductorship as the opportunity to realise the long-term ambition of appointing an Irish person to the post. Gerard Victory told the author at the time that, with the only other possible candidate, Proinnsías Ó Duinn, now working as Principal Conductor of the RTÉCO, he was under considerable 'political' pressure from the RTÉ Authority to appoint Pearce, and that he had succeeded in effecting a compromise by means of an interim co-principal arrangement. This was to prove highly unsatisfactory. In retrospect, Pearce's appointment as 'co-principal' was ill-advised, but at the time it illustrated the notion both within and outside RTÉ that the orchestra should have an Irish principal conductor (the first since Michael Bowles, thirty years previously) – which was part of the larger ambition for the creation of a national orchestra. But it also demonstrated the view (whether valid or not) that at the same time Pearce somehow needed to be phased into the post under the kindly tutelage of Rosen. This is ironic, given that both men had studied with the same teacher, the legendary conducting coach Hans Swarowsky. It could, however, be regarded as patronising and even insulting to Pearce who, in my personal view, suffered from that kind of nuance in what appeared to be a trial period during which, in his person, the nation's musical prowess was being judged.

Charles Acton had previously taken a negative view of Pearce's musicality when he had called his work 'dull', with an 'inability to express the spirit of the music',[39] but after Pearce had spent a year in Vienna studying privately with Swarowsky he was deeply impressed, his review being headed 'RTÉSO responds to new vibrancy': 'Judging by the Dvořák symphony [no. 8] the effect has been electrifying. Purely technically, it was a pleasure to watch the more purposeful gestures, the far greater independence of the hands and a new air of inner assurance … He was able to communicate with the orchestra and do so with authority. In performance, any orchestra always does its best to meet the conductor; on an occasion like this, where the conductor is really giving, the orchestra receives the authority and gives back rewardingly'.[40] He was also

---

38 'Ciaran Carty's Arts Page', *Sunday Independent*, 8 October 1978. Sidney Torch (1908–90) was the conductor of the BBC Concert Orchestra's 'Friday Night Is Music Night' 1953–72. **39** *Irish Times*, 6 March 1965. **40** *Irish Times*, 22 September 1969.

able to identify one of Pearce's undisputed strengths as a conductor, in which he far outstripped Rosen: his ability to accompany a concerto soloist.[41]

Nevertheless, Pearce had already had a difficult relationship with the RTÉSO which was made even more fraught when, at the time of his appointment as co-principal, he said 'It's often been said that an orchestra is like a big bunch of school children and there's some truth in this. By and large, no matter what sort of standards they have, if they can kick to touch, if they can give as little of themselves as possible, they will. There are very few who are giving their "all" all the time, unless the conductor is demanding it'.[42] In this interview with Ciaran Carty, which was supposed to be laudatory – and which began 'With the appointment of Colman Pearce to join Albert Rosen as co-principal ... music in Ireland finally comes of age' – Pearce in fact destroyed any chance that 'his' orchestra would greet this promotion of an Irishman with any measure of support, let alone enthusiasm. It was not so much the reference to 'school children' that was unwise – although this on its own 'grabbed the headlines' in that day's gossip – but the entire tenor of the interview, which had already pitted Pearce-against-the-rest at the beginning of this new relationship. At the top of the article, the point had already been made that the 'musical renaissance' in Ireland had its begrudgers, and 'Pearce's appointment appears to have encountered vague rumours of opposition, particularly within the orchestra'. Pearce's response was that 'I haven't worked with the orchestra for twelve years without getting to know the rough and the smooth. I'm well aware that not everyone is pleased ... My disappointment is in direct proportion to whether they're Irish or not. I think it's shortsighted of some Irish musicians in the orchestra to react against me and to keep looking to outsiders for principal conductors. All over the world orchestras are appointing their own nationalities as principals ... I intend to do the job, whether the majority of the orchestra like me or not. I hope to get very fine results and to make people who are dilatory in giving credit where credit is due to realise the error of their ways'. The appointment was, in fact, a poisoned chalice, since Pearce could not have refused it without signalling the end of his career in Ireland, and yet he was aware that a significant number of the orchestra believed, from its previous experience of his conducting, that he was not, at that time, the right person for the position. It would only be in the 1990s that a direct indication of the orchestra's preferences for its principal conductor could be canvassed and communicated formally to management.

Based on his previous experience with the RTÉSO, Pearce told Ciaran Carty that 'one would like to have the feeling that the orchestra was a close

---

41 *Irish Times*, 26 February 1968: the occasion was a performance by Mindru Katz of the Schumann piano concerto. **42** *Sunday Independent*, loc. cit.

knit team, always with a big majority saying, Yes we'll do this. But this isn't the case, unfortunately'. Compounding the injury he had already caused, he went on: 'The standard will have to go up. It can't remain static or go back'. Commenting on the need to travel more within Ireland, he thought 'They have become too settled, too sedate … A lot of them don't realise how soft [the schedule] is. And there is danger in this complacency. They need a shaking up here every now and again'.

The article caused outrage among the orchestra, leading to a decision by most of its members that they would not stand (as is conventional) when Pearce came on stage to conduct his first concert as Principal. It is probably best to say that the way that the interview was conducted was naïve on the parts of both Carty and Pearce, in that its consequences could have been foreseen and the profile it hoped to achieve could have been presented in a better light.

Pearce's intention was 'to create a sense of unity and a sense of team spirit' and to 'develop areas of orchestral work that haven't been touched too much before, namely on the contemporary front. I would do more rococo period of Haydn and Mozart'. Given that his views, as expressed in this interview, were to cause a severe breakdown in his relations with the RTÉSO, Pearce must have known that 'the standard' of that relationship could only go up.

If Pearce saw himself as another 'builder-conductor', his task would be that much more difficult, not least because his interview had carried an implicit criticism of Albert Rosen's style as principal conductor. Unfortunately, Charles Acton made unflattering comparisons – whether intended or not – between Rosen and Pearce. Thus in November 1980 he wrote of Pearce's direction of the Dvořák Requiem, 'Inherently it seems strange that with such an authority in Czech music in general and Dvořák in particular as Albert Rosen being co-principal conductor … the other co-principal … Mr Pearce, should undertake this work out of all the vast choral literature.'[43] He found the ensemble between the soloists in the Requiem uneven: 'A deeply experienced conductor would have nursed them and their intonation. Mr Pearce was making a good job of shaping the work, but must carry the blame'. A week later, Acton was writing of Rosen's next concert: 'The whole concern was a great occasion, and I could not help feeling that Mr Rosen was unintentionally demonstrating to us that some co-principal conductors are more principal than others.'[44] Such criticism was hardly helpful to Pearce, who was appointed full principal in 1981 – a move which had been anticipated ever since the question of an Irish appointment had been mooted. Although it was clear that the majority of the orchestra was trenchantly opposed to the appointment – a view which Victory had conveyed to his 'political' bosses within RTÉ – he had no alternative but to proceed.

43 *Irish Times*, 17 November 1980. 44 *Irish Times*, 24 November 1980.

Pearce held the position until 1983, probably a shorter period than he had anticipated back in 1979. Despite his well deserved reputation for promoting contemporary composers such as Bruno Maderna, Andrzej Panufnik (who became a personal friend), Humphrey Searle, Renato de Grandis, Leonardo Balada and Isang Yun (both with the RTÉSO and with his chamber group, the 'Ulysses Ensemble'),45 critics, audiences and the musicians themselves have had an ambivalent response to his musical impulses. Perhaps Ian Fox summed up Pearce's difficulties when he wrote: 'He never seemed to make the position really his own.'46

THE RTÉ CONCERT ORCHESTRA

In the late 1970s several events brought the RTÉLO to a new stage of its development. In 1974 it had moved into its new home in Studio 1, in the recently completed custom-built Radio Centre at the RTÉ headquarters in Donnybrook, a south-city suburb of Dublin. Although, with the passing years, the studio would prove less than satisfactory, at that time it was commodious, dedicated to the orchestra's use, technically equipped to the highest standards, and provided ancillary facilities which had not been available in the O'Connell Hall. Then in 1978 its fortunes were transformed with the decision to rename it as the RTÉ Concert Orchestra – thus signalling its emergence from the studio to a more platform-based role – and its first permanent Principal Conductor was appointed in the person of Proinnsías Ó Duinn, who had been working as Choral Director with the RTÉ Singers since 1974 and would remain with the RTÉCO on a permanent basis until the end of 2002.

Immediately, the new partnership made itself obvious to its public by undertaking a summer season at the Royal Marine Hotel, Dún Laoghaire and by moving into territory previously regarded as that of the Symphony Orchestra, with concerts as part of the latter's subscription series at the Gaiety Theatre and, later, at the NCH. In doing so, it proved in public what had always been known over the airwaves, that its hallmark was its versatility, that, as its publicity brochures claimed, it played 'everything from Handel to

---

45 The 'Ulysses Ensemble' gave many important performances, many of them premières, under the auspices of 'Summer Music at Carroll's', sponsored by the tobacco company P.J. Carroll and Company. Pearce's impact with contemporary music was such that in 1977 Charles Acton found himself looking back to the regular appearance of unusual and contemporary works in the 1950s and remarking that 'what little we have now seems to come from the concerts Colman Pearce conducts': *Irish Times*, 20 June 1977. The work in question was 'Rhapsodie Vardar' (1922/28) by Pancho Vladigerov (1899–1978). 46 *Sunday Tribune*, 11 November 1993. Thereafter, Pearce was principal guest conductor with the Bilbao symphony before becoming Principal Conductor and Music Director of the Mississippi Symphony for a twelve-year period.

*Table R: Works by Irish composers performed by the RTÉ Symphony Orchestra
and RTÉ Light Orchestra, 1969–78*

Derek Ball (b. 1949)
Four Chimaerae	1970	14.09.71		
Movement		04.11.69		

Gerald Barry (b. 1952)
Lessness	1972	05.02.74	03.02.78	
All the Dead Voices	1975	03.02.78		

Arnold Bax (1883–1953)
Tintagel	1919	29.05.70	18.06.76	
The Garden of Fand	1916	03.07.70		
Into the Twilight	1908	11.06.71		

Seóirse Bodley (b. 1933)
Divertimento	1961	05.01.70	05.01.73	25.06.76
Chamber symphony	1964	07.01.69		
Never to have lived is best	1965	08.01.71		
Configurations	1967	26.01.69		
Meditations on lines of Patrick Kavanagh	1971	30.06.72	02.07.72	
Ceathrúintí Mháire Ní Ógáin	1973	07.06.74		
A Small White Cloud Drifts over Ireland	1975	05.01.76	06.02.77	

Brian Boydell (1917–2000)
In Memoriam Mahatma Gandhi	1948	05.10.69	10.05.72	18.02.73
Violin Concerto	1953/54	23.01.70		
Wooing of Etáin, suite no. 2	1954	13.02.72		
Megalithic Ritual Dances	1956	16.07.76		
Meditation and Fugue	1956/57	24.04.70	05.05.72	
Mors et vita	1961	24.06.72		
Symphonic Inscapes	1968	26.01.69	13.07.73	23.11.75
Richard's Riot	1968	10.02.74		
Jubilee Music	1976	03.10.76	09.09.77	

John Buckley (b. 1951)
Taller than Roman Spears	1977	26.07.78		

Frank Corcoran (b. 1944)
Two Meditations for speaker and Orchestra	1973	06.09.74	28.02.75	
Chamber Symphony	1976	15.06.76		

Edgar Deale (1902–99)
Four Facets – Padraic Colum	1967	17.06.75		

Raymond Deane (b. 1953)
Sphinxes	1972	03.09.74	04.07.75	

Roger Doyle (b. 1949)
Four Sketches	1969	30.01.73		

Arthur Duff (1899–1956)
Suite for strings	1955	17.10.75		

Michele Esposito (1855–1929)
Irish Symphony	1902	16.03.69		

Howard Ferguson (1908–99)

Overture for an occasion	1952/3	20.11.77		

Aloys Fleischmann (1910–92)

Three Songs	1937	04.11.69		
Cornucopia	1970	11.06.71		
Sinfonia Votiva	1977	06.01.78		

Bernard Geary (b. 1934)

Provocations	1960	12.02.74		

John Gibson (b. 1951)

Lament for Children	1974	14.06.74	19.07.78	

Herbert Hamilton Harty (1879–1941)

Fair Day	1904	30.09.75		
Comedy Overture	1906	15.03.70		

T.C. Kelly (1917–85)

Piano concerto	1960	16.03.69		

John Kinsella (b. 1932)

Cello concerto	1967	06.06.69		
Montage II	1970	12.01.71	11.02.73	
Rondo	1969	05.01.70	25.03.77	
A Selected Life	1973	04.06.76		

J.F. Larchet (1884–1967)

By the Waters of Moyle	1957	10.03.74		

Daniel McNulty (1920–96)

Piano concertino	1964	14.11.69		

Philip Martin (b. 1947)

Terpsichore	1977	05.07.78		

Frederick May (1911–85)

Scherzo	1933	30.01.72		
Spring Nocturne	1937	26.09.75		
Sunlight and Shadow	1955	23.07.71	24.09.74	24.11.74
		09.03.76*		

E.J. Moeran (1894–1950)

In the Mountain Country	1921	02.07.71	23.10.72	
Violin concerto	1941	--.--.70	08.07.75	15.10.78
Overture for a Masque	1944	09.10.77		
Sinfonietta	1944	16.06.70	16.01.77	17.01.77

Havelock Nelson (1917–96)

Sinfonietta	1950	21.01.73		

Proinnsías Ó Duinn (b. 1941)

Symphony	1971	17.01.71		

Seán Ó Riada (1931–71)

Olynthiac Overture	1955	07.02.71	26.05.72	
The Banks of Sullane	1956	05.03.72	04.06.76	
Nomos no. 1	1957	20.02.72		
Mise Eire	1959	22.01.78		
Nomos no. 2	1963	23.11.71	07.01.72	
Seoladh na nGamhna	1959	24.04.72	11.11.73	

A.J. Potter (1918–80)

Rhapsody under a High Sky	1950	09.03.75	24.06.77	

Overture to a Kitchen Comedy	1950	03.10.71	26.02.78	21.06.74
Concerto da chiesa	1952	20.09.74		
Variations on a Popular Tune	1955	25.07.69		
Fox and Geese	1957	04.11.69		
Careless Love	1959	12.07.74		
Fantasia concertante	1959	20.06.72		
Gamble, No Gamble	1961	13.06.72		
Suite for Cardinal Fleury	1969	04.11.69		
Sinfonia de Profundis	1969	23.03.69	08.11.70	09.11.70
		06.01.78		
Sodaz suite	1973	13.01.76	18.02.79	
John Purser (b. 1942)				
Intrada	1966	18.01.70		
Charles Villiers Stanford (1852–1924)				
Overture, Shamus O'Brien	1896	03.03.74		
Comedy Overture		15.03.70		
Irish Rhapsody no. 4	1913	14.06.74		
Eric Sweeney (b. 1948)				
Canzona	1972	05.01.74	07.11.76	
Gerard Victory (1921–95)				
Ballade	1963	08.06.73		
Voyelles	1966	09.01.70		
Accordion concerto	1967	16.05.69		
Four Tableaux	1968	23.11.69		
Praeludium	1968	22.05.70		
Miroirs	1969	21.09.71		
Jonathan Swift – a symphonic Portrait	1970	24.06.72	13.07.73	
Overture, Cyrano de Bergerac	1970	14.03.71	25.02.72	
Piano concerto no. 2	1972	18.11.73		
Tetragon	1972	03.06.77		
Canto e symboli	1973	12.10.75	10.10.76	
Three Idylls		08.01.74		
Olympic Festival Overture	1975	13.03.77		
Sailing to Byzantium	1975	03.03.78		
Symphony no. 2	1977	17.05.78		
Raymond Warren (b. 1928)				
Symphony no. 1	1965	19.06.70		
Symphony no. 2	1969	24.06.72		
James Wilson (b. 1922)				
Symphony no. 1	1960/66	04.06.71		
A Woman Young and Old	1966	16.10.70	06.01.78	
Le bateau ivre	1971	15.10.72		
Irish Songs		30.08.74		
Symphony no. 2	1975	23.07.76		

*and on European tour: 12.03.76; 16.03.76; 18.03.76; 21.03.76; 27.03.76; 28.03.76

Summary: 34 composers (of whom, 27 living), 100 works, 141 performances

Humperdinck and from Lerner and Loewe to Lloyd Webber'. Ó Duinn had put a stamp on the orchestra's public profile with further concert seasons at the Royal Hospital, Kilmainham, but it was not until the 1990s that it finally emerged from the shadow of the NSO, whose concert seasons it supplemented during the latter's holidays and opera seasons. When it began to give its own seasons of defined concerts at the NCH, and moved to become the resident orchestra for the DGOS, it at last acquired its own identity and destiny as far as the public was concerned.

Because of its versatility, it is impossible to define the work of the RTÉCO in the same way that we can immediately grasp the symphonic repertoire of the NSO. Baroque, classical and romantic, film music, 'pop', opera, ballet, musicals, jazz – the gamut of almost every musical style means that it is always moving between genres and therefore difficult to arrest in any particular mode. For this reason it has collected accolades from a broad range of leading musicians with whom it has worked. Thus Irish tenor Frank Patterson wrote: 'I have had the distinct pleasure of working with the ... RTÉ Concert Orchestra on many occasions. Ireland should be very proud of its wonderful musicians and the RTÉ Concert Orchestra is a shining example of excellence, versatility and music-making.' Welsh tenor Dennis O'Neill: 'Having sung with the RTÉ Concert Orchestra for many years, I feel a genuine affection for them. As always with broadcasting orchestras, their workload and public responsibilities are enormous – no group in Europe does the job better or with better spirit'. American conductor Elmer Bernstein: 'I have had the pleasure of conducting the RTÉ Concert Orchestra in concert and film scoring at various times during the past twelve years. Our performance of the Ó Riada was one of the highlights of the past decade for me. The RTÉ Concert Orchestra plays with superb musicianship and sensitivity.' Irish singer Colm Wilkinson, star of *Les Misérables*: 'Working with this orchestra has always been a source of great pride and joy to me. Ladies and gentlemen, you are the best.' And film composer Carl Davis: 'The RTÉ Concert Orchestra performed my score for *The Four Horsemen of the Apocalypse* with immense panache and intelligence. It was a thrilling night for everybody.'

The most effective way of demonstrating this versatility, therefore, is through its programming over successive years. A typical programme from a concert at the Gaiety in 1980 indicates the operatic repertoire at its fingertips, which had been learnt as the pit orchestra at Wexford from the opera festival's inception in 1951 up to 1958; the soloists and chorus were Dennis O'Neill (tenor), Mary Sheridan (soprano), Colette McGahon (mezzo-soprano) and William Young (bass) with the Glasnevin Musical Society and the Renaissance Consort:

Overture, *Giovanna d'Arco* – Verdi
Habañera from *Carmen* – Bizet
'O Soave fanciulla' from *La bohème* – Puccini
'Va pensiero' from *Nabucco* – Verdi
'Ein Mädchen oder Weibchen' from *Die Zauberflöte* – Mozart
'Non più andrai' from *Le nozze di Figaro* – Mozart
'Una furtiva lagrima' from *L'elisir d'amore* – Donizetti
Easter Hymn from *Cavalleria rusticana* – Mascagni
'D'amore sull'ali Rosee' and 'Miserere' from *Il trovatore* – Verdi
'Avant de quitter ces lieux' from *Faust* – Gounod
'Soave sia il vento' from *Così fan tutte* – Mozart
'Nessun dorma' from *Turandot* – Puccini
'O ma lyre immortelle' from *Sappho* – Gounod
'Vedi! Le fosche notturne' from *Il trovatore* – Verdi
Opening of Act III of *Rigoletto* – Verdi

The following year the RTÉCO had moved into the NCH, with programmes which included Haydn's 'Bear' symphony, followed by its principal
clarinettist, John Finucane,[47] in the Nielsen concerto and a second part with
a similar group of operatic numbers. 1982 saw the RTÉCO in a Mozart/
Schubert season which featured the Mozart Sinfonia Concertante for violin
and viola with two members of the Academica Quartet, Ruxandra Colan and
Constantin Zanidache, as soloists.

A feature of the move to the NCH by both orchestras was the ability to give
lunchtime concerts for office workers in the highly populated vicinity of Earlsfort
Terrace and St Stephen's Green, presented by a compère such as Fionn O'Leary,
Bernadette Comerford or Máire nic Gearailt, and featuring a wide range of items
from the classical repertoire, as well as more popular items such as 'Man of La
Mancha' and 'The Impossible Dream'. The classical gamut was by no means the
exclusive province of the RTÉSO, since on 27 May 1986 we find the RTÉCO
playing Dvořák's Slavonic Dance no. 7, the Romance from 'The Gadfly' by
Shostakovitch, Ruby Ashley as soloist in Hummel's 'Introduction, Theme and
Variations' for oboe, Sibelius' 'Andante festivo' for strings, Boyce's fifth symphony and Suppé's overture 'Morning, Noon and Night'.

In the meantime, another major milestone in the RTÉCO's progress was
marked in 1980 by its US tour – presented by Columbia Artists who billed the
orchestra as the 'Irish Light Orchestra of Dublin' and 'The Official National
Television and Radio Concert Orchestra of Ireland' – with soloists Joan
Merrigan and Austin Gaffney, playing 63 concerts in 75 days, largely to appre-

---

47 Finucane became principal clarinet in the NSO in 1997, in succession to Brian O'Rourke.

ciative capacity audiences. As in the case of the RTÉSO, exposure to a foreign audience is a touchstone of whether an orchestra can communicate its musical skills and enthusiasm to people who are unfamiliar with their style, their repertoire or their presentation, rather than the home aficionados who may have become too accustomed to these elements to appreciate them fully.

The programme for the tour included Ó Duinn's theme music for RTÉ's epic dramatisation of James Plunkett's *Strumpet City*; Potter's 'Finnegan's Wake' and 'Rosc Catha'; Victory's 'Gaelic Galop'; Noel Kelehan's 'The Return of the Islander' and arrangements of 'The Raggle-Taggle Gypsy', 'The Rollickin' Irishman' and 'The Fairy Reel'. Merrigan sang 'Ireland, Mother Ireland' and 'The Castle of Dromore', Gaffney sang 'Boolavogue' and 'The Palatine's Daughter', and together they sang 'The Stutterin' Lovers'.

In the programme, Gerard Victory rose to the spirit of the occasion:

> Gold, they say, does not grow on trees. In spite of the legendary crock of the leprechaun, gold is not found all that easily in Ireland, but music certainly is; often, it seems to have sprung up of its own accord, so great is the wealth of our folk melody from the past. Nor is this tradition of the past only. Irish songwriters and composers are still flourishing and creating both serious and light music in great measure. It is with a sense of great satisfaction therefore that RTÉ presents its Irish Light Orchestra featuring Irish music from just a few of the many styles of dance, ballad, patriotic song and gentle lament for which Ireland is justly famous.[48]

Proinnsías Ó Duinn was not the only conductor to work with the RTÉCO, although he conducted the majority of its concerts. Owain Arwel Hughes, better known as a choral conductor, took the rostrum in October 1986 for a concert of 'Russian Favourites' which included Glinka's overture to *Russlan and Ludmilla*, another performance of Shostakovitch's 'Gadfly', Rimsky Korsakov's 'Sheherazade' and Rachmaninov's second piano concerto, with Philip Martin as soloist. (Hughes returned in 1989 for a performance of the Verdi Requiem.) A week later, Albert Rosen was in command with 'Tchaikovsky Favourites', including the fantasy-overture 'Romeo and Juliet', the 'Marche Slave', the suite from 'Swan Lake', the '1812' overture and Joanna Gruenberg as soloist in the first piano concerto.

By this time, Audrey Park had succeeded Colin Staveley as leader of the RTÉSO and had in turn been succeeded by Teresa Costello and (briefly) Martin Loveday before Alan Smale moved over from his position as co-leader of the Symphony. He would remain for ten years until he returned to the now NSO

48 Columbia ESI-100 B.

during the terminal illness of Audrey Park, and was succeeded by Michael d'Arcy (a former RTÉ Musician of the Future) and later Thérèse Timoney.

The RTÉCO undertook its second tour abroad in 1987, with a short visit to the UK, with concerts in Liverpool, Birmingham and, on St Patrick's Day, London's Albert Hall. In 1992 it returned to the UK with a five-centre tour (Wolverhampton, Sunderland, Nottingham, Brentwood and Ashton-under-Lyme) with flautist James Galway as soloist which, however, was not as successful as its previous venture as far as audience sizes were concerned, despite the attraction of the charismatic Galway.

Further tours to the USA and Canada followed in 1997, 1998 and 1999, under the heading 'Spirit of Ireland', the first with ten concerts including Toronto, New York, Atlanta and Miami.

The populist approach to concert-giving by both the RTÉSO/NSO and the RTÉCO broadened considerably in 1989 with two new initiatives. The first, 'Summer Sounds', was a series at the NCH by the RTÉCO in August 1989 with three successive nights dedicated to 'The Music of Shaun Davey' ('Granuaile' and 'The Brendan Voyage'), followed by 'The Music of Andrew Lloyd Webber' (again, three successive nights), 'Symphony in Rhythm' presented by Johnny Dankworth, 'Music of the Eighties' and finally 'Music for Middlebrows', a translation from radio to stage of Des Keogh's long-running radio programme of that name, which returned for a further series later in the year. The second was of much greater extent – 'Carrolls RTÉ Proms',[49] a sophisticated yet light-hearted panorama staged in a massive marquee ('the event in the tent') on the front lawn at RTÉ's Donnybrook headquarters. 'The Pavilion', as it was called, saw a timorous inaugural four-concert season which grew over the years. In 1991 it included not only the RTÉCO and NSO (conducted by Bryden Thomson in his last public performance, only days before his death) but also the Ulster Orchestra under Yan Pascal Tortelier. With a change of sponsor to the Bank of Ireland, 1992 saw a substantial widening of its scope, including a complete stage performance of Verdi's *Rigoletto* and a second visit by the Ulster Orchestra; in 1993, the Ulster Orchestra appeared again, plus the Ferenc Liszt Chamber Orchestra, a 'Musical Extravaganza – A Tribute to Cameron Mackintosh' (the producer of so many spectacular musicals on Broadway and elsewhere), and, specially for young people, 'The Romps'.

In 1990 the RTÉCO demonstrated a further bonus conferred by the move to the NCH when, as was usual during the period when the NSO moved to Wexford for the opera festival, it occupied the NSO's place on the NCH stage. October/November 1990 was the subject of an 'Eastern European Season' with concerts featuring the music of Dvořák (Carnival Overture, Cello Concerto

49 The name of the series reflected the sponsorship by P.J. Carroll and Company.

[soloist Robert Cohen] and 'New World' symphony), and Russian composers (including Rachmaninov's 'Paganini Rhapsody' with soloist Nikolai Demidenko).

Table 5: The RTÉ Concert Orchestra, 1996

1st Violins	*2nd Violins*	*Violas*	
Michael d'Arcy	Elizabeth MacNally	Padraig O'Connor	
Michael Healy	Paul O'Hanlon	Ruth Mann	
Mircea Petcu	Roisin Cavanagh	Thomas Kane	
Pamela Forde	Mairead Nesbitt	Michelle Lalor	
Sunniva Fitzpatrick	Arthur McIver		
Eileen Murphy	Donal Roche		
Ruth Murphy			
Jennifer Murphy			

Cellos	*Basses*		
David James	Martin Walsh		
Catherine Behan	Seamus Doyle		
Hilary O'Donovan			
Delia Lynch			

Flutes/Piccolo	*Oboes*	*Clarinets*	*Bassoons*
Elizabeth Petcu	Peter Healy	Michael Seaver	John Leonard
Gareth Costello	David Agnew	Jean Duncan	Carole Block
Ann Macken			

Horns	*Trumpets*	*Trombones*	*Tuba*
David Carmody	Bernard McNeill	David Weakley	James Kavanagh
Declan McCarthy	David Martin	John Tate	
Feargal O'Ceallachain	Patrick Kennedy		
Mary Curran			

Timpani	*Percussion*		
Richard O'Donnell	Tony Kavanagh		
Paul McDonnell			

A NATIONAL CONCERT HALL

Running parallel to the establishment and growth of the RTÉSO from the 1940s to the 1980s was the question of whether Ireland would ever build a national concert hall, which might or might not be the home of the RTÉSO.[50]

---

50 Eimear Ó Broin informed the author (interview, 3 May 2002) that Gerard Victory expected that the RTÉSO would be removed from RTÉ's control when the NCH came into existence.

It was acknowledged that the Phoenix Hall, due to its size, would never be more than a radio studio with accommodation for a small audience, however fondly it is remembered by those who benefited from the free concerts on Fridays and (until terminated by Tibor Paul) Tuesdays. There was never much enthusiasm for its successor, the SFX Hall, although it did have a much larger capacity, and had witnessed some remarkable performances, including three that I mentioned in my preface: Minchev's Brahms concerto, Messiaen's 'Turangalîla' and Lutosławski conducting his cello concerto with Heinrich Schiff. To provide a suitable permanent home for the acknowledged national symphony orchestra, and to provide a national – or at least a municipal – concert hall in Dublin, were twin ambitions which only occasionally coincided.

The history – or saga – of repeated attempts to provide Dublin with an adequate concert hall stretches back beyond the birth of 2RN's orchestra, however: when the city's main concert venues were the Antient Concert Rooms in Great Brunswick (now Pearse) Street and the hall of the Royal (later National) University which had been built as a concert hall at the time of the Exhibition of 1865 and eventually became the NCH.[51] To go back no further than 1900, the *Musical Times* reported that T.W. Russell, MP, had voiced the need for such a hall at an agm of the Feis Ceoil.[52] In 1908 Michele Esposito said (with the support of Vincent O'Brien and Edward Martyn) 'what a great advantage it would be to those who are anxious to be present at concerts, with distinguished artists and a full orchestra, to have a building which would accommodate two or three thousand people'.[53] In 1912 Vincent O'Brien (later Music Director of RÉ) said 'there are a lot of musical schools in Dublin and there is no culminating point in the form of a large hall in which to produce modern musical works with all the necessary detail'.[54]

Moving forward to the 1930s, we encounter the first occasion on which the idea of a home for the RÉ orchestra and the provision of a concert hall coincided. This involved the purchase or lease of the Rotunda buildings which had been built in the 1700s for the purpose of raising funds for the maternity hospital by means of entertainment, and thus had a tradition of public access for concerts and was at that time (and still is) the home of the Gate Theatre. This complex incorporated a large circular chamber, not unlike the Round Room of the Mansion House, where the RÉ orchestra had already performed, but the scheme would have seen the erection of a new hall as an addition to the existing complex.[55] The proposal met with severe resistance from within P&T, since the secretary, P.S. O'Hegarty believed that 'the general principle of sub-

51 Cf. Pine and Acton, *To talent alone*, pp. 96–7, 357–8. 52 *Musical Times*, 1 December 1900. 53 Quoted in Andrew Marsh [John O'Donovan] 'If Music be the Food of Promises', *Irish Press* 16 December 1970. 54 *Evening Herald*, 21 February 1912. 55 This scheme is described in detail in Brian Kennedy, op. cit., pp. 41–3, 46–9, 72, 107–8, 112, 146–7.

sidising places of amusement, whether theatres or concert halls or stadia, no matter how highbrow or desirable in themselves, seems to me to be entirely bad'.[56] With the express interest of de Valera, investigation of the proposal proceeded, but then in 1937 met with opposition from Finance: 'Although interest in music must have increased enormously, public attendances at Symphony Concerts, and consequently the necessity for such public concerts, has become smaller and will continue to decline. Is it any part of the State's duty to resuscitate a Victorian form of educational recreation[?].'[57]

With the appointment of P.J. Little as Minister for P&T, the project was re-directed to the Capitol Theatre, where RÉ's concerts took place from 1943. Once again, it was resisted by Finance: 'Of its nature, cultural development is a slow process, and State efforts to promote it may be regarded as very successful indeed if a generation from now they have produced such a widespread appreciation of music as would be necessary to give the Capitol Theatre project even a moderate chance of success.'[58] Thus, within or between government departments, a serious division of opinion existed as to whether Ireland was ready for such a hall, or had been severely deprived for many decades. In any case, the purchase price of £65k was regarded as prohibitive and the project once more lapsed. P.J. Little suggested a development in the Iveagh Gardens (to the rear of the present NCH and of Iveagh House) but this too was shot down on financial grounds. (It would resurface when the broader outlines for the conversion of the NCH were being drawn.) The accession to power of the first coalition government in 1948 saw the definitive end of the Rotunda project as well as that to re-locate the RÉ studios at a site in Stillorgan, near to their present location. Shortly after leaving office, Little (who had wanted to build a concert hall in Dublin for the Philharmonic Orchestra and a German-type concert-house for the radio symphony),[59] told the Dáil that a 2,000-seat hall 'would be able to give the country what it deserves in the way of adequate and first-class music and would remove a blot from ... our civilisation, because there is really no country of the standard of education of Ireland which has not got a decent concert hall in its capital'.[60] The response of the new Minister, James Everett, was that 'If we are to go in for building schemes, our first duty should be to provide sanatoria for the poor patients in the country who are in need of them, and houses for those who have no accommodation and not go in for ... fancy building such as cinemas or halls.'[61]

Little saw such a development as essentially taking place 'in co-operation with the radio'. His was not the only view, however. Others considered that Dublin needed not only a concert hall but also a municipal orchestra – serious

56 Ibid., p. 41. 57 Ibid., p. 43. 58 Ibid., pp. 47–8. 59 Information from Eimear Ó Broin. 60 DD. 112, 20 July 1948, col. 832. 61 Ibid., col. 891.

pressure had been put on the previous government in 1936 to give support to the Dublin Philharmonic to prevent its demise and to supply just such a want. Radio accommodation for a radio orchestra, perhaps with a purpose-built hall, as a separate undertaking, which should not be confused with the issue of a venue for public concerts, was envisaged by some who would be involved with the RÉSO (such as Eimear Ó Broin).

Despite the formation of the MAI, with the creation of a concert hall as one of its express objectives, the matter remained dormant until 1952, when discussion in the columns of *The Bell* drew attention once more to this lacuna in Dublin's cultural life, and the MAI set up its subsidiary company, Concert and Assembly Hall Ltd. The incoming Fianna Fáil government in 1953 (with Erskine Childers as P&T's minister) briefly revived the general idea, but again financial considerations made it unviable.

Meanwhile the MAI persevered with fund-raising ventures which were artistically extremely rewarding, regardless of the amounts raised. When the MAI began its fund-raising campaign at the start of 1960, Charles Acton wrote in the *Irish Times* that 'a concert hall can only come from our personal and individual efforts' which would 'prove that we actively *want* a national concert hall. It is no good our sitting down and saying that "They" or "the Government" should do something about it.'[62] At that point, the MAI's target was a site on the corner of Nicholas and High streets, and, having assured itself that Radio Éireann would transfer there from the Phoenix Hall, work actually started on site clearance. Acton commented that 'as the music in the new hall will be physically accessible only to those within an hour or so's run from Dublin, it may not seem at first to be a *national* asset. But we must remember that such a structure will lead to more and better broadcasts'. Reviewing the inaugural concert of the MAI campaign in the Theatre Royal (which included A.J. Potter's ballet suite 'Careless Love'), Acton commented that 'in the right hands, our own national orchestra, the RÉSO, can compare favourably with those distinguished visiting orchestras which have appeared there recently'.[63]

As we have seen, Tibor Paul (who saw in the Concert Hall campaign a publicity vehicle for himself and the orchestra) gave a Beethoven festival with the RÉSO (at the Olympia Theatre) in 1961, causing Charles Acton to observe that 'last night's event ... again emphasised our need of a concert hall, for the acoustics of the Olympia for orchestral music are most unfortunate. The first violins and cellos were heard as they should be, but only they. Wind chords which clearly balanced string ones in loudness appeared as echoes; loud *toned* trumpet notes were soft of *volume*; full *sforzandos* had to be understood and

62 *Irish Times*, 14 January 1960. 63 *Irish Times*, 16 January 1960.

sometimes timpani notes could not be heard in spite of knowledge that they were there all right'.[64] The observation helps us to understand the fate of the RTÉSO, giving its public concerts for almost thirty years in the Gaiety Theatre, where the proscenium arch contributed to acoustic problems almost as serious as those complained of here by Acton, and causing him and others frequently to ask when audiences might hear the full orchestra 'playing in the same room' as themselves.

The following year, the MAI (*recte* Concert and Assembly Hall Ltd.) ran a Concert Hall Fortnight including a Tchaikovsky night and a Wagner night by Paul and the RÉSO; the renowned Bach specialist, Rosalind Tureck, gave a series of recitals, and in May 1963 Artur Rubinstein gave a solo piano recital at the Theatre Royal. In January of that year, the government announced a donation of £100,000 to the MAI which, in the opinion of the *Irish Times*, 'redeem[ed] it from the charge of neglecting a cultural grievance that has been aired since the State began'.[65] The donation was tied in to a plan by the MAI to attract a further £150,000 from Dublin Corporation and to raise £300,000 by public subscription.

It seemed that a breakthrough was imminent, but the assassination of US President John F. Kennedy in November 1963 gave a sharp twist to the narrative, as the government announced the idea of a concert hall, commemorating Kennedy, and thus gave cause for the resurrection of this plan: the site proposed was the military barracks at Beggars Bush, Haddington Road, Dublin, the designer would be Raymond McGrath, who had been the architect for the abortive plan for the Rotunda gardens and was now Principal Architect at the Office of Public Works. A nine-person Oireachtas committee was established to investigate, and McGrath visited several halls in Europe, being accompanied by Tibor Paul on his visit to the Berlin Philharmonic.[66]

McGrath's plan was for a combined Concert and Conference Centre, with a large (Kennedy) hall of 1,850 seats, with a 'distinguished guest suite' of forty seats, and a smaller (McCormack) hall of 460 seats, plus a suite of conference rooms, fifty-eight 'back-up' rooms for conference administration, bars, restaurants and a four-level foyer/exhibition space, with full backstage facilities including rehearsal rooms and broadcasting and recording facilities. The stage of the 'Kennedy' hall would accommodate an orchestra of 120, with 200 choir places, with the lower part being lowered hydraulically to create a pit space for eighty players.

64 *Irish Times*, 14 March 1961. 65 *Irish Times* (second leader), 16 January 1963. 66 Nevertheless, Concert and Assembly Hall Ltd. continued to raise its own funds, bringing the Swedish tenor Nicolai Gedda, then aged forty, in 1965 (accompanied by Geoffrey Parsons) and that same year János Fürst and the Irish Chamber Orchestra played in its support.

By 1967, the Beggars Bush site had been abandoned in favour of the Phoenix Park, aggravating public opinion as to 'what the Hall will, or may, do to the Park',[67] with the architectural correspondent of the *Irish Times*, the music-loving Patrick Delany, voicing his disapproval on environmental grounds. Again, budgetary problems led to the postponement of the scheme in 1968 and, in 1974, the announcement by Richie Ryan (Minister for Finance in the Fine Gael/Labour coalition government) of its abandonment and of the government's decision, as an alternative and much less costly measure, to convert the Great Hall of UCD in Earlsfort Terrace into a concert hall (which would effectively mean a modernisation of what had originally been built as one). The chief architect would be Michael O'Doherty of the Office of Public Works (whose wife, Moya O'Grady, was a member of the RTÉSO cello section). Thus the forty-year involvement of the government with plans for a concert hall in Dublin culminated in a debate which concentrated the minds of interested parties as well as the general public, on the issues of whether Ireland really wanted, or needed, such a hall, and where it might be sited, as well as that of whether a refurbishment was a satisfactory alternative to a purpose-built hall.

That latter question had been answered by P.J. Little, who had been convinced of the rightness of the Rotunda scheme: speaking in opposition in 1948, he told the Dáil 'that the only real answer is to have a proper concert hall ... the Rotunda to be regarded as a *foyer* or a place where various public functions could take place'.[68] Conversion of an existing theatre or cinema would always be a halfway measure and would probably have insufficient seats. At the time of the government announcement, the Arts Council stated that 'while [the conversion of the Great Hall of UCD] may effect a needed improvement in the accommodation available for the Radio Orchestras, [it] will provide none of the essential ancillary accommodation for activities other than small orchestral concerts. By appearing to the general public to provide a reasonably satisfying compromise, the proposed conversion will ensure that for a long time to come it will remain commercially impossible to give Irish people the opportunity of hearing the great European orchestras and top-ranking artists'.[69] Coincidentally, in 1977 two Dáil deputies, Seán Moore (Fianna Fáil, Dublin South-East) and David Andrews (Fianna Fáil, Dún Laoghaire-Rathdown), introduced parliamentary questions regarding the Rotunda site as a potential concert hall, while on the same order of business future taoiseach Charles Haughey asked Richie Ryan's parliamentary secretary, Michael Begley,

---

67 *Irish Times*, 15 September 1967. In 2002 a site in the Phoenix Park was again being mooted as part of a project by the Department of Arts, Culture and the Gaeltacht to build a new NCH in that area. 68 DD. 112, 20 July 1948, cols. 831–2. 69 Quoted in *Counterpoint* (July 1974).

whether he was satisfied 'from the point of view of situation, that Earlsfort Terrace is satisfactory for a national concert hall? Is there sufficient space around it to provide all the amenities, facilities and parking that are necessary in that context?'[70]

In March 1974, just before the government announcement concerning the siting of the NCH, Eimear Ó Broin made a trenchant point about the broadcasting nature of the RTÉSO – and about broadcasting itself – in the context of concert reviews. He believed that a large radio concert studio, costing less than the 'Kennedy Hall', on the model of some European venues which he knew well, would be the most appropriate new home for the RTÉSO as a 'national radio symphony orchestra'. He complained that, in his reviews, Charles Acton 'seems to have been invariably relatively unconcerned with the finished product which is the result of the artistic collaboration between the musical and technical staffs of RTÉ, nor does he appear to consider the much larger unseen radio audience ... to whom the RTÉSO's output is primarily directed. (He has on occasion described the presence of microphones as a "barricade of ironmongery".) ... While he is, of course, entitled to a view of musical performance more firmly rooted in the traditional nineteenth-century concept of the concert hall, Mr Acton, I trust, will allow for other views consistent with an awareness of the immense possibilities afforded by the intelligent application of modern radio technology.'[71] Ó Broin was thus making an important cultural – and indeed political – distinction not only between the 'live' concert and that heard (either directly or in recording) by the radio audience (which could effectively be two different receptions of the same performance), but also between the concept of concert hall performance and the uses of modern radio technology in which, as a staff member of RTÉ, who had worked in radio houses throughout Europe, he was intensely knowledgeable and passionately interested.

The 1974 announcement, as reported by Geraldine Kennedy of the *Irish Times* ('Music Patrons Scorn Plan to Use UCD Great Hall'), 'was attended by an angry group representing musical interests in Ireland, who claimed that the Government had sold the nation's birthright for a mess of potage'.[72] Among them was Olive Smith, now chair of the MAI, who said 'The whole proposal is ridiculous ... Call it a studio hall for the Symphony Orchestra and not a concert hall for Ireland'. Kennedy reported that although the Minister had stated that the government's decision was acceptable to the Oireachtas all-party com-

---

70 DD. 296, 26 January 1977, cols. 205–6; Begley stated that 'the Government have not finally decided on the form which the alternative memorial to the late President Kennedy will take'. 71 *Irish Times*, 11 March 1974. Ó Broin made the further point (*Irish Times* 5 April 1974) that provision of facilities for external broadcasting in the Kennedy Hall were 'of the relay type and not, as in a radio concert studio, the central content of the design'. 72 *Irish Times*, 10 May 1974.

mittee, the Fianna Fáil members had issued a statement that they found the proposal unacceptable, but that they had 'saved the country from having the Kennedy name attached to this face-saving venture'. Maurice Dockrell (Fine Gael) and David Thornley and Noël Browne (Labour) had missed the meeting at which the committee apparently agreed to the proposal, and Thornley subsequently described it as 'a ludicrous architectural and artistic abortion of the original concept'.[73] Raymond McGrath was reported as having told the Minister for Finance that 'adaptation of the Great Hall would be a misguided operation which would be bound to postpone indefinitely the consideration of the city's real need for a hall of an adequate size'.[74]

From the point of view of broadcasting, one major defect of the present NCH is that, at the planning stage, no provision was made for camera positions, so that whenever a concert is televised, seats must be removed, daïses erected, and lighting introduced which is extremely troublesome to both players and audience. The practice of televising the regular symphony concerts, which was undertaken in the early years of the NCH, has been almost completely abandoned, but cameras and the consequent disruption remain a feature of special events of national significance such as the Dublin International Piano Competition and the Veronica Dunne Singing Competition.

Nevertheless, perceived exclusively from the perspective of the NSO, the NCH has, since 1981, provided it with a home immeasurably more convenient and comfortable than the SFX, and one in which its full year-round seasons of concerts can be given, thus raising its profile as a resident orchestra and consolidating its audience.

The first acoustic test was made in the NCH on 8 July 1981, featuring the orchestra's leader, Audrey Park, as soloist in the first Bruch concerto and, as the move towards the RTÉSO's new home looked more likely, the final concerts were given at the Gaiety in March (at the traditional closure of the Subscription Concert season) and in the SFX in July, as the orchestra wound down for its summer vacation. The acoustic test had revealed a too-long reverberation time which had to be adjusted before the State Opening on 9 September, when Colman Pearce conducted the specially commissioned third symphony, 'Ceol', by Seóirse Bodley (with text by Brendan Kennelly) and Beethoven's choral symphony (Violet Twomey soprano, Bernadette Greevy contralto, Louis Browne tenor and William Young bass, with Our Lady's Choral Society). Three months later, Charles Acton recorded that 'acoustically it remains a puzzle. It is certainly a great deal better than anything we have had before, but it still has serious problems ... The result ... is of lovely warmth for soft sounds, but a gonglike effect of a build-up of sound with loud sounds making an unpleasant jumble, whether

73 *Irish Times*, 15 May 1974. **74** *Irish Times*, 3 May 1974.

with choir, orchestra or solo piano. The effect is less downstairs than upstairs, but even downstairs it is unpleasant'.[75]

CHARLES ACTON AND THE 'IRISH TIMES' (3)

In the years 1979–81, developing his earlier theme of 'What's Wrong With The RTÉSO?', Charles Acton penned several major criticisms of RTÉ's broadcasting policies with regard to music. The RTÉ-published *Irish Broadcasting Review* carried his 'Who Does the Educating?' in its issue for autumn/winter 1979.[76] Addressing the question of subliminal (rather than explicit) 'education-by-exposure', Acton said 'I am extremely worried about RTÉ's deeply pervasive musical education ... done by those who do not even know (I hope) that they are debauching a nation's musical taste'. The 'centre of [his] anxiety and accusation' was the predominance of 'pop' to the detriment of both classical and traditional music:

> If one switches on RTÉ Radio at random, as I do almost every time I get into my car, the music that comes out is normally some form of pop. There is some traditional music, and we know that it is still profoundly part of the Irish people in spite of RTÉ's pop conditioning, but hardly any other sorts of music except in special ghetto programmes. This is an unusually musical nation. It is also, perhaps, a more thinking and mature nation than many others, especially outside the cities. But do the most potent moulders of opinion and taste, those who devise broadcasting for the entertainment and interest of the young – and it is also a startlingly youthful nation at the moment – have to choose the worst music to go with the best in other fields?[77]

Acton was particularly worried about radio programmes such as 'That's Entertainment' (presented by Morgan O'Sullivan, and a forerunner of Mike Murphy's 'The Arts Show' and 'Rattlebag' presented by Myles Dungan), which tended to ignore classical music and which had recently included an item on former Beatle George Harrison as its only musical feature. 'If this steady conditioning of the future nation to childish forms of just one of the arts is not to continue, then the Music Department must come out from the ghetto into

---

75 *Irish Times*, 17 December 1981. **76** The authors of *Sit down and be counted* had said 'The greatest single need in the country is education and re-education ... The means of access to ['high' culture], education, must be universally available before they will be universally demanded on radio and television. That they are not available is damnable': p. 178, p. 280. **77** *Irish Broadcasting Review*, 6 (autumn/winter 1979).

which it has allowed itself to be confined, and demand to have some influence on the sort of music purveyed by the station as a whole ... Music is the one field where most of RTÉ's unconscious pressures are downwards'.[78]

Acton's personal judgement – that the music of George Harrison did not deserve to be taken seriously, or to be placed on a par with a discussion of *Hedda Gabler* – may be wrong or at least arguable (certainly in my own opinion) but the crux of his argument leads us to enquire whether or not the Music Department had 'allowed itself' to become a ghetto. In the complexity of the development of different and disparate departments in the Radio Division, section heads liked to rely on the simplicity of chains of command which compartmentalised their responsibilities. Thus, while the Director of (classical) Music would meet his opposite numbers responsible for drama, variety, documentaries, current affairs and light entertainment at the regular editorial committee, there was no real possibility of permeation between departments (other than between Music and Drama), and the only effective method of influencing programme output in other areas was *via* the person at the pinnacle of radio programming, the Controller (later, Director) of Programmes (Radio). While Acton was no doubt completely right to say what he did, it was no more systemically possible for RTÉ's Music Department to influence radio output from any other area than it was to establish a presence in television.

Acton returned to RTÉ's programming policy in December 1979, now explicitly referring to 'the triumph of RTÉ's apparent intentions to debauch the musical taste of the nation'. This, he considered, was due to

> a *trahison des clercs* on the part of the heads of the station, most of whom have high tastes themselves, but personal convictions that the People have not or are incapable of having; to a similar *trahison* on the part of advertising people who will say, of course they love Schoenberg, but no one else does; and to a succession of bright, more or less young middle-aged producers and personalities of good education in most other fields who suffer from musical illiteracy and subnormal musical education.[79]

Two years later, insisting that 'taste is formed by exposure', he was again asserting that 'the high-ups in RTÉ are either genuinely ignorant of the facts or totally indifferent to their cultural responsibilities, even to those spelt out in the Broadcasting Acts ... No one wants to add late Beethoven quartets to Gay Byrne, but there is an immense amount of short bits and pieces, from ancient and modern, from the medieval to Bodley, from Ó Riada to de Bromhead, which exposure in ordinary programmes would help to make popular'.[80]

---

78 Ibid.   79 *Irish Times*, 28 December 1979.   80 *Irish Times*, 15 May 1981.

Here again, the authors of *Sit Down and Be Counted* helpfully provide instances of the context in which Acton was writing. 'Culture is every activity of the human person, living in community, that enlarges, enriches and deepens the common human experience of that community and its members. Community is as much an urban as it is a rural reality'.[81] Citing cuisine, politics, sport and religion as elements in a people's culture, they stated, following Douglas Hyde, that 'a nation's language, literature, art and philosophy' were the 'levels of cultural activity' without which 'the common life' would 'grow obese and wither, would corrupt and lose direction, would eventually become sterile, lose vitality and finally disintegrate'.[82] Acknowledging that there must be 'a principle of hierarchical importance', they nevertheless provided an argument for the fabric of broadcasting to contain both the weft and the warp, the élitist and the populist, for which Acton fought so strenuously.

Turning to concert programming, Acton opined that while Albert Rosen (now sharing the principal conductorship with Colman Pearce) had 'given us a large number of major performances', there was no 'firm impression of overall programme planning or direction' – 'there seems to have been an emptiness at the centre because there has not been any discernible pattern'.[83] It would not be until the appointment of Bryden Thomson as Principal Conductor 1984–7 that such a pattern would emerge, with his symphony cycles of Bruckner, Nielsen and others, which were revelatory, educational and artistically triumphant.

In 1980, celebrating twenty-five years as music critic of the *Irish Times*, Acton said that in the 1950s 'we were exploring the orchestral music of this century and of the byways of other centuries too … My impression is that we now hear our orchestra so seldom each year in live performances that we get neither the basic repertoire nor the new and the strange … There is too little excitement.'[84] He returned to this point in July 1981 when he observed that, under Fachtna Ó hAnnracháin's directorship, a range of continental and British conductors (Franci, Mander, Patanè, Zecchi, Schmidt-Isserstedt, Eckerberg, Matzerath, Balkwill) had performed

> a fantastic range of unusual and modern music. Admittedly we had in the 'fifties little serial and avantgardiste music, but we had an extraordinary amount of interesting modern music from all sorts of European composers, as well as the certainty that, if an Irish composer produced a competent work, it would have at least one hearing … Indeed, in those days, with sixty or more orchestral concerts a year, I, who was delighted with so much unfamiliar exploration, found myself worrying about the regular repertoire.[85]

---

81 *Sit down and be counted*, p. 278. 82 Ibid. 83 *Irish Times*, 15 May 1981. 84 *Irish Times*, 7 November 1980. 85 *Irish Times*, 10 July 1981.

Acton attributed the decline to Tibor Paul's cessation of the Tuesday evening concerts and to 'a concentration on spectaculars ... As a result, the former adventurousness disappeared, the impression of year round programme planning evaporated, and the effective number of public orchestral concerts was drastically reduced'.

> There should be about 65 evenings when our orchestra should be play-
> ing to us in the NCH ... If so, then round the year, they should be able
> to give us, each year, the standard masterpieces ... a great deal of music
> of our own day (including several performances at close intervals of
> important Irish works) and the rarities of the past that we want to hear.[86]

In April, he had asked 'Will RTÉ's top administration now give Dr Gerard Victory and his music department whatever is needed to work out a real new policy, to carry it out and to organise a real, continuing organisation able to plan everything ahead and put through its plans, in place of the hand-to-mouth life that seems characteristic of nearly all its radio and television work?'[87] Now, in July 1981, he became the first critic to ask publicly: 'Has the time now come to extract them [the RTÉSO] from RTÉ administratively?'[88]

The article had begun: 'This is written without consulting Dr Gerard Victory or Richard Pine or Lindsay Armstrong, the people who have the oner-ous job of planning the RTÉSO's programmes and appearances, of running their concerts, of running the new concert hall in which they will be appear-ing'. This was an excellent example of Acton creating a context in which it appeared that the three persons mentioned somehow had a joint responsibil-ity for the tasks mentioned – a context which of course did not exist. Victory had the first responsibility (the orchestral programmes), I was in charge of pub-lic appearances, and Armstrong, who had been seconded from the RTÉSO (in which he had been an oboeist) to be the manager of NICO, had recently been appointed manager of the NCH. Acton's clever suggestion that we were, jointly, a triumvirate is, in retrospect, risible: he could not have known that, with the appointment of Fred O'Donovan as Chairman of both the NCH and the RTÉ Authority, a political situation had built up within both organisations in which O'Donovan had identified Victory, Pine and Armstrong as the three main obstacles to the implementation of his own artistic policy, which was rumoured to include the transfer of the RTÉCO, rather than the RTÉSO, to the NCH as a 'house orchestra' in the style of many provincial German towns, as a way

---

86 Ibid. 87 *Irish Times*, 16 April 1981. 88 *Irish Times*, 10 July 1981. The following year Ray Comiskey would ask whether a radical rethinking of RTÉ's finances 'could mean the hiving off of the orchestras to, say, the NCH, or the creation of an autonomous body to run them': *Irish Times*, 27 April 1982.

of maximising audiences – colloquially known as 'bums on seats'. At one meeting Victory had protested that RTÉ had a responsibility to educate audiences by presenting unfamiliar music, including contemporary works. O'Donovan's reaction was explosively contemptuous: the public would pay for Mozart and Tchaikovsky, 'fiddles and flutes' as he put it. The meeting did nothing to assure the RTÉ Music Department that the one person responsible for the operation of both RTÉ itself and the NCH had a sympathetic ear.

Within two weeks of the State Opening of the NCH on 9 September 1981, Armstrong, who had found it impossible to work with O'Donovan, had resigned;[89] in March 1982 Gerard Victory announced his resignation from RTÉ with effect from the following September; and in January 1983 I agreed to a transfer from the Music Department to a new role in Public Affairs. While it could not be said that the three departures were inextricably linked, any more than it could be said that the three posts were administratively connected, there is no doubt but that considerable pressure was exerted on senior management at the highest level within RTÉ to procure the changes in the Music Department which would remove the obstacles to a more populist approach to the strategic deployment of the orchestras.

With Victory's departure from RTÉ (with a contract commissioning several large-scale works including his requiem 'Ultima Rerum' [1984]), Acton was able to return to the question of music management in RTÉ. Having written in February 1982 that 'our hearts must bleed for Gerard Victory and John Kinsella and Jane Carty and all the other people in the Music Department who are dedicatedly trying to run a music broadcasting service',[90] a month later Acton was saluting Victory as 'a man of enormous energy, underneath the calm, friendly and invariably courteous exterior', who had pioneered the Twentieth-Century Festival, encouraged Jane Carty in her work for young musicians, and who 'is certainly a European, and a world person, being president of the UNESCO Rostrum of Composers'. 'If he has had faults, they have been the reflections of his virtues, one of the chief of which has been loyalty. He is magnificently loyal to the people in his department and … has fought for the RTÉSO as a tigress for her cubs.' Acton hoped that 'that sensitive musician and fine composer, John Kinsella' would succeed him, but warned that 'he will face a lot of problems', urging that the new director must extend his area of influence to all radio activity and to television.[91]

When it became apparent to Victory that after his resignation the post of Director would be diminished to 'Head of Music', he remonstrated with Michael Carroll, Director of Radio:

---

89 In January 1982 Lindsay Armstrong was appointed Director of the RIAM. **90** *Irish Times*, 12 February 1982. **91** *Irish Times*, 12 March 1982.

The practice in almost all national radio stations even in smaller countries has been to have a reasonably impressive title for the prime music
spokesman. In a country especially with a late-developing music structure, a spokesman must act internationally with a feeling and image of
authority and conviction, not just as an area manager but as an approved
expert, able to voice a convinced and definitive opinion … RTÉ has had
to strive very hard to maintain its unique musical standing vis-à-vis the
various music organisations and sectional interests in this country. A
spokesman of authority is necessary in this regard to maintain and justify RTÉ's position and to satisfy all these interests that justice and fair-
ness is being exercised. That greater criticism and dissatisfaction exter-
nally have not arisen has been to a great extent due not just to my own
efforts as a person but to the weight and conviction of the post I have
held. The importance of the post has made me the recipient of considerable singled-out comment in the Press and elsewhere but it is a burden which any holder of this office must bear and respond to effectively
and firmly if RTÉ's status is to remain impressive'.[92]

Five months later, Acton was announcing 'Succession Problems', since no
procedure had been put in place for selecting Victory's successor.

It is now, in mid-1982, that the RTÉ Music Director and the RTÉSO
principal conductor-designate [Bryden Thomson would become principal conductor at the end of 1983] must get down to the planning
board. It is *now* that programmes, soloists, guest conductors must be
planned … At the end of the first and therefore tentative and experimental year of the National Concert Hall, it looks as if the topmost brass
of RTÉ could not care less about this crucial job at the most important
time for Irish music during this century.[93]

After another two months, Acton reported that, in the continued absence
of any announcement regarding the filling of the vacant post, he had written
to the Director-General of RTÉ (now George Waters, the former Director of
Engineering) and had received the reply that 'We propose to advertise for a
new Head of our Music Department as soon as our income permits. When
that will be I am not in a position to say'.[94] A further two months went by, and
in December 1982 Acton was addressing an open letter to Fred O'Donovan:

For half a year, John Kinsella, as Deputy Director, has been carrying
on, but, at a time when far-reaching plans are being made and policies

92 Victory to Carroll, 15 February 1982.   **93** *Irish Times*, 30 July 1982.   **94** George Waters to
Charles Acton, quoted in 'Directorless Dilemma', *Irish Times*, 24 September 1982.

laid down for the next five years or more, a deputy must be reluctant to arrogate the prospective powers of his future principal and therefore leave the latter powerless to put forward his own policies and ideas. You could, Fred, suggest, perhaps, to George Waters that if there is no need to have a Director of Music, there is no need to have a Director-General and that he might retire leaving the station in the hands of the deputy DG ... The single most important musical job in our whole island is the Director of Music of RTÉ. It is he who will plan for the next quinquennium, if not the next decade, what the various groups of RTÉ musicianers will be doing; what the punters will want to listen to; what Irish composers will compose .... Dear Fred, please do not let the present vacuum persist.95

These newspaper incursions by Charles Acton into the sphere of policy in broadcasting and music performance served to set the scene for their later discussion in an even more public arena, as the chief tensions and dichotomies which he identified in the 1970s and early 80s became major sources of irritation and embarrassment to RTÉ in the 1990s. After his retirement I recorded three conversations with him concerning his career, which were broadcast on RTÉ FM3 (and repeated) in 1990 as interval talks during symphony concerts, as a result of which he heard that an RTÉ radio producer had said it was 'a disgrace' that someone who had been critical of RTÉ, who was 'no friend of this institution', should have been accorded such a distinction. Acton wrote to the producer in question: 'I was always, from the 1940s, a friend of your institution. But, being a friend of your institution imposes a duty on a critic of making honest comments and trying to persuade its powers-that-be to do even better. I laboured long in the vineyard to help RÉ/RTÉ, especially at times when others were taking very dim views ... You may not have liked what I wrote for a third of a century, but it is possible that you may find that others may write less sympathetically about RTÉ and the NSO'.96

---

95 *Irish Times*, 30 December 1982. 96 Acton to (name withheld) 12 November 1990 (Acton Archive). And when he felt that his successor, Michael Dervan, was doing less than he might to probe the administrative difficulties surrounding the financial cuts caused by the government 'cap' on advertising revenue, he told him in the course of a long letter: 'You are a critic with a job to express opinions and to *care* ... It seems to me that the job of the senior music critic of the country's one really important paper is to CARE about music ... and support the good efforts of all the others who care and work. People are telling me that it seems to them that you do *not* care a tinker's cuss if music in Ireland dies or is destroyed because it is getting no advocacy from the most important music writer in the whole country, the critic of the I.T. I know that you do care, and only hope that you will confound those people by writing so': Acton to Dervan, 2 October 1990 (Acton Archive).

Table T: RTÉ Symphony Orchestra, State opening of the National Concert Hall, 9 September 1981

Principal Conductor: Colman Pearce; Chief Guest Conductor: Albert Rosen

1st Violins	*2nd Violins*	*Violas*
Audrey Park	Jack Leydier	Archie Collins
Alan Smale	Vanessa Caminiti	Thomas Kane
Sheila O'Grady	Joan Miley	Elizabeth Csibi
Timothy Kirwan	Michael McKenna	Kathleen Green
Clodagh Vedres	Carlos Assa-Munt	John Adams
Anna Kane	Keith Packer	Maureen Carolan
Catherine Briscoe	Claire Crehan	Miriam Lynch
Raymond Griffiths	Arthur Nachstern	Christine McKevitt
Elias Maguire	Yvonne Donnelly	
Helen Briscoe	Mary O'Hanlon	
Katherine Smale		
David McKenzie		

Cellos	*Basses*
Roland Saggs	Helmut Engemann
Robert Pierce	Wolfgang Eulitz
Darine ní Mheadhra	Herbert Nowak
Linda Kelly	David Daly
Thomas Kelly	Eamonn Williams
Niall O'Loughlin	
Paula O'Callaghan	
Una Keenan	

Flutes	*Oboes*	*Clarinets*	*Bassoons*
William Dowdall	Albert Solivérès	Brian O'Rourke	Michael Jones
Madeleine Berkeley	Helmut Seeber	Sydney Egan	Dieter Prodöhl
Deirdre Brady	Patricia Harrison	James Daly	Michael Rogers

Horns	*Trumpets*	*Trombones*	*Tuba*
Patrick McElwee	Joszef Csibi	Seán Cahill	Hartmut Pritzel
Harriet Huxley	Szabolcs Vedres	Francis Hughes	
David Carmody	Graham Hastings	Phil Daly	
Thomas Briggs			
Colin Block			
Nicola Jukes			

Timpani	*Percussion*	*Harp*
Martin Metrustry	Noel Eccles	Síle Cuthbert
Angela Boot		
Stephen Keogh		

CHAPTER 7

A time for change, 1982–97

Perhaps the most difficult point concerning the history of RTÉ's music activity in the period since 1982 is its complexity. The central factor in those decades has been the question mark over the status of the NSO and its relationship with RTÉ. This in turn calls into question the entire history of R(T)É's involvement in music-making, since the evolution of the NSO has never been as straightforward as that of the RTÉCO, its functions were never clearly defined until RTÉ tabulated its Strategy for the Performing Groups in 2004, and its future has mostly been a matter of aspiration rather than a carefully plotted critical path. The professionalisation and internationalisation of the NSO, and of music administration in general, has been more intense in this period than in any since the 1940s and 50s; the questions that have been asked of RTÉ, and which RTÉ has asked itself, in relation to its performing groups, have been more searching than any since the establishment of its two orchestras in that period; the internal structures of the organisation as a whole have been re-established, affecting the way the music department carries out its work and relates to other parts of the whole; and the intimate connection between music and politics became even more evident, as financial crises forced RTÉ to interrupt planned developments in music and to precipitate a debate concerning – and confusing – the artistic, managerial and economic dimensions of its music policies.

The history of the period 1982–97 would not give cause for such confusion were it not for this complexity. A concatenation of events, over most of which RTÉ had little or no control, such as the imposition of the 'cap' on its advertising revenue, and the abrupt resignation of a principal conductor, had an almost devastating effect on a situation over which it *did* have extensive control, namely the designation and direction of its performing groups. One cannot look at any one of the major events in the period in isolation, nor can one appreciate the situation at which RTÉ had arrived in 1994–6 (the time of the PIANO report), without understanding where it had come from, institutionally. Properly speaking, the stabilisation of RTÉ, its achievement (under Bob Collins as Director-General) of a slimmer, more streamlined entity, more alert to its future in cultural and financial terms, belongs to a period after, and is addressed in the Postscript. But moves in that direction can be detected in the way that RTÉ addressed the challenges directed at it by Michael D. Higgins as minister with responsibility for broadcasting in the Fianna Fáil/Labour/ Democratic Left coalition government's Green Paper on Broadcasting of 1995 and in its mid-wifery of Teilifís na Gaeilge (later TG4) leading up to its launch in 1996.

Internationally, it was a period of debate about the *raison d'être* of the public service broadcasting systems, set up in the 1920s as media of communication for national cultures and national political agendas. Of these systems, globally speaking, Seán MacRéamoinn would say 'institutionally we have become spastic and culturally we have lost our way'.[1] It is perhaps only when one sees such an institution in an environment that is potentially, if not actually, hostile, and for which its own evolution has not adequately prepared it, that the fragility of such a concept as music and broadcasting, seen within the totality of that environment, becomes evident, its discussion fraught with tangential and apparently unrelated issues that complicate one's perspective even further.

From the perspective of participants like Fachtna Ó hAnnracháin and Eimear Ó Broin, or commentators like Charles Acton, who had 'grown up' with the broadcasting system in what today seems like a monophonic environment, and who had an association with R(T)É lasting into the 1980s, there were conceptual routes to understanding and relating to the system that were unavailable to younger and harsher critics such as Michael Dervan, or to the newer players joining the orchestras after the expansion of the NSO in 1990. A cultural and informational gap, which it has been part of the purpose of the present study to identify and to bridge, separates those whose interest in 'serious' music began in the 1970s or later: the system itself, without realising it, became qualitatively different, and different questions are now asked of it, different expectations are imposed on it, and different methods of evaluation are employed in assessing its performance.

One conceptual difficulty that has persisted since the establishment of RTÉ in 1962 (and can be traced in detail from the very origins of 2RN/RÉ) is the obstacle in the way of RTÉ's involvement in the development of the arts and arts education – and many other areas of public concern – due to its position as a semi-state body governed under legislation by a statutory authority. Just as, within RTÉ itself, radio and television existed as almost hermetically sealed units, so RTÉ itself remains isolated from the chief agencies for cultural development such as the Arts Council and the Department of Education. Its linkage with the Department of Arts and Culture (by reason of its minister having additional responsibility for broadcasting) was serendipitous, creating no chan-

---

1 S. MacRéamoinn, in Holde Lhoest, report of Council of Europe Symposium, Liège, 1981.

nels of intercourse on non-broadcasting matters, and came to an end in 2002, with the re-shaping of departmental responsibilities which saw broadcasting returning to the remit of a minister for communications.

This is not a unique situation. RTÉ's isolation has left it in an ironical position with regard to any attempt to establish an overall perspective on musical life, or any other aspect of Irish society. When in 1975–6 the Arts Council and the Gulbenkian Foundation commissioned the eminent British architect Sir James Richards (assisted by project director Millicent Bowerman) to conduct a survey of 'Provision for the Arts', he had observed that

> There has been controversy for a long time about the RTÉ symphony orchestra. It is … in effect the national orchestra. The question is whether it should be treated as such and supported by Government funds (channelled presumably through the Arts Council) rather than sponsored as at present by RTÉ.[2]

However, his report made no recommendation on this point to back up this observation. An in-depth review of 'Provision for the Arts', having devoted several paragraphs to a description of RTÉ's activities in the field of music and opera, could make no stronger recommendation than that 'permanent liaison should be established between the staff of RTÉ and the Arts Council'. The report merely repeated what RTÉ itself had been saying in the 1960s, and which would be raised again in the 1990s. Surveying the *status quo* seemed to be more important than making thorough-going recommendations about the future, in areas to which the Arts Council was not central.

In 1979 Ciarán Benson recommended that 'the Arts Council must from now on monitor educational policy. It must establish a right of comment, and it must seek representation for the arts on any advisory or other committee whose recommendations may influence the development of the arts in education'. He advised that the council should undertake continual liaison with, among others, RTÉ and the Department of Education.[3] As an aspiration, this was admirable; as an expectation, it disregarded the institutional quarantine in which most state agencies exist.

The peripherality of RTÉ to central decision-making in the arts continued to be underlined in 1987, when the Fine Gael/Labour coalition government (soon to go out of office) published 'Access and Opportunity: a White Paper on Cultural Policy'. The only consideration given to RTÉ's cultural output or policy was a paragraph within the section devoted to the then Department of

2 J.M. Richards, *Provision for the arts*, pp. 30–1. **3** C. Benson, *The place of the arts in Irish education*, pp. 128–9.

Communications, which referred *en passant* to the two orchestras as 'part of the nation's cultural assets'.[4] In its 'Summary of Proposed Action in the Cultural Field' it stated that 'the objectives of cultural policy will be taken fully into account by RTÉ in its broadcasting policy',[5] yet, short of giving the minister mandatory powers to direct RTÉ to incorporate those objectives into its broadcast output, there was no indication of how it might do so, other than by adhering to its responsibilities as already laid down in the Broadcasting Acts.

These brief examples highlight the fact that, in the period with which we are concerned in this chapter, RTÉ's isolation was accentuated, rather than reduced, by the gravity of the manoeuvres that it was expected to make in order to maintain its centrality in Irish society and cultural life. Its performance in the field of orchestral development, its reaction to adverse financial positions, its artistic vision, were subject to the personalities, persuasions and perspectives of its own administrators, of politicians and civil servants, and of vocal critics who often did not communicate with any level of sophistication and who often did not understand one another.

AN INTERNATIONAL PERSPECTIVE

The 1980s and 90s were decades of considerable change internationally, as all levels and sectors of society – politicians, civil servants, arts administrators, sociologists, social workers, community groups and the citizens in the streets – moved towards a new understanding of the role and status of culture in their lives. The Victorian paternalism of the concept of 'leisure' had given way, in the wake of the second world war, to a new kind of paternalism, with the state as provider of facilities and opportunities for its citizens, the models being G.M. Keynes's Arts Council of Great Britain and, in France, André Malraux's 'Museum without Walls'. This 'democratisation of culture' was mirrored in Ireland by the 1951 Arts Act which established the Arts Council (An Comhairle Ealaíon) as such a provider. RTÉ, at that time struggling to ensure the survival of its orchestras, had only a tangential relationship to such developments. Like most national broadcasters in Europe, it had been set up as a monolithic structure and thus its broadcasting function – however much it impinged on the lives of listeners and viewers – could not easily be integrated into the stream of activity which would gradually divert the flow of 'democratisation of culture' towards a new concept: 'cultural democracy'.

Ireland as a whole also suffered from a gap in its learning experience in the late 1960s, when the seeds of 'cultural democracy' were sown throughout

---

4 *Access and opportunity*, p. 49.   5 Ibid., p. 87.

Europe and the USA in the confrontation between students and authority in Britain, France and, most notably, at Berkeley, California. The birth of the civil rights movement in Ireland (and the political crisis of the 'Arms Trial' in 1970–1) subsumed whatever cultural impetus there might have been, into the overriding political imperative to rescue a submerged 'nationalist' minority in Northern Ireland from the hegemony of unionism. Political and social energies were focussed on issues such as housing and the franchise. Cultural identity was, if anything, assumed to be an implicit part of social and community identity, with the right to self-determination and, indeed, human dignity, as its driving force. The only tangible effect on musical activity of events in Northern Ireland was the cessation of visits there by the RTÉ orchestras.

The appearance in 1969 of *Sit Down and Be Counted* had given anyone interested in the question of identity and communication the opportunity to continue the debate within RTÉ that had occasioned the resignations of its three authors; but it failed to excite such a debate in society at large. The issues were fundamental to Irish society: the question of identities – social, cultural, economic – and of how the new medium of television was to be employed in the portrayal, sustenance and development of those identities. That they were not widely debated can be only partially explained by the continuing antipathy of the still dominant Catholic Church to the idea of the media as vectors of social change; it was also partly due to the 'innate conservatism' of the organisation itself, many of whose personnel still operated under a civil service mentality. It would not be until the proposal was voiced to establish a second television channel that questions would arise as to what 'Irish' television entailed and required.

What has this to do with music, classical or otherwise? Those who remained within RTÉ sat down and allowed themselves to be counted as subscribers to the general editorial policy of a station which could certainly see more crises on the horizon (especially in the perennial minefield of current affairs) but which sought a middle-of-the-road approach to output, with technical excellence rated more highly than cultural self-determination (which perhaps explains why the top echelons of RTÉ have traditionally been populated mainly by accountants and engineers rather than programme-makers). Obvious exceptions to this were the filming of James Plunkett's *Strumpet City* (1980) and Thomas Flanagan's *The Year of the French* (1981), but in music, on both radio and television, little change occurred, simply because no serious questions were being asked about the content of music programmes or the manner of their presentation. The 'politics' of music did not arise until the next major clash between the political and the broadcasting worlds in 1990.

This might have been expected to change when, in the late 1970s, the exponents of 'cultural democracy' suggested that a participatory lifestyle, with its emphasis on the involvement of citizens in decision-making which affected their cultural and social lives, was preferable to a top-down 'democratisation' which merely authorised the widespread distribution of cultural opportunities.

However, a conservative organism such as RTÉ was unlikely to respond to such a challenge, although there was no explicit attempt to resist it – indeed, the present writer was given considerable freedom to engage internationally in the study and promotion of 'cultural democracy', one element of which was termed *schwellenangst* or 'fear of thresholds', signifying reluctance on the part of young people to subscribe to traditional art forms or, literally, to enter the institutions in which they were to be found and, instead, seeking alternative cultural forms.[6] Alienation from cultural norms would, of course, in time affect the numbers of young people attending, for example, the conventional symphony concert.

But there was little evidence of programme makers taking up such challenges and thereby creating an upward momentum that would attract the attention, and sympathy, of the administration. Without a challenge to the relationship between composers, performers and audience, policy and its execution would be left in the hands of those who considered that 'more of the same' was the way forward. In 1987 the editor of *Music Ireland*, Michael Dervan (who had just become music critic of the *Irish Times*) expressed the view that 'The image of the RTÉ Music Department, as communicated by radio, is still by and large fuddy-duddy and inward-looking, and the department conveys little sense of enthusiasm about the works and performances it presents'.[7]

It is helpful, therefore, to look at the broadcasting function from another, also international, angle: the discussions within the EBU of the changing nature of the old-style broadcasting orchestras, which broadened in the 1980s to encompass areas of concern which had hitherto been neglected or unnoticed, the most pressing of which is the health of orchestral members within the context of their working environment. It may seem ironic that in 1984 the EBU was still sponsoring discussion on 'the future of *radio* orchestras', as if the presence of television had no impact on their existence. A symposium held that year, attended by representatives of sixteen broadcasting organisations responsible for thirty-six of the fifty-two radio orchestras within the EBU remit, resolved that more public performances, involving more contemporary music, appearing on television and in commercial recordings, was the way to safeguard their 'necessary and vital contribution to musical culture'.[8] As with so many international gatherings, the resolutions reflected a consensus which followed the line of least resistance, and was less than the sum of the parts of the individual contributions. While Michael Casey, representing RTÉ and Ireland,

---

6 Cf. R. Pine, 'Cultural democracy' (1982). 7 *Music Ireland*, 2/8 (September 1987). 8 L. Salter (rapporteur), 'Symposium', p. 72.

seemed satisfied with the progress of the two orchestras, other speakers, from countries where the broadcasting orchestras lived side by side, and in competition, with other symphony orchestras, referred to 'a state of permanent crisis', especially in relation to the need to stimulate 'progressive musical trends' (as in France); in Germany, there was a 'peaceful co-existence' of the radio and municipal orchestras, and in Sweden competition was regarded as a stimulus; in the Netherlands a wholesale revision and rationalisation of cultural affairs was making redundancies among musicians, and Robert Ponsonby, head of music at the BBC, referred to the sweeping cuts that had been made by his organisation in the past four years, observing (as would Pierre Boulez in his contribution to the debate, quoted above p. 427) that 'it [is] curious that what militated against the achievement of the highest standards by radio orchestras [is] the fact that they worked for broadcasting organisations'.9

Robert Wangermée, director of the French-language service in Belgium, adverting to the ubiquitous financial difficulties of public service broadcasters and the growth in commercial competition, warned that

> the public service system is justified only if it refrains from likening itself to its competitors and making its own programming uniform with theirs … One of the roles of the radio orchestra is to contribute towards a certain democratisation of musical life, by leaving the radio studio, by seeking out new audiences, possibly in venues other than bourgeois concert-halls hallowed by time. It is also necessary to invent appropriate techniques of presentation which, free of didacticism, will allow music to be appreciated in all its beauty.10

(Simon Taylor, as general manager of RTÉ's performing groups, would voice similar possibilities when addressing the PIANO review group.)

Of particular interest was the contribution by a specialist in health, Dr Jacques Sporcq of French-language Belgian broadcasting, who analysed current research into the ergonomics of orchestras as influenced negatively by environmental factors and positively by 'valorizing' factors. The former – lighting, air-conditioning, humidity, seating, legibility of music – were responsible for a higher rate of absenteeism among musicians than among other types of workers. Psychological factors induce lassitude and mental fatigue; conversely, good relations with colleagues and the conductor can stimulate 'the feeling of participating in cultural creation and its diffusion'.11 This contribution provoked a debate about work satisfaction, stress, hearing difficulties, the need for early retirement, and the general agreement that 'orchestras are very fragile communities'.12

9 Ibid. p. 23. 10 Ibid., pp. 32–3. 11 Ibid., pp. 63–7. 12 Ibid., p. 68.

In 1987 Friedrich Nowottny, Director-General of Westdeutscher Rundfunk, published a short paper 'On the relationship between broadcasting and culture' which, *inter alia*, urged that public service broadcasting had a responsibility to facilitate experimental art. He also observed that to maintain the traditional forms of art-music was a valid continuing function because most of these musical genres (the classical and romantic symphonic repertoire, light music of past and present) 'have been neglected by the commercial market for years because they are financially unrewarding'. But he also alerted broadcasters to a fact that would not receive serious attention in Ireland for a further decade: that there is a 'close connexion between the private cultural market and the media market' which was 'not a matter of competition but of complementarity'.[13]

Simultaneously, European broadcasters met to discuss the problems related to contemporary composition and, in particular, how to create new and appreciative audiences for new music, when listenership surveys indicated an almost *nil* audience: could such surveys determine the fate of minority interests? Although RTÉ would have followed these discussions with interest and, perhaps, a certain feeling of helplessness, it is only in very recent years that the Music Division has actively sought to engage audiences with a series of 'new music' initiatives which acknowledge the centrality of the contemporary composer, and the creative process, to the survival of the orchestra as a concept.

An international discussion of the nature of public service broadcasting in an increasingly commercialised and politicised world, which has radio orchestras as its focus, and which expressed concern for the well-being of players both singly and as a 'community' was, in fact, timely. The health issues discussed at the EBU Symposium have taken an important place on the agenda of modern orchestra management, and international conferences on 'Health and the Musician' have become almost commonplace: a survey of fifty-six orchestras, reported in 1997, revealed that stress was the most common health problem experienced by orchestral musicians, with problems relating to the behaviour of conductors proving to be a major cause of stress, and others bearing out very closely the findings of Dr Sporcq. 70% of musicians suffer from anxiety that affects their performance, and 32% suffer from chronic anxiety.[14] Conditions recognised twenty years ago as 'horn-player's palsy, cellist's dermatitis, cor anglais player's thumb and cymbal-player's shoulder',[15] are now being further investigated from the perspective of both medical and musical management, and neurological conditions such as 'focal dystonia', the single biggest cause of musi-

13 F. Nowottny, 'On the relationship between broadcasting and culture' (1987). 14 Source: 'Health and the musician', RTÉ Personnel memo, 1 April 1997. 15 Cf. T. Ziporyn, 'Pianist's cramp to stage fright: the medical side of music making' (1984).

cians' career termination, 'overuse syndrome',[16] and breathing and embouchure problems among wind and brass players, are becoming better understood.[17]

It is against this background of growing international concern for, and understanding of, the problems of music in broadcasting that the artistic and managerial dimensions of RTÉ's role in the last twenty years must be explored. The general review of RTÉ by Stokes Kennedy Crowley, the subsequent internal soul-searching and the political and cultural fall-out of the 1990 Broadcasting Act, all in their own way adopted the flavour of these problems and led towards the formation and report of the PIANO group with which this chapter ends.

JOHN KINSELLA AND CATHAL MacCABE AS HEADS OF MUSIC

Gerard Victory's tenure as Director of Music did not exhibit the overt – even brash – qualities of his predecessor in programme-building or the engagement of visiting soloists, but, as a composer himself, he nevertheless encouraged conductors such as Colman Pearce to introduce new works on a regular basis, besides supporting the many choral societies in Ireland by means of large-scale oratorios such as Haydn's 'The Seasons' or 'The Creation', Sullivan's 'The Golden Bowl' or Tippett's 'A Child of Our Time'. By contrast, the tenure of the now down-graded post of Head of Music by John Kinsella from 1983 to 1988,[18] and by Cathal MacCabe from 1988 to 1997, appears less distinguished, despite the fact that public concerts returned, quite substantially, to a format that favoured the 'cycle' of symphonies by Beethoven, Nielsen, or Bruckner. While outwardly music-making gave the public a certain degree of heightened awareness, within the Music Department a situation was developing which would ultimately give rise to the severe difficulties it would face in the light of the internal 'Sexton report' and the public scrutiny of the PIANO report.

Interviewed in August 1983 by James Maguire, an *Irish Times* deputy critic, Kinsella was described as 'a most unbureaucrat-like bureaucrat'. 'I want a situation where to play in the orchestra is a real source of pride', Kinsella told Maguire. Anticipating the advent of Bryden Thomson as principal conductor, he said 'I find myself in tune with him on most things. We have a similar outlook on areas like repertoire and methods of getting audiences in. I would see that his major contribution would be to raise the essentials. As a fresh influ-

---

16 Cf. H.J.H. Fry, 'The treatment of overuse syndrome in musicians', *Journal of the Royal Society of Medicine*, 81 (October 1988).   **17** Cf. F.H. Leffert et al., 'Hand difficulties among musicians' (1983); and M.P. Sheehy and C.D. Marsden, 'Writer's cramp – a focal dystonia' (1982).   **18** The appointment was initially for three years, extended for a further three, the Director of Personnel telling Kinsella that 'the post is one which the Authority believes should not be held on a permanent basis': Conor Sexton to Kinsella, 12 April 1983.

Table V: Works by Irish composers performed by the RTÉSO and RTÉCO,
1979–1988

Gerald Barry [b. 1952]				
Sur les pointes	1981	08.01.86		
Of Queen's Gardens	1986	22.05.87		
Arnold Bax [1883–1953]				
Tintagel	1919	22.07.79	22.07.81	
Summer Music	1920	08.07.86		
Seóirse Bodley [b. 1933]				
Music for strings	1952	28.02.82		
Movement for orchestra	1956	29.06.84	10.06.87	
Salve Maria Virgo	1957	30.09.79	01.10.79	
Divertimento	1961	26.02.82		
Symphony no. 2	1980	09.01.81	06.01.84	
Symphony no. 3	1981	09.09.81	10.09.81	
Celebration Music		24.09.84		
Brian Boydell [1917–2000]				
In Memoriam Mahatma Gandhi	1948	20.06.79	10.02.80*	
Wooing of Etáin, suite 2	1954	09.03.83	09.07.85	
Megalithic Ritual Dances	1956	--.09.80		
Elegy and capriccio	1956	09.01.86		
Symphonic Inscapes	1968	13.11.87		
Concertino grosso per vestibulo basso	1982	31.12.82		
John Buckley [b. 1951]				
Taller than Roman Spears	1977/86	20.06.86		
Fornocht do chonac thu	1980	29.07.81	30.09.87	01.10.87
Symphony no. 1	1988	03.06.88		
Philip Cogan [1748–1833]				
Piano concerto no. 2	1795	20.03.81		
Frank Corcoran [b. 1944]				
Symphonies of symphonies of wind instruments	1981	17.11.82	18.11.82	09.11.87
Shaun Davey [b. 1948]				
Brendan Voyage	1979	20.03.83	19.04.85	
Pilgrim Suite	1983	19.04.85	15.06.76	
Raymond Deane [b. 1953]				
Embers	1973/79/81	16.01.85	17.01.85	
Enchainement	1982	19.07.85		
Thresholds	1987/91	31.12.87		
Séamus de Barra [b. 1955]				
Pezzo capriccioso		22.07.86		
Jerome de Bromhead [b. 1945])				
Venti eventi	1978	09.03.88		
Symphony no. 1	1985	05.01.86		
John Field [1782–1837]				
Piano concerto no. 2	1811	09.01.81		

Aloys Fleischmann [1910–1992]
Sinfonia Votiva	1977	05.06.87		
Ómós don Phiarsach	1979	18.11.79		
The Táin	1981	15.10.82		
Time's Offspring	1985	13.11.85	14.11.85	05.07.88

Bernard Geary [b. 1934]
Time's Delights	1982	23.11.83

Herbert Hamilton Harty [1879–1941]
Irish Symphony	1904/15/24	09.05.86	
Fair Day		30.10.82	
Violin concerto	1908	07.10.79	
With the Wild Geese	1910	20.03.81	30.10.82
Children of Lir	1938	09.11.87	
In Ireland	1915	06.08.85	

Noel Kelehan [b. 1938]
Three pieces for percussion and Orchestra	1983	06.01.84

T.C. Kelly [1917–85]
Rhapsody on Children's Themes		20.03.81
Harp fantasia	1958	06.08.85

John Kinsella [b. 1932]
Montage II	1970	15.09.82
Symphony no. 1	1984	27.09.85
A Selected Life	1973	14.01.79
Rhapsody on a poem by Francis Ledwidge	1987	20.05.87

J.F. Larchet [1884–1967]
Dirge of Ossian & MacAnanty's Reel	1940	23.07.85		
Dirge of Ossian	1940	15.02.81		
March	1955	16.09.86		
By the Waters of Moyle	1957	16.02.83	17.02.83	27.05.85

Daniel McNulty [1920–96]
Divertimento	1957	26.05.87

Philip Martin [b. 1947]
Marban	1980	06.11.80
Through Streets Broad and Narrow	1980	31.03.82
Piano concerto no. 1	1986	19.02.88

Frederick May [1911–85]
Scherzo	1933	20.07.83	24.01.86	
Spring Nocturne	1937	18.05.83	21.07.83	24.01.86
Songs for Prison	1941	14.05.82		
Sunlight and Shadow	1955	23.03.83	26.09.84	

E.J. Moeran [1894–1950]
Lonely Waters	1932	16.06.87

Havelock Nelson [1917–96]
In Venezuela		24.08.84

Seán Ó Riada [1931–71]
Olynthiac overture	1955	14.09.84

Work	Year			
Seoladh na nGamhna	1959	--.09.80		
The Banks of Sullane	1956	04.10.81	05.10.81	18.11.86
		19.11.86	20.11.86	
Nomos no. 1	1957	20.01.88	21.01.88	
Nomos no. 2	1963	26.04.87		
Nomos no. 4	1958	26.04.87		
A.J. Potter [1918–80]				
Overture to a Kitchen Comedy	1950	06.07.84		
Rhapsody under a High Sky	1950	20.01.80	21.1.80	
		25.02.80**	30.03.84	
Sinfonia de Profundis	1969	01.07.81		
Céad Míle Bienvenues	1972	13.05.84	30.05.85	
Sodaz Suite	1973	18.02.79		
Symphony no. 2	1976	29.06.83		
Brent Parker [b. 1933]				
Piano concerto no. 2	1974	19.09.79		
Charles Villiers Stanford [1852–1924]				
Overture, Shamus O'Brien	1896	24.10.81		
Arthur Sullivan [1842–99]				
Irish Symphony	1866	20.03.81	03.02.88	
Overture di ballo	1870	10.06.85		
Eric Sweeney [b. 1948]				
Canzona	1972	06.07.83		
Symphony no. 1	1977	05.09.79	06.01.84	05.02.88
The World A-Hunting is		08.06.84		
Circles	1985	09.01.86		
Gerard Victory [1921–95]				
Overture, Cyrano de Bergerac	1970	18.06.86		
Harp concerto	1971	18.07.79		
From Renoir's Workshop	1973	04.03.79	11.11.83	
Olympic Festival Overture	1975	10.03.80***		29.07.87
Three Irish Pictures	1980	--.10.81		
Six Epiphanies of the Author	1981	05.02.82		
Il Ricorso		--.09.80		
Ultima Rerum	1981	02.03.84	17.03.88	
Old Person's Guide to the Orchestra	1982	31.12.82		
Symphony no. 3	1984	19.07.85		
William Vincent Wallace [1812–65]				
Overture, Lurline	1847	01.07.86		
James Wilson [b. 1922]				
Le bateau ivre	1971	09.05.86		
Cello concerto	1984	19.07.85		
Irish Songs		04.06.85		
Umbrage	1982	31.12.82		

*and on European Tour, 1980, 4 and 14 March; ** and on European Tour, 1980, 5, 12, 13, 15,17 March; ***and on European Tour, 1980, 10, 18 and 22 March.

Summary: 35 composers (of whom, 23 living), 99 works, 150 performances

ence I think he will build a far more cohesive orchestra'.[19] It was an affinity which was not to last.

Kinsella is a quiet, self-effacing person, little given to temper and not at all to flamboyance, devoted to chamber music, whose interest in larger musical forms had not been much in evidence until the time of his retirement from RTÉ. He had joined RTÉ in 1968, with chamber music as his main remit, having previously worked in industry as a computer programmer. He became assistant Head of Music in 1972 and deputy Director in 1979. Self-taught as a composer, he had written two string quartets and three works for chamber orchestra by the time he joined RTÉ, and, up to the time that he succeeded Gerard Victory, he had added five orchestral works to his *oeuvre* (including a symphony and a violin concerto) and a third string quartet. During his time as Head of Music, a second symphony, a second violin concerto and a sinfonietta were his main productions. On retirement he started to compose symphonies in what might be described as a prodigious and deeply impressive manner – he had written eight by the end of 2003, six of them in the five years since retirement, besides a cello concerto and a fourth string quartet.

Kinsella's distinction as an administrator was his calm manner of addressing any problem, and the even tenor with which he conducted office business. Three factors may have influenced the somewhat jaundiced attitude with which he seemed to approach his new duties. The first and second preceded his appointment: one was his frustration at the protracted timescale of its announcement, coupled with the fact that it was not made immediately clear to him that the post had been down-graded from 'Director' to 'Head';[20] the second was the fact that, succeeding Victory – a far more extrovert and outspoken character – he might be inhibited by public perceptions of his decision-making. To have engaged Thomson as principal conductor, in the terms already quoted, implied a return to the 'builder-conductor' concept, and equally implied a softly-softly approach that would, if possible, eschew any demonstrativeness. The third factor was the attempt by three members of the Academica Quartet

---

19 *Irish Times*, 6 August 1983. **20** One reason for the delay in appointing a successor to Victory was a decision that the post would be re-named 'Head of Music'. The delay in regularising John Kinsella's function had, to the knowledge of the author, caused him considerable personal stress, and this was hardly lessened by the diminishing of the status of the post – which, it was mooted, was due to the fact that Tibor Paul's tenure had damaged the prestige of the position and that no action had been possible at the time of Victory's appointment. When, therefore, Charles Acton published an 'Open Letter to John Kinsella' congratulating him on his appointment as 'Director of Music' and describing the post as 'the most important job in music in Ireland and, obviously just about the most difficult and frustrating' the frustration must have been immediately palpable. In urging Kinsella to 'beaver away' at the inclusion of the RTÉSO in television programming, however, Acton must have known that he was asking the impossible. Acton – and perhaps Kinsella himself – cannot have known that Gerard Victory was aware of the intention of downgrading the post following his retirement.

to abandon the fourth, which was a very upsetting episode in Kinsella's career and one which he handled with utterly professional aplomb and correctness, even though he found it a personally distasteful experience.

The general frustration which the music department experienced in its dealings with anyone above the level of Controller of Radio also affected Kinsella badly. In 1986, the RÉSO had recorded Bruckner's early symphony (known as 'the nought' or '*Die Nullte*' which preceded his published, numbered symphonies [nos. 1–9]); at that time it was not represented in the gramophone catalogue. Kinsella wanted to gain *kudos* for RTÉ and the RTÉSO by issuing this recording but, by the time approval had been granted, two other commercial recordings had been issued, by orchestras more likely to grab the musical headlines, and the initiative fell by the wayside.

An example of John Kinsella's reticence as an administrator was his reluctance to speak out authoritatively as Head of Music, although he had told the Director-General, before his appointment was confirmed, that he saw as a priority 'the standard of music teaching in Ireland which is low and is not producing musicians of sufficient calibre ... The music academies must be taken to task and this I would see as one of my first moves as Director'.[21] In 1985–6 the present writer was commissioning editor of a series of pamphlets published by RTÉ under the general title 'Issues in Broadcasting', which were intended to demonstrate the commitment of individual members of staff to aspects of broadcasting and thus reflect the fact that, within RTÉ's various cadres of employment, people existed who had more in mind than merely their day-to-day functions.[22] The series would, it was hoped, impress decision-makers such as TDs, and improve RTÉ's public profile. As part of this series, John Kinsella was commissioned to write on 'Music and Broadcasting'. His contribution was anodyne and far too brief for publication. It mentioned the issues of music's absence from television, the role of radio in respect of contemporary music, the lack of appropriate music education, the uneconomic use of the Symphony Orchestra for opera and, most significantly of all, whether the RTÉSO should become the National Symphony Orchestra: 'It may be time for the child to leave home!'.[23] But it did not address any of these issues in any determined way: it simply stated the case and left the liability for dealing with the situation to other parties. It was, in that sense, characteristic of Kinsella's reluctance to engage in polemics which might divert energies from more constructive or even routine applications, and it indicated the lack of integration between the

---

21 Kinsella to DG, 3 March 1983. Kinsella appears to have been unaware even at this late stage that the title of the post would be changed. 22 Of which seven were issued: on information policy, leisure, technology, the representation of unemployment, audience research, community television and community radio. 23 'Music and Broadcasting', 41pp. typescript; all subsequent quotations from the conversation between the author and John Kinsella are taken from this source.

Music Department and the rest of the organisation, which had so affected Kinsella at meetings of the editorial board (see above, p. 21).

In order to develop the points made in this short statement, John Kinsella was asked to record an interview which was subsequently heavily edited for publication.[24] In the course of this interview he was asked whether the day might come 'when RTÉ will successfully make an overture to the state to take over the funding and administration of [what is effectively] the national symphony orchestra?', to which he replied: 'The day may come when that may be regarded as necessary but I see nothing wrong with the step if RTÉ deems it necessary. It would be a very logical step. It would be ... acknowledging the reality of the situation. But the loser all round would be RTÉ itself, because the orchestras and the drama groups are actual adornments on RTÉ, they're living proof of enlightened thinking'. If that step were taken, in Kinsella's view RTÉ could then develop a sixty-strong multi-purpose radio orchestra, and the putative NSO would become a reflection of 'the nation's own view of itself, and the nation's own self-respect'.

At one point in the interview, Kinsella's frustration developed into a tirade which made one aware of how heated and passionate he could become, if sufficiently provoked:

> Could you foresee such a thing happening here as a festival of modern Irish opera [such as took place in Finland], with audiences in such numbers that they can't all be accommodated? The fact that we haven't got a publishing industry, the fact that we haven't got a recording industry, the fact that when you read the section on music in *Facts about Ireland*,[25] you get such a sketchy misleading article which in no way recognises the totality of the facts. It's the *ignorance* of the subject ... The ignorance is enormous and the lack of belief in what's possible is enormous. It's almost total ... There's no currency in music at all in general thinking. There's a suspicion of it almost. And yet on the other hand the organisation, RTÉ itself, can be so enlightened ... In a more general sense, however, the country is very blinkered musically. The education system pushes music onto the sidelines and that's where the fault lies.

When asked to what use the media at RTÉ's disposal could be put, in order to overcome such ignorance, his reply was somewhat complacent: 'That's what we are doing – making good music available'. And, when pressed for his personal view of his role, Kinsella seemed unable or unwilling to perceive himself as *engagé*, as the Head of Music, and even if he were, the fact that Music had no remit for television activity closed off the departmental mind from that area.

---

24 The pamphlet was in fact never published, due to the decision within RTÉ Public Affairs to draw the series to a close. 25 An official handbook published by the Department of Foreign Affairs.

His sense of powerlessness cannot have been lessened by RTE's statement the following year, that he would thenceforth be reporting not only to the Director of Radio Programmes for his management of the performing groups, but to a newly created 'Controller, Music Programming' for the department's broadcast output; this was his eventual successor, Cathal MacCabe.

In the period 1984–7, with Bryden Thomson as Principal Conductor, Kinsella programmed enticing concerts which featured Beethoven or Tchaikovsky symphonies as a lure to attract audiences to the NCH, which was still a slightly unknown quantity for concert-goers, especially those who had been accustomed to a weekly concert at the SFX, free of charge. As full houses became more normal, he was encouraged to proceed with more adventurous items, such as the Nielsen and Bruckner symphony cycles, and hoped to be looking at a different structure of concert programme which moved away from the 'overture-concerto-symphony' framework towards, for example, concert performances of opera, which were proposed by Thomson's successor, János Fürst.

It has been generally believed that the increasing distance between Kinsella and Thomson led to the decision in 1987 not to renew the latter's contract, a situation that was regarded by many concert-goers as inexplicable, in view of Thomson's obvious popularity. But the fact that Thomson himself appeared to be deeply embittered, obscured the reality of his contractual situation: that he had been engaged originally on a two-year contract which had been extended by a third year, and that he had known from the outset that the appointment was for a maximum of three years, on foot of Kinsella's expressed policy of changing gear by means of the different musical personalities and interests of a series of principal conductors.

Thomson's musical and popular success with his repertoire (including a Bruckner cycle that introduced many listeners to this composer for the first time – and which was repeated by the NSO under Gerhard Markson in 2002–3) had captured the imagination of all concerned, and he had won the esteem of the orchestra. In a sense, the partnership of himself and Kinsella could have been as distinguished as was that of Albert Rosen and Victory, in marrying administrative acumen with podium brilliance and discipline. If it had not been policy on Kinsella's part to introduce regular changes in the principal conductorship, it would be difficult to understand why he would want to dispense with the services of someone who, in the tradition that RTÉ had maintained for forty years, had spent his working life demonstrably building up orchestras in the broadcasting field. In fact, Kinsella asked Thomson, as his contract neared completion, if he would consider returning as principal conductor in three, or six, years' time – a possibility that appears not to have been pursued.[26]

26 J. Kinsella, interview with the author, 19 November 2003, for information in the two preced-

Cathal MacCabe was also an unusual choice as Head of Music. In contrast to Kinsella, he was more outward-looking and -going, yet his proven skills as (in his free time) a freelance director of musicals throughout Ireland (in addition to a degree in music) did not seem to equip him for the administrative burden of the post, nor for the diplomacy necessary in dealing with musicians and their unions. When the time came for him to speak on RTÉ's behalf at the PIANO hearing, he appeared to make the case for retention of the NSO, yet disavowed any responsibility for its appearance on television. One observer in fact thought that he was 'gently detaching the orchestra from RTÉ, partly through touring, partly through hiring it out for recording and freelance work'.[27]

Shortly after his appointment, the cutbacks occasioned by the 'cap' on RTÉ's income put him in the unwelcome position of having to make decisions as to where the savings required in the Music Department were to be effected. As we have seen, the axe fell on chamber and choral music rather than on the orchestras, although the planned expansion of the NSO had to be halted. MacCabe's decade as Head of Music should have seen RTÉ putting in place a framework that could embrace the overall needs of its performing groups and enunciating it by way of policy. That it did not do so was a cardinal factor in creating the environment in which the PIANO review group would take RTÉ to task for its apparent neglect of those groups.

PRINCIPAL CONDUCTORS

The period 1987–93 was exceptionally difficult for the RTÉSO/NSO, due to the problems that RTÉ encountered with its principal conductors, and which were the major factor in the orchestral instability that persisted to the end of the century. The orchestra had warmed to Bryden Thomson, and there had been a tangible rise not only in the standard of its playing but also in the atmosphere of its concerts. The personality of a principal conductor is, arguably, the chief ingredient in the chemistry of his relationship with the orchestra: a personable conductor without musicality, or a thoroughly efficient conductor without charm, will not, in most circumstances, establish that rapport and, while their joint music-making may be enjoyable for them and for their audience, it will not achieve that sense of 'lift' that communicates itself to the audience and tells them that a very special kind of music-making is taking place, that they are witnessing an excitement within the orchestra, as well as a high level of musical achievement, that promises to invest concerts under this particular *maestro* with zest and zeal.

ing paragraphs. **27** Antony Thorncroft, 'Band with a voice of its own', *Financial Times*, 3 February 1997.

This is seldom achieved, however. 'Charisma' is probably the term most frequently applied to the personality who can create that chemistry and, when it is combined with the rare musicality of a great artist, it can be legitimately used to describe a few of the hundreds of conductors who have worked with the RTÉSO/NSO. In the author's opinion and experience, of the conductors who have spent significant periods of time with the RTÉSO/NSO only Albert Rosen combined that charisma and musicianship to such an extent that one felt one was in the presence of a great musical personality. (From an earlier period, no doubt Jean Martinon also conveyed this same personal quality.) Others came and went and one witnessed certain moments, or even sustained periods, of great music-making, but in Rosen's case his thirty-year association with the orchestra demonstrated this consistently.

One such 'moment' occurred in 1979 with the visit by the young Spanish conductor Garcia Navarro (another pupil of Swarowsky). A prizewinner at the conducting competition at Besançon in 1967, he had been music director of the Valencia Symphony and at that time had the same post with the Portuguese radio symphony; he went on to establish an impressive career as a conductor of opera in Lisbon, Madrid and Stuttgart before his early death in 2002. His performance in Dublin evoked such a level of response from both audience and orchestra that a large majority of the latter signed a petition requesting his immediate appointment as principal conductor.[28] If such an appointment had been made, RTÉ might in time have looked back on Navarro as yet another 'star' with whose early career it had been associated, but it was also possible that, to paraphrase, 'one concert doesn't make a principal conductor'. The slimness of Rosen's platform acquaintance with the orchestra before his appointment is the only instance of a subsequent successful partnership. When János Fürst succeeded Bryden Thomson, a complaint was received from a lecturer in music in TCD who argued that standards had dropped as a result of the change: 'a conductor who is prepared to work over long periods with the orchestra is needed: one who is concerned with the projection of the music rather than of himself'.[29]

Sad examples of the opposite end of the spectrum of music-making from that of Navarro were the concerts conducted in Dublin by the Israeli, Yuval Zaliouk, in 1979, and the Mexican, Enrique Batiz, in 1980. Zaliouk, who had won first prize at Besançon in 1967, directed the Toledo Symphony 1980–9; Batiz founded the State of Mexico Symphony and directed it 1971–82 and the Mexico City Philharmonic 1982–9. Both conductors have distinguished inter-

---

28 Navarro's programme, on 28 January 1979, was: Falla, 'El Amor Brujo' and Tchaikovsky's sixth symphony, with Cristina Ortiz as soloist in Mozart's piano concerto K.271. 29 Letter to RTÉ Music Department, 10 March 1988 (name of writer withheld).

national careers and recording achievements. Yet in Dublin, both conductors appeared to be quite unable to grasp their music, and unable to communicate with either soloists or orchestra, and both concerts were the nearest to musical disasters that the author can recall over a ten-year period.

Bryden (Jack) Thomson (1928–91) was Scottish by birth and did not begin musical studies until the age of fifteen. After studying with Hans Schmidt-Isserstedt, he started his career as a conductor as deputy to Ian Whyte with the BBC Scottish Symphony. He moved on to Norwegian Opera and the Royal Opera in Stockholm (where he conducted Stravinsky's *The Rake's Progress* in the Bergman production, and where he developed his love of the Scandinavian repertoire). He returned to Scotland in 1958 as associate conductor with the Scottish National, and became principal conductor of the BBC Northern (later BBC Philharmonic) in 1968. From 1977 to 1985 he was music director of the Ulster Orchestra (during the first year of his tenure in Dublin he still held his post in Belfast), and his experience with these regional orchestras (including a year's association with the BBC Welsh SO) recommended him to RTÉ as the right person to succeed Colman Pearce in 1984 at the end of the latter's three-year contract. He had the demonstrable capacity to build an orchestra's musical strengths and, in addition, to give it a sense of its own importance: in Belfast, he had recorded all Harty's orchestral works on the Chandos label, thus succeeding not only in resurrecting Harty's reputation as a composer but also gaining worldwide recognition for the Ulster Orchestra. It would be part of his unrealised ambitions for the RTÉSO to introduce it, also, to an international recording label.

David Wright has written that 'Jack knew what he wanted from orchestras. This occasionally brought him into conflict with some individuals and administrators, earning him a reputation for being peppery',[30] but that is a common phenomenon among conductors who are determined to get the best from 'their' orchestra. We will see that, in the case of Kees Bakels, it was an insuperable problem, mainly due to the fact that, unlike Thomson, Bakels did not have the diplomatic ability to make an unanswerable case.

Thomson acknowledged that he was an old-fashioned conductor, in the sense that his main interest lay in the classical and romantic repertoire: 'The majority of people love to leave a concert whistling a tune'.[31] Before he took up his appointment he saw that the main emphasis of his work with the orchestra would be on rhythm and intonation, but gave evidence that he would not adopt the draconian attitude to the players that would be demonstrated by János Fürst or attempted by Bakels: 'I'd like to think that as a conductor I'd be

30 'Bryden Thomson', *Classical Music on the Web* http://www.musicweb.uk.net/thomson/index.htm.
31 B. Thomson, interview with Ronit Lentin, *Irish Times*, 14 May 1983.

a useful member of an orchestra, a colleague, not a tyrant, although if I can achieve things only in a tyrannical way, that's the way it's going to be.'³² And he announced his intention of basing his programmes thematically, presenting the complete Beethoven, Sibelius, Nielsen, Tchaikovsky and Dvořák symphonies, 'leaving contemporary and unusual music to guest conductors'.³³ This was part of the strategy that he had adopted in previous posts to maximise audiences and to create a sense among them that the orchestra was *theirs*. At the end of his tenure he was pleased to be able to say that 'it has been a privilege to have been able to better the playing standards of the orchestras without changing any of the personnel'.³⁴ He had learned from his mentor, Ian Whyte, that the basic skills an orchestra must possess are: 'play in time, play in tune and give me a good sound'.³⁵

While Thomson was anxious, on taking up his appointment, not to be seen to criticise his predecessors, towards the end of his tenure he referred more critically to the problems he had encountered with rhythm and intonation, and a 'psychological' problem with players' self-esteem. Thomson took sectional rehearsals which, conventionally, are regarded as a sign that musical discipline within the orchestra is less than good. Given what has already been said about the need for varying styles of principal conductors, Thomson could be regarded as more of a 'builder-conductor' than a 'star', even though his personal style allowed him to be flamboyant and demonstrative on the podium and even though audiences recognised, and applauded, his showmanship. His choice of repertoire during his first year, to which he referred as a time of 'musical purge', represents a series of 'training targets', with the approval of John Kinsella who also saw them as popular programming to maximise audiences: 'The Beethoven [cycle] was … more in a sense a training area for the orchestra than a musical thing, because everybody knows the Beethovens but they are difficult to bring off'. After the cycles by Tibor Paul, twenty years had passed before this area of the repertoire was addressed in a learning fashion. 'They can give a lot, this band, when they're turned on.'³⁶ As Charles Acton observed: 'He is using music whose notes his orchestra must know virtually by heart in order to help them to get to know his ways and in order to make them into a really cohesive instrument … and he is using the superb leadership of Audrey Park to weld a style of the strings'.³⁷

There was a not-so-subtle irony in Acton's review, one year later, of a concert by János Fürst, when it was already rumoured that the latter was to suc-

32 Ibid.   33 Thomson was not interested in contemporary music in general, although he did express an interest in, and liking for, the music of Berg, Henze, Lutosławski and Ligeti: Philip Hammond, 'Bryden Thomson: A Sense of Direction', *Soundpost*, 1 (April–May 1981).   34 In interview with Michael Dervan, *Music Ireland*, 1/6 (June 1986).   35 Ibid.   36 Ibid.   37 *Irish Times*, 7 June 1984.

ceed Thomson: 'There is a great difference between being a guest conductor and being a principal conductor. The former can put on a stunning perform-ance provided the latter has trained and shaped an orchestra and given it a per-sonality. In just over a year Bryden Thomson has trained the RTÉSO already as no one has since Jean Martinon a third of a century ago ... Therefore, János Fürst was able to give us an electrifying concert.'[38]

After Thomson's death, Michael Dervan wrote that, after fifteen years under Rosen and Pearce, the orchestra was 'poor in discipline and often unsure in intonation. Musical style and the finer points of orchestral practice tended to be dealt with through a smothering cover-up of all-purpose emotion'[39] – a crit-icism that we have seen him level at Rosen and which was far less merited by Pearce. Thomson, Dervan believed, was slow to win the orchestra's sympathies: 'they acknowledged the solidity of his conducting technique, his reliability ... They spoke of the feeling of security they felt when playing under him. They spoke with respect of the fineness of his ear. But they also spoke of a lack of feeling in his work. They missed the high emotional drama they were familiar with ... They complained of the sharpness of his tongue, and some, it must be said, complained because they were having to work just that much harder.'

After three years, Thomson could claim that audiences were increasing because it was said generally that orchestral standards had risen: 'I've got the players to the degree where they are now more aware of what orchestral play-ing is about'.[40] As a publicist, working in both directions to raise the orchestra's confidence in itself and to raise audiences' confidence in the orchestra, 'the first thing is to support and increase the public awareness of what the orchestra con-tribute to musical life in Dublin'. As Michael Dervan reported, 'he believes that audiences should feel for their orchestra as followers do for their local football team'.[41] As the self-proclaimed supporter of the orchestra, achieving heights of public acclaim that he had previously sought and found for the Ulster Orchestra, Thomson found RTÉ management less than satisfactory in supporting *him*. Having learned that his contract would not be renewed, and that he would be succeeded by János Fürst, Thomson expressed bitterness that his contribution to the RTÉSO had not been better appreciated. 'Had I known I was only going to be in Dublin for three years, I might not have bothered coming. I might just have said, yes I'll come as a guest conductor', retaining his position in Belfast. 'I'm not a political animal really ... Knowing how pretty direct I am ... I am amazed at how well I have got on in this rather stinking, rotten, vicious, world of musical politics'.[42] As we have seen, however, Thomson *did* know in advance that his appointment was for a maximum of three years, and was actually engag-ing in a form of musical politics in suggesting otherwise.

38 *Irish Times*, 8 May 1985. 39 *Irish Times*, 22 November 1991. 40 Ibid. 41 Ibid. 42 Ibid.

The world of musical politics was much kinder to his successor, János Fürst. It seems to have been an extraordinary step on John Kinsella's part to contemplate the appointment of a conductor who, as a member of the RTÉSO, had been subject to disciplinary action, who had been one of the causes of disruption between the orchestra and its principal conductor, and who had peremptorily vacated his post as leader to become leader of another orchestra. From leader of the Ulster Orchestra he had become its assistant conductor under Sergiu Commissiona,[43] developing the skills he had discovered as the founder of the Irish Chamber Orchestra, and he later worked with the RLPO and the RPO before obtaining principal posts at Malmö, Aalborg and the Marseilles Opera and Philharmonic. Fürst had conducted half a dozen concerts as a guest, between 1977 and 1986, and had been very well received, his Hungarian spirit reminding audiences of the *élan* of Tibor Paul. Despite his past record as a member of the RTÉSO, the present move was of a different order, and no one in RTÉ Personnel mentioned previous disturbances, most likely because no one remembered them, and Kinsella himself was not aware of the exact historical details.[44]

On a superficial level, his sentimental return to the orchestra which had given him his first job as the most junior of violinists, and to the country which, in his own words, had given him his 'first real home',[45] was full of the emotion of rediscovering a lost treasure. 'In this age of philistine behaviour patterns art is one of the very few living things left to put a civilised face on humanity. I believe it [the RTÉSO] has a great function, even in a country which cannot afford it. Can you afford not to afford it?'[46]

Fürst's insistence on artistic matters was also evident in his plan to perform all the Mahler symphonies (except the eighth, which calls for too large forces), and to record his 'Lieder eines fahrenden Gesellen' and 'Kindertotenlieder' with Bernadette Greevy: 'I find it an absolute scandal that the woman who has been one of the foremost exponents of Mahler, not just here but elsewhere, has never recorded those pieces. And I think we owe it to her, to a distinguished career, we owe it to make this while it can still be done.'[47]

Fürst said before taking up his position that, because the orchestra was in good shape ('My predecessor has done a marvellous job'), he did not anticipate any major upheavals, although there were some problems to be sorted out.[48] But in practice he wanted some far-reaching changes. This was an exam-

43 Commissiona had succeeded Maurice Miles as principal conductor of the Ulster Orchestra. **44** J. Kinsella, interview with the author, 19 November 2003. **45** Interview with Michael Dervan, 'Full Cycle', *Music Ireland*, 2/1 (December 1986–January 1987). **46** Ibid. **47** Ibid. Greevy recorded these works with the RTÉSO and Fürst in 1987 (RTÉ catalogue 107) – the disc also included 'Blumine', a movement deleted by Mahler from the original version of his first symphony. **48** Ibid.

ple of what Pat O'Kelly has referred to as Fürst's recruitment 'due to his particular skill as a string specialist' which was 'necessary at that time to strengthen
this side of the orchestra's development'.[49] O'Kelly believes that Fürst's relationship with the orchestra deteriorated, to the point where he asked to be
released from his contract: this is not strictly true but, although he did in fact
serve the full three years, he did cancel a number of concerts towards the end
of his tenure – seven, in fact, in July 1988, principally on health grounds.[50]
Certainly his attempt to achieve relocation of certain players did contribute to
his unpopularity with the orchestra, but his difficulties with management were
probably more serious. Fürst in fact told Michael Dervan in mid-1989 that 'it
was a job he should never have accepted'.[51] Feeling, like his predecessor, that
he had been 'very badly used', he complained that he had no power to formu-
late policies, and expected that his successor would experience the same problems 'unless the format is changed'. The orchestra was apathetic, which he
attributed to management attitudes: 'When people feel they are not led properly, they have no aim. People who have no aim, they amble. And ambling is
not a terribly nice occupation … You feel this atmosphere "why bother?"'. At
the time of his appointment he had said that 'the term "principal conductor"
is a misnomer: he prefers to think of himself as Music Director and in charge
of policy. Ideally, he would like somebody to kick both him and the orchestra
out of RTÉ … because then he could have his own staff and make the orchestra the national and prestigious orchestra it could and should be'.[52] Such sentiments would hardly endear him to a Music Department which already had a
Head (if not Director) of Music, but his idea of the RTÉSO withdrawn from
RTÉ was of course gaining currency all through this period. At the time of his
departure, referring to the pending appointment of a general manager for the
performing groups (which, as we shall see, was envisaged as a step preparatory
to a separation of some kind), he said that the appointee would find an inherent problem: 'The orchestra is a kind of nuisance. It is not an organic part of
the nation's culture.' He meant that he thought *RTÉ* regarded the orchestra as
a 'nuisance', a point which Charles Acton had pursued in the 1970s with Gerard
Victory, and which was a major difficulty in John Kinsella's dealings with his
opposite numbers.

   Pat O'Kelly is certainly correct in stating that Fürst's 'resignation' marked
a deepening of RTÉ's problems, in identifying the appropriate artistic personnel to entrust with the orchestra's development'.[53] Ian Fox's judgement,
three years after Fürst's departure, was that 'he showed a surprising lack of tact

49 P. O'Kelly, *The National Symphony Orchestra*, n.p. **50** Cf. interview with Michael Dervan, *Irish Times*, 26 September 1988. **51** *Irish Times*, 20 May 1989. **52** Interview with 'Sarah Hamilton' (Carol Acton), *Hibernia*, May 1987. **53** P. O'Kelly, op. cit., n.p.

and some arrogance in dealing with his old colleagues, raising many hackles in attempts to reorganise the players. Not a happy reign'.[54]

THE 'SEXTON REPORT'

As part of an overall internal review of RTÉ, conducted by Conor Sexton (Director of the Activity Review Unit, and previously Director of Personnel), attention was focussed on music in a document dated January 1989 entitled 'The Music Department – A Time For Change'.[55] Sexton's report was the fourth milestone in the evolution of the NSO, since he identified the RTÉSO as such, and argued for its redefinition on a completely new administrative basis, paving the way for the eventual structure that today sees the NSO separately managed but remaining within RTÉ.

John Kinsella had recently taken early retirement in order to concentrate on composition, and his position was vacant: he was succeeded by Cathal MacCabe, with responsibility for all music output on Radio 1, Radio 2 and FM3. At that time, the overall music budget was over £3.5m of which the RTÉSO accounted for £2.1m and the RTÉCO approximately half of that figure. 'There are some within RTÉ who are of the view that the organisation cannot indefinitely continue to maintain two orchestras, a string quartet and a number of choirs ... Expenditure of this magnitude inevitably comes into account whenever the somewhat uncertain financial prospects of RTÉ are examined, and questions are raised as to the "value for money" obtained by RTÉ from this level of ongoing investment'.[56] In the context of the overall finances of RTÉ, Sexton was no doubt correct to sound such a warning, since the establishment of the Activity Review Unit had itself been occasioned by a scathing external review by management consultants Stokes Kennedy Crowley, once it was realised that the funding of RTÉ, and its internal structures, required a major overhaul. Sexton continued 'It is argued that RTÉ does not in fact need any or all of the performing groups to meet its broadcasting requirements ... When viewed from a purely financial standpoint and from the narrow angle of RTÉ's "needs" there is no answer to this argument and it is quite impossible to justify spending £3.5m p. a. on the Performing Groups'. This can not have made easy reading for members of the Music Department, especially when, towards the end of his analysis, Sexton said 'There is fairly general agreement within the Music Department that it is not great when it comes to financial management. The heart frequently rules the head, and proj-

---

54 *Sunday Tribune*, 11 November 1993.   55 C. Sexton, 'The Music Department – a time for change'.   56 Ibid., p. 2.

ects which have no real prospect of paying for themselves, let alone generating a surplus, are frequently undertaken.'[57]

However, as Sexton was quick to admit, 'That, of course, is not the whole story'. Having thus shocked the Music Department into mental action,[58] Sexton went on to put the case for 'public service', stating that

> RTÉ could not in present circumstances consider any significant reduction in its involvement in the provision of 'live' music, concerts, recitals, etc., unless some other body was available and willing to assume this role. To do so would be to undermine almost everything which is happening in the serious music world in Ireland – a prospect which could not be contemplated.[59]

Throughout the review, Sexton maintains the tone of someone not entirely sympathetic to the Music Department, but who realises that, in the absence of 'some other body', RTÉ was hoist with the petard of its history as the 'onlie begetter' of these groups, and therefore as a parent who could not in all decency divest itself of them. At the time of the planning and implementation of the NCH, there had been some speculation that the transfer of the RTÉSO from its erstwhile home at the SFX would be the right transitional moment for the orchestra to become the 'National Symphony Orchestra' in name as well as in function, but this had not been pursued, and there is a note of both regret and defiance in Sexton's observation that the orchestras' role as 'radio orchestras' had been transformed by the advent of the NCH, which 'has significantly changed the relationship between the orchestras and the public'.[60] Here I must enter a personal *caveat*: Sexton's statement that because admission to the SFX concerts was free, 'they were not essentially public concerts' may be conceptually correct, but his review entirely omitted the existence, since 1941, and in particular since 1953, of the Public (Subscription) Concerts at the Gaiety Theatre. As Concerts Manager in the years 1974–83, I am acutely conscious of the 'relationship' between concert-goers and the musicians, so much so that I personally knew almost all the subscribers (who in 1975 amounted to 100% of the audience)[61] and very distinctly had a working relationship with a large

57 Ibid., p. 22.   58 The publication of 'the Sexton reports', as they were commonly called, in relation to any department which he investigated, were anticipated with trepidation; in the case of the Music Department 'A time for change' was met in some cases with fierce resistance, one member of staff writing a response, 'The Music Department is alive and well', which it demonstrably was not.   59 'A time for change', p. 3.   60 Ibid. In 1988 Gemma Hussey, then Fine Gael TD for Wicklow and a former minister for (variously) education, labour and social welfare, had called for the establishment of a National Orchestra as part of the NCH complex. 'It is no longer the business of a broadcasting company ... to run a National Orchestra': Fine Gael press release, 21 July 1988.   61 Following the season for which 100% of seats were sold on a subscription basis, the

proportion of them. Thus Sexton's statement 'Concerts can no longer be planned or treated as essentially studio recordings or live broadcasts' did not hold true of the transfer from the SFX: at the least, RTÉ operated a dual system in the years 1953–80, whereby studio concerts at the SFX ran in tandem with the twelve-concert 'public' or 'subscription' series in autumn/winter at the Gaiety, four of which were repeated in Cork and usually one each in Limerick and Galway. Sexton went some way towards compounding that confusion by observing that, since the establishment of the NCH, 'we have failed to reconcile the sometimes conflicting demands of the paying audience and the requirement that the radio audience be provided with the widest possible range of classical music'.[62]

Rather than argue for a curtailment of the RTÉSO, however, Sexton acknowledged that at the NCH it had become clear that it was under-strength, and asked 'what can be done to increase the size of this orchestra and how the additional cost involved can be met'.[63] He identified certain strengths and weaknesses in the existing management structure and recruitment procedures: 'The RTÉSO has been described as the "jewel in the crown" of RTÉ,[64] ...[but] is not however an institution without flaws and these need to be addressed in a systematic manner'.[65] New recruits were needed and older players needed to be retired. 'It would appear that new conditions of employment are required ... The responsibility for dealing with an issue of this kind must be clearly allocated. As of now there is uncertainty as to who precisely should take the necessary steps. Some see it as a matter for the Principal Conductor while others see it as the responsibility of the management of the Music Department.'[66] Here Sexton had correctly identified an inbuilt confusion (not always helped by the Personnel Division) that had allowed a deterioration in the quality of playing because no one seemed willing, able or empowered to address the issue. 'The overriding impression which I have gained is of an orchestra which is not at present in bad shape but which is not going in any particular direction, is essentially treading water, expecting change but cautious about the possible price which may have to be paid for such change'.[67] Ever the diplomat in the business of delivering bad news, Sexton recognised that 'there is within the orchestra a group of very practical people who fully understand the situation in which they find themselves, who can provide a leadership role and who, if encouraged, will assist in finding solutions to the problems'.[68] This would become evident in the thoughtful role played by the orchestra committee with the PIANO group.

Concerts Manager was instructed to limit pre-bookings to 80% of seats, thus retaining the remainder for sale on a per-concert basis. **62** Ibid., p. 6. **63** Ibid., p. 4. **64** Cf. R. Pine, 'The jewel in the crown', *RTÉ Guide*, 13 January 1989. **65** 'A Time For Change' p. 4. **66** Ibid. **67** Ibid., p. 5. **68** Ibid.

Furthermore, Sexton went so far as to echo Michael Dervan's view of two years previously, in stating that the Music Department had no 'clear vision and consensus as to what it is seeking to achieve and how effective it is in meeting that objective'.[69] He rightly saw conductors as crucial to the sense of direction 'but who probably require assistance in the development of a coherent brief and an agreed plan as to what needs to be done'. The missing ingredient in Sexton's assessment, up this point, is the concept of artistic direction, and its absence from his deliberations on how to resolve the dichotomy between broadcasting and performance – and that between the roles of a Principal Conductor and of a Music Director – is probably the single most significant factor in the lead-up to the PIANO review five years later since, by not addressing the issue of continuity, he allowed the ambiguity to remain. Nevertheless, Sexton delivered a damning indictment of the lack of artistic direction at that time in his statement: 'We should ideally have working for us either on staff or as an agent a person who is *au fait* with what is happening in the wider world of international music, who will be aware of the up and coming stars either as conductors or as soloists';[70] the fact that the Music Department did *not* have someone of this calibre can be traced to the fact that Gerard Victory had invariably allowed the initiative for proposing visiting conductors and soloists to remain with the London artists' agencies, whose incoming literature dominated his attention in making such decisions.

In respect of the RTÉCO, Sexton again raised the question of whether RTÉ could afford 'an embarrassment of riches',[71] but, as in the case of the SO, agreed that it was 'too good a flagship to abandon' – although here, too, one detects a wistful air of 'if only …' Without mentioning the DGOS seasons of opera in Dublin and Cork, Sexton recommended that the CO should take the place of the SO at the 'Wexford Music Festival' [*sic*].[72]

In respect of the Vanbrugh String Quartet (appointed in 1986) Sexton demonstrated a remarkable lack of judgement: while acknowledging that the Quartet 'is clearly of a high standard judging by the international success which it has achieved' he suggested that 'it is perhaps time to assess the value of the service which it provides. It is an expensive undertaking for RTÉ to finance and it would be important to establish that the Cork music-going public or RTÉ or both are getting the best possible return for this investment … It is difficult to see … why … they seem to be unavailable for the next 4–5 months … Their priorities may need to be redefined'.[73] Since the Vanbrugh's international touring commitments – which were part of their contractual understanding with RTÉ – to say nothing of their international stature, were a major factor in their retention by RTÉ, it appears disingenuous of Sexton to have

69 Ibid., p. 20. 70 Ibid., p. 20. 71 Ibid., p. 9. 72 Ibid., p. 11. 73 Ibid., p. 14.

taken such an invasive tone with regard to the Quartet's priorities, and may have contributed to the barely concealed indignation expressed by the Quartet in its submission to PIANO.

Sexton's major recommendation was that the Performing Groups should be separated from the broadcasting functions of the Music Department, under a General Manager, and that the RTÉSO should be renamed as the National Symphony Orchestra and built up to full strength.[74] There should be separate administrators for the RTÉSO, RTÉCO and the choirs. Commercial recordings should be pursued for the purpose of prestige rather than profit: 'If there are people in the Music Department who regard this type of activity as being too commercial it might be explained to them that it is not with a view to profit that it is being pursued but with a view to promoting the orchestra'.[75] Promotion itself was ill-co-ordinated, and needed to be assigned to a single area of responsibility.

As a result, the renaming of the RTÉSO/NSO was announced six months later; Gareth Hudson was appointed General Manager to oversee the Performing Groups, and on his first day in office was told by the DG (Vincent Finn) that he had an extra budget of £300k, enabling him to take the immediate decision to recruit 21 new players to bring the NSO up to full strength of 93 players.[76] The announcement concerning the NSO stated that 'RTÉ has reassessed the status and identity of the Symphony Orchestra as part of its ongoing review of its public service responsibilities and had decided to reaffirm its commitment to orchestral activity by guaranteeing the future of the RTÉ Symphony Orchestra and establishing it as Ireland's national symphony'.[77] A further six months on, when the NSO gave its inaugural concert, RTÉ said that 'this activity confirms RTÉ's determination to fulfil a public service obligation not only over the airwaves but also in the concert hall and in the community … Building on the established strengths of the RTÉ Symphony means that the human and musical resources of a fine and mature ensemble, with its huge collective experience, can be harnessed to the realisation of this new initiative'.[78]

However, not everything that had been envisaged by Conor Sexton was achieved, and Hudson's short-lived tenure was marked on 23 March 1990 by

---

74 This was consonant with similar contemporaneous moves in other broadcasting companies: the orchestra of RIAS (Berlin) became the Deutsches Symphonie Orchester; the BBC Welsh Symphony became the BBC National Symphony of Wales; and the Radio-Télévision Luxembourg SO became the Orchestre Philharmonique du Luxembourg. Ironically, as a Scottish writer observed, where 'music and politics' conspired to attempt the removal by the BBC of its Scottish orchestra, in RTÉ it was intended to enhance and retain the NSO: Keith Bruce, 'Out to play for more than national identity', *The Herald* (Glasgow) 12 February 1997. **75** 'A time for change', p. 15. **76** G. Hudson, interview with the author, 5 August 2003. **77** RTÉ press release, 28 July 1989, written by the present author. **78** RTÉ concert programme, 5 January 1990, written by the present author.

his memorandum to all Music Department personnel and other senior figures within RTÉ, signalling his frustration with the lack of provision and the lack of foresight in relation to the development of what he referred to as 'truly national groups'[79] and incorporating a five-year plan to ameliorate the situation. He began with an analogy:

> A few years ago, Aer Lingus faced a major problem. International noise regulations were fast outlawing their four BAC 1–11 jets which were at least 25 years of age. The decision was simple, either the aircraft would have to be scrapped or some means found to make them quieter. Considerable investigation into the aircraft took place during which it was found that they were superbly built and showed no traces of corrosion, unlike the newer Boeing 737s which were becoming known as the 'Datsuns' of aviation! The decision was made that appropriate action should be taken (i.e. the fitting of engine hushkits) that would satisfy the regulations and keep the jets flying into the 90s and possibly beyond.
>
> In 1989 the RTÉ Authority faced a similar problem though the origin was 'sound' of a different kind. The RTÉ Symphony Orchestra was in a rut both musically and financially. The decision was between scrapping the orchestra or finding some way of altering the way the orchestra was run to allow the development of music making that would bear comparison on an international level. The decision went in favour of retaining the orchestra, restructuring the management and providing funds to add 22 positions to the orchestra, making a strength of 93 players. This, along with a new profile for all the Performing Groups was to prove RTÉ's commitment to provide Public Service not only on the airwaves but in the concert halls of Ireland and elsewhere. All this quite rightly brought critical acclaim to the station, it was indeed a milestone in Irish musical history. This document is intended to map out plans required to complete the project and realise the hopes and aspirations of RTÉ in relation to its Performing Groups. To use the Aer Lingus example, we have the 'hushkits' but they are built on to a structure which is in many ways antique …
>
> Of course, it could be said that RTÉ merely wants its Groups simply to 1) run more efficiently 2) bring in more revenue by playing to larger houses 3) have a higher public profile. These targets are being attained already but they are a long way from the aspirations of running truly national groups. It is time to ask RTÉ of its <u>true</u> hopes for musical performance; what does it really want? …The following pages do

79 G. Hudson to Head of Music, 23 March 1990, 26 pp.

not include options, they are essential plans for those parts of Ireland's musical future which RTÉ has elected to lead and manage.

Hudson was looking back to the 'Sexton Report', stating that RTÉ was not fulfilling the commitment it had given, and, looking forward, anticipating the PIANO Review Group. And he was both putting a gun to RTÉ's head and paving the way for his own resignation. Every point he made – for example, that 'RTÉ cannot boast that it "runs Ireland's National Orchestras" and then not provide adequate trained personnel' – anticipated the criticisms voiced to PIANO, that there were too few, under-professionalised staff in its music administration. He called for a NSO Concert Director and a Marketing/ Development Officer; for more extensive touring ('regional concerts *have* to increase in number if we are a truly national orchestra'); augmentation of, and more concerts by, the RTÉCO; higher salaries; more support for the RTÉ Vanbrugh String Quartet; and a more strategic approach to educational work by all the performing groups: 'we desperately need a way of guiding our audiences through the musical maze to end with a situation where they have a love affair with live music, and not just children either. Why shouldn't our Orchestras/Choirs perform in factories? ... We must consider putting one or preferably both orchestras on the road for at least one week per year for the performance of Schools concerts'.

On the artistic issue of soloists and conductors, he looked back to the period when 'RTÉ hired some of the finest continental conductors available', continuing 'In the 1970s the quality of conductors deteriorated, it was very much the time of "swaps". An Irish conductor would be exported say to France with a copy of a latest Irish opus e.g. "Chaos in the Chicken Run". Six months later a French maestro of often dubious quality would be imported with an accompanying symphony "La Guerre dans la maison poulet". Everyone was happy, except of course the audience.' Hudson, although making a valid point, was being unfair, since the 'swaps' to which he referred were mainly those under the EBU 'Let Us Know the Names' series, where a tripartite arrangement saw an Irish conductor working with (say) a Turkish orchestra and incorporating a work by an Italian composer with a Greek soloist, while in Dublin the RTÉSO would be conducted by a Norwegian in a programme including a French work and featuring a Finnish soloist. As an exchange mechanism it was probably too clumsy, and it did result in the inclusion of conductors 'of dubious quality', but RTÉ, as an active member of the EBU, could hardly refuse to take part.

As far as Irish soloists were concerned, Hudson took a brave and intelligent step:

I am putting an end to the sort of expectation that exists among certain Irish soloists that they *deserve* engagements because of some past triumph or because they believe in lobbying. The NSO exists to serve the public, not the artist. It cannot possibly reflect 'all Irish artists' and 'all Irish composition'. My aim is to be entirely selfish for the Orchestra, only when the NSO is of truly international status will Ireland be able to glow in the Orchestra's reflected glory. Such glory is not achieved by arguments such as 'But I must have a quota of RTÉ concerts' – 'I sang for the Pope' or 'my uncle is in the Senate, you must have an engagement for me'.[80]

Hudson betrayed a lack of confidence about the 'access path' to RTÉ's more 'serious' music when he wrote: 'On so many occasions at a "Music for Fun" family concert I have been asked by parents "our children really enjoyed that, would you recommend that they come to the Symphony Orchestra next week to hear Bodley's First Symphony and Strauss' Death and Transfiguration?" I have sometimes found myself saying, "No, don't take them to the Symphony Orchestra" – it doesn't give you a great feeling of salesmanship.'

He ended on a suicidal note: 'Do my plans coincide with the aspirations of senior RTÉ personnel[?] If not, where do we diverge? Should I be encouraged or slapped on the wrist[?]'

Commenting on the latter point of Hudson's memorandum regarding a work by a contemporary Irish composer, Michael Dervan, as editor of *Music Ireland*, observed that

> To understand the full implications ... one need only shift the scene of action to the world of the theatre rather than the world of music: management at the Abbey disparaging Irish writing in general? management at the Abbey acknowledging the folly of highlighting Irish works or works with Irish connections ...? management at the Abbey being ashamed of having the work of Irish playwrights to offer to parents whose children had been fired with enthusiasm by an educational project at the Abbey?[81]

The response of Kevin Healy, Director of Radio, was that 'I believe our immediate priority, however, is to consolidate our position now that the orches-

---

80 This echoed a note from Fürst to RTÉ producer Jerome de Bromhead (12 December 1985): 'As far as I am concerned I would *always* give priority to Irish artists (resident in Ireland or elsewhere) but they *must* be of a certain standard, otherwise we do no service to either them or us. Working with the Symphony Orchestra must be really the "top of the tree" – at least that is the way I see it'. **81** 'The screw tightens', *Music Ireland*, 5/10 (November 1990).

tra is being brought up to strength. We should learn to walk before we can run and before any additional investment can be made, we need to satisfy ourselves that the best use is being made of the already substantial additional resources which have been invested by RTÉ in the performing groups. It should be a source of concern to all of us that in spite of the additional revenue which has been allocated we are already running substantially over budget.'[82]

If Hudson was frustrated by the slowness of progress, the political bomb-shell in the form of the announcement by Ray Burke, Minister for Communications, that he was placing a limit or 'cap' on the amount that RTÉ could earn from advertising, caused widespread disorder throughout the organ-isation. Some had expected that the RTÉCO would be axed, which would at least ensure the survival of orchestral and choral music, even in the face of los-ing such a valuable group. In the Music Department, it was seen not merely as a reversal of the planned expansion (costing £300k) but requiring a further reduction in current expenditure of approximately £200k. Hudson was not only instructed by Healy and MacCabe to cease recruitment immediately, but also to inform the Vanbrugh Quartet that it was being taken off the pay-roll (a measure which was later partially rescinded).[83] In addition, the RTÉ Chamber Choir was to be disbanded and the RTÉ Chorus discontinued. By September 1990, a month before the 'cuts' were to take effect, Hudson had told the orches-tras that flexibility would be expected, with players moving between the orches-tras as required, which some saw as the introduction of the 'pool' system whereby orchestras would be constituted from the totality of players, accord-ing to the numbers and combinations required by each programme (a concept that had been developed, with difficulty, by Boulez with the BBCSO and had been voiced for many years in RTÉ by Eimear Ó Broin). Michael Dervan even went so far as to assert, erroneously, that the episode was being manipulated by RTÉ 'to bring about a conflict which will lead inexorably to the real target situation: the disbanding of one of the orchestras'.[84]

The decisions caught the popular imagination, since supporters of the Chamber Choir formed a 'Friends of the Choral Arts' which mobilised pub-lic opinion: *Irish Times* columnist Nuala Ó Faoláin, admitting that she had not previously known what a chamber choir actually was, found, after hearing the choir's arguments and understanding the circumstances of its bursaried mem-bers, that its suspension was a 'poignant waste of gifted young people who have to have training so as to become professionals'.[85]

Cathal MacCabe was in the unenviable position on 26 September 1990, the day after the 'cuts' had been announced, of hosting a reception to greet the

82 Healy to Hudson, 30 March 1990. 83 Hudson, interview with the author, 5 August 2003. 84 'The screw tightens'. 85 *Irish Times*, 10 December 1990.

NSO's concert schedule for 1991. He explained that, given the amount that had to be cut from the budget, he had looked for 'the least worst ways' to effect the reductions. 'We have said [to senior management] that we can't keep targeting musicians every time there are economies. Musicians are not like other people ... You can't cut back in the same way you can cut back in other areas.' He looked to the negotiations over flexibility to enable the organisation 'to write *Finis* over this business of constantly targeting musical groups for economies .... The situation is not that we can't afford to have a string quartet or that we can't afford to have a chamber choir or we can't afford to have a chorus. It is that we're not allowed to afford to do it.'[86]

The 'cuts' provoked widespread criticism of this demonstration of the vulnerability of music-making to the political process, with the RDS Music Sub-Committee pointing out that RTÉ had been faced with resolving a problem not of its own making, with no indication from government as to how the situation would be dealt with, should RTÉ fail to find solutions.[87] RTÉ's proposal for flexibility also resulted in a short-term, and extremely rare, industrial action involving the suspension of some players in early 1991.

In the face of this development, Hudson resigned, to take up a similar position with BBC Scotland.[88] An unsigned news item in the *Irish Times* stated that his resignation 'is being interpreted in some quarters as reflecting the difficult, if not impossible task which faces any general manager in coping reasonably with the cutbacks which have been imposed on the music department at RTÉ'.[89] It was almost the only media statement that accepted the difficulty faced by RTÉ: while criticism of how it arrived at its decisions on the economies to be made could be validly levelled at the Music Department and its bosses, it was seldom that the cutbacks in general were recognised as being totally outside RTÉ's control.

But RTÉ's corporate identity was saved at that time by the two-edged sword of the advertising 'cap', which both inhibited increased expenditure on the performing groups and, therefore, gave it an excuse not to engage with Hudson on what he hoped would be 'open debate as to the future'. Instead, an internal debate took place, which would soon become a matter of public notice, as to whether one or other of the orchestras might be disbanded, in order to alleviate the financial crisis caused by the 'cap'. If the RTÉCO were dissolved, it could provide extra players who might then supply the numbers necessary to fulfil the commitment to bring the NSO up to full strength. Hudson had spo-

---

86 Quoted in *Music Ireland*, 5/9 (October 1990). 87 Letter to the Editor, *Irish Times*, 20 November 1990: the sub-committee consisted of Anthony Hughes, Enid Chaloner, Ian Fox, Síle Larchet-Cuthbert, Bernadette O'Rahilly, Seán Tinney, Betty Minchin Clarke, Nancy Larchet, Col. Fred O'Callaghan and Kevin Roche. 88 Although he would return to RTÉ in later years in roles relating to the RTÉCO. 89 *Irish Times*, 17 November 1990.

ken of RTE's desire for flexibility and mobility within and between the orchestras, and with the 'cap' RTÉ moved towards cost-cutting measures involving new work practices. This might involve an extension of the practice whereby, during the Wexford opera season, some members of the RTÉSO had joined forces with the RTÉCO, in order to avoid the employment of casual freelance players for individual events. When this was resisted by the musicians' union, SIPTU,[90] RTÉ suspended the members of both orchestras for a fortnight in January/February 1991, resulting in the cancellation of some concerts. The conflict was resolved largely to the musicians' satisfaction, especially since it secured the retention of both orchestras at not less than their current strength.[91]

The cuts seem to have galvanised Proinnsías Ó Duinn (as Principal Conductor of the RTÉCO) into action, since he spent a great deal of 1990–1 urging the administration to improve the conditions of the RTÉCO. At first sight, some of his proposals appear idiosyncratic, such as his urgent suggestion that the orchestra's workload on television should be reduced, or that it should be broadcast on Radio 1 rather than FM3, but on inspection his views were sound: as regards television, he asserted that 'the generally undemanding technical and musical role … means that exclusive exposure to this work results in an orchestra that is close to brain dead'.[92] His view on FM3 was that, by transferring all music from Radio 1, the orchestra had lost its regular listenership: 'The majority of non-Radio 2 listeners in this country are the middle-of-the-road type who hear our music purely because they turn on Radio 1 and leave it there. They are not the enthusiasts who consciously retune for a period of "culture". In the past we gained many new followers for our orchestras through our Radio 1 broadcasts. They were particularly important for our provincial listeners and the programmes laid the foundation for our box office attendance at our live provincial concerts.'[93] A few months previously, Gareth Hudson had referred to the fact that Ó Duinn 'has on several occasions spelt out the hopeless situation of what to date has been RTÉ's most successful ensemble. The RTÉCO, a highly committed and integrated group, is simply unable to appear in public without significant augmentation.'[94] At a time when a merger of the two orchestras was being considered, O'Duinn advised an increase in the size of the RTÉCO to forty-five, using the large budget for augmentation (£70k) to pay salaries instead.[95] It was essential, in Ó Duinn's view, that the RTÉCO should

---

90 SIPTU had become the union representing the musicians in the two RTÉ orchestras after the winding up of IFMAP in 1985; in January 2003 SIPTU announced the establishment of a separate Musicians' Union of Ireland. 91 During the suspension, members of the NSO played a concert in Galway under their own auspices and at their own expense, and another in the NCH featuring Frank McNamara's 'Beatlesymphony'. 92 Ó Duinn to MacCabe, Kevin Healy and Simon Taylor, 4 April 1991. 93 Ibid. 94 Hudson to Head of Music, loc. cit. 95 Ó Duinn to Director-General, 3 August 1990 (Music Department file).

follow the NSO in prioritising its public performances, and it was therefore crucial that a policy be put in place to effect that, so as to boost morale among the orchestra's members. That the RTÉCO, under Ó Duinn (who was succeeded as principal conductor in 2003 by Laurent Wagner), should be capable of renewing its reputation for versatility after fifty years of variable existence, can be demonstrated by its recent work with musicians such as glass harmonica player Alasdair Malloy, composer/conductors Robert Lamb and Ron Goodwin, and singer Jack L, besides continuing its lunchtime concerts at the NCH with 'Summer Classics' which give a platform to young performers such as Iona Petcu, and new music such as Ronan Guilfoyle's piano concerto (played by Conor Linehan), and, in 2001, the return of 'Music for Fun – the Next Generation!'

THE NATIONAL SYMPHONY ORCHESTRA

That János Fürst was succeeded by George Hurst, who has been described as 'an old-style martinet', is one of the greatest mysteries and one of the deepest causes of mistrust between orchestra and management in the history of the NSO. Before his retirement, John Kinsella had been asked by the DG (Vincent Finn) and the Director of Radio (Michael Carroll) what steps he would advise on the appointment of a successor to Fürst. He gave them three options: to take no immediate action, and to leave the decision to the new Head of Music; to invite Albert Rosen to return for a one-year 'lap of honour', thus allowing the Head of Music to take stock of the situation; or to appoint the visiting conductor who had made the most impression in the recent past. They chose the latter option, and by general agreement that conductor was George Hurst.[96]

Of Romanian and Russian extraction (né Herskovich), Hurst studied at the Royal Conservatory in Toronto, earning a living as an arranger for the orchestras of the Canadian Broadcasting Corporation. He became professor of composition at the Peabody Conservatory, simultaneously studying conducting with Pierre Monteux. After the second world war he had engagements with the LPO (including concerts on its first tour to the USSR in 1956), became (like Bryden Thomson after him) conductor of the BBC Northern in 1958, with a brief to turn it into a larger band, and in 1968 moved to the Bournemouth Symphony to start the Sinfonietta, declining the principal conductorship of the Symphony when it was offered on the death of Silvestri.

Hurst had worked with the orchestra twice previously, in 1980 and 1982. Both experiences had been traumatic for the orchestra, since Hurst's attitude in rehearsals was meticulous to the point of obsession. Reviewing his per-

96 John Kinsella, interview with the author, 19 November 2003.

formance of Berlioz' 'Symphonie fantastique' on his first appearance, Charles Acton said: 'From the beginning, Mr Hurst not only secured a beautiful balance in the orchestra, but kept on revealing little touches of Berlioz's genius for scoring that normally go unnoticed. He shaped the music beautifully.'[97] Such a review demonstrates how an objective report from the auditorium can mask the traumas of rehearsal; normally, as we have seen Acton observe before, an orchestra will rise to a conductor who communicates his authority: on this occasion Hurst's rehearsals had been fraught with resentment at his methods by some key members of the orchestra, and in such circumstances it would have been understandable if he had failed to achieve his end result, but it was precisely the *authority* to which the orchestra responded, rather than his musical judgements.

His reputation as an orchestral trainer preceded him, since several of the players in the NSO had attended his summer courses at Canford in the UK. That he should give his inaugural concert on 5 January 1990, the day on which the RTÉSO officially became the National Symphony Orchestra, was widely regarded, both inside and outside the orchestra, as a calculated insult on RTÉ's part (for which John Kinsella was unfairly regarded as being responsible), since at this much-vaunted stage in its development it seemed quite inappropriate that it should be seen to be in the hands of a trainer, on a new learning curve, rather than associated with a 'star' whose presence would indicate that the orchestra, too, was in the ascendant. Possibly RTÉ's decision to install Hurst at this point was misguided, since it did send out the wrong signals: either the RTÉSO merited the change of title, or it required a further training period. But with a planned expansion of twenty-one new players, the balance of the orchestra was bound to change, and it was Hurst's task to weld it once more into a unity. 'I want to see Ireland getting the orchestra it deserves.'[98] Even though the decision on Hurst's appointment preceded that on the expansion of the RTÉSO, on this inaugural occasion there were grounds for Michael Dervan's observation that 'he ... managed over a four-day rehearsal period to weld the new ensemble into an impressively cohesive body'.[99] Dervan also commented on the fact that many of the new faces were on trial, and asked how many of them might still be on the platform at the end of the recruitment phase; he could hardly have known that the same uncertainty of trial-and-error had characterised the enlargement of the RÉSO over forty years previously.

Conductors seem to have a habit of denigrating their predecessors in the most telling way. In Hurst's case, he referred to the growth in orchestra numbers as essential for performing larger works such as the Mahler symphonies

97 *Irish Times*, 13 October 1980. **98** Interview with Wendy Fitzgerald, *Magill*, February 1990.
99 *Irish Times*, 8 January 1990.

– the same symphonies that had been the centrepiece of Fürst's conductorship, thus suggesting that that series had been artistically sub-standard.

Hurst's keyword at that time was *fulfilment*, by which he meant the process of teaching players singly and collectively to learn music thoroughly, so as to realise their potential. 'When you do this you enter into a different phase of playing ... It's learning not just the sequence of notes but the *meaning* of the notes. Not just the dynamic background but the nuances.'[1] The decision to programme three Brahms symphonies in his first year was indicative of Hurst's intention to saturate the players with the densest part of the repertoire, in order to make that learning experience as intense as possible.

This, in his opinion, required more rehearsals-per-concert than the NSO schedule permitted, and he immediately met resistance from the music department on this issue, which was probably the principal reason for his abrupt resignation, only fourteen months into his contract. No doubt the financial cutbacks of 1990–1, with their obvious effect on orchestral recruitment, contributed to his frustration, but if he could not be permitted to do, on his own terms, the job for which he had been hired there was no point continuing, even though he would have been well aware that, by opting out so suddenly, he was creating a hiatus that would be difficult to mend, although he did return to the orchestra for its German tour in 1992, for which he had also been contracted.

Hurst's resignation in fact precipitated a crisis both musically and managerially which would be as evident as a gaping wound for the next three years, since it not only left the fledgling NSO without a principal conductor, but also indicated that there was a gap between RTÉ's ambitions for the NSO and its means of achieving them. Since there was, at that point, no chief guest conductor to step into the breach (Albert Rosen having relinquished the post), the NSO was, artistically, rudderless. An approach to Bryden Thomson to return as principal conductor was frustrated by his death (which also necessitated a replacement for the concerts for which he had been engaged in 1992). Cathal MacCabe, as Head of Music, was also coping with the resignation of Gareth Hudson, and RTÉ was therefore confronted by a management deficit at precisely the time when the organisation needed to be strong in wisdom, foresight and diplomacy.

As the search for a successor got under way, the members of the NSO made it clear that they should be more closely involved in the selection procedure. Attention focussed on a Dutch conductor, Kees Bakels, who was beginning to work with the NSO at this stage, conducting in July 1991 and being re-engaged for the following November. Hudson's successor, Simon Taylor, later told Kevin

1 Ibid.

Healy that 'We were all in agreement that he had many of the qualities that we were looking for and he expressly stated that whilst he had some reservations about various sections of the orchestra he was happy to take it on as it was.'[2] After Bakels' third concert, in May 1992, a formal offer was made and accepted and, with some *élan*, Bakels' appointment was promulgated. It was the beginning of what became known as 'the Bakels *débâcle*'. It is no pleasant task to explain – let alone justify – to the most senior figure in one's division, how a catastrophe had occurred, and Taylor somewhat haplessly told Healy, 'There had for some years been very definite problems with various key positions in the orchestra and as previous Principal Conductors had either refused to tackle these or come to grief in trying to do so, it was decided that the time had come to try to solve those problems in advance of the new principal conductor taking up his duties'. Bakels at first said that he was willing to work with the players whom he considered unsatisfactory, but when the time came for the Nielsen symphonies to be recorded commercially for the Naxos label, he expressed particular reservations about the brass sections. The outcome was that Naxos agreed to another conductor being engaged (Adrian Leaper) and Bakels withdrew from the concerts which were the prelude to the recording dates. He also withdrew from the short tour to Britain by the NSO in February 1993. Bakels had in fact gone back on the assurances that he had given, and had stated categorically that he would not commence as Principal Conductor until certain key players had been replaced. These were in the strings and brass sections. When the problems proved intractable, RTÉ issued a statement on 25 January 1993, that

> Mr Bakels has expressed reservations about the present composition of the orchestra, reservations which RTÉ has made every reasonable effort to accommodate. Already substantial changes have been made to continue the raising of standards within the orchestra with the full recognition and support of the players but further changes could not be made at this stage because of RTÉ's responsibilities to its staff. Over the last number of years huge strides have been made to develop and foster the national and international reputation of the orchestra to an extent where it is undertaking an extensive series of recordings with one of the world's largest classical music recording companies.

But the sense of 'responsibility' was masking a deeper difficulty: that RTÉ had failed to confront the anxieties voiced by P.S. O'Hegarty in the 1930s, and by León Ó Broin in the 1940s, that musicians are *different* by virtue both of

---

2 Taylor to Healy, 29 January 1993, RTÉ Music Department file.

their temperament and of the nature of their work, and therefore cannot be regarded as run-of-the-mill civil (or public) servants. The system had not taken into account that employment of musicians required different standards, procedures and conditions. Taylor continued: 'As there has been over the years no precedent for coping with orchestral players whose standard has either slipped or been overtaken by the rest of the orchestra, the process of dealing with the brass situation has been very tortuous'. He pointed out that Bakels' insistence was due to the fact that, in his eyes, his artistic integrity was being undermined by RTÉ's refusal to meet his demands, and had to acknowledge a systemic problem that had never been addressed, dating back to the origins of the RÉSO itself: 'There are fundamental flaws in the way in which RTÉ musicians are employed that have been exposed.' These flaws, which were inherent in the overall RTÉ system, would remain until, with the establishment of Music as a separate division in 1997–8, it was possible to put in place a completely new set of working procedures and conditions.

In the meanwhile, it was becoming clear to the public that the re-naming of the RTÉSO, with all that that entailed, had fallen foul of political events (the imposition of the 'cap') and of a lack of political and artistic vision within Radio. It was not adequate to announce an enlargement and a new designation, without having thought through the implications. Bakels' behaviour may well have been, in the long term, a bonus for RTÉ in opening its eyes to some organisational shortcomings, but it also helped to suggest that RTÉ was not in fact the best custodian of this particular national asset. To announce the re-designation of the RTÉSO, to claim it as the 'national orchestra' which it had always been, was in fact to draw attention to fundamental issues, greatest of all being: what *was* a national orchestra – what did it represent, and how should it be administered? As Niall O'Loughlin, a member of the NSO cello section, was to tell the PIANO group, 'a nation gets the orchestra it deserves'.[3]

At the time that RTÉ announced the dis-appointment of Kees Bakels, a series of public comments drew attention to the fact that the crisis in the NSO was due to much more than a personality issue: Brian Boydell pointed out the paucity of Irish works in the schedule,[4] which was to cause Irish composers to mobilise their colleagues in Aosdána in an initiative which led directly to the setting up of PIANO. Michael Dervan, analysing the 1993 schedule, commented on the lack of the thematic programming that had characterised Bryden Thomson's concerts. He got to the heart of the matter when he observed: 'That men as temperamentally and artistically diverse as … Thomson … Fürst …

---

3 N. O'Loughlin, at the oral sessions of PIANO 19 November 1994 (PIANO Archive).   4 Letter to the Editor, *Irish Times* 15 December 1992: his own 'In Memoriam Mahatma Gandhi' was the only Irish work scheduled for 1993.

Hurst and … Bakels should encounter such wide-ranging problems suggests that RTÉ's management style is not finely adjusted to the specialised workings of the "national cultural asset" which the orchestra set out to be'. Devastatingly, he quoted Cathal MacCabe's statement in 1991: 'a principal conductor is just a conductor who conducts rather more concerts than anybody else'.[5] At the time that this comment was first made, serious questions were raised privately within the Music Department as to his suitability to lead it, such was the perplexity of staff that MacCabe could see the role of principal conductor through such myopic lenses. He had added to that remark, 'The fact that we don't have a principal conductor is not a disaster – it's a decision – if I wanted a principal conductor I would be able to appoint one.'[6]

In the meantime, the now extra-urgent matter of actually appointing a principal conductor continued, as disquiet in the orchestra grew, and standards and morale fell. Kasper de Roo, from Holland, had conducted the orchestra twice in 1989, and was considered a 'safe bet' by many. Bearing in mind the upsets with the last three principals, the NSO members balloted for a successor, choosing de Roo decisively over other candidates with whom they had worked successfully in recent months, including Matthias Bamert, Adrian Leaper, Takuo Yuasa, Jerzy Maksimiuk, Raymond Leppard, Franz Paul Decker and even Albert Rosen.

De Roo came from a musical family (his father had been Director of the Netherlands Opera) and began his career as a bassoonist in the Rotterdam Philharmonic and the Concertgebouw, working under conductors such as Eugene Ormandy, Klaus Tennstedt, Carlo Maria Giulini and Rafael Kubelík; he had won the Besançon Young Conductors' Competition in 1980. He had been working with the Stuttgart State Orchestra 1987–91, before moving to Innsbruck to direct both the city's symphony orchestra and the opera company of the Tyrol Landestheater. He, too, saw room for improvement in the NSO: 'they play with a lot of energy and precision and really make music. There is a big potential quality in the capacity of the players.'[7] He had further concerts with the NSO in 1993 and 1994, before officially taking up his three-year post (later extended to mid-1998) in November of that year.

Interviewing de Roo on the eve of his first concert with the NSO since the news of his appointment, Michael Dervan found that 'he doesn't talk with the firmness of artistic resolve' of Bakels, or 'to be animated by projects as intensely concentrated as those of the late Bryden Thomson', that he was 'admirably clear in detailing the past, but altogether more vague about the specifics of the

5 *Irish Times*, 12 January 1993; the interview, with Arminta Wallace, originally appeared in the *Irish Times* on 30 March 1991. 6 *Irish Times*, 30 March 1991. 7 Interview with Ian Fox, *Sunday Tribune*, 11 November 1993.

future'. He observed that 'the eyes and ears of the musical world will be focused with special acuity ... tomorrow night [25 February 1994] to find out if the new man's work on the podium is likely to provide the inspirational force to lift the NSO out of the artistic free-fall into which it has so scandalously been allowed to drift over the last few years.'[8]

De Roo's three-and-a-half-year term was, in fact, artistically solid, with 'this dapper little Dutchman',[9] as Ian Fox described him, establishing a good working relationship with the players and leading them through an undistinguished and basic repertoire in which a further period of consolidation could be undertaken, in a spirit of what Dervan called 'literalness and coolness'.[10] Like the direction of RTÉ's music policy in these years, it was unspectacular, even unimaginative.

It was only in 1998, with the appointment of Alexander Anissimov, that the NSO and their audiences encountered a new principal who had the Slavonic musicality and artistic flamboyance that had been so much a part of Albert Rosen's 'charisma'. Since this takes us outside the chronological boundary of this chapter, Anissimov's 'reign' and that of his successor, Gerhard Markson, will be briefly considered in the Postscript.

TOURING RESUMED

In 1992, twelve years after its last European appearance, the NSO, under George Hurst, undertook a modest tour of Germany, visiting Wolfsburg, Kiel, Wilhelmshaven, Emden, Witten, Erlangen, Stuttgart, Ingolstadt, Leverkusen and Bielefeld. The relatively minor status of the venues was belied by the boost which orchestral morale received from its reception. The tour programme included Eric Sweeney's 'Dance Music' (introduced in three venues by the composer), Hindemith's 'Symphonic Metamorposes', Spohr's 'Concertante no. 2' for violin and harp (Christoph Poppen and Ursula Holliger), Brahms' 'St Anthony Variations' and second symphony, and Shostakovich's tenth symphony. In contrast to the RTÉSO's 1980 tour, the absence of any Irish soloist is noteworthy.

Reviewers tended to express reservations about the orchestra's ability to settle down in the opening works, but were almost unanimous in their praise for the Brahms and Shostakovich symphonies; in Bielefeld (where the orchestra had already played in 1980), the concert was regarded as 'of superlative

---

8 Interview with Michael Dervan, *Irish Times*, 24 February 1994. The concert featured Philip Martin's new harp concerto (soloist Andreja Maliř), Stravinsky's 'Firebird' suite, Kodály's 'Dances of Galanta' and Schubert's third symphony. 9 *Sunday Tribune*, 11 November 1994. 10 *Irish Times*, 28 November 1994.

Table V: National Symphony Orchestra, Inaugural Concert, 5 January 1990

Principal Conductor: George Hurst; Chief Guest Conductor: Albert Rosen

1st Violins	*2nd Violins*	*Violas*
Audrey Collins	Jack Leydier	Seamus O'Grady
Clodagh Vedres	Vanessa Caminiti	Thomas Kane
Timothy Kirwan	Joan Miley	Kathleen Green
Catherine Briscoe	Carlos Assa-Munt	Margaret Adams
Anna Kane	Keith Packer	John O'Mahony-Adams
Camilla Gunzl	Audrey McAllister	Neil Martin
Claire Crehan	Elias Maguire	Randal Devine
Catherine McCarthy	Mary Wheatley	
Breige McGoldrick		

Cellos	*Basses*
Aisling Drury Byrne	Helmut Engemann
Lindsay Martindale	Wolfgang Eulitz
Dairne ní Mheadhra	Herbert Nowak
Niall O'Loughlin	Seamus Doyle
Rosemary Elliot	
Paula O'Callaghan	
Linda Kelly	
Steven Wise	

Flutes	*Oboes*	*Clarinets*	*Bassoons*
William Dowdall	Matthew Manning	Brian O'Rourke	Michael Jones
Madeleine Staunton	Patricia Corcoran	Paul Roe	Michael Rogers
Deirdre Brady	Helmut Seeber	Fintan Sutton	Dieter Prodöhl

Horns	*Trumpets*	*Trombones*	*Tuba*
Lesley Bishop	Josef Csibi	Seán Cahill	Hartmut Pritzel
Fergus O'Carroll	Szabolcs Vedres	Francis Hughes	
Ian Dakin	Graham Hastings	Seán Fleming	
Thomas Briggs			
David Atcheler			

Timpani	*Percussion*	*Harp*
Martin Metrustry	Noel Eccles	Andrea Malíř
Angela Boot		

standard', with a 'particularly sensitive understanding' of Brahms' 'deep emotions',[11] and in Wolfsburg Hurst came across as 'a fundamentally solid maestro'[12] and also conducted 'with absolute sovereignty'[13] – in Erlangen, the sovereignty had become 'careful'.[14] In Kiel, 'it was thrilling to follow how incisively

[11] *Neue Westphälische Zeitung*, 5 October 1992. [12] *Wolfsburger Nachrichten*, 25 September 1992.
[13] *Wolfsburger Allgemeine Zeitung*, 24 September 1992. [14] *Erlanger Nachrichten*, 30 September 1992.

Table W: National Symphony Orchestra, Golden Jubilee Gala, 14 February 1998

1st Violins	*2nd Violins*	*Violas*
Alan Smale	David McKenzie	Adele Govier
Elaine Clark	Vanessa Caminiti	Cheremie Allum
Clodagh Vedres	Keith Packer	Seamus O'Grady
Timothy Kirwan	Elias Maguire	Margaret Adams
Catherine Briscoe	Mary Wheatley	John O'Mahony-Adams
Anna Kane	Cornelia Sexton	Neil Martin
Claire Crehan	Fiona McAuslan	Randal Devine
Catherine McCarthy	Rosalind Brown	Helena Plews
Patrick Fitgerald-Mooney	Paul Fanning	Aine O'Neill
Ting-Zhong Deng	Joanne Fleming	Margaret Lutz
Audrey McAllister	Dara O'Connell	Niamh Nelson
Anne-Marie Twomey	Melanie Briggs	Cliona O'Driscoll
Anne Harte	Evelyn McGrory	
David Clark	Joan Miley	
Brona Fitzgerald		
Kathryn McKeggie		

Cellos	*Basses*
Aisling Drury Byrne	Dominic Dudley
Niall O'Loughlin	Wolfgang Eulitz
Linda Kelly	Waldemar Kozak
Peter Hickey	Chris Long
Stephen Sensbach	Mark Jenkins
Una Ní Chanainn	Aura Stone
Claire Fitch	Daniel Whibley
Siobhan Lynch	Edward McNally
Benedict Rogerson	
Adrian Gallagher	

Flutes/Piccolo	*Oboes/Cor Anglais*	*Clarinets*	*Bassoons*
William Dowdall	Matthew Manning	John Finucane	Michael Jones
Madeleine Staunton	Síle Daly	Paul Roe	Robert Dulson
Catriona Ryan	Susanne Schluanus	Fintan Sutton	Hilary Macken
		Susanne Brennan	

Horns	*Trumpets*	*Trombones*	*Tuba*
Lesley Bishop	Graham Hastings	Gavin Roche	Conor O'Riordan
Fergus O'Carroll	Killyan Bannister	Brendan Kennedy	
Ian Dakin	Thomas Rainer	Seán Fleming	
Tom Briggs	Eoin Daly		
David Atcheler	Colm Byrne		
	Vivienne Johnston		
	Niall O'Connor		
	Helen Mackle		

Mandolin	*Timpani*	*Percussion*	*Harp*
Liam Kennedy	Martin Metrustry	Richard O'Donnell	Andrea Maliř
		Angela Dakin	
		Paul Maher	

the musicians fashioned the distorted stylistic disguises of the [Shostakovich]'.[15] Several reviewers commented (as they had in 1980) on the surprising level of women players (compared to a continental orchestra). In Wilhelmshaven the NSO was 'a compact orchestra with an appealing tone culture' whose Brahms symphony 'lacked refinement';[16] in Emden it 'played ... in a most discriminating manner' and its Brahms proved it 'a first class orchestra' giving 'among the most beautiful [and] varied concerts in the last few years'.[17] In Erlangen, the strings were generally greeted for their sonority and velvety tone, whereas the brass was found to be occasionally 'coarse'; in Stuttgart, reviewers found the reverse to be the case.

The following year, a short outing to Leeds, Liverpool and Belfast, while artistically successful, met with very poor houses, but in 1996 the NSO's touring fortunes were redeemed with an invitation to Hong Kong, at the behest of Naxos chief, Klaus Heymann, which saw six concerts in seven days at the Hong Kong Culture Centre Concert Hall. These included Chinese repertoire and film music, conducted by Long Yu from Shanghai, and 'Classics for Leisure', 'A Seat at the Opera' and 'Dancing on the Green', all with Gerhard Markson. As Pat O'Kelly remarked, 'the nature of the tour and its programme was untypical and it showed the versatility of the NSO in a very wide ranging series of unusual events'.

A year later, the NSO returned to Britain, for concerts in Edinburgh, Glasgow and London's Royal Festival Hall with Barry Douglas playing Beethoven's fourth piano concerto, and also including Ravel's 'Mother Goose' suite, Stravinsky's 'Firebird', Kodály's 'Háry János' and Gerald Barry's 'Flamboys', originally commissioned by TCD for its quatercentenary.[18] Two British journalists, previewing the tour, commented that part of the motive for the tour was 'to prove that there is more to Irish culture than Daniel O'Donnell and Riverdance', and that 'we need reminding ... that the musical life of the Emerald Isle encompasses more than tourist-brochure ceilidhs awash in Guinness and Murphy's',[19] thus suggesting that the impact of Irish classical performance on the British mind had been less than thorough. Despite its diplomatic mission, however, reviewers were not impressed, Raymond Monelle commenting in *The Independent* that Barry's 'Flamboys' was 'in tune with the general impression of this concert ... not much fun',[20] and Barry Millington, in *The Times*, finding little to say of the RFH concert, either good or bad, except for the Barry, which he found 'unpleasant'.[21]

15 *Kieler Nachrichten*, 25 September 1992. 16 *Wilhelmshavener Zeitung*, n.d. 17 *Emden Zeitung*, n.d. 18 Flamboys – thick wicks dipped in wax – were seventeenth-century torches. 19 Keith Bruce, *The Herald* (Glasgow), 12 February 1997, Christpopher Lambton, *The Guardian Guide*, 15–21 February 1997. 20 *Independent Tabloid*, 18 February 1997. 21 *Times*, 21 February 1997.

COMMERCIAL RECORDINGS

In 1992, RTÉ entered into a recording contract with Naxos, the most extensive and comprehensive classical budget catalogue in the world, which has seen the NSO and RTÉCO, as well as the choirs and Vanbrugh String Quartet, making discs of both popular and less well-known works for Naxos and its associate label, Marco Polo.

According to an interview given by Cathal MacCabe to Antony Thorncroft of the *Financial Times*, it was part of MacCabe's strategy for gaining an international reputation for the newly renamed NSO,[22] and coincided with its German tour of that year. This had been an unrealised ambition for many Directors/Heads of Music and principal conductors, only one of whom, Milan Horvat, actually saw a pair of widely distributed discs by the then RÉSO, issued by Decca and aimed at the US market: 'New Music from Old Erin' volumes 1 and 2, with sleeves depicting a thatched cottage, haystack and donkey and cart, featured Boydell's 'Megalithic Ritual Dances', Bodley's 'Music for Strings', Duff's 'Irish Suite', Kelly's 'Three Pieces for Orchestra', Larchet's 'Dirge of Ossian and Macananty's Reel', Potter's 'Variations on a Popular Tune' and three movements from May's 'Suite of Irish Airs'.[23] Another, 'Ireland, Mother Ireland', with Our Lady's Choral Society, appeared in 1964 on the Argo label.

For the domestic market, Gael-Linn issued several discs including 'Ceolta Éireann' and 'Ceol na hÉireann' (including Potter's first 'Fantasia Éireannach' with the RÉLO and Eimear Ó Broin),[24] and 'Ceol Potter' (Potter's arrangements of traditional tunes played by the RTÉCO under Colman Pearce).[25] Ó Riada had his three film scores recorded by Gael-Linn,[26] as well as 'Ceol na Laoi'.[27] RTÉ itself issued a disc of the RTÉCO under Ó Duinn,[28] and a commemorative disc of the first US tour by 'Irish Light Orchestra of Dublin' was issued by Columbia.[29] Several other selections of short, atmospheric pieces found their way onto market-led productions such as EMI's 'Gems from the Irish Airwaves', 'The Best of Ireland's Music Heritage', 'The Best of Ireland's Music' and HMV's 'Amhrán Dochais' (Song of Hope), almost all billing the performers as 'Irish National Orchestra'.[30] It is thus clear that the RÉLO had much better prospects of reaching an international market, due to the attractiveness of its repertoire. (RRE issued the RÉLO's and Dermot O'Hara's inaugural performance of Balfe's *The Rose of Castille* from the Wexford festival.)[31]

22 'Band with a voice of its own', *Financial Times*, 3 February 1997. 23 Decca DL 9843 and DL 9844. 24 Gael-Linn CEF 004 (works by Beckett, Bodley, Duff, Friel and Ó Riada) and CEF 019 (Ó Riada alone). 25 Gael-Linn CEF 034. 26 *Mise Éire* (CEF 002) and *An Tine Bheo* (GL 12) with the RTÉSO, both conducted by the composer, and *Saoirse?* (CEF CD 134) with the RTÉCO conducted by Elmer Bernstein. 27 GL 14. 28 RTÉ 57. 29 Columbia ESI – 100B. 30 EMI STAL (1) 1003; EMI Talisman STAL 6025; EMI CLP 3530; HMV IP 1302. 31 RRE 191/2.

It seemed to confirm Antony Thorncroft's observation that 'It is perhaps Ireland's great musical tradition which has held back orchestral music there'.[32]

In the early 1970s a short-lived label, the New Irish Recording Company, purported to offer a medium for the recording and distribution of Irish compositions, and issued a limited number of discs, including the RTÉ String Quartet in works by Kinsella and Victory,[33] and Bodley,[34] and an orchestral disc with Boydell's 'Symphonic Inscapes' and Victory's 'Jonathan Swift – a Symphonic Portrait' (RTÉSO with Albert Rosen),[35] but the venture ended before several other recordings could be issued.

Thus the potential for exploiting classical performances by the RTÉSO, and of bringing Irish compositions to international attention, was severely restricted. In 1981 the author (as a member of the Music Department) attempted to rectify this situation through a contract with Polydor, which would have seen a number of archive recordings, by all the RTÉ performing groups, promoted by means of a scheme similar to that supported by the Welsh Arts Council for the 'Composers of Wales' series on the Argo label. This was to have been spearheaded by an actuality recording of the première of Bodley's 'Ceol' (symphony no. 3) from the State Opening of the NCH, with an archive recording of Potter's 'Sinfonia de Profundis' on the obverse,[36] but due to a series of administrative difficulties the project foundered, the initial disc being issued privately but never commercially available. With the sole exception of the Mahler recording of 1987 (RTÉSO, János Fürst and Bernadette Greevy) referred to above, and the recording of Balfe's *The Bohemian Girl* in 1991 on the Argo label,[37] no other significant exposure was accorded to RTÉ's performing groups until the Naxos contract was put in place.

Opening the doors to worldwide distribution instantly made the NSO part of the marketplace which included such frequently played orchestras as the Oslo Philharmonic under Mariss Jansons but, in addition, it made it possible for the RTÉ/Naxos discography to embrace the widest possible repertoire. As previously mentioned, the NSO under Adrian Leaper undertook the complete Nielsen symphonies,[38] and went on to record the Tchaikovsky Suites (with Stefan Sanderling)[39] and (with Andrew Penny) the complete symphonies of Malcolm Arnold,[40] which the composer preferred to a previous cycle by the LPO. Harty was represented by his 'Irish symphony', 'With the Wild Geese' and 'In Ireland' (NSO and O'Duinn),[41] and Stanford by his Requiem (conducted by Adrian Leaper) and 'The Veiled Prophet' (conducted by Colman

32 Thorncroft, *Financial Times*, loc. cit. 33 NIRC 002. 34 NIR 006. 35 NIRC 011. 36 RTÉ 56. 37 Argo 433 324–2. 38 Naxos 8.550743 (symphonies 4 and 5), 8.550825 (symphonies 2 and 3) and 8.550826 (symphonies 1 and 6). 39 8.550644 and 8.550728. 40 8.553406 (symphonies 1 and 2), 8.553739 (symphonies 3 and 4), 8.552000 (symphonies 5 and 6), 8.552001 (symponies 7 and 8) and 8.553540 (symphony no. 9). 41 8.554732.

Pearce with Virginia Kerr as soprano soloist).[42] Two opera productions, from the Wexford Festival, followed: Rubinstein's *The Demon* (Alexander Anissimov)[43] and Pacini's *Saffo* (Maurizio Benini),[44] together with a studio recording of Verdi's *Aida* (Rico Saccani).[45] Meanwhile, the RTÉCO (sometimes billed as the RTÉ Sinfonietta) was embarking on the first complete recording of Wallace's *Maritana* (with Proinnsías Ó Duinn),[46] several discs of incidental music by Sullivan (with Andrew Penny),[47] and, with Richard Hayman, discs of Duke Ellington, Simon and Garfunkel and Burt Bacharach.[48]

Of considerable significance in relation to RTÉ's long association with Irish composers has been the 'Irish Composers Series' on the Marco Polo label, initially with financial support from the Arts Council, which includes discs devoted to Brian Boydell,[49] A.J. Potter,[50] James Wilson,[51] Gerald Barry,[52] Frank Corcoran,[53] Raymond Deane,[54] and Philip Martin,[55] Victory's cantata 'Ultima Rerum',[56] Kinsella's third and fourth symphonies,[57] Robert Lamb's cantata 'The Children of Lir' conducted by the composer,[58] Bodley's fourth and fifth symphonies (conducted by Colman Pearce),[59] and John Buckley's first symphony and organ concerto (soloist Peter Sweeney).[60] In this series, the RTÉ Vanbrugh quartet recorded Fleischmann's piano quintet (with Hugh Tinney, piano) coupled with May's quartet.[61]

As a result of the slowing down of the Naxos publication schedule, another, smaller, label, Black Box, emerged as a champion of Irish composers, and as a result the RTÉ Vanbrugh Quartet recorded Ian Wilson's 'Towards the Far Country', 'Winter's Edge' and 'Capsizing Man'.[62] The Vanbrugh have also recorded Raymond Deane's 'Brown Studies' for Black Box,[63] and, for Chandos,

42 8.223580/1. **43** 8.223781.2. **44** 8.223884. **45** 8.660033.4 **46** 8.554080.1 **47** Sullivan, Ballet Music: 8.223460; Incidental Music 1 ('The Merchant of Venice', 'Henry VIII', 'The Sapphire Necklace', 'Overture in C'), 8.223461; Incidental Music 2, Macbeth, *King Arthur, Merry Wives of Windsor*, 8.223635; Victoria and Merrie England (ballet), 8.223677. **48** 8.990053, 8.990052 and 8.990051. **49** 'In Memoriam Mahatma Gandhi', 'Megalithic Ritual Dances', 'Masai Mara' and the violin concerto (Maighread McCrann), NSO, Colman Pearce: 8.223887. **50** Overture to a Kitchen Comedy, Finnegan's Wake, Variations on a Popular Tune, Fantasia Gaelach no. 1, and Sinfonia de Profundis, NSO conducted by Robert Houlihan: 8.225158. **51** 'Menorah' (viola concerto, soloist Constantin Zanidache), 'Pearl and Unicorn' (soloist Alan Smale) and Concertino for orchestra, NSO conducted by Colman Pearce: 8.225027. **52** 'Diner', 'Sur les pointes', 'Of Queen's Gardens', 'Chevaux de frise', 'Flamboys' and 'Hard D', NSO conducted by Robert Houlihan: 8.225006. **53** Second, third and fourth symphonies, NSO conducted by Colman Pearce: 8.225107. **54** 'Quaternion' (soloist Anthony Byrne), 'Krespel's concerto' (soloist Alan Smale) and oboe concerto (soloist Matthew Manning), NSO conducted by Colman Pearce: 8.225106. **55** 'Beato Angelico', piano concerto no. 2 (composer as soloist) and harp concerto (soloist Andrea Malíř), NSO conducted by Kasper de Roo: 8.22384. **56** Virginia Kerr, Bernadette Greevy, Adrian Thompson, Alan Opie, RTÉ Philharmonic Choir, RTÉ Chamber Choir, Cór na nÓg RTÉ, NSO, Colman Pearce: 8.223532.3. **57** 8.223766, conducted by Proinnsías Ó Duinn. **58** 8.554407. **59** 8.225157. **60** 8.223876, NSO conducted by Colman Pearce. **61** 8.223888. **62** BBM 1031; 'Winter's Edge' has also appeared (also with the RTÉ Vanbrugh String Quartet) on the Chandos label: CHAN 9295. **63** BBM 1014.

Boydell's second quartet and Kinsella's third.[64] Their recording of Moeran's string quartet in A appeared in 1998,[65] with his Fantasy Quartet and second string quartet.[66]

Critical commentary on the Naxos output overall has been very encouraging, with Edward Greenfield opining that, in Arnold's symphony no. 9, Andrew Penny 'draws not just a concentrated, consistently committed performance from the Irish players, but a warmly resonant one, with the strings sounding glorious and brass consistently brilliant',[67] while, in relation to his first and second symphonies, Joe Staines considered that 'The [NSOI] are particularly good at making sense of Arnold's quixotic changes of mood, and the way he sets up internal tensions within a work by brilliant orchestral colouring'.[68] In 2003 the NSO's recording of symphony no. 4 by Joly Braga Santos, under Alvaro Cassuto, won the Orchestra and Concerto CD premiere award at the Cannes Classical Awards.

THE 'PIANO' REVIEW

In June 1994 Michael D. Higgins, TD, Minister for Arts, Culture and the Gaeltacht (with responsibility for broadcasting) established a review group, PIANO ('Provision and Institutional Arrangements Now for Orchestras and Ensembles') to consider the evolution of the RTÉ orchestras with regard to both their broadcasting and non-broadcasting functions, and the extent to which those were compatible; to make recommendations on programming policy with special regard to the role of Irish composers; to quantify the resources available to the orchestras; and to consider whether Ireland needed an additional, regionally-based, orchestra. (The latter term of reference was considered to have been superseded by the announcement in the meantime of the re-constitution of the existing NICO as the Irish Chamber Orchestra [the title of the ensemble originally founded by Janos Fürst in the 1960s] and its relocation in Limerick in association with the University of Limerick, serving in particular the needs of the western seaboard.)

The group was chaired by John O'Conor, recently appointed Director of the RIAM, and included John Horgan, a human resources expert working with Guinness Peat Aviation (and a former chairman of the Labour Court); Loretta Keating, pianist and director-chair of the Irish Youth Orchestra; John Kinsella, composer and recently retired as Head of Music at RTÉ; and Geraldine O'Grady, violinist and former guest leader of the RTÉSO.

64 CHAN 9295; Kinsella's third quartet had previously been recorded by the RTÉ Academica quartet, coupled with Buckley's first, on the Goasco label: GXX 002–4. **65** ASVDCA 1045. **66** ASVDCA 1045. **67** *Gramophone* May 1996. **68** *Classic CD* June 1996.

Table X: Works by Irish composers performed by the RTÉSO/NSO and RTÉCO,
1989–1998

Michael William Balfe (1808–70)				
The Bohemian Girl	1843	13.01.91		
Highlights from:		05.08.94	06.08.94	
		20/21/22.09.96		
Gerald Barry (b. 1952)				
Chevaux-de-Frise	1988	28.06.91		
Flamboys	1991	14.05.91	15.05.91	14.02.97
Of Queen's Gardens	1986	23.02.95		
Walter Beckett (1914–96)				
Dublin Symphony	1990	10.09.91		
Seóirse Bodley (b. 1933)				
The Palatine's Daughter		17.03.92		
A Small White Cloud Drifts				
over Ireland	1975	02.05.97		
Symphony no. 4	1991	22.02.94		
Brian Boydell (1917–2000)				
Shielmartin Suite	1959	19.08.97		
Megalithic Ritual Dances	1956	12.09.97		
In Memoriam Mahatma Gandhi	1948	05.11.93		
Masai Mara	1988	04.07.89	21.11.97	
John Buckley (b. 1951)				
A Thin Halo of Blue	1990	26.01.92	24.02.94	
Organ concerto	1992	26.06.92		
Rivers of Paradise		18.09.93	19.09.93	18.02.94
Maynooth Te Deum	1995	16.11.95	17.11.95	
Rhona Clarke (b. 1958)				
Everything passes	1997	05.08.97		
Shaun Davey (b. 1948)				
Relief of Derry Symphony		21.07.91	20.05.97	
Granuaile		09.09.92		
Brendan Voyage		20.05.97		
Gulliver	1994	--.--.95		
Raymond Deane (b. 1953)				
Thresholds	1987/91	10.09.91		
Krespel's Concerto	1990	04.04.97		
Oboe concerto	1994	21.04.95		
Séamus de Barra (b. 1955)				
Pezzo capriccioso		22.06.93		
Overture to a Slapstick Comedy		28.06.94		
John Field (1782–1837)				
Piano concerto no. 2	1811	29.10.93		
Piano concerto no. 3	1811	21.07.91		
Aloys Fleischmann (1910–92)				
Elizabeth McDermott Roe	1944	22.06.93		
Lament for strings		09.09.92		
5 Dances from The Táin	1981	07.03.91		

Philip Flood (b. 1964)				
Kicking Down	1993	22.02.94		
Stephen Gardner (b. 1958)				
Wallop	1996	24.01.97	23.07.98	
Ronan Guilfoyle (b. 1958)				
Concerto for jazz guitar trio	1993	24.02.94		
Herbert Hamilton Harty (1879–1941)				
In Ireland	1915	12.09.97		
Field Suite	1939			
Fair Day	1904	17.02.92	09.09.92	01.01.96
In the Antrim Hills & Fair Day		19.02.93		
Michael Holohan (b. 1956)				
Cromwell	1994	23.02.95		
Leaves of Glass	1995	03.10.95		
The Lost Land	1996	06.03.97		
Marian Ingoldsby (b. 1965)				
Overture	1994	17.02.95		
Fergus Johnston (b. 1959)				
Samsara	1991	14.06.91		
Flute concerto	1996/7	17.01.97		
T.C. Kelly (1917–85)				
Carolan Suite	1978	17.02.92		
John Kinsella (b. 1932)				
Festive Overture	1995	01.01.96		
Dawn		29.10.93		
Symphony no. 2	1988	27.09.89		
Violin concerto no. 2	1989	09.03.90		
Symphony no. 3	1990	10.09.91	09.01.98	
Symphony no. 4	1991	20.11.92		
Symphony no. 5	1992	18.02.94		
Symphony no. 6	1993	02.02.96		
Jubilee Fanfare	1997	14.02.98		
Robert Lamb (b. 1931)				
Children of Lir	1994	01.07.94		
J.F. Larchet (1884–1967)				
By the waters of Moyle	1957	16.11.94		
Charles Lennon (b. 1935)				
Famine Suite		--.--.95		
Philip Martin (b. 1947)				
Through Streets Broad and Narrow	1980	12.09.97		
Piano concerto no. 2	1991	21.06.91		
Harp concerto	1993	25.02.94		
Beato angelico	1990	--.06.90		
Frederick May (1911–85)				
Spring Nocturne	1937	24.11.95	29.11.95	01.12.95
Sunlight and Shadow	1955	22.11.96	13.03.98	
E.J. Moeran (1894–1950)				
Rhapsody no 3	1943	07.07.98		

Cello concerto	1945	14.03.90		
Gráinne Mulvey (b. 1966)				
Diverge and merge	1997	06.02.98		
Padraig O'Connor (b. 1940)				
Introspect		17.08.93		
3 Yeats settings		26.02.95		
Proinnsías Ó Duinn (b. 1941)				
Stuff and Nonsense		05.01.97	12.01.97	
Jane O'Leary (b. 1946)				
Islands of Discovery	1991	17.07.92	19.07.92	
Mirror Imaginings	1991	23.02.95		
Seán Ó Riada (1931–71)				
Slán go Maigh		17.02.92	09.09.92	
Mise Eire	1959	21.07.91	29.10.93	
A.J. Potter (1918–80)				
Finnegan's Wake	1957	31.12.91	17.03.92	17.03.94
Amhran Dochais		17.03.94		
Overture to a Kitchen Comedy	1950	12.09.97		
Charles Villiers Stanford (1852–1924)				
Overture, Shamus O'Brien	1896	17.02.92		
Irish Rhapsody no. 6	1922	12.06.98		
Irish Rhapsody no. 1	1902	12.09.97		
Requiem	1897	12.09.97		
Arthur Sullivan (1842–1900)				
Overture di Ballo	1870	31.12.95		
Eric Sweeney (b. 1948)				
Deirdre	1989	06.04.90		
Dance Music	1990	11.09.92	23.02.95	
Fiachra Trench (b. 1941)				
Summer Suite		03.08.93		
Gerard Victory (1921–95)				
From Renoir's Workshop	1973	25.11.94	17.03.95	
Gaelic Galop		17.03.92		
Ave Scientia		28.11.95	30.11.95	
3 Irish Pictures		12.09.97		
Concerto alla grecque		23.02.95		
Olympic Festival Overture	1975	14.02.98		
Ultima Rerum	1981	11.12.92		
Symphony no. 4	1988	12.07.91		
Ómós don Uachtarán	1990	16.11.90		
William Vincent Wallace (1812–65)				
Maritana	1845	15.09.95	16.09.95	22.09.95
		23.09.95		
Highlights from		05.08.94	06.08.94	
Bill Whelan (b. 1950)				
Seville Suite	1991	24.02.92	11.11.93	
Ian Wilson (b. 1964)				
Rich Harbour	1995	21.06.96		

James Wilson (b. 1922)

Concerto giocoso	1998	12.06.98	
Triple concerto 'For Sarajevo'	1996	12.12.97	
Angel II	1988	18.05.90	
Menorah	1989	22.02.94	
Concertino for orchestra	1993	15.04.94	12.04.96

Patrick Zuk (b. 1968)

Ritual Dance	1994	13.12.96

Summary: 43 composers (31 living), 102 works, 136 performances

Although the review group was not required to allocate blame or to find fault, it cannot be denied that, in terms of the musical world, its status was similar to that of a tribunal of enquiry, receiving written submissions and conducting a public hearing, assessing the relevance and significance of existing structures and the import of practices and transactions. The principal requirement of the Minister was that the group should

> review the roles as they have evolved of the performing groups in RTÉ with particular reference to the extent to which the broadcasting and non-broadcasting demands are compatible and to make whatever recommendations it considers desirable regarding the organisational arrangements that would enhance the development of the groups.[69]

It was widely bruited at the time that the formation of the group had been brought about at the insistence of John Kinsella who, as Head of Music, had experienced much professional frustration in his administration of the NSO, and who, it was said, had, as his firm objective, the separation of the NSO from RTÉ. There is no concrete evidence to substantiate that widespread belief, although it has been confirmed to the author by one member of the review group that, in his opinion, Kinsella had this as his principal aim. Kinsella himself agrees that his experience as Head of Music had made him realise that the RTÉSO (as it still was during his occupancy of the position)

[69] *The PIANO Report*, p. iv.

enjoyed a precarious position within the politics – musical and otherwise – of RTÉ, and we have seen his frustration and sense of alienation at the attitude of some of his colleagues, that the Symphony Orchestra might be 'expensive and irrelevant':

> As you may imagine this was quite hard to take, having to constantly defend and justify the cause of great music within RTÉ itself. Ultimately I began to debate back, on the grounds that it was being made clear to me RTÉ was perhaps not now the correct place from which a major art form should be administered ... as it had obviously changed in character from the organisation which had had the cultural vision to form the music groups in the first place. These actions [the 1990 'cuts'] led to the formation of a cross-disciplinary group within Aosdána who met with Ray Burke and subsequently with Michael D. Higgins to seek to protect the position of classical music. Public meetings were also held which were attended by prominent people within classical music to protest at what RTÉ had done and groups met for a long time afterwards which helped in the survival of the National Chamber Choir and the Vanbrugh Quartet. After the Aosdána meeting with Michael D. Higgins it was agreed that our group would summarise our meeting with him and I added my addendum to that, giving my view as an ex-RTÉ employee with insights into the situation.[70]

Kinsella's thinking from 1986 – that it might be time 'for the child to leave home' – had clearly received a sharp nudge as it bore in on him that a radical change in RTÉ's mindset had separated it from the environment in which the orchestra had originally been conceived and grown. By the mere process of evolution, which had seen radio put aside, as energies were concentrated on the establishment of television, and then the growth of the single radio channel to a second national channel, and a third frequency which was shared by Raidió na Gaeltachta and the classical service on FM3, the enormous budget for Music seemed anomalous, considering the marginalised status of that part of the service which had originally been central.

The Aosdána approach to the ministers had been based on its concern for the reducing level of RTÉ airtime devoted to Irish compositions, but this had developed in the light of what was seen as the increasing vulnerability of an entire art form. In his personal addendum, Kinsella had said that, in his view, RTÉ had acted in such a way as to make the Performing Groups more and

70 J. Kinsella, e-mail to the author, 8 November 2003.

more irrelevant in the scheme of things, that the general public found it unusual that a broadcasting organisation should be responsible for the majority of events at the NCH, but that he believed that there would always be a place for a multi-purpose broadcasting orchestra.[71]

With these beliefs, it is understandable that Kinsella's behaviour during the group's oral hearing pointed towards the separation of the NSO from RTÉ. It was also expected that the members of the NSO would themselves put forward a case for separation, which they did not in fact propose. It is ironic that Conor Sexton, in pointing the way forward, had advocated the separation of the per-forming groups in a new department within RTÉ, and had expected Kinsella, as the then Head of Music, to administer this, shedding his other duties in order to concentrate on building up the groups.

The PIANO group received written and oral submissions from a wide vari-ety of organisations and individuals, including RTÉ, the two RTÉ orchestras (represented by SIPTU), the RTÉ/National Chamber Choir(s), the RTÉ Philharmonic Choir, the Vanbrugh String Quartet, Proinnsías Ó Duinn, the Association of Irish Composers, the Contemporary Music Centre, DGOS Opera Ireland, Wexford Festival Opera, the NCH, Music Network, the RIAM and the DIT College of Music.

The irony of the group's work was the fact that almost every submission of consequence pointed to the educational system as the root problem of music in Ireland – an irony because music education was not within the group's terms of reference nor, of course, within the remit of the Minister who had established it. In their submissions, the Arts Council's Music Officer and the NCH had referred, respectively, to the 'parlous' and 'abysmal' state of music education in Ireland.[72] As John O'Conor observed in his Foreword to the group's report,

> unless an audience is educated properly through our schools there will not be a sufficient number of people capable of appreciating the per-formers and composers of the future ... The proposals for the reform of music at Junior and Leaving Certificate levels ... [are] heartening, but the problem of music education at Primary Level remains. Anything we propose must be overshadowed by the lack of action on the recom-mendations made in the Benson Report of 1979 and the 'Deaf Ears?' report of 1985.[73]

---

71 J. Kinsella to M.D. Higgins, 26 July 1993, communicated to the author, November 2003.
72 The Arts Council's submission spoke of the 'parlous state of music education' (Dermot McLoughlin to PIANO 14 November 1994) and the NCH submission (p. 3) referred to 'the abysmal state of music in the Irish educational system' (PIANO Archive). 73 *PIANO Report*, p. i. In 1985 Donald Herron wrote *Deaf ears?: a report on the provision of music education in Irish schools* which highlighted the extreme fragility and paucity of such provision, which contribute to the dif-

While therefore educational matters were not conceived as part of its deliberations, the weight of the submissions made it necessary for the group to address the issues raised. The submission by the RIAM, for example, called for the establishment of a national training orchestra as a way of resolving difficulties which, as have been evident in the course of this book, are persistent irritants and obstacles to the recruitment of adequately trained Irish musicians.[74]

This served to highlight the fact that, as John O'Conor put it, 'it was said both that the terms of reference were too wide and that the terms of reference were too narrow to deal with the situation of classical music in Ireland at the present time'.[75]

The latter point was made particularly strongly by Niall Doyle (later, Director of Music at RTÉ) in the submission by Music Network, the Arts Council-funded organisation responsible for developing a nationwide linkage of venues and locally-based organisations capable of stimulating interest in concert tours and in the wider appreciation of music. Its submission devoted much of its space to its criticism of the group's terms of reference, arguing that to confine the review to the role of RTÉ and to orchestral provision was 'dangerous', and urging that the review should also address 'the enormous gaps in provision for music in other areas of musical life ... in addition [to] and in conjunction with RTÉ's role in and provision for music'.[76] The converse idea, that the terms of reference were too wide, originated in the general impression, already mentioned, that the sole item on the group's agenda was the relocation of the NSO, a point which was very clear to one member of the group, John Horgan.[77]

In the Introduction to its Report, the group acknowledged the role of Radio Éireann in establishing the orchestras and in making music a cornerstone of the broadcasting schedule, but stated explicitly that 'with the advent of television, radio – in the view of many professional broadcasters – became the poor relation' and continued:

ficulties of would-be Irish professional musicians. **74** In 1979 Ciarán Benson, acknowledging that 'the establishment of a new conservatoire, although desirable, is financially unrealistic at present', had proposed the now-familiar but never-achieved collaboration of the RIAM and the colleges of music in Dublin, Cork and Waterford to establish a 'Music Training Board ... to provide a conservatoire training for advanced young musicians', and had gone on to identify RTÉ's recruitment needs for its orchestras: C. Benson, *The Place of the Arts*, pp. 110–11. **75** *PIANO Report*, p. i. **76** Music Network submission to PIANO, 23 September 1993 p. 4 (PIANO Archive). **77** 'From the terms of reference it was clear to me that the NSO was the big item and that all the others were peripheral by comparison': J. Horgan, e-mail to the author, 14 November 2003. Horgan, while a member of the PIANO group, had voiced his personal opinion (at the Merriman Summer School) that 'it was entirely inappropriate that the Government should continue to delegate the running of a cultural institution as important as the [NSO] to any organisation whose primary purpose was not musical': *Irish Times*, 23 August 1996.

> The fact that our only fully professional orchestras, our only profes-
> sional string quartet, and until recently our only semi-professional cham-
> ber choir are located within a department within a division (Radio) of
> a large organisation is a cause for concern. If the development of these
> groups as national institutions is to be realised then change must be seri-
> ously considered.[78]

This represented the most serious question-mark ever placed over RTÉ's
ability and entitlement to administer Ireland's national symphony orchestra
and its responsibility for its development. For seventy years the assumption
had been planted within RTÉ and the 'civil service mind' generally, that the
national broadcaster was the natural custodian of the national orchestra – an
assumption which closely echoed Eimear Ó Broin's contention that broadcasting was the principal if not the only function of such an orchestra, and/or
that responsibility for non-broadcasting orchestras, whether municipal, regional
or national, lay elsewhere.

Simultaneously, another view had developed – not necessarily antagonistic
but perhaps complementary to the first – that such an orchestra had outgrown
the environment in which it had been conceived and that, particularly, over
the past forty years, as its professional status and commitments increased, it
should be given its own separate identity and destiny. This challenged the
implicit assumption that broadcasting – and public concerts by a broadcasting
orchestra – was synonymous with music-making, since it highlighted the fact
that music-making, and the needs and demands of public audiences, had developed beyond the point at which it could be satisfied by radio and/or television.
Furthermore, the dismantling of RTÉ's monopoly situation, with deregulation
of what had previously been termed 'pirate' radio, and the creation of an
Independent Radio and Television Commission, parallel to the RTÉ Authority,
meant that, in the minds of at least some, RTÉ could no longer, automatically
and without question, be regarded as the *national* broadcaster.

Whereas, during the mid-1960s, RTÉ had seriously questioned whether it
could afford either the financial commitment or the responsibility for managing such an asset, now – at least behind the scenes – it vigorously rebutted the
notion of separation, making a strenuous case for retention of the NSO. Since,
however, the terms of reference of PIANO did not explicitly ask the group to
consider whether the NSO should or should not be part of RTÉ, RTÉ's own
submission could only address this threat to its integrity by way of subliminal
argument, and this had the effect of making that argument appear complacent,
which is certainly the impression given to many by the oral presentations made

78 *PIANO Report*, p. vi.

by Kevin Healy (Director of Radio) and Cathal MacCabe (Head of Music) at
the public hearing in November 1994.

Thus, RTÉ's own submission was a matter-of-fact statement of the background to the performing groups, emphasising the role they played in the community, and giving valuable financial information not only about its funding
of the performing groups, but also making comparisons with other orchestras
and other broadcasting organisations.

As far as RTÉ's view of the NSO was concerned, 'a search for excellence is
pursued in recruitment, the calibre of conductors and soloists … The artistic
heights which an orchestra can achieve are predicated by the calibre of conductor which it can afford and attract. The NSO, increasingly, is attracting
better and better conductors and RTÉ intends continuing this trend.'[79] As we
shall see, this was a point on which there was severe disagreement.

Point by point, RTÉ set out its case in respect of each of the terms of reference of the review group: each performing group in turn, the Naxos/Marco
Polo recording contract, the consideration of Irish composers, regional and
international touring – without addressing the real (but hidden) question of
whether the NSO should be separated from its mother organisation. Its submission overall stressed two significant factors: that RTÉ's music activity had
to be seen within the overall broadcasting context in which RTÉ was under
severe financial pressure, and that 'RTÉ is now operating in a totally different
broadcasting environment from that which obtained when the Authority was
established [1960].'[80]

The financial information provided showed that almost £5 million was spent
annually on the performing groups, of which approximately £2.75m was allocated to the NSO – this in addition to the invisible costs of central services (i.e.
those provided within RTÉ but outside the Music Department). The NSO's
marketing budget was a mere £15k, compared to £200k for the BBCSO (which
had an overall budget of twice the NSO's), or £100k for the Ulster Orchestra
(which had a marginally smaller overall budget than the NSO). The orchestral budget of RTÉ was 24% of its total radio budget as compared with 4.4%
at the BBC, 5.6% at Radio France, and 16.5% at Finnish Radio.

A clerical error in the list of presentations to be made at the oral hearings
on 19 and 20 November 1994 indicates how the hierarchies within RTÉ can
be misunderstood by those unfamiliar with them: the first party listed to appear
was 'The RTÉ Authority', but in fact the three representatives who appeared
before the review panel were the Director of Radio, Kevin Healy, and two
members of the Music Department: Cathal MacCabe (Head of Music) and
Simon Taylor (who had succeeded Hudson as General Manager of the

79 RTÉ submission to PIANO, September 1994, pp. 3–4 (PIANO Archive).   **80** Ibid., p. 10.

Performing Groups). Their presentation, while affirming their own, and RTÉ's, commitment to the maintenance and development of the performing groups, indicated the systemic problems encountered when one section of an organisation has needs and expectations which are different from those of the organisation as a whole. In particular, the issue of salaries raised the intractable case that not only was RTÉ restricted at that time by a governmental restraint of 3% on pay increases, but also the relativities which had permeated the situation regarding pay and conditions for the RTÉ workforce as a whole would, as on previous occasions, prevent the musicians from receiving a pay increase in isolation. It was underlined by Cathal MacCabe's statement: 'You're talking to the wrong people'[81] – meaning that all employees of semi-state companies were bound by the same restrictions and that not only did the Music Department or the Radio Division as a whole have no role to play in the matter of RTÉ salaries, but that RTÉ itself was powerless to act outside the terms of the national wage agreements.

This led Loretta Keating to broach the question of whether, therefore, the NSO would fare better if it were separated from RTÉ: although all present at this discussion appeared to anticipate the question, there had been no explicit reference in any form to separation as an issue on the table. In reply, Kevin Healy said that 'If the orchestras can find a benefactor who will pay them substantially more money and give them the security that RTÉ has given them since the year dot – 1947 for the Symphony Orchestra – I wouldn't blame the players for looking at it.'[82] But as far as the *status quo* was concerned, MacCabe (who had been asked by John Horgan whether RTÉ would be prepared to fund the orchestras but not administer them) stated: 'RTÉ intends to continue to run a symphony orchestra. If someone decides that they would like to fund a symphony orchestra in some other way or take the title of "National Symphony Orchestra" and run it some other way, that's a matter of considerable concern, but RTÉ is committed to run a symphony orchestra which it hopes will continue to be called the National Symphony Orchestra.'[83] This was supplemented by Kevin Healy's observation (which of course constituted the crux of the perceived difficulty) that 'RTÉ took a decision in 1988 that the NSO would become a public performance orchestra and that broadcasting would become secondary – broadcasting would be the "carrier of the signal" and the same is true of the Concert Orchestra.'[84] At this point in the proceedings John Kinsella, emphasising that he was primarily representing Irish composers, restricted himself to the observation that 'it is my own personal view that some kind of

---

81 Cathal MacCabe, oral statement at PIANO hearing, 19 November 1994 (PIANO Archive).
82 Kevin Healy, oral statement at PIANO hearing, 19 November 1994 (PIANO Archive).
83 C. MacCabe, ibid. 84 K. Healy, ibid.

legal underpinning of the existence of the music groups is necessary',[85] thus signalling an issue to which he would return in questioning the representatives of the NSO.

As far as appearances by the performing groups on television were concerned, Cathal MacCabe – who, as a member of the Radio Division, had no televisual function – said that while the orchestras appeared in the televised 'Proms' seasons, this did not make attractive television, and was very expensive to produce.[86] In addition, he pointed out that it was technically very difficult 'to get ninety people into a studio' and achieve interesting programming, and that the relevant decision-makers in Television provided a regular classical slot on Sunday afternoons on Network2, mostly with less expensive, bought-in programmes: the costs of televising an NCH concert were in the region of £50–60k, and 'the Controller would say "I can buy the Berlin Philharmonic for that"'.[87] He acknowledged that, apart from meetings relevant to specific television programming involving the orchestras, there was no regular scheduled meeting between the Music Department and Television.

On programming policy, Simon Taylor said that while special one-off events at large venues, such as *Aida* or Mahler's Eighth Symphony at the Point Theatre, could attract capacity audiences, it was difficult to make a series (such as the NSO subscription concerts) attractive. (The NSO and the RTÉCO were at that time averaging 65% and 75% seat occupancy respectively.) 'What we have been exercising our minds on in recent times is how do we make the regularity of a symphony orchestra concert not become humdrum, the ordinariness of a symphony concert – how do we develop an excitement with the symphony concerts? Changing the time of the concerts, changing the day of the concerts, changing the dress, lighting it like a rock concert, changing the programme, playing Tchaikovsky 1812 more regularly, these are all difficult questions to answer. The one thing you can never do easily is ask people who aren't there why they aren't there.'[88]

In his oral presentation John Swift, Secretary of the Education Branch of SIPTU (to which the RTÉ orchestras were now affiliated), blamed the level of salaries for the high turnover in players, pointing out that the starting salary for a rank-and-file player was less than the average industrial wage; while the official NSO strength was 88 players at that stage, he asserted that the actual

---

85 John Kinsella, comment at PIANO hearing, 19 November 1994 (PIANO Archive). **86** This view has been expressed by many, including Bob Collins both as Director of Television and subsequently as Director-General. The search for an effective means of portraying an orchestral concert was perhaps envisaged by the authors of *Sit down and be counted* when they wrote (p. 277): 'Technology is no longer *necessarily* ugly and brutal. It has unparalleled means to provide us with an environment of grace and beauty, if it could find the vision, hold it steadily in focus and summon the will to realise it'. **87** C. MacCabe, ibid. **88** Simon Taylor, ibid.

number employed by RTÉ was only 74 (the remainder being deputies or temporaries), and he queried the seat occupancy at concerts, claiming that it was currently between 25% and 50%.

It was a matter of some speculation that the written submission by the NSO fell short of the expected call for its complete separation from RTÉ. While it argued that at present it worked within 'inappropriate organisational structures' in which it had no confidence, and that management lacked appropriate artistic knowledge or expertise, the NSO stated its wish to be 'attached' to RTÉ, with its own independent board of management, within the overall RTÉ structure, which would be jointly responsible to the Minister for Arts and the RTÉ Authority.[89] This was the cause of some confusion, since it was difficult to see exactly how such a structure could be made viable – a point that would be emphasised by John Kinsella in discussion. (Geraldine O'Grady noted that 'In conversation Alan [Smale, leader of the NSO] said that there were mixed feelings in the orchestra about the idea of leaving RTÉ. The main worry would be possible insecurity. They feel … that changing governments and different priorities could make their position precarious.')[90]

The NSO also took up the question of the quality of conductors and soloists, which would also feature in the NCH's submission: observing that the post of Principal Conductor had been vacant for three years after the abrupt resignation of George Hurst, and that the post of Principal Guest Conductor was still vacant after four years, the orchestra said 'for the greater part of the season the orchestra is in the dubious hands of a succession of largely uninspiring conductors … It seems that little consideration is given to the number of available and able conductors who would be stimulating to the orchestra and, indeed, attractive to the audience.'[91] In the search for a new Principal, 'most candidates had been seen only once or twice in a number of years and it was widely felt that this was insufficient to form any sort of reliable impression of a particular applicant'[92] – unlike the situation in the 1940s when guest conductors had been 'resident' for a number of weeks, and whose rapport with the orchestra could therefore be closely monitored over a series of concerts.

Furthermore, the NSO argued, 'concert programming is lacking in imagination, balance, shape and focus, and this is contributing to low attendance at

89 SIPTU, NSO submission to PIANO, September 1994, pp. 3–4 (PIANO Archive). 90 Geraldine O'Grady, ms. note on verso of letter to her from Alan Smale, 1 August 1994 (PIANO Archive). 91 SIPTU, NSO submission to PIANO p. 8 (PIANO Archive). 92 Ibid. Geoffrey Spratt made the same point more scathingly: 'a string of young, inexperienced "foreign" conductors using the orchestras to practise their craft and giving not only nothing in return, but actually contributing to the overall decline of standards and morale' – G. Spratt, submission to PIANO 25 September 1994 (PIANO Archive).

concerts with yet another adverse effect on the morale of the players'.[93] That the NSO considered it necessary to spell out the need for better programming is salutary:

> The influence it [programming] has on the life and success of the orchestra must first be recognised ... The music the orchestra plays is of prime importance in its relationship with its public audience, and this relationship is at the very heart of an orchestra's life. Good orchestral programming demands many skills: a thorough knowledge of music is obvious, but it also demands accounting skills and the ability to stamp a concert season, or longer term programme, with a sense of direction and a balance between entertainment and education, and between stability and surprise.[94]

It would have been difficult for artistic management in RTÉ to have followed the thematic success of Bryden Thomson's seasons, but the NSO drew explicit attention to these, which had reached their 'zenith' with his cycles of Sibelius, Nielsen, Bruckner and Beethoven, which created 'a huge upsurge of interest in the orchestra. It was a time when the orchestra and audience built that special trust which is so necessary if one is to programme anything more than Tchaikovsky and Beethoven'.[95] The expression 'special trust' indicates how far the NSO accepted that the personality and aura of a conductor played a very significant part in establishing that relationship between orchestra, conductor and audience which succeeded in maintaining audience figures and, on the admittedly rare occasions of 'zenith', in eliciting what is commonly called 'rapturous applause'.

The orchestra attributed its falling standards to 'the construction and marketing of the programmes the orchestra plays', which in turn led to 'the present situation where the orchestra cannot even fill the Concert Hall playing Tchaikovsky's Fifth Symphony'.[96] It pointed out that in the previous three years there had been major gaps in the standard repertoire, and that the main figures of twentieth-century music had been almost totally ignored, although works by living Irish composers had fared better, with performances of works by Barry, Boydell, Buckley, de Barra, Hayes, Johnston, Kinsella, Martin, Jane O'Leary, Sweeney, Victory and (James) Wilson. However, it criticised the fact that 'RTÉ does not seem to understand that it is not sufficient simply to perform these works, the public must also be persuaded to come and listen.'[97]

Moving outwards from this latter point, 'the NSO suggests that, as part of its public service mandate, education should be one of its key roles and a cen-

93 Ibid., p. 10.   94 Ibid.   95 Ibid., p. 11.   96 Ibid.   97 Ibid., p. 12.

tral reason for its very existence',[98] and identified sections of the population who should be targeted for special attention.

> With imagination and hard work, many orchestras have expanded their audience and their reach into the general community. For example, it should be possible to organise concerts with an educational purpose, such as 'Meet the Composer' to promote new works; open rehearsals; a series of informal concerts of standard works to draw in new audiences; and, on the more practical side of things, to establish a 'Friends of the NSO' type of organisation. Whatever form it takes, anything that involves the public more closely in the life of the orchestra makes the orchestra truly belong to the public.[99]

In conclusion, the NSO tried to answer a point which readers of this volume may already be asking themselves: 'The Review Group may well be puzzled by the apparent contradiction between, on the one hand, the very many difficulties currently confronting the orchestra and, on the other hand, the fact that, somehow, the NSO has overcome such obstacles with consistent performances of outstanding merit' – another point on which there was clearly room for disagreement. 'For an explanation, we may turn to the remarkable dedication of the musicians; the extraordinary pride that they take in their role as NSO members, echoes of which abound in our submission; their utter conviction that the NSO can develop into one of the leading orchestras of the world, contributing much to the cultural and commercial life of the country, and, finally, their fervent hope that the Minister's initiative in establishing this Review will culminate in the realisation of their worthy objectives … The orchestra is now at a crossroads. It can struggle on as it is, barely fulfilling its role in Irish society or it can be rejuvenated on the lines that have been suggested.'[1]

The chief difference between the NSO's submission and that by RTÉ is in the vigour and imagination of the language employed by the former. It was as if the NSO was prepared to come out of its corner, fighting for its survival, while RTÉ sat in its own corner, unable for a fight, or even to engage constructively in discussion which might alleviate the NSO's anxieties and realise some of its ambitions. That would be an unfair summary of the situation, however, since it is clear to the author that, personalities aside, RTÉ was unaware of exactly how critical was the position in which it was placed, was unprepared for the demonstration of vituperative comment that indicated, from so many quarters, that its music policy – or lack of it – was such a burning matter of public concern, and, above all, was systemically incapable of dealing with such

98 Ibid., p. 23. 99 Ibid. 1 Ibid., p. 33.

a major point of contention without involving much higher levels of its hier-archy than it was prepared to venture forward.

The representatives of the NSO at the oral hearing – William Dowdall, chair of the artistic committee (and principal flute), Fiona McAuslan (violin) and Niall O'Loughlin (cello) – indicated as frankly as possible, and in the face of intense questioning, that this problem had concerned their members very deeply. Dowdall, referring to the establishment of the PIANO group as 'the most sig-nificant initiative since the founding of the Radio Éireann Symphony Orchestra', stated that the NSO's members were 'aggressively interested in the future of *our* orchestra ... Many members of the NSO could play in any orchestra in the world but have made a conscious decision to remain in this country with the ambition that some day we will be an orchestra of international reputation and stature. This ambition is eminently attainable'.[2] Referring to the expectations raised by the 'Time For Change' document, he asked (as had Gareth Hudson before him) 'Have these expectations been recognised? Is enough being done to realise the expectations raised by such an important change in policy?'

When asked by John O'Conor whether the orchestra wished 'to stay under the umbrella of RTÉ?,' Dowdall replied 'Yes.' The NSO wanted to see a Board 'that can control its activities. We have always operated in RTÉ based on the goodwill of RTÉ and we have no argument against RTÉ'. But one priority – with the experience of the 'cap' at their immediate shoulder – was to guaran-tee security of funding.

Niall O'Loughlin then made the significant point that there was 'an evolv-ing relationship', and that one priority was to establish 'what the country needs' – thus bringing to the fore the evolving nature of the NSO itself.[3] Fiona MacAuslan acknowledged 'We do see the dichotomy of what we are asking – we want an independent set-up but we want to be part of RTÉ ... The way forward has to be an organisational change but we need this link as well.'[4]

The artistic vision of the orchestra members was clear from John O'Conor's next question (what did the NSO see as its priority?) and William Dowdall's reply: 'The NSO being moved much more into the mainstream of European music-making'.[5] He had pointed out that there was insufficient touring – the NSO had not played in a European capital since 1980 – and that it was not necessary to undertake two-week tours if the orchestra could play once a year in one or more large European cities with discriminating audiences.

It was now John Kinsella's turn to question the NSO representatives, and he asked 'If the future of the performing groups was underpinned by legisla-

2 W. Dowdall, oral statement to PIANO hearing, 19 November 1994 (PIANO Archive). 3 Niall O'Loughlin, oral statement to PIANO hearing, 19 November 1994 (PIANO Archive). 4 Fiona MacAuslan, oral statement to PIANO hearing, ibid. 5 W. Dowdall, ibid.

tion, whether that might alter your thinking as regards vulnerability?'[6] To which Dowdall replied:

> What is needed is something that will specify a minimum level of funding from licence fee or equivalent income ... We do need a lot more investment in the orchestra ... On a management level there is a lot of goodwill in RTÉ. This seems to change with a change of wind. If a new Authority comes next May,[7] we could find the opposite. We would like to see if at all possible – by the creation of this Board which would be answerable to the RTÉ Authority and also answerable to the Minister for Arts and Culture – a sort of balance or co-responsibility.[8]

MacAuslan followed this by saying

> As an orchestra we've always wanted legislation of whatever sort to underpin our existence and our viability. The elements we saw as having a specific interest to the orchestra were: RTÉ from broadcasting; the national interest through the Department [of Arts and Culture]; and an orchestral interest from ourselves. That was the prime motivating factor in looking at the idea of a Board. We would be moving away from the idea that RTÉ has a sole interest in running the NSO because there are other very important elements that should come into play. The struggle is how far out do we move? ... This is a developing subject among ourselves at the moment ... to actively find what legislation and organisational structures are right for the NSO.[9]

John Kinsella pressed the point by asking how such a Board could solve the specific problems of pay, conditions of service and early retirement, to which Dowdall responded 'We haven't really found any answer at the moment. We are looking for more expertise. We aren't management consultants. Maybe by moving the orchestra into a more independent position within RTÉ and with a guaranteed budget and the freedom to exercise that budget ... We are really asking *you* if that is possible'. To which MacAuslan added: 'One thing we're absolutely sure of is that we're not going to get these things sorted out where we are, and that was one of the driving forces to look at moves. Maybe we're too restricted in ourselves, in the way we look at things, to come up with a specific answer but we do know that we need a move of some sort to create the structure that will allow for all these things'.

6 J. Kinsella, comment, ibid. 7 The term of office of the then RTÉ Authority expired on 31 May 1995. 8 W. Dowdall, oral statement to PIANO hearing, 19 November 1994 (PIANO Archive). 9 F. MacAuslan, ibid.

Perhaps Dowdall's comment, 'We are really asking *you* if that is possible', gave a new impetus to, as well as an exit from, the difficulty of the admitted 'dichotomy', since John Kinsella was forthright in his opinion that the proposed half-way Board was not viable. Thus, in a letter of clarification sent after the oral hearing, John Swift stated that 'if this proposal is impossible to achieve, SIPTU would favour the establishment of the NSO as a completely independent and unique national institution, with its own Board and staff.'[10] It should be noted that this was the only point at which any such establishment was formally and officially proposed in the course of the PIANO review – it had not been part of either its written or its oral submission, but it was the – admittedly belated – statement that some had hoped for from the inception of the PIANO review.

The leader of the NSO, Alan Smale, stated that the players felt underpaid and undervalued, and that there was a relentlessness about the schedule which led to stress and ill-health; there was a need for time off and rotation among the more senior positions. Working within the orchestra, Smale was aware of both the tensions and the rewards of working with a range of visiting musicians; he put forward the view that

> the orchestra … has improved on all counts since my time in Ireland [1976] and there is a freshness, commitment and total lack of professional cynicism to the music-making here which is remarked upon by all visiting musicians and conductors.[11]

Whereas in London, for example, players specialised in one branch of music, in Ireland the lack of specialisation was an advantage, allowing orchestral musicians to teach, and to play chamber music and contemporary works. He wanted a better public perception of classical music, and better recognition of the orchestra's status:

> We are ambassadors for the country when we travel abroad as much as the Irish football team or traditional music groups, and we feel that this is not recognised enough. Much could be done in education to put this right. Classical music for too long has been seen as a minority interest, instead of the birthright of every Irish citizen, and an essential part of the country's moral and spiritual well-being.[12]

In oral presentation Smale's thesis became even more emotional than it was in writing: music was 'a deeply spiritual matter – at the risk of embarrassing

---

10 J. Swift to J. O'Conor, 23 November 1994 (PIANO Archive).   11 A. Smale to Geraldine O'Grady, 1 August 1994 (PIANO Archive).   12 Ibid.

myself – it is not a vague intellectual interest and it is not a minority interest
… It allows us to tap into a life-force that is within us and can communicate
to our audience'. This was 'not always recognised by the media, by our management or by the public at large'.[13]

Smale himself expressed no opinion regarding the proper location or status of the NSO, other than to urge better promotion of the orchestra's activities, and better working conditions.

In its turn, the RTÉCO, pointing out that its concert-giving had increased
from a figure of eight concerts in 1979 to eighty in 1994, also asked for its re-
establishment as an 'autonomous unit' within RTÉ, complaining of the lack
of accountability and professionalism in the present administrative structure,
and in addition calling for a proper base for its activities and more efficient
schedule planning.[14] In oral hearing the point was underscored: 'We are highly
trained. We have to be experts in our field' – and therefore management should
have the necessary complementary skills. 'We would like to have our own concert series in our own home that is our identity'.[15]

As permanent Principal Conductor of the RTÉCO, Proinnsías Ó Duinn
stated in his submission that, since his appointment in 1978,

> my aspiration for both the musicians in the orchestra and my fellow
> countrymen was that every opportunity should be grasped to transform
> the orchestra from a studio based unit to one which would perform in
> concert, live, to the people of our country. By either broadcasting such
> performances direct or recording them for future transmission, RTÉ
> would satisfy the needs of the national broadcasting station and fill an
> enormous social and cultural void.[16]

Ó Duinn observed that the orchestra's improvement over the past sixteen
years, in terms of quality and versatility, in 'chang[ing] its role and image to such
a phenomenal degree' had been due to the musicians' determination and willingness 'to dramatically change the work practice without insisting on productivity agreements at every turn'.[17] Progress had, however, been impeded by inadequate budgets for national touring and, above all, by the fact that the RTÉCO
had no home of its own which could also function as a performance space.

At the oral hearing he pointed out that he had experience of both a radio-
based orchestra (as in Iceland) and a national orchestra governed by a Board
(as in Ecuador) and judged that on balance 'I'm not sure that the orchestras

13 A. Smale, oral statement to PIANO hearing, 19 November 1994 (PIANO Archive). 14 SIPTU,
RTÉCO submission to PIANO, September 1994 (PIANO Archive). 15 Ruth Mann, RTÉCO,
oral statement to PIANO hearing, 19 November 1994 (PIANO Archive). 16 P. Ó Duinn submission to PIANO, 12 September 1994 (PIANO Archive). 17 Ibid.

can be served better under another régime.' Nevertheless, 'the Concert Orchestra has progressed in what it is aspiring to do, faster than any other group within RTÉ and the budget, which was never adequate in the first place, is miles out of focus'. Studio 1 in the Radio Centre, to which the RTÉLO had moved in 1974, was 'incorrect' as far as air conditioning, lighting and acoustics were concerned.[18]

The RTÉ Vanbrugh String Quartet, in a very diplomatically worded submission, reviewed the past four years, during which it had been placed on less than half-pay as a reaction to the advertising 'cap', and then re-instated. As a group with an extra-broadcasting function implicit in its contract with RTÉ – to participate actively in the musical life of Cork – and as an ensemble of world class which frequently worked internationally, the quartet was in a strong position to exert influence on the way PIANO perceived RTÉ music management. Throughout its detailed observations, the quartet repeatedly referred to 'our administrators' as having shown less than adequate attention to the non-musical needs of the quartet, especially in areas such as on-air promotion, and complained that RTÉ's Cork offices had shown no interest in its existence.[19] The members of the quartet were clearly deeply worried at the lack of administrative support for their music-making, but equally one can detect their concern that they should not jeopardise an environment which made that music-making so worthwhile and rewarding. Cork provided them with that working environment, but also contributed to their sense of isolation from any branch of RTÉ that might make valuable connections with their work.

Serious concern was aroused by the submissions by the RTÉ Chamber Choir, the National Chamber Choir (with which it was virtually identical) and the RTÉ Philharmonic Choir. The latter's statement read:

> This is the tenth anniversary of the RTÉ Philharmonic Choir. Instead of rejoicing and celebrating this fact, feelings of hurt, uncertainty and low morale exist widely among choir members ... We believe that shortcomings in management, communication and consultation have made it extremely difficult for the choral director to perform his functions in a way that is satisfactory and meaningful to him.[20]

The RTÉ Chamber Choir and the National Chamber Choir added to this sense of anxiety and confusion, not only in their written submissions but in their presentations at the oral hearing, which left many with a sense of bafflement and not a little amusement as they attempted to explain the circumstances

18 P. Ó Duinn, oral statement to PIANO hearing, 19 November 1994 (PIANO Archive).
19 RTÉ Vanbrugh String Quartet submission to PIANO [n.d.] (PIANO Archive).
20 RTÉ Philharmonic Choir, submission to PIANO September 1994 (PIANO Archve).

in which the same seventeen people existed symbiotically under both nomen-
clatures, and with the same conductor in the same premises, but insisted that
they were two totally different entities. Underlining their sense of grievance,
however, was the same problem of how they felt they had been treated by RTÉ
management – especially during the cutbacks caused by the 'cap' – and their
feeling of commitment to the Choral Director.[21]

Possibly the oral presentation by the National Chamber Choir's administrator, Karina Lundström, contained the most succinct summary of the perceived crisis within the performing groups as a whole when she said:

> Radical change is needed to end the present monopoly. Monopolies by
> their very nature are generally bad for industry. The classical music
> industry is no different in this respect from any other. RTÉ is not and
> should not be made the sole responsibility to supply almost all the
> nation's classical music employment.[22]

Her presentation brought to the fore the fact that (as we have seen in chapter 5) the position of the choral director, Colin Mawby, had become extremely
ambiguous and precarious, due mainly to two factors: firstly, Mawby's perception of RTÉ management as being unsupportive of him and his proposals,
and insufficiently appreciative of the nature of choral music and choral artists;
and secondly, RTÉ's perception of Mawby as a member of management with
responsibility for administrative efficiency and acumen as well as artistic direction, who was not demonstrating sufficient commitment to the organisational
ethos but was, instead (as it saw him) displaying disloyalty to his employer.

Wryly, Mawby's own submission to PIANO stated that 'the views expressed
are my own and in no way reflect those of RTÉ'.[23] That was hardly surprising,
since he stated at the outset that

> RTÉ is no longer a fit custodian of these unique and important national
> assets [the performing groups] … RTÉ has little policy towards its
> Choral Groups, no understanding of their dynamic, and no genuine
> interest in their performing standard. Historical circumstances have
> enabled RTÉ to assume an almost monopolistic control of Irish pro-

21 SIPTU, RTÉ Chamber Choir submission to PIANO, September 1994; Karina Lundström,
National Chamber Choir submission to PIANO , September 1994: the NCC submission also
referred to the larger picture, expressing the hope that the review would bring about 'the radical
change that is needed to bring classical music in Ireland to the level of excellence that can be
achieved' (p. 2) (PIANO Archive).   22 K. Lundström, oral statement to PIANO hearing, 19
November 1994 (PIANO Archive).   23 C. Mawby to Maura Eaton (secretary of the review group),
15 September 1994 (PIANO Archive).

fessional music. This is an unhealthy situation that calls for urgent amendment ... All in RTÉ's Choral Groups look forward with eager anticipation to the Review Group's recommendations because we have suffered considerably from RTÉ management's arrogant and short-sighted behaviour. Its attitudes are no longer acceptable.[24]

Based primarily on what he perceived as an arbitrary and irresponsible decision in 1990 to disband the choral groups, which clearly rankled at the depths of his artistic being, Mawby argued for the removal of all performing groups from RTÉ's control, but continuing to be funded from the licence fee, with RTÉ mandated to transmit their performances. He recommended that the RTÉ Chamber Choir be subsumed into the National Chamber Choir and that the Philharmonic Choir be re-named the National Symphony Chorus.

In his oral presentation to PIANO Mawby was as outspoken as he was on paper, making, in the minds of several observers, the case for his own dismissal. He stated that in 1990 he had not been officially informed that the RTÉ Chamber Choir had been suspended, nor in 1993 had he been told that it had been restored. Making a case for the restoration of a professional choir (as had pertained with the RTÉ Singers) he said:

> I find it utterly unacceptable that in a civilised country an important profession which is so much a part of our heritage should be treated in this disgraceful way ... Singing is so much a part of our heritage and our culture. Singing is such a fine expression of human nature – human love, human hate – and yet we condemn the very people who can do this to earn their living outside the country. I personally find that shameful.[25]

Summing up his differences with management, he said 'I am a musician. My job is making music. I'm not an administrator although I have to do that. I'm not a manager, although I have to do that.'

Those working outside RTÉ who made submissions ranged from the tactful and positive to those who adopted the same tone as Colin Mawby. Thus Gerard Gillen, professor of music at St Patrick's College, Maynooth,[26] who acknowledged RTÉ's co-operative attitude in regard to the Dublin International Organ Festival, observed the terms of reference of the review group when he said:

> There is much evidence to suggest that the demands of the NSO as the state's premier performing body and its remit as the national broad-

---

24 Ibid. 25 C. Mawby, oral statement to PIANO hearing, 19 November 1994 (PIANO Archive). 26 Today, NUI Maynooth.

casting orchestra have produced tensions which have resulted in a serious *malaise* permeating the entire performing body at present. This *malaise* appears to be due to the following: (a) an apparent serious lack of artistic direction and coherence in programme planning; (b) the absence of an inspiring permanent *maestro*.[27]

He recommended the separation of the NSO from RTÉ.

The National Concert Hall made a strong case for its own involvement in NSO decision-making, pointing out that

> because the NSO plays such a vital and important role in the image and satisfaction ratings of the NCH it is a matter of serious concern to us if there is any decline in attendance at its concerts or any perceived lack of confidence in its programming or in the content or scheduling of them. Of equal concern is any perceived lack of stature in its conductors or in the choice of soloists with whom it plays. Unfortunately, there has been a perceptible fall in attendance at NSO performances over the past year. This worrying decline in attendance figures has implications not alone for a fall in the revenue of the NSO and the NCH but in terms of audience loyalty, confidence and respect for both organisations. Arguably, the decline in audience acceptance of NSO programme offerings is not good for the morale of the orchestra membership either.[28]

The NCH, calling for 'ongoing and progressive programming, aimed at embracing a wide audience', voiced an open criticism of RTÉ's management structures when it said

> The NSO is at some disadvantage in that it is but part of the musical responsibilities of RTÉ and so far it has not operated under the kind of dedicated management and operational structures that an orchestra of national stature needs.[29]

This was tantamount to saying that the re-establishment of the RTÉSO as the NSO in 1990 should have been accompanied by a restructuring of the Music Department so as to provide the NSO with its own dedicated administration with appropriate skills. The NCH went further, clearly showing its awareness of the needs of orchestral musicians:

> We suggest that the review group include in their work specification an examination of the main determinants of overall orchestral quality ...

---

27 G. Gillen submission to PIANO, 20 September 1994 (PIANO Archive). 28 NCH submission to PIANO, November 1994 (PIANO Archive). 29 Ibid.

issues such as morale, motivation, and the implications of reward structures on commitment and the attraction or retention of musical talent
… Inherent in the assignment given to the PIANO review group is the
challenge to discover the catalysts that might drive a new phase in the
development of classical and other musical performance in Ireland.[30]

However, the most strident and outspoken version of these criticisms came
from Geoffrey Spratt, recently appointed Director of the Cork School of Music
and formerly a lecturer in music at UCC, Director of the Cork International
Choral Festival and a noted choral conductor. Echoing the tone set by Colin
Mawby, Spratt declared

Over the last few years, RTÉ has proven itself to be unfit beyond all
measure to fulfil the range and depth of responsibilities which are concomitant with the administration of chamber music groups, choirs –
amateur and professional – and orchestras … The RTÉ administration
is, at its very best, incompetent, unprofessional and lacking appropriate
vision … The catalogue of ineptitude and incompetence on the existing administrative front is simply too horrendous and well known to
detail … They have failed the musicians, they have failed the audiences
who listen to them, and they have failed the taxpayers whose money
they have not used in the best manner possible … Because the situation
is so serious – both in terms of extent and depth – it would be my contention that it is not only too late, but also impossible, to 'restore' matters within the framework of RTÉ. In my opinion, the only solution is
to take these groups away from RTÉ and establish an independent body
of the highest calibre to oversee their every need.[31]

It was clear that, across the spectrum of public, private and professional
opinion, the view had been formed that RTÉ was giving inadequate support
to, and consideration of, the NSO at the very least, as well as appearing to lack
a policy for choral music. The falling audiences and lack of musical excitement
in the choice of programmes and artists were one palpable cause of unrest
among audiences, with concomitant reduction in orchestral morale, while
informed criticism of RTÉ's music policy had identified more deep-rooted
causes of the *malaise* mentioned by Gerard Gillen.

The PIANO report commented on the fact that, following the retirement
of Gerard Victory, the change of title from 'Director' to 'Head' 'reflected …
the diminished status of music within the RTÉ organisational structures'.[32]

30 Ibid. 31 G. Spratt submission to PIANO, 25 September 1994 (PIANO Archive). 32 *PIANO*

The hierarchy within RTÉ Radio Division, and the relationship between Radio, the Directorate-General and the Authority, would not have been known to many outsiders, but the representatives of RTÉ's Music Department who spoke at the public sessions, Cathal MacCabe and Simon Taylor, would have been the focus of attention as far as attempting to express RTÉ's less than convincing policies towards its performing groups was concerned.

Even though the NSO itself had not put forward separation as its principal proposal, the main recommendation of the review group, delivered in January 1996, was that the NSO should be re-established by legislation and managed by a sixteen-member Board of Directors appointed by the Minister for the Arts, with representatives from RTÉ, the Arts Council, the Association of Irish Composers, the NCH, the putative IAPA,[33] and to include performers and concert-goers in order to make the Board as representative as possible of all 'stakeholders'.

This was a position on which John O'Conor found himself initially unable to agree: from his experience of the demise, for financial reasons, of several American orchestras, he had strong reservations about the vulnerability of the NSO, if it was withdrawn from the shelter of RTÉ, and on this he clearly empathised with the dilemma expressed by the NSO representatives. (Conversely, John Kinsella argued that, in a country with only one full-sized symphony, that risk did not exist.) However, O'Conor was anxious to avoid a situation where he, as Chairman, would issue a minority report and, finally persuaded by the argument that the rates of musicians' pay were below acceptable levels, he agreed to subscribe to a unanimous report, even though he privately continued to experience, and express, his misgivings.[34]

On 29 January 1996, when launching the report, Michael D. Higgins stated that its implications required him to allow time for RTÉ, the Arts Council and the Minister for Education to consider them and to consult with him. In the Dáil, Síle de Valera (Fianna Fáil, Clare), the opposition spokesperson on the arts, suggested that an independent unit within RTÉ (as proposed by both the Sexton Report and the NSO itself) was the more practical way forward for the NSO, and took the opportunity to urge the Minister to confer with his opposite num-

---

Report, p. 2. **33** The proposed establishment of IAPA [Irish Academy for the Performing Arts] was not announced until 1997–98 but it was envisaged as part of the *PIANO Report* (pp. 53–4). After protracted negotiations, it was announced in 2002 that the proposal would not proceed in its current form: cf. R. Pine, 'In Dreams Begins Responsibility'. **34** Interviews with John O'Conor, 1 September 2003 and with John Kinsella, 19 November 2003. At least one member of the group, John Horgan, continued to voice his view that the NSO should be removed from RTÉ, submitting to the Department of Communications' Forum on the RTÉ Charter that 'it is even more urgent now that steps should be taken to this end. The continuing uncertainty surrounding RTÉ due to technological and political paradigm shifts in broadcasting practice and thinking will inevitably lead to the demise of all large state controlled broadcasters across Europe'.

ber in Education to discuss the future of music education at primary and secondary levels, as well as the setting up of a conservatoire. Higgins confirmed that he was in the process of discussions with the Minister for Education.[35]

It was a process that fell by the wayside, as, a year later, the coalition government of Fine Gael, Labour and Democratic Left went out of office, and Síle de Valera herself was appointed minister with responsibility for broadcasting and culture, in the incoming Fianna Fáil/Progressive Democrat coalition government. The searching investigation of the condition of the RTÉ orchestras, in particular, resulted in no direct action whatsoever being taken, and as far as governmental attitudes are concerned, the NSO remains in a limbo from which it may never emerge. It is unlikely that any future government would take the action recommended by the PIANO review unless it were prompted to do so by a groundswell of public opinion.

By making public for the first time the contents of the written and oral submissions to the PIANO group, this chapter has been able to establish a modern-day perspective on the way in which RTÉ's performing groups were originally conceived and established, on the way that their working environment has changed over the fifty-five years of the RÉSO and RÉLO; fifty of the professional choir; and forty-five of the string quartet; and on the changing relationship with management in both artistic and strategic terms.

Althouth the PIANO experience was a harsh one for RTÉ as an organisation (especially in the light of the preconceptions of at least some of the participants) and although its findings, due to political change, were not implemented, most of the elements in both the 'Sexton' and PIANO reports have since been put in place, with, consequently, a much improved level of understanding, respect and synergy between artists and management. RTÉ's new policy for management, briefly described in the Postscript, and its increasing concern for the role of composition in contemporary society, have halted the haemorrhage of trust that had characterised the previous two decades, and have allowed the organisation to regain much of the recognition it achieved in the 1940s, 50s and 60s as a positive and dynamic facilator for music-making.

35 DD. 461, 14 February 1996, cols. 1295–6.

Postscript

In 1926 no one knew (or could have known) what the phenomenon of radio would mean to Irish culture and society, and no one could foresee the role that music would occupy in their development. Many of the elements in the 'Policy, Strategy and Initiatives' for the RTÉ Performing Groups, finalised in early 2004, might have been considered self-evident in 1926, so great is the necessity, at certain historical nodes, of re-inventing the wheel. The chief elements in the 2004 policy were regionalisation, engagement with new music, and education. RTÉ's stated policy was:

> To engage, enrich and entertain the widest audience, through live performance, broadcasting, recordings and new technologies, and through education and community initiatives;
>
> to create music and musical experiences of the highest possible quality;
>
> to present the best of music of the past and present, with a particular emphasis attached to Irish music.
>
> Underlying these policies ... is the core principle of seeking the greatest possible interaction and engagement between composers, performers and audience.

Right from the start, Vincent O'Brien, and after him Michael Bowles, wanted to get out from behind the studio microphones to address a living audience, but almost eighty years went past before it was possible, and necessary, for RTÉ to articulate a policy in such terms that would keep faith with both concert audiences and radio listeners. (It was the first explicit statement of such policy since the establishment of the RÉSO and the RÉLO had been announced in 1947, and represents the fifth and most recent milestone in RTÉ's understanding of the NSO and, of course, of its other performing groups.) That a newly-appointed Director of Music should realise this necessity underlines the fact that these elements of RTÉ's music activity have been self-evident over the decades, and therefore assumed to be in no need of articulation. Only in the dichotomous decades, when it seemed that RTÉ wanted to retreat from concert-giving, in favour of predominantly radiophonic activity, was that outward-looking perspective lost. Certainly, neither Tibor Paul, Gerard Victory, John Kinsella nor Cathal MacCabe would have hesitated to express this view if they had thought it necessary. It took the crises of the PIANO report and the financial abyss into which RTÉ was staring for most of the 1990s, to evoke a statement of RTÉ's sense of musical direction which recognises the totality of performing groups, their administration, their audiences, and the composers of today and tomorrow. The major difference between the radio orchestra which has become today's NSO, and the other broadcasting orchestras established in Europe in the 1920s and '30s is that, in most cases, the cities in which those orchestras were set up already had at least one orchestra of professional standard, whereas Dublin did not. Very few of those European broadcasting orchestras have found themselves obliged to act also as a civic or even national orchestra. With hindsight, to found what would inexorably become the NSO may have been an error of judgement, but it was an unavoidable error which set the founders on a path which they followed with astonishing determination and diplomacy. The resistance offered by figures such as Maurice Gorham and Roibéard Ó Faracháin, not only to their own Music Department but also to ministers like Erskine Childers, was perhaps also due to the same deprivation of music education and appreciation which, I have suggested, affected the judgements of John Kinsella's colleagues in the 1980s. Yet it did not prevent the evolution of two orchestras and other performing groups, even though it may have inhibited the evolution of a supporting policy for their development.

It is a sign of the ponderous nature of such a large organisation that RTÉ should have succeeded, but at a slow and episodic pace, in putting in place most of the recommendations of the 'Sexton' and PIANO reports, and thereby righting the faults and imbalances identified by them. It is also a sign of the presence of music and politics in each others' lives that the revenue 'cap' of 1990–4 precipitated such inter-related crises and forced an awareness of the vulnerability of performance to the financial constraints which R(T)É's music-making has almost always succeeded in surmounting.

That politics and music continue to be inter-related was made clear when, subtly but unequivocally, the Sinfonia Varsovia appeared as musical ambassadors in Dublin in 2003, to persuade Irish citizens to 'listen to Poland' – a country rich in both musical tradition and political division, trying to find its way in a new Europe of diversity and yet cohesion. It reminded me of the poignant occasion twenty-one years previously, when violinist Wanda Wiłkomirska, a member of Solidarity and ex-wife of Poland's then deputy prime minister, Mieczyslaw Rakowski, announced on arrival at Dublin Airport that she was defecting to western Europe. By the time our car had reached Dublin city, a strategy had been put in place to deal with this extra-musical factor in that weekend's concert-giving. The following three days – with international news interviews, and an appearance on the 'Late, Late Show', in addition to her performance of the

Khatchaturian concerto – were some of the most moving, as well as the most unusual, that a Concerts Manager can expect to encounter, and it underlined, as did the Polish chamber orchestra, that there is both a strength and a fragility in musical politics, as there is in political music. RTÉ, in its espousal of new music (for example, John Kinsella's sixth symphony, to which the subtitle is 'The Birmingham Six') and in its negotiation of established patterns of music-making and music administration, encounters these factors on a daily basis, as part of what is today called 'the Irish music industry'.

Perhaps the most disturbing and ambiguous aspect of the contemporary focus on the 'Irish music industry' is its studied ignorance of 'classical' music. The first significant exploration of the economic relevance of the performing arts in Ireland was a report commissioned by the Arts Council from John O'Hagan and Christopher Duffy of TCD, published in October 1987: *The Performing Arts and the Public Purse: an economic analysis*. This effectively excluded RTÉ from its considerations, arguing that, since RTÉ's funding was not derived from the Arts Council or from government, 'a separate study on the role of the RTÉ orchestra, both within RTÉ and the performing arts industry as a whole' was required.[1] The PIANO Report can be considered as the most far-reaching consideration of the NSO to date, but it made little attempt to locate the orchestra within the broad context of 'the performing arts industry', so that O'Hagan's and Duffy's suggestion has yet to be pursued.

The next thrust in this direction was a brief 'Submission to government' entitled *The Irish Music Industry – Turnpike or Boreen on the Sound Superhighway of the 21st Century [?]* commissioned from Simpson Xavier Horwath Consulting in 1993. Although the report was illustrated by two full-page out-of-date photographs of the NSO and also featured one of Colman Pearce,[2] its text contained no word about classical music except a passing reference to 'the prolific output of modern classical works'[3] – the works, and their authors, were unspecified. Its emphasis was on creativity and on job- and wealth-creation, and, while it carefully did not focus on any specific area of music composition or performance, the predominance of images of Enya, Bill Whelan, U2, Shaun Davey, Clannad and Van Morrison suggested that the main categories of activity were in the more popular segments of the market. The emphasis on recordings, exports and tourism also suggested that the regular performance of classical music by the RTÉ performing groups would not be a major plank in any subsequent investigation of the 'Irish music industry'.

The initial 'submission' by Simpson Xavier Horwath gave no indication of its sponsors, but it was followed by *A Strategic Vision for the Irish Music*

---

1 *The performing arts and the public purse*, p. 8.   2 A large number of the orchestral players featured in these photographs had either retired from RTÉ, or had died, before the date of publication. 3 *The Irish music industryj turnpike or boreen on the sound superhighway of the 21st century*, p. 4.

Industry (1994) to which many organisations were party.[4] A cardinal point embedded in both documents was the statement that 'Ireland is synonymous with music'[5] – a sentiment current from the time of Giraldus Cambrensis. Yet the economic relevance and potential of music, and the implications of technological change, had not been addressed in any significant detail up to that point. As one of the authors of the report observed to the present writer, 'music to many is seen as little more than entertainment, and not an "industry" which supports or sustains *real* jobs'.[6] Again, the 'flavour' of the report is coloured by two parallel equations: that music is 'a form of cultural expression which is a defining national characteristic'; and music is 'an internationally traded service'.[7] These suggest that the 'Irishness' of Irish music-making also defines the nature of the 'service' to be 'traded', which we have seen as a point of comment by many critics overseas.

Despite the careful avoidance by the authors of the report of identifying, or discussing, any one area of music activity or any one genre, one cannot escape the conclusion that if classical music were to be discussed in detail, in terms of both composition and performance, it would fit much more closely into the category of 'boreen' than into that of 'turnpike'.

While the report contained a section describing RTÉ as 'the country's largest consumer by far, and the means by which the largest proportion of the Irish radio listening and television watching public access music',[8] it had little observation, and no recommendations, to make on the subject of RTÉ's music policy. RTÉ was excluded from the list of 'groups' which should 'address particular issues and ... adopt co-ordinated strategies'.[9]

The core activity of the NSO is the delivery of live performances on most Friday nights to an audience of up to 1160 people, which are usually broadcast by Lyric fm to a nationwide audience of maybe another 1–200,000 – which makes it almost irrelevant in terms of the overall 'Irish music industry' with its emphasis on 'value-added', sales to tourists and export audience reach. Its international audience, accessed mainly through its commercial recordings, may constitute a minor module in the notion of an export market, but hardly compares with the exportability of the myriad of Irish music recordings available worldwide, while its occasional appearances outside Ireland cannot compare (or be compared) with either the international tours of Irish groups such as U2 or the Chieftains, or the spurious 'Irish' groups which proliferate in Europe (especially Germany), many of whose members are not Irish, or from Ireland, at all.

4 Commissioned by Irish Music Rights Organisation, the Mechanical Copyright Protection Society, the Contemporary Music Centre, the Association of Irish Composers, the Performing Rights Society and others. 5 *A strategic vision for the irish music industry*, p. 1. 6 Ronan King (Simpson Xavier Horwath) to the author, 7 March 1994. 7 *A strategic vision*, p. 1. 8 Ibid., p. 7. 9 Ibid., p. 63.

One of the chief recommendations of this report was the establishment of a 'Music Industry Task Force', which eventually materialised as the Music Board of Ireland in 2001. It set about its work with two documents: the first, by Goodbody Economic Consultants, was *Economic Significance of the Irish Music Industry*, and the second was entitled *Shaping the Future: a strategic plan for the development of the music industry in Ireland*. The figures contained in the economic analysis indicate how small is the classical music sector: live performances generated a revenue of €144.6m (30% of the total value of the 'Irish music industry') and the number of performers was estimated at 6,215 (or 70% of those employed in the industry). RTÉ's total income from concerts and recordings would amount to significantly less than one per cent, and its 150+ musicians and ancillary staff are a mere fraction of employment in the total industry. This report agreed with the author of the *Strategic Vision* quoted above, to the extent that it commented: 'to some extent, music is a hidden industry with understanding of its structure and complexities the preserve of a few. This needs to be addressed, if the industry is to gain access to finance and support services that other more well-defined sectors enjoy'.[10]

In its analysis of the situation of the Irish music industry, the Music Board identified four main areas: creation (composers and performers); facilitators (management); production (concert promotion) and distribution (concerts, media).[11] As I observed in my Introduction, RTÉ's Music Division, without reference to any other sector within the organisation, encapsulates all of these activities. It thus holds within itself the roles of developing musical talent, its commercial exploitation, arrangement of live performances, and provision of administration and technical support. Thus, the most recent attempt to address the complexity of the Irish music industry reveals that that entire industry is reflected in miniature by a single division in RTÉ, which has effectively been thus constituted since 1941.

When, therefore, Michael Dervan asserted that 'RTÉ sees its problems in terms of money and structure [b]ut the biggest issue it faces in the area of music is actually about artistic issues',[12] he was asking RTÉ, and all those who are eligible to express an interest in the management of its performing groups, to prioritise between 'money and structures' (which, we have seen, are considered a primary concern by the authors of these reports) and 'artistic issues' (which appear *not* to be a major concern of those reports). As this study hopes to have shown, financial and structural preoccupations are a *sine qua non* of an organisation such as that within which these performing groups have grown up, and with which they have such intimate and complex relationships.

---

10 *Economic significance of the irish music industry*, p. ix.   11 *Shaping the future*, p. 3. The Board's work terminated in mid-2004   12 *Irish Times*, 4 March 2003.

Today, an arts manager is a recognisable type of professional, who was unavailable in the dangerous days when these early administrators were setting out to achieve what they saw as the best route through the particular terrain of the Irish civil service, with its sloughs and its firmer ground. But s/he occupies a similar position, as a middle-man between the State and the artist/audience.[13] To reconcile management skills with an artistic orientation remains a personal matter for each arts manager, and a leadership challenge for a director who has to make a team out of a disparate amalgam of such individuals. It remains true to say that 'there has been little investment in management training for the arts and heritage [sector] in Ireland and even less in training customised to the particular needs of those working in this sector'.[14] As the author of that statement, Paula Clancy, observes, 'arts managers in Ireland have come to their present positions from a variety of backgrounds, with diverse educational and occupational histories ... Management of organisations is typically a task which is tacked on to arts-related skills'.[15] The torsion between managerial skills and musical interests/motivations can, of course, either provide the energy and synergy that drives such a team or, conversely, put a brake on its artistic momentum, to such an extent that the performance of accountancy functions becomes more important than the performance of Renaissance madrigals and the twenty-first century avant-garde.

In February 1998, on the eve of the NSO's fiftieth-birthday concert, Michael Dervan stated his opinion that that season's schedule 'lacks the essential thread of imaginative programming and choice of artist that is so needed to invigorate a body that has become weighed down by poor artistic input and developmental neglect. The imminent arrival of [Alexander] Anissimov [as Principal Conductor] and a new director of music could be the signal for change'.[16] Two months later, RTÉ announced the appointment of Niall Doyle, formerly Director of Music Network, to the newly restored position of Director of Music in RTÉ. The repositioning of the post, after its demotion since 1982–3, was accompanied by the removal of the Music Department from Radio Division, where it had remained since the restructuring of RTÉ in 1962–6, and its establishment as a Division in its own right, with its chief officer reporting immediately to, and working with, the Director-General.

After Doyle's appointment, public consultation meetings were held throughout Ireland, which indicated that the public at large wanted more regional appearances by the performing groups, more new music, more educational programmes and greater use of the groups on television.

---

13 Cf. Paula Clancy, op. cit., pp. 1, 69. 14 Ibid., p. 12. 15 Ibid., pp. 41, 46. 16 *Irish Times*, 13 February 1998.

One of the first developments was an 'Agreement between RTÉ and SIPTU in respect of orchestral musicians' productivity/regrading'. This agreement, dated December 1999, following so closely on the heels of the PIANO report, recognised that RTÉ and the musicians would 'create ... a climate and a set of conditions in which the Performing Groups can go on developing as the unique national institutions that they are', and reflected 'a renewed and enhanced capacity to service more fully and lead the nation's musical development'. The aspiration, which is reflected in all the developments since undertaken by the Performing Groups, was underpinned by a new financial settlement by means of which an increase in the musicians' salaries was all-inclusive, thus eliminating any possibility of negotiation and dissension over extra payments, as had been the case, for example, with the opera seasons, foreign tours and commercial recordings.

This long overdue recognition of the status of music in Irish broadcasting removed many factors of imbalance. It erased the notion that music was exclusively a radiophonic activity, and concomitantly it took the Music Department away from the radio balance sheet: henceforward, the cost of music would be charged to the organisation as a whole. It brought those responsible for planning music activity into the higher echelons of general planning and development, thus eliding at least one hierarchical layer in the chain of command. Twenty years after Seán Tinney's assessment of the orchestras' status and conditions, it enabled the future of the Performing Groups to be considered on the same terms as that of any other division within RTÉ, and, along with subsequent restructuring of administration at all levels and in all areas of RTÉ, it made Music Division responsible for its own conceptual and financial future. The working relationship between the Director of Music and the Director-General facilitates – and indeed necessitates – a perspective on the development of RTÉ's presence and activity in the overall context of Irish music-making, which can ensure the optimum deployment of resources and will identify RTÉ as a public service broadcaster and as a continuing player in Ireland's musical life both at home and abroad.

With the celebrations in 1998 to mark the half-century of both the NSO and the RTÉCO, a new confidence was evident in everything to do with the Performing Groups. Despite negative developments in the 1990s, such as the phasing out of the RTÉ Chamber Choir and the departure of its Choral Director, Colin Mawby, and the episode of the PIANO report with the strongly angled possibility that the NSO might be removed from RTÉ, the forward momentum of Music Division, in both artistic and fiscal matters, has been marked and successful.

The fact remains, however, that, as Pierre Boulez has pointed out since at least the 1980s,[17] the symphony orchestra can be, and often is, regarded as an anachronism. As a centenary history of the LSO asks:

---

17 Cf. Boulez' contribution to the EBU symposium reported by Lionel Salter, op. cit.

> Does the symphony orchestra have a future? Will there always be a mar-
> ket for a large ensemble of musicians, quaintly attired as if for some
> sedate nineteenth-century ball, playing music that was mostly written
> more than a hundred years ago to connoisseurs who sit in rapt and con-
> templative silence? Can this ritual continue in an age when a thousand
> different varieties of entertainment are beamed or cabled into our homes
> at the flick of a remote-control? ... How can these venerable institu-
> tions – custodians and curators of so much great music of the past, and
> (one hopes) catalysts for so much yet to be written – break through the
> psychological, social, geographical and financial barriers that seem to
> deter the vast majority of people ... from going to concerts or buying
> classical recordings?[18]

New concepts within RTÉ, such as employment of the internet to deliver
music services, first in traditional music with *CeolNet* and later in classical music
with *ClassicNet*,[19] have thoroughly modernised one of the world's oldest media,
reaffirming its centrality in social life today. Commercial recordings by all the
Performing Groups continue to proliferate on the Naxos and Marco Polo
labels. The NSO made its first tour of the USA, 'to enormous popular and
critical acclaim' (as the clichés have it) in 2003, while in 2001 and 2003 respectively it had residencies in Kerry and Donegal, led by conductors David Brophy,
Robert Houlihan and James Cavanagh, which saw it engaging with local school
groups and individuals to foster an appreciation of music and music-making
in areas which it had never previously visited.

With the rationalisation – and stabilisation – of the position regarding RTÉ's
income from licence fees in 2002–3,[20] 'the context of assessing RTÉ's output has
changed radically', in the words of Niall Doyle.[21] The RTÉ submission which
secured the increase in the licence fee contained seven points from Music
Division, one of which was a significant increase in the number of commissions
it could offer. 'Radical change' was thus not merely one of managerial competence or potential, but intricately linked to artistic change, which has seen developments in RTÉ's relationship with contemporary music similar to those in the
1970s and 80s with the Dublin Twentieth-Century Festival, and unmatched since
then. Of special significance is the fact that Doyle's strategy is intended to
increase the level and manner of engagement with composers and composition.

---

18 R. Morrison, *Orchestra: the LSO*, pp. 225, 244. **19** One of the author's last assignments in RTÉ
was to select, from the Sound Archives, 200 hours of classical music which would feature on
ClassicNet; at the time of writing, this facility had yet to become available to the public. **20** The
successive ministers with responsibility for broadcasting granted an increase in the licence fee from
€70 to €107 in 2001 and from €107 to €150 in 2003. **21** N. Doyle, interview with the author,
19 May 2003, which is the source of all subsequent attributions to Doyle.

Doyle's view, that broadcasting and live performance 'to a large degree over-lap', and that there is 'a challenge to make them sit together comfortably and to see in what manner they can produce more than the sum of their parts', was matched by William Eddins' view, on his appointment as chief guest conduc-tor with the NSO, that 'What really excites me is that this is a radio band – that I have the chance to perform orchestral music live over radio. That just doesn't happen in America these days'.[22] Perhaps this signifies the full circle of understanding of the nature of the NSO. In Doyle's perspective, the rela-tionship was exemplified in RTÉ's first 'Living Music Festival' of 2002 at the new Helix auditorium in Dublin,[23] in that it not only served its live audience but lives on, beyond the event, in its broadcast and archived recordings. To see a symphony orchestra as primarily a 'resource bank',[24] with a planned partic-ipation in the life of its community, rather than as purely a performing group, would be an easier role for ensembles such as the NSO and RTÉCO than for many other traditional 'combinations', precisely because the organisational and cultural resources are already at their disposal.

However, Doyle himself shared the personal view of Bob Collins (expressed when the latter was Controller of Television) that the televising of concerts is 'boring', and that music on television should be 'musically engaging'.[25] The challenge here is 'how to make music sing and dance on the medium'. To this end, he wanted to see short stylish concerts and magazine programmes and documentaries which are semi-educational and semi-informational, 'with built-in access paths to the music'. In this he follows Gareth Hudson (above, pp. 550–2) in wanting to create such 'access paths' without exhibiting any of Hudson's apparent dilemma.

Preceded by two successive 'Music Now!' festivals of new Irish music, pro-moted by RTÉ and the CMC in 1994–5 (which were intended to fill the *lacuna* which had existed for the previous eight years, since the demise of the Twentieth-Century Festival), the 'Living Music Festival' in 2002 and 2004 had as its artistic director Raymond Deane, who had been a trenchant critic of RTÉ's programming policy in relation to new works. He observed that the Festival was not, strictly speaking, a 'ghetto', 'another cozy get-together for trendy élitists, another carnival to satiate us in advance of a few more lean years'. He noted the presence in the RTÉ regular concert schedules of works by Varèse, Boulez, Messiaen, Schnittke, Carter and Adams, and the inclusion of modern works in four of the RTÉ Vanbrugh Quartet's next five tours:

22 *Encore: the newsletter of the RTÉ Music Division*, 6 (October 2002). Eddins is Resident Conductor with the Chicago Symphony.   **23** The Helix performing arts centre is an integral part of Dublin City University.   **24** Cf. R. Morrison, op. cit. p. 232.   **25** Cf. R. Morrison, op. cit., p. 179: 'Television has an inbuilt abhorrence of orchestras, for the obvious reason that they are, on the whole, static and visually boring beasts'.

'While few commentators have been more critical than myself of RTÉ's musical policies down the years, I am heartened by this evidence that the national broadcaster is taking its responsibilities seriously'.[26] A major landmark in 2000 was Lyric fm's 'Gerald Barry Festival' over five nights at the NCH and four other main venues, which was the first such extended recognition of a single Irish composer.

Yet one of the perennial problems facing RTÉ in this regard is *education*: while, by definition, all music programming is, in the widest sense, 'educational', broadcasting is 'a tributary of a broad stream' rather than the stream itself, and *cannot* – in Doyle's view – be 'the lead partner'. As the Music Board's *Shaping the Future* observed, lack of music education continues to hamper budding performers from reaching their goals, or even from deciding what those goals should be, and the board's announcement that it would seek a partnership which could provide locally-based education points in a direction that RTÉ might also choose to take, given the confidence generated by its NSO residencies.[27] An initiative launched by Music Network in June 2003 – 'A National System of Local Music Education Services' – which recommended the establishment of a partnership-based, cost-effective network of music teachers, parallel to the music education available within the schools system, may offer a viable alternative to the schools system which has so demonstrably failed; at the time of writing, it has yet to be implemented.

An educational ploy which indicated how far music and technology can work together was 'The Toy Symphony' devised by Tod Machover, of the MIT Media Lab Europe (then based in Dublin) which had its world première in a series of workshops at the Ark Cultural Centre for Children (Dublin), culminating in a concert at the NCH with the NSO. High-tech 'music toys' developed by Machover – 'beatbags' and 'music shapers', which the children learned to squeeze in order to produce and compose musical sounds – were accommodated by a compositional tool, 'Hyperscore', and employed to produce the concert which also featured internationally acclaimed violinist Joshua Bell (who is also Adjunct Professor at MIT) playing a 'hyperviolin'.

One of the most far-reaching developments in the delivery of music *via* the medium of Irish radio has been the existence of Lyric fm as a 24-hour classical music channel since 1 May 1999, evolving out of the previous part-time FM3, and described by Michael Dungan as having a mission 'of making up for lost time' in the sense of providing a musical menu which was unavailable to most listeners up to that point.[28] Part of that mission is to journey 'into that

---

26 'An Irishman's Diary', *Irish Times*, 19 October 2002. 27 *Shaping the future*, pp. v, vii. 28 M.Dungan, 'A messenger with fresh news', *New Music News*, May 2000.

void of unknown which Lyric has the opportunity – and perhaps the artistic obligation – to explore'.

The arrival of Lyric, originally conceived as a 'music and arts channel', which was rapidly defined as almost exclusively music (and talk about music), has generated considerable debate about the content that such a channel should carry and about the style of presentation. At its inauguration, Michael Dervan, observing that the schedule was markedly different from that envisaged at its inception, wrote that it followed 'not the public service ideals of BBC Radio 3 but rather those of the unashamedly commercial Classic FM', and asserted that 'the new service is not primarily aimed at music lovers'.[29] By contrast, and a year into Lyric's new life, Seamus Crimmins, its first director, would say 'I don't like the elitism that surrounds classical music. I think it can be for everyone if they want to listen. I suppose Lyric is trying to mormalise classical music'.[30]

Lyric quickly discovered that it had attracted (as one would expect in a 24-hour schedule) many housewives who had previously given their listening allegiance to Classic fm (broadcast from the UK), but who now preferred (as many told the author) to hear introductions and announcements in an Irish accent. But it also brought itself to the attention of motorists who were attracted to short works, or individual movements from longer works, which entertained during car journeys including the morning trip to, and the evening trip from, work.

The success of Crimmins in securing the services of current affairs broadcaster Éamonn Lawlor as an 'anchor-man' in the early evening schedule with 'Into the Evening' was a major coup, while the consolidation of many of the finest contributors to the existing FM3 schedule, such as Donald Helme and Tim Thurston, with new voices such as Aideen Gormley, into a visible and dependable schedule, immediately earned it a sizeable slice of the overall radio cake, at a time when RTÉ's share on other channels was in danger of diminishing. Lyric's participation in events such as the RTÉ Vanbrugh Quartet's West Cork Chamber Music Festival has earned it a strong public profile both within and without the music community, and its 'ABC#' educational series, presented by composer John Buckley, has proved an instant success.

Since 1999 the audience has fluctuated, partly due to constant revamping of the schedule and the movement of radio personalities from one time-slot to another, but by the time Crimmins handed over the reins in 2003 to Aodhán Ó Dubhghaill, it had settled into a 'niche' with a plateau listenership.

One of the most striking developments during the past decade has been the rising level of accomplishment of the NSO. Reading the reviews by Charles Acton and others from the 1950s to the 1990s, one is struck by the fact that

---

29 *Irish Times*, 20 April 1999. **30** Interview with Eileen Battersby, *Irish Times*, 20 April 2000.

orchestral standards have fluctuated dramatically for no obvious reason. In some instances, critics have observed that the absence of the Principal Conductor has resulted in less satisfactory performances under the batons of other staff conductors or of visitors; in others, a visiting conductor may appear to have raised the standard of performance to a height not usually attained under more normal or regular conditions.[31] This is a problem less likely to arise with the RTÉCO which, despite the broader range of its repertoire, has experienced a much greater degree of consistency under its own Principal Conductor, Proinnsías Ó Duinn 1978–2002.

This fluctuation has not been entirely due to the changing musical personalities of the conductors appearing in succession, week after week, on the podium, or to their chemistry with the orchestral personnel, but that has obviously been a major factor which in turn has been reflected in repertoire. Between the departure of Bryden Thomson in 1987 and the advent of Gerhard Markson in 2001 this tendency to a fluctuation in performing standards (or the discernible results of performance styles) continued to be very noticeable, particularly during periods of uncertainty regarding the occupancy of the principal conductorship, as we have seen in respect of János Fürst, George Hurst, and the non-present Kees Bakels. A series of performing peaks was evident during the tenure of Alexander Anissimov, who found favour with both orchestra and audiences, the latter once again expressing surprise that he was not retained as principal for a longer period. With the situation in 2003 of the retention of Gerhard Markson as Principal Conductor, and, in association, Anissimov as 'Conductor Emeritus', William Eddins as Principal Guest Conductor and David Brophy as Assistant Conductor,[32] a stable of conducting acumen provided a plateau on which one could expect to meet a musical *persona* and artistic achievement from the NSO which had never previously been evident on a consistent basis. Other conductors working with the RTÉ orchestras, such as Robert Houlihan (described by the *Irish Times* in 1990 as 'a young conductor with fire in his belly')[33] and the newly appointed principal conductor of the RTÉCO, Laurent Wagner, also added significantly to the

---

31 John O'Donovan put this in his idiosyncratically irreverent style when he wrote: 'If you choose to view the relationship between orchestra and conductor as a counterpart to the relationship between husband and wife, you will understand how even the best of conductors can become a burden to players for much the same reason as housewives become restless and irritable with the continued presence in their kitchen of a husband on holiday. Without this clue to what can happen behind the scenes you would be puzzled to understand why the RTÉ Symphony Orchestra could after two months with quite a competent conductor perpetrate a ghastly performance of some work you'd expect them to shine in, and how on the other hand they could put up a smashing show with some charlatan, much as the wives of handsome and brilliant men have been observed to brighten considerably in the presence of a duffer who enjoys the transient advantage of novelty': L. McRedmond (ed.), *Written on the wind* (1976), p. 146. 32 Succeeded in 2004 by Gavin Maloney. 33 *Irish Times*, 20 July 1990.

national and international talent available, and it was noticeable that in 2003 Michael Dervan drew attention to the approach of the NSO and Gerhard Markson to symphonies by Haydn and Mozart, works which have largely dropped out of its repertoire but which are an essential training ground for the 'builder-conductor' that RTÉ clearly recognises in Markson.[34]

In 1976 and 1980, when I had the privilege of organising the first and second European tours of the then RTÉSO, attitudes to Europe itself were as much in evidence as concern over the financial outcome of the tours or their musical content. Even though, in the revelational symphony programmes of the 1940s and 50s, Irish audiences had become aware of the *music* of Europe, in the 1970s, for many of the orchestra, 'Europe' as an *idea* was an unknown place, where language and cuisine might become dangerous barriers to the business of concert-giving. So too for the RTÉCO when it toured the USA in 1980.[35] In the twenty-first century, neither orchestra has any conceptual difficulty in setting out for Europe, the USA or Hong Kong. Yet, despite this international exposure – enormously increased by RTÉ's recording contracts with the Naxos/Marco Polo label – it still cannot be said that RTÉ's music-making is 'internationally traded' as part of the Irish music industry, to use a contemporary buzz-word.

Nevertheless, the NSO's first tour to the USA, in early 2003, indicates how in some ways perception of Irish music-making internationally has not changed since the RTÉSO's first foray to London in 1966. Playing in 10 venues including Florida, Charlotte (North Carolina), Worcester (Massachusetts), and concluding at the Avery Fisher Hall, New York, the orchestra, under Gerhard Markson, presented two Irish works, by Jane O'Leary and Ian Wilson, the main items being Stravinsky's 'Firebird' and Brahms' first symphony.

The tour was undoubtedly aided by the fact that the soloist, John O'Conor (playing Beethoven's third and fourth concertos) is well-known in the US, and was thus able to draw an audience who might not otherwise want to hear an Irish symphony orchestra: as a writer in the *Palm Beach Daily News* put it: 'considering Ireland is not known for being a country of classical music lore, it was a surprising delight to hear the [NSO],'[36] while another, in the Worcester *Telegram and Gazette* told her readers that 'the orchestra is based in Dublin, a city better known for its literary than its musical legacy'.[37] Thus, common preconceptions as to the nature of Irishness and Irish culture were once more dis-

34 Author's interview with Martyn Westerman, former Executive Director of the NSO, 5 November 2002. 35 Cf. Harry White, address at the inauguration of the National Library of Ireland's Music Library Project, 29 May 2003: 'Ireland's long agony of debate about her own identity has impeded her access to the discourse of European musical culture.' 36 Bryce Seliger, 'Ireland's National Symphony soars with "Firebird"', *Palm Beach Daily News*, 4 April 2003. 37 Jennifer Weininger, *Telegram and Gazette*, 14 April 2003.

pelled, as the opinions of British and continental critics in the 1970s and 80s were confirmed by their American counterparts: Willa Conrad, of the New Jersey *Star-Ledger*, found that 'the orchestra, though as disciplined and clean as any other modern major ensemble, has a sense of airiness to its string sound, too much graininess in its brass playing, and pure, bubbling wind playing, particularly in the flute section. The mixture of the two – a conductor with a calm yet warm podium style and an orchestra with a touch of earthy unevenness in its sound – tended to illuminate the score of Brahms' First Symphony, giving it a chewy vigour that was appealing'.[38] It is worth remarking that, over a quarter of a century, with a succession of principal conductors of varying musical characters, and with a considerable turnover of players in all sections, such similar opinions can be expressed about the particular qualities that constitute the RTÉSO/NSO's own musical character.

In 2003, Michael Dervan, commenting on the fortunes – or lack of them – of classical music during the brief era of the 'Celtic Tiger', reviewed the position of RTÉ as follows: 'with two orchestras, a string quartet, a number of amateur choirs [two] and a heavy investment in the professional National Chamber Choir, RTÉ is the major player in Irish musical life' – a fact that has been the *raison d'être* of the present study, and one that has been evident, in Dervan's terms, since at least 1958/59, when the string quartet was added to RTÉ's musical pack. 'It pats itself on the back – as well it might, given the level of its investment – but it behaves as a monopolist, just as Aer Lingus used to and Eircom still wants to. It dictates to most everybody it deals with, with pretty sorry results in recent years through friction with Wexford Festival Opera, the NCH and the loss of the proposed residency by the RTÉ Concert Orchestra at the Helix.'[39] Dervan would hardly maintain that RTÉ should follow the policy – or lack of it – which was allowed to prevail in the 1940s and 1950s, when outside bodies appeared to dictate the availability of the RÉ performing groups and the price-tags attached thereto: the detachment of the NSO from Wexford, the renegotiation of the contract for the NSO's residency at the NCH, and the breakdown of negotiations for that of the RTÉCO at the Helix – a disappointment for all who had hoped that this was the end of the long search for an adequate home for it – were all indications that RTÉ does not operate in a vacuum and recognises that, in addition to its responsibility in fiscal matters, it no longer holds a monopoly over any form of music-making on the island of Ireland.

If the NSO were a completely separate, independent entity, its personnel and its management structure would probably not be unlike the present, but

38 Willa J. Conrad, 'Something to share', *Star-Ledger*, 14 April 2003.   39 *Irish Times*, 4 March 2003.

without existing lines of communication to the supervening authority of RTÉ. Instead, it would become subject to a different set of reporting relationships, a different kind of accountability, and a different vulnerability to the winds of cultural and financial change. The environment would change, but the realities would remain constant. That, however, does not in itself constitute an argument for the retention by RTÉ of the NSO.

Looking back at the personalities who have largely been responsible for the major developments in the existence of the performing groups at present within RTÉ, we find a curious mixture of civil servants (T.J. Kiernan, P.S. O'Hegarty, León Ó Broin), administrators from a variety of backgrounds in the arts (Fachtna Ó hAnnracháin, Róibéard Ó Faracháin, Charles Kelly, Maurice Gorham, Gerard Victory, John Kinsella) and musicians who also performed administrative functions (Vincent O'Brien, Michael Bowles, Tibor Paul): together, these and others who were purely, or almost entirely, engaged in music-making (such as successive principal conductors of the orchestras and choirs) have constituted a historical tapestry which, whatever its rights or wrongs, and however much it may be 'an Irish solution to an Irish problem' (or even simply an Irish problem without a solution), cannot be undone. Whether the threads of that historical tapestry continue to live in its culture of management, is the subject of another study.

Bibliography

Acton, Charles, 'Seán Ó Riada: the next phase', *Eire–Ireland* 2/4, 1967.
——, 'Interview with Seóirse Bodley', *Eire–Ireland* 5/3, 1970.
——, 'Interview with Brian Boydell', *Eire–Ireland* 5/4, 1970.
——, 'Interview with A.J. Potter', *Eire–Ireland* 5/2, 1970.
——, 'An interview with Seán Ó Riada', *Eire–Ireland* 6/1, 1971.
——, 'What's wrong with the RTÉSO?', *Irish Times*, 19, 20 and 21 March 1974.
——, 'Who does the educating?', *Irish Broadcasting Review* no. 6 (autumn/winter 1979).
Andrews, C.S., *Man of no property* (Dublin: Mercier Press, 1982).
Barry, Malcolm, *Counterpoint* (December 1980–January 1981).
——, *Soundpost* 16 (October–November 1983).
Bartók, Béla, *Collected essays* (London: Faber and Faber, 1976).
Bax, Arnold, *Farewell my youth and other writings*, ed. Lewis Foreman (repr. London: Scolar Press, 1992).
Beckett, Brian, 'Tested teaching' in Pine and Acton (eds.), *To talent alone* (1998).
Benson, Ciarán, *The place of the arts in Irish education* (Dublin: Arts Council, 1979).
Bowles, Michael, *The art of conducting* (New York: Doubleday, 1959).
——, 'Hands across the musical border', *Irish Times*, 15 February 1972.
——, 'The birth of the R.É.S.O.', *Irish Times*, 6 February 1973.
Boydell, Brian, 'The future of music in Ireland', *The Bell* 16/4 (January 1951).
——, 'Orchestral and chamber music in Dublin', in A. Fleischmann, *Music in Ireland* (1952).
Bracefield, Hilary, 'The Northern composer: Irish or European?' in Devine and White (eds.), *Irish Musical Studies 4*.
Breathnach, Breandán, *Folk music and dances of Ireland* (Dublin: Talbot Press, 1971).
Briggs, Asa, *The history of broadcasting in the United Kingdom*, vol. 1, *The birth of broadcasting, 1896–1927* (Oxford: Oxford University Press, 1961).
Byers, David, 'Norman Hay', *Soundpost* 6 (February–March 1982).
Cathcart, Rex, *The most contrary region: the BBC in Northern Ireland, 1924–1984* (Belfast: Blackstaff Press, 1984).
Clancy, Paula, *Managing the cultural sector: essential competencies for managers in arts, culture and heritage in Ireland* (Dublin: Oak Tree Press/UCD, 1994).
Collins, Derek, 'Music in Dublin, 1800–1848' in Pine and Acton (eds.), *To talent alone* (1998).
Cooke, Jim, *A musical journey, 1890–1993: from Municipal School of Music to Dublin Institute of Technology* (Dublin: College of Music 1994).
Cox, Gareth, and Klein, Axel (eds.), *Irish Musical Studies 7: Irish music in the twentieth century* (Dublin: Four Courts Press, 2003).
Cox, Gareth *et al.*, *The life and music of Brian Boydell* (Dublin: Irish Academic Press, 2003).
Daly, Karina, *Tom Walsh's opera: a history of the Wexford Festival, 1951–2004* (Dublin: Four Courts Press, 2004).
Deale, Edgar, *Catalogue of contemporary Irish composers* (Dublin: Music Association of Ireland, 1968/1973).
Deane, Raymond, 'The honour of non-existence – Classical composers in Irish society' in G. Gillen and H. White (eds.), *Irish Musical Studies 3*.

——, 'Identity on parade', *Journal of Music in Ireland* 3/5 (July–August 2003).

Deane, Séamus, 'Remembering the Irish future', *The Crane Bag* 8/1 (1984).

——, 'Synge and heroism' in S. Deane, *Celtic revivals: essays in modern Irish literature, 1880–1980* (London: Faber and Faber, 1985).

de Barra, Séamus, 'The music of Aloys Fleischmann: a survey' in Ruth Fleischmann (ed.), *Aloys Fleischmann*.

de Paor, Paschal, 'The development of electroacoustic music in Ireland', in Cox and Klein (eds.), *Irish Musical Studies 7*.

Devine, Patrick and Harry White (eds.), *Irish Musical Studies 4: The Maynooth International Musicological Conference 1995, selected proceedings part 1* (Dublin: Four Courts Press, 1996).

Donoghue, Denis, 'The future of Irish music', *Studies* 44 (spring 1955).

Dowling, Jack, Leila Doolan and Bob Quinn, *Sit down and be counted: the cultural evolution of a television station* (Dublin: Wellington, 1969).

Fanning, Ronan, *The Irish Department of Finance, 1922–58* (Dublin: Institute of Public Administration, 1978).

Fleischmann, Aloys, 'The outlook of music in Ireland', *Studies* 24 (March 1935).

——, 'Ars nova: Irish music in the shaping', *Ireland Today* 1 (1936).

——, 'The music of E.J. Moeran', *Envoy* 4/16 (March 1951).

—— (ed.), *Music in Ireland: a symposium* (Cork: Cork University Press, 1952).

——, 'Appreciation: Seán Ó Riada's *Nomos II*', *Eire–Ireland* 7/3 (1972).

Fleischmann, Ruth (ed.), *Aloys Fleischmann (1910–1992): a life for music in Ireland remembered by contemporaries* (Cork: Mercier Press, 2000).

Flood, W.H. Grattan, *A history of Irish music* (Dublin: Browne and Nolan, 1913).

Friel, Brian, *Dancing at Lughnasa* (London: Faber and Faber, 1990).

Gorham, Maurice, *Forty years of Irish broadcasting* (Dublin: Talbot Press, 1967).

Government of Ireland, *Access and opportunity: a White Paper on cultural policy* (Dublin: Stationery Office, 1987).

Graydon, Philip, 'Modernism in Ireland' in Cox and Klein (eds.), *Irish Musical Studies 7*.

Groocock, Joseph, *A general survey of music in the Republic of Ireland* (Dublin: Foras Éireann, 1961).

Harris, Bernard and Grattan Freyer (eds.), *Integrating tradition: the achievement of Seán Ó Riada* (Ballina: Irish Humanities Centre, 1981).

Harty, Herbert Hamilton, *Early memories*, ed. by David Greer (Belfast: Queen's University, 1979) .

Heaney, Séamus, *Preoccupations* (London: Faber and Faber, 1980).

Henebry, Richard, *Irish music* (Dublin, 1903).

Herron, Donald, *Deaf ears?: a report on the provision of music education in Irish schools* (Dublin: Arts Council, 1985).

Hofstede, Geert, *Cultures and organizations: software of the mind* (London: McGraw-Hill, 1991).

Horgan, John, *Irish media: a critical history since 1922* (London: Routledge, 2001).

——, *Broadcasting and public life: RTÉ news and current affairs* (Dublin: Four Courts Press, 2004).

Kearney, Richard (ed.), *The Irish mind: exploring intellectual traditions* (Dublin: Wolfhound Press, 1985).

Kelly, Charles, 'Look back in pleasure' in L. McRedmond (ed.), *Written on the wind* (1976).

Kelly, J.S., 'The political, intellectual and social background to the Irish literary revival', PhD thesis, University of Cambridge, 1971.

Kennedy, Brian P., *Dreams and responsibilities: the State and the arts in independent Ireland* (Dublin: The Arts Council n.d. [1990]).

Kennedy, S.B., 'Introduction' to *Paul Henry* (Dublin: National Gallery of Ireland, 2003).

Kenyon, Nicholas, *The BBC Symphony Orchestra, 1930–1980* (London: BBC, 1981).

Kingston, Warren, *Strengthening the management culture* (London: Sigma, 1994).

Klein, Axel, 'Irish composers and foreign education: a study of influences' in P. Devine and H. White (eds.), *Irish Musical Studies 4*.

——, 'Roots and directions in twentieth-century Irish art music' in Cox and Klein (eds.), *Irish Musical Studies 7*.

——, *Irish classical recordings: a discography of Irish art music* (Westport, Conn: Greenwood Press, 2001).

Larchet, John F., 'A plea for music' in W. Fitzgerald (ed.), *The voice of Ireland* (1923).

Lasswell, Harold, 'The structure and function of communication in society', in L. Bryson (ed.), *The communication of ideas* (New York: Harper and Row, 1948).

Leffert, F.H. *et al.*, 'Hand difficulties among musicians', *Journal of the American Medical Association* 249 (1983).

Loveland, Kenneth, 'Composers in search of a national identity', *Counterpoint* (October 1972).

Lynch, Charles, 'The concert pianist in Ireland', in Fleischmann (ed.), *Music in Ireland* (1952).

McCarthy, Marie, 'Music education and the quest for cultural identity in Ireland, 1831–1989', PhD dissertation, University of Michigan, 1990.

——, 'Music education in the emergent nation state' in Pine (ed.), *Music in Ireland* (1998).

——, *Passing it on: the transmission of music in Irish culture* (Cork: Cork University Press, 1999).

McCormack, W.J., *Fool of the family: a life of J.M. Synge* (London: Weidenfeld and Nicolson, 2000).

McRedmond, Louis (ed.), *Written on the wind: personal memories of Irish radio, 1926–76* (Dublin: RTÉ/Gill and Macmillan, 1976).

MacRéamoinn, Seán, 'Foreword' in Harris and Freyer (eds.), *The achievement of Seán Ó Riada*.

Mäkelä, Tomi (ed.), *Music and nationalism in 20th-century Great Britain and Finland* (Hamburg: von Bockel Verlag, 1997).

Marcus, Louis, 'Seán Ó Riada and the Ireland of the Sixties' in Harris and Freyer, *The achievement of Seán Ó Riada*.

Martyn, Edward, 'The Gaelic League and Irish music', *Irish Review* 1 (March 1911–February 1912).

May, Frederick, 'Music and the nation', *Dublin Magazine* 11/3 (July–September 1936).

——, 'The music of Aloys Fleischmann', *Father Mathew Record* 42/12 (December 1949).

——, 'The composer in Ireland' in Fleischmann (ed.), *Music in Ireland*.

——, 'Radio Éireann Symphony concerts' in Fleischmann (ed.), *Music in Ireland*.

——, 'First performances of works by Irish composers, 1935–1951' in Fleishmann (ed.), *Music in Ireland*.

Morrison, Richard, *Orchestra: The LSO: a century of triumph and turbulence* (London: Faber and Faber, 2004).

Murphy, Michael, 'Moniuszko and musical nationalism in Poland' in White and Murphy (eds.), *Musical constructions of nationalism* (2001).

Music Board of Ireland, *The economic significance of the Irish music industry* (Dublin: Music Board of Ireland, 2001).

——, *Shaping the future* (Dublin: Music Board of Ireland, 2001).

Nowottny, Friedrich, 'On the relationship between broadcasting and culture', *EBU Review, Programmes, Administration, Law* 33/1 (January 1987).

O'Boyle, Seán, *The Irish song tradition* (Dublin: Gilbert Dalton, 1976).

Ó Braoin, Donnchadh, 'School music' , *Irish School Weekly* 77, 15 May 1926.

Ó Braonáin, Séumas, 'Seven years of Irish radio' *The Leader* 1 January 1949.

——, 'Music in the broadcasting service' in Fleischmann (ed.), *Music in Ireland.*

Ó Broin, Eimear, 'Music and broadcasting' in Pine (ed.), *Music in Ireland.*

Ó Broin, León, *Just like yesterday: an autobiography* (Dublin: Gill and Macmillan, n.d. [1986]).

O'Byrne, Robert, *Hugh Lane, 1875–1915* (Dublin: Lilliput Press, 2000).

Ó Canainn, Tomás, *Traditional music in Ireland* (Cork: Ossian Press, 1978/1993).

——, *Seán Ó Riada: his life and work* (Cork: Collins Press, 2003).

O'Conor, John, 'Towards a new academy' in Pine (ed.), *Music in Ireland.*

—— *et al.* [PIANO Review Group], *The PIANO Report: report of the review group PIANO presented to the Minister for Arts, Culture and the Gaeltacht, Mr Michael D. Higgins, T.D.,* January 1996.

O'Donovan, John 'Music on the air' in Louis McRedmond (ed.), *Written on the wind* (1976).

Ó Gallchobhair, Éamonn, 'The cultural value of festival and feis' in Fleischmann (ed.), *Music in Ireland.*

——, 'Academies and professors', *Ireland To–day* 2 (1937).

O'Hagan, John and Duffy, Christopher, *The performing arts and the public purse* (Dublin: The Arts Council, 1987).

Ó hAnnracháin, Fachtna, 'Choral singing in Ireland', in Fleischmann (ed.), *Music in Ireland.*

——, 'Introduction' to Pat O'Kelly, *The National Symphony Orchestra of Ireland.*

O'Kelly, Pat, *The National Symphony Orchestra of Ireland, 1948–1998: a selected history* (Dublin: Radio Telefís Éireann, 1998).

O'Neill, Joseph, 'Music in Dublin' in Fleischmann (ed.), *Music in Ireland.*

Ó Riada, Seán, *Our musical heritage*, ed. T. Kinsella (Fundúireacht an Riadaigh/Dolmen Press, 1982).

Ó Séaghda, Barra, 'Harping on', *Graph* 3/3, summer 1999.

O'Sullivan, Mary, 'The legacy of Michele Esposito', MA thesis, St Patrick's College, Maynooth, 1991.

Page, John, 'A post-war symphony: Frank Corcoran's Symphony no. 2' in Cox and Klein (eds.), *Irish Musical Studies* 7.

Petrie, Charles, 'Introduction' to *The complete collection of Irish music* edited by C.V. Stanford, (London: Boosie, 1902–5).

Pine, Richard, 'Cultural democracy' in *The development of cultural policies in Europe* (Helsinki: Finnish National Commission for UNESCO, no. 24, 1982).

—— (ed.), *Music in Ireland, 1848–1998* (Cork: Mercier Press, 1998).

——, *2RN and the origins of Irish radio* (Dublin: Four Courts Press, 2002).

——, 'In dreams begins responsibility', *Journal of Music in Ireland* 2/3, March–April 2002.

—— and Acton, Charles (eds.), *To talent alone: the Royal Irish Academy of Music, 1848–1998* (Dublin: Gill and Macmillan, 1998).

Praeger, Jeffrey, *Building democracy in Ireland: political order and cultural integration in a newly independent nation* (Cambridge: Cambridge University Press, 1986).

Quinn, Antoinette, *Patrick Kavanagh: a biography* (Dublin: Gill and Macmillan, 2001).

Quinn, Bob, *Atlantean: Ireland's North African and maritime heritage* (London: Quartet, 1986; repub. as *The Irish Atlantean: Ireland's oriental and maritime heritage*: Dublin: Lilliput Press, 2004).

——, *Maverick: a dissident view of broadcasting today* (Tralee: Brandon, 2001).

Radio Éireann Yearbook 1948.

Radio Éireann Handbook 1955.

Rainbow, Bernarr, *The land without music* (London: Novello, 1967).

Richards, J.M., *Provision for the arts* (Dublin: Arts Council & Gulbenkian Foundation, 1976).

Richman, Barry, 'Significance of cultural variables', *Academy of Management Journal* 8/4 (December 1965).

Ryan, Joseph, 'Nationalism and Irish music' in White and Gillen (eds.), *Irish Musical Studies* 3.

——, 'Nationalism and music in Ireland', PhD thesis, NUI Maynooth, 1991.

——, 'The tone of defiance', in White and Murphy (eds), *Musical Constructions of Nationalism.*

Saddlemyer, Ann, 'Synge's soundscape', *Irish University Review* 22/1 (1992).

——, *Becoming George: the life of Mrs W.B.Yeats* (Oxford: Oxford University Press, 2002).

Salter, Lionel (rapporteur), *EBU: Symposium on the future of radio orchestras: Frankfurt 2–4 April 1984* (Geneva: EBU, 1984)

Schmitz, Oscar, *Das land ohne musik* (1920).

Sealy, Douglas, 'Seán Ó Riada: man or mask?', *Soundpost* 5 (December 1981–January 1982).

Sexton, Conor, 'The Music Department – a time for change' (RTÉ: RTÉ Activity Review Unit, 1989).

Sheehan, Helena, *Irish television drama: a society and its stories* (Dublin: RTÉ, 1987).

——, *The continuing story of Irish television drama: tracking the tiger* (Dublin: Four Courts Press, 2004).

Sheehy, Jeanne, *The rediscovery of Ireland's past: the Celtic revival, 1830–1930* (London: Thames and Hudson, 1980).

Sheehy, M.P. and Marsden, C.D., 'Writer's cramp – a focal dystonia', *Brain* 1982, 105.

Simpson Xavier Horwath Consulting, *The Irish music industry – turnpike or boreen on the sound superhighway of the 21st century* (Dublin: Simpson Xavier Horwath, 1993).

——, *A strategic vision for the Irish music industry* (Dublin: Simpson Xavier Horwath, 1994).

Smith, Gus, *Love and music: the glorious history of the Dublin Grand Opera Society, 1941–1998* (Dublin: Atlantic Publishers, 1998).

——, *Dr Tom's festival legacy* (Dublin: Atlantic Publishers, 2001).

Smith, Pamela, *Towards a policy and action plan for opera* (Dublin: Arts Council, 2002).

Stanford, C.V., *Pages from an unwritten diary* (London: Edwin Arnold, 1914).

—— and C. Forsyth, *A history of music* (London: Dent, 1925).

Stewart, Andrew, *LSO at 90: from Queen's Hall to the Barbican Centre* (London: London Symphony Orchestra, 1995).

Sutton, David, *Memories cast in stone: the relevance of the past in everyday life* (Oxford: Berg, 1998).

Taylor, Michael, 'An interview with Brian Boydell' in Cox *et al.* (eds.), *The life and music of Brian Boydell.*

Travers-Smith, Hester, 'A musical league for Dublin', *Irish Statesman* 1 (26 July 1919), p. 119.

Vallely, Fintan (ed.), *The companion to Irish traditional music* (Cork: Cork University Press, 1999).

Vedin, Bengt-Arne, *Corporate culture and creative management* (Bromley: Chartwell-Bratt, 1985).

Verba, Sidney, 'Conclusion: comparative political culture' in L. Pye and S. Verba (eds.), *Political culture and political development* (Princeton NJ: Princeton University Press, 1965).

Victory, Gerard, 'Ó Riada on radio' in Harris and Freyer (eds.), *The achievement of Seán Ó Riada.*

——, 'What broadcasting contributes to music in Ireland', *Irish Broadcasting Review* 5, summer 1979.

Warner, Malcolm, 'Culture, organizational behaviour and human resource management: a critique' (University of Cambridge, Research Papers in Management Studies, no. 217, 1995).

White, Harry, 'Music and the literary imagination' in Gillen and White (eds.), *Irish Musical Studies 3*.

——, 'The conceptual failure of music education', *The Irish Review* 21 (Autumn/Winter 1997).

——, *The keeper's recital: music and cultural history in Ireland, 1770–1970* (Cork: Cork University Press.

——, 'Nationalism, colonialism and the cultural status of music in Ireland', in White and Murphy (eds.), *Musical constructions of nationalism*.

——, 'The divided imagination: music in Ireland after Ó Riada' in Cox and Klein (eds.), *Irish Musical Studies 7*.

—— and Gillen, Gerard (eds.), *Irish Musical Studies 3: Music and Irish cultural history* (Irish Academic Press, 1995).

—— and Murphy, Michael (eds.), *Musical constructions of nationalism: essays on the history and ideology of European musical culture, 1800–1945* (Cork: Cork University Press, 2001)

Wright, David, 'Gerard Victory', *Classical music on the web* http://www.musicweb.uk.net/victory/index.htm

——, 'Seán Ó Riada', *Classical music on the web* http://www.musicweb.uk.net/oriada/index.htm

Ziporyn, T., 'Pianist's cramp to stage fright: the medical side of music making', *Journal of the American Medical Association* 1984, 252, pp. 985–9.

Zuk, Patrick, 'Music and Nationalism', *Journal of Music in Ireland* 3/5, July–August 2003.

Index